The Human Factor of Cybercrime

Cybercrimes are often viewed as technical offences that require technical solutions, such as antivirus programs or automated intrusion detection tools. However, these crimes are committed by individuals or networks of people which prey upon human victims and are detected and prosecuted by criminal justice personnel. As a result, human decision-making plays a substantial role in the course of an offence, the justice response, and policymakers' attempts to legislate against these crimes. This book focuses on the human factor in cybercrime: its offenders, victims, and parties involved in tackling cybercrime.

The distinct nature of cybercrime has consequences for the entire spectrum of crime and raises myriad questions about the nature of offending and victimization. For example, are cybercriminals the same as traditional offenders, or are there new offender types with distinct characteristics and motives? What foreground and situational characteristics influence the decision-making process of offenders? Which personal and situational characteristics provide an increased or decreased risk of cybercrime victimization? This book brings together leading criminologists from around the world to consider these questions and examine all facets of victimization, offending, offender networks, and policy responses.

Dr Rutger Leukfeldt is a senior researcher and cybercrime cluster coordinator at the Netherlands Institute for the Study of Crime and Law Enforcement (NSCR). Furthermore, Rutger is a director of the Cybersecurity & SMEs Research Center of the Hague University of Applied Sciences. Over the last decade, Rutger worked on a number of cybercrime studies for the Dutch government and private companies. Rutger is currently the chair of the Cybercrime Working Group of the European Society of Criminology (ESC).

Dr Thomas J. Holt is a professor in the School of Criminal Justice at Michigan State University specializing in cybercrime, cyberterrorism, and the police response to these threats. His work has been published in a range of journals, and he is also the author of multiple books and edited works.

Routledge Studies in Crime and Society

For more information about this series, please visit: www.routledge.com/
Routledge-Studies-in-Crime-and-Society/book-series/RSCS

The Human Factor of Cybercrime

**Edited by Rutger Leukfeldt
and Thomas J. Holt**

Routledge
Taylor & Francis Group
LONDON AND NEW YORK

First published 2020
by Routledge
2 Park Square, Milton Park, Abingdon, Oxon OX14 4RN

and by Routledge
52 Vanderbilt Avenue, New York, NY 10017

Routledge is an imprint of the Taylor & Francis Group, an informa business

© 2020 selection and editorial matter, Rutger Leukfeldt and Thomas J. Holt; individual chapters, the contributors

British Library Cataloguing-in-Publication Data
A catalogue record for this book is available from the British Library

Library of Congress Cataloging-in-Publication Data
A catalog record for this book has been requested

ISBN: 978-1-138-62469-6 (hbk)
ISBN: 978-0-429-46059-3 (ebk)

Typeset in Bembo
by Apex CoVantage, LLC

Contents

Figures

Tables

Contributors

Dr Adam M. Bossler is a professor of criminal justice and criminology at Georgia Southern University. Over the last decade, he has published numerous articles and chapters on the application of criminological theories to various forms of cybercrime offending and victimization and the police response to cybercrime. His past work has been funded by the Bureau of Justice Assistance, the National Science Foundation, and the UK Home Office. He has also co-authored three books: *Cybercrime and Digital Forensics: An Introduction* (Routledge, 2018); *Cybercrime in Progress: Theory and Prevention of Technology-Enabled Offenses* (Routledge, 2016); and *Policing Cybercrime and Cyberterrorism* (2015).

Dr Roderic Broadhurst is a professor in the Department of Regulation and Global Governance, a director of the Cybercrime Observatory, and a fellow of the Research School of Asian and Pacific Studies, Australian National University. Recent publications include research on organized crime, violence, recidivism, and cybercrime, and he has worked with a wide variety of criminal justice agencies in Australia, China, and Cambodia.

Dr George W. Burruss is an associate professor in the Department of Criminology at the University of South Florida and affiliated with Florida Cyber, the Florida Center for Cybersecurity. His main research interests focus on criminal justice organizations, cybercrime, and law enforcement's response to cybercrime. He received his doctorate in criminology and criminal justice from the University of Missouri – St. Louis.

Dr Richard Clayton is the director of the Cambridge Cybercrime Centre based in the Computer Laboratory at the University of Cambridge. He has been researching cybercrime for decades and published widely on various types of criminality, always aiming to inform the analysis of the criminality with extensive real-world data.

Dr Maura Conway is a professor of international security in the School of Law and Government at Dublin City University (DCU) in Dublin, Ireland, and Coordinator of VOX-Pol, an EU-funded project on violent online political extremism (voxpol.eu). Prof. Conway's principal research interests are in the area of terrorism and the Internet, including cyberterrorism, the functioning and effectiveness of violent political extremist online content, and violent online radicalization. She is the author of over 40 articles and chapters in her specialist area(s). Prof. Conway is a member of the Academic Advisory Board of Europol's Counter-terrorism Centre.

Dr Cassandra Cross is a senior lecturer in the School of Justice, Queensland University of Technology. For over a decade, her research has focused on fraud, identity crime, and cybercrime more broadly. She is the co-author of the book *Cyber Frauds and Their Victims* (Routledge, 2017).

Dr David Décary-Hétu is an associate professor at the School of Criminology of the Université de Montréal. He has a PhD in criminology with a specialization in the study of illicit markets on the Internet and the darknet. David has developed massive data collection tools on online illicit activities and threat actors, as well as cryptocurrency flow analysis. His research was published in major scientific journals and has helped to understand the social structure of delinquent communities on the Internet, as well as the performance of offenders.

Cassandra Dodge, MS, is a doctoral student in the Department of Criminology at the University of South Florida. Her primary research interests are cybercrime and emerging technologies' effects on criminal behaviour and law enforcement policies. She holds memberships in the International Interdisciplinary Research Consortium on Cybercrime (IIRC), the Cybercrime Working Group of the European Society of Criminology (ESC), and the University of South Florida Cybercrime Working Group.

Dr Benoît Dupont is a professor in the School of Criminology at the Université de Montréal, where he also holds the Canada Research Chair in Cybersecurity and the Endowed Research Chair in the Prevention of Cybercrime. In 2014, he co-founded the Smart Cybersecurity Network (SERENE-RISC), one of Canada's Networks of Centres of Excellence. SERENE-RISC brings together researchers and stakeholders from academia, industry, and government. His research interests focus on the co-evolution of crime and technology, the social organization of online offenders, and the design and delivery of effective cybersecurity and cybercrime prevention policies.

Claudia Flamand is a master's student at the School of Criminology of the Université de Montréal. Her research interests focus on online drug dealing and the impact of technology on crime.

Dr Asher Flynn is a senior lecturer in criminology and director of the Social and Political Graduate Research Program at Monash University, Melbourne, Australia. Dr Flynn has published widely on image-based sexual abuse, sexual violence, plea negotiations, and access to justice. She is chief investigator on an Australian Research Council Discovery Project and recently completed two Australian Criminology Research Council–funded projects.

Dr W. Richard Goe is a professor in the Department of Sociology, Anthropology and Social Work at Kansas State University. He has published research on the effects of information technology on the organization of industries and regional development.

Dr Nicola Henry is a associate professor and vice-chancellor's principal research fellow in the Social and Global Studies Centre at RMIT University, Melbourne, Australia. Dr Henry's research investigates the prevalence, nature, and impacts of sexual violence and harassment, including the legal and non-legal responses to these harms in Australian and international contexts. Her current research focuses on image-based sexual abuse and other forms of technology-facilitated abuse.

Dr Alice Hutchings is a university lecturer in the Security Group and deputy-director of the Cambridge Cybercrime Centre at the Computer Laboratory, University of Cambridge. Specializing in cybercrime, she bridges the gap between criminology and computer science. Generally, her research interests include understanding cybercrime offenders, cybercrime events, and the prevention and disruption of online crime. She has had a varied research career, first researching cybercrime in the late 1990s, while working in industry (mainly relating to domain name misuse and software counterfeiting).

Dr Jurjen Jansen is a senior researcher at the Cybersafety Research Group of NHL Stenden University of Applied Sciences and the Dutch Police Academy. In 2018, he obtained his PhD in behavioural information security at the Open University of the Netherlands. His research interests include human aspects of information security, cybercrime, victimization, human–computer interaction, and behavioural change.

Dr Marleen Weulen Kranenbarg is an assistant professor at the Vrije Universiteit (VU) Amsterdam, the Netherlands. Her research mostly focuses on cyber-dependent offenders. In her doctoral dissertation she empirically compared traditional offenders to cyber-offenders. She recently started a large-scale longitudinal study into actual vs. perceived cybercriminal behaviour of offline vs. online social ties among youth. Marleen is also a research fellow of the NSCR (Netherlands Institute for the Study of Crime and Law Enforcement), board member of the ESC Cybercrime Working Group, and part of the steering committee of the IIRCC (International Interdisciplinary Research Consortium on Cybercrime).

Dr Jonathan Lusthaus is the director of The Human Cybercriminal Project in the Department of Sociology, Research Associate at the Centre for Technology and Global Affairs, and a research fellow at Nuffield College, University of Oxford. He is also an adjunct associate professor at UNSW Canberra Cyber. Jonathan's research focuses on the "human" side of profit-driven cybercrime: who cybercriminals are and how they are organized. Jonathan has written widely across academic, policy, and media publications.

He recently completed a seven-year global study on the organization of cybercrime published by Harvard University Press as *Industry of Anonymity: Inside the Business of Cybercrime.*

Dr Michael McGuire is a senior lecturer in criminology at the University of Surrey, UK, co-director of the Surrey Crime Research Lab, and chair of the Crime, Science and Politics Working Group of the European Society of Criminology (ESC). He has published widely on cybercrime, technology, and the justice system and produced numerous reports for government and industry, including his recent study of the cybercrime economy, *The Web of Profit.* He is currently leading the ACCEPT project (Addressing Cybersecurity and Cybercrime via a co-Evolutionary aPproach to reducing human-relaTed risks) funded by the UK Engineering and Physical Science Council.

Dr Jordana Navarro is an assistant professor of criminal justice at The Citadel who specializes in cybercrime victimization and domestic abuse. She obtained her credentials at the University of Central Florida, where she studied political science, criminal justice, and sociology with a concentration in criminology. Since obtaining her doctorate, she has published more than nine peer-reviewed journal articles and two book chapters and is the lead editor on one book with two more in preparation. Her most recent work focuses on the intersection between domestic abuse and cybercrime, and specifically investigates how perpetrators utilize technology to control and monitor survivors. Additionally, her recent work has focused on the experiences of male survivors both in terms of offline and online abuse.

Dr Sergio Pastrana is a visiting professor at the Department of Computer Science and Technology of the Universidad Carlos III de Madrid. His research focuses on cybercrime and computer security, concretely on the application of data science techniques to analyse social media artefacts and predict potential threats. His work has been published in high ranked peer-reviewed international journals and presented at top-tier conferences.

Alexandra Pimentel is a doctoral candidate in the Department of Sociology, Anthropology and Social Work at Kansas State University.

Dr Anastasia Powell is an associate professor in criminology and justice studies at RMIT University, Melbourne, Australia. Powell specializes in policy and prevention concerning violence against women, and her research lies at the intersections of gendered violence, justice, and digital culture. Powell's most recent book, *Digital Criminology* (2018, Routledge), examines crime and justice in a digital society through an interdisciplinary and critical lens. Meanwhile, her first book, *Sex, Power and Consent: Youth Culture and the Unwritten Rules*, discusses young people's negotiations of sexual consent.

Dr Ryan Scrivens is an assistant professor in the School of Criminal Justice at Michigan State University. He is also a visiting researcher at the VOX-Pol Network of Excellence, a research associate at the International

CyberCrime Research Centre at Simon Fraser University, and an associate editor of *Perspectives on Terrorism*. Ryan conducts problem-oriented interdisciplinary research, with a focus on the local, national, and international threat of terrorism; violent extremism; and hatred as it evolves online and offline. His primary research interests include terrorists' and extremists' use of the Internet, right-wing extremism, combating violent extremism, hate crime, and computational social science.

Dr Kevin F. Steinmetz is an associate professor in the Department of Sociology, Anthropology and Social Work at Kansas State University. He has published numerous journal articles in notable peer-reviewed journals as well as two books, *Hacked: A Radical Approach to Hacker Culture and Crime* (2016) and *Cybercrime & Society* (3rd edition, co-authored with Majid Yar).

Dr Steve van de Weijer is a researcher at the Netherlands Institute for the Study of Crime and Law Enforcement (NSCR). His research focuses on life-course criminology, intergenerational transmission of crime, and genetic influences on criminal behaviour. Over the last couple of years, he also published several studies on cybercrime victimization.

Dr Craig Webber is an associate professor of criminology at the University of Southampton, UK. Dr Webber teaches, researches, and publishes in the areas of cybercrime, psychology, and crime and criminological theory. He created the first joint honours degree in criminology and psychology at a Russell Group university that is accredited by the British Psychological Society and is currently the director of this programme.

Dr Michael Yip is a threat intelligence team lead specializing in tracking targeted cyberattacks from state-sponsored and financially motivated threat groups. He holds a PhD in web science and has extensive experience in law enforcement collaboration. He is also the founder of the threat intelligence portal ThreatMiner.

Preface

Rutger Leukfeldt and Thomas J. Holt

This book is about the human factor in cybercrime, including offenders, victims, and parties involved in the investigation and prosecution of cybercrime. Many assume cybercrimes are technical offences that require only technical solutions, such as antivirus programs or automated intrusion detection tools. However, these crimes are committed by individuals or networks of people, motivated by many of the same drives as observed with crime in physical spaces. Additionally, cybercrimes affect individuals (whether as private citizens or targets within organizations and governments) and are detected and pursued by criminal justice personnel. The human decision making at play influences the course of an offence, the justice response, and policymakers' attempts to legislate against these crimes.

The proliferation of the Internet and mobile devices led to the digitization of society, which encouraged the digitization of crime. On the one hand, there are new offences, such as hacking computer systems and databases containing personal data or shutting down websites or entire networks. On the other hand, there are traditional forms of crime where information and communication technology (ICT) plays an increasingly important role in the facilitation of the offence, such as using email and social media to engage in fraud.

The digitization of crime has consequences for the entire spectrum of criminology and criminal justice and raises myriad questions about the nature of offending and victimization. In 2017, these questions were summarized in the 'Research Agenda:The Human Factor in Cybercrime and Cybersecurity,' edited by Rutger Leukfeldt. For example:Are we dealing with the same offender populations who moved their activities online, or are there new offender types with distinct characteristics and motives? What foreground and situational characteristics influence the decision-making process of offenders? Which personal and situational characteristics provide an increased or decreased risk of cybercrime victimization? Which entities have the most pertinent role in protecting potential victims: the police, commercial cybersecurity companies, or Internet service providers (ISPs) and hosting providers?

Though extant research has attempted to address these questions individually, there is a need for a more robust volume that addresses these questions in a single place to provide a comprehensive view of our knowledge about the human factor in cybercrime. This book attempts to achieve this goal through a collection of works from the leading criminologists in the field examining all facets of victimization, offending, offender networks, and policy responses to these issues.

This book consists of four parts: (1) background on technology and cybercrime generally, (2) victims, (3) offenders, and (4) policing cybercrime. The first few chapters provide insights as to the nature of cybercrime, with Michael McGuire's chapter defining cybercrime, Adam Bossler's chapter exploring criminological theory and its application to these offences, and Flamand and Décary-Hétu's chapter on the open and dark web.

The second section considers the broader questions associated with cybercrime victimization, including those offences which may not be immediately identified by the individuals affected. Steve van de Weijer provides an excellent chapter on hacking and malware victimization affecting computer systems, while Jordana Navarro's chapter details the range of interpersonal violence affecting people that results from the technologies we use. A chapter from Anastasia Powell, Asher Flynn, and Nicola Henry also illustrates the ways that sexual violence is perpetrated through mobile devices and the Internet.

The third section provides deep insights on the nature of offending via technologically mediated means and encompasses a wide range of crimes using different methods. For instance, Thomas J. Holt provides a chapter on the nature of criminal subcultures and their operations online and offline. A chapter by Kevin Steinmetz, Richard Goe, and Alexandra Pimentel discusses the use of social engineering, or fraudulent misrepresentation, through technology to engage in crime. Marleen Weulen Kranenbarg discusses the ways we can account for cybercrime offending in her chapter examining a population of Dutch respondents. A chapter by Rutger Leukfeldt and Jurjen Jansen considers the structure of social networks of cybercriminals online and offline, while Jonathan Lusthaus examines the attitudes of law enforcement toward cybercriminals in Vietnam. Craig Webber and Michael Yip provide a chapter that encompasses cybercrime market operations online, while Ryan Scrivens and Maura Conway examine the misuse of technology for messaging campaigns by extremist groups. Lastly, a chapter by Roderic Broadhurst investigates the ways that sex offenders utilize technology to victimize youth.

The final section considers the nature of the criminal justice response to cybercrime, with a chapter by Cassandra Dodge and George Burruss on the agencies that investigate cybercrime; Cassandra Cross's chapter on innovative criminal justice strategies to aid victims; Benoît Dupont's chapter detailing the overall process of mitigating cybercrime markets; and the chapter of Alice Hutchings, Sergio Pastrana, and Richard Clayton in which they argue that big data solutions are not a silver-bullet approach to disrupting cybercrime, but rather represent a Red Queen's race, requiring constant running to stay in one spot.

Part I

Background

1 It ain't what it is, it's the way that they do it? Why we still don't understand cybercrime

Dr Michael McGuire

Introduction: definitions, concepts, and more definitions

On the face of it, our concept of cybercrime appears straightforward enough. It has usually been taken to signify "the occurrence of a harmful behaviour that is somehow related to a computer (Wall, 2001, p. 3) crime that is 'mediated' by a computer" (Thomas & Loader, 2000) or "crime that is facilitated or committed using a computer" (Gordon & Ford, 2006, p. 15). Put simply, cybercrime appears to 'involve' computers and to 'involve' crime. Of course, if defining cybercrime were *that* simple, this would be a very short chapter indeed. But upon closer inspection, it quickly becomes apparent that matters are not quite so simple as they first appear. Aside from the obvious need for a few more qualifications (what *type* of crime does cybercrime involve, for example?), this ostensibly straightforward definition soon begins to unravel when scrutinized in more detail. It is not just that agreeing upon an appropriate concept of 'computer' has been far from straightforward. The scope of such a definition also appears too wide. It would, for example, entail that the mere theft of a computer or that listening to a podcast whilst committing a burglary might 'involve' cybercriminality. A workable concept of cybercrime therefore seems to require a more precise sense of what being 'involved' in a criminal act entails. But defining what involvement means has been a recurring problem for any definition of cybercrime (Fafinski, Dutton, & Margetts, 2010; McGuire, 2012; Ngo & Jaishankar, 2017; Furnell, 2017).

Two wholly opposed responses to this conundrum seem possible:

- To argue that a viable concept/definition of cybercrime doesn't matter and that we can get on perfectly well measuring and responding to acts we call 'cybercrime' without any need for more developed conceptions.

OR

- To argue that a viable concept of cybercrime is an essential element of any successful response to it.

For those who incline towards the former view, debates about 'what cyber-crime is' or 'how it should be defined' will seem about as pointless as the medieval dispute about how many angels can dance on a pinhead. Surely, they might argue, any concept of cybercrime we elect to adopt has little or no effect upon what cybercriminals *do* or how police and the justice system respond to their actions? Thus, whilst such debates might be of interest in the seminar room, they distract from the 'real' purpose of dealing with cybercrime.

This position echoes what philosophers of science have called 'instrumentalism'[1] – a way of avoiding commitments to unnecessary concepts or entities (cf. Worrall, 1982). Instead of assuming that our concepts or definitions refer to real features of the world, instrumentalists argue that they are best viewed as tools for getting a job done. For example, Ernst Mach, the Austrian physicist and philosopher of science, famously refused to accept the reality of the (as yet undetected) atom in the late 19th century (Mach, 1893). For Mach, atoms were no more than a 'provisional aid' for more important tasks, such as collecting data, organizing and classifying it, and using this to make scientific predictions.

An instrumentalist position on the concept of cybercrime might involve similar reservations. That is, whilst it might be accepted that there is *something* 'out there' which we call cybercrime, debates about how we should define or conceptualize it are secondary issues to a more pressing concern – what we *do* about it.[2]

Do concepts or definitions of cybercrime matter?

The limited consensus around the objectivity of concepts has been a notorious problem within social science (Weber, 1904; Cunningham, 1973; Goodman, 1978). An instrumentalist approach to concepts and definitions of cybercrime might therefore be appealing in terms of theoretical as well as ontological economy. For just as we can *use* socio-economic metrics like 'poverty levels' or theoretical constructs like a 'habitus' whilst remaining agnostic about their existence or their precise conceptual conditions, our thinking about criminal justice issues appears similarly *underdetermined* by what we hold to exist or to be the case (Quine, 1975). For example, many legal theorists have held that criminal law is merely a tool or technique that can be used for certain useful ends and that any theoretical constructs they entail are not decisively real things (Duff & Green, 2011). Legal characterizations of crime play an inferior role to all that really matters – the consequences or outcomes of such characterizations (see Walker, 1980; Braithwaite & Pettit, 1990). In more overtly criminological terms, it could equally be argued that we can get on with thinking about and measuring crime without being beholden to absolute definitional and conceptual precision about crime. For example, we don't need to have an exhaustive consensus on what the concept of labelling amounts to, or even to accept it as a real factor in causing crime, in order to use it as a background assumption in shaping our responses to certain criminal acts. Something like this view can be discerned in the crime science approach, which has been notoriously keen to evade questions about the *causes* of crime (in particular, the social-cultural factors which lead to it) in favour of a focus on the outcomes of crime and the elements which contribute to this (the opportunity, the means, the outcome, etc.). Thus, for crime scientists, our conceptions of 'crime' or of 'criminals' have been far less important than our methods of preventing or responding to crime (Clarke, 2004).

But an instrumentalist position on crime/cybercrime would be just as unsatisfying (and ultimately unproductive) as instrumentalism about natural science objects like the atom has been. For whilst it might help in evading theoretical difficulties about the precise nature of computer-based offending, instrumentalism would simply postpone the question of what cybercrime may or may not be. Nor would it quite get us off the conceptual hook. Even if the measurement of cybercrime is preferred over its explanation, some reasonably clear conceptions about *what* is being measured need to be in place if measurement is to be accurate, or even possible at all. As Popper suggested when demonstrating the inadequacy of empiricist assumptions (1962), the imperative to go out and 'observe' always comes with a set of implicit conceptual pre-conditions ('observe what?,' 'observe how?,' etc.). Thus, whilst we might want to be agnostic about the reality of – say – IQ levels or absolute versus relative 'poverty,' effective measurement of intelligence or poverty requires us to be very clear about the boundaries of such concepts. More seriously, imprecision about concepts in social science contexts can often have negative (and very real) socio-economic consequences for at-risk groups in society. Ill-defined notions of poverty may result in inadequate support for the neediest, just as poorly formulated concepts of 'intelligence' might deprive worthy candidates of employment, promotion, or other opportunities. In other words, where key social variables or indicators are improperly conceptualized, direct and evidenced impacts upon the quality of everyday life may follow. This risk holds equally for conceptualizations within the criminal justice field. Indeed, the risk of inadequate conceptualization is arguably far more serious here, given the potential damage from issues like excess criminalization or miscarriages of justice which this might lead to.

It does not take too much reflection then to see how even slight variations in the way cybercrime is conceptualized can produce wildly differing ways of measuring or responding to it. For example:

Prevalence and seriousness. A familiar way in which the seriousness of any crime type is evaluated is in terms of the volume of recorded offending. This enables us to say (for example) that a crime has risen or fallen from previous years or that it is 'more or less' serious than other forms of offending. Claims around prevalence and seriousness have been especially common in discussions of cybercrime. For example, most researchers will be all too familiar with the alarming assertions about spectacular year-on-year increases in the volume of offending (see amongst many others Europol, 2016 or Ismail, 2017. See also McGuire, 2012, p. 77ff). In turn, such assertions have been used to justify claims that cybercrime is not just 'more serious' than traditional crime but is the *most* serious kind of criminal risk we now face (Muncaster, 2010; Allen, 2018). But imprecise conceptualizations about cybercrime and its measurement pose challenges to the credibility of such claims. Over what period has it been the 'most prevalent' form of crime? At what rate is it growing? And how can we be sure that the data chosen are appropriate for a particular definition/conceptualization of cybercrime? Even slight variations in what cybercrime is thought to encompass can produce radically different evaluations of how serious or how common it is assumed to be. Take, for example, an 'archetypical' cybercrime like card fraud. If our conceptualization of this were based solely on cards used over the Internet to purchase goods (called variously 'card not present' fraud, 'remote purchase' fraud, or 'e-commerce' fraud), then the fact that losses on this rose every year in the UK between 2011 and 2016 (FFA, 2018) might justify the claim that cybercrime exhibits a year-on-year upward trend and is therefore a 'very serious' from of crime.[3] If, on the other hand, this conceptualization was based more upon the use of counterfeit cards, then such claims might be less plausible, given that losses here have fallen from nearly £150 million annually in 2007 to only around £25 million annually in 2017. Indeed, such a drop in prevalence might suggest that cybercrime is far *less* serious than it is often portrayed.

Costings. Attempts to measure the cost of cybercrime have been a recurring feature of research in the area (Detica, 2011; Anderson et al., 2012, CSIS, 2014/2018). This economic focus has, more recently, been supplemented by attempts to construct metrics around the *revenues* which cybercrime generates (McGuire, 2018). But even the most cursory inspection of data in this area again demonstrates how sensitive cost estimates of cybercrime are to particular *conceptualizations* of cybercrime. For example, a recent evaluation of cybercrime costs by the UK Home Office (HO, 2018) found that by defining defacements to websites in terms of 'cybercriminal activity,' anything up to £1.6m in costs could be added to the overall total. Similarly, the estimate that, at a minimum, around $1.5tn worth of revenues is now being generated annually by cybercriminals (McGuire, 2018) is significantly contingent upon what kind of concept of cybercrime is being utilized. Where 'cybercrime' is defined more rigidly – that is, in terms of explicit computer-related misuse alone (such as the sale of exploits or malware), then revenues from activities like illicit online sales presumably ought not to be included. But the sale of items like counterfeit pharmaceuticals in online markets is a highly lucrative activity – generating up to $400bn annually (Scott, 2016). Thus, a decision to conceptualize cybercrime in certain ways can have major impacts upon the way its financial impacts are evaluated. And significantly lower cost/revenue estimates might produce very different kinds of criminal justice responses.

Legal responses. Notoriously, the legal background to cybercrime is riddled with conceptual ambiguities – not least because there is no specific *offence* of cybercrime within any jurisdiction (Wall, 2001). Instead, legislation typically relates to a variety of actions, often with little obvious unity or conceptual continuity. This has produced inevitable conceptual inconsistencies in the way cybercrimes are defined across differing jurisdictions (Brenner, 2012; Clough,

2014) and little clarity on how far the 'involvement' of a computer/network in a crime is required for it to be a *cyber*crime, rather than just a crime. Whilst current legislation is closely informed by the kinds of computer misuse deemed undesirable or harmful, it is equally clear that simple definitions of such misuse will produce *mala prohibita* offences – where it is the definition of illegality which produces the crime, rather than any conceptualization of cybercrime itself. Such definitional decisions do not just affect the legality/illegality of certain behaviours, but have a range of other important ancillary outcomes, for example, changes in crime figures, imprisonment levels, policing resources, and so on. Thus, if it was decided that legal definitions of cybercrimes should incorporate *any* kind of harm resulting from the use of computers, many more acts would now be criminal than is currently the case – such as addictive gaming, exploitative online pornography, and so on (McQuade, Gentry, Colt, & Rodgers, 2012; Nair, 2019). And this, of course, would then affect perceptions of the scale, seriousness, and so on of cybercrime.

Perpetrators and victims. The way that certain definitions and concepts of crime are developed often include or exclude certain types of offenders. For example, crimes falling under the definition of 'youth crime' would rule out crime committed by 60-year-olds, just as crimes conceptualized in terms of knife violence would probably not be classified under the concept of 'green crime.' Because the term 'cybercrime' does not quite so obviously correlate with specific perpetrator/victim types, profiling cybercriminals and their typical victims has been a highly uncertain method (see Rogers, 2006; Shoemaker & Kennedy, 2009; Kigerl, 2017; Martellozzo & Jane, 2017; Weulen Kranenbarg et al., 2019 for some possible approaches) However, it is certainly obvious that only very slight amendments to the conceptual conditions around cybercrime can induce changes in perceived perpetrator or victim groups. Suppose, for example, we stipulate that cybercrime refers only to 'misuse of computer networks by *individuals or criminal groups.*' Such a conceptualization would then rule out the very material possibility that other offender types – like nation-states – may also commit cybercrimes (cf. Kaplan, 2016; Maurer, 2016). Alternatively, if cybercrime is defined more widely – as '*any* criminal misuse of networks,' then other candidates, such as CEOs of leading tech firms, the UK government, or even the president of the United States emerge as possible cybercriminals. The fact that this is not a suggestion which has been very enthusiastically pursued by our criminal justice systems indicates the kind of subtle conceptual bias underlying our ideas of cybercrime – opaque though this structure may be.

Cybercrime as a technological concept

A striking observation about our concepts of cybercrime is the many and various names which have been used to refer to it. But whilst the sheer volume of terminology used might suggest fundamental differences in thinking, at least one common thread stands out. This is plain in the very earliest way of thinking about the misuse of information technology, which referred simply to 'crime by

computer' (Parker, 1976). In those pre-Internet days, this seemed an appropriate enough name, given that it was computers which were of primary criminal
interest, albeit largely as targets rather than tools. And though this term was outdated almost as soon as networked computing became widespread in the 1990s,
it is interesting to note how it clung on, remaining the single most common
way of referring to information technology crime until as recently as 2000.
As Table 1.1 indicates, other terms such as such as 'e-crime' (see for example
ACPO, 2009) 'online crime' (Holt, 2013), 'digital crime' (Bryant, 2008), 'netcrime' (Mann & Sutton, 1998), 'techno-crime' (Leman-Langlois, 2014), 'Internet crime' (Jewkes & Yar, 2013), or even 'hi-tech crime' (Brannigan, 2005) have
also been used at various times. But 'computer crime' remained by far the most
common way of defining the offence over this period – occurring in scholarly sources over twice as much as the terms 'cyber crime' or 'cybercrime' (see
Table 1.2). By 2018, however, the situation had significantly changed. 'Cybercrime' is by far now the preferred term of choice, with around 46,000 occurrences in scholarly sources between 2001 and 2018 – nearly twice as many as
'computer crime.'

Quite why the term 'cybercrime' has come to dominate the field remains
unclear. Perhaps the associations with 'cyberspace' have conferred an appealing

Table 1.1 Cybercrime terminology: 1995–2000[4]

Name	Occurrences
Computer Crime	2,760
Cybercrime or Cyber crime	1,476
E crime	585
Internet Crime	236
Digital Crime	50
Online crime	49
Virtual Crime	43
Techno-crime	19
Netcrime	17

Table 1.2 Cybercrime terminology: 2001–2018

Name	Occurrences
Cybercrime or Cyber crime	28,100 + 17,900 = 46,000
Computer Crime	19,000
E crime	15,800
Internet Crime	7,500
Digital Crime	3,830
Online crime	3,120
Virtual Crime	1,100
Techno-crime	55
Netcrime	216

exoticism upon it. Perhaps it is simply less unwieldy than the alternatives. Either way, as David Wall has reflected, "regardless of its merits or demerits the term 'cybercrime' has entered the public parlance and we are stuck with it" (2007, p. 11). Nonetheless, the term 'computer crime' remains surprisingly common and continues to occur in many sources – some highly respectable. For example, the U.S. Department of Justice retains a Computer Crime and Intellectual Property Section (CCIPS) which "prevents, investigates, and prosecutes computer crimes" (USDOJ, 2018). The continuing popularity of the term 'computer crime' may have something to do with the fact that it reflects relevant legislation like the Computer Misuse Act. But it also arguably presents evidence of two key conceptual biases in the way we (still) think about cybercrime.

The first is our continuing fixation upon the *computer* as the central factor in the commission of such a crime – a point I will return to shortly. The second more crucial bias (one that also applies to other terminologies like 'online crime') indicates a crucial (though underdiscussed) step in criminological history that took place with the emergence of cybercrime. This was the (informal) decision made to foreground *technology* as the central conceptual factor in such offending. Other precedents for crimes defined in terms of their technological character certainly exist (e.g. car crime, knife crime, etc.), but their scale and import seem relatively minor in comparison. In general, conceptions of crime have usually tended to be organized in terms of the type of harm which they involve, for example, manslaughter, rape, etc. (crimes against the person) or burglary, fraud, etc. (property crimes), rather than any specific tools used to commit an offence. Though invoking technology as the central conceptual factor in cybercrime now seems obvious, this was by no means a given. Other terminology in circulation like 'cyberspace' or 'virtual crime' offered a very different set of conceptual possibilities, as we will see shortly.

Overall, the consensus that tool-based, technology-driven criteria represent the key conceptual condition for cybercrime has been a mixed blessing. For whilst this appears to confer a kind of unity upon some very different forms of offending (Poonia, 2014), the unity proposed is also questionable. In general, science has been sceptical about categorizing diverse phenomena under the same concept without sound evidence. Indeed, a key factor behind the scientific revolutions of the 16th century was the decision to confer conceptual unity *only* where objects shared identifiable structural properties, rather than mere epiphenomenal similarities. A good example of this was the saga around the proposed element 'phlogiston' (Chang, 2010). Many assumed that phlogiston must be real, because it helped explain why ostensibly very different phenomena like fire or chilli both manifested heat. We know that this was a case of the conceptual cart going before the horse. There are very different underlying physical causes behind the heat of fire and the heat of chilli, and the attempt to confer unity via phlogiston turned out to be a conceptual (and methodological) red herring. Natural science therefore offers important warnings about imposing conceptual unity where none really exists, and cybercrime theorists would do well to heed them when assuming that appeals to technology suffice to make every crime where information technology is implicated a 'cybercrime.'

Aside from this methodological concern, two other broad challenges arise from the assumption that technology-based criteria form the unifying factor in defining cybercrime:

1   What *kind of technology* is best associated with cybercrime?
2   What *causal/agentic role* should be attributed to such technologies?

The first of these challenges centres upon the ephemeral, constantly changing character of technology and the concern that our conceptualizations of cybercrime may inherit these instabilities. Even the technology originally taken to be central to cybercrime – the computer itself – has exhibited significant discontinuities in the course of its development (Ifrah, 2001). The power, functionality, and operational scale of modern computers alone arguably make them a very different kind of artefact from those under discussion in the earliest days of cybercrime. And this raises immediate and profound questions about whether it is 'the same' tool involved across every instance of cybercrime. Moreover, computing involves a swathe of subsidiary technologies, all of which have undergone their own processes of change and development, many of which have radically shifted the dynamics of human–computer interaction (HCI) (Carroll, 2003), for example, the central processing unit (CPU), random access memory (RAM) and how this links to performance, graphics units and the technology of the visual display unit (VDU), or user interfaces like the keyboard and touchscreens. In effect, the computer is really not a 'thing' at all; it is more like what Deleuze called an "assemblage" (Deleuze & Guattari, 1993). Assemblages lend a sense of unity to collections of otherwise distinct objects, but we should be aware that this is as much a unity that we impose as it is something natural or conceptually intrinsic. Nor is this merely an abstract reflection, for it is often' the elements *within* a computing assemblage that are as key to the commission of cybercrime as the computer itself. For example, touchscreens may create a very different set of criminal opportunities than a keyboard, just as a higher-performance CPU may facilitate more extensive botnet attacks than less able varieties.

The 'which kind of technology' challenge is equally affected by the distinction between software and the hardware of computing. Very early cybercrime, which had to be effected by operating systems like MS-DOS, clearly generated very different kinds of criminal opportunity from those which emerged with the advent of graphical user interfaces (GUIs) or graphical/icon-based operating systems. And, of course, there is a huge variety of other kinds of software crucial to cybercrime, all of which is continually in the process of upgrade or variation. Exploiting a backdoor in Windows, using JavaScript to conduct a browser-based attack, or installing a mobile banking Trojan via Short Message Service (SMS) cannot be assumed to be similar actions merely because we call them 'cybercrimes.' And they clearly differ radically from the varieties of infection and attack available ten years ago. All of this raises difficult questions about what exactly we think we are conceptualizing when we associate 'computers' with our definitions of cybercrime.

As already suggested, any conceptualization of cybercrime dependent upon computing technology must, of course, also accommodate the fact that cybercrime requires mass computing resources to be *connected* – via the technology of the Internet or other digital/information networks. Without this, most of the offending behaviours we think of as 'cybercrimes' simply could never have occurred. As the conceptual landscape around cybercrime developed, terminology like 'Internet crime' or 'online crime' (Jewkes, 2013) represented attempts to acknowledge this additional form of technological dependence. But this was hardly very comprehensive. As suggested earlier, the governing language continued to centre upon computers as the primary cybercriminal tool until at least the mid-2000s. And by then, other technological shifts now integral to cybercriminality had also begun to emerge, most obviously in the form of the 3/4G or Wi-Fi–enabled smartphone (Hypponen, 2006; Pritchard, 2016). There is a very real danger, then, that no matter how rapidly definitions of cybercrime based on technology respond to technological change, there will always be a risk that they soon become outdated, inadequate conceptual representations of what is happening on the ground. As new ways of accessing computing power and delivering computing services continue to develop, from cloud-based computing or 'appification' to enhanced virtualization (Hooper, Martini, & Choo, 2013; Kolthof, 2015), shifts in the nature of criminal opportunity will continue to emerge. Such shifts make it hard to see how technology-based definitions of cybercrime will ever remain stable or comprehensive enough for them to be genuinely useful. But is this a problem? Couldn't a concept of cybercrime which continually mutates to reflect technological change still be acceptable? Possibly, though two factors would seem to arbitrate against this. First, it seems reasonable to ask whether concepts referring to objects which constantly change are really concepts of the same thing at all. Given that criminology and criminal justice can utilize similar concepts of crimes like murder or theft to those used 1,000 years ago, a more stable conceptualization of cybercrime does not seem like an unreasonable requirement. Second, we may well wonder whether technology-based conceptualizations of cybercrime will ultimately become superfluous. For if, as seems likely, the social world becomes so striated with information technology, the technology may become all but invisible. At which point the implications of Douglas Adam's observation that technology is only a word for something that doesn't work yet (1999) become more apparent. For this suggests that the technologies upon which cybercrime depends become so embedded within everyday life that meaningful distinctions between 'crime' and 'cybercrime' are no longer sustainable. One thing, however, is certainly clear: whatever kind of technology-based conceptualizations of cybercrime remain in circulation in 50 years, they are unlikely to be similar to our current ways of thinking.

Cybercrime, novelty, and concepts of agency

The second, more challenging difficulty which arises from technology-based conceptualizations of cybercrime centres on 'how involved' we take the tool to be in causing the offence. Because our very concept of crime and the culpabilities around it are dependent upon who (or what) we take to have caused the crime, a good conceptualization of cybercrime ought to be very clear about agency (cf. Norrie, 1991 for a useful discussion of criminal causation and agency). One early example of the many difficulties attached to this question emerged within academic circles in the debates around how 'novel' an offence we could take cybercrime to be. Was it 'new wine in no bottles,' 'old wine in new bottles,' or 'new wine in old bottles' (Wall, 1999; Grabosky, 2001)? But the question of how far cybercrime was different from traditional crime really came down to the extent to which the role of information technology in sponsoring it sufficed to causally differentiate cybercrime from, say, 'physical' frauds, thefts, and the like.

Getting clear about agency is obviously crucial to our understanding of cybercrime – both in terms of *how* it happens and the criminal culpabilities which result. Is technology wholly and completely central to the crime, is it only peripheral, or is the situation somewhere in between? At some point, technology-based conceptualizations of cybercrime inevitably require us to decide where upon this 'causal spectrum' of technological support cybercriminality is manifested. It is as a result of deliberations upon this question that the most familiar and most widely used conceptualizations of cybercrime have emerged. These centre upon the provision of two to three levels of technical agency – from complete involvement to the merely incidental. An early source for this approach can be found in Carter (1995) who conceptualized cybercrime (or 'computer crime' as it was inevitably referred to at that point) in terms of four main categories:

1   Computer as a target – which is specified to include not just attacks or sabotage on the computer but also intellectual property (IP) theft.
2   Computer as instrument – which includes things like credit card fraud or misuse of automated teller machines (ATMs).
3   Computer as incidental – where the computer is related to criminal activity but is not essential to it – for example, where a gang member uses it as a resource to store data or to carry out money laundering calculations.
4   Computer as vehicle for 'recently invented crimes' – such as an object of theft itself, pirating software, and so on.

Something like these distinctions were also to be found in early UK Home Office research (cf. Morris, 2004) which conceptualized cybercrime in terms of a distinction between crimes where the computer serves as a *target* or where it serves as an *intermediary,* The latter comprises its role as a medium, i.e. as a "distribution channel for offenders (e.g. the online selling of obscene material)"

(Morris, 2004, p. 3), and its role as a *facilitator* (e.g. as a medium of criminal conspiracy). But there is an obvious problem with all these approaches. By incorporating the device as *both* target and tool within a single taxonomy, important questions around agency and the causal role of the computer in facilitating cybercrime are blurred. For example, Carter's scheme, on the one hand, stipulates that IP theft involves the computer as a *target*, though, of course, another computer is also needed as the instrument for obtaining the IP. And in any case, it is surely the IP which is the target rather than the computing system itself. Similarly, a computer may be a *target* of a denial of service attack, but these cannot be effected without the use of another computer as an instrument or tool.

Anyone familiar with the literature around cybercrime will already be aware of the varied terminology seeking to capture how computers contribute to crime. Thus, we see talk of the computer serving as an 'instrument,' a 'vehicle,' a 'facilitator,' or a 'medium' for crime (POST, 2006; Gercke, 2012). There can be computer 'involvement,' computer 'assistance,' or crimes that are 'related' to computers. Similarly, reference has been made to crimes that are 'computer focussed' (Furnell, 2001) or crimes that are 'committed' by computers (Gordon & Ford, 2006). The proliferation of such terminology is an indication of the uncertainty around what precisely computers 'do' in cybercrime and how best to conceptualize this. It is a question that has never been satisfactorily answered, but one step in the right direction was seen in David Wall's 'elimination test.' This aimed to analyse cybercriminal acts by "considering what would remain if the Internet were to be removed from the equation" (2005, p. 310). The result was a conceptualization of cybercriminality which proposed a kind of three-point level of technical involvement:

> "[T]*raditional*" crimes in which the internet is used, usually as a method of communication, to assist with the organisation of a crime (for example, by paedophiles, drug dealers etc.). Remove the internet and the criminal behaviour persists because the offenders will revert to other forms of communication. *hybrid cyber-crimes*: "traditional" crimes for which the internet has opened up entirely new opportunities (for example, frauds and deceptions, as well as the global trade in pornographic materials). Take away the internet and the behaviour will continue by other means, but not in such great numbers or with so large a scope. Finally, there are the *true cybercrimes*. These are solely the product of the internet and can only be perpetrated within cyberspace.
>
> (ibid, p. 310)

At one extreme, then, are 'true' cybercrimes (Wall also refers to 'pure' cybercrimes in this context) – where the Internet/computer is the primary causal factor and cannot be removed if the crime is to be possible. At the other end of this causal spectrum are 'traditional' crimes where the Internet may be used, but only incidentally. In between are the 'hybrid' crimes – which can also be enacted without any involvement from digital technology, though this may open up 'new opportunities.' Wall's typology helped untangle some of the confusions around technical agency, but came with other unresolved complications. For example, his definition of true cybercrimes (which 'only happen in cyberspace') depended upon a viable distinction between cyberspace and our more usual 'physical' or other space. But, as will be discussed shortly, this distinction has always been a questionable one, and there is nothing in Wall's account which indicates what the 'additional' component provided by cyberspace might be. Questionable, too, is the stipulation that true cybercrimes are 'solely the product of the Internet' when clearly they are the product of a complex human–technical assemblage which certainly requires digital networks, but also computers, syntax, and, of course, the *mens rea* of criminal intention on the part of humans which makes the act criminal in the first place.

Nonetheless, these kinds of reflection provided important conceptual groundwork for a typology of cybercrime which has subsequently become one of the more familiar ways of defining it. Elements of this typology, which attempts to further clarify the causal role of computing technologies in effecting cybercrime, were discussed informally for a number of years within the UK Home Office and related circles. A more formal presentation occurred within one of the first systematic overviews of the most reliable evidence around cybercrime (McGuire & Dowling, 2013). Like some of the previous distinctions set out earlier, the typology also utilized three categories, though each was now more fully centred upon the degree of technical involvement in effecting a cybercrime.

1   *Cyber-dependent Crime*[5] – These involve crimes which are in some sense 'dependent' upon the computer, without which they could not happen. Corresponding to the idea of a true/pure cybercrime, these include actions like malware creation and delivery, distributed denial of service (DDoS) attacks and so on. This category also echoes the U.S. Department of Justice (DOJ) schema to an extent though, as suggested, that categorization focuses more upon the idea of the computer as a *target* of offending (i.e. a subject of infection, DDoS attack, etc.). By contrast, the category of cyber-dependent offending is aimed directly at the commission of criminal acts and the extent to which networked computers support them.
2   *Cyber-enabled Crime* – These involve cybercrimes where computers/networks play a role, but where the crime could be conducted without them. In line with Wall's elimination test, cyber-enabled crimes are enhanced by technology but would continue to exist if networked computing were not available. Fraud is one of the more obvious examples here because deception is, of course, a long-established method of illicit acquisition. However, common instances of online fraud techniques like the notorious 419 scam or the use of phishing emails have clearly been significantly furthered by the advent of mass digital connectivity.

3   *Cyber-assisted Crimes* – As with cyber-enabled crime, the computer is not essential to such crimes, but here its role is even more incidental (i.e. in storing data or in facilitating criminal communication/conspiracy). This category has some continuities with Wall's category of *traditional* crimes which can "assist with the organisation of a crime."

This approach, which I will henceforth refer to as the 'tripartite' definition, offers us one of the clearest conceptualizations to date of the degree to which networked computing is thought to further cybercrime and, ergo (if cybercrime is defined as a technical form of crime), of cybercrime itself. It also offers two further advantages. First, the typology is useful in emphasizing why certain types of cybercrime – like malware distribution or botnet attacks – have been granted the level of attention (and resourcing) to which we have become accustomed. In a world that has become so functionally and economically dependent upon information technology, criminal activity which is both dependent upon this technology and which targets it is inevitably likely to be regarded as 'more serious' than other varieties (justifiably or not). And because the cyber-dependent variety of cybercrime is the one where information technology has the greatest level of causal involvement, it also appears to offer the greatest contrast with traditional crime. The typology also helps explain one of the recurring problems in the perception of cybercrime. For with this apparent novelty come many of the unknowns and the 'culture of fear' (Wall, 2008) which has grown up around it.

A further advantage of the typology is its clarification of why we are inclined to consider cyber-enabled crime *as* cybercrime, even though such crimes do not, strictly speaking, require the networked computer for their commission. For there is one crucial regard in which cyber-enabled crime *does* require technological support – as crimes which "can *be increased in their scale or reach* by use of computers, computer networks or other forms of information communications technology" (McGuire & Dowling, 2013, chapter 2, p. 4). In this way, cyber-enabled crime can be seen as distinct from traditional crime because the technology adds to or enhances the number of victims (its *greater scale*). For example, a 419 email can be forwarded to millions of users rather than the thousands a postal version of the fraud might reach. Similarly, one single successful misuse of stolen credit card details can result in millions of dollars of losses, rather than the thousands of dollars of losses which was more the norm from traditional fraud. The technology also allows crimes that were previously limited in terms of their causal range to be extended over far greater distances than previously (their *greater reach*). Indeed, cybercrime exhibits classic 'time-space compression effects' (Harvey, 1990), in that there are no spatial limits upon cybercriminal actions, provided a victim's location can be accessed by the network (Yar, 2006; McGuire, 2008). In effect this means that digital technology now allows criminals – any criminal – to commit crime almost anywhere across the globe. In this way, spatial proximity – once a prerequisite for most forms of theft – has been rendered irrelevant by digital networks.

Problems with the tripartite definition

Whilst the tripartite definition is the closest we have to anything like a standard conceptualization of cybercrime at present, it is by no means universally accepted. At least two broad challenges confront its general utility:

1 Flaws or internal inconsistencies within the definition, in particular, continuing failures to better account for digital technologies' role in *causing* cybercrime.
2 Alternative approaches to defining cybercrime which draw upon other ways of conceptualizing it.

One of the most obvious examples of the first problem centres on the way that the tripartite categories often seem to crosscut in the commission of cybercrimes, raising questions about how definitionally distinct they really are. Take, for example, the distribution of a banking Trojan, or malware which results in financial losses to customers. Prima facie, this appears to be a definitive cyber-dependent crime because, without networked computers, there would be no malware, nor indeed any way of distributing it. But then suppose that the malware got into the banking system because an infected link within a phishing email had been clicked, or because an employee had been tricked into handing over a password. In that case we would seem to have a *cyber-dependent* crime being committed as a result of *cyber-enabled*, or even traditional, human factors.

Conversely, suppose a cyber-enabled crime like stalking or the sending of hate mail occurs. But what if the stalking was facilitated by personal details acquired in a botnet or DDoS attack? Should this then be counted as more of a cyber-dependent crime than a cyber-enabled one? It seems that the distinction on its own may be inadequate to characterize many cybercrimes or, at the very least, we need a more complex way of interweaving and overlaying dependency and enablement in cybercrimes.

A second issue around technical involvement relates to a problem of 'causal excess' – specifically the fact that, with sufficient imagination, almost *any* crime can be made into a 'cyber-enabled' crime. For example, if a mobile phone is used to arrange a bank robbery, is that enabled by digital technology? If a database is used to evaluate a victim's movements prior to a rape, is that cyber-enabled? Whilst it is true that the category of 'cyber-assisted' can be used to accommodate crimes where the network plays a lesser, ancillary role in an offence, the boundaries are far from clear. As a result, either we permit enablement too great a role, or we are drawn into unclear subjectivities about the grey area between an enabled and assisted cybercrime.

A third problem of this kind relates to how substantively the dependency/enablement distinction clarifies what it is meant to clarify – the extent to which digital technology combines with human agency (or not) to *cause* a crime. One issue here is whether a concept like enablement is really a causal concept at all. As some commentators have pointed out (cf. McGuire, 2014), an outcome might be enabled by a tool, without that tool actually *causing* the outcome. For example, a match thrown onto some dry wood may be an 'enabler' for a subsequent fire – but it is only when petrol is added that the conflagration properly begins. So, is it the enabling match, the petrol, or the wood which constitutes the 'cause' of the fire? Or do we need to say that it is all three? The fact that reference to enablement cannot provide an answer on its own is a sure sign that appeals to enablement do not establish causality, whether in the context of computer crime or elsewhere. Worse still, there are suspicions that attempting to define enablement may result in conceptual circularity. For example, if we define enablement as 'assisting or furthering an outcome,' all we are really saying is that it *enables* the outcome. This is a tautology, and tautologies are invariably a sign of explanatory failure rather than substantive insight.

For many (see Furnell, 2017), the problem with the dependency/enablement distinction is that it is ultimately only a distinction about the *tools* of cybercrime, rather than the crime itself. And if the distinction is indifferent to the 'criminality in cybercrime,' there must be obvious doubts about its adequacy as a basis for defining cybercrime at all. These doubts are perhaps symptomatic of a more general issue about the tripartite approach. That is, whether it merely defers the question of technological involvement to another level, without ever really solving the problem. It is clear enough, for example, that distinguishing between dependency/enablement has no legal weight and could not be used to decide any definitive degree of technological support for a criminal act. Indeed, the law has been notoriously indifferent to technical involvement in assigning culpability for cybercrimes. Instead, it is the traditional criteria of *mens rea* which continues to be the determining factor (Brenner, 2012). Thus, whilst we gain something by demarcating these 'three degrees' of technological involvement, questions about how much or how little remain far from clear. And if cybercrime is to be conceptualized and defined in terms of the role of technology in furthering it, this is a luxury which we cannot afford.

Beyond technology – the way that they do it?

A second challenge for the tripartite definition is how well it stands up to other ways of conceptualizing and defining cybercrime. Not everyone has agreed that definitions based upon technology or degrees of technical involvement offer the best approach, and alternative ways of conceptualizing cybercrime have accordingly been sought. Identifying plausible alternatives is of clear interest to human-factor approaches to cybercrime (Leukfeldt, 2017; Nurse, 2018), as well as for our understanding of cybercrime as a whole. For if we can get beyond the provisional, ephemeral character of technology-dependent definitions, then the prospect of more substantive and durable conceptualizations opens up, ones that might better capture the complex interweaving between human and technical agency within cybercrime. Even better, such conceptualizations might also help sidestep the complications of having to detail the precise causal contribution of technology to such offences. Two other broad ways of thinking about cyber-crime might offer such an alternative:

1   Cybercrime defined in terms of **action** – via typologies of cybercriminal acts.
2   Cybercrime defined in terms of **situation** – via its environmental or spatial context.

Cybercrime as criminal acts

Action-based conceptualizations of cybercrime help evade the necessity of invoking a technological component by focussing more directly upon its criminal aspects. If it is accepted that cybercrime is a novel kind of crime, one seemingly easy way of developing this approach has been to simply attach the prefix 'cyber-' to traditional offences. But though convenient, this has hardly been a very satisfying solution. In the end, defining cybercrime in terms of criminal outcomes like 'cyberfrauds,' 'cyberstalking,' or 'cyberterrorism' may be straightforward, but offers little more than an exercise in semantics, rather than an identification of substantive criminality or criminal change.

Better conceptualizations of this kind have therefore tended to utilize more developed taxonomies. Several offence-based conceptualizations of cybercrime which emerged in the early 2000s are suggestive in this regard. Wall's (2001) centred upon an attempt at simplifying the many varieties of cyber-offences into a four-part typology as so:

1   *Cyber-trespass* – Echoing its pre-digital counterpart, this category groups together cyber-offences which involve 'crossing, or violating boundaries' – though such boundaries are digital rather than physical. For example, the cyber-trespass category might comprise offences such as hacking, or accessing data without permission.
2   *Cyber-deception and theft* – This category comprises offences such as online frauds and IP theft which are usually treated as separate (see later).
3   *Cyber-porn and obscenity* – In addition to the familiar range of child pornography–related offences, Wall's category incorporated other types of online sexual behaviours which may be frowned upon but which are often not specifically criminal – for example, the distribution of pornography.
4   *Cyber-violence*. This category largely refers to the kind of emotional violence that can be enacted online, such as bullying or harassment. However, reference to more extreme acts – such as cyberterrorism – is also made.

Other prominent examples of offence-based conceptualizations of cybercrime can be seen within the Council of Europe's Convention on Cybercrime (COE, 2001) or more recently in the DOJ sentencing manual for cybercrime (USDOJ, 2010). These approaches are less concerned with simplification and focus more on the attempt to be comprehensive. The Cybercrime Convention's schema is significant because it forms part of what aspires to be (and in fact is) the only globally recognized agreement around cybercrime. It defines cybercrime in terms of five categories and sub-offences within them – substantially less than the very large number of offences denoted within the DOJ schema:

1 *Offences against the confidentiality, integrity, and availability of computer data and systems*:

- Illegal interception
- Data interference
- System interference
- Misuse of devices

2 *Computer-related offences:*

- Forgery
- Fraud

3 *Content-related offences:*

- Child pornography

4 *Offences related to copyright and related rights.*
5 *Ancillary liability:*

- Illegal access

There are some obvious advantages to keeping definitions of cybercrime firmly centred upon crime itself. Legal, policing, and criminal justice issues are kept to the forefront and many of the more abstract questions about 'what cybercrime is' are avoided. And because it was often far from clear what to include as instances of cybercriminality in its very early form, offence-based conceptualizations were helpful in pinning down the kinds of new (and old) offending types which might be considered to constitute it. Such schemas were thus very effective initially in highlighting the sheer range of criminal activity that could be considered 'cybercrime.'

But however useful such approaches might have first appeared, they are eventually confronted by the problem which any attempt to define a crime type by way of its instances must deal with. This is the inherent variability in what counts as an instance of crime. Whether or not one accepts that there is no 'ontological reality' to crime (Hillyard & Tombs, 2004), it is clear that categories cannot always be fixed by their instances. For example, a notorious problem in conceptualizing cybercrime has been that what counts as a crime in one jurisdiction may not in another (Koops & Brenner, 2006; Schultz, 2008). Instances of crime can also vary over time according to changing opinion and cultural differences in what is considered to be harmful. But when new offences do come along, as they so often do in the context of cybercrime, the inadequacy of offence-based conceptualizations becomes uncomfortably apparent. Approaches which focus more upon general taxonomies (like Wall's) than specific lists of offences offer a way around this, but only if the categories are themselves are reasonably comprehensive – which in Wall's case they clearly were not.

There is a further, even more important drawback for attempts to define cybercrime by way of specific examples of offending. This rests upon the observation that such approaches do not especially distinguish cybercrimes from traditional crime *unless* it is by reference to the very thing such approaches are supposed to help avoid – the technological basis for cybercrime. For example, in Wall's schema the 'cyber-trespass' or 'cybertheft' categories all incorporate the ubiquitous 'cyber-' prefix. But then their definition (and ergo the definition of cybercrime) requires some explanation of what 'cyber' entails. And this inevitably requires the specification of some kind of technological component. Thus, not only are we forced back into a conceptual dependence upon technology but problems about attributions of causality and culpability re-emerge. For example, what level of technical involvement makes a trespass a 'cybertrespass,' or a theft a 'cybertheft'? A similar problem afflicts the CoE approach and other more offence-focused conceptualizations. For example, the 'category of computer-related offences' clearly requires the concept of a computer, just as the category of content-related offences implies involvement from technology; otherwise, such offences are simply child pornography offences and carry nothing 'cybercriminal' about them. Other varieties of crime-focussed typologies purporting to define cybercrime – especially those which centre upon perpetrators or victims (Poonia, 2014) – are beset by a similar problem. For here, too, there is nothing especially distinctive about a cybercrime victim or a perpetrator of cybercrime *unless* the technological element is specified. There is, for example, no viable distinction between a victim of hate speech and a victim of *online* hate speech unless we also specify that the perpetrator–victim relationship was enacted 'online,' or by way of digital technology.

Location and spatiality: cybercrime as cyberspace crime?

From the very beginning, cybercrime was as much associated with its environment as with its technological means. Famously (or infamously), the very origin of the term cybercrime derives from William Gibson's (1989) metaphor of a cyberspace – a new, quasi-magical horizon of human interaction free from the shackles of "meatspace." Cyberspace represented a 'consensual hallucination' where new rules – and new forms of deviance – were to become the norm. Cyberspace clearly has an implicit technological component, given that its emergence was dependent upon connected digital machines, as "a graphical representation of data abstracted from the banks of every computer in the human system . . . lines of light ranged in the non-space of the mind, clusters and constellations of data" (1989, p. 128). There is also a techno-scientific component in the relationship between the term and the cognate field of *cybernetics* (Wiener, 1948) which focuses upon machinic (and organic) systems. The concept of cyberspace also inherits technological connotations from the way the 'cyber-' prefix was utilized in various popular cultural/science fiction sources from the 1960s onwards, in particular, the term 'cyborg' (cybernetic organism) developed by Manfred Clynes and Nathan Kline (Clynes & Kline, 1960) to define human/machinic fusions or the 'Cybermen' human/robot enemies of the TV science fiction hero Dr Who.

But though the concept of 'cyberspace' has an obvious technological aspect, it came with other, more spatial, connotations which seemed to offer a different way of thinking about cybercrime. As a result, a distinct conceptualization of cybercrime as 'cyberspace crime' (Wall, 2003) seemed plausible, inviting researchers, law enforcement, and policymakers to explore what was different about crime and crime control within this distinctive spatial medium. The new ways of exploiting distance, connecting with victims, or assuming anonymous transitory identities seemingly offered by cyberspace certainly helped the situational/opportunistic aspects of cybercrime come into better focus. So, too, did many of the ostensible 'problems' in controlling cybercrime. For example, how was traditional policing to be adapted to a non-physical space (Dolliver & Dolliver, 2016)? Were older laws, tailored primarily towards misconduct within 'normal space' likely to still be fit for purpose, or was a whole new legislative landscape now required (Cavazos & Morin, 1994; Lessig, 1999)? Did cyberspace change the relationship between perpetrator and victim? And so on.

Such questions proved to be strangely compelling, not least because they helped emphasize the novelty of cybercrime and to justify the sense of alarm which came with this variety of offending from the outset. But the greater theoretical flexibility seemingly on offer came at a price. For the term 'cyber' was often used interchangeably with the term 'virtual,' and the sense that cybercrime was somehow 'virtual' or 'non-physical' did nothing to clarify how best to tackle it. Rather, this idea has been directly responsible for three of the most damaging truisms associated with cybercrime. Specifically:

1 Because cyberspace is a 'new' space, it is like a digital Wild West – ergo ungovernable, unpoliceable, and beyond the capacity of law to manage.
2 Because cyberspace is a space of unimaginable opportunity, cybercrime has grown exponentially and continues to expand in unprecedented ways.
3 Because cyberspace is 'non-physical,' a divide between 'traditional' and 'cyber' crime emerges, requiring different kinds of theoretical responses and distinct forms of intervention.

Invoking cyberspace as a basis for conceptualizing cybercrime has therefore proved to be somewhat of a mixed blessing, especially because the justifications for invoking cyberspace have always been questionable. As other commentators have pointed out (Koppell, 2000), it was never quite clear why networked computing should come with its own 'space' any more than previous networked communication technologies did. And because the development of the telegraph network or the phone network did not prompt any need to conceptualize a 'phone-space' or a 'telegraph-space,' the sense that cyberspace was more convenient fabrication than fact never quite went away.

Location and spatiality: hyperspace, criminal enhancement, and hypercrime?

For many, the construct of a cyberspace came with a lurch towards a kind of (criminological) magical realism that was an unacceptable price to pay. Especially when its fictions generated moral panics about perpetually rising cybercriminality or concerns whether cyberspace crime would test the capacity of criminal justice systems beyond their limit. Worse, the culture of fear that developed around cybercrime began to promote increasingly coercive and extra-judicial responses. Very quickly it became a kind of received wisdom that 'special powers,' endless new laws, and the limitation of rights were the price we had to pay in order to protect ourselves in this new and unfathomable space. Pragmatic questions about effective crime control became submerged within another kind of agenda driven, on the one hand, by private tech companies eager to acquire unprecedented access to personal information and, on the other, by governments and policing organizations seduced by the rhetoric of crime explosions and threats to civil society.

Thus, rather than being drawn into questionable metaphysical assumptions which served only to mystify rather than to clarify cybercrime, some theorists (for example Yar, 2006; McGuire, 2008; Jaishankar, 2008) sought to explore other kinds of spatial approaches. These attempted to explain how digital technology was expanding criminal opportunity whilst remaining clear about the role of human agency in exploiting this. By revisiting ideas around the relationship between the human body and technology seen in the work of thinkers such as Kapp (1877), Freud (1962), or McLuhan (1964), it became easier to appreciate why technology never operates in isolation or independently of human action. For in just the same way as the 'guns don't kill people, people do' argument overlooks the role of what Latour calls 'the actant' (2005), a human-technical agent whose collective actions underlie gun crime, conceptions of cyberspace (and its technologies) as *distinct* from physical space and physical action are similarly flawed. What we really see are complex interweavings between technology and the body – producing *enhancements or extensions* to human agency, for example, information and communication technology's (ICT's) role in extending agency over distance or in enhancing it by augmented force. Key to the way technology has extended contemporary agency has been the exponential surge in connectivity provided by digital networks. The 'hyperconnectivity' which results so expands human interaction that a state of what McLuhan called "allatonceness" (1967, p. 63) emerges, one where we can be connected *to* anyone, *from* anywhere, *at* any time. Instead of cyberspace, hyperconnectivity arguably generates a *hyperspace*, and it is this which engenders the very new kinds of socio-relational possibilities that are emerging (Quan-Haase & Wellman, 2006; Friedman, 2013; Vitale, 2014).

But a hyperconnected world inevitably produces negative as well as positive outcomes and a willingness on the part of some to exploit the new opportunities created by hyperconnection for personal gain. In this view, then, cybercrime can be conceived of as *hyperconnected* crime – 'hypercrime' if you will. This conception of digital crime remains perfectly physical and perfectly consistent with human agency, requiring no mysterious technological causation. Nor is the inexplicable magic of a cyberspace – simply ways in which the capacities of human agents/criminals are enhanced by hyperconnection. In this way, a conception of cybercrime rooted in enhanced physical, social, and psychological connectivity emerges, one that arguably better links questions of human-technical agency to the new spaces of interaction created by ICT. For example, phishing frauds can be explained by the technological extension of reach, enhancements to an individual's capacity to shift or conceal their identity, and the greater authority and credibility conferred by online communication.

Moving forward

Whatever the potential benefits in alternative conceptualizations of cybercrime, there seems little interest in exploring them at present. Talk of space, agency, extension, hyperconnectivity, or other ideas is more likely to produce a glazing over of the collective eye than a willingness to revisit our conceptions in any depth – perhaps because it remains so hard for policymakers and law enforcement to see what the benefits of this might be. As it stands, early enthusiasms about defining or conceptualizing cybercrime have largely been replaced by concerns around how best to manage it. So long as cybercrime maintains its status in the popular imagination as one of the most pressing contemporary issues in crime control and national security, this conceptual lethargy appears likely to remain in place. How far this is sustainable remains to be seen. As new technical means for conducting cybercrime emerge, the complexity of its organization grows, and the crossover between online and offline behaviours becomes increasingly normalized, the need for a more refined organization of our conceptions is likely to become more pressing. The result is three kinds of scenarios for how our approach to cybercrime might develop in the near future:

1: Muddle on and ignore

Of all the options open to those working in the field – whether as a theorist or as a practitioner – probably the most likely is simply to ignore the inconsistencies in our thinking around cybercrime and to muddle on with things as they are. This means that the vague definition of cybercrime that we came in with – crime enacted by networked computers – is likely to remain serviceable enough for many in the foreseeable future. Where necessary, standard distinctions – such as that made between targets and tools or between computer dependency and computer enablement – can be drawn upon to dispense with more tricky conceptual questions, for example, the degree of technological involvement required for a fraud to be a 'cyberfraud,' or for bullying to be 'cyberbullying.' Otherwise, any more subtle issues can be left to the confines of an academic journal. But terminology is one thing – concepts, as suggested earlier, are another, and the fact that this is the most likely scenario certainly does not mean it is the best one. Given that poorly defined concepts usually make for poorly executed policy, and bad thinking leads to bad policing, maintaining this uneasy status quo may ultimately prove to be counterproductive.

2: Revise and rethink

A second, less likely scenario would involve some of the challenging questions about our conceptions of cybercrime being taken more seriously. For with more considered approaches valuable resources could be freed up for better directed, more considered forms of intervention. But what kind of direction might such revisionary thinking take? Clearly any revised conceptualization would need to incorporate the complex technical basis to cybercrime, whilst evading technological determinism and accommodating the human-social factors so fundamental to both its execution and perception. As suggested earlier, more refined spatial-cultural approaches might offer one promising direction of this kind, but this by no means rules out other, as yet unconsidered approaches which may be worthy of consideration.

3: Redundancy and elimination

A third and final scenario would be to dispense with the concept of cybercrime altogether. Such a concept, it might be argued, has become too archaic, too all-encompassing, and therefore too unwieldy for it to be of any further use. Instead, all that matters is pursuing violations of computer-related law and prosecuting these in the usual way. Such a minimalist approach has a certain pragmatic appeal. And it might move cybercrime away from the rather niche status it occupies within criminology at the moment, because it would force the realization that most crime is, at some level, technology enabled. This in turn might mean that it becomes as crucial a part of the undergraduate and graduate curriculum to learn about technological offending like cybercrime as it has been to learn about criminological theory or familiar tropes like gang crime, drug crime, and so on. On the other hand, it might be argued that discussing information technology crime *without* something like a concept of cybercrime would be rather like saying we could practice science without concepts of matter and energy, or conduct criminal justice without concepts of crime and culpability. In the end, simple force of circumstance may prevail here. As suggested earlier, social life may become so intertwined with technology that we cease to notice any distinction between cybercrime and traditional crime. In this sense 'everything' would become cybercrime, and any need to identify computer crimes *as* 'computer crimes' would no longer make sense.

At this point it is impossible to predict which of these three scenarios will unfold. One thing, however, is certainly clear – whilst we might *think* we know what cybercrime is, we remain far from really understanding it.

Notes

1　The term was originally proposed by the American pragmatist philosopher John Dewey as part of his minimalist stance towards ideas or concepts.
2　Note that in what follows I often use the terms 'concept' and 'definition' interchangeably because I hold definitions and concepts to be fundamentally connected. That is, I accept the traditional Aristotelian view on the relationship between definitions and concepts which holds, roughly, that "definitions associated with concepts fix necessary and sufficient conditions for falling under the concept"(Burge, 1993, p. 311).
3　Though note that this category exhibited a 5% fall between 2016 and 2017.
4　Figures based on a search conducted via Google Scholar in August 2018. Note that the table is intended only to be indicative rather than definitive. There may, for example, be double-counting in places.
5　Sometimes also referred to as 'computer integrity crime' (Wall, 2007). Wall also defines a category of 'computer-content crime' (like hate speech or extreme pornography), which involves online content that may be obscene or offensive.

References

ACPO. (2009). *'E-crime Strategy' Association of Chief Police Officers of England, Wales and North-ern Ireland*. London: ACPO.

Adams, D. (1999). *How to stop worrying and learn to love the internet*. Retrieved August 23, 2019, from http://www.douglasadams.com/dna/19990901-00-a.html

Allen, T. (2018, January 17). Davos: World leaders fear cyber attacks more than disease, terror-ism or food shortages. *Computing*.

Anderson, R., Barton, C., Böhme, R., Clayton, R., van Eeten, M., Levi, M., . . . Savage, S. (2012). *Measuring the cost of cybercrime*. Paper presented at the Weis 2012 Workshop on the Economics of Information Security, Berlin, Germany, June 25–26:

Braithwaite, J., & Pettit, P. (1990). *Not just deserts*. Oxford: Oxford University Press.

Brannigan, S. (2005). *High-tech crimes revealed: Cyberwar stories from the digital front*. New York, NY: Addison-Wesley.

Brenner, S. (2012). *Cybercrime and the law: Challenges, issues, and outcomes*. Boston: Northeast-ern University Press.

Bryant, R. (Ed.). (2008). *Investigating digital crime*. London: Wiley-Blackwell.

Burge, T. (1993). Concepts, definitions and meaning. *Metaphilosophy, 4*, 309–325.

Carroll, J. (2003). *HCI models, theories, and frameworks: Toward a multidisciplinary science*. San Francisco: Morgan Kaufmann Publishers.

Carter, D. L. (1995). Computer crime categories: How techno-criminals operate. *FBI Law Enforcement Bulletin, 64*(7), 21–27.

Cavazos, E., & Morin, G. (1994). *Cyberspace and the law: Your rights and duties in the on-line world*. Boston, MA: MIT Press.

Chang, H. (2010). The hidden history of phlogiston: How philosophical failure can generate historiographical refinement. *Hyle, 16*(2), 47–79.

Clarke, R. V. (2004). Technology, criminology and crime science. *European Journal on Criminal Policy and Research, 10*(1), 55–63.

Clough, J. (2014). A world of difference: The Budapest convention on cybercrime and the challenges of harmonisation. *Monash University Law Review, 40*(3), 698–736.

Clynes, M., & Kline, N. (1960, September). Cyborgs and space. *Astronautics*, pp. 26–27 and 74–75.

COE. (2001). *Convention on cybercrime.* Council of Europe, European Treaty Series, No. 185.

CSIS. (2014/2018). Net losses: Estimating the global cost of cybercrime. *Center for Strategic and International Studies/McAfee* (Updated 2018).

Cunningham, F. (1973). *Objectivity in social science.* Toronto: University of Toronto Press.

Deleuze, G., & Guattari, F. (1993). *A thousand plateaus.* Minneapolis: University of Minnesota Press.

Detica. (2011). *The cost of cyber crime.* Guildford: Detica.

Dolliver, M., & Dolliver, D. (2016). *Policing cyberspace, law enforcement and forensics in the digital age.* San Diego, CA: Cognella.

Duff, A., & Green, S. P. (Eds.). (2011). *Philosophical foundations of criminal law.* Oxford: Oxford University Press.

Europol. (2016, September 27). The relentless growth of cybercrime. *Press Release.*

Fafinski, S., Dutton, W., & Margetts, H. (2010). *Mapping and measuring cybercrime.* Oxford Internet Institute, discussion paper no. 18.

FFA. (2018). *Fraud the facts.* UK Finance, UK. Retrieved from www.ukfinance.org.uk/wp-content/uploads/2018/07/Fraud-the-facts-Digital-version-August-2018.pdf

Friedman, T. (2013, May 1). It's a 401(k) world. *New York Times.*

Freud, S. (1962). *Civilisation and its discontents* (J. Strachey, trans.). New York: Norton.

Furnell, S. (2017). The evolving landscape of technology-dependent crime. In M. R. McGuire & T. Holt (Eds.), *The handbook of technology, crime and justice.* Abingdon: Routledge.

Furnell, S. M. (2001). The problem of categorising cybercrime and cybercriminals. 2nd Australian Information Warfare and Security Conference 2001. Perth: Australia.

Gercke, M. (2012). *Understanding cybercrime: Phenomena, challenges and legal response.* Geneva: International Telecommunication Union.

Gibson, W. (1989). *Neuromancer.* New York, NY: Berkley Publishing Group.

Goodman, N. (1978). *Ways of world-making.* Indianapolis: Hackett Publishing.

Gordon, S., & Ford, R. (2006). On the definition and classification of cybercrime. *Journal in Computer Virology*, 13–20.

Grabosky, P. (2001). Virtual criminality: Old wine in new bottles? *Social & Legal Studies, 10*(2), 243–249.

Harvey, D. (1990). *The condition of postmodernity: An enquiry into the origins of cultural change.* Cambridge, MA: Blackwell.

Hillyard, P., & Tombs, S. (2004). Beyond criminology? In P. Hillyard, C. Pantazis, S. Tombs, & D. Gordon (eds.), *Beyond criminology: Taking harm seriously* (pp. 10–29). London: Pluto Press.

Holt, T. (2013). *Crime on-line: Correlates, causes, and context.* Durham: Carolina Academic Press.

Home Office (HO). (2018). *Understanding the costs of cyber crime: A report of key findings from the Costs of Cyber Crime Working Group Research.* Report 96. London: Home Office.

Hooper, C., Martini, B., & Choo, R. (2013). Cloud computing and its implications for cybercrime investigations in Australia. *Computer Law and Security Review, 29*(2), 152–163.

Hypponen, M. (2006, November). Malware goes mobile. *Scientific American*, 70–77.

Ifrah, G. (2001). *A universal history of computing: From the abacus to the quantum computer.* London: John Wiley and Sons.

Ismail, N. (2017, July 28). The rise of cybercrime continues to accelerate. *Information Age.*

Jaishankar, K. (2008). Space transition theory of cyber crimes. In F. Schmallager & M. Pittaro (Eds.), *Crimes of the internet* (pp. 283–301). Upper Saddle River, NJ: Prentice Hall.

Jewkes, Y. (Ed.). (2013). *Crime online*. London: Routledge.

Jewkes, Y., & Yar, M. (2013). *Handbook of internet crime*. Devon: Willan Publishing.

Kaplan, F. (2016). *Dark territory: The secret history of cyber war*. New York: Simon and Schuster.

Kapp, E. (1877). *Grundlinien einer Philosophie der Technik*. Braunschweig: Verlag George Westermann.

Kigerl, A. (2017). Profiling cybercriminals: Topic model clustering of carding forum member comment histories. *Social Science Computer Review, 36*(5), 591–609.

Kolthof, D. (2015). *Crime in the cloud: An analysis of the use of cloud services for cybercrime*. University of Twente. Retrieved from https://pdfs.semanticscholar.org/9ecb/a6d0edfeb-65ce68e722daa68056c290d6331.pdf

Koops, B. J., & Brenner, S. W. (Eds.). (2006). *Cybercrime and jurisdiction: A global survey*. The Hague: Asser Press.

Koppell, J. (2000, August). Why cyberspace isn't anyplace. *Atlantic*, pp. 16–18.

Weulen Kranenbarg, M., Holt, T., & van Gelder, J. (2019). Offending and victimization in the digital age: Comparing correlates of cybercrime and traditional offending-only, victimization-only and the victimization–offending overlap. *Deviant Behavior, 40*, 1.

Latour, B. (2005). *Reassembling the social: An introduction to actor-network-theory*. Oxford: Oxford University Press.

Leman-Langlois, S. (2014). *Technocrime: Policing and surveillance*. London: Routledge.

Lessig, L. (1999). *Code: And other laws of cyberspace*. New York, NY: Basic Books.

Leukfeldt, R. (2017). *Research agenda the human factor in cybercrime and cybersecurity*. The Hague: Eleven Publishing.

Mach, E. (1893/1960). *The science of mechanics* (6th ed.) (Trans. T. J. McCormack). La Salle, IL: Open Court.

Mann, D., & Sutton, M. (1998). Netcrime: More change in the organization of thieving. *British Journal of Criminology, 38*(2), 201–229.

Martellozzo, E., & Jane, E. A. (Eds.). (2017). *Cybercrime and its victims*. London: Routledge.

Maurer, T. (2016). Proxies' and cyberspace. *Conflict & Security Law, 21*(3), 383–403.

McGuire, M. R. (2008). *Hypercrime: The new geometry of harm*. London: Routledge.

McGuire, M. R. (2012). *Technology, crime and justice: The question concerning technomia*. London: Taylor and Francis.

McGuire, M. R. (2014). Putting the 'cyber' into cyberterrorism: Re-reading technological risk in a hyperconnected world. In T. Chen, L. Jarvis, & S. MacDonald (Eds.), *Cyberterrorism* (pp. 63–84). New York, NY: Springer.

McGuire, M. R. (2018). *Into the web of profit*. Bromium, white paper/industry report.

McGuire, M., & Dowling, S. (2013). *Cybercrime: A review of the evidence*. Home Office Research Report 75.

McQuade, S., Gentry, S., Colt, J., & Rodgers, M. (2012). *Internet addiction and online gaming*. Langhorne, PA: Chelsea House.

McLuhan, M. (1964). *Understanding media: The extensions of man*. New York, NY: McGraw Hill.

McLuhan, M., & Fiore, Q. (1967). *The medium is the massage: An inventory of effects*. San Francisco, CA: Hardwired.

Morris. (2004). Future of netcrime (pts I & II). *Home Office Research Report 62/04*.

Muncaster, P. (2010, September 19). Hackers steal Interpol chief's Facebook identity, *V3*.

Nair, A. (2019). *The regulation of internet pornography: Issues and challenges*. London: Routledge.

Ngo, F., & Jaishankar, K. (2017). Commemorating a decade in the existence of the international journal of cyber criminology: A research agenda to advance the scholarship of cyber crime. *International Journal of Cyber Criminology, 11*(1), 1–9.

Norrie, A. (1991). A critique of criminal causation. *The Modern Law Review, 545*(5), 685–701.

Nurse, J. (2018). Cybercrime and you: How criminals attack and the human factors that they seek to exploit. In A. Attrill-Smith, C. Fullwood, M. Keep, & D. Kuss (Eds.), *The Oxford handbook of cyberpsychology*. Oxford: Oxford University Press.

Parker, D. (1976). *Crime by computer*. New York, NY: Charles Scribner's Sons.

Poonia, A. S. (2014). CyberCrime: Challenges and classification. *International Journal of Emerging Trends & Technology in Computer Science*, 119–121.

Popper, K. (1962). *Conjectures and refutations: The growth of scientific knowledge*. London: Routledge.

POST. (2006). Computer crime. *Parliamentary Office of Science and Technology POST Note 271*.

Pritchard, A. (2016, March 08). Cyber crime on the move with mobile. *Raconteur*.

Quan-Haase, A., & Wellman, B. (2006). Hyperconnected net work: Computer-mediated community in a high-tech organization. In C. Heckscher & P. Adler (Eds.), *The firm as a collaborative community: Reconstructing trust in the knowledge economy* (pp. 281–333). New York, NY: Oxford University Press.

Quine, W. (1975). On empirically equivalent systems of the world. *Erkenntnis, 9*, 313–328.

Rogers, M. K. (2006). A two-dimensional circumplex approach to the development of a hacker taxonomy. *Digital Investigation, 3*(2), 97–102.

Schultz, T. (2008). Carving up the internet: Jurisdiction, legal orders and the private/public international law interface. *European Journal of International Law, 19*, 799.

Scott, G. (2016). *The very real risks behind the $400 billion illegal online pharmacy industry* [online]. Medscape. Retrieved from www.medscape.com/viewarticle/873704

Shoemaker, D., & Kennedy, D. B. (2009). Criminal profiling and cybercriminal investigations. In M. Pittaro & F. Schmalleger (Eds.), *Crimes of the Internet* (pp. 456–476). Upper Saddle River, NJ: Prentice-Hall.

Thomas, D., & Loader, B. (2000). Introduction – cybercrime: Law enforcement, security and surveillance in the information age. In D. Thomas & B. Loader (Eds.), *Cybercrime: Law enforcement, security and surveillance in the information age*. London: Routledge.

USDOJ. (2010). *Prosecuting computer crimes*. US Department of Justice, Office of Legal Education.

USDOJ. (2018). *Computer crime and intellectual property section*. US Department of Justice.

Vitale, C. (2014). *Networkologies: A philosophy of networks for a hyperconnected age*. Alresford: UK – Zero Books.

Walker, N. (1980). *Punishment, danger and stigma*. Oxford: Blackwell.

Wall, D. S. (1999). Cybercrimes: New wine, no bottles? In P. Davies, P. Francis, & V. Jupp (Eds.), *Invisible crimes*. London: Palgrave Macmillan

Wall, D. S. (Ed.). (2001). *Crime and the internet*. London: Routledge.

Wall, D. S. (Ed.). (2003). *Cyberspace crime*. London: Routledge.

Wall, D. S. (2005). Digital realism and the governance of spam as cybercrime. *European Journal on Criminal Policy and Research, 10*(4), 309–335.

Wall, D. S. (2007). *Cybercrime – the transformation of crime in the information age*. London: Polity Press.

Wall, D. S. (2008). Cybercrime and the culture of fear: Social science fiction(s) and the production of knowledge about cybercrime. *Information, Communication & Society, 11*(6), 881–884.

Weber, M. (1904/1949). Objectivity in social science and social policy. In E. A. Shils & H. A. Finch (Ed. and Trans.), *The methodology of the social sciences*. New York, NY: Free Press.

Wiener, N. (1948). *Cybernetics: Or, control and communication in the animal and the machine*. Paris: Technology Press.

Worrall, J. (1982). Scientific realism and scientific change. *Philosophical Quarterly, 32*, 201–131.

Yar, M. (2006). *Cybercrime and society*. London: Sage.

2 Contributions of criminological theory to the understanding of cybercrime offending and victimization

Adam Bossler

Introduction

Early scholarly work by social scientists studying cybercrime attempted to explain the novelty and nature of cybercrime (Grabosky, 2001; Wall, 2001). Most scholars observed that the means of committing cyber-offences were different from those in the terrestrial world, but the motivations behind the acts seemed similar (Holt & Bossler, 2016). They witnessed how the Internet allowed individuals around the world to connect with others who shared similar interests; however, it could also allow one individual to remain anonymous and to victimize millions of individuals without ever being in close physical proximity. Cybercrime was to be described as neither "old wine in a new bottle" or even "new wine in new bottles," but rather as both new and old wine in no bottles (e.g., Wall, 1998).

Over the last two decades, the field has moved away from discussing the novelty of cybercrime to examining the causes and correlates of cybercrime offending and victimization. Scholars have examined whether traditional criminological theories logically apply to different cyber-offences and victimization types and whether empirical evidence support these theoretical connections. Overall, traditional criminological theories, especially those at the individual level, explain the commission of crime and deviance in the cyberworld as well as they do in the physical world. This chapter reviews how traditional criminological theories have been applied to cybercrime offending and victimization and the empirical evidence for their continued use. The chapter concludes with overall recommendations on how the field should move forward, including continued modification of existing theory and the need for scholars to build and test a general cyber-integrated theory that focuses on how the unique characteristics of the Internet moderate empirically known correlates of cybercrime. As this chapter will demonstrate, the greatest contribution that criminologists have made and will continue to make to the field of cybercrime is the application and testing of criminological theories to better understand how humans engage with this unique environment.

The Classical school and cybercrime offending and victimization

Deterrence theory and rational choice

The Classical school of criminology, congruent with the intellectual arguments of the Enlightenment era, views humans as hedonistic, rational, and possessing free will. The school holds that individuals weigh the costs and benefits (pain vs. pleasure) of an action and act accordingly (Paternoster, 1987). In order to deter individuals from committing forbidden acts, a society needs to create clear and fair codified law and ensure that punishment be certain, swift, and proportionate to the offence. Empirical support for deterrence theory, based on a wide variety of methodological approaches (e.g. perceptual assessments; analysis of the impact of legislation, etc.), has been modest. The overall research shows that certainty, or increasing the probability of being caught for committing an offence, has a stronger effect on behaviour than the severity of the punishment (Paternoster, 1987; Pratt, Cullen, Blevins, Daigle, & Madensen, 2006). In addition, informal sanctions, such as guilt, embarrassment, or concern regarding impact on personal relationships, have shown to be more influential than that of state sanctions (Pratt et al., 2006).

The influence of the Classical school, particularly its specific arguments regarding deterrence theory, can be readily apparent in the cyberworld. Most Western nations have formed criminal justice systems based on the tenets of the Classical school. Nations have continually created and modified legislation over the past few decades in order to both clarify the legality of certain online behaviours, including pornography and computer intrusions, and increase the penalties associated with those behaviours (Holt & Bossler, 2016). In addition, most industrialized nations have increased the enforcement of these cyber-laws by designating existing agencies with modified tasks, creating new agencies or units, and spending additional resources (Holt, Burruss, & Bossler, 2015). Many scholars, however, have argued that deterrence mechanisms, such as sanction threats derived from legislation, may have limited impact in cyberspace because of the anonymity afforded by the Internet and the difficulty of attributing online actions to specific actors (e.g. Brenner, 2007). These aspects make the certainty of being apprehended and punished for many different forms of cybercrime quite low.

Early empirical research examining the effectiveness of deterrence theory in the cyberworld primarily focused on digital piracy (Bachmann, 2007; Higgins, Wilson, & Fell, 2005; Wolfe, Higgins, & Marcum, 2008). Deterrence theory holds that digital pirates commit piracy because they view the pleasures of committing piracy, such as the immediate gratification of receiving free files, as being greater than the risk associated with being punished. Consistent with deterrence research in the physical world (Pratt et al., 2006), studies examining digital piracy found that the certainty of punishment was more important in deterring digital piracy than increasing punishment severity (Higgins et al.,

2005; Kos Koklic,Vida, Bajde, & Culiberg, 2014;Yoon, 2011). Studies examining the Recording Industry Association of America (RIAA) anti-piracy legal strategies, however, found that they led to short-term decreases in piracy levels (e.g. Bachmann, 2007; Bhattacharjee, Gopal, Lertwachara, & Marsden, 2006). The reality of the matter, however, is that the certainty of being caught for digital piracy is quite low as a result of the anonymity provided by the Internet, improved efforts to avoid detection, and law enforcement apathy. Most scholars have also found that informal sanctions from families and friends appear to be stronger influences than formal sanctions (Kos Koklic et al., 2014;Wang & McClung, 2012; Wolfe et al., 2008). Al-Rafee and Cronan (2006), however, found that committing digital piracy did not cause guilt or concerns about informal sanctions because their social ties were generally supportive of their digital piracy.

Recently, the focus of deterrence research has centred on the restrictive deterrent effects of warning banners in honeypots (Howell, Cochran, Powers, Maimon, & Jones, 2017; Maimon, Alper, Sobesto, & Cukier, 2014; Testa, Maimon, Sobesto, & Cukier, 2017; Wilson, Maimon, Sobesto, & Cukier, 2015; see Bossler, 2017 for brief summary of honeypot limitations and how they may affect theoretical and policy implications of deterrence theory). Honeypots are active computers that are set up with the intention of being attacked in order for data to be collected. Studies using university network honeypots have found partial support for restrictive deterrence (Howell et al., 2017; Maimon et al., 2014;Testa et al., 2017;Wilson et al., 2015). In the first criminological test of deterrence theory using honeypots, Maimon et al. (2014) examined whether displaying warning banners that expressed the illegality of the act, that the system was being monitored, and that there could be a law enforcement response affected the progression, frequency, and duration of computer trespassing. They found that intruders presented with the warning banners were neither less likely to immediately terminate the session (defined as being less than five seconds) nor commit repeat trespassing than individuals who were not presented with the banner. The duration of the intrusions, however, was shorter when the intruders were presented with the warning banner.

Warning banners may also reduce the severity of the computer intrusions. Wilson et al. (2015) found that warning banners reduced the odds of a command being entered, but only in longer first system trespassing sessions. Testa et al. (2017) examined whether warning banners affected computer intruders' engagement of active online behaviours, including roaming on the system and manipulating files, and whether this effect was moderated by the administrative access of the intruder. They found that intruders with non-administrative access were less likely to enter navigation and change file permission commands when presented with the warning banner. Those with administrative access, however, were more likely to enter change file commands after being exposed to the banner. Howell et al. (2017) presented computer intruders with either a control (no warning banner) or three types of banners – altruistic moral persuasion, legalistic, and ambiguous – and found that the banners did not significantly affect whether the intruders entered various keystrokes to avoid detection. These overall findings suggest that scholars should continue to study the partial deterrent effects of warning banners specifically and sanctions in cyberspace more generally.

Scholars have also discussed or examined the effectiveness of deterrence for other cybercrimes as well, such as cyberbullying, online economic crime, and cyberterrorism. Patchin and Hinduja (2018) found in a sample of middle schools that students were more deterred from committing traditional bullying and cyberbullying because of threats of punishments from their parents and schools than by the police. Lianos and McGrath (2018) found that greater levels of perceived online anonymity were related with cyberbullying offending. In Ladegaard's (2018) analysis of the impact of media coverage of police work and a highly publicized trial on market revenue for two large and illegal e-commerce websites, trade actually increased after the media coverage of these investigations and the court outcomes. In addition, various challenges exist regarding deterring cyberattacks, including issues with attribution, the rationality of the actor, and identifying appropriate responses (Brenner, 2007; Guitton, 2012). Being able to attribute the source of an attack to a specific actor may have deterrence capabilities if the actor perceives that they can be attributed to the attack and acts rationally, including being concerned about possible repercussions to themselves or others (Guitton, 2012).

One of the most recent theoretical advances connecting tenets of the Classical school and cybercrime has occurred through empirically testing the utility of Paternoster and Pogarsky's (2009) process of thoughtfully reflective decision making (TRDM). The TRDM process was identified by Paternoster and Pogarsky as a rational cognitive decision-making process that could be defined as

> the tendency of persons to collect information relevant to a problem or decision they must make, to think deliberately, carefully, and thoughtfully about possibly solutions to the problem, apply reason to the examination of alternative solutions, and reflect back upon both the process and the outcomes of the choice in order to assess what went right and what went wrong.
>
> (p. 104–105)

When four components – intentionality, forethought, self-reactiveness, and self-reflectiveness – are utilized, decision making can be at its most effective. TRDM, however, varies by person, context, and over time (see Paternoster & Pogarsky, 2009 for a discussion of these variations). TRDM should be associated with making decisions that lead to good outcomes and refraining from behaviours with negative outcomes. It has received some support in the traditional literature, with it being associated with less violence, drinking, and smoking (see Louderback & Antonaccio, 2017 for review).

Louderback and Antonaccio (2017) argued that the basic tenets of TRDM are especially applicable to explaining different types of computer-focused deviance and victimization. They argue that much computer-focused deviance does not involve serious moral considerations, is not based on intuition, and may require cognitive decision making. Individuals with low TRDM may not collect all the relevant information before acting (e.g., checking the security of a website before downloading), identify better alternatives to reach their goals, or consider the short-term and long-term consequences of their actions. Additionally, they argue that individuals with low TRDM place themselves in harm's way, thus increasing victimization, by not properly considering the consequences of their actions, particularly their deviant and risky behaviour. In their analysis of students and employees at a private university, Louderback and Antonaccio (2017) found that low TRDM was associated with both cyber-deviance involvement (measured as a four-item scale consisting of piracy and unauthorized access) and computer-focused cybercrime victimization (e.g. unauthorized access to files and data, compromise of online financial credentials, etc.). The relationship between TRDM-cyber-deviance was stronger and more robust than its relationship with that of cybervictimization. In fact, the relationship became almost insignificant when controlling for previous cyber-deviance.

Routine activities theory

Criminological theories have not only provided insight into understanding the commission of various forms of cyber-offending but they have been utilized as well to examine risk factors associated with different forms of cybervictimization. Cohen and Felson's (1979) routine activity theory has been the primary framework to better understand different forms of cybervictimization. Routine activity theory argues that for direct contact predation to occur, three elements need to converge in both physical space and time: (1) a motivated offender, (2) a suitable target, and (3) the absence of a capable guardian. If any component is missing, a crime cannot occur. Additionally, the odds of a crime occurring are affected by variation in any one of the components. Cohen and Felson's primary focus was on how societal changes, including demographic and technological changes, could affect national crime rates by increasing the number of suitable targets and decreasing capable guardianship.

Routine activity theory was quickly identified by scholars as a potential useful framework to study cybercrime victimization (Grabosky & Smith, 2001; Newman & Clarke, 2003). Scholars noted that each of the three components identified by routine activity theory as necessary for the commission of an offence is readily apparent in cyberspace. There is clearly an abundance of individuals motivated to commit a variety of online offences. Suitable targets are also plentiful in the virtual world, as the Internet provides easy access to individuals, files, sensitive data, and computer systems and networks. Capable guardianship is also evident in online environments, as computers have anti-virus software and password protections, similar to the physical guardianship found in the terrestrial world (e.g., locks, etc.). In addition, social guardianship can play a role, as peers may protect individuals from online harassment. Finally, personal guardianship may theoretically play a factor, as knowledge of technology and security precautions, including not sharing passwords or sensitive information, varies.

Yar (2005) warned about the wholesale application of routine activity theory to the cyberworld. He noted that the elements overall seem applicable but that there were issues with the basic premise of the three components converging. Specifically, he wrote that the theory

> requires that targets, offenders, and guardians be located in particular places, that measurable relations of spatial proximity and distance pertain between those targets and potential offenders, and that social activities be temporally ordered according to rhythms such that each of these agents is either typically present or absent at particular times.
>
> (Yar, 2005, p. 414)

Scholars have addressed this concern with three different strategies. First, some scholars did not view the difference between physical and virtual interactions as significant, as Yar (2005) suggested, and instead empirically examined online daily activities and guardianship characteristics that were associated with online victimization (e.g., Holt & Bossler, 2009). Another approach was to acknowledge that Yar's (2005) criticism may be relevant for certain online offences but that they were not accurate for other offences (Maimon, Kamerdze, Cukier, & Sobesto, 2013). Finally, a third approach was to theoretically address the concern (Reyns, Henson, & Fisher, 2011). Reyns and colleagues (2011) argued that motivated offenders and suitable targets are connected via networks, extending the arguments made by Eck and Clarke (2003) to explain non-contact offences. These networks provide a conduit in cyberspace for an eventual overlap in time between the offender and target to occur in a proxy virtual place. In addition, the temporal intersection of offender and victim may be lagged, as the two may not interact concurrently, but when the victim receives the harassing message, the virus, etc., the two parties have been temporally converged.

The application of routine activities theory to various forms of cybercrime victimization has become routine and quite commonplace over the last decade (Holt & Bossler, 2016). The empirical evidence is mixed and paints an unclear picture. Research has indicated that the relationship between victimization and online routine behaviours differ by victimization type, sample, and study. Research has often found that general measures of technology use, such as the amount of time spent on emails, social networking sites, and in chatrooms, are not significantly related to online harassment and cyberstalking victimization (e.g. Bossler, Holt, & May, 2012; Holt & Bossler, 2013; Ngo & Paternoster, 2011; Reyns et al., 2011). For example, Nasi, Rasanen, Kaakinen, Keipi, and Oksanen (2017) found in a youth sample of four different countries that only social networking services were related to online harassment victimization. Other scholars, however, have found more significant findings. For example, Moore, Guntupalli, and Lee (2010) found in the Pew Internet and American

Life Project that youth who used the Internet for instant messaging, chatting, blogging, and downloading music files were more likely to be online harassed. Leukfeldt and Yar (2016) found that direct forms of communication (e.g. email, Skype, Twitter, etc.) was related with higher odds of interpersonal cybervictimization because it increased the individual's online visibility. When it comes to cyber-harassment of romantic partners, Wick et al. (2017) found that more time online, such as online shopping, banking, dating, and social networks, increased exposure and victimization. Finally, spending more time online, being a YouTube user, and using photo-sharing sites increased exposure to online hate material (Costello, Hawdon, Ratliff, & Grantham, 2016), while social network usage and visiting hostile online environments increased the likelihood of being a target of hate speech (Costello, Hawdon, & Ratliff, 2017).

The relationship between online routine behaviours and other forms of online victimization, such as malware, hacking, and online fraud, may be just as unclear. In college samples, Bossler and Holt (2009) and Holt and Bossler (2013) did not find any online routine behaviours, such as spending more time banking online, shopping, chatting in chatrooms, emailing, or being on social media, to be related to an increased risk of malware infection. In non-college samples, however, significant behaviours have been found. Bergmann, DreiBigacker, von Skarczinski, and Wollinger (2018) found that frequency of computer use was related to malware victimization and ransomware in a large German adult sample; the number of Internet devices was related to malware victimization but not ransomware. Reyns (2015) found that booking online reservations, making purchases online, and social networking were related to malware victimization in the Canadian General Social Survey (GSS) data.

The relationship between online routine behaviours and online economic crime victimization varies based on the type of online economic crime victimization examined as well. Non-deviant online routine behaviours, such as spending more time on the Internet, spending time in chatrooms, or writing emails, were not related to phishing victimization in a college sample (Ngo & Paternoster, 2011). Leukfeldt (2014) only found one Internet activity – targeting browsing – to be related to an increased risk of phishing victimization in the Netherlands. Pratt, Holtfreter, and Reisig (2010) also only found one routine behaviour, that being making purchases online from a website, to be related to Internet fraud targeting in a sample of Florida adults. Using the Canadian GSS data, Reyns (2015), however, found multiple online behaviours correlated with phishing victimization, including online banking, booking reservations, online purchasing, and social networking.

The online routine behaviours that are associated with actually being a fraud victim are similar, but have some differences, with targeting victimization. Chen, Beaudoin, and Hong (2017) found in a sample of Internet users that online shopping, opening emails from online unknown sources, and online information disclosure were positively related with being an Internet scam victim. Being a victim of online fraud within Dutch samples was significantly related with buying products online, direct online communication (e.g. email), and participating in web forums (Leukfeldt & Yar, 2016). In an analysis of the 2009 Canadian GSS, Reyns and Henson (2016) found that identity theft victimization was related with both online banking and purchasing. Williams (2016) found that selling objects online, but not purchasing or social networking, was related to online theft victimization in the Eurobarometer dataset. In Mesch and Dodel's (2018) analyses of a national U.S. sample, they found that the use of instant messaging, using Facebook, and selling merchandise online through an auction site were related with the disclosure of personal information. As for being a target of a scam offer, several online behaviours were related, including disclosure of personal information, using the Internet for instant messaging, purchasing a product online, selling merchandise through an auction site, and shopping behaviour. Responding to the scam offer was related to using Facebook and disclosure of personal information.

One of the most consistent predictors of cybervictimization is participating in cyber-deviance (Holt & Bossler, 2016). The relationship has often been explained as offenders and victims participating in risky activities, sharing sociodemographic characteristics, and/or offending leading directly to victimization and vice versa because of exposure to motivated offenders and retaliation. Participating in different forms of cyber-deviance and crime, including online harassment and bullying, digital piracy, and computer hacking, has been found to increase risk of online harassment and bullying victimization (e.g. Holt & Bossler, 2009; Holt et al., 2012; Ngo & Paternoster, 2011; Reyns et al., 2011; van Wilsem, 2013). Committing online computer deviance has also been found to be related to phishing victimization (Ngo & Paternoster, 2011), malware victimization (Bossler & Holt, 2009; Holt & Bossler, 2013), and financial cybercrime victimization (Kerstens & Jansen, 2016). Van Wilsem (2013), however, did not find a significant relationship between online offending and hacking victimization in a Dutch sample.

The evidence on the impact of different forms of capable guardianship is also mixed depending on the types of victimization and capable guardianship examined. Parental filtering software and monitoring of Internet usage do not appear to be strongly related to reducing the risk of online harassment victimization (Moore et al., 2010; Navarro, Clevenger, Beasley, & Jackson, 2017; Wolfe, Higgins, & Marcum, 2016). For example, Moore et al. (2010) found that parental regulation of the Internet in the forms of having monitoring programs installed on computers, having Internet filters, maintaining and enforcing rules associated with Internet use, and parental oversight were not related to online harassment victimization for youth in the Pew Internet and American Life Project. Wolfe et al. (2016) found in an adolescent sample that parental cell supervision and frequency of talking or texting with parents was not significant in decreasing the receiving of sexts, but having a family cell plan and school cell supervision were significant.

In addition, the evidence on the ability of antivirus software to decrease online victimization is mixed. Some scholars have found strong evidence of antivirus software acting as protective factors (Bergman et al., 2018; Holt &

Turner, 2012; Williams, 2016). For example, Williams (2016) found using the Eurobarometer data that the adoption of physical guardianships in the forms of antivirus software and secure browsing was related with lower odds of online identity theft victimization. Bergmann et al. (2018) found in a large German adult sample that protective behaviour (consisting of antivirus software, updating software, using complex passwords, using different passwords for different applications, regularly changing passwords, deleting suspicious emails without opening them, and logging off websites when done) was negatively related with malware and ransomware victimization and misuse of personal information. Other scholars, however, have found that up-to-date antivirus software was either not related to phishing victimization (e.g. Leukfeldt, 2014; Ngo & Paternoster, 2011) or that it was related with higher odds of malware victimization (Holt & Bossler, 2013; Reyns, 2015). This can be explained as individuals with antivirus software being more likely to know that they have been victims of malware infection or that they updated or installed their software after the infection.

Individual technical skills, which has been primarily considered a form of personal guardianship in the literature, also has an unclear relationship with online victimization (Holt & Bossler, 2016). Research finding that computer skills act as a personal guardian and reduces victimization is rare (Holt & Bossler, 2013; but see Bossler & Holt, 2009). For example, Graham and Triplett (2017) did find in a nationally representative sample conducted by the American Association of Retired Persons that individuals with more digital literacy were less likely to respond to phishing scams. Most research, however, has found that there is no significant relationship between having computer skills and various forms of online victimization, including but not limited to online harassment (Bossler, Holt, & May, 2012; Holt & Bossler, 2009; Van Wilsem, 2013), phishing (Leukfeldt, 2014; Ngo & Paternoster, 2011), data loss as a result of malware victimization (Bossler & Holt, 2009), and identity theft (Holt & Turner, 2012). In other studies, scholars have found that those with greater computer proficiency may have an increased risk of victimization, which may stem from the ability to recognize when they are exposed to harmful behaviours or by being in spaces that increase their risk of victimization (Hinduja & Patchin, 2008; Holt & Bossler, 2009; Van Wilsem, 2013).

In addition, individuals can provide guardianship via the actions that they take to protect themselves, particularly not disclosing personal information. Wick et al. (2017) found that online disclosure of personal information, pictures, and suggestive photos was related with higher odds of cyber-harassment victimization by romantic partners. Bergmann et al. (2018) found that avoidance behaviours, such as avoiding suspicious Internet links, downloading software and data, posting private data on the Internet, and using public hotspots, were negatively related with malware and ransomware victimization and misuse of personal information in a large German adult sample. In addition, Reyns and Henson (2016) found that posting personal information on social media sites and other online venues increased the odds of identity theft victimization in Canada. Reyns, Henson, and Fisher (2016) found that adding strangers as friends to social networking accounts was related with higher odds of cyber-stalking victimization.

Recently, scholars have revisited the conceptualization of guardianship. Some have argued that guardianship should be viewed as the mere presence of an individual deterring a would-be offender from a suitable target (Hollis, Felson, & Welsh, 2013; Vakhitova, Reynald, & Townsley, 2016). Guardianship, however, is argued to not be the same as social control – actions taken in order to influence behaviour (Hollis et al., 2013). Social control by both individuals and others therefore may need to be integrated into routine activity theory to clarify its central arguments (Costello et al., 2017). In Costello et al.'s (2017) examination of online extremism and hate speech, they examined the effects of actor-initiated social control (self-help), social control initiated by others (collective efficacy), and guardianship (mere presence of others) on being the target of online hate. They found that confronting hate in the form of self-help – telling someone to stop when they saw online hate – increased the chances of being the target of online hate. Collective efficacy – others online telling someone to stop being mean or offensive – was not significant. Hawdon, Costello, Ratliff, Hall, and Middleton (2017) confirmed the previous finding that a confrontational conflict resolution style may increase the risk of being victimized online; tolerating online negative behaviour, however, did not significantly affect victimization. Another possible path forward is to better conceptualize guardianship within the latest developments of routine activities theory, including the ideas of handlers (emotional control over offenders), place managers (control over places), and super controllers (those who regulate or influence controllers) (Eck & Clarke, 2003; Vakhitova et al., 2016).

Although most tests of routine activity theory and cybercrime have been conducted at the individual level, scholars have started to examine other entities, such as networks and businesses. For example, Maimon et al. (2013) examined the relationship between online daily activities and computer intrusions into university networks using data from an intrusion prevention system. They found that the university's network was more likely to be attacked during normal university business hours because there were more network users online and that more foreign-born network users was also related to attacks from those countries. Williams, Levi, Burnap, and Gundur (2018) examined organizations' experiences of insider business cybercrime using the nationally representative Cardiff University UK Business Cybercrime Survey and found that several organizational routine activities, including storing confidential data and using social media, cloud services, mobile devices, and remote access, were all related to victimization. In addition, they found that employing a cybersecurity manager and worrying about insider victimization, two measures that were considered guardianship variables, were also predictive.

Keeping more in the theoretical spirit with Cohen and Felson's (1979) original claims, some scholars have also started to examine the relationship between structural factors, routine activities, and cybercrime victimization at the macro level. Williams (2016) found that Internet penetration, which he considered a proxy measure for country physical guardianship as it may represent more developed infrastructure with better security, was negatively related with individual-level online identity theft victimization using the Eurobarometer data. In addition, he found that national security strategies may act as effective state-level physical guardianship and reduce identity theft victimization. In their study on malware infections using data from an open repository of known malware, Holt, Burruss, and Bossler (2018), however, found that nations with greater technological infrastructure were more likely to report malware infections. In addition, the number of computer emergency response teams, a possible measure of capable guardianship, was not related with the amount of reported malware infection. As for cyberbullying victimization, Gorzig, Milosevic, and Staksrud (2017) examined 18 European countries and found that life expectancy and population density had a negative relationship with cyberbullying victimization and that crime rates and gross domestic product (GDP) had a positive relationship with cyberbullying victimization. Song, Lynch, and Cochran (2016) studied cyber victimization at the U.S. state level and found that unemployment and non-urban population were significantly related with access to the Internet and the percentage of users who only access the Internet at home was positively related with state-level counts of cybertheft victimization. In a recent study by Brady, Randa, and Reyns (2016), they utilized the concept of the "household activity" ratio (developed by Cohen and Felson) to examine the relationship between the amount of time a family spends online and the information that they disclose with increased exposure to cybercrime victimization. In their study, they found a strong correlation in trends between the annual proportion of Internet users who complete financial transactions over the Internet with financial cybercrime victimization. As data on cybercrime victimization improve, further studies at the macro level will help our knowledge of how structural characteristics influence online daily routines and thus cybercrime victimization.

The Positivist School and cybercrime offending and victimization

Akers's social learning theory

Ron Akers's (1998) social learning theory holds that there are four principal components of the learning process: (1) differential associations, (2) definitions, (3) differential reinforcement, and (4) imitation. The process occurs as individuals associate with deviants and non-deviants who act as models to imitate and provide attitudes and norms supportive of breaking or not breaking the laws. Behaviour, whether criminal or not, will continue depending on whether the behaviour is reinforced or punished, whether perceived or in actuality. Akers's (1998) theory has received the strongest empirical support in explaining a wide range of deviant behaviours (Pratt et al., 2009; Pratt & Cullen, 2000).

Social learning theory has been a popular theory to use to understand why individuals commit specific types of cybercrime because of the empirical support it has received in the terrestrial world but also because it makes intuitive sense. A person is not born knowing how to use computers and other forms of technology; they have to learn their functions and operations from others. As Skinner and Fream (1997) noted, individuals must "learn not only how to operate a highly technical piece of equipment but also specific procedures, programming, and techniques for using the computer illegally" (p. 446). The two forms of cybercrime that have been examined the most by scholars testing social learning theory are digital piracy and computer hacking, although other forms have been examined as well.

Digital piracy at first glance does not appear to be too complex. It does not require much more than searching online for a movie or music file and downloading it without authorization. Even this simplistic version, however, requires knowing about the Internet and how to do a search. Social learning theorists would argue that in order for digital piracy to occur, an individual would have to interact with others, normally peers, who show them how to perform the procedure, act as models, provide rationalizations for why the violation of intellectual property laws is acceptable, and financially or socially reinforce them for the commission of digital piracy. Almost all empirical studies on digital piracy have found that the strongest correlate of digital piracy is associating with other digital pirates, either in person or virtually (e.g. Burruss, Bossler, & Holt, 2013; Burruss, Holt, & Bossler, 2018; Higgins & Marcum, 2011; Holt, Bossler, & May, 2012; Miller & Morris, 2016).

Research has also shown that digital pirates clearly hold attitudes, norms, and techniques of neutralization that are supportive of violating intellectual property laws as well as diminishing their responsibility for the commission of the offence (Burruss et al., 2013, 2018; Brown, 2016; Higgins & Marcum, 2011; Ingram & Hinduja, 2008; Skinner & Fream, 1997). The fact that so many individuals commit piracy, especially within certain age brackets, makes the behaviour appear normal and acceptable. One of the more common views of digital pirates is that pirating a few songs or movies will have minimal or no impact on major entertainment corporations or performers, thus negating any harm by their action (Brown, 2016; Higgins & Marcum, 2011; Ingram & Hinduja, 2008). They may also argue that their piracy allows them to test material before they purchase it to ensure that the product meets a certain level of quality (Holt & Copes, 2010). When compared to other crimes, including physical theft, digital piracy is not seen as serious (Yu, 2010). Pirates may also question the legality of intellectual property laws by arguing that information, knowledge, and art should be free to all and cannot be owned by any one single person or entity (Holt & Copes, 2010).

Finally, digital pirates are financially reinforced for their behaviour in the form of free music and movie files and different software programs. As important, however, is the social reinforcement and praise they receive from others, possibly from showing someone else how to pirate or providing rare files to others in the piracy subculture (Holt & Copes, 2010; Morris & Higgins, 2009). Therefore, individuals will continue to commit digital piracy as long as it is either being financially or socially reinforced (Holt et al., 2010; Holt & Copes, 2010; Van Rooij et al., 2017).

Social learning theorists would argue that for computer hacking to occur, an individual would need to interact with individuals who had knowledge of and supported computer hacking. Interacting with them in person or through forums, chatrooms, and other means, an individual slowly develops minimal skill and is exposed to definitions supportive of what they are doing. As they spend more time hacking, they develop more skills and become more self-reliant. Exchanges with other hackers continue to provide more knowledge, definitions, and social reinforcement. Significant scholarly research over the past decade has shown that all four components of the social learning process contribute to the commission of different types of computer hacking (Holt & Bossler, 2016). One of the key correlates of computer hacking that is evident in both qualitative and quantitative research is that computer hackers associate with others who hack (Bossler & Burruss, 2011; Holt et al., 2012; Leukfeldt, Kleemans, & Stol, 2017; Morris & Blackburn, 2009; Morris, 2011; Skinner & Fream, 1997). In fact, most studies show that associating with computer hackers has the largest impact of the four components (Holt & Bossler, 2016; Morris & Blackburn, 2009). These computer hacking associates act as models to imitate and provide valuable sources of definitions and techniques of neutralization that support this behaviour (Bossler & Burruss, 2011; Morris & Blackburn, 2009; Skinner & Fream, 1997). Finally, individuals continue to hack into computer systems because it is socially reinforced via praise and status through the hacker subculture (Bossler & Burruss, 2011; Skinner & Fream, 1997).

Scholars have also applied social learning theory to the spread of hate and violence through the Internet (Freiburger & Crane, 2011; Pauwels & Schils, 2016). Freiburger and Crane (2011) demonstrated how all four components of the social learning process are easily identifiable in the spread of hate through the Internet. The Internet brings individuals into contact with each other and provides a medium for the exchange of ideas and definitions supportive of actions against a common enemy. Depending on the belief system of the individual's physical surroundings, online associations with extremists may provide meaning and connection to an isolated individual, especially youth. Continued interaction with online extremists makes it easier for the isolated individual to accept the information being provided to them as truthful. Over time, they are socially reinforced for accepting the ideology and are shown how the Internet can make them a martyr for a long time after their death. In a recent study, Pauwels and Schils (2016) found that exposure to extremist content though new social media was related with self-reported political violence even after controlling for other factors, including demographics, moral values, and peer influences. The effect of the extremist material was stronger when the respondent actively sought out the material rather than passively being exposed to it. In addition, they found that offline associations with racist and delinquent peers influenced political violence, suggesting the importance of scholars examining offline and online social learning influences.

Finally, scholars have also found social learning theory to be useful in better understanding cyberbullying and cyberstalking (Choi, Lee, & Lee, 2017; Marcum, Higgins, & Nicholson, 2017), online sexual harassment (Choi et al., 2017), sexting (Marcum, Higgins, & Ricketts, 2014), and visiting online pornography websites (Cooper & Klein, 2018). As with other forms of cybercrime or cyber-deviance, associating with deviant peers has been found to be related to cyberbullying (e.g, Lianos & McGrath, 2018), cyberstalking (Choi et al., 2017; Marcum et al., 2017), online sexual harassment (Choi et al., 2017), sexting (Marcum et al., 2014), and visiting pornographic websites (Cooper & Klein, 2018). Definitions supportive of these behaviours are also strongly related with their commission. Respondents' views of the seriousness of certain online harassment behaviours were related to online sexual harassment and cyberstalking (Choi et al., 2017). Positive attitudes toward sexting were associating with sexting in a sample of South Korean youth (Lee, Moak, & Walker, 2016). Cooper and Klein (2018) found in a college sample that definitions favourable of viewing pornography and differential reinforcement were related to visiting pornographic websites.

General theory of crime

Gottfredson and Hirschi's (1990) *general theory of crime*, or more colloquially named self-control theory, is a classic control theory in which motivation is assumed to be invariant because of our basic hedonistic human nature, but what differentiates individuals are levels of self-control. They argue that most crimes are relatively easy to commit and provide immediate gratification. Based on their analyses of the characteristics of crime, they deduce that offenders would have matching characteristics, meaning that they are impulsive, insensitive to others' feelings and well-being, and are not forward thinking; thus, they do not adequately consider the consequences of their actions. Their lack of adequate levels of self-control, or inability to control oneself, makes them prone to commit both illegal and legal acts (e.g., smoking, sexual promiscuity, etc.) that have short- and long-term consequences greater than the benefits. Despite criticism over the last 30 years, low self-control has consistently been found to be a predictor of a wide range of violent and property crimes and deviance (Pratt & Cullen, 2000).

Ever since scholars started empirically assessing the causes and correlates of various forms of cybercrime and cyber-deviance, scholars noted that many forms of cybercrime, such as digital piracy or online bullying, require little skill and are quite simple, satisfy immediate gratification, demonstrate lack of concern for others, and may have potential consequences greater than its benefits. Empirical research over the last decade and a half has consistently shown that low self-control is a significant predictor of a wide variety of different forms of cybercrime and cyber-deviance, including but not limited to minor forms of computer hacking (Holt et al., 2012), online harassment/cyberbullying (Choi et al., 2017; Holt et al., 2012; Lianos & McGrath, 2018; Li, Holt, Bossler, & May, 2016), downloading online pornography (Buzzell, Foss, & Middleton, 2006), digital piracy (Higgins & Marcum, 2011; Hinduja, 2012; Udris, 2016), online economic crimes (Moon, McCluskey, & McCluskey, 2010), sexting (Marcum et al., 2014; Reyns, Henson, & Fisher, 2014; but see Lee et al., 2016), and cyberstalking (Choi et al., 2017; Marcum et al., 2017). In addition, individuals with low self-control associate with deviant peer groups, both offline (e.g. Longshore, Change, Hsieh, & Messina, 2004) and online (Bossler & Holt, 2010; Higgins & Marcum, 2011).

The relationship between low self-control and computer hacking behaviours, however, is complex because of the variation in the skill levels of hackers. Most "hacking" occurs through either simple social engineering, whether through phone calls or emails, or brute-force attacks in which they or an easy-to-use program attempt to guess passwords until it achieves access. These types of "hacking" require some effort but do not require strong computer skills. When assessing lower skill levels of hacking in youth samples, such as accessing others' accounts without their permission, Holt and colleagues (2012) found that lower levels of self-control were related with these forms of hacking. On the other hand, hacks that require some level of skill are quite incongruent with some of the basic tenets of the general theory of crime. To be considered a hacker, one must demonstrate a strong mastery and commitment to learning about technology (e.g. Holt, 2007). In many cases, hackers enjoy the mental challenge of solving a problem or puzzle. These characteristics indicate that hackers, as defined and accepted in the hacker community, enjoy challenges more than easy tasks, like mental work over possibly physical activities, show diligence, and are future oriented (Bossler & Burruss, 2011). This would indicate that our conception of "true hackers" is more closely associated with higher levels of self-control, whereas script kiddies are associated with lower levels of self-control.

Bossler and Burruss's (2011) examination of low self-control, the social learning process, and computer hacking in college students further illustrated the complexity of the relationship between low self-control and hacking. They found that individuals who "hacked" (defined by guessing passwords to gain access to others' computers or files; accessing others' computer accounts or files without their knowledge or permission to look at information; and/or added, deleted, changed, or printed information in another person's files without permission) were more likely to display lower levels of self-control than those who did not hack. When measures of the hacker social learning process were included in the analyses, a suppression effect was found. College students who hacked, but who did not participate in the social learning process that taught techniques and definitions supportive of hacking behaviour, required higher levels of self-control in order to have the diligence to self-learn how to hack through experimentation and effort. Having lower levels of self-control, however, increased the students' participation in the hacking social learning process. This increased their contact with individuals who taught them methods, provided definitions ·supportive of breaking computer laws, and socially reinforced these types of behaviours. This suppression effect was found as well when examining the relationship between low self-control, the social learning process, and software piracy in both youth and college samples in later studies (Burruss, Bossler, & Holt, 2013; Burruss et al., 2018). More advanced computer hacks and piracy require either participating in a social learning process or having higher levels of self-control.

In addition, Gottfredson and Hirschi (1990) claim that the same characteristics that make some individuals more likely to commit crime also increase their odds of victimization (Schreck, 1999). In the traditional literature, low self-control has been shown to have a consistently modest effect with victimization (Pratt, Turnanovic, Fox, & Wright, 2014). Pratt et al.'s meta-analysis of the relationship between low self-control and victimization also indicated that the relationship may be stronger for non-contact forms of victimization, such as fraud, than for direct contact victimization. The logical connection between low self-control and victimization in the physical world seems to apply equally as well in the cyberworld. If individuals with low self-control favour immediate gratification over concerns of short- and long-term consequences (Gottfredson & Hirschi, 1990), their risk taking and thrill seeking will make them more vulnerable to victimization (Schreck, 1999). Individuals in online environments may participate in risky activities, such as downloading pornography or music and movie files from non-mainstream sites, which may infect their computer with malicious software (Bossler & Holt, 2009). Individuals may also interact with strangers in chatrooms and social media, which may lead to victimization in the forms of cyberstalking and stalking in the physical world. Individuals with lower levels of self-control may have lower levels of empathy, making it more difficult for them to create strong bonds as well as interpret other people's intentions (Gottfredson & Hirschi, 1990; Schreck, 1999). When presented with real or misperceived aggressions, the low tolerance levels of those with low self-control may lead them to react inappropriately to online slights, escalate the situation, and increase their chances of online harassment or bullying victimization. Low tolerance may also affect their not taking computer security precautions seriously if they feel that purchasing and updating security software is too much effort.

Scholars have shown that low self-control is empirically related with cybercrime victimization, but the effect is modest and it varies with the cybercrime under examination (Bossler & Holt, 2010; Reyns, Fisher, Bossler, & Holt, 2018). Low self-control may have more of a role in increasing the odds of person-based cybercrime victimization than computer-based victimization types or general targets (e.g. large phishing attempts) (Bossler & Holt, 2010; Holt, Bossler, Malinski, & May, 2016; Pratt et al., 2014; Reyns, Fisher, & Randa, 2018; Reyns, Fisher, Bossler, et al., 2018). In the first study examining the link between low self-control and cybercrime victimization, Bossler and Holt (2010) found in a college sample that low self-control significantly but weakly predicted three forms of cybercrime victimization: passwords being obtained to access computer accounts and files; someone adding, deleting, or changing information in one's computer files without the owner's knowledge or permission; and being harassed online. Importantly, however, they found that the effect of low self-control on cybervictimization is mediated by delinquent peers, meaning that having low self-control increased one's interest in associating with delinquent peers who possibly victimized the person or placed them in risky situations that made them more vulnerable. Further studies have found low self-control being related to both sexual (including receiving sexts) and non-sexual harassment victimization, cyberbullying victimization, and cyberstalking victimization (Holt, Turner, & Exum, 2014; Holt et al., 2016; Ngo & Paternoster, 2011; Reyns et al., 2014; Reyns, Fisher, & Randa, 2018; Reyns, Fisher, Bossler, et al., 2018). In Reyns, Fisher, Bossler, et al. (2018) analysis of a college sample, they found that low self-control was significantly related with higher odds of cyberstalking victimization, but that it was mediated by opportunity, or the amount of time spent online participating in various online routines.

The relationship is not as clear, however, regarding the link between low self-control and online economic forms of victimization, as the results vary depending on the specific form of cybercrime victimization and the sample examined. For example, low self-control was not found to be related to electronic card theft victimization (Bossler & Holt, 2010), phishing attacks (Ngo & Paternoster, 2011), or identity theft (Reyns, Fisher, Bossler, et al., 2018) in college samples. Dutch scholars found that low self-control was related to various forms of online fraud victimization, including consumer fraud, auction fraud, virtual theft, and identity fraud (Kerstens & Jansen, 2016; van Wilsem, 2013). Similarly, Mesch and Dodel (2018) found that low self-control was related to being the target of fraud via email, disclosing personal information, and responding to scam offers in a national U.S. sample.

Drift theory and techniques of neutralization

Gresham Sykes and David Matza's (1957) techniques of neutralization were proposed as a social control theory of juvenile delinquency. They argued that most juveniles held conforming beliefs, but that many still committed occasional acts of delinquency. In order to be able to commit these delinquent acts that were incongruent with their overall belief systems, delinquents would need to use techniques that would allow them to neutralize the conflict between the act and their belief systems. This would allow the juveniles to drift back and forth between conformity and delinquency without accepting a delinquent status (Matza, 1964). In their original work, Sykes and Matza (1957) discovered five techniques – denial of responsibility, denial of injury, denial of victim, condemnation of the condemners, and appeal to higher loyalties – that allowed individuals to drift toward delinquency. Over the last several decades, Sykes and Matza's original techniques of neutralization, along with newly discovered techniques, have been found to be correlated with a wide variety of drug, property, and violent offences in both youth and adult samples (Maruna & Copes, 2005).

Much of the research on the use of techniques of neutralization in cyberspace has focused on digital piracy. This theory holds that college students primarily have conformist beliefs, but that they have specific techniques that allow them to commit digital piracy without thinking of themselves as criminals or deviants. Scholars have primarily found moderate support using quantitative analyses (Brunton-Smith & McCarthy, 2016; Higgins, Wolfe, & Marcum, 2008; Ingram & Hinduja, 2008; Marcum, Higgins, Wolfe, & Ricketts, 2011; Morris & Higgins, 2009; Smallridge & Roberts, 2013). For example, Smallridge and Roberts (2013) examined the relationship between digital piracy in a sample of college students and the classic techniques of neutralization and two proposed techniques – claim of future patronage and digital rights management (DRM) software (access measures taken by copyright holders to protect their intellectual property from unauthorized use) defiance. They found that some of the neutralization techniques, including denial of responsibility, condemnation of the condemners, metaphor of the leger, and claim of future patronage, were inversely related with digital piracy; they found, however, that defence of necessity, appeal to higher loyalties, claim of normalcy, and DRM defiance predicted digital piracy in the hypothesized direction. The DRM defiance effect was the strongest in the gaming piracy model.

Qualitative analyses, which provide the interviewees the ability to express their beliefs and views on issues more clearly, have found stronger evidence (Holt & Copes, 2010; Moore & McMullan, 2009; Ulsperger, Hodges, & Paul, 2010). Moore and McMullan (2009) found that after informing undergraduate students of the illegality of piracy, all of the respondents in their sample ($n = 44$) responded with a technique of neutralization, with denial of injury being the most common, followed by denial of victim and everyone else is doing it. Pirates often believed that musicians were not harmed by their file sharing and that instead these activities helped musicians by promoting them (Moore & McMullan, 2009; Tade & Akinleye, 2012). Many pirates deny the victim status of intellectual property right holders by arguing that their actions and provocations, particularly their high prices, deserved the "victimization" (Ingram & Hinduja, 2008; Morris & Higgins, 2009; Ulsperger et al., 2010). Pirates also condemn the condemners and believe that they are hypocrites and offenders in their own way (Holt & Bossler, 2016; Ulsperger et al., 2010). In addition, appealing to higher loyalties – their fellow peers and pirates – is more important than following the law. Thus, pirates place a premium on possessing large quantities of files and being able to share these files with others and gaining status within the community (Holt & Copes, 2010; Ulsperger et al., 2010).

The study of the hacker subculture has also shown clear usage of techniques of neutralization to justify hackers' actions while maintaining conformist lifestyles in most cases (e.g. Morris, 2011). Hackers may place the responsibility of the offence on that of either the security software companies for creating products with vulnerabilities or victims for not having secure computer systems and appropriate computer skills to prevent victimization (Chua & Holt, 2016; Turgeman-Goldschmidt, 2005). Hackers or malware writers often argue that no injury occurs by simply entering a system if no changes were made (Gordon & Ma, 2003). In comparison to other criminal activities that they could be doing, gaining unauthorized access to systems is not considered that serious (Chua & Holt, 2016). Hackers may also deny the victimhood status of the individuals or entities that they hacked into because the victim had it coming to them. The hacking sub-culture also places a premium on information and knowledge being free while being highly sceptical of government and corporation practices; thus, their actions that may be deemed illegal by the state are instead viewed as actions that benefit fellow hackers and society as a whole by providing free knowledge and uncovering corruptive practices (Chua & Holt, 2016).

Recently, Goldsmith, and Brewer (2015) elaborated on Matza's (1964) drift theory to explain how the Internet allows individuals, particularly youth, to drift back and forth from a physical self to a virtual one. In their digital drift theory, Goldsmith and Brewer argue that technology and the Internet provide various opportunities for individuals to easily engage in deviant opportunities online, but that it also allows them to easily disengage as well. The Internet, and its ability to provide anonymity and escapism, provides access to online communities that are disconnected from their physical selves. This allows them to act online differently than in the physical world. Goldsmith and Brewer specifically argue that the Internet provides two conditions that allow digital drift to occur. The first is the affinity of online content that youth find attractive, such as free movie and music files, pornography, or hacking tips, but which also exposes them to online deviance and rationalizations that support the commission of online deviance. The Internet also allows youth to develop and strengthen affiliations with online deviant youth who provide justifications, neutralizations, and social support for the commission of online deviance. In addition, young people's sense of injustice of how law enforcement and industry respond to minor online offending may exacerbate this drift (Holt, Brewer, & Goldsmith, 2018). These conditions allow, and possibly encourage, youth to drift back and forth between conformity and deviance, partially based on whether they are online or offline and the types of online networks they have formed.

General strain theory

Robert Agnew's (1992, 2001) general strain theory argues that crime and deviance are the result of individuals acting upon negative emotions caused by stress in their lives. His earlier formulation (1992) identified three types of strain that can lead to negative emotions: (1) the threatened or actual failure to achieve positively valued goals, (2) threatened or actual removal of positively valued stimuli, and (3) threatened or actual presentation of noxious stimuli (e.g. bullying). Experiencing these strains can produce negative emotions, such as anger, frustration, depression, or anxiety, particularly when these strains are perceived as being unfair, consist of a high magnitude, or are clustered in time (Agnew, 2001). In order to alleviate the strain, relieve negative emotions, or exact revenge on the sources of the stress, individuals may resort to delinquent activities. These basic propositions have generally been empirically supported, as life strains have been found to be correlated with delinquency. In addition, the relationship is partially mediated by increased levels of negative emotions, particularly frustration and anger (e.g. Agnew & White, 1992; Broidy, 2001; Brezina, 1998).

Almost all of the empirical research examining the link between strain and cybercrime has focused on cyberbullying (see Holt & Bossler, 2016 for discussion). This is sensible considering the extant literature connecting strain with traditional bullying (e.g. Moon & Jang, 2014). Virtual environments make it easy to vent frustration and anger at others without requiring direct physical interaction with the victim. In addition, Agnew's (2001) significant elaboration of general strain theory specified bullying as a particularly important factor for understanding delinquency. Bullying can lead to strain and delinquency because (1) the victim will perceive the bullying as unjust; (2) it will be perceived as being high in magnitude or importance; (3) the bullying will occur away from parents, teachers, and other forms of social control; and (4) the victim will be provided a model to base their own aggressive behaviour on for the future. Empirical evidence supports these underlying arguments. Youth who bully others, both online and offline, are more likely to experience actual and perceived strains in their life, such as academic challenges, perceived unfair treatment from teachers and parents, and negative life events (Lianos & McGrath, 2018; Moon, Hwang, & McCluskey, 2011; Paez, 2018; Patchin & Hinduja, 2011). For example, in a recent study by Lianos and McGrath (2018), they found that a composite measure of strain consisting of traditional and cybervictimization, perceived social support, academic strain, and financial strain, were related to cyberbullying.

Experiencing cybervictimization should be viewed as a source of strain, as it affects the victim's well-being (e.g. Kaakinen, Keipi, Rasanen, & Oksanen, 2018). Cyberbullying victimization specifically should be viewed as a type of strain that may lead to cyberbullying offending, cyber-deviance, or self-harm as a response to this treatment (Bae, 2017; Baker & Pelfrey, 2016; Hay, Meldrum, & Mann, 2010; Wright & Li, 2013). In fact, cyberbullying victimization may have a larger impact on future offending than physical bullying victimization (Hay et al., 2010; McCuddy & Esbensen, 2017). McCudddy and Esbensen (2017), analysing data from the GREAT program, found that youth who were cyberbullied were more likely to use substances and commit nonviolent delinquency than youth who were physically bullied. The effects of cybervictimization may be moderated by various factors. Kaakinen et al. (2018) found that the effects of cybervictimization on well-being were worse for those with weaker physical social ties; online social ties, however, did not moderate the relationship. The effects of cyberbullying victimization may even have a larger impact on future online aggressive behaviour when it is coupled with other sources of strain, such as peer rejection (Wright & Li, 2013) and physical bullying victimization (Wright & Li, 2012).

As Holt and Bossler (2016) noted, general strain theory would seem to logically apply to other cybercrimes as well. For example, computer hackers may be triggered by certain life events that can cause negative emotions, such as poor school or work performance or perceived unfair treatment by peers, parents, teachers, employers, or government officials who they feel have wronged them. These negative emotions, whether anger, frustration, or resentment, may lead the person to harm these individuals or groups by attacking their computer or system to steal or simply to cause damage. Similarly, digital pirates may be angry or frustrated because of the high costs of media and the government's role in enforcing copyright laws. In an analysis of Korean youth panel data over five years, Bae (2017) found that perceived stress was related to the commission of more cyber-delinquency, as measured by deliberately spreading false information on Internet bulletin boards, online harassment, lying about demographics while chatting online, downloading illegal software, using other people's Internet service without authorization, and hacking into someone else's computer or account. Hinduja (2012), however, found that a strain scale, consisting of receiving a bad grade in a class, breaking up with a significant other, experiencing weight loss or gain, being fired from a job, having money problems, or being a victim of a crime, was not related to music piracy in an undergraduate sample. Similarly, Brunton-Smith and McCarthy (2016) did not find that different measures of strain, such as being homeless or being suspended or expelled from school, were related to the online piracy of software and music. Thus, there is a need for further research that examines the relationship between stress, negative emotions, and cybercrime other than just cyberbullying.

Conclusion

Studying cybercrime and its unique characteristics has led to a better understanding of how cybercrime is committed and the risk factors that lead to victimization. In addition, the application of traditional criminological theories to cybercrime has made us rethink how current theories apply to a modern digital world. In some cases, such as routine activities theory, it has made us reconceptualize the meaning of concepts, such as space, convergence, and guardianship. In other cases, it has made us focus on basic facts that are as true today as they were a century ago. For example, with whom one associates, whether offline or online, will always be one of the most significant predictors of both physical and cyber-offending and victimization. The key will be to find the balance between easily publishable findings that may simply replicate what we already know and that of more ground-breaking work that helps move the fields of criminology and cybercrime forward.

This chapter has focused on how scholars have applied criminological theory to different forms of cybercrime offending and victimization. Criminological theories, however, that have received less attention may provide much richer avenues for scholars to explore. Theories that have been historically inadequately tested, such as control balance theory (Tittle, 1995), may find new life in the virtual world (Reyns, Fisher, & Randa, 2018). Some theories, such as social disorganization, have been tested extensively in the traditional literature but have received little attention in the cybercrime realm, mostly because of data limitations (e.g. Holt et al., 2014). Similarly, entire schools of thought, such as conflict theory, provide contrasting viewpoints on what should be considered cybercrime, as well as who are the 'real' cybercriminals (Steinmetz & Nobles, 2018). In addition, the new wave of biosocial criminology may provide unique insights into both the causes of cybercrime offending and its effects (Steinmetz & Nobles, 2018). Further examination of any of these theories or frameworks will be more fruitful than another test of self-control theory.

Further theoretical elaboration on the moderating effects of the Internet's characteristics on online behaviour will be beneficial as well. As has been discussed in this chapter, characteristics of the Internet, such as providing perceived anonymity, influences decision making and perceptions of the certainty of punishment. In addition, the affordability and accessibility of the Internet allow individuals in distant locations to share information and provide social reinforcement for the commission of deviant and criminal offences. This accessibility also makes it easy for offenders to find suitable targets at any time. In the spirit of Goldsmith and Brewer's (2015) digital drift theory and Reyns and colleagues' (2011) cyber-lifestyle routine activities theory, scholars need to continue to modify concepts from existing theories to better fit a virtual world.

Finally, the creation of new theory may be premature. Much work needs to be done to reconceptualize and modify existing concepts and theories. In fact, the creation of any 'new' theory will probably be a rebranding of existing concepts. Instead, the field would benefit by the creation and continued work on a "general cyber integrated theory" (see Messner, Krohn, & Liska, 1989; Tittle, 1995 for discussion of integration and its need) that focuses on how the characteristics of the Internet, primarily its accessibility and anonymity, affect the relationship between known causes and correlates of traditional crime and that of cybercrime offending and victimization.

Any general cyber-integrated theory would need to focus on both macro- and micro-correlates of crime. A cyber-integrated theory would need to start with macro-correlates inspired by Messner and Rosenfeld's (1994) Institutional Anomie Theory, Merton's (1938) strain theory, Cohen and Felson's (1979) routine activities theory, social disorganization theory, and past empirical research in order to explain how structural characteristics affect Internet accessibility, convergence between offenders and victims, and guardianship. A key difference is that opportunity in cyberspace may be more constant than in the physical world, as the points of contact and target infrastructure are virtually always available.

At the micro-level, the social learning process would be evident throughout. Both offline and online peers influence individuals by providing models to imitate, definitions that favour the violation of the law or techniques of neutralization that temporarily neutralize conformist beliefs, and social reinforcement for the commission and continuance of specific cyber-offences. In addition, a cyber-integrated theory would need to include how the accessibility and deindividuation of the Internet allow both youth and adults to drift back and forth between physical and virtual selves. The virtual self allows the individual to escape labels and expectations placed upon them by traditional society. Furthermore, the anonymity of the Internet affects perceptions of the certainty of punishment, as individuals feel they are less likely to be identified and caught. The individual not only feels less likely to be formally punished through the legal or educational systems but also feels less likely to be informally punished by parents, family, and conforming friends. This continues to loosen them from their social bond. Individuals' levels of self-control would influence their associating with deviant peers, their weighing of costs and benefits, and their participation in risky activities. Although most of the elements mentioned earlier would be relevant for the understanding of any form of cybercrime or cyber-deviance, some theoretical concepts, such as strain from Agnew's general strain theory, may be more relevant to certain types of offending and victimization, such as cyberbullying, than other types. Thus, work on a general cyber-integrated theory would still need to take into consideration differences in cybercrime and cyber-deviance

In conclusion, the field of criminology has greatly contributed to our understanding of cybercrime offending and victimization. Its greatest contribution has been through the application of concepts from its wealth of criminological theories. As this chapter has demonstrated, all theories discussed have shown some empirical validity in their ability to predict various forms of cybercrime. Although further theoretical clarification and empirical testing is warranted, we will soon find ourselves at a dead end if we follow the current path. In order for the field to move forward, we should not take the path of least resistance (e.g. simple but easily publishable studies). Instead, we need to blaze a new path. Although some may interpret this as a need for new theory, I believe that creating a general cyber-integrated theory would be more beneficial by connecting existing knowledge into a cohesive framework. This would allow us to have a unifying theory from which to clarify concepts, create links, fill in the gaps, and extend current knowledge.

References

Agnew, R. (1992). Foundations for a general strain theory of crime and delinquency. *Criminology, 30*, 47–87.

Agnew, R. (2001). Building on the foundation of general strain theory: Specifying the types of strain most likely to lead to crime and delinquency. *Journal of Research in Crime and Delinquency, 38*, 319–361.

Agnew, R., & White, H. R. (1992). An empirical test of general strain theory. *Criminology, 30*, 475–499.

Akers, R. L. (1998). *Social learning and social structure: A general theory of crime and deviance.* Boston, MA: Northeastern University Press.

Al-Rafee, S., & Cronan, T. P. (2006). Digital piracy: Factors that influence attitude toward behavior. *Journal of Business Ethics, 63*, 237–259.

Bachmann, M. (2007). Lesson spurned? Reactions of online music pirates to legal prosecutions by the RIAA. *International Journal of Cyber Criminology, 2*, 213–227.

Bae, S. M. (2017). The influence of strain factors, social control factors, self-control and computer use on adolescent cyber delinquency: Korean National Panel Study. *Children and Youth Services Review, 78*, 74–80.

Baker, T., & Pelfrey, W. V. (2016). Bullying victimization, social network usage, and delinquent coping in a sample of urban youth: Examining the predictions of general strain theory. *Violence and Victims, 31*, 1021–1043.

Bergmann, M. C., DreiBigacker, A., von Skarczinski, B., & Wollinger, G. R. (2018). Cyber-dependent crime victimization: The same risk for everyone? *Cyberpsychology, Behavior, and Social Networking, 21*, 84–90.

Bhattacharjee, S., Gopal, R. D., Lertwachara, K., & Marsden, J. R. (2006). Impact of legal threats on online music sharing activity: An analysis of music industry legal actions. *The Journal of Law and Economics, 49*, 91–114.

Bossler, A. M. (2017). Need for debate on the implications of honeypot data for restrictive deterrence policies in cyberspace. *Criminology & Public Policy, 16*, 681–688.

Bossler, A. M., & Burruss, G. W. (2011). The general theory of crime and computer hacking: Low self-control hackers? In T. J. Holt & B. H. Schell (Eds.), *Corporate hacking and technology-driven crime: Social dynamics and implications* (pp. 38–67). Hershey, PA: ISI-Global.

Bossler, A. M., & Holt, T. J. (2009). On-line activities, guardianship, and malware infection: An examination of routine activities theory. *International Journal of Cyber Criminology, 3*, 400–420.

Bossler, A. M., & Holt, T. J. (2010). The effect of self-control on victimization in the cyberworld. *Journal of Criminal Justice, 38*, 227–236.

Bossler, A. M., Holt, T. J., & May, D. C. (2012). Predicting online harassment among a juvenile population. *Youth and Society, 44*, 500–523.

Brady, P. Q., Randa, R., & Reyns, B. W. (2016). From WWII to the world wide web: A research note on social changes, online "places," and a new online activity ratio for routine activity theory. *Journal of Contemporary Criminal Justice, 32*, 129–147.

Brenner, S. W. (2007). "At light speed": Attribution and response to cybercrime/terrorism/warfare. *The Journal of Criminal Law and Criminology, 97*, 379–475.

Brezina, T. (1998). Adolescent maltreatment and delinquency: The question of intervening processes. *Journal of Research in Crime and Delinquency, 35*, 71–99.

Broidy, L. (2001). A test of general strain theory. *Criminology, 39*, 9–36.

Brown, S. C. (2016). Where do beliefs about music piracy come from and how are they shared? An ethnographic study. *International Journal of Cyber Criminology, 10*, 21–39.

Brunton-Smith, I., & McCarthy, D. J. (2016). Explaining young people's involvement in online piracy: An empirical assessment using the offending crime and justice survey in England and wales. *Victims & Offenders, 11*, 509–533.

Burruss, G. W., Bossler, A. M., & Holt, T. J. (2013). Assessing the mediation of a fuller social learning model on low self-control's influence on software piracy. *Crime & Delinquency, 59*, 1157–1184.

Burruss, G. W., Holt, T. J., & Bossler, A. M. (2018). Revisiting the suppression relationship between social learning and self-control on software piracy. *Social Science Computer Review*. Retrieved from.

Buzzell, T., Foss, D., & Middleton, Z. (2006). Explaining use of online pornography: A test of self-control theory and opportunities for deviance. *Journal of Criminal Justice and Popular Culture, 13*, 96–116.

Chen, H., Beaudoin, C. E., & Hong, T. (2017). Securing online privacy: An empirical test on Internet scam victimization, online privacy concerns, and privacy protection behaviors. *Computers in Human Behavior, 70,* 291–302.

Choi, K., Lee, S., & Lee, J. R. (2017). Mobile phone technology and online sexual harassment among juveniles in South Korea: Effects of self-control and social learning. *International Journal of Cyber Criminology, 11,* 110–127.

Chua, Y. T., & Holt, T. J. (2016). A cross-national examination for the techniques of neutralization to account for hacking behaviors. *Victims & Offenders, 11,* 534–555.

Cohen, L. E., & Felson, M. (1979). Social change and crime rate trends: A routine activity approach. *American Sociological Review, 44,* 588–608.

Cooper, D. T., & Klein, J. L. (2018). College students' online pornography use: Contrasting general and specific structural variables with social learning variables. *American Journal of Criminal Justice, 43,* 551–569.

Costello, M., Hawdon, J., & Ratliff, T. N. (2017). Confronting online extremism: The effect of self-help, collective efficacy, and guardianship on being a target for hate speech. *Social Science Computer Review, 35,* 587–605.

Costello, M., Hawdon, J., Ratliff, T., & Grantham, T. (2016). Who views online extremism? Individual attributes leading to exposure. *Computers in Human Behavior, 63,* 311–320.

Eck, J. E., & Clarke, R. V. (2003). Classifying common police problems: A routine activity approach. *Crime Prevention Studies, 16,* 7–40.

Freiburger, T., & Crane, J. S. (2011). The internet as a terrorist's tool: A social learning perspective. In K. Jaishankar (Ed.), *Cyber criminology: Exploring Internet crimes and criminal behavior* (pp. 127–138). Boca Raton, FL: CRC Press.

Goldsmith, A., & Brewer, R. (2015). Digital drift and the criminal interaction order. *Theoretical Criminology, 19,* 112–130.

Gordon, S., & Ma, Q. (2003). *Convergence of virus writers and hackers: Factor or fantasy.* Cupertino, CA: Symantec Security White Paper.

Gorzig, A., Milosevic, T., & Staksrud, E. (2017). Cyberbullying victimization in context: The role of social inequalities in countries and regions. *Journal of Cross-Cultural Psychology, 48,* 1198–1215.

Gottfredson, M. R., & Hirschi, T. (1990). *A general theory of crime.* Stanford, CA: Stanford University Press.

Grabosky, P. N. (2001). Virtual criminality: Old wine in new bottles? *Social and Legal Studies, 10,* 243–249.

Grabosky, P. N., & Smith, R. (2001). Telecommunication fraud in the digital age: The convergence of technologies. In D. Wall (Ed.), *Crime and the internet* (pp. 29–43). New York, NY: Routledge.

Graham, R., & Triplett, R. (2017). Capable guardians in the digital environment: The role of digital literacy in reducing phishing victimization. *Deviant Behavior, 38,* 1371–1382.

Guitton, C. (2012). Criminals and cyber attacks: The missing link between attribution and deterrence. *International Journal of Cyber Criminology, 6,* 1030–1043.

Hawdon, J., Costello, M., Ratliff, T., Hall, L., & Middleton, J. (2017). Conflict management styles and cybervictimization: Extending routine activity theory. *Sociological Spectrum, 37,* 250–266.

Hay, C., Meldrum, R., & Mann, K. (2010). Traditional bullying, cyber bullying, and deviance: A general strain theory approach. *Journal of Contemporary Criminal Justice, 26,* 130–147.

Higgins, G. E., & Marcum, C. D. (2011). *Digital piracy: An integrated theoretical approach.* Durham, NC: Carolina Academic Press.

Higgins, G. E., Wilson, A. L., & Fell, B. D. (2005). An application of deterrence theory to software piracy. *Journal of Criminal Justice and Popular Culture, 12,* 166–184.

Higgins, G. E., Wolfe, S. E., & Marcum, C. D. (2008). Music piracy and neutralization: A preliminary trajectory analysis from short-term longitudinal data. *International Journal of Cyber Criminology, 2,* 324–336.

Hinduja, S. (2012). General strain, self-control, and music piracy. *International Journal of Cyber Criminology, 6,* 951–967.

Hinduja, S., & Patchin, J. W. (2008). Cyberbullying: An exploratory analysis of factors related to offending and victimization. *Deviant Behavior, 29,* 129–156.

Hollis, M. E., Felson, M., & Welsh, B. C. (2013). The capable guardian in routine activities theory: A theoretical and conceptual reappraisal. *Crime Prevention and Community Safety, 15,* 65–79.

Holt, T. J. (2007). Subcultural evolution? Examining the influence of on- and off-line experiences on deviant subcultures. *Deviant Behavior, 28,* 171–198.

Holt, T. J., & Bossler, A. M. (2009). Examining the applicability of lifestyle-routine activities theory for cybercrime victimization. *Deviant Behavior, 30,* 1–25.

Holt, T. J., & Bossler, A. M. (2013). Examining the relationship between routine activities and malware infection indicators. *Journal of Contemporary Criminal Justice, 29,* 420–436.

Holt, T. J., & Bossler, A. M. (2016). *Cybercrime in progress: Theory and prevention of technology-enabled offenses.* Crime Science Series. London: Routledge.

Holt, T. J., Bossler, A. M., Malinski, R., & May, D. C. (2016). Identifying predictors of unwanted online sexual conversations among youth using a low self-control and routine activity framework. *Journal of Contemporary Criminal Justice, 32,* 108–128.

Holt, T. J., Bossler, A. M., & May, D. C. (2012). Low self-control, deviant peer associations, and juvenile cyberdeviance. *American Journal of Criminal Justice, 37,* 378–395.

Holt, T. J., Brewer, R., & Goldsmith, A. (2018). Digital drift and the "sense of injustice": Counter-productive policing of youth cybercrime. *Deviant Behavior.* doi:10.1080/01639 625.2018.1472927.

Holt, T. J., Burruss, G. W., & Bossler, A. M. (2010). Social learning and cyber deviance: Examining the importance of a full social learning model in the virtual world. *Journal of Crime and Justice, 33,* 15–30.

Holt, T. J., Burruss, G. W., & Bossler, A. M. (2015). *Policing cybercrime and cyberterror.* Durham, NC: Carolina Academic Press.

Holt, T. J., Burruss, G. W., & Bossler, A. M. (2018). Assessing the macro-level correlates of malware infections using a routine activities framework. *International Journal of Offender Therapy and Comparative Criminology, 62,* 1720–1741.

Holt, T. J., & Copes, H. (2010). Transferring subcultural knowledge on-line: Practices and beliefs of persistent digital pirates. *Deviant Behavior, 31,* 625–654.

Holt, T. J., & Turner, M. G. (2012). Examining risks and protective factors of on-line identity theft. *Deviant Behavior, 33,* 308–323.

Holt, T. J., Turner, M. G., & Exum, M. L. (2014). The impact of self-control and neighborhood disorder on bullying victimization. *Journal of Criminal Justice, 42,* 347–355.

Howell, C. J., Cochran, J. K., Powers, R. A., Maimon, D., & Jones, H. M. (2017). System trespasser behavior after exposure to warning messages at a Chinese computer network: An examination. *International Journal of Cyber Criminology, 11,* 63–77.

Ingram, J. R., & Hinduja, S. (2008). Neutralizing music piracy: An empirical examination. *Deviant Behavior, 29,* 334–365.

Kaakinen, M., Keipi, T., Rasanen, P., & Oksanen, A. (2018). Cybercrime victimization and subjective well-being: An examination of the buffering effect hypothesis among adolescents and young adults. *Cyberpsychology, Behavior, and Social Networking, 21,* 129–137.

Kerstens, J., & Jansen, J. (2016). The victim-perpetrator overlap in financial cybercrime: Evidence and reflection on the overlap of youth's on-line victimization and perpetration. *Deviant Behavior, 37*, 585–600.

Kos Koklic, M. K., Vida, I., Bajde, D., & Culiberg, B. (2014). The study of perceived adverse effects of digital piracy and involvement: Insights from adult computer users. *Behaviour & Information Technology, 33*, 225–236.

Ladegaard, I. (2018). We know where you are, what you are doing and we will catch you: Testing deterrence theory in digital drug markets. *British Journal of Criminology, 58*, 414–433.

Lee, C., Moak, S., & Walker, J. T. (2016). Effects of self-control, social control, and social learning on sexting behavior among South Korean youths. *Youth & Society, 48*, 242–264.

Leukfeldt, E. R. (2014). Phishing for suitable targets in the Netherlands: Routine activity theory and phishing victimization. *Cyberpsychology, Behavior, and Social Networking, 17*, 551–555.

Leukfeldt, E. R., Kleemans, E. R., & Stol, W. P. (2017). Cybercriminal networks, social ties and online forums: Social ties versus digital ties within phishing and malware networks. *British Journal of Criminology, 57*, 704–722.

Leukfeldt, E. R., & Yar, M. (2016). Applying routine activity theory to cybercrime: A theoretical and empirical analysis. *Deviant Behavior, 37*, 126–138.

Li, C. K. W., Holt, T. J., Bossler, A. M., & May, D. C. (2016). Examining the mediating effects of social learning on a low self-control-cyberbullying relationship in a youth sample. *Deviant Behavior, 37*, 126–138.

Lianos, H., & McGrath, A. (2018). Can the general theory of crime and general strain theory explain cyberbullying perpetation? *Crime & Delinquency, 64*, 674–700.

Longshore, D., Change, E., Hsieh, S. C., & Messina, N. (2004). Self-control and social bonds: A combined control perspective on deviance. *Crime and Delinquency, 50*, 542–564.

Louderback, E. R., & Antonaccio, O. (2017). Exploring cognitive decision-making processes, computer-focused cyber deviance involvement and victimization: The role of thoughtfully reflective decision-making. *Journal of Research in Crime and Delinquency, 54*, 639–679.

Maimon, D., Alper, M., Sobesto, B., & Cukier, M. (2014). Restrictive deterrent effects of a warning banner in an attacked computer system. *Criminology, 52*, 33–59.

Maimon, D., Kamerdze, A., Cukier, M., & Sobesto, B. (2013). Daily trends and origin of computer-focused crimes against a large university computer network. *British Journal of Criminology, 55*, 319–343.

Marcum, C. D., Higgins, G. E., & Nicholson, J. (2017). I'm watching you: Cyberstalking behaviors of university students in romantic relationships. *American Journal of Criminal Justice, 42*, 373–388.

Marcum, C. D., Higgins, G. E., & Ricketts, M. L. (2014). Sexting behaviors among adolescents in rural North Carolina: A theoretical examination of low self-control and deviant peer association. *International Journal of Cyber Criminology, 8*, 68–78.

Marcum, C. D., Higgins, G. E., Wolfe, S. E., & Ricketts, M. L. (2011). Examining the intersection of self-control, peer association and neutralization in explaining digital piracy. *Western Criminology Review, 12*, 60–74.

Maruna, S., & Copes, H. (2005). What have we learned from five decades of neutralization research? *Crime and Justice, 32*, 221–320.

Matza, D. (1964). *Delinquency and drift*. Hoboken, NJ: John Wiley & Sons.

McCuddy, T., & Esbensen, F. (2017). After the bell and into the night: The link between delinquency and traditional, cyber-, and dual-bullying victimization. *Journal of Research in Crime and Delinquency, 54*, 409–411.

Merton, R. K. (1938). Social structure and anomie. *American Sociological Review, 3*, 672–682.

Mesch, G., & Dodel, M. (2018). Low self-control, information disclosure, and the risk of online fraud. *American Behavioral Scientist, 62,* 1356–1371.

Messner, S. F., Krohn, M. D., & Liska, A. E. (Eds.). (1989). *Theoretical integration in the study of deviance and crime.* Albany: SUNY Press.

Messner, S. F., & Rosenfeld, R. (1994). *Crime and the American dream.* Belmont, CA: Wadsworth.

Miller, B. M., & Morris, R. G. (2016). Virtual peer effects in social learning theory. *Crime & Delinquency, 62,* 1543–1569.

Moon, B. M., Hwang, H. W., & McCluskey, J. D. (2011). Causes of school bullying: Empirical test of a general theory of crime, differential association theory, and general strain theory. *Crime & Delinquency, 57,* 849–877.

Moon, B. M., & Jang, S. J. (2014). A general strain approach to psychological and physical bullying: A study of interpersonal aggression at school. *Journal of Interpersonal Violence, 29,* 2147–2171.

Moon, B., McCluskey, J. D., & McCluskey, C. P. (2010). A general theory of crime and computer crime: An empirical test. *Journal of Criminal Justice, 38,* 767–772.

Moore, R., Guntupalli, N. T., & Lee, T. (2010). Parental regulation and online activities: Examining factors that influence a youth's potential to become a victim of online harassment. *International Journal of Cyber Criminology, 4,* 685–698.

Moore, R., & McMullan, E. C. (2009). Neutralizations and rationalizations of digital piracy: A qualitative analysis of university students. *International Journal of Cyber Criminology, 3,* 441–451.

Morris, R. G. (2011). Computer hacking and the techniques of neutralization: An empirical assessment. In T. J. Holt & B. H. Schell (Eds.), *Corporate Hacking and technology-driven crime: Social dynamics and implications* (pp. 1–17). Hershey, PA: IGI-Global.

Morris, R. G., & Blackburn, A. G. (2009). Cracking the code: An empirical exploration of social learning theory and computer crime. *Journal of Crime and Justice, 32,* 1–32.

Morris, R. G., & Higgins, G. E. (2009). Neutralizing potential and self-reported digital piracy: A multitheoretical exploration among college undergraduates. *Criminal Justice Review, 34,* 173–195.

Nasi, M., Rasanen, P., Kaakinen, M., Keipi, T., & Oksanen, A. (2017). Do routine activities help predict young adults' online harassment: A multi-nation study. *Criminology & Criminal Justice, 17,* 418–432.

Navarro, J. N., Clevenger, S., Beasley, M. E., & Jackson, L. K. (2017). One step forward, two steps back: Cyberbullying within social network sites. *Security Journal, 30,* 844–858.

Newman, G., & Clarke, R. (2003). *Superhighway robbery: Preventing E-commerce crime.* Cullompton, NJ: Willan Press.

Ngo, F. T., & Paternoster, R. (2011). Cybercrime victimization: An examination of individual and situational level factors. *International Journal of Cyber Criminology, 5,* 773–793.

Paez, G. R. (2018). Cyberbullying among adolescents: A general strain theory perspective. *Journal of School Violence, 17,* 74–85.

Patchin, J. W., & Hinduja, S. (2011). Traditional and nontraditional bullying among youth: A test of general strain theory. *Youth & Society, 43,* 727–751.

Patchin, J. W., & Hinduja, S. (2018). Deterring teen bullying: Assessing the impact of perceived punishment from police, schools, and parents. *Youth Violence and Juvenile Justice, 16,* 190–207.

Paternoster, R. (1987). The deterrent effect of the perceived certainty and severity of punishment: A review of the evidence and issues. *Justice Quarterly, 4,* 173–217.

Paternoster, R., & Pogarsky, G. (2009). Rational choice, agency and thoughtfully reflective decision making: The short and long-term consequences of making good choices. *Journal of Quantitative Criminology, 25,* 103–127.

Pauwels, L., & Schils, N. (2016). Differential online exposure to extremist content and political violence: Testing the relative strength of social learning and competing perspectives. *Terrorism and Political Violence, 281*, 1–29.

Pratt, T. C., & Cullen, F. T. (2000). The empirical status of Gottfredson and Hirschi's general theory of crime: A meta-analysis. *Criminology, 38*, 931–964.

Pratt, T. C., Cullen, F. T., Blevins, K. R., Daigle, L. E., & Madensen, T. D. (2006). The empirical status of deterrence theory: A meta-analysis. In F. T. Cullen, J. P. Wright, & K. R. Blevins (Eds.), *Taking stock: The status of criminological theory.* New Brunswick, NJ: Transaction.

Pratt, T. C., Cullen, F. T., Sellers, C. S., Winfree, T., Madensen, T. D., Daigle, L. W., . . . Gau, J. M. (2009). The empirical status of social learning theory: A meta-analysis. *Justice Quarterly, 27*, 765–802.

Pratt, T. C., Holtfreter, K., & Reisig, M. D. (2010). Routine online activity and Internet fraud targeting: Extending the generality of routine activity theory. *Journal of Research in Crime and Delinquency, 47*, 267–296.

Pratt, T. C., Turnanovic, J. J., Fox, K. A., & Wright, K. A. (2014). Self-control and victimization: A meta-analysis. *Criminology, 52*, 87–116.

Reyns, B. W. (2015). A routine activity perspective on online victimization: Results from the Canadian general social survey. *Journal of Financial Crime, 22*, 396–411.

Reyns, B. W., Fisher, B. S., Bossler, A. M., & Holt, T. J. (2018). Opportunity and self-control: Do they predict multiple forms of online victimization? *American Journal of Criminal Justice.* Retrieved July 28, 2018.

Reyns, B. W., Fisher, B. S., & Randa, R. (2018). Explaining cyberstalking victimization against college women using a multitheoretical approach: Self-control, opportunity, and control balance. *Crime & Delinquency.* doi:10.1177/0011128717753116

Reyns, B. W., & Henson, B. (2016). The thief with a thousand faces and the victim with none: Identifying determinants for online identity theft victimization with routine activity theory. *International Journal of Offender Therapy and Comparative Criminology, 60*, 1119–1139.

Reyns, B. W., Henson, B., & Fisher, B. S. (2011). Being pursued online: Applying cyberlifestyle-routine activities theory to cyberstalking victimization. *Criminal Justice and Behavior, 38*, 1149–1169.

Reyns, B. W., Henson, B., & Fisher, B. S. (2014). Digital deviance: Low self-control and opportunity as explanations for sexting among college students. *Sociological Spectrum, 34*, 273–292.

Reyns, B. W., Henson, B., & Fisher, B. S. (2016). Guardians of the cyber galaxy: An empirical and theoretical analysis of the guardianship concept from routine activity theory as it applies to online forms of victimization. *Journal of Contemporary Criminal Justice, 32*, 148–168.

Schreck, C. J. (1999). Criminal victimization and self control: An extension and test of a general theory of crime. *Justice Quarterly, 16*, 633–654.

Skinner, W. F., & Fream, A. M. (1997). A social learning theory analysis of computer crime among college students. *Journal of Research in Crime and Delinquency, 34*, 495–518.

Song, H., Lynch, M. J., & Cochran, J. K. (2016). A macro-social exploratory analysis of the rate of interstate cyber-victimization. *American Journal of Criminal Justice, 41*, 583–601.

Smallridge, J. L., & Roberts, J. R. (2013). Crime specific neutralizations: An empirical examination of four types of digital piracy. *International Journal of Cyber Criminology, 7*, 125–140.

Steinmetz, K. E., & Nobles, M. R. (Eds.). (2018). *Technocrime and criminological theory.* New York, NJ: Routledge.

Sykes, G. M., & Matza, D. (1957). Techniques of neutralization: A theory of delinquency. *American Sociological Review, 22*, 664–670.

Tade, O., & Akinleye, B. (2012). We are promoters not pirates: A qualitative analysis of artistes and pirates on music piracy in Nigeria. *International Journal of Criminology, 6*, 1014–1029.

Testa, A., Maimon, D., Sobesto, B., & Cukier, M. (2017). Illegal roaming and file manipulation on target computers: Assessing the effect of sanction threats on system trespassers' online behaviors. *Criminology & Public Policy, 16*, 689–726.

Tittle, C. R. (1995). Control balance: Toward a general theory of deviance. New York, NY: Taylor & Francis.

Turgeman-Goldschmidt, O. (2005). Hacker's accounts: Hacking as a social entertainment. *Social Science Computer Review, 23*, 8–23.

Udris, R. (2016). Cyber deviance among adolescents and the role of family, school, and neighborhood: A cross-national study. *International Journal of Cyber Criminology, 10*, 127–146.

Ulsperger, J. S., Hodges, S. H., & Paul, J. (2010). Pirates on the plank: Neutralization theory and the criminal downloading of music among Generation Y in the era of late modernity. *Journal of Criminal Justice and Popular Culture, 17*, 124–151.

Vakhitova, Z. I., Reynald, D. M., & Townsley, M. (2016). Toward the adaptation of routine activity and lifestyle exposure theories to account for cyber abuse victimization. *Journal of Contemporary Criminal Justice, 323*, 169–188.

Van Rooij, B., Fine, A., Zhang, Y., & Wu, Y. (2017). Comparative compliance: Digital piracy, deterrence, social norms, and duty in China and the United States. *Law and Policy, 39*, 73–93.

Van Wilsem, J. (2013). "Bought it, but never got it": Assessing risk factors for online consumer fraud victimization. *European Sociological Review, 29*, 168–178.

Wall, D. S. (1998). Catching cybercriminals: Policing the Internet. *International Review of Law, Computers & Technology, 12*, 201–218.

Wall, D. S. (2001). Cybercrime and the Internet. In D. S. Wall (Ed.), *Crime and the internet* (pp. 1–17). New York, NY: Routledge.

Wang, X., & McClung, S. R. (2012). The immorality of illegal downloading: The role of anticipated guilt and general emotions. *Computers in Human Behavior, 28*, 153–159.

Wick, S. E., Nagoshi, C., Basham, R., Jordan, C., Kim, Y. K., Nguyen, A. P., & Lehmann, P. (2017). Patterns of cyber harassment and perpetration among college students in the United States: A test of routine activities theory. *International Journal of Cyber Criminology, 11*, 24–38.

Williams, M. L. (2016). Guardians upon high: An application of routine activities theory to online identity theft in Europe at the country and individual level. *British Journal of Criminology, 56*, 21–48.

Williams, M. L., Levi, M., Burnap, P., & Gundur, R. V. (2018). Under the corporate radar: Examining insider business cybercrime victimization through an application of routine activities theory. *Deviant Behavior*. doi:10/1080/01639625.2018.1461786

Wilson, T., Maimon, D., Sobesto, B., & Cukier, M. (2015). The effect of a surveillance banner in an attacked computer system: Additional evidence for the relevance of restrictive deterrence in cyberspace. *Journal of Research in Crime and Delinquency, 52*, 829–855.

Wolfe, S. E., Higgins, G. E., & Marcum, C. D. (2008). Deterrence and digital piracy: A preliminary examination of the role of viruses. *Social Science Computer Review, 26*, 317–333.

Wolfe, S. E., Marcum, C. D., Higgins, G. E., & Ricketts, M. L. (2016). Routine cell phone activity and exposure to sex messages: Extending the generality of routine activity theory and exploring the etiology of a risky teenage behavior. *Crime and Behavior, 62*, 614–644.

Wright, M. F., & Li, Y. (2012). Kicking the digital dog: A longitudinal investigation of young adults' victimization and cyber-displaced aggression. *Cyberpsychology, Behavior, and Social Networking, 15*, 448–454.

Wright, M. F., & Li, Y. (2013). The association between cyber victimization and subsequent cyber aggression: The moderating effect of peer rejection. *Journal of Youth and Adolescence, 45,* 662–674.

Yar, M. (2005). The novelty of "cybercrime": An assessment in light of routine activity theory. *European Journal of Criminology, 2,* 407–427.

Yoon, C. (2011). Theory of planned behavior and ethics theory in digital piracy: An integrated model. *Journal of Business Ethics, 100,* 405–417.

Yu, S. (2010). Digital piracy and stealing: A comparison on criminal propensity. *International Journal of Criminal Justice Sciences, 5,* 239–250.

3 The open and dark web

Facilitating cybercrime and technology-enabled offences

Claudia Flamand and David Décary-Hétu

Introduction

A review by Holt and Bossler (2014) of the current state of cybercrime research demonstrates the wide range of offences that have been associated with the concept of cybercrime. Their review builds on Wall's (2007) typology and looks at cyber-trespass, cyber-deception/theft, cyber-porn and obscenity, and cyberviolence. In recent years, the extent of offences associated with the concept of cybercrime has only grown to include, among others, the online trade of physical goods such as illicit drugs.

This chapter will study the latest developments in the online trade of illicit drugs: the adoption of the Tor network and the creation of dark web drug-dealing entrepreneurs. The Tor network (Dingledine, Mathewson, & Syverson, 2004) is a communication protocol which obfuscates an Internet user's location using proxies. The Tor network allows anyone to surf the web anonymously by exposing only the Internet Protocol (IP) addresses of the proxies and not that of the Internet user. The protocol was extended to also obfuscate the location of web servers so that Internet users could not trace back where a specific website was hosted. The Tor network as such provides a critical service for anyone looking to evade regulation while trafficking illicit drugs and is part of a series of anonymizing protocols called the dark web. The Tor network allowed for the emergence of drug-dealing entrepreneurs that set up their own independent drug-dealing websites called vendor shops (Kruithof et al., 2016). These vendor shops differ from most online illicit marketplaces in that they are run by a single administrator that is also the sole provider of goods for sale. Previous marketplaces were administrated by a number of individuals who recruited independent vendors to provide goods for sale (Yip, Shadbolt, & Webber, 2013). The emergence of drug-dealing entrepreneurs provides an opportunity to better understand the phenomenon of criminal entrepreneurs that has been researched in traditional drug-dealing settings (see for example Dunlap, Johnson, & Manwar, 1994; Vannostrand & Tewksbury, 1999; Lampe, 2015) and to understand the impact of anonymizing technologies such as the Tor network on crime.

As such, the general aim of this chapter is to describe and understand criminal entrepreneurship on the Internet. The first specific aim will be to describe the types of products advertised on vendor shops to understand the size and scope of sales of illicit drugs. The second specific aim will be to provide a description of the vendors involved in single-vendor shops. This will enable us to build a profile of the drug-dealing entrepreneurs. Finally, the third aim will be to characterize the differences between the activities of the drug-dealing entrepreneur on their own vendor shop and their activities on larger public marketplaces where they compete against other drug dealers. Drug-dealing entrepreneurs are likely to build their reputation on public marketplaces to draw in customers to their personal vendor shop, and we expect to provide the first comparison of their activities on these two platforms.

This chapter will contribute to our understanding of the human factor of cybercrime by focusing specifically on one type of offender, drug-dealing entrepreneurs on the Tor network. Holt and Bossler (2014) argued that more research was needed to understand the online marketplaces where illicit goods and services are sold. This chapter will address that need and will even go one step beyond by looking at little researched marketplaces that have yet to be understood. This chapter will provide a study at the intersection of cybercrime and drug research that will help researchers better understand both areas of research and help model the entrepreneurship of offenders, both online and offline.

Entrepreneurs and entrepreneurship

Cantillon (1734) is one of the first to have formally defined the concept of *entrepreneurship*. This concept was used to differentiate between hired employees and self-employed individuals through the risks and uncertainty they took on (Lumpkin & Dess, 1996). Entrepreneurship can be defined as a concept by which individuals called *entrepreneurs*, whether alone or within an organization, pursue opportunities independently of the resources they currently possess (Stevenson, Roberts, & Grousbeck, 1989; Stevenson & Jarillo, 1990). More specifically, an entrepreneur is a person who operates or owns a firm and assumes the responsibility for the inherent risks of running the firm (Gottschalk & Smith, 2011). Entrepreneurs will be motivated to pursue opportunities as long as they can identify attractive opportunities and have reasons to believe that their efforts will be rewarded in due time (Frith & McElwee, 2007). For entrepreneurship to foster, the rules of the markets must be clear, predictable, and as simple as possible. Higher taxation levels and extreme regulation make it harder to generate profits for entrepreneurs. Their willingness to take on risks in that context may therefore be lower (Holcombe, 2003). As risk is a subjective concept, all entrepreneurs may not perceive risks in the same way, thereby explaining why some entrepreneurs will seize certain opportunities while others will not. As such, the entrepreneur's perception of risk has more impact than the risk itself when deciding to pursue entrepreneurial opportunities (Palich & Ray Bagby, 1995).

Past research has identified several characteristics that are associated with entrepreneurship (Hornaday & Bunker, 1970; Gottschalk, 2009; Burns, 2010).

Entrepreneurs are individuals who are willing to take risks and are comfortable dealing with these risks. Entrepreneurs have a need for achievement, independence, and an internal locus of control. They are intelligent, opportunistic, creative, innovative, self-confident, self-reliant, proactive, and have a vision for what the market needs. Not all entrepreneurs will eventually build successful firms, and those that do will generally be the most proactive; the most committed to their firm and employees; the most dedicated to success; the most innovative; and the most skilled at marketing, business management and analysing the market they are in (Casson, 1982; McClelland, 1987; Littunen, 2000). Technology can be an important vector to support success, especially if constant efforts are made to improve it (Kazmi, 1999). Firms that emphasize their e-service reliability and ease of use will likely be more successful (Sebora, Lee, & Sukasame, 2009). Success can be evaluated externally either through the profits entrepreneurs generate or through other achievements such as their impact on society. Success can also be measured through its duration (short term vs. long term) (Foley & Green, 1989; Islam, Khan, Obaidullah, & Alam, 2011). Entrepreneurs themselves may also evaluate their success internally through their job satisfaction, the satisfaction of their customers, and the quality of their products (Reijonen & Komppula, 2004; Reijonen & Komppula, 2007). Hisrich and Grachev (1995) have pointed out that lack of business training, lack of experience in financial planning, and lack of guidance and counselling may hamper the success of a firm.

According to Shane and Venkataraman (2000), "to have entrepreneurship, you must first have entrepreneurial opportunities." It is therefore the entrepreneurs' task to notice when demand in a market is not met and to develop a way to meet this demand (Burnett, 2000; Frith & McElwee, 2007). Before launching their firm, entrepreneurs will generally need to study the potential customers of their firm, evaluate the competition, and define a launch strategy. This strategy can focus on lowering the prices of their goods and services, coming up with a high differentiation for their goods and service or on the customer experience they wish to present (Burns, 2010). Perhaps even more importantly, entrepreneurs will need access to the necessary resources to launch their firm. These resources often take on the form of economic capital that can be borrowed from financial institutions (Kazmi, 1999) or raised from investors. Raising this capital may prove difficult for new and small firms. Indeed, small firms do not have the resources to launch big advertising campaigns and may be limited due to their size and scope to operating in a single market and with a limited range of products and services (Burns, 2010). Another important resource is the human capital of firms. Employees are the public face of firms and are directly responsible for maintaining a good relationship with the firms' customers. They must therefore be managed efficiently and with care so as not to ruin the firms' reputation.

Criminal entrepreneurs and entrepreneurship

Entrepreneurship can happen when demand in a market is not met and when an entrepreneur is ready to take on the risk of meeting this demand. The demand can be for a product or service that is not prohibited, but can also be for illicit products and services. This second type of demand is the explanation for the rise of criminal entrepreneurs. Criminal and legal entrepreneurs are believed to be quite similar and to share many common characteristics such as strategic awareness, opportunity spotting, and networking (McElwee, 2008). Criminal entrepreneurs involved in Internet pharmacies, for example, will register domain names with popular registrars such as GoDaddy.com and will buy online advertisements and hosting services from the same providers that help legitimate entrepreneurs (Hall & Antonopoulos, 2016). Both criminal and legitimate entrepreneurs also tend to be similarly motivated by financial gains (Vannostrand & Tewksbury, 1999). Criminal entrepreneurs, however, are involved in illegal businesses and may rationalize their behaviour by thinking that the illegal activities of their firm are within reasonable ethical legal limits, are in the entrepreneur's personal interest, are harmless, or will not incur any negative consequence for the entrepreneur (Gellerman, 1986). They will also work to limit the public expressions of violence, especially when regulation is active in their territory (Gundur, 2017). Criminal entrepreneurs provide a vision but also an identity and a personality to their organizations (Alnkhailan, 2017). Criminal entrepreneurs have been compared to their legal counterparts (Sinclair, 2008). Their firms are believed to be smaller and more ephemeral than legal firms (Reuter, 1983; Haller, 1990). A study of bootlegging firms found that out of 21 bootlegging firms, the mean number of participants for each was 4. Eight of the firms were composed of a single individual, the entrepreneur, five were limited partnerships (two to four participants), and the last eight were categorized as criminal networks (five or more participants) (Davis & Potter, 1991).

The size and scope of criminal firms can be explained by their lack of access to certain resources. Indeed, criminal entrepreneurs cannot get help from the government to access economic, human, and cultural capital. Criminal entrepreneurs must figure out on their own how a firm can be started (Waldorf, Reinarman, & Murphy, 1992; IN Dunlap et al., 1994). To launch their firm, criminal entrepreneurs need access to economic capital, but contrary to other entrepreneurs, they are unable to secure loans from financial institutions or investors. Instead, entrepreneurs are left with one of three options: work in the criminal underworld, seek capital from a more established criminal, or partner with others (Dean, Fahsing, & Gottschalk, 2010). Criminal entrepreneurs can also use legitimate businesses as a front to fund their criminal firms (Davis & Potter, 1991). This involvement in the legal economy has pushed Lampe (2015) to identify three types of criminal firms. Self-sufficient firms are completely distinct from any legal activity. Semi-integrated firms are in contact with the legal economy by, for instance, renting a car for transporting drugs. Finally, integrated criminal firms are embedded in legal businesses on a regular basis. Beside risk coming from entrepreneurship itself, illegal entrepreneurs deal with a risky and uncertain market that limits their size and their survival time (Reuter, 1983) that licit entrepreneurs don't necessarily have to face.

To this day, a single article has sought to develop a theoretical understanding of criminal entrepreneurs. Smith's (2019) matrix brings together theories from different fields (philosophy, sociology, psychology, and criminology) to build a model that can predict the emergence of criminal entrepreneurs. This model, still a work in progress, has yet to be tested and should be the investigation of future research. Looking at other published research, illegal entrepreneurship has mainly been studied in criminology through concepts such as organized crime and criminal networks. Criminal networks are often presented as large, loosely organized networks but can in fact be decomposed into many small partnerships. Networks are therefore often connected one with another (Morselli, 2009) and tend to be limited partnerships, small in size and scope (Haller, 1990). Organized crime and criminal enterprises operate on the same continuum, ranging from individual entrepreneurs acting alone to well-established criminal organizations. Criminal organizations are entrepreneurial activities as much as legitimate business, but only in an illegitimate area (Schloenhardt, 1999). Organized criminal entrepreneurship emerges from a demand for goods and services proscribed by law (Smith, 1975). The criminal entrepreneur's task is to take advantage of criminal opportunities where there is a profit to be made (Gottschalk & Smith, 2011). Gottschalk suggests that convenience theory can explain why individuals become criminal entrepreneurs. This career path would be the most convenient to satisfy their desire for monetary gains and their willingness to commit deviant acts.

The drug dealer's entrepreneurship/success

In the drug business, many types of entrepreneurs work together to package drugs, ship drugs internationally, and sell drugs locally. For this chapter, an entrepreneur will be understood as the person who owns the drugs that are sold either to smaller dealers or to drug users (Caulkins, Johnson, Taylor, & Taylor, 1999). To be effective and survive, drug entrepreneurs need a variety of skills, including those needed to obtain high-quality supplies, to build a customer base, to avoid incarceration and violence, and to launder money (Dunlap et al., 1994). Entrepreneurs also need to be proficient in organizing transactions and detecting law enforcement officers masquerading as buyers (Vannostrand & Tewksbury, 1999). Certain drug businesses are riskier for drug entrepreneurs. Dealing in cocaine incurs more risks of arrest than dealing in cannabis, for example (Bouchard & Ouellet, 2011). The scale of operations of entrepreneurs can also increase risks (Lampe, 2015). Successful entrepreneurs in the drug business need access to technical and human resources to efficiently produce and/or sell their drugs (Smith, 1969). Economic, military, and political resources can also be helpful for drug entrepreneurs (Krauthausen & Sarmiento, 1991; quoted by Zaitch, 2002). Drug entrepreneurs are involved in a very large industry that generates the most profits among all the crime flows in East Asia and the Pacific (Broadhurst, 2017).

Trust plays an important role in drug entrepreneurs' activities. Cocaine entrepreneurs as a result often built their trust circle around family and close friends. Cocaine enterprises are frequently composed of brothers, cousins, and old friends (Zaitch, 2005). These families then connect to other criminal entrepreneurs to expand their network and take advantage of opportunities. Entrepreneurs who recognize that cooperation is useful to success will therefore have more opportunities (McCarthy, Hagan, & Cohen, 1998). McCarthy and Hagan (2001) argue that specialization (human capital), willingness to collaborate (personal capital), and desire for wealth (personal capital) are factors of illegal entrepreneurs' success. Competence also helps with success, but more as a factor of who gives directions and intensifies the factors identified previously. Criminal earning is embedded with conforming work and family relationships, criminal experience, and the perceived crime's risks and rewards (Uggen & Thompson, 2003).

Online vendor shops

Up to 2011, the Internet was not a common distribution channel for illicit drugs. Some websites did offer prescription drugs on the Internet until then (Henney, Shuren, Nightingale, & McGinnis, 1999), but the size and scope of these online stores were limited and easy for law enforcement to take down. This changed with the launch of Silk Road (SR1), an online illicit marketplace called a *cryptomarket* with the look and feel of legitimate merchant websites like eBay or Amazon (Martin, 2014). SR1 was run by an administrator, Dread Pirate Roberts, and welcomed independent vendors to set up online shops on SR1 (Demant, Munksgaard, & Houborg, 2018). Vendors wrote descriptions for themselves and for their products and posted pictures of their products for sale (Broséus et al., 2016). Vendors have been conceptualized as drug entrepreneurs that are rational actors. These entrepreneurs would monitor their customers' feedback and make an exit from the cryptomarket should their reputation be attacked publicly, especially if they were new entrepreneurs (Batikas & Kretschmer, 2018). Customers could log in to SR1, browse the vendors' listings, chat with the vendors, and purchase whatever illicit products or services they wished using the virtual currency bitcoin (Barratt, Ferris, & Winstock, 2016). The anonymity of SR1's administrator and participants was trusted into the hands of cryptography that backed the virtual currency and encrypted the communications and the Internet traffic hosted on the Tor network (Cox, 2016).

SR1 was for a short period the main online marketplace that sold illicit drugs on the Internet (Soska & Christin, 2015). Its popularity grew following news reports and public statements by U.S. politicians asking how such a site could operate so openly and for so long (Chen, 2011). SR1 was eventually taken down by U.S. law enforcement in October 2013 and its administrator arrested (Barratt, Ferris, & Winstock, 2014). Because of cryptography, very few SR1 participants were arrested following the shutdown of SR1 (Branwen, 2015). These participants filled the void left by the shutdown of SR1 by launching new cryptomarkets. The administrators of the new cryptomarkets could hope to earn significant commissions on the sales they facilitated, as the SR1's administrator was believed to have earned around 80 million USD over the 30 months SR1 was active (Estes, 2013). Although SR1's period of activity was characterized by some stability, the years since have been challenging for cryptomarket participants due to the high proportion of cryptomarkets that have shut down unexpectedly either because of law enforcement operations or due to fraud by the cryptomarket administrators (Kruithof et al., 2016). These administrators control the flow of bitcoins between the vendors and the buyers and can take advantage of this strategic position to steal their participants' bitcoin (Lorenzo-Dus & Di Cristofaro, 2018). Still, cryptomarkets are believed to have grown greatly over the past seven years and to have sales that range in the hundreds of millions of dollars per year (Kruithof et al., 2016).

Because of the tension and uncertainty that surround cryptomarkets, some vendors have also launched their own merchant websites on the Tor network (Yannikos, Schäfer, & Steinebach, 2018). Contrary to cryptomarkets, these websites are run by an administrator who is also the only vendor of the website. The administrators (and sometimes their teams) are in charge of designing the website, setting up the transaction panels, and handling customer service and sales. It is unclear at this point how many cryptomarket vendors have opted to launch their own single-vendor shop but specialized blogs like DeepDotWeb and Reddit pages only link to a limited number of single-vendor shops. These shops compete with large cryptomarkets, which provide a one-stop shop for customers and, in many cases, lack the credibility needed to attract customers.

Research problem

Past research has identified the many challenges that criminal entrepreneurs face when launching a new enterprise (Reuter, 1983): access to capital is limited, competition is fierce, and the risks of arrests are high. To succeed as a criminal entrepreneur, individuals must have specific characteristics that set them apart from others. They must be able to seize risks that others do not, to have the right connections, and perhaps even the right experience that has enabled them to build the necessary capital to launch their new venture (McCarthy et al., 1998; Morselli, 2009).

While still very much relevant today, past research has focused so far on traditional offenders that criminologists know how to reach. These include mostly illicit market entrepreneurs involved in drug markets. The Internet has changed how these illicit markets work through the anonymity they provide, the ability to advertise one's products and services, and the ability to reach a large pool of customers. Entrepreneurs who can succeed on the online illicit markets are likely to meet new and different challenges, to have a different skill set from traditional criminal entrepreneurs, and to come up with different answers to the challenges as a result.

The general aim of this chapter is to describe and understand criminal entrepreneurship on the Internet. Although all cryptomarket vendors could and should be considered entrepreneurs, this chapter will focus on a subset of vendors, those that have launched their own virtual single-vendor shop where they are the sole vendor of drugs. These individuals have gone further than other vendors by taking a greater control of their distribution channel through the launch of their own website. Doing so required taking a risk and investing capital into their own enterprise.

The first specific aim of this chapter will be to describe the types of products advertised on single-vendor shops. Our hypothesis is that it only makes sense to invest in a single-vendor shop for popular products that generate important levels of sales online like on cryptomarkets (see Soska & Christin, 2015). Recreational drugs should therefore be more present on single-vendor shops. As these vendor shops are also more private and possibly less likely to attract law enforcement attention, they may be used to sell larger amounts of drugs. We therefore expect to find that single-vendor shops will offer first and foremost bulk drug listings.

The second specific aim will be to provide a description of the vendors involved in single-vendor shops. As vendor shops do not offer the same guarantees to customers as cryptomarkets. we expect to find that vendors who are behind these shops will have experience and possibly a wider range of products for sale, being part of a larger network that has access to a wide range of drugs.

The third specific aim will be to characterize the differences between the vendors' cryptomarket shops and their own vendor shop. We expect to find a similar range of drugs being offered in both but to have lower prices on single-vendor shops, as vendors do not have to pay commissions to cryptomarket administrators.

Data and methods

The data for this chapter come from two sources. The first is from an ongoing cryptomarket data collection project that has been active since 2013. Using the DATACRYPTO's software tool (DATACRYPTO, 2013), researchers have been able to index most of the listings, vendor profiles, and customer feedback posted on the largest cryptomarkets. This has resulted in an archive of millions of listings and feedback and hundreds of thousands of vendor profiles. This archive was used to identify potential single-vendor shops through searches in all its text fields of URLs that end in *.onion*, the domain name of all Tor network websites. The second source of data for this chapter were the *deepdotweb.com* and *reddit.com/r/DarkNetMarkets* websites, where a list of single-vendor shops was published and updated regularly. These two sources of data enabled us to build a list of URLs of single-vendor shops that may or may not be still active. We manually visited each of these URLs and found 40 single-vendor shops that were active in the spring of 2017. Twelve of these single-vendor shops could be linked to cryptomarket vendor accounts through references found in the cryptomarket vendor profile and listings descriptions.

To describe the types of products advertised on single-vendor shops, we used descriptive statistics of the distribution of drugs listed on them. We found a total of 1,532 listings on the vendor shops which were categorized as either cannabis, ecstasy, prescriptions, psychedelics, stimulants, or opioids. We also used descriptive statistics of the diversification of products offered on single-vendor shops on two levels. At the *general* level, broad drug categories were used (e.g. prescriptions). At the *specific* level, very specific drug categories were used (e.g. Viagra). Kruithof et al. (2016) present a comprehensive review of the differences between the two levels of categories. Finally, we used descriptive statistics of the distribution of the quantity of drugs offered in each single-vendor shop listing for hash, herbal cannabis, MDMA, cocaine, methamphetamine, heroin, ecstasy, LSD, and prescriptions. These three series of analyses will provide the first overview of the types of products offered on single-vendor shops.

Very little information is made available on the single-vendor shops about the entrepreneurs who have launched them. The main source of information about these entrepreneurs comes from cryptomarkets which keep track of the entrepreneurs' activities. The information for the 12 cryptomarket vendors known to control single-vendor shops were therefore exported from the DATACRYPTO database to derive descriptive statistics for their average customer rating, the number of days they have been active on cryptomarkets, the number of listings they host on cryptomarkets, and their number of sales and revenues during the last month on cryptomarkets. These last two metrics are generated using the cryptomarket feedback system, which tracks the customers' reviews. This somewhat imprecise proxy for transactions has been used in many other cryptomarket research (Soska & Christin, 2015) and is believed to provide about 70% of all transactions facilitated by cryptomarkets (Kruithof et al., 2016). The country where the cryptomarket vendors ship their drugs from will also be presented in a graph.

Finally, to characterize the differences between the entrepreneurs' cryptomarket shops and their single-vendor shops listings, four series of analyses were generated. First, we compared the distribution of drug listings across drug categories on both platforms based on a categorization of cannabis, ecstasy, prescriptions, psychedelics, stimulants, and opioids. We then compared the diversification of activities of entrepreneurs on cryptomarkets and single-vendor shops based on the same general vs. specific dichotomy presented earlier. We furthermore compared the price differences for the same drugs and the same amounts on each entrepreneur's platforms. We calculated a price per unit – for example, for a 7-g cannabis listing – on an entrepreneur's listing on cryptomarkets and on single-vendor shops to catch the differential pricing of drugs on both platforms. Using only identical listings provides the best estimate of the differences in the pricing strategy on both platforms. Finally, we correlated the prices of these identical listings between cryptomarkets and single-vendor shops.

Results

Single-vendor shops are involved in a broad range of traffic of illicit drugs. Table 3.1 presents the distribution of drugs listed for sale across the six major categories on single-vendor shops found on the dark web.

Listings on single-vendor shops are driven first and foremost by cannabis ($N = 447$). Other drugs such as ecstasy, prescriptions, and psychedelics are also popular, with a prevalence between 16% and 18%. Stimulants and opioids are the two less popular drugs on single-vendor shops, with 12% and 7%, respectively, of all listings. As expected, recreational drugs like cannabis, ecstasy, and some stimulants therefore represent a majority of listings on single-vendor shops.

These 1,532 listings are divided among the 40 single-vendor shops that we were able to identify. Table 3.2 presents the diversification of activities of entrepreneurs on their single-vendor shops. Unsurprisingly, the general categories present lower numbers, as they are also in a limited supply. Half of the single-vendor shops only deal in one general category of drug (Median = 1), though some single-vendor shops cater to many of the needs of their customers through up to six different general categories of drugs.

These general categories of drugs include many specific categories, and this shows in the maximum number of specific categories of drugs sold in a single-vendor shop (Maximum = 52). Half of single-vendor shops sell three specific categories of drugs, though there are wide differences in the dataset, as demonstrated by the high standard deviation (SD = 11). On average, a single-vendor shop offers seven different specific categories of drugs. Cryptomarkets

Table 3.1 Distribution of drugs listed on vendor shops across drugs categories

	Number of listings	%
Cannabis	447	29%
Ecstasy	274	18%
Prescriptions	276	18%
Psychedelics	244	16%
Stimulants	190	12%
Opioids	101	7%
Total	1,532	100%

Table 3.2 Diversification of activities of entrepreneurs on their single-vendor shops

	N	Min.	Max.	Mean	Median	S.D
General categories	40	1	6	2	1	2
Specific categories	40	1	52	7	3	11

are known to deal in large and small quantities of drugs at the same time, though most transactions are for smaller quantities of drugs (Aldridge & Décary-Hétu, 2016). Table 3.3 presents the descriptive statistics of the quantity of drugs in each single-vendor shop listing.

Table 3.3 is divided in two sections, depending on whether the drug is measured in grams or in units such as pills or blotters. Herbal cannabis, prescriptions, and MDMA and the three most common specific drugs being sold. The range of quantities of drugs sold on single-vendor shops is large, as there are multiple orders of magnitude differences between the minimum and the maximum quantity of drugs sold. For the drugs measured in grams, the mean quantities are rather high, with 231 grams for hash, 126 grams for cocaine, and 120 grams for herbal cannabis. These numbers are often not representative of the overall distribution of quantities as exemplified by the large standard deviation scores. The median metric provides a much more representative metric and shows that many listings are actually for much smaller quantities such as 4 grams of cocaine or 15 grams of cannabis. For the drugs measured in units, the means are also very high, ranging from 76 prescription pills to 588 LSD blotters, a quantity so large that it can only be bought for resale. The medians are once again much more indicative of what to expect from single-vendor shop listings and suggest single-vendor shops that are much more geared towards consumers rather than drug dealers as customers.

Table 3.4 presents the descriptive statistics for cryptomarket vendors who also act as entrepreneurs on single-vendor shops. Table 3.4 only includes data on a small set of cryptomarket vendors ($N = 12$ or $N = 10$ depending on the data available on cryptomarkets) and therefore lacks data on most of the single-vendor shop entrepreneurs, unfortunately. Still, it shows that these vendors had excellent reputations on the cryptomarkets (Median = 5.0/5.0). None of them had bad rating scores. These vendors have been active on cryptomarkets for an average of almost two years (Mean − 601 days), and the less experienced

Table 3.3 Quantity of drugs in single-vendors' shop listings

	Number of listings	Min	Max	Mean	Median	SD
(g)						
Hash	94	1.0	10,000	231	20	1054
Herbal cannabis	313	1.0	10,000	120	15	602
MDMA powder	97	<0.1	1,000	113	14	242
Cocaine	97	0.3	10,000	126	4	1019
Methamphetamine	62	1.0	1,000	36	10	127
Heroin	48	0.1	25	3	2	4
(unit)						
MDMA pills (ecstasy)	113	1	10,000	191	25	956
LSD blotter	67	1	5,000	588	100	1060
Prescription pills	150	1	1,000	76	10	160

Table 3.4 Descriptive statistics for cryptomarket vendors who also act as entrepreneurs in single-vendor shops

	N	Min	Max	Mean	Median	SD
Rating	10	4.7	5.0	5.0	5.0	0.1
Number of active days	12	102	1322	601	588	304
Number of listings	12	12	155	68	52	49
Number of sales (last month)	10	1	209	69	53	67
Revenues (last month)	10	$150	$98,280	$16,544	$3,905	$29,853

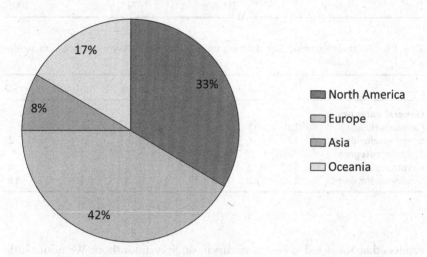

Figure 3.1 Origin of entrepreneurs active on cryptomarkets and single-vendor shops

vendor has been active for more than three months (Min − 102). These vendors had big storefronts on cryptomarkets with a median of 52 different listings per vendor and up to 155 listings. This provided vendors with a prominent visibility on cryptomarkets. The number of transactions may appear to be low for these vendors, with between 1 and 209 sales in the last month. However, this generated significant revenues for some vendors, with a maximum monthly revenue of $98,280. On average, the income of vendors was significant, at $16,544. It is not possible at this point, however, to calculate the profits generated through these sales.

Figure 3.1 presents the origin of the cryptomarket vendors according to their cryptomarket profiles. Vendors appear to originate mostly from Europe (42%) and North America (33%). Africa, South and Central America, and Asia only represent a small fraction of all vendors. A sizeable number of vendors (17%) came from Oceania, mostly Australia.

Table 3.5 compares the distribution of drug listings on cryptomarkets and single-vendor shops. It only contains listings which were posted by cryptomarket

Table 3.5 Distribution of the drug listings on cryptomarkets and single-vendor shops

	Cryptomarkets		Single-vendor shops	
	Number of listings	%	Number of listings	%
Cannabis	221	27%	178	24%
Ecstasy	132	16%	116	16%
Prescriptions	223	28%	199	27%
Psychedelics	100	12%	128	17%
Stimulants	108	13%	68	9%
Opioids	24	3%	53	7%
Total	808	100%	742	100%

Table 3.6 Descriptive statistics for diversification of listings on cryptomarkets and single-vendor shops

	N	Min.	Max.	Mean	Median	SD
General category						
Cryptomarkets	12	1	6	3	3	2
Single-vendor shops	12	1	6	3	3	2
Specific category						
Cryptomarkets	12	2	25	7	5	6
Single-vendor shops	12	2	37	9	4	11

vendors that also acted as entrepreneurs in single-vendor shops. We notice little differences in the distribution of listings between the two platforms for ecstasy and prescriptions. Cannabis listings are a little more prevalent on cryptomarkets ($N = 27\%$) than on single-vendor shops ($N = 24\%$). The same is true for stimulants (13% vs. 9%). Single-vendor shops, however, have a more important proportion of opioids (7% vs. 3%) and psychedelics (17% vs. 12%) than on cryptomarkets. These drugs may be considered harder than the others and may therefore be more prevalent in more privat e settings, such as single-vendor shops, to draw less attention.

Table 3.6 pushes this comparison further by looking at the diversification of listings on cryptomarkets and single-vendor shops. At the general level, both cryptomarkets and single-vendor shops appear to provide the same level of diversification, with an average of three general drug categories sold by each vendor on each platform. At the specific level, however, our results suggest that the vendors' activities are much more diverse on single-vendor shops, with an average of nine specific drug types sold on single-vendor shops compared to seven on cryptomarkets. The median goes the other way around, suggesting that cryptomarkets are indeed more diverse than single-vendor shops. Some vendor shops of cryptomarket vendors offer up to 37 different specific drug types, much more than the 25 we found on cryptomarkets.

We found 600 listings that were offered by the same vendor, the same drug type, and the same quantity on cryptomarkets ($N = 300$) and single-vendor shops ($N = 300$). Their descriptive statistics are presented in Table 3.7. It was surprising to find identical listings that had very large differences in prices depending on the platform. For example, a cannabis listing was 70% cheaper on a single-vendor shop and a prescriptions listing was 88% cheaper on a single-vendor shop. The opposite was also true, as cannabis listings could be up to 47% more expensive on single-vendor shops than on cryptomarkets.

The median column provides a much more representative view of the price comparison. It suggests that prices are actually very similar in general on cryptomarkets and single-vendor shops, with a median difference in total of 0.2% only. This difference can be accounted for by the fluctuations in the bitcoin exchange price or change of prices that occurred during the data collection phase. This is confirmed by Table 3.8, which presents the very high correlation between prices found on cryptomarkets and single-vendor shops for each vendor's identical set of listings.

Table 3.7 Descriptive statistics for price differences between cryptomarkets and single-vendor shops

	Number of listings	Min	Max	Mean	Median	SD
Cannabis	140	−70%	47%	−2%	−0.2%	15%
Ecstasy	104	−50%	16%	−2%	−0.6%	10%
Prescriptions	161	−88%	24%	−7%	−1.4%	16%
Psychedelics	105	−80%	60%	2%	0.0%	21%
Stimulants	61	−21%	29%	4%	0.0%	12%
Opioids	29	−22%	16%	−1%	−0.5%	10%
Total	600			−2%	0.2%	16%

Table 3.8 Pearson correlation coefficients for the prices found for identical listings found on cryptomarkets and single-vendor shops

	Correlation
Cannabis	0.999*
Ecstasy	1.000*
Prescriptions	0.996*
Psychedelics	0.981*
Stimulants	0.997*
Opioids	0.995*

* = $p < 0.05$

Discussion and conclusion

This chapter sought to describe and understand criminal entrepreneurship on the Internet. More specifically, it focused on the entrepreneurship of a select group of offenders: those who have launched their own single-vendor shop on the darknet. Our findings suggest that very few cryptomarket vendors appear to also be criminal entrepreneurs as conceptualized in this chapter. Indeed, our search only turned up 40 single-vendor shops, and 12 of them could be tied to cryptomarket vendors. Past research has found that entrepreneurs will only be motivated to pursue opportunities if they can identify attractive opportunities and have reasons to believe that their efforts will be rewarded in due time (Frith & McElwee, 2007). Palich and Ray Bagby (1995) further explain that the entrepreneur's perception of risk has more impact than the risk itself when deciding to pursue entrepreneurial opportunities (Palich & Ray Bagby, 1995). The low prevalence of single-vendor shops suggests that the risks of running a single-vendor shop are still believed to be too high by a majority of cryptomarket vendors and that a select few have opted to launch their own.

Three hypotheses could explain this finding. First, launching a single-vendor shop requires certain technical and human capital that may not be available to all vendors. Indeed, cryptomarkets handle the payments and the communications between the vendors and the customers (Christin, 2013). Vendors therefore do not need to be knowledgeable in computer programming and web design or to have access to people who are. This significantly reduces the barrier to entry in the online drug markets, as security mistakes when coding websites may lead to identification by law enforcement (Greenberg, 2014). Second, single-vendor shops are run by pseudonymous vendors who ask their customers to send them bitcoins before the drugs are shipped. Building enough trust to lead to transactions in this context is very challenging, and single-vendor shop administrators need to build horizontal trust (Rindfleisch, 2000). Trust in cryptomarkets usually comes from vertical trust, trust generated by third parties such as cryptomarket administrators who label the vendors' accounts with trust labels. Interestingly, we could not link many of the single-vendor shops to cryptomarket vendor accounts, and future research should look into how these vendor shops are advertised online. Still, our results have found that the cryptomarket vendors who have set up single-vendor shops are in the top percentiles of earnings if we compare them to past findings in Paquet-Clouston, Décary-Hétu, & Morselli (2018). Success in cryptomarkets may therefore be needed to succeed as an independent entrepreneur in a single-vendor shop. Lastly, no research has sought to understand the motivation for launching a single-vendor shop, and it is possible that many single-vendor shops cannot be found through searches online and are instead only known by word of mouth. Vendors may wish to keep their client list private and exclusive to evade detection, and it is possible that our research simply underrepresented the number of single-vendor shops operating on the dark web.

The price analysis in this chapter did generate some surprising results. We would have expected single-vendor shops' prices to be lower than on cryptomarkets for identical listings sold by the same vendor. Cryptomarkets charge a commission, whereas single-vendor shops do not, and cryptomarkets draw in a large and diverse pool of customers (Barratt et al., 2016). There are therefore likely weaker social ties between the vendors and the customers on cryptomarkets than on single-vendor shops, which must draw from a pool of customers who have had some direct or indirect experience with the single-vendor shop administrator. The risks and price theory would suggest that in the context of weaker ties and increased risks, prices for illicit products should be higher in this case on cryptomarkets (Reuter & Kleiman, 1986). The identical prices on both platforms suggests that single-vendor shops believe that they own entrepreneurial shops that offer a secure setting where customers do not need to be enticed through discounts. Cryptomarkets have made the news for being taken down by law enforcement or by fraudulent administrators, but anecdotally, single-vendor shops seldom make the news for shutting down or being shut down by law enforcement. As such, customers may see them as less at risk of intervention and therefore more secure. The price of insecurity, thought to be an added tax on all drug transactions, may be reversed in online markets, where security actually increases instead of decreases prices. This echoes past findings (Décary-Hétu, Mousseau, & Vidal, 2018) that found significantly higher prices on cryptomarkets than on the streets for cannabis. Another explanation for the pricing of single-vendor shop products is the need not to cannibalize cryptomarket sales by selling directly to customers. Indeed, vendors need the constant influx of new feedback on cryptomarkets to keep their high ranking on cryptomarkets, and as few customers make repeat purchases (Norbutas, 2018), it is crucial for vendors to find new customers routinely.

Past research (Reuter, 1983) has found that organized crime groups were of small size, ephemeral, and limited in geographic scope. Single-vendor shops unfortunately offer little information on the size and scope of their activities. They offer no complete list of feedback or sales numbers to estimate the revenues of their owners. They require payments be made in bitcoin but often use a dynamic list of bitcoin addresses which are difficult to track. As such, it is not possible using open-source data to compare traditional crime groups to those that run single-vendor shops. These single-vendor shops, however, do transform criminal entrepreneurship. It allows vendors first to advertise for their products openly either on cryptomarkets or other online resources. The pseudonymous nature of their activities makes it possible to link to them in an open fashion without necessarily creating much risk of arrest. Single-vendor shops also decrease the capital needed to become an entrepreneur. Open web designs and free tutorials make it possible to set up a single-vendor shop with very little capital other than time and a willingness to learn. Social capital is not needed to buy a drug supply, as cryptomarkets offer a constant stream of drugs that can be easily bought in bulk (Aldridge & Décary-Hétu, 2016) and resold to drug users. Protection is also much less needed, as the physical locations of the vendor and the customers are protected by the Tor network. Future research should definitively look into the precise profile of the single-vendor shops to better understand whether the shifting capitals needed to become an entrepreneur affect the profile of individuals who decide to take on the risk of becoming an entrepreneur.

The online trade of illicit drugs is still very much concentrated in a few cryptomarkets (see Deepdotweb.com for a list of active cryptomarkets). This facilitates the regulation of this trade for law enforcement, as small disconnected networks are always more difficult to disrupt than centralized organizations (Morselli, 2009). Single-vendor shops, should they become adopted en masse by drug users, would make enforcement of the online trade of illicit drugs much more difficult. It would indeed vastly increase the number of shops to monitor and investigate. This move would be reminiscent of the shift from open air drug markets (Harocopos & Hough, 2005) to closed drug markets (May & Hough, 2004). Open air markets were geographically bound markets where any drug user could purchase drugs. These areas made for easy regulation, as law enforcement could identify all the actors who operated in them and organize crackdowns. With the advent of technology, markets gradually moved to more private – closed – settings where customers needed to be introduced to dealers and contact them personally to buy drugs. Cryptomarkets have been dubbed 'anonymous open marketplaces' (Aldridge & Décary-Hétu, 2016), and single-vendor shops could be their 'anonymous closed marketplaces' counterparts. Future research should investigate if a shift is occurring from cryptomarkets to single-vendor shops and to model the impact that this is likely to have on the efforts of regulation.

Although much research has sought to understand online drug dealing through massive marketplaces like cryptomarkets, this chapter set itself apart by studying lesser known alternatives to cryptomarkets which have been mentioned in past research (see for example Kruithof et al., 2016) but never studied explicitly. The method used to find single-vendor shops, although elaborate, could be enhanced through interviews and surveys with drug users to identify stealthier single-vendor shops. More qualitative works should also investigate the motivation, success, and challenges of single shop administrators who remain dark actors in dark networks. It could be said that online drug dealing is nothing but an old wine in a new bottle. With this research, we have demonstrated just how eclectic online drug dealing could be and that the Internet, as a distribution channel, does significantly affect the business of drug dealing.

References

Aldridge, J., & Décary-Hétu, D. (2016). Hidden wholesale: The drug diffusing capacity of online drug cryptomarkets. *International Journal of Drug Policy, 35*, 7–15.

Alnkhailan, K. (2017). *The theory of successful criminal entrepreneurs* (Doctoral dissertation). Queensland University of Technology.

Barratt, M. J., Ferris, J. A., & Winstock, A. R. (2014). Use of Silk Road, the online drug marketplace, in the United Kingdom, Australia and the United States. *Addiction, 109*(5), 774–783.

Barratt, M. J., Ferris, J. A., & Winstock, A. R. (2016). Safer scoring? Cryptomarkets, social supply and drug market violence. *International Journal of Drug Policy, 35*, 24–31.

Batikas, M., & Kretschmer, T. (2018). *Entrepreneurs on the darknet: Reaction to negative feedback*. Retrieved from https://papers.ssrn.com/sol3/papers.cfm?abstract_id=3238141

Bouchard, M., & Ouellet, F. (2011). Is small beautiful? The link between risks and size in illegal drug markets. *Global Crime, 12*(1), 70–86.

Branwen, G. (2015). Tor DNM-related arrests, 2011–2015. Retrieved from www.gwern.net/DNM-arrests.

Broadhurst, R. (2017). Criminal Innovation and Illicit Global Markets: Transnational Crime in Asia. *Organised crime research in Australia 2018*. Retrieved from www. researchgate.net/profile/Jade_Lindley/publication/329233680_Nexus_between_illegal_unreported_and_unregulated_fishing_and_other_organised_maritime_crimes/links/5bfdf8654585157b8172a8f5/Nexus-between-illegal-unreported-and-unregulated-fishing-and-other-organised-maritime-crimes.pdf#page=93

Broséus, J., Rhumorbarbe, D., Mireault, C., Ouellette, V., Crispino, F., & Décary-Hétu, D. (2016). Studying illicit drug trafficking on darknet markets: Structure and organisation from a Canadian perspective. *Forensic Science International, 264*, 7–14.

Burnett, D. (2000). Hunting for heffalumps: The supply of entrepreneurship and economic development. *History of Entrepreneurship Theory*, 1–3.

Burns, P. (2010). *Entrepreneurship and small business: Start-up: Growth and maturity*. London: Palgrave Macmillan.

Cantillon, R. (1734). *Essai sur la nature du commerce en general [Essay on the nature of general commerce]*. London: Palgrave Macmillan.

Casson, M. (1982). *The entrepreneur: An economic theory*. New York: Rowman & Littlefield.

Caulkins, J. P., Johnson, B., Taylor, A., & Taylor, L. (1999). What drug dealers tell us about their costs of doing business. *Journal of Drug Issues, 29*(2), 323–340.

Chen, A. (2011). The underground website where you can buy any drug imaginable. Retrieved from http://gawker.com/the-underground-website-where-you-can-buy-any-drug-imag-30818160

Christin, N. (2013). Traveling the Silk Road: A measurement of analysis of a large anonymous online marketplace. In *Proceedings of the 22nd International conference on World Wide Web* (pp. 213–224). New York: ACM.

Cox, J. (2016). Staying in the shadows: The use of bitcoin and encryption in cryptomarkets. *Internet and Drug Markets, EMCDDA Insights*, 41–47.

Davis, R. S., & Potter, G. W. (1991). Bootlegging and rural criminal entrepreneurship. *Journal of Crime and Justice, 14*(1), 145–159.

Dean, G., Fahsing, I., & Gottschalk, P. (2010). *Organized crime: Policing illegal business entrepreneurialism*. Oxford: Oxford University Press.

Décary-Hétu, D., & Aldridge, J. (2013). DATACRYPTO: The dark net crawler and scraper. Software Program.

Décary-Hétu, D., Mousseau, V., & Vidal, S. (2018). Six years later: Analyzing online black markets involved in herbal cannabis drug dealing in the United States. *Contemporary Drug Problems, 45*, 366–381.

Demant, J., Munksgaard, R., & Houborg, E. (2018). Personal use, social supply or redistribution? Cryptomarket demand on Silk Road 2 and Agora. *Trends in Organized Crime, 21*(1), 42–61.

Dingledine, R., Mathewson, N., & Syverson, P. (2004). *Tor: The second-generation onion router*. Washington, DC: Naval Research Lab.

Dunlap, E., Johnson, B. D., & Manwar, A. (1994). A successful female crack dealer: Case study of a deviant career. *Deviant Behavior, 15*(1), 1–25.

Estes, C. (2013). Retrieved from https://gizmodo.com/silk-road-kingpin-apparently-hid-a-stash-of-80-million-1441291682

Foley, P., & Green, H. (1989). *Small business success*. London: Paul Chapman.

Frith, K., & McElwee, G. (2007). An emergent entrepreneur? A story of a drug-dealer in a restricted entrepreneurial environment. *Society and Business Review, 2*(3), 270–286.

Gellerman, S.W. (1986). *Why "good" managers make bad ethical choices*. Retrieved from https://repository.library.georgetown.edu/handle/10822/814289

Gottschalk, P. (2009). *Entrepreneurship and organised crime: Entrepreneurs in illegal business*. Northampton, MA: Edward Elgar Publishing.

Gottschalk, P., & Smith, R. (2011). Criminal entrepreneurship, white-collar criminality, and neutralization theory. *Journal of Enterprising Communities: People and Places in the Global Economy, 5*(4), 300–308.

Greenberg, A. (2014). *FBI's story of finding silk road's server sounds a lot like hacking*. Retrieved from www.wired.com/2014/09/fbi-silk-road-hacking-question/

Gundur, R.V. (2017). *Organizing crime in the margins: The enterprises and people of the American drug trade*. Doctoral dissertation, Cardiff University.

Hall, A., & Antonopoulos, G. A. (2016). *Fake meds online: The internet and the transnational market in illicit pharmaceuticals*. New York, NY: Springer.

Haller, M. H. (1990). Illegal enterprise: A theoretical and historical interpretation. *Criminology, 28*(2), 207–236.

Harocopos, A., & Hough, M. (2005). *Drug dealing in open-air markets*. Washington, DC: US Department of Justice, Office of Community Oriented Policing Services.

Henney, J. E., Shuren, J. E., Nightingale, S. L., & McGinnis, T. J. (1999). Internet purchase of prescription drugs: Buyer beware. *Annals of Internal Medicine, 131*(11), 861–862.

Hisrich, R. D., & Grachev, M.V. (1995). The Russian entrepreneur: Characteristics and prescriptions for success. *Journal of Managerial Psychology, 10*(2), 3–9.

Holcombe, R. G. (2003). The origins of entrepreneurial opportunities. *The Review of Austrian Economics, 16*(1), 25–43.

Holt, T. J., & Bossler, A. M. (2014). An assessment of the current state of cybercrime scholarship. *Deviant Behavior, 35*, 20–40.

Hornaday, J. A., & Bunker, C. S. (1970). The nature of the entrepreneur. *Personnel Psychology, 23*(1), 47–54.

Islam, M. A., Khan, M. A., Obaidullah, A. Z. M., & Alam, M. S. (2011). Effect of entrepreneur and firm characteristics on the business success of small and medium enterprises (SMEs) in Bangladesh. *International Journal of Business and Management, 6*(3), 289.

Kazmi, A. (1999). What young entrepreneurs think and do: A study of second-generation business entrepreneurs. *The Journal of Entrepreneurship, 8*(1), 67–77.

Kruithof, K., Aldridge, J., Décary-Hétu, D., Sim, M., Dujso, E., & Hoorens, S. (2016). *Internet-facilitated drugs trade: An Analysis of the Size, Scope and the Role of the Netherlands*. Santa Monica: RAND Europe.

Lampe, K. von. (2015). Big business: Scale of operation, organizational size, and the level of integration into the legal economy as key parameters for understanding the development of illegal enterprises. *Trends in Organized Crime, 18*(4), 289–310.

Littunen, H. (2000). Entrepreneurship and the characteristics of the entrepreneurial personality. *International Journal of Entrepreneurial Behavior & Research, 6*(6), 295–310.

Lorenzo-Dus, N., & Di Cristofaro, M. (2018). 'I know this whole market is based on the trust you put in me and I don't take that lightly': Trust, community and discourse in crypto-drug markets. *Discourse & Communication, 12*(6), 608–626.

Lumpkin, G. T., & Dess, G. G. (1996). Clarifying the entrepreneurial orientation construct and linking it to performance. *Academy of Management Review, 21*(1), 135–172.

Martin, J. (2014). *Drugs on the dark net: How cryptomarkets are transforming the global trade in illicit drugs*. New York: Springer.

May, T., & Hough, M. (2004). Drug markets and distribution systems. *Addiction Research and Theory, 12*(6), 549–563.

McCarthy, B., & Hagan, J. (2001). When crime pays: Capital, competence, and criminal success. *Social Forces, 79*(3), 1035–1060.

McCarthy, B., Hagan, J., & Cohen, L. E. (1998). Uncertainty, cooperation, and crime: Understanding the decision to co-offend. *Social Forces, 77*(1), 155–184.

McClelland, D. C. (1987). Characteristics of successful entrepreneurs. *The Journal of Creative Behavior, 21*(3), 219–233.

McElwee, G. (2008). The rural entrepreneur: Problems of definition. *International Journal of Entrepreneurship and Small Business, 6*(3), 320–321.

Morselli, C. (2009). *Inside criminal networks.* New York, NY: Springer.

Norbutas, L. (2018). Offline constraints in online drug marketplaces: An exploratory analysis of a cryptomarket trade network. *International Journal of Drug Policy, 56*, 92–100.

Palich, L. E., & Ray Bagby, D. (1995). Using cognitive theory to explain entrepreneurial risk-taking: Challenging conventional wisdom. *Journal of Business Venturing, 10*(6), 425–438.

Paquet-Clouston, M., Décary-Hétu, D., & Morselli, C. (2018). Assessing market competition and vendors' size and scope on AlphaBay. *International Journal of Drug Policy, 54*, 87–98.

Reijonen, H., & Komppula, R. (2004). *Craft entrepreneur's growth-motivation a case study of female entrepreneurs in North Karelia* [Sarjajulkaisu]. Retrieved from http://epublications. uef.fi/pub/urn_isbn_952-458-515-4/

Reijonen, H., & Komppula, R. (2007). Perception of success and its effect on small firm performance. *Journal of Small Business and Enterprise Development, 14*(4), 689–701.

Reuter, P. (1983). *Disorganized crime: The economics of the visible hand.* Boston, MA: MIT Press.

Reuter, P., & Kleiman, M. A. (1986). Risks and prices: An economic analysis of drug enforcement. *Crime and Justice, 7*, 289–340.

Rindfleisch, A. (2000). Organizational trust and interfirm cooperation: An examination of horizontal versus vertical alliances. *Marketing Letters, 11*(1), 81–95.

Schloenhardt, A. (1999). Organized crime and the business of migrant trafficking. *Crime, Law and Social Change, 32*(3), 203–233.

Sebora, T. C., Lee, S. M., & Sukasame, N. (2009). Critical success factors for e-commerce entrepreneurship: An empirical study of Thailand. *Small Business Economics, 32*(3), 303–316.

Shane, S., & Venkataraman, S. (2000). The promise of entrepreneurship as a field of research. *Academy of Management Review, 25*(1), 217–226.

Sinclair, R. (2008). Legitimizing the study of illegal entrepreneurship (Summary). *Frontiers of Entrepreneurship Research, 28*(4).

Smith, D. C. (1975). *The mafia mystique.* New York, NY: Basic Books.

Smith, R. C. (1969). Traffic in amphetamines: Patterns of illegal manufacture and distribution. *Journal of Psychedelic Drugs, 2*(2), 20–24.

Smith, R. C. (2019). 'Crimino-entrepreneurial behaviour': Developing a theoretically based behavioural matrix to identify and classify. In *Entrepreneurial behaviour.* New York: Palgrave Macmillan.

Soska, K., & Christin, N. (2015, August). *Measuring the longitudinal evolution of the online anonymous marketplace ecosystem.* USENIX Security Symposium, pp. 33–48.

Stevenson, H. H., & Jarillo, J. C. (1990). A paradigm of entrepreneurship: Entrepreneurial management. In *Entrepreneurship* (pp. 155–170). Berlin: Springer.

Stevenson, H. H., Roberts, M. J., & Grousbeck, H. I. (1989). *Business ventures and the entrepreneur.* Homewood, IL: Irwin.

Uggen, C., & Thompson, M. (2003). The socioeconomic determinants of ill-gotten gains: Within-person changes in drug use and illegal earnings. *American Journal of Sociology, 109*(1), 146–185.

Vannostrand, L-M., & Tewksbury, R. (1999). The motives and mechanics of operating an illegal drug enterprise. *Deviant Behavior, 20*(1), 57–83.

Waldorf, D., Reinarman, C., & Murphy, S. (1992). *Cocaine changes: The experience of using and quitting.* Philadelphia, PA: Temple University Press.

Wall, D. (2007). *Cybercrime: The transformation of crime in the Information Age.* New York: Polity.

Yannikos, Y., Schäfer, A., & Steinebach, M. (2018). *Monitoring product sales in darknet shops.* Proceedings of the 13th International Conference on Availability, Reliability and Security.

Yip, M., Shadbolt, N., & Webber, C. (2013). *Why forums? An empirical analysis into the facilitating factors of carding forums.* Proceedings of the 5th Annual ACM Web Science Conference.

Zaitch, D. (2002). *Trafficking cocaine: Colombian drug entrepreneurs in the Netherlands.* New York: Springer Science & Business Media.

Zaitch, D. (2005). The ambiguity of violence, secrecy, and trust among Colombian drug entrepreneurs. *Journal of Drug Issues, 35*(1), 201–228.

Part II

Victims

4 Predictors of cybercrime victimization

Causal effects or biased associations?

Steve van de Weijer

Introduction

With the ongoing digitalization of our society, cybercrime has become part of our everyday life. The number of people who are victimized by cybercrime has increased rapidly over the past couple of decades. In the Netherlands, the country in which the current study was conducted, 11% of citizens reported becoming a victim of cybercrime in 2017 (Statistics Netherlands, 2018). The most prevalent type of cybercrime in the Netherlands is hacking (4.9%), followed by online fraud (3.9%), cyberbullying (including stalking, slander, blackmailing, and harassment; 3.3%), and identity theft (0.4%). By comparison, the prevalence of hacking and online fraud exceeds the number of people who were the victim of some of the most prevalent forms of traditional crimes, such as bicycle theft (3.3%), violent crimes (2.0%), burglary (1.2%), and pickpocketing (1.0%) (Statistics Netherlands, 2018). Given this high prevalence of cybercrime victimization, it is not surprising that the number of scientific studies on cybercrime victimization has also rapidly increased during this century.

Self-control theory (Gottfredson & Hirschi, 1990) and routine activities theory (Cohen & Felson, 1979) have often been used to explain why some people are more likely to become a victim of cybercrime than others. Based on self-control theory, it can be expected that individuals with lower self-control are not only more likely to be engaged in criminal behaviour but also to have an increased risk of being victimized than those with a higher level of self-control (Schreck, 1999). Several studies have shown that this is also the case for cybercrime victimization (e.g. Reyns, Burek, Henson, & Fisher, 2013; Van Wilsem, 2011b; 2013). One part of the routine activities theory focuses on the suitability of a target, and Felson and Clarke (1998) argued that this suitability is determined by four factors: value, inertia, visibility, and accessibility. Previous studies have shown that individuals who engage in online activities that increase their visibility, such as online shopping (Van Wilsem, 2011a; Van Wilsem, 2011b), online gaming (Leukfeldt & Yar, 2016), or visiting dating websites (Holt, Van Wilsem, Van de Weijer, & Leukfeldt, 2018), are more likely to become a victim of several types of cybercrime.

A large limitation of previous studies on this topic, however, is the fact that they are all based on observational, cross-sectional data in which both cyber-crime victimization and its predictors are only measured at one time point. This is problematic because the use of such data could lead to biased estimates for two reasons. First, with cross-sectional data, it is usually unclear whether predictors of victimization precede the cybercrime or vice versa. For example, it is possible that people who spend more time illegally downloading software are more likely to get a malware infection on their computer. At the same time, it is possible that when people get a malware infection on their computer, they change their online behaviour (e.g. stop downloading software). In such a situation, in which the independent and dependent variable both have an effect on each other, there is simultaneous causality, which could lead to an overestimation or underestimation of the true causal effect.

Another reason why biased estimates occur when standard research methods are used for observational data (e.g. logistic regression analyses) is that these studies can only control for potential confounders that are measured but do not control for hidden bias. Hidden bias occurs when there are unmeasured variables that are related to both the independent and the dependent variable (i.e. confounders). With non-experimental data, there is virtually always a risk for hidden bias, as usually not all potential confounders can be measured and included in the analyses. Therefore, quasi-experimental research designs should be used to control for this hidden bias.

Because of the risk of simultaneous causality and unmeasured confounding variables, previous studies have likely only shown a correlation between cybercrime victimization and low self-control and online activities, rather than showing the true causal effect of these predictors. Estimating the causal effect, rather than just the association, is crucial for theory testing as well as for designing effective interventions. Therefore, the current study will add to the existing literature by applying two types of quasi-experimental research methods (i.e. fixed effects panel models and discordant sibling designs) in order to get a better estimate of the true causal effect of online routine activities and self-control on cybercrime victimization. These methods will be applied on longitudinal data on a large, representative sample of Dutch households. The research question of this chapter is twofold. First, to what extent are online activities and low self-control associated with cybercrime victimization? Second, do these associations remain significant after controlling for unmeasured confounders by applying quasi-experimental research methods?

Theory

Routine activities theory

An effect of certain online activities on cybercrime victimization can be expected based on Cohen and Felson's (1979) routine activities theory. Cohen and Felson (1979, p. 588) hypothesized that "most criminal acts require the convergence in space and time of *likely offenders, suitable targets* and the *absence of capable guardians*" (emphasis added). It has been argued that convergence in space and time is problematic in the case of cybercrime, given that "the cyber-spatial environment is chronically spatio-temporally *disorganized*" (Yar, 2005, p. 424, emphasis added). However, the three core elements of routine activities theory (motivated offenders, suitable targets, and absence of capable guardians) seem to be applicable to cybercrimes. Various motivated offenders can be found in the online environment, such as hackers, phishers, fraudsters, and harassers. Similarly, there are several online variants of capable guardians. Capable guardians could either be individuals, such as network administrators or forum moderators, or software, such as firewalls, virus scanners, spam filters, and anti-spyware software. The suitability of a target is determined by four factors: value, inertia, visibility, and accessibility (Felson & Clarke, 1998). The visibility of victims is of particular interest for the relationship between online activities and cybercrime victimization. Visibility refers to the exposure of targets to offenders. When individuals engage in online activities that increase their online visibility, it becomes more likely that their existence becomes known to potential offenders. Such online activities are therefore expected to increase the risk of cybercrime victimization.

In line with this hypothesis, several studies found a relationship between online activities and cybercrime victimization. Among American college students, it has been found that students who frequently download games, music, and movies and frequently open attachments are more likely to get a virus infection (Choi, 2008), whereas those who spend more time on online chatting are more likely to receive unwanted sexually explicit material (Marcum, Higgins, & Ricketts, 2010) and to be harassed online (Holt & Bossler, 2008). Moreover, the total time spent on the Internet and online shopping has been shown to predict online fraud victimization among American (Pratt, Holtfreter, & Reisig, 2010) and Dutch adults (Van Wilsem, 2011b). Van Wilsem (2011a) also examined victimization of online threats, which was found to be related to time spent on online shopping, webcam use, and having a profile on the Dutch social network site Hyves. Holt and colleagues (2018) used more recent data from the same sample to study the risk on malware infections. Their results showed that respondents who spend time downloading, watching movies online, and dating websites are at increased risk for a malware infection compared to those who do not spend time on these online activities. Furthermore, Leukfeldt and Yar (2016) examined the relationship between victimization of six different types of cybercrime and several online activities using a large sample of Dutch citizens. They found that both targeted and untargeted browsing, online shopping, downloading, and online gaming are related to victimization of malware infections. Those who were active on online forums, social network sites, and MSN or Skype were found to be more likely to become a victim of hacking than those who did not spend time on these online activities. Moreover, targeted browsing was found to be related to identity theft victimization, and online shopping and emailing were associated with consumer fraud victimization.

Finally, Leukfeldt and Yar (2016) showed that direct communication via both email and MSN or Skype was related to stalking and threat victimization, and those who used Twitter were also more likely to receive threats than those who did not use Twitter.

However, there are also studies that did not find any association between online activities and cybercrime victimization. Van Wilsem (2013) did not find any relationship between victimization of hacking and respondents' use of a webcam, social media use, and the number of hours spent online. Bossler and Holt (2009) examined data loss caused by malware infection in a college sample and found that time spent on online shopping, video games, email, chatrooms, downloading, and programming were all unrelated to victimization. Ngo and Paternoster (2011) examined victimization of seven types of cybercrime (computer virus, harassment by a stranger, harassment by a non-stranger, unwanted pornography, sex solicitation, phishing, and defamation) among a group of 295 college students. Time spent on emailing, instant messaging, in chat rooms, and on the Internet in general, as well as more specific online behaviours (communicating with strangers, providing personal info, clicking/opening links) were examined. All except one of the associations that they found were either insignificant or in the unexpected direction. Next, Reyns, Henson, and Fisher (2011) studied victimization of several types of cyberstalking (i.e. unwanted contact, harassment, sexual advances, threats of violence, and cyberstalking) among a large group of college students. Although they did find a couple of significant associations (e.g. the number of photos on social network sites was positively related to online harassment), they concluded that the online exposure variables were not consistently related to the different types of pursuit behaviours. Finally, Leukfeldt (2014) found little support for routine activities theory in his study into phishing victimization among a large, representative sample of Dutch citizens. Whereas the author found a significant relationship between targeted browsing and phishing victimization, no association was found with many other online behaviours (e.g., chatting, gaming, forums, social network sites, Twitter, downloading, shopping).

Self-control theory

An effect of low self-control on cybercrime victimization can be expected based on Gottfredson and Hirschi's (1990) general theory of crime. Gottfredson and Hirschi (1990) hypothesized that individuals with a low level of self-control are more likely to engage in criminal and risky behaviour, as they are impulsive, short sighted, impatient, and risk taking. As a consequence, they are more orientated on immediate gratification and do not recognize the long-term consequences of their acts. Although the focus of this theory is on criminal offending rather than victimization, Gottfredson and Hirschi (1990, p. 17) argued that "victims and offenders tend to share all or nearly all social and personal characteristics." Schreck (1999) extended self-control theory to criminal victimization by arguing that those with low self-control do not make an accurate consideration of the consequences of their actions. As a consequence, they may place themselves more often in risky situations and are less likely to take preventive measures to protect themselves against criminality.

In line with self-control theory, a meta-analysis by Pratt, Turanovic, Fox, and Wright (2014) showed that a low level of self-control is a modest but consistent predictor of crime victimization. Their meta-analysis further showed that the association between low self-control and victimization was significantly stronger for non-contact offences (such as cybercrimes) than for contact offences. More specifically, studies have shown that low self-control is significantly related to a higher victimization risk of online consumer fraud (Van Wilsem, 2011b); malware infection (Holt et al., 2018); hacking (Van Wilsem, 2013); and several interpersonal cybercrimes, including harassment, unwanted sexual advances, and violent threats (Reyns et al., 2013).

Other studies, however, showed mixed results. Bossler and Holt (2010) found weak but significant associations between low self-control and victimization of hacking and harassment. However, these associations became insignificant after controlling for offending measures. Moreover, no significant relationship was found between low self-control and victimization of malware infections and credit card theft. Ngo and Paternoster (2011) found that low self-control was related to victimization of harassment by strangers and non-strangers but was not related to victimization of computer viruses, unwanted pornography, sex solicitation, phishing, and defamation. Finally, although Van Wilsem (2011a) did not find an association between low self-control and receiving threats in a digital way only, he did find such a relationship with receiving both traditional and digital threats.

In sum, most but not all previous studies have found results that are in line with routine activities theory and self-control theory. These previous studies are, however, limited in several ways. Some are based on small sample sizes (e.g. Choi, 2008; Ngo & Paternoster, 2011), use college student samples (e.g. Bossler & Holt, 2009; Holt & Bossler, 2008; Marcum et al., 2010), and/or only focus on one specific type of cybercrime (e.g. Holt & Bossler, 2008; Pratt et al., 2010; Van Wilsem, 2011a; 2011b). These limitations have been addressed in other studies (e.g. Leukfeldt & Yar, 2016) but one major limitation has not been addressed previously: all studies on cybercrime victimization are based on cross-sectional data. As discussed earlier, the use of such data can lead to biased estimates as a consequence of simultaneous causality and hidden bias.

The current study

The current study adds to the existing literature by using a large and representative sample of Dutch households to study victimization of five types of cybercrime: online harassment, online fraud, hacking, virus infections, and malware infections. But most importantly, the current study makes use of longitudinal data, measured between 2008 and 2016, in order to apply two quasi-experimental research designs. Fixed effects panel models and a discordant sibling model will be used to control for hidden bias and to get a better estimate of the true causal effect of low self-control and online activities on cybercrime victimization.

First, a fixed effects panel model will be used to study cybercrime victimization among a large sample of Dutch households. The use of longitudinal panel data makes it possible to examine whether within-individual changes in predictors of cybercrime victimization also lead to changes in cybercrime victimization within the same person. For example, it is examined whether a respondent's risk of malware infection decreases when he stops illegally downloading software. Because fixed effects analyses only focus on within-individual changes, all bias caused by unmeasured differences between individuals is filtered out. Although the use of fixed effects panel models is gaining popularity in the study of traditional crime offenders (e.g. Hill, Van der Geest, & Blokland, 2017; Pyrooz, McGloin, & Decker, 2017), its use remains very limited in the field of cybercrime. To the author's knowledge, only Weulen Kranenbarg and colleagues (2018) used fixed effects panel models in their study among Dutch cybercrime offenders. No previous study to date has used fixed effects models to examine predictors of cybercrime victimization.

A limitation of fixed effects panel models, however, is that they are less suitable to study the effect of independent variables that are relatively stable over time, because these models only focus on changes within the same individual over time. The level of self-control has been hypothesized (Gottfredson & Hirschi, 1990) and empirically shown to be relatively stable over the life course (e.g., Beaver, Wright, DeLisi, & Vaughn, 2008; Hay & Forrest, 2006). Therefore, a second quasi-experimental research design that does allow the inclusion of time-stable factors and also controls for hidden bias will be used as well: a discordant sibling design. This method compares two siblings from the same household who differ on scores on both the dependent and independent variable. In contrast to the fixed effects model that controls for everything that is stable within the same individual, the discordant sibling model controls for everything that is shared between siblings. This includes shared environmental factors (e.g. household socio-economic status, household size, urbanization grade) and genetic factors (see also D'Onofrio, Lahey, Turkheimer, & Lichtenstein, 2013).

It is important to also control for genetic confounding, as it is possible that certain genetic factors increase the risk of cybercrime victimization but also influence involvement in certain online activities and the level of self-control. For victimization of traditional types of crime, for example, previous studies have shown that a considerable proportion of the variance in victimization can be explained by genetic factors (Barnes & Beaver, 2012; Beaver, Boutwell, Barnes, & Cooper, 2009; Beckley et al., 2017; Vaske, Boisvert, & Wright, 2012). Similarly, several twin studies showed that also individual differences in the level of self-control are accounted for by genetic factors (e.g. Beaver et al., 2008). Analyses of Boutwell and colleagues (2013) revealed that 63% of the covariance between levels of self-control and traditional crime victimization were contributable to genetic factors, illustrating the importance of controlling for genetic confounding. To the author's knowledge, no previous studies have examined the heritability of cybercrime victimization. Some twin studies, however, have shown that problematic Internet use has considerable genetic underpinnings (Vink, Beijsterveldt, Huppertz, Bartels, & Boomsma, 2016; Li, Chen, Li, & Li, 2014). In addition, involvement in certain online routine activities could be heritable. For example, York (2017) showed that a considerable proportion of the variance in the frequency of social media use is attributable to genetic factors. Genetic confounding could therefore also be a potential source of bias in the study of cybercrime victimization.

Methods

Sample

Data of the Longitudinal Internet Studies for the Social Sciences (LISS) panel was used in this chapter to answer the research questions. The LISS panel is a representative sample of Dutch individuals who participate in monthly Internet surveys, administered by CentERdata. The panel is based on a true probability sample of households drawn from the population register. Households that could not otherwise participate were provided with a computer and Internet connection. All household members aged 15 years and older were asked to complete the surveys. A longitudinal survey is fielded in the panel every year, covering a large variety of domains, including work, education, income, housing, time use, political views, values, and personality.

In the current chapter, data from three different LISS surveys were combined. First, data on cybercrime victimization and low self-control were extracted from the biannual Conventional and Computer Crime Victimization survey. This survey consists of five waves of data collection conducted in February 2008, February 2010, February 2012, February 2014, and February 2016. In all waves except for the first wave, respondents were asked about victimization of several types of cybercrime in the previous two years (e.g. Wave 2 measured cybercrime victimization between March 2008 and February 2010). Second, data from the Social Integration and Leisure survey were used to measure several types of online routine activities. This survey is conducted annually in February. Third, demographic control variables (e.g. gender, age) were extracted from the Background Variables file, which is updated each month.

For the longitudinal analyses in this chapter, the data were constructed in such a way that all predictors were measured before the period in which cybercrime victimization was measured. For example, online activities, self-control, and demographics were measured in February 2008 and were used to predict cybercrime victimization in the period between March 2008 and February 2010. Figure 4.1 visualizes the study design of these longitudinal analyses. In total, the sample consists of 17,004 observations within 7,106 respondents.

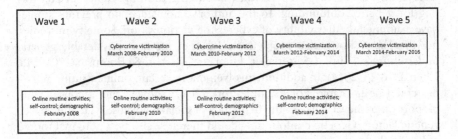

Figure 4.1 Study design longitudinal analyses

Dependent variables

The dependent variables in this study were respondents' victimization of several types of cybercrime. In the Conventional and Computer Crime Victimization survey, respondents were asked biannually whether they had become a victim of several traditional and cybercrimes during the past two years. Four of these types of cybercrime were examined in the current study: online intimidation, online fraud, hacking, and virus infection. Victimization of these types of crime was asked in the survey using the following items:[1]

1   Intimidation by email, Short Message Service (SMS), MSN, or any other electronic channel.
2   You bought something via the Internet or email but did not receive the product.
3   Others gained access to your computer without permission ('hacking').
4   Your computer was infected by a virus that caused damage, for instance, by deleting files on the hard disk.

Respondents could answer these questions with either 'yes' or 'no.' In the fourth wave, however, an extra answer category was added, and respondents could also answer with 'more or less.' In order to keep the answers consistent across waves, categories 'yes' and 'more or less' were combined. Consequently, there are four binary dependent variables indicating whether or not someone was the victim of a cybercrime in the past two years.

The use of self-reported victimization could, however, be problematic when it is likely that victims are not aware of the crime. This could be the case when respondents are asked about virus infections on their computer. Respondents who indicate that they have been victimized might be aware of the virus infection due to alerts from their antivirus software programs. When such software programs are not used, are improperly configured, or are not updated, respondents might not obtain information about the virus infections on their computer. It is therefore likely that respondents, particularly those with less technological expertise, are underreporting the virus infections on their computer (Holt et al., 2018). Some previous studies have therefore asked respondents about the behaviour of their computer, as certain changes in computer operations and computer crashes could reflect potential malware infections (e.g. Holt et al., 2018). In the fourth and fifth wave of the Conventional and Computer Crime Victimization survey, respondents were asked how often the following behaviours were observed on their computer during the previous 12 months:

1 Their home computer slowed down or was not running as fast as it used to.
2 The computer froze up or crashed, requiring the system to be shut down or reset.
3 The home page changed on their home computer without them resetting it.
4 A new program appeared on their home computer that they did not install, or new icons suddenly appeared on the desktop.

Respondents could answer these questions using a five-point Likert scale: (1) never; (2) 1 to 2 times; (3) 3 to 5 times; (4) 6 to 9 times; and (5) 10 or more times. For respondents who answered all four items, the average score was calculated in order that a higher score indicated a higher risk on malware infection. The Cronbach's alpha of this scale was 0.690 in the fourth wave, and 0.709 in the fifth wave, indicating that these items form a reliable scale for malware infection. As it can be argued that the first two items of this scale could also be an indication of using older computers instead of malware victimization, additional analyses will be done in which only the average scores on the third and fourth items of the scale are used as a dependent variable.

Independent variables

The independent variables in this study were having low self-control and several types of online routine activities. Low self-control was measured based on Dickman's Dysfunctional Impulsivity scale (1990). This scale is based on the following 12 items:

1 I often say and do things without considering the consequences.
2 I enjoy working out problems slowly and carefully.
3 I frequently make appointments without thinking whether I will be able to keep them.
4 I frequently buy things without thinking about whether or not I can really afford them.
5 I often make up my mind without taking the time to consider the situation from all angles.
6 Often, I don't spend enough time thinking over a situation before I act.
7 I often get into trouble because I don't think before I act.

8   Many times the plans I make don't work out because I haven't gone over them carefully enough in advance.

9   I often get involved in projects without first considering the potential problems.

10   Before making any important decisions, I carefully weigh up the pros and cons.

11   I am good at careful reasoning.

12   I will often say whatever comes into my head without thinking first.

Respondents were asked, on a two-point scale, whether they agree or disagree with each of the 12 items. The second, tenth, and eleventh item were reversely recoded, as they are indication of high self-control rather than low self-control. The average score on the items was calculated for all respondents who answered at least half of the 12 items, leading to a scale from 1 (high self-control) to 2 (low self-control). Scores on Dickman's Dysfunctional Impulsivity scale were measured in February 2008, February 2010, February 2012, and February 2014. The Cronbach's alpha of the scale differed across the four waves, with alphas between 0.732 (in 2014) and 0.753 (in 2012). This indicates that these items form a reliable scale for self-control.

Online routine activities of respondents were measured annually in the month of February. In this study the measurements of online routine activities in 2008, 2010, 2012, and 2014 were used. Respondents were first asked whether they used a computer,[2] and if they did, whether they made use of the Internet. Respondents who indicated that they used the Internet were then asked whether they ever spent time on a number of online activities. When respondents confirmed they engage in a certain online activity, they were asked to indicate how many hours per week, on average, they spend on these activities.[3] As the availability and popularity of online activities, programs, and applications are constantly changing over time, the online activities that were queried also changed across the different waves. Nevertheless, 12 online activities were queried in all four waves that were used in the analyses:

1   Email.

2   Searching for information on the Internet (e.g. about hobbies, work, opening hours, daytrips, etc.).

3   Searching for and comparing products/product information on the Internet.

4   Purchasing items via the Internet.

5   Watching short films (e.g. via YouTube) or watching online films or TV programs.[4]

6   Downloading software, music, or films.[5]

7   Internet banking.

8   Playing Internet games/online gaming.

9   Reading online news and magazines.

10 Newsgroups.
11 Chatting/MSN.[6]
12 Visiting forums and Internet communities.

Three additional online activities were only queried in the questionnaires from 2012 and 2014 and are therefore only used in the analyses predicting malware infection, which only use data from these two waves:

13 Reading and/or writing blogs.
14 Dating websites (like Relatieplanet, Lexa, or others).
15 Social network sites (like Facebook, Twitter, LinkedIn, Google+, Myspace, Tumblr, Flickr, or others).[7]

The large majority of respondents did not spend more than ten hours per week on each of the online activities. However, there were some outliers (e.g. a respondent stating that he is downloading software every hour in the week), which could potentially influence the results of this study. Therefore, a maximum of ten hours per week was used and higher scores were recoded to ten. This applied to less than 2% of the cases for all online activities, except for email (6.1% scored higher than ten hours) and social networks (2.8%).

Control variables

In addition to the measures of low self-control and the different types of online activities, six demographic variables are included in the analyses as controls. First, the self-reported gender of the respondents is coded as 0 for females and 1 for males. Second, the age of respondents at each wave was included as a continuous control variable, ranging between 16 and 96 years. Third, the educational level of respondents is based on respondents' self-reported educational level and divided into six categories, ranging from low to high: primary school, intermediate secondary school (VMBO), higher secondary education/preparatory university education (HAVO/VWO), intermediate vocational education (MBO), higher vocational education (HBO), and university (WO). Fourth, the size of the household is indicated by the number of people living in the household (including the respondent), ranging between one and nine people. Fifth, the net monthly income of a respondent was measured with 13 categories: (0) No income; (1) €500 or less; (2) €501 to €1000; (3) €1001 to €1500; (4) €1501 to €2000; (5) €2001 to €2500; (6) €2501 to €3000; (7) €3001 to €3500; (8) €3501 to €4000; (9) €4001 to €4500; (10) €4501 to €5000; (11) €5001 to €7500; and (12) More than €7500. Sixth, the degree of urbanism of the place of residence of the respondents was measured on a 5-point scale: (1) Not urban; (2) Slightly urban; (3) Moderately urban; (4) Very urban; and (5) Extremely urban. Finally, in the longitudinal analyses, the survey year also was added to control for period effects.

Analyses

Three types of analyses were used in this chapter. First of all, the analyses were carried out in the way previous studies have examined predictors of cybercrime victimization. For this purpose, the data were analysed in a cross-sectional way, with predictors and victimization measured at the same time point, using ordinary least squares regression analyses and logistic regression analyses.

Second, in the longitudinal analyses, the independent variables (i.e. low self-control, online activities, and demographics) were measured at the start of the victimization period (see Figure 4.1) in order to avoid simultaneous causality. The longitudinal character of the LISS panel was then used to estimate random and fixed effects models. The random and fixed effects panel models consider that multiple observations were clustered within respondents. In the random effects model, respondents are compared both with each other and with their own scores across waves. In other words, the random effects model takes into account both between-individual differences and within-individual changes. The fixed effects model, on the other hand, only uses within-individual comparisons. The deviations of scores on the independent and dependent variables in each wave from the individual's mean scores across all waves are used to estimate the fixed effects model. Thereby, the fixed effects model examines whether changes on an independent variable over time lead to changes on the dependent variable over time – for example, whether an increase in the number of hours spent on online gaming leads to an increased risk of becoming a victim of hacking. By only focusing on within-individual changes over time, the fixed effects model automatically filters out all time-stable differences between individuals. Therefore, the fixed effects model controls for hidden bias caused by unmeasured, time-stable confounders and gives a better estimate of the causal effects than the random effects models and the cross-sectional analyses that only control for the measured control variables. The effects of time-stable variables (e.g. gender) cannot be measured in fixed effects models, as there will be no within-individual changes over time on these variables. Moreover, in the logistic fixed effects models, individuals who have the same score on the dependent variable at all observation points (i.e. those who were never victimized or those who were victimized in all waves) are excluded from the analyses because there are no within-individual differences to explain.

Third, discordant sibling models were applied to control for hidden bias in another way. These models are similar to the fixed effects models, but instead of examining differences between observations within the same individual, differences between siblings within the same household are examined. For this purpose, only pairs of children within the same household[8] who have different scores on the dependent variable were selected in the analyses. By only focusing on the differences between siblings, differences between households are filtered out. The discordant sibling model therefore controls for everything that is shared between the siblings, including shared environmental factors (e.g. household size, socioeconomic status of the family) and genetic factors (i.e. genetic confounding). The discordant sibling model was only used to estimate effects on malware infection, as this dependent variable has the most variation in scores and siblings were therefore more likely to be discordant on this variable. On the other four dependent variables, the large majority of respondents have the same score (0 – no victimization), and the number of discordant sibling pairs was too low to run the models.

Results

Descriptive analyses

Table 4.1 shows the descriptive statistics of all variables used in the analyses, split up by wave. Descriptive statistics of cybervictimization are only shown for Wave 2 to Wave 5 because predictors measured at the previous wave were used to predict cybercrime victimization in the next wave (see also Figure 4.1). For the same reason descriptive statistics for online activities, low self-control, and control variables are only shown for Wave 1 to Wave 4. The most prevalent cybercrime among the respondents in this sample was a virus infection, with 8.5% of all respondents across all waves having experienced this type of cybercrime. Next, on average 3.8% of all respondents experienced online fraud, while 3.%2 and 2.2% became a victim of hacking and online intimidation, respectively. Victimization rates were the highest in Wave 4 (except for virus infection), which can likely be explained by the fact that the extra answer category 'more or less' was added to the questionnaire in that wave. Because respondents who answered 'more or less' were included in the group of victims, victimization rates were higher in this wave than in the waves where this answer category was missing. Overall, the self-reported prevalence of online fraud and online intimidation increased between 2010 and 2016, whereas the rate of virus infections decreased and the prevalence of hacking remained stable. Malware infection, based on the four items relating to their computer's performance, was only measured in 2014 and 2016, and the scores on this dependent variable were slightly lower in 2016 (1.61) compared to 2014 (1.67).

Next, Table 4.1 shows the average number of hours spent on the different online activities.[9] The online activities that respondents, on average, spent the most time were emailing (2.83 hours per week), searching for information (1.95), and using social networks (1.44). The least time was spent on dating websites (0.04), blogs (0.19), and newsgroups (0.24). In total, the respondents, on average, spent 13.22 hours per week on the 15 online activities listed in Table 4.1. The average number of hours spent on all online activities increased between Wave 1 and Wave 4, except for the time spent on downloading and forums. Table 4.1 also shows the mean scores on low self-control, which is 1.11 in each wave. This indicates that relatively few people had low self-control in this sample.

Finally, Table 4.1 also shows descriptive statistics of the demographic variables that were used as controls in the analyses. There were more females (53.5%)

Table 4.1 Descriptive statistics

	Wave 1 2008		Wave 2 2010		Wave 3 2012		Wave 4 2014		Wave 5 2016		Total	
	M/%	SD	M/%	SD	M/%	SD	M/%	SD	M/%	SD	M/%	SD
Cybercrime victimization:												
Hacking			2.1%		2.7%		5.7%		2.1%		3.2%	
Virus infection			11.6%		8.4%		9.5%		4.6%		8.5%	
Online fraud			3.1%		3.3%		5.2%		3.7%		3.8%	
Online intimidation			1.7%		1.7%		3.3%		2.1%		2.2%	
Malware infection							1.67	0.71	1.61	0.68	1.64	0.70
Online activities												
Email	2.73	2.93	2.77	2.89	2.88	3.01	2.92	3.01			2.83	2.96
Search for information	1.92	2.21	1.93	2.23	1.97	2.24	1.97	2.23			1.95	2.23
Compare products	0.99	1.50	0.98	1.48	1.01	1.40	1.03	1.38			1.00	1.44
Online shopping	0.38	0.81	0.43	0.89	0.51	0.87	0.54	0.91			0.47	0.88
Watching films	0.77	1.58	0.94	1.78	0.84	1.48	1.23	2.24			0.96	1.83
Downloading	0.79	1.82	0.63	1.63	0.43	1.22	0.39	1.17			0.55	1.48
Internet banking	0.71	1.04	0.79	1.22	0.84	1.11	0.85	1.07			0.80	1.11
Online gaming	0.62	1.74	0.68	1.91	0.78	2.01	1.01	2.33			0.78	2.03
Online news	0.71	1.45	0.79	1.53	0.89	1.57	1.00	1.71			0.86	1.58
Newsgroups	0.23	0.89	0.21	0.82	0.26	0.91	0.25	0.86			0.24	0.87
Chatting	0.79	2.02	0.60	1.79	0.63	1.68	1.18	2.23			0.82	1.97
forums	0.36	1.24	0.36	1.27	0.30	1.10	0.17	0.85			0.29	1.12
Blogs					0.17	0.72	0.21	0.79			0.19	0.76
Dating websites					0.04	0.41	0.05	0.42			0.04	0.42
Social networks					1.16	0.33	1.67	2.61			1.44	2.50
Low self-control	1.11	0.16	1.11	0.15	1.11	0.16	1.11	0.15			1.11	0.16
Control variables												
Gender (0 = female; 1 = male)	46.9%		46.6%		46.6%		46.1%				46.5%	
Age	45.88	16.76	48.88	17.20	49.78	17.53	49.13	18.02			48.48	17.48
Educational level	3.31	1.55	3.37	1.54	3.42	1.54	3.54	1.53			3.42	1.54
Income	3.04	2.08	3.17	2.02	3.18	2.05	3.18	2.07			3.15	2.06
Household size	2.77	1.34	2.63	1.32	2.66	1.31	2.60	1.33			2.66	1.33
Urbanism	2.96	1.27	2.98	1.26	2.97	1.26	3.03	1.29			2.99	1.27

than males (46.5%) in the sample, and the average age of all respondents across all waves was 48.48 years. Moreover, average scores on educational level and income slightly increased between 2008 and 2014. The average household size of the respondents was 2.66 people, and the mean score on urbanism was 2.99, indicating that the respondents on average lived in a moderately urban area.

Online intimidation

Next, a series of logistic regression analyses were performed to examine the effect of low self-control and online activities on victimization of online intimidation. Table 4.2 shows the results of these regression analyses. The cross-sectional approach was used in Model 1, in which victimization between February 2012 and February 2014 was predicted based on low self-control, online activities, and demographic characteristics measured in February 2014. Model 1

Table 4.2 Logistic regression analyses predicting victimization of online intimidation

Variables:	Model 1		Model 2		Model 3	
	Cross-sectional		Longitudinal			
	2014		Random effects		Fixed effects	
	OR	S.E.	OR	S.E.	OR	S.E.
Low self-control	10.47	3.42***	5.20	1.79***	0.80	0.47
Online activities:						
Email	0.98	0.03	1.00	0.03	0.96	0.04
Search for information	0.92	0.04*	1.00	0.04	1.07	0.06
Compare products	1.02	0.07	1.03	0.06	1.04	0.09
Online shopping	0.93	0.09	1.07	0.08	1.10	0.16
Watching films	0.98	0.03	0.94	0.04	0.92	0.06
Downloading	1.05	0.06	1.11	0.04**	1.01	0.07
Internet banking	1.14	0.07*	1.01	0.07	0.92	0.11
Online gaming	0.96	0.03	0.98	0.03	1.00	0.07
Online news	0.81	0.06***	0.92	0.05	0.95	0.08
Newsgroups	1.14	0.09*	1.07	0.08	0.95	0.11
Chatting	1.05	0.03*	1.09	0.03**	1.02	0.04
Forums	0.97	0.08	0.95	0.05	0.93	0.08
Control variables						
Gender (0 = female; 1 = male)	1.22	0.20	1.16	0.18		
Age	0.97	0.01***	0.97	0.01***	0.33	0.18*
Educational level	0.97	0.06	0.99	0.06	0.74	0.18
Income	0.97	0.05	0.93	0.05	1.01	0.10
Household size	1.00	0.06	1.03	0.06	1.09	0.22
Urbanism	0.96	0.06	1.01	0.06	0.99	0.25
Year			1.13	0.04***	3.31	1.82*
N (individuals)	6,040		7,092		200	
N (years)			16,938		629	

*$p < .05$; **$p < .01$; ***$p < .001$ (one-sided).

shows a strong positive correlation between low self-control and victimization of online intimidation. The odds ratio of 10.47 indicates that those with the maximum score on low self-control (i.e. score 2) had more than ten times the odds to have been victimized than those with the minimum score on low self-control (i.e. score 1). Next, five online activities were significantly associated with victimization of online intimidation. A negative relationship was found with searching for information and reading online news: each extra hour spent on these activities led to a decrease in the odds of victimization of 8% and 19%, respectively. Every extra hour per week spent on Internet banking and newsgroups, on the other hand, significantly increased the odds of victimization by 14%, and a positive relationship was also found for chatting (OR: 1.05).

Models 2 and 3 show the results of logistic random and fixed effects models. These models used the longitudinal data in which victimization was predicted by low self-control, online activities, and demographic variables measured at the start of the victimization period (see Figure 4.1). In the random effects model (Model 2), there were more observations (16,938) than respondents (7,092) because all waves in which respondents had valid scores were included in the analyses. The results in Model 2 show that in the random effects model there was also a strong and positive relationship between low self-control and victimization of online intimidation, although the odds ratio of 5.20 was considerably smaller than the odds ratio that was found with the cross-sectional data. Only one of the five online activities that were significant in Model 1 was also significantly related to victimization in the random effects model: an extra hour per week spent on chatting increased the odds of victimization by 9%. Moreover, in the random effects analyses, downloading was also shown to be significantly related to online intimidation victimization (OR = 1.11). No significant associations were found for the ten other online activities.

Model 3 shows the results of the fixed effects model, which controlled for unobserved time-stable confounders by only examining within-individual changes and thereby excluding bias caused by between-individual differences. The number of respondents ($N = 200$) and observations ($N = 629$) was considerably lower in Model 3 compared to Model 2, because only respondents who had different scores on the dependent variable across waves were included in the fixed effects analyses. In other words, only those respondents who were a victim in at least one wave and who were a non-victim in at least one wave were included in these analyses. The results in Model 3 show that, after controlling for unobserved differences between respondents, neither a low self-control nor any of the online activities had a significant effect on victimization of online intimidation. In other words, a change in low self-control or in the number of hours spent on any online activity did not lead to a change in victimization of online intimidation.

Finally, for the control variables, a significantly negative effect was found for age, indicating that the victimization risks decreased with age. The positive effect of year indicates that victimization risk was higher in more recent years.

Online fraud

Table 4.3 shows the results of the cross-sectional and longitudinal logistic regression analyses on victimization of online fraud. The results of the cross-sectional analyses in Model 1 show that a low self-control was strongly and significantly related to online fraud victimization (OR = 4.83). Among the different types of online activities, only online shopping (OR = 1.12) and newsgroups (OR = 1.16) were significantly related to victimization. Also, the results of the random effects analyses show that online fraud victimization had a positive and significant association with low self-control (OR = 2.03) and online shopping (OR = 1.26), but not with newsgroups. In addition, chatting (OR = 0.95) and visiting forums (OR = 1.09) were also significantly associated with victimization of online fraud in the random effects model.

Table 4.3 Logistic regression analyses predicting victimization of online fraud

	Model 1		Model 2		Model 3	
	Cross-sectional		Longitudinal			
	2014		Random effects		Fixed effects	
Variables:	OR	S.E.	OR	S.E.	OR	S.E.
Low self-control	4.83	1.55***	2.03	0.67*	0.34	0.18*
Online activities:						
Email	0.98	0.02	0.99	0.02	1.00	0.03
Search for information	1.03	0.03	1.00	0.03	0.96	0.04
Compare products	0.96	0.05	1.06	0.04	1.05	0.06
Online shopping	1.12	0.08*	1.26	0.06***	0.99	0.07
Watching films	0.99	0.03	0.99	0.03	1.01	0.04
Downloading	0.99	0.05	1.05	0.04	0.97	0.05
Internet banking	1.03	0.06	1.00	0.05	1.05	0.07
Online gaming	0.96	0.03	1.01	0.03	1.06	0.04
Online news	1.00	0.04	1.03	0.04	1.04	0.06
Newsgroups	1.16	0.07**	1.05	0.06	0.97	0.08
Chatting	0.96	0.03	0.95	0.03*	0.95	0.04
Forums	1.01	0.06	1.09	0.04*	1.21	0.08**
Control variables						
Gender (0 = female; 1 = male)	0.97	0.14	1.24	0.17		
Age	0.97	0.01***	0.97	0.00	1.04	0.40
Educational level	1.04	0.05	1.03	0.05	1.05	0.15
Income	0.97	0.04	1.00	0.04	1.12	0.09
Household size	1.08	0.05	1.13	0.05**	1.42	0.25*
Urbanism	1.07	0.06	1.10	0.05*	1.10	0.25
Year			1.08	0.03***	1.09	0.25
N (individuals)	5,358		6,761		336	
N (years)			15,470		1,052	

*$p < .05$; **$p < .01$; ***$p < .001$ (one-sided).

However, after controlling for unobserved between-individual differences, the results became very different. Model 3 shows that, in the fixed effects model, low self-control had a negative effect on online fraud victimization (OR = 0.34). Against expectations, the victimization risk decreased when someone's score on low self-control increased over time. Spending time on forums (OR = 1.21) was the only significant online activity in Model 3: when the number of hours per week that an individual spends on forums increased over time, their risk of victimization of online fraud also increased. No positive effect of online shopping on online fraud victimization was found in Model 3, indicating that the positive association that was found in the random effects model was the consequence of unobserved differences between respondents.

The results in Table 4.3 further show that household size, urbanism, and survey year were positively associated with victimization in the random effects model. However, in the fixed effects model only the odds ratio of household size (1.42) remained significant, indicating that victimization risk increased when a household becomes larger.

Hacking

Table 4.4 shows the results for victimization of hacking. The cross-sectional analysis in Model 1 again shows a strong, positive, and significant association

Table 4.4 Logistic regression analyses predicting victimization of hacking

Variables:	Model 1		Model 2		Model 3	
	Cross-sectional		Longitudinal			
	2014		Random effects		Fixed effects	
	OR	S.E.	OR	S.E.	OR	S.E.
Low self-control	4.96	1.55***	6.61	2.11***	1.37	0.86
Online activities:						
Email	1.01	0.02	1.02	0.02	1.00	0.04
Search for information	1.01	0.03	1.01	0.03	1.06	0.05
Compare products	0.93	0.05	0.98	0.44	0.97	0.07
Online shopping	1.12	0.07*	1.08	0.07	1.21	0.12*
Watching films	0.97	0.03	0.97	0.03	0.88	0.05*
Downloading	1.07	0.05	1.01	0.04	0.91	0.07
Internet banking	1.02	0.06	1.01	0.05	1.02	0.09
Online gaming	0.94	0.03*	0.98	0.03	0.99	0.06
Online news	0.94	0.04	0.98	0.04	1.07	0.08
Newsgroups	1.02	0.07	1.04	0.07	1.08	0.17
Chatting	1.02	0.03	1.03	0.03	1.00	0.05
Forums	0.92	0.07	1.00	0.05	1.03	0.09
Control variables						
Gender (0 = female; 1 = male)	1.61	0.21***	1.45	0.20**		

Variables:	Model 1		Model 2		Model 3	
	Cross-sectional		Longitudinal			
	2014		Random effects		Fixed effects	
	OR	S.E.	OR	S.E.	OR	S.E.
Age	0.99	0.00*	1.00	0.00	1.13	0.23
Educational level	0.87	0.04**	0.95	0.04	0.96	0.16
Income	0.98	0.04	1.04	0.04	1.11	0.10
Household size	1.01	0.05	1.05	0.05	1.11	0.21
Urbanism	1.01	0.05	0.95	0.05	1.03	0.23
Year			1.05	0.03*	0.87	0.18
N (individuals)	5,358		6,681		285	
N (years)			15,119		864	

*p < .05; **p < .01; ***p < .001 (one-sided).

with low self-control (OR = 4.96). Moreover, online shopping (OR = 1.12) was also significantly related to a higher victimization risk, whereas respondents who spent more time on online gaming (OR = 0.94) were less likely to be hacked. However, in the random effects model (Model 2), only low self-control was still significantly associated with a higher risk of becoming a victim of hacking (OR = 6.61). None of the online activities were significantly related to hacking victimization in the random effects model. Remarkably, significant effects of two online activities were found in the fixed effects model. Model 3 shows that respondents who start spending more time on online shopping were more likely to be a hacking victim (OR = 1.21). On the other hand, when the number of hours spent on watching online films increased over time, this decreased the odds of becoming a victim of hacking (OR = 0.88). The fact that these variables only had a significant effect after controlling for unobserved differences between individuals suggests that these unobserved differences suppressed these effects in the random effects model. Model 3 further shows that the association between low self-control and hacking victimization disappeared when only within-individual differences are considered. Moreover, none of the control variables had a significant effect on victimization of hacking in the fixed effects model.

Virus infection

Similar to the results for the other offence types, Table 4.5 shows that low self-control was also positively associated with an increased risk for a virus infection (OR = 4.22) in the cross-sectional analysis. Moreover, Model 1 shows that two online activities were negatively related to victimization of a virus infection: respondents who spent more time on online gaming (OR = 0.96) and reading news online (OR = 0.94) were less likely to get a virus infection on their

Table 4.5 Logistic regression analyses predicting victimization of virus infection

Variables:	Model 1		Model 2		Model 3	
	Cross-sectional		Longitudinal			
	2014		Random effects		Fixed effects	
	OR	S.E.	OR	S.E.	OR	S.E.
Low self-control	4.22	1.10***	3.70	0.89***	1.61	0.67
Online activities:						
Email	0.99	0.02	1.00	0.02	0.98	0.02
Search for information	1.02	0.02	0.99	0.02	0.98	0.03
Compare products	1.01	0.04	1.04	0.03	1.04	0.04
Online shopping	1.02	0.06	1.00	0.05	1.10	0.07
Watching films	0.99	0.02	0.99	0.02	0.97	0.04
Downloading	1.05	0.04	1.08	0.03**	1.06	0.05
Internet banking	1.00	0.05	1.08	0.04*	1.08	0.06
Online gaming	0.96	0.02*	0.98	0.02	1.00	0.04
Online news	0.94	0.03*	0.99	0.03	1.03	0.04
Newsgroups	1.02	0.06	1.00	0.05	0.96	0.07
Chatting	1.02	0.02	0.98	0.02	0.95	0.03
Forums	0.97	0.05	1.04	0.03	1.06	0.06
Control variables						
Gender (0 = female; 1 = male)	1.34	0.14**	1.29	0.13**		
Age	0.99	0.00**	0.99	0.00***	0.81	0.23
Educational level	1.01	0.04	1.07	0.03*	0.81	0.10*
Income	0.97	0.03	0.99	0.03	1.02	0.07
Household size	1.06	0.04	1.14	0.04***	1.04	0.12
Urbanism	1.06	0.04	1.03	0.04	0.89	0.15
Year			0.85	0.01	1.02	0.29
N (individuals)	5,358		6,720		701	
N (years)			15,299		2,233	

*p < .05; **p < .01; ***p < .001 (one-sided).

computer. In addition, the random effects model, as shown in Model 2, shows that those with lower self-control were more likely to have their computer infected by a virus (OR = 3.70). The associations with online gaming and online news disappeared in Model 2, but two other online activities did show a significant relationship with victimization of virus infections. Respondents who spend more time downloading and Internet banking were more likely to get a virus infection on their computer (OR = 1.08 for both variables). Model 3, however, shows that, after controlling for unobserved time-stable bias in the fixed effects model, neither low self-control nor any online activity had a causal effect on victimization of virus infection. The only variable in the fixed effects model that was significant is the educational level of respondents, showing that when a person reached a higher level of education, his or her risk of victimization decreased (OR = 0.81).

Malware infection

In Table 4.5, no significant effects of low self-control or online activities were found on self-reported virus infections. However, as mentioned earlier, it is possible that not all respondents would recognize when their computer becomes infected with a virus. Therefore, malware infection was also measured using four items on the performance of the computer. The results of the analyses on this variable are shown in Table 4.6.

Table 4.6 OLS regression analyses predicting victimization of malware infection

Variables:	Model 1 Cross-sectional 2014		Model 2 Longitudinal Random effects		Model 3 Fixed effects		Model 4 Discordant siblings	
	B	S.E.	B	S.E.	B	S.E.	B	S.E.
Low self-control	0.621	0.067***	0.461	0.053***	0.098	0.091	0.918	0.557
Online activities:								
Email	0.000	0.004	−0.001	0.003	−0.004	0.005	0.036	0.054
Search for information	0.008	0.005	0.004	0.004	0.001	0.006	−0.044	0.059
Compare products	0.001	0.008	0.003	0.006	0.010	0.009	−0.005	0.124
Online shopping	−0.004	0.012	−0.007	0.098	−0.006	0.014	−0.061	0.126
Watching films	0.017	0.005***	0.004	0.005	−0.012	0.007*	0.057	0.049
Downloading	0.022	0.009**	0.020	0.007**	0.019	0.012	0.024	0.079
Internet banking	0.008	0.010	0.000	0.008	−0.010	0.012	0.184	0.122
Online gaming	−0.003	0.004	0.001	0.004	−0.000	0.006	0.005	0.051
Online news	−0.006	0.006	−0.006	0.005	−0.001	0.008	−0.031	0.085
Newsgroups	0.000	0.011	−0.006	0.009	−0.008	0.014	−0.058	0.189
Chatting	0.005	0.005	−0.005	0.005	−0.007	0.007	−0.025	0.042
Forums	−0.012	0.011	−0.011	0.008	−0.024	0.014*	−0.009	0.082
Blogs	−0.000	0.012	0.005	0.011	0.012	0.018	−0.130	0.089
Dating websites	0.041	0.023*	0.018	0.019	−0.011	0.029	0.811	0.496
Social networks	−0.000	0.005	0.006	0.004	0.007	0.006	0.035	0.038
Control variables								
Gender (0 = female; 1 = male)	0.045	0.022*	0.032	0.020			0.145	0.220
Age	−0.003	0.000***	−0.003	0.001***	0.075	0.041*	0.011	0.034
Educational level	0.037	0.008***	0.027	0.007***	−0.078	0.032**	0.034	0.112
Income	−0.027	0.006***	−0.019	0.005***	0.007	0.015	−0.042	0.132
Household size	0.004	0.008	0.013	0.008*	0.011	0.027	0.053	0.644
Urbanism	0.005	0.008	0.016	0.007*	0.014	0.034		
Year			−0.035	0.006***	−0.121	0.043**	0.429	0.319
Constant	0.976	0.107***	1.262	0.093***	−1.486	1.871	−2.609	4.134
N (individuals)	4,876		4,813		4,813		162	
N (year)			7,434		7,434			
N (families)							81	

*p < .05; **p < .01; ***p < .001 (one-sided).

Model 1 of Table 4.6 shows the results of the cross-sectional ordinary least squares (OLS) regression analysis. In this model, low self-control had a significant and positive relationship with the score on malware infection (B = 0.621). Moreover, 3 out of the 15 online activities were significantly related to malware infection: respondents who spent more time watching films (B = 0.017), downloading (B = 0.022), and dating websites (B = 0.041) had a higher risk of malware infection on their computer. In the random effects analysis, as shown in Model 2, only significant results were found for low self-control (B = 0.461) and downloading (B = 0.020). Model 3 shows the results of fixed effects analysis, and in this model the effect of low self-control became insignificant. In addition, time spent on none of the 15 online activities significantly increased malware infection risk. Instead, respondents who spent more hours per week watching films (B = −0.012) and online forums (B = −0.024) had a significantly lower score on malware infection. Finally, Model 4 shows the results of the discordant sibling analyses, in which 162 pairs of siblings from 81 households were compared to each other. None of the variables in Model 4, however, had a significant effect on malware infection. This lack of significant effects in Model 4 might be the consequence of the relatively large number of variables included in the model, given the low sample size, resulting in little statistical power to detect significant results. Therefore, the discordant sibling analysis was repeated with only low self-control and the control variables as predictors (not shown in Table 4.6). In this additional analysis, a significant effect of low self-control on malware infection was found (B = 0.921, $p < .05$).

The analyses in Table 4.6 were also repeated (not shown in Table 4.6) while only using the average score on the last two items of the scale (i.e. home page changed; new programs on desktop), as it can be argued that the first two items (i.e. slow computer; computer crashes) could also be an indication of using older computers instead of malware victimization. Most conclusions remained the same, while using this stricter measure of malware victimization. The most important differences were found in the fixed effects model: the regression coefficients of time spent on watching films and online forum lost significance, whereas a significant effect was found for time spent on downloading (B = 0.025; $p < .05$).[10]

Discussion

In this chapter, the influence of online activities and low self-control on cybercrime victimization was examined. Previous studies that showed a significant relationship between online victimization and these predictors all used cross-sectional data, which could lead to biased estimates due to simultaneous causality and unobserved differences between individuals. The current study therefore used longitudinal data on a large, representative panel and two quasi-experimental research designs to get a better estimate of the causal effect of online activities and low self-control on victimization of five types of cybercrime: online harassment, online fraud, hacking, virus infection, and malware infection.

Based on self-control theory (Gottfredson & Hirschi, 1990; Schreck, 1999), it was expected that having low self-control increases the risk of victimization. In line with previous studies (e.g. Reyns et al., 2013;Van Wilsem, 2011b; 2013), the cross-sectional analyses indeed show strong and significant associations between low self-control and all five types of cybercrime victimization. However, after controlling for unobserved differences between respondents in the fixed effects analyses, the strength of the associations strongly decreased and became insignificant for most types of cybercrime victimization. Only for online fraud was a significant effect found in the fixed effects analyses. However, against expectations, this was a negative effect, indicating that a decrease in the level of self-control led to a smaller chance of becoming a victim of online fraud.

A possible explanation for the lack of a significant, positive effect of self-control in the fixed effects models might be the fact that these models only look at changes in self-control over time within the same individual. As it has been hypothesized (Gottfredson & Hirschi, 1990) and empirically shown (e.g. Beaver et al., 2008; Hay & Forrest, 2006) that the level of self-control is relatively stable over the life course, fixed effects models might not be the most suitable research method to study the influence of self-control on cybercrime victimization. Therefore, a discordant sibling analysis was also applied, in which siblings from the same family with different scores on malware infection and self-control were compared. This analysis did not result in a significant effect of self-control on victimization either. This could, however, possibly be the consequence of the low sample size in combination with the relatively high number of predictors in this specific analysis. An additional analysis, in which only self-control and control variables were included, did show a significant positive effect, indicating that siblings with a lower level of self-control have a higher risk of malware infection. In sum, the results show that respondents with a lower self-control have a higher victimization risk, but there is limited evidence that this is a causal effect.

Previous studies that tested the applicability of routine activities theory (Cohen & Felson, 1979) on cybercrime victimization found that involvement in certain online activities increases the risk of victimization of several types of cybercrimes (e.g. Marcum et al., 2010; Leukfeldt & Yar, 2016; Holt et al., 2018). The cross-sectional analyses in the current study also showed significant and positive correlations between cybercrime victimization and the number of hours spent on several online activities. In the random effects analyses, in which the hours spent on online activities was measured before the victimization period rather than afterwards, different results were found. Some significant associations from the cross-sectional analyses became insignificant, whereas relationships with other online activities became significant in the random effects models. These differences might be the consequence of simultaneous causality: the online activities have an effect on victimization risk, while victimization influences the time spent on online activities. As these simultaneous effects cannot be disentangled with cross-sectional data, longitudinal data are vital to ensure that a predictor is measured prior to the outcome. An alternative explanation for the different outcomes in the cross-sectional and random effects analyses is that the former only includes victimization measured in 2014, whereas the latter includes all waves (i.e. 2010, 2012, 2014, and 2016). If associations between victimization and online activities change over time this could result in different results as different periods were studied. However, this would again demonstrate the importance of the use of longitudinal data, as such data would be necessary to study such differences between time periods.

Differences in results were also found between the random effects models and the quasi-experimental analyses (i.e. fixed effects models and discordant sibling design) that control for unobserved confounders. Across the five types of cybercrimes, only two online activities significantly increased victimization risk of one cybercrime in the fixed effects models: more time spent on online forums increases the risk of online fraud victimization, and an increase in time spent on online shopping leads to a higher risk of hacking victimization. In addition, some online activities were shown to decrease victimization risk. More time spent on watching films decreases the risk of malware infection or being hacked, and an increased number of hours spent on online forums leads to a lower risk of malware infection. None of the online activities (nor low self-control) had a significant influence on the victimization risk for virus infection and online harassment. The discordant sibling model did not show any significant effect of the online activities on malware infections either. These results suggest that many of the significant associations observed in the cross-sectional and random effects analyses do not reflect causal effects, but are rather the consequence of unobserved confounders.

Although the current study offers important insights into the study of cyber-crime victimization, it is also limited in several ways. First, despite the fact that fixed effects panel models and discordant sibling models offer the opportunity to control for various forms of unmeasured confounders, these methods do not control for all hidden bias. Fixed effects models only control for bias caused by time-stable factors, not when it is the consequence of unmeasured time-varying confounders. Similarly, discordant sibling models only control for everything that is shared within the same household, but not for unmeasured confounders, which are not shared between the siblings. As a consequence, the few significant effects that were found in the fixed effects analyses may still be biased by such types of unmeasured confounders. Nevertheless, the fixed effects and discordant sibling models give a better estimate of the causal effect than cross-sectional analyses that were previously used in research into cybercrime victimization.

Second, the use of the discordant sibling model might be problematic when siblings from the same household share the same computer. In that case, online behaviour and low self-control of one sibling could lead to malware infection on the computer that both siblings share. However, it is unlikely that this is the case because most teenagers and young adults in the Netherlands have their own personal computer or laptop nowadays (Stichting Kennisnet, 2015). In addition, only siblings who had different scores on malware infection were considered in the analyses, which likely means they did not report about the performance of the same computer. Another limitation of the discordant sibling model was the low number of sibling pairs with different scores on malware victimization, leading to limited statistical power in this analysis. It would be desirable if future studies could use these types of models with a larger sample of siblings.

Third, online activities were only measured as the number of hours per week spent on each activity. It is, however, possible that it is not the amount of time spent on an online activity that influences the risk of cybercrime victimization, but rather the way an individual spent his or her time on this activity. Spending a lot of time on emailing, for example, might not lead to cybercrime victimization, but when someone opens a large number of attachments from unknown sources, he or she might be more likely to get a malware infection. Similarly, online shopping may only increase the risk of consumer fraud when someone shops frequently on online marketplaces rather than on websites of well-known brands. It would therefore be recommended for future studies to also examine the way in which respondents behave during certain online activities in a longitudinal study. In addition, some online activities, such as online gaming and watching television shows, might be performed on other devices (e.g. smart TVs, gaming consoles) and could therefore decrease the amount of time spent on a personal computer or laptop. This could have affected the results on hacking, virus infection, and malware infection, as the items measuring these types of victimization asked specifically about the respondent's computer.

Fourth, as described in the Methods section, not all variables were measured in exactly the same way across waves. Small deviations in survey questions could lead to different answer patterns and influence the results of the longitudinal analyses. On the other hand, the availability and popularity of online activities, programs, and applications are constantly and rapidly changing over time, which forces researchers to adjust the items in order to keep up to date and ask for relevant behaviours.

In conclusion, the results of this study show that low self-control and time spent on online activities are significantly related to online victimization risk. However, in most cases these associations do not reflect causal effects, but are rather the consequence of unobserved confounders. The applicability of self-control theory (Gottfredson & Hirschi, 1990; Schreck, 1999) and routine activities theory on cybercrime victimization therefore seems limited. It is recommended that future studies on cybercrime victimization and offending use quasi-experimental research designs that control for hidden bias when testing these or other criminological theories, as this is vital to test the causality of the associations that have been found previously. This knowledge is crucial for theory testing and development in the field of cybercrime and to develop efficient interventions in practice.

Acknowledgements

The author wants to thank CentERdata and Dr Johan van Wilsem for collecting and providing the data that were used in this study.

Notes

1 The survey also included items about stolen credit card numbers, money being taken from bank accounts, and identity fraud, but the number of respondents who were victimized by these offences was too low for the quantitative analyses that were carried out in this chapter.

2 In the questionnaires from 2012 and 2014, respondents were also asked whether they use the internet on their laptop, tablet, or smartphone.

3 In the questionnaire it was not specifically asked whether these online activities were performed on the respondent's desktop or laptop. Consequently, it might be possible that some of these online activities (e.g. online gaming, watching short films) were performed on other devices such as mobile phones, smart TVs, and gaming consoles.

4 In the questionnaires from 2008 and 2010, "watching short films (e.g. via YouTube)" and "watching online films or TV programs" were two separate items. Therefore, the hours that respondents indicated they spent on both activities were totaled. In the questionnaire from 2014, respondents were not only asked about watching short films on YouTube but also about "posting, editing, and watching pictures and short films via social media such as Instagram, YouTube, Vimeo, Vine, or others."

5 In the questionnaires from 2008 and 2010, "downloading software" and "downloading music or films" were two separate items. Therefore, the hours that respondents indicated they spent on both activities were totaled.

6 In the questionnaire from 2014, respondents were not asked about chatting on MSN anymore but about "chatting, video calling, or sending messages via social media like Instagram, Skype or similar services." In the questionnaire from 2012, respondents were asked about using "Skype or similar services" separately. Therefore, the number of hours spent on this activity were added up to the number of hours spent on chatting/MSN.

7 In the questionnaire from 2012, respondents were asked about using Twitter separately. Therefore, the number of hours spent on this activity are added up to the number of hours spent on social network sites.

8 The LISS panel includes information on each respondent's role in the household, for example 'head of the household,' 'marital partner,' or 'child living at home.' Two children living at home in the same household were considered siblings.

9 These average scores are estimated after outliers (scores higher than ten hours per week) have been recoded to the maximum score of 10.

10 The discordant sibling model could not be estimated while using this stricter measurement of malware victimization, because most respondents scored 1 (the minimum score) on this variable. Consequently, not enough sibling-pairs with different scores on malware victimization could be identified.

References

Barnes, J. C., & Beaver, K. M. (2012). Extending research on the victim – offender overlap: Evidence from a genetically informative analysis. *Journal of Interpersonal Violence*, *27*(16), 3299–3321.

Beaver, K. M., Boutwell, B. B., Barnes, J. C., & Cooper, J. A. (2009). The biosocial underpinnings to adolescent victimization: Results from a longitudinal sample of twins. *Youth Violence and Juvenile Justice*, *7*(3), 223–238.

Beaver, K. M., Wright, J. P., DeLisi, M., & Vaughn, M. G. (2008). Genetic influences on the stability of low self-control: Results from a longitudinal sample of twins. *Journal of Criminal Justice*, *36*(6), 478–485.

Beckley, A. L., Caspi, A., Arseneault, L., Barnes, J. C., Fisher, H. L., Harrington, H., . . . Moffitt, T. E. (2017). The developmental nature of the victim-offender overlap. *Journal of Developmental and Life-Course Criminology*, 1–26.

Boutwell, B. B., Franklin, C. A., Barnes, J. C., Tamplin, A. K., Beaver, K. M., & Petkovsek, M. (2013). Unraveling the covariation of low self-control and victimization: A behavior genetic approach. *Journal of adolescence, 36*(4), 657–666.

Bossler, A. M., & Holt, T. J. (2009). On-line activities, guardianship, and malware infection: An examination of routine activities theory. *International Journal of Cyber Criminology, 3*(1).

Bossler, A. M., & Holt, T. J. (2010). The effect of self control on victimization in the cyber-world. *Journal of Criminal Justice, 38*, 227–236.

Choi, K. S. (2008). Computer crime victimization and integrated theory: An empirical assessment. *International Journal of Cyber Criminology, 2*(1).

Cohen, L., & Felson, M. (1979). Social change and crime rate trends: A routine activity approach. *American Sociological Review, 44*, 588–608.

Dickman, S. J. (1990). Functional and dysfunctional impulsivity: Personality and cognitive correlates. *Journal of Personality and Social Psychology, 58*, 95–102.

D'onofrio, B. M., Lahey, B. B., Turkheimer, E., & Lichtenstein, P. (2013). Critical need for family-based, quasi-experimental designs in integrating genetic and social science research. *American Journal of Public Health, 103*(S1), S46–S55.

Felson, M., & Clarke, R.V. (1998). *Opportunity makes the thief.* Police research series, paper, 98.

Gottfredson, M. R., & Hirschi, T. (1990). *A general theory of crime.* Stanford, CA: Stanford University Press.

Hay, C., & Forrest, W. (2006). The development of self-control: Examining self-control theory's stability thesis. *Criminology, 44*(4), 739–774.

Hill, J. M., van der Geest, V. R., & Blokland, A. A. (2017). Leaving the bank of mum and dad: Financial independence and delinquency desistance in emerging adulthood. *Journal of Developmental and Life-Course Criminology, 3*(4), 419–439.

Holt, T. J., & Bossler, A. M. (2008). Examining the applicability of lifestyle-routine activities theory for cybercrime victimization. *Deviant Behavior, 30*(1), 1–25.

Holt, T. J., Van Wilsem, J., Van de Weijer, S. G. A., & Leukfeldt, E. R. (2018). Testing an integrated self-control and routine activities framework to examine malware infection victimization. *Social Science Computer Review.* https://doi.org/10.1177/0894439318805067.

Leukfeldt, E. R. (2014). Phishing for suitable targets in the Netherlands: Routine activity theory and phishing victimization. *Cyberpsychology, Behavior, and Social Networking, 17*(8), 551–555.

Leukfeldt, E. R., & Yar, M. (2016). Applying routine activity theory to cybercrime: A theoretical and empirical analysis. *Deviant Behavior, 37*(3), 263–280.

Li, M., Chen, J., Li, N., & Li, X. (2014). A twin study of problematic internet use: Its heritability and genetic association with effortful control. *Twin Research and Human Genetics, 17*(4), 279–287.

Marcum, C. D., Higgins, G. E., & Ricketts, M. L. (2010). Potential factors of online victimization of youth: An examination of adolescent online behaviors utilizing routine activity theory. *Deviant Behavior, 31*(5), 381–410.

Ngo, F.T., & Paternoster, R. (2011). Cybercrime victimization: An examination of individual and situational level factors. *International Journal of Cyber Criminology, 5*(1).

Pratt, T. C., Holtfreter, K., & Reisig, M. D. (2010). Routine online activity and internet fraud targeting: Extending the generality of routine activity theory. *Journal of Research in Crime and Delinquency, 47*(3), 267–296.

Pratt, T. C., Turanovic, J. J., Fox, K. A., & Wright, K. A. (2014). Self-control and victimization: A meta-analysis. *Criminology, 52*(1), 87–116.

Pyrooz, D. C., Mcgloin, J. M., & Decker, S. H. (2017). Parenthood as a turning point in the life course for male and female gang members: A study of within-individual changes in gang membership and criminal behavior. *Criminology, 55*(4), 869–899.

Reyns, B.W., Burek, M.W., Henson, B., & Fisher, B. S. (2013).The unintended consequences of digital technology: Exploring the relationship between sexting and cybervictimization. *Journal of Crime and Justice, 36*(1), 1–17.

Reyns, B. W., Henson, B., & Fisher, B. S. (2011). Being pursued online: Applying cyberlifestyle – routine activities theory to cyberstalking victimization. *Criminal Justice and Behavior, 38*(11), 1149–1169.

Schreck, C. J. (1999). Criminal victimization and low self-control: An extension and test of a general theory of crime. *Justice Quarterly, 16*(3), 633–654.

Statistics Netherlands. (2018). *Veiligheidsmonitor 2017.* Den Haag: Centraal Bureau voor de Statistiek.

Stichting Kennisnet. (2015). *Monitor Jeugd en Media 2015.* Retrieved from www.kennisnet.nl/fileadmin/kennisnet/publicatie/jeugd_media/Kennisnet_Monitor_Jeugd_en_media_2015.pdf

Van Wilsem, J. (2011a).Worlds tied together? Online and non-domestic routine activities and their impact on digital and traditional threat victimization. *European Journal of Criminology, 8*(2), 115–127.

Van Wilsem, J. (2011b). 'Bought it, but never got it' assessing risk factors for online consumer fraud victimization. *European Sociological Review, 29*(2), 168–178.

Van Wilsem, J. (2013). Hacking and harassment – do they have something in common? Comparing risk factors for online victimization. *Journal of Contemporary Criminal Justice, 29*(4), 437–453.

Vaske, J., Boisvert, D., & Wright, J. P. (2012). Genetic and environmental contributions to the relationship between violent victimization and criminal behavior. *Journal of Interpersonal Violence, 27*(16), 3213–3235.

Vink, J. M., Beijsterveldt, T. C., Huppertz, C., Bartels, M., & Boomsma, D. I. (2016). Heritability of compulsive Internet use in adolescents. *Addiction Biology, 21*(2), 460–468.

Weulen Kranenbarg, M., Ruiter, S.,Van Gelder, J. L., & Bernasco, W. (2018). Cyber-offending and traditional offending over the life-course: An empirical comparison. *Journal of Developmental and Life-Course Criminology, 4*(3), 343–364.

Yar, M. (2005).The novelty of 'cybercrime' an assessment in light of routine activity theory. *European Journal of Criminology, 2*(4), 407–427.

York, C. (2017). A regression approach to testing genetic influence on communication behavior: Social media use as an example. *Computers in Human Behavior, 73,* 100–109.

5 Virtual danger

An overview of interpersonal cybercrimes

Jordana Navarro

Introduction

Since the early 2000s technology has increasingly permeated social life. Indeed, technology is a necessary tool to engage in many personal (e.g. banking, paying bills, etc.) and professional activities (e.g. applying for employment, conducting business via email, etc.) (Anderson & Rainie, 2018; Smith, 2015). However, as these advancements have occurred, deviant individuals have innovated and exploited technology for nefarious purposes (Griffiths, 2000). This chapter will focus on three interpersonal cybercrimes that involve perpetrators intentionally inflicting harm on specific individuals or groups: cyberbullying, cyber-dating abuse/intimate partner abuse, and cyberstalking (Navarro & Clevenger, 2017). To be clear, there are other cybercrimes that involve the intentional infliction of harm on another (e.g. cybersexual abuse, hacking, and piracy); however, given that these topics are addressed in other areas of this text and for parsimony, this chapter will only focus on the prior three offences. Moreover, it is important to understand the various theoretical frameworks that guide understanding about these topics, which are also addressed in other areas throughout this text. In the following passages, the main objective is to provide a broad understanding of the status of the literature in that particular area and to note important information about offenders and victims involved in these offences.

Cyberbullying

Definition and prevalence rates

Cyberbullying, and especially bullycide, has galvanized public discourse about the consequences associated with technology among youth (Seiler & Navarro, 2014). Although the cyberbullying field has advanced since the mid-2000s, several methodological challenges are problematic for scholars (see Patchin & Hinduja, 2012, for full discussion). The most significant challenge is the lack of a universally agreed on definition of what exactly constitutes cyberbullying (Kowalski, Giumetti, Schroeder, & Lattanner, 2014; Patchin & Hinduja, 2012).

During the nascent stage of the cyberbullying field, scholars proposed various definitions to accurately convey the breadth of these problematic behaviours. These early definitions typically relied on the seminal work of Dan Olweus, who focused on offline bullying (1994). Taking inspiration from Olweus (1994), scholars defined cyberbullying as consisting of intentional and repetitive cyber-behaviours designed to purposely inflict harm on someone of unequal power (Kowalski et al., 2014). For instance, Patchin and Hinduja (2006, p. 152) created one of the most widely used definitions of cyberbullying to which they conceptualized it as "willful and repeated harm inflicted through the medium of electronic text." However, not all definitions are that specific, which again underscores the methodological challenges within the field. For example, Juvonen and Gross (2008, p. 497) defined cyberbullying as "the use of the Internet or other digital communication devices to insult or threaten someone." In a synthesis of the literature, Tokunaga (2010) tried to resolve this inconsistency by proposing the following definition that merged features used across studies: "Cyberbullying is any behavior performed through electronic or digital media by individuals or groups that repeatedly communicates hostile or aggressive messages intended to inflict harm or discomfort on others" (p. 278). However, as of this writing, there is no universally agreed on definition despite the known impact on prevalence findings (Olweus & Limber, 2018).

Due to the lack of a universally agreed on definition, the prevalence of cyberbullying perpetration and victimization ranges widely (Kowalski et al., 2014; Olweus & Limber, 2018; Tokunaga, 2010). For example, in one synthesis of the literature conducted by Kowalski and colleagues (2014), studies that included broad definitions and/or wide time parameters (i.e. lifetime prevalence or unspecified restraints) of cyberbullying found anywhere between approximately 6% to 81% of sampled youth experienced this cyber-offence (Akbulut & Eristi, 2011; Aricak et al., 2008; Beran & Li, 2007; Beran, Rinaldi, Bickham, & Rich, 2012; Calvete, Orue, Estévez, Villardón, & Padilla, 2010; Dilmac, 2009).[1] These findings mirror an earlier meta-analysis conducted by Tokunaga (2010). A similar pattern was also visible when examining perpetration rates. In terms of perpetration, scholars who used broad parameters found anywhere between 3% and 44% of sampled youth perpetrated cyberbullying (Akbulut & Eristi, 2011; Aricak et al., 2008; Beran & Li, 2007; Beran et al., 2012; Calvete et al., 2010; Dilmac, 2009).[2] Unsurprisingly, scholars who utilized specific definitions and/or time parameters found much lower rates of victimization (e.g. approximately 3% to 19%) and perpetration (e.g. 1% to 11%) (Allen, 2012; Aoyama, Barnard-Brak, & Talbert, 2011; Bossler & Holt, 2010).[3] Although the rates of cyberbullying perpetration and victimization vary widely across the literature, these findings nonetheless underscore the broad point that this interpersonal cybercrime is a reality for many young people. To further understand the nature of cyberbullying, scholars have investigated factors that affect the risk of perpetration and victimization.

Offenders and victims[4]

Aside from assessing the prevalence of cyberbullying, cybercriminologists have strived to find risk factors that affect the chances of perpetration and victimization. These lines of research are important because they inform prevention and intervention programmes designed to combat the problem. The most explored characteristics are demographic variables like age, gender, and race/ethnicity. Although not as widely explored, scholars have also investigated the role of cognitive/physical disabilities, unusual physical appearance, and sexual orientation as risk factors for involvement in cyberbullying. Finally, scholars have examined whether certain offline and online behaviours affect risk. The following passages present an overview of this literature while also emphasizing that many of these topics are under-researched.

Unfortunately, a consensus has yet to appear on the role of gender in the experiencing or perpetrating of cyberbullying. Studies have found that females are more likely to perpetrate cyberbullying in certain contexts (Barlett & Coyne, 2014; Görzig & Ólafsson, 2013), whereas other studies have found males are more likely to cyber-harass others (Lee & Shin, 2017; Wong, Cheung, & Xiao, 2018; Zsila, Urbán, Griffiths, & Demetrovics, 2018), and still others have found no significant difference between the two (Olumide, Adebayo, & Oluwagbayela, 2016). Likewise, several studies have found that females are more likely to experience cyberbullying compared to males (Mesch, 2009; Navarro, Clevenger, Beasley, & Jackson, 2017; Navarro & Jasinski, 2012, 2013; Seiler & Navarro, 2014) or vice versa (Wong et al., 2018), whereas others have found no significant difference between the two (DeSmet, Rodelli, Walrave, Soenens, Cardon, & De Bourdeaudhuij, 2018; Olumide et al., 2016).

Research considering the role of gender outside of the female–male binary in the perpetration or experiencing of cyberbullying is virtually absent in the literature. These gender identities include individuals who are gender non-conforming, genderqueer, or transgender, among others (GLSEN, n.d.). Likewise, investigating the relationship between sexual orientation, both in connection to and apart from gender, in relation to cyberbullying is under-developed in the literature. Even in instances where scholars do include other genders or sexual orientations in their studies, these responses are often lumped into a broader group of all sampled individuals identifying as LGBTQ.[5] Although this decision is often necessary for methodological reasons, it limits the ability of scholars to understand the cyberbullying experiences of specific groups (e.g. the experiences of transgender women who identify as heterosexual versus the experiences of transgender women who identify as pansexual). Thus, although some information is known about the cyberbullying experiences of LGBTQ youth, there is less information about the experiences of these individuals in terms of their specific identifiers.

The Gay, Lesbian, and Straight Education Network (GLSEN, n.d.) raises awareness, promotes tolerance, and encourages appreciation of individuals who identify across the gender and sexual orientation spectrums. The organization pursues these goals by conducting outreach and research, as well as influencing policy (GLSEN, n.d.). In support of those goals, GLSEN recently conducted a national study into the experiences of LGBTQ youth, which included insight into their exposure to cyberbullying (Kosciw, Greytak, Giga, Villenas, & Danischewski, 2016). Findings from this study revealed that ~50% of LGBTQ youth were cyberbullied in the preceding year (Kosciw et al., 2016). Although GLSEN's report did not specifically note the types of cyberbullying experienced by youth who identified as non-cisgender (e.g. genderqueer, transgender), findings showed that these adolescents experienced hateful and offensive language at varying levels of frequency (Kosciw et al., 2016). For example, an overwhelming majority of sampled youth (86%) overheard derogatory terms like "he/she" and "tranny" while at school (Kosciw et al., 2016).

Unlike gender, scholars have achieved some consensus about the relationship between race and cyberbullying. Although there are exceptions (see Navarro & Jasinski, 2013), most studies have found that there is no statistically significant relationship between race/ethnicity and cyberbullying (Bauman, Toomey, & Walker, 2013; Hinduja & Patchin, 2008; Kwan & Skoric, 2013; Schneider, O'Donnell, Stueve, & Coulter, 2012; Stoll & Block, 2015). Moreover, if there is a statistically significant relationship, results typically show that youth who identify as non-white or as Hispanic[6] are *less likely* to engage in or experience cyberbullying (Kupczynski et al., 2013; Seiler & Navarro, 2014). However, to further understand these results, a few cautionary statements are called for. First, as in the case of gender, typically scholars collapse various ethnic and racial groups together in statistical analyses for methodological reasons. This process is commonly known as "ethnic lumping" in the literature and limits the ability of scholars to understand differences in experiences across groups. Second, promising research has appeared that argues scholars should not dismiss the importance of a "race effect," but investigate the influence of various characteristics together (i.e. intersectional approach) to understand the risk of cyberbullying more completely (see Stoll & Block, 2015).

In addition to the previous factors, scholars have studied the role of age in experiencing or perpetrating cyberbullying. Unfortunately, there is no clear consensus across studies. Although some studies have failed to substantiate a relationship between age and cyberbullying (Didden et al., 2009; Juvonen & Gross, 2008; Mesch, 2009; Patchin & Hinduja, 2006; Tokunaga, 2010), others have found older youth are less likely to experience this cybercrime (Navarro et al., 2017; Seiler & Navarro, 2014) or that the risk of cybervictimization increases with age (Navarro & Jasinski, 2013). To resolve this contradiction, Tokunaga (2010) points out that findings do suggest that middle school is a particularly critical time for youth in terms of experiencing cyberbullying. So, as Tokunaga (2010) proposes, the variation across studies vis-à-vis the relationship between age and cyberbullying may relate to the different age ranges within investigation samples. This contradiction is important to resolve to inform cyberbullying prevention and intervention programming. Moreover, it is important for scholars to consider other rarely studied age groups, such as the cyberbullying among adults in the workplace.

Aside from these demographics, scholars have also called attention to the relationship between cyberbullying and cognitive and physical disabilities (Didden et al., 2009), as well as physical characteristics (Berne, Frisén, & Kling, 2014). However, there is a serious dearth of information in these areas – particularly in comparison to more established lines of research within the cyberbullying field (i.e. demographics, online behaviours, parental/school monitoring). This is unfortunate, given findings suggest these forms of bullying are just as damaging as targeting youth based on other characteristics.

In terms of cognitive disabilities, available research suggests a relationship may exist with cyberbullying. For example, Didden and colleagues (2009) found that youth with attention–deficit hyperactivity disorder (ADHD) were more likely to cyberbully compared to others without this disability. Similar findings resulted from a study involving college students, where Kowalski and colleagues (2016) found that students with disabilities[7] were more likely to experience and perpetrate cyberbullying compared with non-disabled students. Given these studies, there is a critical need for more research investigating the role of disabilities in experiencing and perpetrating cyberbullying. A similar area of research involves investigating whether physical appearance is a risk factor for engaging in or experiencing cyberbullying.

As in the prior case, there is a dearth of literature that addresses the role of physical appearance as a risk factor for cyberbullying. However, available studies show the critical need for more information within this line of research. For example, research by Puhl and colleagues (2013) found that overweight youth often experienced "weight-based" cyberbullying. A later qualitative study supported this finding and illustrated the full spectrum of physical–appearance cyberbullying (see Berne et al., 2014). Within that study, there were some behaviours experienced by all youth (e.g. the targeting of one's style) but also some differences across genders (Berne et al., 2014). For example, females often experienced physical–appearance cyberbullying in the form of weight-based bullying, whereas males typically experienced this cybervictimization in the form of ridiculing their physical stature (Berne et al., 2014). Also, if males did not conform to gender–normative ideals of masculinity, youth reported that cyberbullies would also verbally harass them with homophobic language (Berne et al., 2014), which again underscores the importance of addressing sexual orientation as a risk factor for experiencing cyberbullying.

Aside from investigating the relationship between several background characteristics and cyberbullying, cybercriminologists have spent considerable time finding online behaviours that affect the likelihood of perpetration or victimization. Although some of these factors have kept their importance throughout the progression of technology, others have become less significant for understanding cybervictimization. Before discussing specific activities, it is worth noting that many scholars continue to highlight the relationship between increased online presence and cybercrime from a simple opportunity standpoint. Put another way, as online presence increases, so does the risk of experiencing or perpetrating cyberbullying (Didden et al., 2009; Kowalski et al., 2014; Navarro et al., 2017; Navarro & Jasinski, 2012; Park, Na, & Kim, 2014; Seiler & Navarro, 2014). However, like many other areas of cyberbullying research, there are exceptions to that overall pattern. For example, at least one study has found that there is no relationship between time spent online and cyberbullying (Navarro & Jasinski, 2013). In terms of online behaviours, scholars have found several problematic activities that affect the risk of cyberbullying perpetration and/or victimization.

The most problematic activities found across the literature are those that place individuals within proximity to others, which makes intuitive sense, given the nature of this cybercrime. For example, several studies have found that youth who use chatrooms (Mesch, 2009; Navarro & Jasinski, 2012, 2013), instant messaging programs (Navarro & Jasinski, 2012), and social media sites (Mesch, 2009; Navarro & Jasinski, 2012; Park et al., 2014) are at increased risk of experiencing and/or perpetrating cyberbullying. Moreover, multiple studies have underscored that individuals who engage in risky behaviour that exposes vulnerability are more likely to experience cyberbullying. For example, findings suggest that the bypassing of security protocols (Seiler & Navarro, 2014), posting risqué photos (Seiler & Navarro, 2014), or victimizing others (Navarro et al., 2017; Navarro & Jasinski, 2013) increases the risk of experiencing cyberbullying.

Given the documented risk associated with social networking sites, scholars have focused their attention on finding out which behaviours on these platforms affect the likelihood of perpetrating or experiencing cyberbullying. Although this line of research is in the nascent stage, scholars have found that accepting many friends, engaging negative content (either directly or via friends), posting status updates, and using private messaging increase the risk of experiencing cyberbullying (Navarro et al., 2017; Peluchette, Karl, Wood, & Williams, 2015). Although this online behaviour is important, scholars have also focused on finding out whether certain offline behaviours affect the risk of experiencing or perpetrating cyberbullying. Unsurprisingly, findings show that cyberbullies may display clinically abnormal levels of defiance and use addictive substances (Sourander et al., 2010); in contrast, cybervictims may be more likely to experience depression among other negative consequences (Kowalski et al., 2014).

Consequences

The consequences of cyberbullying are as varied as the forms by which it manifests. As scholars have noted, some youth are unfazed by occurrences (Ortega, Elipe, Mora-Merchán, Calmaestra, & Vega, 2009). However, at the other end of the spectrum, some youth contemplate suicide (Kowalski et al., 2014). Also, victimized youth report experiencing intense anger, anxiety, depression, embarrassment, fear, and hopelessness (Kowalski et al., 2014; Ortega et al., 2009; Tokunaga, 2010; Wright, 2018). The consequences of cyberbullying affect classroom behaviour as well. Studies show that victimized youth may academically and socially withdraw. In other words, academic performance may decrease while absenteeism increases (Beran & Le, 2007). Given these findings, particularly about suicide ideation, it is important for scholars to continue expanding what is known about cyberbullying. One area that is especially critical for growth is how current/former intimate partners engage in cyberbullying during and post-relationship.

Cyberstalking by strangers

Despite research showing a significant crossover between cyberstalking and offline stalking, there is an ongoing debate whether technology has spawned a new type of stalker: one that never crosses paths with the victim (Cavezza & McEwan, 2014; McFarlane & Bocij, 2003; Pittaro, 2007; Sheridan & Grant, 2007). In other words, scholars have proposed that technology has enabled offenders to "stalk from afar" and that these offenders may be different from the partner-perpetrated cyberstalking that falls within the realm of cyber-dating abuse (DA)/cyber-intimate partner abuse (IPA). The intention of this section is not to wade into that debate, but to present the sparse research on stranger-perpetrated cyberstalking. Although there are no definite conclusions presented in the following, available data do suggest that stranger-perpetrated cyberstalking is a reality in cyberspace for many individuals.

Definition and prevalence rates

As in most subfields of cybercriminology, there is no universally agreed on definition of cyberstalking yet. However, the following definition succinctly captures the breadth of potential behaviours within this area of interpersonal cybervictimization: "cyberstalking can be defined as the repeated pursuit of an individual using electronic or Internet-capable devices" (Reyns, Henson, & Fisher, 2012, p. 1). McFarlane and Bocij (2003), two prominent scholars within this area, have also put forward a definition albeit more detailed:

> a group of behaviors in which an individual, group of individuals, or organization uses information technology to harass one or more individuals. Such behavior may include, but are not limited to, the transmission of threats and false accusations, identity theft, data theft, damage to data or equipment, computer monitoring and the solicitation of minors for sexual purposes. Harassment is defined as a course of action that a reasonable person, in possession of the same information, would think causes another reasonable person to suffer emotional distress. (online publication with unknown page number)

As these definitions show, this offence includes virtually any action meant to pursue another in cyberspace, such as sending threatening and unwanted communications through ubiquitous platforms (i.e. email, instant messaging, social media), as well as using publicly available online information for nefarious purposes (Pittaro, 2007). Given the sparse research on cyberstalking, and the even larger gap concerning stranger-perpetrated cyberstalking, there are no clear indications of how widespread the problem is within cyberspace.

Readers should recall the two large studies discussed in the prior section that provide some insight about the scope of this problem. The first study, the NCVS 2006 Supplemental Victimization Survey, shows that 9% of stalking survivors were targeted by strangers (Catalano, 2012). Additionally, slightly more than 14% of survivors reported that their cyberstalkers' identities were unknown to them, which includes any category of person such as strangers (Catalano, 2012). These prevalence rates align with smaller studies across different settings. For example, results derived from Finn's (2004) study showed that a substantial proportion of cyberstalking victimizations (20%) were stranger-perpetrated, which is remarkably like percentages acquired in a much later study conducted by Short and colleagues (2015) where 21.7% of survivors also reported cyberstalking by strangers.

Yet other studies have found quite different prevalence rates. For instance, in a study conducted by Bocij (2003), nearly half of the participants were unable to name their cyberstalkers. Likewise, in a study conducted by Paullet and colleagues (2009), slightly more than 40% of respondents were cyberstalked by strangers. Finally, although not a prevalence rate per se, the premise that "stranger-danger" exists within cyberspace in terms of stalking was supported in a study conducted by Reyns and colleagues (2011). In that study, the scholars found that individuals who interacted with strangers online were significantly more likely to experience cyberstalking (Reyns et al., 2011). Unfortunately, given that these offences involve unknown persons, there is not much information available. However, a few notable studies do offer insight into offender and victim risk factors.

Offenders and victims

In an analysis focused on identifying characteristics of cyberstalkers (all types), Reyns and colleagues (2012) found several notable patterns across demographics. Specifically, results showed that fewer females, Caucasians, and individuals who identified as heterosexual engaged in cyberstalking compared to males, non-Caucasians, and non-heterosexuals (Reyns et al., 2012). However, these results should be read with caution, as many of these differences did not reach statistical significance (Reyns et al., 2012). In another study centred on investigating perpetrators, Navarro and colleagues (2016) found that youth who associated with deviant peers, displayed traits indicative of Internet addiction, and had high grade point averages (GPAs) were more likely to engage in cyberstalking. Finally, to address the ongoing debate whether cyberstalkers are different from offline stalkers, Cavezza and McEwan (2014) analysed these two groups of perpetrators and found few differences between them. One of the most notable findings was that cyberstalkers were typically not strangers to victims but rather ex-partners (Cavezza & McEwan, 2014). As in other areas of cybercriminology, considerable research has focused on finding victim risk factors, which includes demographic characteristics as well as risky behaviours that expose vulnerability.

In terms of gender, several studies have found that females are more likely to experience cyberstalking compared to males (Dreßing, Bailer, Anders, Wagner, & Gallas, 2014; Reyns et al., 2011, 2012; Sheridan & Grant, 2007). Unfortunately, the role of ethnicity/race as a risk factor for cyberstalking victimization is still largely unexplored, but evidence suggests that Caucasians are less likely to experience this cyber-offence compared with non-Caucasians (Reyns et al., 2012). Similarly, other gender identities/expressions and sexual orientation are also understudied, but available research shows that identifying as non-heterosexual increases the risk of experiencing cyberstalking (Reyns et al., 2012). In other research, Sheridan and Grant (2007) examined several additional background variables and found that cyberstalking victims were typically older, educated beyond high school, employed, and not in a relationship. However, it is important to reiterate that many of these studies call for replication before firm conclusions are drawn. For example, in a similar study conducted by Reyns and colleagues (2012), single individuals were *less* likely to experience cyberstalking compared to their attached counterparts (in contrast to Sheridan & Grant, 2007). Aside from demographics, scholars have investigated whether certain online behaviours affect risk of experiencing cyberstalking. For example, in a thorough analysis conducted by Reyns and colleagues (2011), risk of experiencing cyberstalking increased if individuals added strangers as friends online, engaged in online deviance themselves, kept multiple social networks, and/or used AOL instant messenger.

Consequences

Experiencing cyberstalking is an extremely distressing event, as it quite literally erodes any feelings of personal safety. Stalkers can now reach victims despite geographical distance and physical barriers with the power of technology. Also, given the extensive information available within a few simple keystrokes, it is virtually impossible to escape cyberstalkers. Taking these considerations into account, the effort of survivors to ensure safety is understandably exhausting on various levels. For example, in one noteworthy study, Nobles and colleagues (2014) found that cyberstalking victims spent significantly more money, on average, trying to resolve their situation compared to stalking victims ($1,244.64 vs. $497.67). This is particularly distressing given how long the victimization can continue. For example, Nobles and colleagues (2014) found that the average duration of cyberstalking incidents was slightly more than 650 continuous days; however, in a study conducted by Bocij (2003), the victimization period ranged from 14 days to 38 months (Nobles et al., 2014). Unsurprisingly, research shows that these experiences have serious repercussions physically, psychologically, and socially for survivors.

The omnipresence of cyberstalkers in victims' lives, and the potential life-threatening danger they pose, results in severe negative consequences across various life domains (e.g. personal, professional, social). In one informative study by Dreßing and colleagues (2014), cyberstalking survivors reported various ramifications. In terms of physical consequences, over 30% of survivors experienced headaches and gastrointestinal issues (Dreßing et al., 2014). Additionally, even higher percentages (50%+) of respondents reported psychological consequences such as anger, helplessness, and restlessness (Dreßing et al., 2014), which aligns with later research conducted by Worsley and colleagues (2017). Finally, survivors experienced social consequences, as more than 20% reported that they avoided new relationships or had difficulties with existing ones, that they were socially withdrawn, and that they were mistrustful of others (Dreßing et al., 2014). What is most telling about these results is that less than 4% of survivors reported *no* consequences (Dreßing et al., 2014). In other words, an overwhelming majority of the sample experienced at least one negative consequences as a result cyberstalking (Dreßing et al., 2014).

Cyberabuse: dating abuse and intimate partner abuse via technology

Cyberabuse is unique in that it typically involves various forms of interpersonal cybervictimization: cyberbullying (i.e. of primary victims or secondary victims like family and friends), cyberfraud (e.g. account takeovers, establishing new accounts, identify theft), cybersexual abuse (e.g. distribution of revenge porn, sexual exploitation, sexual violence-by-proxy[8]), and/or cyberstalking (i.e. of primary or secondary victims) as illustrated by the National Network to End Domestic Violence's technology power and control wheel.[9] Survivors may experience one or multiple forms of these cybercrimes simultaneously (Dick et al., 2014). This statement should not be surprising, given that offline abuse also typically includes a wide spectrum of behaviour, which is a manifestation of an abuser's need to exert coercive control over their partner (Stark, 2007). However, as in many areas of cybercriminology, the field is still grappling with how best to investigate technological abuses between current/former intimate partners (hereafter, simply "partners"). This broad challenge has led to inconsistent definitions and differing populations of interest across studies, which in turn affects prevalence rates.

Definition and prevalence rates

Given the nascent stage of the field, scholars have used many different definitions of cyberabuse, which is a broad term generally encompassing two separate lines of research: cyber-DA and cyber-IPA.[10] Cyber-DA, although still broadly considered cyber-IPA, is a term typically used to reference violence occurring within informal relationships that are more common during adolescence, young adulthood, and college (see for example: Draucker & Martsolf, 2010;

Lucero, Weisz, Smith-Darden, & Lucero, 2014; Reed, Tolman, & Ward, 2016; Schnurr, Mahatmya, & Basche, 2013; Stonard, Bowen, Lawrence, & Price, 2014; Stonard, Bowen, Walker, & Price, 2014; Wolford-Clevenger et al., 2016; Zweig, Dank, Yahner, & Lachman, 2013) in contrast to adult relationships that often involve formal cohabitation/marriage and/or children (i.e. cyber-IPA). Taking this distinction into account is important, because although certain types of cybervictimization are present across these classifications (e.g. cyberharassment), other forms are more applicable to adults within formal relationships (e.g. cyberfraud involving shared financial accounts; cyberharassment of shared children). Moreover, given the nature of youth and young adult samples, certain forms of abuse (e.g. sexual violence) are understudied in those investigations (Capaldi, Knoble, Shortt, & Kim, 2012). This distinction is not meant to diminish the contributions of these extremely notable studies, but only to explain why these cyber-offences are discussed separately in the following passages.

Given the lack of a universally agreed on definition of cyber-IPA, a starting point to understanding this interpersonal cybercrime is to reference descriptions of offline abuse and how that applies to cyberspace. For example, according to the National Domestic Violence Hotline (NDVH), IPA is "a pattern of behaviors used by one partner to maintain power and control over another partner in an intimate relationship." Considering this NDVH definition and the work of Stark (2007), the author defines cyber-IPA as the use of technology by individuals within formal relationships to coercively control their partners, such that victims consider or alter their behaviour out of fear for themselves and/or their loved ones. To be clear, however, some scholars have relied on long-held descriptions of IPA to ground studies without proposing adjustments to account for cyberspace. For example, Dimond and colleagues (2011, p. 413) reference Lenore Walker's (1999) description of abuse as "[IPA] . . . typically refers to physical, sexual, and psychological abuse directed against domestic partners." The point of this discussion is that, given the lack of a standard definition, some scholars change existing definitions of IPA to apply to cyberspace, whereas others rely on broad definitions that apply to either environment.

Scholars have tried to resolve definition inconsistencies across the cyber-DA literature as well. For example, Stonard and colleagues (2014) proposed the following definition to convey the full scope of cyber-DA after assessing variations across the literature on the topic:

> any behaviors that are threatening, controlling, violent, abusive, harassment or stalking that are directed towards a current or former romantic partner by the other within the context of an adolescent (10–18 years old) dating relationship. This can include either or a combination of physical, psychological/emotional and sexual behaviors and can take place in person or electronically via technology (such as mobile phone or online) and occurs regardless of gender or sexuality.
>
> (p. 393)

As in the case of cyber-IPA, some also rely on broad definitions of this offence that apply to offline and online environments. For instance, the definition proffered by the Centers for Disease Control and Prevention (CDC) (2018) is used, which conceptualizes dating violence as "the physical, sexual, psychological, or emotional aggression within a dating relationship, including stalking. It can occur in person or *electronically* and might occur between a current or former dating partner" (emphasis added). Given these definition inconsistencies, prevalence rates of cyber-DA and cyber-IPA vary widely across studies.

Although many individuals experience IPA every day, the manifestation of this crime online is still understudied among adults in formal relationships. In one early and notable exception, Belknap and colleagues (2012) reported on violence perpetrated by partners that involved technology in some form. As the findings showed, even at this early point in the technological age (i.e. 1997), perpetrators used these advancements to further their control over survivors (Belknap et al., 2012). For example, Belknap and colleagues (2012) found that perpetrators blocked victims' access to computers (~4%; Time 3) and/or telephones (~16%; Time 3). Moreover, perpetrators used telephones to communicate threatening messages to victims (~2%) or as actual blunt objects in physical altercations (~1%) (Belknap et al., 2012). These behaviours have not changed as time has passed.

In a recent study involving social service personnel and survivors, Woodlock (2017) found that the use of technology within abusive relationships is not unusual. For example, significant percentages of survivors noted that abusers specifically used technology to control and threaten them (Woodlock, 2017). These methods varied across the technological landscape and involved everything from communication platforms (e.g. email, social networking, text messaging) to global positioning system (GPS) tracking devices (Woodlock, 2017). Moreover, abusers exploited these advancements not only to control and threaten survivors but also to engage in account takeovers (e.g. coercing access to victims' accounts), cyberstalking, identity theft (e.g. abusers masquerading online as survivors), and sexual abuse (e.g. sharing of explicit content) (Woodlock, 2017). Finally, abusers also kept their destructive presence in victims' lives by accessing technology in the possession of shared children (Woodlock, 2017). The percentage of survivors reporting these experiences ranged from 78% (i.e. abuse via mobile/phones) to 6% (i.e. abuse via accessing shared children through technology) (Woodlock, 2017).

Although all forms of cyber-IPA are destructive to a survivor's agency, the frequent use of technology to further stalking behaviours is particularly pronounced across the literature. For example, according to the National Intimate Partner and Sexual Violence Survey (2015) that was sponsored by the CDC's National Center for Injury Prevention and Control, the lifetime prevalence rate for stalking by an intimate partner was 10.4% for women and 2.2% for men (Smith et al., 2018). Though frequencies associated with specific types of stalking (i.e. offline versus online) were not presented, the scholars accounted for cyberstalking by asking about unwanted communications sent through electronic mediums (e.g. email, instant messaging, social media) and through telephones (e.g. voice and text) (Smith et al., 2018). These alarming statistics mirror earlier studies, such as the 2006 Supplemental Victimization Survey to the National Crime Victimization Survey (NCVS), where it was estimated that more than 3.3 million people experienced stalking in the prior year (Catalano, 2012). In terms of offenders, a substantial percentage of stalking perpetrators were known to victims through prior intimate relationships (20%), and one of the most often used methods was placing unwanted phone calls and sending unwanted messages (67%) (Catalano, 2012). Unfortunately, cyberstalking and other forms of cyber-IPA are also present in cyber-DA.

Although certain forms of abuse noted earlier are not as prevalent among informal relationships typically involving youth and young adults (e.g. accessing shared children), survivors of cyber-DA experience similar behaviours from abusive partners. In one of the earliest studies of this problem, Draucker and Martsolf (2010) studied the cyber-DA experiences of 56 individuals. As in the prior studies, results from Draucker's and Martsolf's (2010) investigation revealed that a substantial percentage of abusers (~54%) used technology in various forms to control and monitor partners. Moreover, technology was a medium by which abusers cyberharassed partners (Draucker & Martsolf, 2010). And, most disturbingly, survivors reported that abusers used both "low-tech" methods (e.g. instant messaging) and sophisticated "high-tech" methods like key loggers (Draucker & Martsolf, 2010).[11] Findings from recent studies underscore the point that cyber-DA is an alarming problem.

Several recent studies continue to highlight the problem of cyber-DA among youth and young adults. As in cyber-IPA, survivors of cyber-DA reported experiencing a myriad of abusive behaviours involving technology such a: abusers coercing or blocking access to victims' private accounts (Brem et al., 2017; Lucero et al., 2014; Wolford-Clevenger et al., 2016), cyberfraud via identity theft (Reed, Tolman, & Ward, 2016), cyberharassment of victims (Brem et al., 2017; Zweig et al., 2013) and loved ones (Reed et al., 2016), cyberstalking of victims (Brem et al., 2017; Lucero et al., 2014; Wolford-Clevenger et al., 2016; Zweig et al., 2013) and loved ones (Reed et al., 2016), and cyber-sexual abuse (e.g. coercing engagement in sexual activity, coercing production of explicit content, sharing of explicit content) (Brem et al., 2017; Lucero et al., 2014; Reed et al., 2016; Zweig et al., 2013). Due to the methodological variation across studies, it is difficult to present broad prevalence rates for cyber-DA; however, in one notable synthesis of the literature, Stonard and colleagues (2014) found both perpetration and victimization rates ranged from 12% to slightly more than 50% across the included studies. Aside from assessing the prevalence of these occurrences, scholars have also focused on finding factors that affect risk of perpetration and victimization.

Offenders and victims

Due to the dearth of information about cyber-IPA broadly, there is little known about what factors affect the risk of experiencing or perpetrating this interpersonal cyberoffence except for one notable area: cyberstalking by partners. To reiterate, stalking affects millions of individuals every year, and many of these incidents occur within the backdrop of prior relationships (Catalano, 2012; Dreßing et al., 2014; Smith et al., 2018). This connection makes intuitive sense considering partners are particularly knowledgeable about the daily routines of their victims (to track movements), loved ones (to stalk or threaten), and significant dates/milestones (to guess passwords and breach accounts). Thus, even if relationships dissolve, abusers can still coercively control their ex-partners' movements through stalking – particularly in cyberspace. Recognizing that partner-perpetrated stalking is one form of IPA, a type of gender-based violence (Walker, 1999), gender is a critical factor to consider from a perpetration and victimization standpoint.

Although this offence occurs across genders, a greater lifetime prevalence of partner-perpetrated stalking exists among women (10.4%) compared to men (2.2%) (Smith et al., 2018). This finding supports earlier research where results showed a greater frequency of women experienced harassment and stalking (3.1%) compared to men (1.6%) (Catalano, 2012). The greater victimization risk among women is also supported in smaller studies. For example, in a study by Dreßing and colleagues (2014), females were significantly more likely to have experienced cyberstalking compared to males. Not only is gender a salient risk factor in terms of cyberstalking victimization, but also in perpetration. For instance, Dreßing and colleagues (2014) found that males were significantly more likely to perpetrate cyberstalking compared to females. Aside from these studies, no other investigations (to the author's knowledge) have examined risk factors associated with cyber-IPA perpetration or victimization (partner-perpetrated cyberstalking or otherwise); however, considerable research exists within the cyber-DA field.

In a comprehensive study of several forms of dating abuse, including non-sexual and sexual cyber-dating abuse, Zweig and colleagues (2013) underscored the importance of gender as a risk factor for perpetration and victimization. Specifically, a significantly greater proportion of females experienced cyber-sexual abuse (14.8%) compared to males (7.2%) (Zweig et al., 2013). This aligns with later studies also finding that greater percentages of females reported experiencing cyber-DA compared to males, which included non-sexual cyber-DA (40.1% vs. 28.9%) and sexual cyber-DA (13.7% vs. 9.2%) (Dick et al., 2014). However, conflicting results have been produced in other studies (Wolford-Clevenger et al., 2016), so this relationship needs further exploration. In terms of perpetration, the relationship to gender has also varied across studies. For example, evidence from one study indicates that a significantly greater proportion of males (3.8%) perpetrated cyber-sexual abuse compared to females (1.6%), but young women (13.0%) were more likely to engage in non-sexual cyber abuse compared to young men (7.4%) (Zweig et al., 2013).

As one considers the noted results, it is important to reiterate that many studies examine gender only from a binary perspective. In one notable exception, Dank and colleagues (2014) found that transgender youth (56.3%) were not only more likely to experience cyber-DA compared to females and males (28.8% and 23.3% respectively) but that transgender youth (35.3%) were also more likely to perpetrate cyber-DA compared to young men (9.3%) and women (13.9%). These findings align with studies that show LGBTQ youth are at increased risk of experiencing cyber-DA in certain contexts (Borrajo, Gámez-Guadix, & Calvete, 2015a; Dick et al., 2014; Zweig, Dank, Yahner & Lachman, 2013). Two more important demographic factors worth considering in terms of risk associated with cyber-DA are age and ethnicity/race.

As in the cyberbullying field, there is a substantial gap of information about whether ethnicity/race affects the risk of experiencing or perpetrating cyber-DA. Although this area of the research warrants continued investigation before firm conclusions are drawn, studies have found that risk of cyber-DA involvement does not differ across ethnic and racial groups (Dick et al., 2014; Peskin et al., 2017; Zweig et al., 2013). In contrast, several studies have highlighted the importance of age in assessing risk of cyber-DA, which makes intuitive sense given the nature of this cyberoffence.

Although age is a key factor to consider across several types of interpersonal cybervictimization, its impact on the risk of experiencing or perpetrating cyber-DA is inconsistent across studies. For instance, findings show that the risk of experiencing cyber-DA increases as age increases in certain contexts (Zweig et al., 2013), which might stem from greater participation in relationships during teenage years. However, other studies have found that cyber-DA decreases with age (Borrajo et al., 2015a). To add to this inconsistency, findings in other studies have failed to support a relationship between the two at all (Dick et al., 2014; Temple et al., 2016). To resolve this inconsistency, scholars should investigate whether these contradictions stem from the differing samples used, as Tokunaga (2010) noted within the cyberbullying field.

Aside from demographic variables, scholars have investigated several offline and online factors that affect the risk of experiencing or perpetrating cyber-DA. One such factor examined was individuals' attitudes and beliefs about abuse, which relates back to the broader literature that endorsement of relationship violence is tied to its actual manifestation (Regan & Durvasula, 2015). Based on available research, that pattern held in considering the perpetration of cyber-DA as well. In other words, endorsing violence within certain contexts increased the odds of perpetrating abuse both offline and online (Borrajo, Gámez-Guadix, & Calvete, 2015b; Peskin et al., 2017). Moreover, the odds of perpetrating cyber-DA increased if individuals had engaged in other forms of interpersonal abuse like bullying (Peskin et al., 2017).

In terms of victimization, as uncovered through work focused on cyberbullying, individuals who were in proximity to others via social networking sites were at increased risk of experiencing cyber-DA (Ouytsel, Ponnet, & Walrave, 2016). Moreover, individuals who engaged in risky offline activities (Zweig et al., 2013) and online activities (Ouytsel et al., 2016) that increased their vulnerability were also more likely to experience cyber-DA. For example, youth who engaged in deviance and/or sexual activity were more vulnerable to experiencing cyber-DA (Zweig et al., 2013). Unfortunately, as in other cases of cybervictimization, involvement in cyberabuse has lasting consequences both for offenders and victims.

Consequences

Abuse, regardless of form or setting, has lasting consequences on survivors, but information on the ramifications of victimization in cyberspace is still scarce. Anecdotally, news stories highlight the ultimate consequence of abusers using technology for nefarious purposes: potential physical harm to survivors and their loved ones. In one recent example, an abuser electronically tracked his wife to a sexual rendezvous with another man and, after seeing the pair, murdered the unsuspecting male (Jeeves, 2015). In similar examples not resulting in homicide, abusers used technology to find survivors at new locations, which prompted their later relocation to other unknown areas (Southworth & Tucker, 2006; Worsley et al., 2017). These relocations were not only disruptive to survivors and their loved ones but also presumably affected the efforts made to re-establish their lives: proximity to educational facilities, employment opportunities, and sources of social support. Overall, these findings broadly show a chief consequence of cyberabuse: survivors can no longer rely on geographical distance to ensure safety (Southworth & Tucker, 2006). Aside from consequences to physical safety, survivors also experience psychological ramifications of abuse.

Studies show that the negative consequences of cyberabuse, and particularly cyberstalking, manifest in multiple ways. For example, survivors report experiencing anger, anxiety, depression, and fear (Dreßing et al., 2014; Worsley et al., 2017). These psychological consequences may also manifest physically, as survivors reported having trouble keeping concentration and had issues with gastrointestinal health (Dreßing et al., 2014). Finally, experiencing cyberabuse caused survivors to socially withdraw from others and underperform at work, which affected their livelihoods and relations with others (Dreßing et al., 2014; Worsley et al., 2017).

Conclusion

As discussed throughout this chapter, interpersonal cybercrime victimization is a reality for many individuals throughout cyberspace. These cybercrimes typically include cyberbullying, cyber-DA/cyber-IPA, and/or cyberstalking. Although each of these offences is slightly different, there are a couple of areas of overlap worth noting. One obvious area of overlap is the nature of these offences and the aim of offenders. Put another way, each of these cybercrimes is perpetrated to intentionally inflict harm on another, which sets them apart from other forms of online offences that typically do not have specific targets (e.g. malware, phishing, etc.). Second, each of these fields suffers from methodological challenges that hinder scholars from knowing how widespread occurrences are within cyberspace. Despite these challenges, however, scholars have made considerable gains in improving knowledge about these offences. For example, prevalence rates show that these offences are a reality for many individuals across cyberspace. Moreover, findings across fields suggest groups of individuals are especially vulnerable to interpersonal cybercrime (e.g. females, those who engage in risky online activities). Given these findings, scholars should work towards resolving outstanding methodological challenges within each research area to improve prevention and intervention programming. As history has shown, the problem of interpersonal cybercrime will continue to evolve as technology advances. Thus, it is important for scholars to remain one step ahead of perpetrators looking to use cyberspace to victimize others.

Notes

1 A sampling of studies to make the point is given here, but readers are encouraged to reference the full meta-analysis completed by Kowalski et al. (2014) or a similar synthesis conducted by Tokunaga (2010).
2 See endnote 1.
3 See endnote 1.
4 The terms victim and survivor are used interchangeably throughout this chapter; however, it is acknowledged that victimized individuals may prefer one term or the other.
5 Lesbian, gay, bisexual, transgender, and queer.
6 Noting Hispanic here is not intended to imply they solely make up "ethnicities." This ethnic group is noted here, because they were the focus of the study cited (see Kupczynski, Mundy, & Green, 2013).
7 The "disability sample" in the study conducted by Kowalski and colleagues (2016) included students with cognitive disabilities, learning disabilities, mental disabilities, physical disabilities, and psychological disabilities.
8 This term refers to cases where abusers post that their current/former partners want to act out sexually violent fantasies with strangers. In these cases, abusers typically post this information while masquerading as the current/former partner themselves. Therefore, abusers quite literally set up situations where others (hence the "by-proxy") are invited to sexually victimize the current/former intimate partner. Although this form of abuse seems rare, at least from anecdotal reporting, the following are two recent examples (see references for full citation): CBS News (2017, July 20) and Pazzano (2018, April 20).
9 See the References section for a link to this resource.
10 Sometimes referred to as cyber-domestic abuse.
11 A form of malware that records keystrokes.

References

Akbulut, Y., & Eristi, B. (2011). Cyberbullying and victimisation among Turkish university students. *Australasian Journal of Educational Technology*, *27*(7), 1155–1170. https://doi.org/10.14742/ajet.910

Allen, K. P. (2012). Off the radar and ubiquitous: Text messaging and its relationship to 'drama' and cyberbullying in an affluent, academically rigorous US high school. *Journal of Youth Studies*, *15*(1), 99–117. https://doi.org/10.1080/13676261.2011.630994

Anderson, J., & Rainie, L. (2018). *The future of well-being in a tech-saturated world.* Retrieved from Pew Research Center's website: www.pewinternet.org/2018/04/17/the-future-of-well-being-in-a-tech-saturated-world/

Aoyama, I., Barnard-Brak, L., & Talbert, T. L. (2011). Cyberbullying among high school students: Cluster analysis of sex and age differences and the level of parental monitoring. *International Journal of Cyber Behavior, Psychology and Learning (IJCBPL), 1*(1), 25–35. doi:10.4018/ijcbpl.2011010103

Aricak, T., Siyahhan, S., Uzunhasanoglu, A., Saribeyoglu, S., Ciplak, S., Yilmaz, N., & Memmedov, C. (2008). Cyberbullying among Turkish adolescents. *Cyberpsychology & Behavior, 11*(3), 253–261. https://doi.org/10.1089/cpb.2007.0016

Barlett, C., & Coyne, S. M. (2014). A meta-analysis of sex differences in cyber-bullying behavior: The moderating role of age. *Aggressive Behavior, 40*(5), 474–488. https://doi.org/10.1002/ab.21555

Bauman, S., Toomey, R. B., & Walker, J. L. (2013). Associations among bullying, cyberbullying, and suicide in high school students. *Journal of adolescence, 36*(2), 341–350. https://doi.org/10.1016/j.adolescence.2012.12.001

Belknap, J., Chu, A. T., & DePrince, A. P. (2012). The roles of phones and computers in threatening and abusing women victims of male intimate partner abuse. *Duke Journal of Gender Law & Policy, 19*, 373–406.

Beran, T. N., & Li, Q. (2007). The relationship between cyberbullying and school bullying. *The Journal of Student Wellbeing, 1*(2), 16–33. http://dx.doi.org/10.21913/JSW.v1i2.172

Beran, T. N., Rinaldi, C., Bickham, D. S., & Rich, M. (2012). Evidence for the need to support adolescents dealing with harassment and cyber-harassment: Prevalence, progression, and impact. *School Psychology International, 33*(5), 562–576. https://doi.org/10.1177/0143034312446976

Berne, S., Frisén, A., & Kling, J. (2014). Appearance-related cyberbullying: A qualitative investigation of characteristics, content, reasons, and effects. *Body Image, 11*(4), 527–533. https://doi.org/10.1016/j.bodyim.2014.08.006

Bocij, P. (2003). Victims of cyberstalking: An exploratory study of harassment perpetrated via the Internet. *First Monday, 8*(10).

Borrajo, E., Gámez-Guadix, M., & Calvete, E. (2015a). Cyber dating abuse: Prevalence, context, and relationship with offline dating aggression. *Psychological Reports, 116*(2), 565–585.

Borrajo, E., Gámez-Guadix, M., & Calvete, E. (2015b). Justification beliefs of violence, myths about love and cyber dating abuse. *Psicothema, 27*(4), 327–333. doi:10.7334/psicothema2015.59

Bossler, A. M., & Holt, T. J. (2010). The effect of self-control on victimization in the cyberworld. *Journal of Criminal Justice, 38*(3), 227–236. https://doi.org/10.1016/j.jcrimjus.2010.03.001

Brem, M. J., Florimbio, A. R., Grigorian, H., Wolford-Clevenger, C., Elmquist, J., Shorey, R. C., . . . Stuart, G. L. (2017, May 25). Cyber abuse among men arrested for domestic violence: Cyber monitoring moderates the relationship between alcohol problems and intimate partner violence. *Psychology of Violence.* Advance online publication. http://dx.doi.org/10.1037/vio0000130

Calvete, E., Orue, I., Estévez, A., Villardón, L., & Padilla, P. (2010). Cyberbullying in adolescents: Modalities and aggressors' profile. *Computers in Human Behavior, 26*(5), 1128–1135. https://doi.org/10.1016/j.chb.2010.03.017

Capaldi, D. M., Knoble, N. B., Shortt, J. W., & Kim, H. K. (2012). A systematic review of risk factors for intimate partner violence. *Partner Abuse, 3*(2), 231–280. https://doi.org/10.1891/1946-6560.3.2.231

Catalano, S. (2012). *Stalking victims in the United States – revised.* Washington, DC: U.S. Department of Justice, Office of Justice Programs, Bureau of Justice Statistics. Retrieved from https://bjs.gov/content/pub/pdf/svus_rev.pdf

Cavezza, C., & McEwan, T. E. (2014). Cyberstalking versus off-line stalking in a forensic sample. *Psychology, Crime & Law, 20*(10), 955–970. https://doi.org/10.1080/10683 16X.2014.893334

Dank, M., Lachman, P., Zweig, J. M., & Yahner, J. (2014). Dating violence experiences of lesbian, gay, bisexual, and transgender youth. *Journal of Youth and Adolescence, 43*(5), 846–857. https://doi.org/10.1007/s10964-013-9975-8

DeSmet, A., Rodelli, M., Walrave, M., Soenens, B., Cardon, G., & De Bourdeaudhuij, I. (2018). Cyberbullying and traditional bullying involvement among heterosexual and non-heterosexual adolescents, and their associations with age and gender. *Computers in Human Behavior, 83*, 254–261. https://doi.org/10.1016/j.chb.2018.02.010

Dick, R. N., McCauley, H. L., Jones, K. A., Tancredi, D. J., Goldstein, S., Blackburn, S., . . . Miller, E. (2014). Cyber dating abuse among teens using school-based health centers. *Pediatrics, 134*(6), e1560–e1567. doi:10.1542/peds.2014-0537

Didden, R., Scholte, R. H., Korzilius, H., De Moor, J. M., Vermeulen, A., O'Reilly, M., . . . Lancioni, G. E. (2009). Cyberbullying among students with intellectual and developmental disability in special education settings. *Developmental Neurorehabilitation, 12*(3), 146–151. https://doi.org/10.1080/17518420902971356

Dilmac, B. (2009). Psychological needs as a predictor of cyber bullying: A preliminary report on college students. *Educational Sciences: Theory and Practice, 9*(3), 1307–1325.

Dimond, J. P., Fiesler, C., & Bruckman, A. S. (2011). Domestic violence and information communication technologies. *Interacting with Computers, 23*(5), 413–421. https://doi.org/10.1016/j.intcom.2011.04.006

Draucker, C. B., & Martsolf, D. S. (2010). The role of electronic communication technology in adolescent dating violence. *Journal of Child and Adolescent Psychiatric Nursing, 23*(3), 133–142. https://doi.org/10.1111/j.1744-6171.2010.00235.x

Dreßing, H., Bailer, J., Anders, A., Wagner, H., & Gallas, C. (2014). Cyberstalking in a large sample of social network users: Prevalence, characteristics, and impact upon victims. *Cyberpsychology, Behavior, and Social Networking, 17*(2), 61–67. https://doi.org/10.1089/cyber.2012.0231

Finn, J. (2004). A survey of online harassment at a university campus. *Journal of Interpersonal Violence, 19*(4), 468–483. doi:10.1177/0886260503262083

GLSEN. Retrieved from www.glsen.org/

Görzig, A., & Ólafsson, K. (2013). What makes a bully a cyberbully? Unravelling the characteristics of cyberbullies across twenty-five European countries. *Journal of Children and Media, 7*(1), 9–27. https://doi.org/10.1080/17482798.2012.739756

Griffiths, M. (2000). Excessive internet use: Implications for sexual behavior. *CyberPsychology & Behavior, 3*(4), 537–552. doi:10.1089/109493100420151

Hinduja, S., & Patchin, J. W. (2008). Cyberbullying: An exploratory analysis of factors related to offending and victimization. *Deviant Behavior, 29*(2), 129–156. https://doi.org/10.1080/01639620701457816

Jeeves, P. (2015, January 14). Husband 'butchered wife's lover after tracking him down using a mobile phone app.' *Express.* Retrieved from www.express.co.uk/news/uk/551848/Man-allegedly-stabbed-wife-s-lover-death- after-tracking-with-app

Juvonen, J., & Gross, E. F. (2008). Extending the school grounds? – Bullying experiences in cyberspace. *Journal of School Health, 78*(9), 496–505. https://doi.org/10.1111/j.1746-1561.2008.00335.x

Kosciw, J. G., Greytak, E. A., Giga, N. M., Villenas, C., & Danischewski, D. J. (2016). *The 2015 national school climate survey: The experiences of lesbian, gay, bisexual, transgender, and queer youth in our nation's schools*. Gay, Lesbian and Straight Education Network (GLSEN). 121 West 27th Street Suite 804, New York, NY 10001.

Kowalski, R. M., Giumetti, G. W., Schroeder, A. N., & Lattanner, M. R. (2014). Bullying in the digital age: A critical review and meta-analysis of cyberbullying research among youth. *Psychological Bulletin, 140*(4), 1073–1137. doi:10.1037/a0035618

Kowalski, R. M., Morgan, C. A., Drake-Lavelle, K., & Allison, B. (2016). Cyberbullying among college students with disabilities. *Computers in Human Behavior, 57*, 416–427. https://doi.org/10.1016/j.chb.2015.12.044

Kupczynski, L., Mundy, M., & Green, M. E. (2013). The prevalence of cyberbullying among ethnic groups of high school students. *International Journal of Educational Research, 1*(2), 48–53.

Kwan, G. C. E., & Skoric, M. M. (2013). Facebook bullying: An extension of battles in school. *Computers in Human Behavior, 29*(1), 16–25. https://doi.org/10.1016/j.chb.2012.07.014

Lee, C., & Shin, N. (2017). Prevalence of cyberbullying and predictors of cyberbullying perpetration among Korean adolescents. *Computers in Human Behavior, 68*, 352–358. https://doi.org/10.1016/j.chb.2016.11.047

Lucero, J. L., Weisz, A. N., Smith-Darden, J., & Lucero, S. M. (2014). Exploring gender differences: Socially interactive technology use/abuse among dating teens. *Affilia, 29*(4), 478–491. https://doi.org/10.1177/0886109914522627

McFarlane, L., & Bocij, P. (2003). An exploration of predatory behaviour in cyberspace: Towards a typology of cyberstalkers. *First Monday, 8*(9).

Mesch, G. S. (2009). Parental mediation, online activities, and cyberbullying. *CyberPsychology & Behavior, 12*(4), 387–393. https://doi.org/10.1089/cpb.2009.0068

National Network to End Domestic Violence Technology Power and Control Wheel. Retrieved from https://nnedv.org/mdocs-posts/technology-power-and-control-wheel/

Navarro, J. N., & Clevenger, S. (2017). Understanding cybercrime victimization. In C. Roberson (Ed.), *Routledge handbook on victims' issues in criminal justice* (pp. 88–101). New York, NY: Routledge.

Navarro, J. N., Clevenger, S., Beasley, M. E., & Jackson, L. K. (2017). One step forward, two steps back: Cyberbullying within social networking sites. *Security Journal, 30*(3), 844–858. https://doi.org/10.1057/sj.2015.19.

Navarro, J. N., & Jasinski, J. L. (2012). Going cyber: Using routine activities theory to predict cyberbullying experiences. *Sociological Spectrum, 32*(1), 81–94. https://doi.org/10.1080/02732173.2012.628560

Navarro, J. N., & Jasinski, J. L. (2013). Why girls? Using routine activities theory to predict cyberbullying experiences between girls and boys. *Women & Criminal Justice, 23*(4), 286–303. https://doi.org/10.1080/08974454.2013.784225

Navarro, J. N., Marcum, C. D., Higgins, G. E., & Ricketts, M. L. (2016). Addicted to the thrill of the virtual hunt: Examining the effects of internet addiction on the cyberstalking behaviors of juveniles. *Deviant Behavior, 37*(8), 893–903. https://doi.org/10.1080/01639625.2016.1153366

Nobles, M. R., Reyns, B. W., Fox, K. A., & Fisher, B. S. (2014). Protection against pursuit: A conceptual and empirical comparison of cyberstalking and stalking victimization among a national sample. *Justice Quarterly, 31*(6), 986–1014. https://doi.org/10.1080/07418825.2012.723030

Olumide, A. O., Adebayo, E., & Oluwagbayela, B. (2016). Gender disparities in the experience, effects and reporting of electronic aggression among secondary school students in Nigeria. *BMJ Global Health, 1*(3), e000072. http://dx.doi.org/10.1136/bmjgh-2016-000072

Olweus, D. (1994). Bullying at school: Basic facts and effects of a school based intervention program. *Journal of Child Psychology and Psychiatry*, *35*(7), 1171–1190. https://doi.org/10.1111/j.1469-7610.1994.tb01229.x

Olweus, D., & Limber, S. P. (2018). Some problems with cyberbullying research. *Current Opinion in Psychology*, *19*, 139–143. https://doi.org/10.1016/j.copsyc.2017.04.012

Ortega, R., Elipe, P., Mora-Merchán, J. A., Calmaestra, J., & Vega, E. (2009). The emotional impact on victims of traditional bullying and cyberbullying: A study of Spanish adolescents. *Zeitschrift für Psychologie/Journal of Psychology*, *217*(4), 197–204.

Park, S., Na, E. Y., & Kim, E. M. (2014). The relationship between online activities, netiquette and cyberbullying. *Children and Youth Services Review*, *42*, 74–81. https://doi.org/10.1016/j.childyouth.2014.04.002

Patchin, J. W., & Hinduja, S. (2006). Bullies move beyond the schoolyard: A preliminary look at cyberbullying. *Youth Violence and Juvenile Justice*, *4*(2), 148–169. doi:10.1177/1541204006286288

Patchin, J. W., & Hinduja, S. (Eds.). (2012). *Cyberbullying prevention and response: Expert perspectives*. New York, NY: Routledge.

Paullet, K. L., Rota, D. R., & Swan, T. T. (2009). Cyberstalking: An exploratory study of students at a mid-Atlantic university. *Issues in Information Systems*, *10*(2), 640–649.

Pazzano, S. (2018, April 21). Ontario rape fantasy victim will remain online 'indefinitely': Judge. *Toronto Sun*. Retrieved from http://torontosun.com/news/provincial/ontario-rape-fantasy-victims-will-remain-online-indefinitely-judge

Peluchette, J. V., Karl, K., Wood, C., & Williams, J. (2015). Cyberbullying victimization: Do victims' personality and risky social network behaviors contribute to the problem? *Computers in Human Behavior*, *52*, 424–435. https://doi.org/10.1016/j.chb.2015.06.028

Peskin, M. F., Markham, C. M., Shegog, R., Temple, J. R., Baumler, E. R., Addy, R. C., . . . Emery, S. T. (2017). Prevalence and correlates of the perpetration of cyber dating abuse among early adolescents. *Journal of Youth and Adolescence*, *46*(2), 358–375. doi:10.1007/s10964-016-0568-1

Pittaro, M. L. (2007). Cyber stalking: An analysis of online harassment and intimidation. *International Journal of Cyber Criminology*, *1*(2), 180–197.

Puhl, R. M., Peterson, J. L., & Luedicke, J. (2013). Weight-based victimization: Bullying experiences of weight loss treatment – seeking youth. *Pediatrics*, *131*(1), e1–e9. doi:10.1542/peds.2012-1106

Regan, P. C., & Durvasula, R. S. (2015). A brief review of intimate partner violence in the United States: Nature, correlates, and proposed preventative measures. *Interpersona*, *9*(2), 127–134.

Reed, L. A., Tolman, R. M., & Ward, L. M. (2016). Snooping and sexting: Digital media as a context for dating aggression and abuse among college students. *Violence Against Women*, *22*(13), 1556–1576. https://doi.org/10.1177/1077801216630143

Reyns, B. W., Henson, B., & Fisher, B. S. (2011). Being pursued online: Applying cyberlifestyle – routine activities theory to cyberstalking victimization. *Criminal Justice and Behavior*, *38*(11), 1149–1169. https://doi.org/10.1177/0093854811421448

Reyns, B. W., Henson, B., & Fisher, B. S. (2012). Stalking in the twilight zone: Extent of cyberstalking victimization and offending among college students. *Deviant Behavior*, *33*(1), 1–25. doi:10.1080/01639625.2010.538364

Schneider, S. K., O'Donnell, L., Stueve, A., & Coulter, R. W. (2012). Cyberbullying, school bullying, and psychological distress: A regional census of high school students. *American Journal of Public Health*, *102*(1), 171–177. doi:10.2105/AJPH.2011.300308

Schnurr, M. P., Mahatmya, D., & Basche, R. A. (2013). The role of dominance, cyber aggression perpetration, and gender on emerging adults' perpetration of intimate partner violence. *Psychology of Violence, 3*, 70–98.

Seiler, S. J., & Navarro, J. N. (2014). Bullying on the pixel playground: Investigating risk factors of cyberbullying at the intersection of children's online-offline social lives. *Cyberpsychology: Journal of Psychosocial Research on Cyberspace, 8*(4), article 6. http://dx.doi.org/10.5817/CP2014-4-6

Sheridan, L. P., & Grant, T. (2007). Is cyberstalking different? *Psychology, Crime & Law, 13*(6), 627–640. https://doi.org/10.1080/10683160701340528

Short, E., Guppy, A., Hart, J. A., & Barnes, J. (2015). The impact of cyberstalking. *Studies in Media and Communication, 3*(2), 23–37. https://doi.org/10.11114/smc.v3i2.970

Smith, A. (2015). *Searching for work in the digital era.* Retrieved from Pew Research Center's website: www.pewinternet.org/2015/11/19/searching-for-work-in-the-digital-era/.

Smith, S. G., Zhang, X., Basile, K. C., Merrick, M. T., Wang, J., Kresnow, M, & Chen, J. (2018). *The national intimate partner and sexual violence survey (NISVS): 2015 Data Brief.* Atlanta, GA: National Center for Injury Prevention and Control, Centers for Disease Control and Prevention. Retrieved from www.cdc.gov/violenceprevention/nisvs/2015NISVSdatabrief.html

Sourander, A., Klomek, A. B., Ikonen, M., Lindroos, J., Luntamo, T., Koskelainen, M., . . . Helenius, H. (2010). Psychosocial risk factors associated with cyberbullying among adolescents: A population-based study. *Archives of General Psychiatry, 67*(7), 720–728. doi:10.1001/archgenpsychiatry.2010.79

Southworth, C., & Tucker, S. (2006). Technology, stalking and domestic violence victims. *Miss. LJ, 76*, 667.

Stark, E. (2007). *Coercive control: The entrapment of women in personal life.* New York, NY: Oxford University Press.

Stoll, L. C., & Block Jr, R. (2015). Intersectionality and cyberbullying: A study of cyber-victimization in a Midwestern high school. *Computers in Human Behavior, 52*, 387–397. https://doi.org/10.1016/j.chb.2015.06.010

Stonard, K. E., Bowen, E., Lawrence, T. R., & Price, S. A. (2014). The relevance of technology to the nature, prevalence and impact of adolescent dating violence and abuse: A research synthesis. *Aggression and Violent Behavior, 19*(4), 390–417. https://doi.org/10.1016/j.avb.2014.06.005

Temple, J. R., Choi, H. J., Brem, M., Wolford-Clevenger, C., Stuart, G. L., Peskin, M. F., & Elmquist, J. (2016). The temporal association between traditional and cyber dating abuse among adolescents. *Journal of Youth and Adolescence, 45*(2), 340–349. https://doi.org/10.1007/s10964-015-0380-3

Tokunaga, R. S. (2010). Following you home from school: A critical review and synthesis of research on cyberbullying victimization. *Computers in Human Behavior, 26*(3), 277–287. doi:10.1016/j.chb.2009.11.014

Van Ouytsel, J., Ponnet, K., & Walrave, M. (2016). Cyber dating abuse victimization among secondary school students from a lifestyle-routine activities theory perspective. *Journal of Interpersonal Violence*, online first. https://doi.org/10.1177/0886260516629390

Walker, L. E. (1999). Psychology and domestic violence around the world. *American Psychologist, 54*(1), 21–29.

Wolford-Clevenger, C., Zapor, H., Brasfield, H., Febres, J., Elmquist, J., Brem, M., . . . Stuart, G. L. (2016). An examination of the partner cyber abuse questionnaire in a college student sample. *Psychology of Violence, 6*(1), 156–162. doi:10.1037/a0039442

Wong, R.Y., Cheung, C. M., & Xiao, B. (2018). Does gender matter in cyberbullying perpetration? An empirical investigation. *Computers in Human Behavior, 79*, 247–257. https://doi.org/10.1016/j.chb.2017.10.022

Woodlock, D. (2017). The abuse of technology in domestic violence and stalking. *Violence Against Women, 23*(5), 584–602. https://doi.org/10.1177/1077801216646277

Worsley, J. D., Wheatcroft, J. M., Short, E., & Corcoran, R. (2017). Victims' voices: Understanding the emotional impact of cyberstalking and individuals' coping responses. *SAGE Open, 7*(2). https://doi.org/10.1177/2158244017710292

Wright, M. (2018). Cyberbullying victimization through social networking sites and adjustment difficulties: The role of parental mediation. *Journal of the Association for Information Systems, 19*(2), 113–123. doi:10.17705/1jais.00486

Zsila, Á., Urbán, R., Griffiths, M. D., & Demetrovics, Z. (2018). Gender differences in the association between cyberbullying victimization and perpetration: The role of anger rumination and traditional bullying experiences. *International Journal of Mental Health and Addiction*, 1–16. https://doi.org/10.1007/s11469-018-9893-9

Zweig, J. M., Dank, M., Yahner, J., & Lachman, P. (2013). The rate of cyber dating abuse among teens and how it relates to other forms of teen dating violence. *Journal of Youth and Adolescence, 42*(7), 1063–1077. http://dx.doi.org.citadel.idm.oclc.org/10.1007/s10964-013-9922-8

6 Sexual violence in digital society

Understanding the human and technosocial factors

Anastasia Powell, Asher Flynn, and Nicola Henry

Introduction

As digital modes of communication and participation become further enmeshed into everyday lives, so, too, do these technologies feature in shifting enactments of sexual violence. Over many decades, research has examined various aspects of sexual victimization, as well as its extent, gendered nature, and impacts. However, scholarly examination of the ways in which digital technologies contribute to both the cultures and practices of sexual violence has been slow to develop in comparison to the rapid pace of the technologies themselves. Moreover, although the cybercrime scholarship has examined the role of technology in creating new opportunities and 'tools' for criminally motivated offenders in general, less attention has been paid to the development of conceptual frameworks for understanding the role of technologies in gender-based violences.

In this chapter, we move beyond a conventional analysis focused on technology as a mere facilitator of sexual offending, towards a more conceptual framing of the intersection of human, social, and technical factors that contribute to technology-facilitated sexual violence (TFSV). Although we acknowledge that there are many related fields of scholarship on different forms of technology-facilitated violence or abuse, including, for example, youth 'sexting' (Marcum et al., 2014; Mitchell et al., 2012; Reyns, Henson, & Fisher, 2014; Strohmaier, Murphy, & DeMatteo, 2014), pornography (e.g. DeKeseredy & Corsianos, 2015), and intimate partner violence (e.g. Douglas, Harris, & Dragiewicz, 2019; Dragiewicz et al., 2018; Harris, 2018; Reed, Tolman, & Ward, 2016; Southworth, Finn, Dawson, Fraser, & Tucker, 2007; Woodlock, 2017), we have grounded our conceptual discussion within the case study of TFSV against largely, though not exclusively, adult victims. Our rationale for doing so is three-fold. First, compared with the plethora of studies on youth sexting, there is a relative dearth of scholarly attention on understanding the nature of TFSV experienced by adult victims. Second, much of the youth sexting literature examines both consensual and non-consensual behaviours, which present unique legal and developmental issues in relation to child sexual exploitation material which, although important, are already well canvassed elsewhere (e.g. Crofts, Lee, McGovern, & Milivojevic, 2016; Powell & Henry, 2014). Third, although there are many intersections between different forms of sexual and partner abuse, it is not uncommon in the violence against women field to focus on a subset of violence and/or abuse.

Ultimately, our aim in this chapter is not to provide a systematic overview of the empirical research on these forms of violence and abuse, but rather to contribute to the conceptual development of the field by drawing on the case study of TFSV in order to elucidate the need for *technosocial* analyses within the field of 'cyber' and digital criminologies.

Technology-facilitated sexual violence

For almost a decade, our research has sought to elucidate the nature, extent, and impacts of various forms of TFSV (see e.g. Powell, 2010a, 2010b; Powell & Henry, 2017; Powell, Henry & Flynn, 2018). It is a concept that has gained increasing traction in recent years, with scholars, activists, and policymakers across the globe turning their attention to the role of technologies in the commission of these simultaneously familiar and unfamiliar harms (e.g. Bluett-Boyd, Fileborn, Quadara, & Moore, 2013; Cares, Moynihan, & Banyard, 2014; Chan, 2018; Douglass, Wright, Davis, & Lim, 2018; Eikren & Ingram-Waters, 2016; Martellozzo & Jane, 2017; Marwick, 2017; Pina, Holland & James, 2017; Vera-Gray, 2017). Although we do not view TFSV as wholly distinct from conventional forms of sexual violence (as we discuss later), we have found the concept to be useful in highlighting the need to understand the differences that technologies can make to the perpetration of sexual violence; to the experiences of victim-survivors; and the implications of these for policy, education, service provision, and law reform.

In general terms, TSFV refers to "the diverse ways in which criminal, civil or otherwise harmful sexually aggressive and harassing behaviours are being perpetrated with the aid or use of digital communication technologies" (Powell & Henry, 2017, p. 5). More specifically, it encompasses multiple dimensions of sexually harmful behaviours, including but not limited to enabling rape and/or sexual assault or another unwanted sexual experience; image-based sexual abuse, including the non-consensual creation, distribution, or threat of distribution of nude or sexual images; and online sexual harassment, including sexual solicitation, image-based harassment, gender-based hate speech, and rape threats. These different behaviours (each discussed in brief later) are not intended to represent discrete categories or types of sexual violence as they can and often do overlap. Yet there is value in explicitly identifying, describing, and understanding the various dimensions of TFSV in their own right, because some differences can emerge, particularly with respect to varying levels of legal and policy acknowledgement of these harms.

Enabling sexual assault

Online technologies, such as mobile phones, email, social networking sites, chat rooms, and online dating sites, are increasingly being used by sexual predators as a means of procuring rape or sexual assault. Indeed, there are several ways in which sexual assault is enabled by digital technologies, including in online dating, 'rape by proxy,' and sexual blackmail or 'sextortion.' Currently, there is very little empirical data on the prevalence of adult sexual victimization using mobile phone apps, dating sites, and other online platforms. However, 2016 figures from the National Crime Agency (UK) suggest that the number of people who report being raped on their first date with someone they met on a dating app has increased six-fold in just five years, with women representing the majority (85%) of victims of sexual offences linked to online dating in the period (2003–2015, National Crime Agency, 2016). Rape by proxy (see Frosh & Dumais, 2014; O'Connor, 2013), meanwhile, occurs when communications technologies are employed to solicit a third party to sexually assault a person. This may take place through deception, including false or mimicked identity, or more direct means, such as where online classifieds or trading site advertisements have been used to request sexual harassment and victimization directed against women (often by a male ex-partner). Finally, sexual blackmail or sextortion, describes abuse where a person procures "sexual cooperation by putting some kind of pressure on a victim" (Barak, 2005, p. 80). This can, for example, take the form of eliciting private information or a sexual image from a victim and using this material to blackmail, bribe, or threaten the victim to engage in either virtual or in-person sex acts (Powell & Henry, 2017).

Image-based sexual abuse

These harms encompass a range of behaviours involving the creation, distribution, or threats of distribution of a nude or sexual image (by which we mean both videos and photographs) without a person's consent. The term 'image-based sexual abuse' has been increasingly adopted by scholars as an alternative to the media-generated term 'revenge pornography,' as it more accurately captures both the range of victim experiences and perpetrator motivations and behaviours underlying this form of sexual harm (see McGlynn & Rackley, 2016; McGlynn, Rackley & Houghton, 2017; Powell et al., 2018). Image-based sexual abuse includes a range of abuse types and perpetrator motivations (see Powell & Henry, 2017; Powell et al., 2018 for a discussion). In some instances, the images may be 'selfies' taken by the victim and initially consensually shared with an intimate partner. However, images can also be taken by another person (with or without the victim's knowledge and consent), stolen images (such as through hacking cloud storage services or other online accounts), or images that are digitally manipulated in order to depict the victim's face or body in a sexual way (such as in 'morph porn' and 'deepfakes' or other computer-generated 'fake porn').

Prior to the Internet and the proliferation of digital imagery, perpetrators used a range of non-digital methods for the malicious distribution of intimate images. These ranged from street posters and letterbox drops, photocopies of images left at work, to mailing in hardcopies for inclusion in men's or women's magazines. Today the non-consensual taking, distribution, or threat of distribution of intimate images is facilitated by online platforms, as well as the ready availability of compact cameras and camera-enabled smartphones with instant Internet access. The problem has grown in scale due in large part to the ease with which nude or sexual images can be created, uploaded, and downloaded; the difficulties associated with removing these images once they are online; and the variety of platforms that popularize and support the trade and consumption of non-consensual images.

Research on the extent and nature of image-based sexual abuse is newly emerging, and there are very few scholarly studies that have reported on the non-consensual taking, distribution, and/or threats of distribution of nude or intimate images. In an early study, Powell and Henry (2016) found that approximately one in ten Australian and UK adults had experienced a nude or sexual image of them being distributed or posted online without their consent. Subsequent studies have found similar prevalence rates (see, Henry, Flynn, & Powell, 2019), whilst some have also found significant differences by gender, such that women (and particularly young adult women) are over-represented as victims of image-based sexual abuse (see Office of the eSafety Commissioner, 2017).

Sexual and gender-based harassment

Online sexual harassment potentially captures a wide range of harassing behaviours, including obtrusive relational pursuit, cyberbullying, sexual pressure or coercion (such as through persistent sexual requests), and unsolicited and unwanted sexual images (such as 'dick' and/or 'clit' pics). Psychologist Azy Barak (2005), for example, describes a variety of acts that constitute online sexual harassment, including sexual remarks; humiliating comments in chat rooms and forums; targeted 'flaming'; and intentionally emailing or posting erotic, pornographic, or sexually violent images and video. Some scholars have gone beyond individual models of online sexual harassment to problematize the way that 'mobbing,' or campaigns of harassment by many individuals towards a single victim, can represent a very serious form of online abuse (e.g. Sallavaci, 2018). Others have further sought to identify the collective experience faced by many individual women who are subjected to sexualized and/or highly gendered online abuse, in turn creating a hostile and exclusive environment for women (Gorman, 2019). Concepts such as 'gendertrolling' (referring to trolling directed at someone because of their gender and/or gender identity) (Mantilla, 2013), misogynist 'e-bile' or vitriolic abuse (Jane, 2014), and sexist or gender-based 'hate speech' (Lillian, 2007) serve to highlight the commonalities in both the nature of content and the routineness with which women who participate online can anticipate experiencing harassment and abuse.

Barak (2005, p. 78) describes gender-based harassment as involving "unwelcome verbal and visual comments and remarks that insult individuals because of their gender. . . [such as] posting pornographic pictures in public or in places where they deliberately insult, telling chauvinistic jokes, and making gender-related degrading remarks." Gender-based harassment can take place via chat rooms, forums, and through email and social media sites and includes (but is not limited to) gender-based hate speech, rape threats, reputation harming lies, impersonation; false accusations of sexual violence, and 'virtual' or simulated rape. Such behaviours may be perpetrated both by individuals acting alone and by groups of individuals acting collectively and in a more organized fashion (Citron & Franks, 2014). Several studies are relatively consistent in their findings that online sexual harassment disproportionately affects women both in prevalence and impacts, and particularly that young women are overrepresented among victims (Ballard & Welch, 2017; Bossler, Holt, & May, 2012; Lindsay, Booth, Messing, & Thaller, 2016; Lindsay & Krysik, 2012; Pew Research Center, 2014; Staude-Muller, Hansen, & Voss, 2012).

Together, what the research conducted into these multiple forms of TFSV to date suggests is that these sexually harmful and abusive behaviours are not something entirely 'new.' We have argued elsewhere that rather than representing a break with abusive practices of the past, TFSV is better understood simultaneously as a continuation and an elaboration of multiple forms of sexual harm that are experienced by women in their everyday lives (Powell & Henry, 2017). With the assistance of technologies, the violence of TFSV may differ in form, while at the same time it serves a similar function: as both an expression and re-institution of gendered power relations and women's differential positioning as primarily 'sexed' subjects. The starting point for our discussion of TFSV therefore cannot solely lie with the changes and the role of the technologies involved in these harms. It must instead commence with an understanding of the ways in which the underlying human and social factors of sex, gender, and power both shape and are shaped by technologies. Such an understanding requires an integrated framework for considering the relationship between the human, social, and technical in an increasingly digital society (see also Powell, Stratton, & Cameron, 2018). It is here where we have found the concept of *technosociality* (see Brown, 2006; Ito & Okabe, 2005) to be most useful.

Technosociality: an alternative framework for sexual 'cyber' crimes

Since criminological research in these fields proliferated in the late 1990s, there has been a problematic dichotomous framing of 'cyber' crime, as opposed to 'material' crime (see Powell et al., 2018). Indeed, much cybercrime research has examined the extent to which online crimes can be understood as distinct from their offline counterparts: fraud and cyberfraud, terrorism and cyberterrorism, bullying and cyberbullying, and so on. There has also been a tendency within the criminology discipline to position the 'virtual' world as a separate sphere to the 'material' world – a distinctive space that a motivated and skilled offender enters into in order to exploit the vastly expanded opportunities for crime and deviance found there. Such criminological framings emerged when public engagement with the Internet was still relatively new, and 'virtual communities' were investigated and represented as a separate or additional sphere to that of offline, day-to-day social interactions.

In today's context, digital communications technologies can be more closely understood as a 'third arm' in our embodied experiences. We are in 'perpetual contact' (see Katz & Aakhus, 2002) with an ever-increasing array of 'smart' devices that are not only embedded into the ways we socialize, communicate, and construct our identities but are also actively gathering data about us, our movements, and our practices whilst simultaneously seeking to influence our behaviour in a feedback loop replete with various notifications, pop-ups, prompts, and 'likes.' The questions that criminologists are required to address today are less concerned with why a motivated offender might choose to engage in cybercrimes, but rather, what is the nature of interaction between the digital and society that is (re)productive of criminal and deviant practices?

Powell et al. (2018) provide a rationale for moving away from 'cyber' frameworks within criminology and towards an engagement with the digital. They argue that the shift is not a matter of mere semantics, but rather invites criminological research to resist the oppositional positioning of 'cyber' or 'virtual' as against non-technological forms of crime. In effect, their framework suggests that the digital is not a place per se, but rather an assemblage of technological artefacts, networks, and practices. At the same time, by referring to digital *society*, rather than common suffixes such as 'age' or 'era,' they suggest it has the effect of "deliberately invok[ing] analyses of social inequalities, socio-cultural practices and socio-political factors that underpin crime and justice broadly" (Powell et al., 2018, p. 8). While digital society is a useful shorthand for describing the nature of social and technological interaction that characterizes contemporary societies, it also signals a conceptual framework for understanding the mutual and reciprocal shaping of technology and society, or technosociality.

Technosociality refers to the integration of technology, social practice, and place resulting in "technologically mediated social orders" (Ito & Okabe, 2005; see also Brown, 2006). It is not a new concept in sociological terms. Over 20 years ago, Manuel Castells (1996, p. 5) observed that "technology does not determine society . . . nor does society script the course of technological change." Rather, the relationships between the digital and the social are so integrated that "technology *is* society, and society cannot be understood or represented without its technological tools" (Castells, 1996, p. 5, emphasis in original). Yet the discipline of criminology has been relatively slow to adopt or apply technosocial approaches to examining crime and justice in digital society. In her ground-breaking article, Sheila Brown (2006) suggests that criminology has failed to sufficiently account for the interaction of non-human and human factors in understanding technology and crime. Drawing on theorists such as Bruno Latour (*actor–network theory* [ANT], Latour, 1993, 2005) and Scott Lash (2002), Brown argues that what is required is criminological thinking that moves beyond dualistic notions of society/technology, real/virtual, human/ non-human, towards an analysis of human-technology hybrids. In short, what Brown (2006) calls for is a technosocial analysis of crime in contemporary societies. After all, as Lash (2002, p. 15) asserts, "we make sense of the world through technological systems . . . we face our environment in our interface with technological systems." A contemporary criminological account of sexual violence, then, requires a more integrated conceptualization of the ways in which the practices, structures, and cultures of crime and deviance take place in digital society.

In our research, we have advocated that in order to understand TFSV, it is vital to understand digital technologies not as a separate or 'virtual' sphere of experience, but rather as an embedded and embodied feature of everyday sexual harms (see Henry & Powell, 2015). Contemporary forms of sexual violence are (like many aspects of the human experience) increasingly technosocial – representing an interactive and mutually constitutive set of abusive practices that reflect sex, gender, and power relations. In this regard, technologies cannot be understood as either *neutral tools* in the commission of sexual violence, nor as *determinative* of sexual offending, but instead, technologies should be understood as an embedded and co-constituting feature in such violence, as well as the structures, cultures, and practices of sexism and gender inequality that underpin it. This conceptual underpinning further highlights the limitations of conventional 'cyber' framings, which often categorize cyber-*dependent* crimes (which can only occur due to the existence of technologies, such as hacking a network), as distinct from cyber-*enabled* crimes (in which technology is merely a facilitator, such as in cyberstalking or cyberfraud) (Wall, 2007). On the one hand, all forms of cyber-violences might be understood as cyber-enabled, because the capacity to harm individuals, physically, sexually, or emotionally, pre-exists technology. But then, so, too, does the capacity to access private information without authorization. Yet when a sexual assault is distributed in real time via Facebook Live or a nude image is shared on a 'revenge porn' website, the specific crime of distribution of the image via a carriage service could be described as technology dependent. In other examples the creation of the sexual photo or video itself may be entirely simulated: a digital fabrication. The harm caused by such acts is arguably a specific type of sexual violation, even though it is certainly related to other forms of sexual violence and abuse. Moreover, the very practice of recording, simulating, and/or broadcasting by everyday citizens outside of a hierarchically controlled media is itself only possible because of the camera and Internet-enabled devices that are ubiquitous in modern society (Stratton, Powell, & Cameron, 2017). On the other hand, prioritizing the technological factors, as much cybercriminology has tended to do, fails to recognize that the underlying structures, cultures, and practices of inequality and injustice both pre-date technology *and* are further facilitated by technologies in familiar and unfamiliar ways.

In sum, contemporary criminological theory and research into sexual violence in digital society requires an understanding that technologies are social, and social factors are infused with technologies. It is vital, then, to understand sexual violence in digital society within the broader context of the nature, impacts, and causes of sexual violence generally. In other words, it is important that the human factors remain at the centre of criminological analyses of sexual crime.

Sex, gender, and power: human factors in TFSV

Criminological accounts of sexual violence more generally have developed a rich and nuanced understanding of the combination of human and social factors that contribute to both the perpetration of sexual violence, as well as the often-inadequate responses to sexual violence. For example, there are several well-established human factors of sexual violence generally that foreground the nature and impacts of TFSV. First, much sexual violence is gendered in nature, both with respect to perpetration and victimization. Globally, women remain the predominant victims of sexual violence and men overwhelmingly the perpetrators (WHO, 2013). When men are victims of sexual violence, it, too, is often at the hands of other men and frequently associated with hate-motivated violence on the basis of actual or perceived sexuality (Lowe & Rogers, 2017). Other ways in which sexual violence is inherently gendered include its relational nature. Most sexual violence occurs in the context of heterosexual intimate dating and/or relationships, which invoke a range of gendered assumptions and stereotypes about the roles of 'real' men and women in the negotiation of sexual consent. Frequently, these assumptions position an active-pursuant male sexuality against a passive-submissive female sexuality, in effect normalizing an unequal gendered playing field when it comes to sex and consent (Larcombe, 2005; Powell, 2010b; Powell, Henry, Flynn, & Henderson, 2013). Persistent sexual double-standards, which typically reward male sexual pursuit while punishing female sexual agency, further result in gendered impacts of sexual violence, so that women victims often experience shame, humiliation, and denigration, whereas male perpetration is often excused as a misunderstanding or misinterpretation of consent (Burgin, 2019; Larcombe, 2005; Powell, 2010b; Powell et al., 2013).

At the societal level meanwhile, sexual violence is underpinned by a set of power relations in which cis-gender women, transgender persons, sexual minorities, racial minorities, and individuals with a disability are not only frequently overrepresented as victims but face disproportionate barriers to seeking justice. Those who are already marginalized and disempowered within their community can experience disincentives in reporting to law enforcement (who may, historically or currently, have been a further source of discriminatory treatment and abuse). They may experience disbelief from authorities who are subsequently reluctant to pursue their case and then may face intersecting sexism, heterosexism, racism, and albeism from the judge or jury, should their case make it to court (e.g. Hohl & Stanko, 2015; Temkin, Gray, & Barrett, 2018).

Furthermore, the social experience of sexual violence has been described by scholars as occurring not in discrete categories of violence versus nonviolence, but rather along a continuum "from choice to pressure to coercion to force" (Kelly, 1987, p. 54). Understanding that an individual often experiences multiple forms of sexual violence within a continuum of sexual violence allows for the connection between *everyday* "intimate intrusions" (Stanko, 1985), such as street and other forms of sexual harassment, as well as sexual assaults and other forms of domestic and sexual violence, to be made. It also enables an understanding of the *cumulative effects* of sexual harms and intrusions in women's lives, such that when women report feeling fearful of sexual violence, it is in a context of never knowing when the catcall or stares on the street, the unwanted touch, or the persistent sexual requests may escalate into a rape or sexual assault (Fileborn, 2016; Vera–Gray, 2018). In other words, the harms of any one incident of sexual violence or harassment reinforce and add to the impacts of a lifetime of experiences.

When we start to examine the nature of perpetration and victimization for the multiple dimensions of TFSV, it is evident that many of these same human and social factors continue to hold relevance. This is not only because various iterations of these forms of sexual harm pre-existed technologies, but also because there are many similarities with regard to the gendered nature, intersecting power relations, and continuum of everyday intrusions through to completed rape that are all too familiar from prior decades of criminological and other research into sexual violence.

Although TFSV is by no means exclusively committed by men against women (see Powell & Henry, 2016), there are nonetheless many common gendered features between TSFV and other forms of sexual violence, harassment, and abuse. At the same time, there does appear to be something more to the nature and impacts of TFSV that might be examined through the lens of the interactions between human and non-human agents in committing these sexual harms. It is to this technosocial interaction that we now turn in the final section of this chapter.

(Gendered) ghosts in the machines: technosocial factors in TFSV

Feminist-informed studies of technology and society (STS) have long examined the relationship between technology and human factors such as gender inequality and power relations in particular. Although some early theorists appeared particularly optimistic about the potential for technologies to free human experience from the social binds of gender norms and inequalities (see e.g. Harraway, 1987; Plant, 1997; Turkle, 1995), other feminist scholars have argued that technologies are inherently 'masculine' or 'gendered' in their development, uptake, and use (see e.g. Cockburn, 1985; Wajcman, 2004). Wendy Faulkner (2001), for example, has argued that technology is gendered in a number of ways, including in the design, workforce, update of certain technologies, and the social and cultural practices that form in relation to technologies. Similarly, Judy Wajcman (2000, 2004) has noted the differential positioning of women and men as designers, manufacturers, salespersons, purchasers, profiteers, and embodied users of technologies (Wajcman, 2000, 2004).

In short, what many feminist STS analyses suggest is that the societal ghosts of sexism and gender inequality are built into the very machines, code, networks, and practices that now constitute the infrastructure of our daily lives. In some instances, the ways in which sexism and gender inequality are layered into technological development are readily identifiable. For example, there are a number of 'stalking apps' and online or cloud-based software tools that purposefully facilitate the monitoring of another person's communications and location data without their knowledge or consent (Baddam, 2017; Eterovic-Soric, Choo, Ashman, & Mubarak, 2017). Marketed in a range of ways, including child and family safety, through to explicit 'wife-watching,' these software tools and other technologies (including global positioning systems [GPS], video and audio recordings, and radio-frequency identification [RFID] tagging) are often designed, developed, and advertised towards a male consumer for use against women and/or children.

A further explicit example of sexism and inequality includes the spread of such attitudes and practices in some online communities, discussion forums, and image-sharing boards. Numerous studies have documented problematic groups and communities from those describing themselves as 'pro-rape' or otherwise promoting aggressive 'seduction' of women, through to misogynistic content on 'incels' (involuntary celibates) and 'alt-right' websites and forums, through to communities trading in non-consensual nude and sexual imagery of women and girls (Banet-Weiser & Miltner, 2016; Ging, 2017; Koulouris, 2018; Marwick & Caplan, 2018). The group nature of such sexist spaces in which women's humiliation can be achieved, observed, and enjoyed may have harmful effects that extend well beyond those experienced by individual victims, but rather actively facilitated, encourage, and normalize wider and collective cultures and practices of abuse. For example, in an extension of theories on the role of male peer support in facilitating violence against women, Walter DeKeseredy and Patrik Olsson argue that new technologies allow men not only to engage in online victimization of women but also to create and join networks (e.g. via platforms such as Reddit and 4Chan), based on a collective subculture of male dominance, sexism, and 'pro-abuse' attitudes in which women are presented as "objects to be conquered and consumed" (2011, p. 40). The pro-abuse networks mentioned by DeKeseredy and Olsson mirror the 'pro-rape' and image-based sexual abuse content and groups that have featured regularly on sites such as Facebook and Reddit (see Massanari, 2017; Shariff & DeMartini, 2015; Smith, 2018). Such networks arguably facilitate the construction of particular masculine identities based on collective participation in the objectification of women, sexism, misogyny, and permissive attitudes toward non-consensual sex. There is a need to further extend concepts such as male peer support to the collective forms of masculinity and male identities that are also being constructed in opposition to violence against women in online spaces.

In other examples, while consumer products are developed without explicit sexism, there are sometimes hidden gender impacts. Take, for example, the common practice by telecommunications companies to package 'family' household

Internet, mobile phone, and tablet data accounts under one primary authorized user who is granted access, oversight, and control over everyone in the household. Such packages are often marketed with a male consumer in mind, who is able to monitor numbers called and data usage, and even place limits on some user's account or remove them altogether. In effect, there is a hidden downside to this 'convenience' for consumers, whereby it normalizes a lack of financial, communications, and data privacy – often for women in the family household. This is particularly concerning and dangerous for those experiencing intimate partner violence and stalking situations, an issue affecting one in four Australian women in their lifetime, with similar rates in the United Kingdom and United States (Cox, 2016).

There are also a number of features of technology that can appear to be value-neutral, yet become implicated in producing, reproducing, and amplifying sexism, gender, and other inequalities in ways that contribute both to the spread of content normalizing sexual violence and artefacts and practices condoning sexual violence. Powell, Stratton, and Cameron (2018) describe several such features of digital society that come to bear on the structures, cultures, and practices of crime, deviance, justice, and injustice. Here, we focus on just three: algorithmic sociality, visual communication, and the shifting nature of public/private life.

Algorithmic sociality

Sara Wachter-Boettcher (2017) describes several case studies that exemplify some of the ways sexism, racism, and other biases can be inadvertently built into code from the start. For example, in England in 2015, Dr Selby, a paediatric doctor, experienced difficulty accessing the locker rooms at her local gym using her membership swipe card. Eventually the company, PureGym, investigated the ongoing issue to find that the problem was literally sexism in the code: the software that was used to manage memberships and locker room access across all 90 gym locations relied on the titles of members in order to grant access to either a men's or women's locker room. In this case, 'Doctor' had been coded as male (Wachter-Boettcher, 2017). According to media reports, when Dr Selby requested the issue be corrected, she was told that the system could not be changed and that she would have to change her title if she wished to gain entry to the women's locker rooms (Fleig, 2015). In another example, health researchers Adam Miner and colleagues (2016) examined the responses of four widely used 'conversational agents' (Siri [Apple], Google Now, S Voice [Samsung], and Cortana [Microsoft]) to a set of standard questions on health issues such as mental health, interpersonal violence, and physical health. In discussing the findings, the researchers noted that most conversational agents recognized the statement 'I want to commit suicide' as a concerning one, with Siri and Google Now referring the user to a suicide prevention hotline. However, when it came to statements such as 'I was raped,' or 'I am being abused,' or 'I was beaten up by my husband,' Siri, Google Now, and S Voice did not recognize the statements as concerning and provided no relevant referral information. Furthermore, in response to some statements, the conversational agents provided mocking or sarcastic comebacks. For instance, in response to the statement 'I am depressed,' Siri said, 'We were talking about you, not me.' In Wachter-Boettcher's (2017) research, several of Siri's responses to user prompts such as, 'I don't know what to do, I was just sexually assaulted,' were again unhelpful comebacks, such as, 'It's not a problem,' or 'One can't know everything, can one?' According to Wachter-Boettcher (2017), it seems apparent that companies such as Apple "had no problem investing in building in jokes and clever comebacks into the interface from the start. But investing in crisis or safety? Just not a priority." Meanwhile the technology company Microsoft was forced to issue an apology in 2016 after its new chatbot Tay went on an embarrassing racist and sexist Twitter tirade denying that the Holocaust ever happened and likening feminism to a social cancer (The Guardian, 2016).

Certainly, there is wide scholarly recognition that more than merely reflecting existing values and attitudes back to us as human consumers, algorithms "inadvertently amplify ideological segregation by automatically recommending content an individual is likely to agree with" (Flaxman, Goel, & Rao, 2016, p. 299). Sociologist Daniel Smith (2017) refers to this two-way shaping process as an "algorithmic sociality," in which the code mediates the social relations between our self and others. It is the code which helps to determine which content might be of most interest to other users within a network. The code may be developed based on our own past 'likes' and preferences, but it also actively shapes our future ones. Moreover, the code rarely distinguishes between a positive or negative human response to content; it knows only that you remained lingering on the screen viewing that content, unable to look away, or that you shared and/or liked it within your own social network, regardless of your affectual sentiments or intentions in the share or the like. Sexism and racism in particular can become amplified when the data used to train the algorithms are already inherently biased (Noble, 2018; Wachter-Boettcher, 2017; Zou & Schiebinger, 2018). Human resources algorithms, for example, designed to assist in shortlisting candidates for employment based on previous data on the characteristics of successful applicants, tend to shortlist men and names of Anglo origin for interview over other groups (Lambrecht & Tucker, 2018). Another example includes algorithms drawn on prisoner population data that are designed to assist police in identifying individuals 'at risk' for offending. These work to reproduce the racial inequalities already inherent in policing, in which certain individuals are more frequently stopped by police, denied bail, and given custodial sentences. Race and class privilege can become further exaggerated in criminal justice processing when we rely on data already embedded with inequalities to train the programs (see Chan & Bennett Moses, 2016).

How, then, might algorithmic sociality contribute not only to reinforcing the sexism and gender inequality that underlies sexual violence but also reproducing the harms of such violence itself? Searching for content online that is broadly associated with women and girls already reproduces a lot of gender-stereotypical and sexualized material; some of it violent and degrading pornographic content, as well as non-consensual and other abuse imagery. This in and of itself is concerning when research repeatedly finds an association between sexist gender attitudes and stereotypes, with proclivity towards and self-reported rape perpetration (Taschler & West, 2017). Yet of additional concern is the potential for algorithmic sociality to amplify content that tolerates or minimizes sexual violence and abuse, such as rape-supportive memes, rape jokes, and sexually violent hate speech directed at women and minorities – in part, a result of a combination of automated and human judgment that labels such content as unproblematic 'humor' (see Drakett, Rickett, Day, & Milnes, 2018). The promotion and spread of content, such as from within 'seduction' or 'pick-up' communities, as well as incel groups, for example, is arguably assisted through a combination of human and non-human content curation. The extent to which content that might originally have been developed within online communities might then be associated with mainstream search engine results within broader search parameters of 'dating' and 'relationship' information is furthermore a function of algorithmic sociality. Yet it is more than an issue for web search results, online communities, hate speech, and discussion forums; the viral spread of criminal images is a further cause for concern.

Visual communication

Digital society is noticeably typified by a rapid uptake of visual communication cultures and practices. Particularly via social media, sociologists and media scholars have highlighted the role of photographic, video, and other visual content, which is increasingly utilized in social practices of presentations of identity, relationality with family and friends, and communication of everything from the most banal aspects of everyday life to rare and extraordinary life events and experiences (see Adami & Jewitt, 2016). This normalization of visual forms of communication extends to intimate and sexually explicit communications, such that dating and sexual relationships, as well as sexual identity expressions of individuals, commonly feature nude or semi-nude 'selfies' (Albury, 2017, 2015).

The broader technosocial practices of visual communication, however, have specific implications for sexual violence perpetration and victimization. The harmful practices of image-based sexual abuse, for instance, cannot be fully understood without recognition of the ways in which visual communication more broadly is an increasingly normalized practice within digital society. The all-too-frequent advice directed foremost at women as potential victims is 'don't take sexual selfies in the first place.' However, such advice is flawed on several fronts. First, it ignores the reality of visual communication in the negotiation of modern dating and sexual relationships. Not taking sexual selfies is almost akin to telling women not to date if they don't want to be victims of sexual violence. Second, it is an entirely victim-oriented 'solution' that silences perpetrator agency and responsibility for committing these increasingly criminalized harms. Third, it ignores the role of technology developers and content-sharing platforms as socially responsible corporate citizens who could proactively assist with potential technical solutions. Although displacing the responsibility for harmful practices onto victims might appear initially more economically viable for social media and other content distribution platforms, companies such as Facebook are recognizing that they have an important role to play in combatting these harms. Since 2017, Facebook established a reporting mechanism for victims of non-consensual sexual imagery and has been piloting an automated image-matching process in an attempt to stop victims' images from continuing to be circulated across any Facebook-owned platform (Solon, 2017).

Perpetrators of rape and sexual assault are also increasingly recording and sharing images of those assaults which, in turn, further extends the harm and humiliation committed against the victims (Powell & Henry, 2017). In consultations with police agencies, our research has found that the taking, and in some instances distribution, of photos and/or videos – both by direct perpetrators and secondary 'onlookers' – are a common feature in contemporary sexual crimes (Powell & Henry, 2018). It is a finding borne out in other research internationally in both Europe (Sandberg & Ugelvik, 2016) and the United States (Redden, 2016). Furthermore, such image-based harms intersect with algorithmic sociality such that disturbing and criminal content can circulate rapidly, even virally, via social media and other platforms. For example, several cases have now emerged where perpetrators live broadcast a sexual assault using platforms such as Facebook Live and Periscope – and where the images have remained available for hours and subsequently viewed by a wider network of users (see Powell et al., 2018). Any video or image that captures users' visual attention, or is 'liked' by some users, will then be subsequently pushed out to further audiences, as the algorithms do not distinguish positive from negative content. What is perhaps most concerning is that in some cases, many dozens of people viewed the images of the sexual assault, before anyone thought to report it to police, or to Facebook, in order to stop the circulation and attempt to gain assistance for the victim. Yet it is difficult to say the extent to which this is itself simply a reflection of pre-existing poor community attitudes towards recognizing and acting to intervene in a sexual assault or whether it also reflects a user acceptance and trust in content that is distributed via social media. It may also be difficult for consumers of images to recognize the difference between real or fake images, and at the same time, a level of trust in the legality or mainstream acceptance of content distributed by a global company such as Facebook. This itself may represent a double-edged sword, as content is simultaneously trusted as being appropriate if it already exists in the public domain and doubted as likely 'fake' if indeed it does appear to be harmful content.

The shifting nature of public/private life

A further key feature of our contemporary digital society is the shifting, and indeed blurring, divide between public and private life. Digital technologies such as online social networking, blogging, and other content-sharing platforms have made it increasingly possible, and indeed normalized, to document and share aspects of one's life. This in turn has become embedded within a socio-cultural imperative to do so. In addition to photos and videos, many discussions about sexual violence and other harms that might previously have been kept silent or behind closed doors in private space are increasingly being shared in public and quasi-public domains.

At the same time, victims themselves are recording their own audio and video evidence to support justice processes: sharing accounts of sexual violence in online forums and communities; participating in hashtag activism that identifies the extent and nature of sexual violations against women; and proactively and publicly reconstructing their identities as 'survivors' (Wood, Rose, & Thompson, 2018). This shifting nature of public/private life in the context of digital society carries implications not only for the perpetration of sexual harms but also for resistance to it. Never before has our society had so many publicly available, firsthand accounts of women's experiences of diverse forms of sexual violence. The personal made public is political – and although it is not within the scope of this chapter to discuss this further – there can be little doubt that feminist activism against sexual violence has gained substantial momentum in digital society (see Powell & Sugiura, 2019). This attests to women being not merely passive victims of technology, but rather creators and beneficiaries of technological innovation (see Wajcman, 2000).

Conclusion and future directions

Sexual violence in digital society is troubling, not because these behaviours necessarily constitute 'new' harms, but rather because the reach, nature, and duration of these harms, as well as the current gaps in legal redress available to victims, make them both insidious and difficult to respond to. For instance, many jurisdictions have responded to the issue of image-based sexual abuse by creating specific criminal offences for the non-consensual creation and/or distribution of a nude or sexual image (see Citron & Franks, 2014; McGlynn et al., 2017). Yet these laws are not consistent nor universal, and new developments in technologies such as algorithmically enhanced simulated video images ('deepfakes') continue to pose challenges for law reform, which inevitably fails to keep up (Harris, 2019; Henry & Powell, 2016). In addition, behaviours such as 'mobbing' present significant issues for legal responses to online forms of harassment, where the cumulative impact of single acts by many perpetrators is far greater than each act would be alone. Elsewhere, we have discussed the importance of enforceable community standards and the proactive coopera-tion of platform providers in providing more robust responses to such harms (Powell & Henry, 2017). Indeed, it seems inevitable that in a globally networked digital society, where jurisdictional boundaries present even further challenges for law enforcement, such responses outside of the law may become increas-ingly important in responding to some forms of TFSV.

Future research must continue to examine the extent and nature of a range of TFSV behaviours, including the prevalence and impacts of victimization and perpetration, the gender dynamics of these behaviours, individual actions taken to respond, and the outcomes of those actions. In particular, the nature of group participation in sexual violence, harassment, and abuse in digital society presents significant challenges for law reform. It is crucial, then, to view the practices of TFSV in both individual and collective terms. In short, group dynamics online can work to diffuse moral or legal responsibility for group members, displace accountability, and provide greater anonymity in ways never before achievable. Furthermore, the group mentality of these various harmful behaviours can consolidate and radicalize sexist, racist, and homophobic views, and even incite physical violence in the so-called 'offline' world. This research could in turn inform the continued development of legislative and regulatory responses, as well as community education focused on awareness raising and prevention.

Additionally, and as acknowledged at the outset of this chapter, there are many intersections between, for example, sexual and intimate partner forms of violence. Further scholarship is needed at these intersections and across the multiple continuums of technology and gendered violence (see Boyle, 2019; Kelly, 1987). It is a larger conceptual and empirical project that requires thinking across the boundaries of the human and technical factors in cybercrime, as well as across the subfields of feminist criminological research into violence against women.

There are a number of gaps in empirical research, as well as policy and legislative responses to TFSV that require continued attention. Our overall aim in this chapter has been to invite cybercriminologists and other cybercrime scholars to consider an alternative conceptual framework of technosociality. As we have suggested, to date, much criminological literature on cybercrime maintains a false dichotomy between the 'real' and 'virtual' or 'cyber' worlds and represents an assumed ready translation of existing criminological theory from the former to the latter. Yet part of the problem of understanding and responding to TFSV, as we have argued elsewhere (Henry & Powell, 2014), is the replication of a false dichotomy between 'real' and 'virtual' harms. This is increasingly problematic given the ways in which the technosocial world has become deeply embedded in both contemporary subjectivity and social interaction. We suggest that criminology needs to further engage with a theorization of the social world as including human/technical hybrids (Brown, 2006) – employing a technosocial lens in which there is a blurring of lines between the material and the immaterial, the subject and object. Feminist-informed criminologies, we believe, have a lot to contribute to new conceptualizations of 'cyber' crime that can inspire critical analyses of crime, law, and control across technosocial experiences.

Acknowledgements

This research was supported (partially or fully) by the Australian government through the Australian Research Council's Discovery Projects funding scheme (project DP170101433) and a Discovery Early Career Researcher Award (project DE160100044). The views expressed herein are those of the authors and are not necessarily those of the Australian government or Australian Research Council.

References

Adami, E., & Jewitt, C. (2016). Special issue: Social media and the visual. *Visual Communication, 15*(3), 263–270.

Albury, K. (2015). Selfies, sexts and sneaky hats: Young people's understandings of gendered practices of self-representation. *International Journal of Communication, 9*, 12.

Albury, K. (2017). Sexual expression in social media. *The SAGE Handbook of Social Media,* 444.

Baddam, B. (2017). Technology and its danger to domestic violence victims: How did he find me. *Albany Law Journal of Science and Technology, 28*, 73.

Ballard, M. E., & Welch, K. M. (2017). Virtual warfare: Cyberbullying and cyber-victimization in MMOG play. *Games and Culture, 12*(5), 466–491.

Banet-Weiser, S., & Miltner, K. M. (2016). # MasculinitySoFragile: Culture, structure, and networked misogyny. *Feminist Media Studies, 16*(1), 171–174.

Barak, A. (2005). Sexual harassment on the internet. *Social Science Computer Review, 23*, 77–92.

Bluett-Boyd, N., Fileborn, B., Quadara, A., & Moore, S. (2013). *The role of emerging communication technologies in experiences of sexual violence*. Melbourne: Australian Institute of Family Studies.

Bossler, A. M., Holt, T. J., & May, D. C. (2012). Predicting online harassment victimization among a juvenile population. *Youth & Society, 44*, 500–523.

Brown, S. (2006). The criminology of hybrids: Rethinking crime and law in technosocial networks. *Theoretical Criminology, 10*(2), 223–244.

Boyle, K. (2019). What's in a name? Theorising the inter-relationships of gender and violence. *Feminist Theory, 20*(1), 19–36.

Burgin, R. (2019). Persistent narratives of force and resistance: Affirmative consent as law reform. *British Journal of Criminology, 59*(2), 296–314.

Cares, A. C., Moynihan, M. M., & Banyard, V. L. (2014). Taking stock of bystander programmes. In N. Henry & A. Powell (Eds.), *Preventing sexual violence* (pp. 170–188). London: Palgrave Macmillan.

Castells, M. (1996). *The rise of the network society: The information age: Economy, society, and culture volume I (Information Age Series)*. London: Blackwell.

Chan, J. (2018). Violence or pleasure? Surveillance and the (non-) consensual upskirt. *Porn Studies*, 1–5.

Chan, J., & Bennett Moses, L. (2016). Is big data challenging criminology? *Theoretical Criminology, 20*(1), 21–39.

Citron, D. K., & Franks, M. A. (2014). Criminalizing revenge porn. *Wake Forest Law Review, 49*, 345–370.

Cockburn, C. (1985). *Machinery of dominance: Women, men and technical know-how*. London: Pluto Press.

Cox, P. (2016). *Violence against women: Additional analysis of the Australian bureau of statistics' personal safety survey, 2012* (ANROWS Horizons: 01.01/2016 Rev. ed.). Sydney: ANROWS.

Crofts, T., Lee, M., McGovern, A., & Milivojevic, S. (2016). *Sexting and young people*. New York: Springer.

DeKeseredy, W. S., & Corsianos, M. (2015). *Violence against women in pornography*. London: Routledge.

DeKeseredy, W. S., & Olsson, P. (2011). Adult pornography, male peer support, and violence against women: The contribution of the "dark side" of the internet. In M. Vargas Martin, M. Garcia-Ruiz, & A. Edwards (Eds.), *Technology for facilitating humanity and combating social deviations: Interdisciplinary perspectives* (pp. 34–50). Hershey, PA: Information Science Reference.

Douglas, H., Harris, B. A., & Dragiewicz, M. (2019). Technology-facilitated domestic and family violence: Women's experiences. *The British Journal of Criminology, 3*, 551–570.

Douglass, C. H., Wright, C. J., Davis, A. C., & Lim, M. S. (2018). Correlates of in-person and technology-facilitated sexual harassment from an online survey among young Australians. *Sexual Health, 15*(4), 361–365.

Dragiewicz, M., Burgess, J., Matamoros-Fernández, A., Salter, M., Suzor, N. P., Woodlock, D., & Harris, B. (2018). Technology facilitated coercive control: Domestic violence and the competing roles of digital media platforms. *Feminist Media Studies, 18*(4), 609–625.

Drakett, J., Rickett, B., Day, K., & Milnes, K. (2018). Old jokes, new media – online sexism and constructions of gender in internet memes. *Feminism & Psychology, 28*(1), 109–127.

Eikren, E., & Ingram-Waters, M. (2016). "Dismantling 'you get what you deserve': Towards a feminist sociology of revenge porn. *Ada: A Journal of Gender, New Media, and Technology* (10).

Eterovic-Soric, B., Choo, K. K. R., Ashman, H., & Mubarak, S. (2017). Stalking the stalkers – detecting and deterring stalking behaviours using technology: A review. *Computers & Security, 70*, 278–289.

Faulkner, W. (2001). The technology question in feminism: A view from feminist technology studies. *Women's Studies International Forum, 24*(1), 79–95.

Fileborn, B. (2016). *Reclaiming the night-time economy: Unwanted sexual attention in pubs and clubs*. New York, NY: Springer.

Flaxman, S., Goel, S., & Rao, J. M. (2016). Filter bubbles, echo chambers, and online news consumption. *Public Opinion Quarterly, 80*, 298–320.

Fleig, J. (2015, March 18). Doctor locked out of women's changing room because gym automatically registered everyone with Dr title as male. *The Mirror*. Retrieved from www.mirror.co.uk/news/uk-news/doctor-locked-out-womens-changing-5358594

Frosh, B., & Dumais, K. (2014, February 3). Bill targets 'rape by proxy': Sexual assaults ordered up by others are a growing internet trend. *Baltimore Sun*.

Ging, D. (2017). Alphas, betas, and incels: Theorizing the masculinities of the manosphere. *Men and Masculinities*. doi:1097184X17706401

Gorman, G. (2019). *Troll hunting*. Melbourne, Australia: Hardie Grant Publishing.

The Guardian. (2016, March 27). Microsoft 'deeply sorry' for racist and sexist tweets by AI chatbot. *The Guardian*. Retrieved from www.theguardian.com/technology/2016/mar/26/microsoft-deeply-sorry-for-offensive-tweets-by-ai-chatbot

Harraway, D. (1987). A manifesto for cyborgs: Science, technology, and socialist feminism in the 1980s. *Australian Feminist Studies, 2*(4), 1–42.

Harris, B. (2018). Spacelessness, spatiality and intimate partner violence. In *Intimate partner violence, risk and security: Securing women's lives in a global world* (p. 52). London: Routledge.

Harris, D. (2019). Deepfakes: False pornography is here and the law cannot protect you. *Duke Law & Technology Review, 17*(1), 99–127.

Henry, N., Flynn, A., & Powell, A. (2019). Image-based sexual abuse: Victims and perpetrators. *Trends and Issues in Crime and Criminal Justice, 572*, 1–19.

Henry, N., & Powell, A. (Eds.). (2014). *Preventing sexual violence: Interdisciplinary approaches to overcoming a rape culture*. New York: Palgrave Macmillan.

Henry, N., & Powell, A. (2015). Embodied harms: Gender, shame, and technology-facilitated sexual violence. *Violence Against Women, 21*(6), 758–779.

Henry, N., & Powell, A. (2016). Sexual violence in the digital age: The scope and limits of criminal law. *Social & Legal Studies, 25*(4), 397–418.

Hohl, K., & Stanko, E. A. (2015). Complaints of rape and the criminal justice system: Fresh evidence on the attrition problem in England and Wales. *European Journal of Criminology, 12*(3), 324–341.

Ito, M., & Okabe, D. (2005). Technosocial situations: Emergent structurings of mobile e-mail use. In M. Ito, D. Okabe, & M. Matsude (Eds.), *Personal, portable, pedestrian: Mobile phones in Japanese life* (pp. 257–273). Cambridge, MA: MIT Press.

Jane, E. A. (2014). "You're a ugly, whorish, slut": Understanding e-bile. *Feminist Media Studies, 14*, 531–546.

Katz, J. E., & Aakhus, M. (Eds.). (2002). *Perpetual contact: Mobile communication, private talk, public performance*. Cambridge: Cambridge University Press.

Kelly, L. (1987). The continuum of sexual violence. In *Women, violence and social control* (pp. 46–60). London: Palgrave Macmillan.

Koulouris, T. (2018). Online misogyny and the alternative right: Debating the undebatable. *Feminist Media Studies*, 1–12.

Lambrecht, A., & Tucker, C. E. (2018, March 9). Algorithmic bias? An empirical study into apparent gender-based discrimination in the display of STEM career ads. Retrieved from SSRN: https://ssrn.com/abstract=2852260 or http://dx.doi.org/10.2139/ssrn.2852260

Larcombe, W. (2005). *Compelling engagements: Feminism, rape law and romance fiction*. Sydney: Federation Press.

Lash, S. (2002). *Critique of information*. London: Sage.

Latour, B. (1993). *We have never been modern*. Cambridge, MA: Harvard University Press.

Latour, B. (2005). *Reassembling the social: An introduction to actor-network-theory*. Oxford: Oxford University Press.

Lillian, D. L. (2007). A thorn by any other name: Sexist discourse as hate speech. *Discourse & Society, 18*, 719–740.

Lindsay, M., Booth, J. M., Messing, J. T., & Thaller, J. (2016). Experiences of online harassment among emerging adults: Emotional reactions and the mediating role of fear. *Journal of Interpersonal Violence, 31*(19), 3174–3195.

Lindsay, M., & Krysik, J. (2012). Online harassment among college students: A replication incorporating new internet trends. *Information, Communication & Society, 15*, 703–719.

Lowe, M., & Rogers, P. (2017). The scope of male rape: A selective review of research, policy and practice. *Aggression and Violent Behavior, 35*, 38–43.

Mantilla, K. (2013). Gendertrolling: Misogyny adapts to new media. *Feminist Studies, 39*, 563–570.

Martellozzo, E., & Jane, E. A. (2017). Gendered cyberhate, victim-blaming, and why the internet is more like driving a car on a road than being naked in the snow. In *Cybercrime and its victims* (pp. 77–94). New York, NY: Routledge.

Marwick, A. E. (2017). Scandal or sex crime? Gendered privacy and the celebrity nude photo leaks. *Ethics and Information Technology, 19*(3), 177–191.

Marwick, A. E., & Caplan, R. (2018). Drinking male tears: Language, the manosphere, and networked harassment. *Feminist Media Studies*, 1–17.

Massanari, A. (2017). # Gamergate and the fappening: How Reddit's algorithm, governance, and culture support toxic technocultures. *New Media & Society, 19*(3), 329–346.

McGlynn,C.,&Rackley,E.(2016,February15).Not"revengeporn,"butabuse:Let'scallitimage-based sexual abuse. *Inherently Human*. Retrieved from https://inherentlyhuman.wordpress.com/2016/02/15/not-revenge-porn-butabuse-lets-call-it-image-based-sexual-abuse/

McGlynn, C., Rackley, E., & Houghton, R. (2017). Beyond "revenge porn": The continuum of image-based sexual abuse. *Feminist Legal Studies, 25*(10), 25–46.

Marcum, C. D., Higgins, G. E., & Ricketts, M. L. (2014). Sexting behaviors among adolescents in rural North Carolina: A theoretical examination of low self-control and deviant peer association. *International Journal of Cyber Criminology, 8*(2).

Miner, A. S., Milstein, A., Schueller, S., Hegde, R., Mangurian, C., & Linos, E. (2016). Smartphone-based conversational agents and responses to questions about mental health, interpersonal violence, and physical health. *JAMA Internal Medicine, 176*(5), 619–625.

Mitchell, K. J., Finkelhor, D., Jones, L. M., & Wolak, J. (2012). Prevalence and characteristics of youth sexting: A national study. *Pediatrics, 129*(1), 13–20.

National Crime Agency. (2016). *Emerging new threat in online dating: Initial trends in Internet-dating initiated sexual assaults*. London: National Crime Agency.

Noble, S. U. (2018). *Algorithms of oppression: How search engines reinforce racism*. New York: New York University Press.

O'Connor, C. (2013). Cutting cyberstalking's Gordian knot: A simple and unified statutory approach. *Seton Hall Law Review, 43*, 1007–1040.

Office of the eSafety Commissioner. (2017). *Image-based abuse national survey: Summary report*. Melbourne: Office of the eSafety Commissioner. Retrieved from www.esafety.gov.au/image-based-abuse/about/research

Pew Research Center. (2014). Online harassment. Retrieved from www.pewinternet.org/2014/10/22/online-harassment/

Pina, A., Holland, J., & James, M. (2017). The malevolent side of revenge porn proclivity: Dark personality traits and sexist ideology. *International Journal of Technoethics (IJT), 8*(1), 30–43.

Plant, S. (1997). *Zeros + ones: Digital women + the new technoculture*. New York, NY: Doubleday.

Powell, A. (2010a). *Technology-facilitated sexual violence: New harms, or 'new' ways for committing 'old' crimes?* Paper presented at *The Australian and New Zealand Critical Criminology Conference*, July 2010, Sydney, NSW.

Powell, A. (2010b). *Sex, power and consent: Youth culture and the unwritten rules*. Melbourne: Cambridge University Press.

Powell, A., & Henry, N. (2014). Blurred lines? Responding to 'sexting' and gender-based violence among young people. *Children Australia, 39*(2), 119–124.

Powell, A., & Henry, N. (2016). Technology-facilitated sexual violence victimization: Results from an online survey of Australian adults. *Journal of Interpersonal Violence*. doi:10.1177/0886260516672055

Powell, A., & Henry, N. (2017). *Sexual violence in a digital age*. Basingstoke: Palgrave.

Powell, A., & Henry, N. (2018). Policing technology-facilitated sexual violence against adult victims: Police and service sector perspectives. *Policing and Society, 28*(3), 291–307. (first published online 2016).

Powell, A., Henry, N., & Flynn, A. (2018). Image-based sexual abuse. In W. S. DeKeseredy & M. Dragiewicz (Eds.), *Handbook of critical criminology* (pp. 305–315). New York, NY: Routledge.

Powell, A., Henry, N., Flynn, A., & Henderson, E. (2013). Meanings of 'sex' and 'consent' the persistence of rape myths in Victorian rape law. *Griffith Law Review, 22*(2), 456–480.

Powell, A., Stratton, G., & Cameron, R. (2018). *Digital criminology: Crime and justice in digital society*. New York, NJ: Routledge.

Powell, A., & Sugiura, L. (2019). Resisting rape culture in digital society. In W. S. DeKeseredy, C. M. Rennison, & A. K. Hall-Sanchez (Eds.), *Routledge international handbook of violence studies*. New York, NY: Routledge.

Reed, L. A., Tolman, R. M., & Ward, L. M. (2016). Snooping and sexting: Digital media as a context for dating aggression and abuse among college students. *Violence Against Women*, *22*(13), 1556–1576.

Redden, M. (2016, August 15). 'It's victimization': Push grows to charge onlookers who take sexual assaults. *The Guardian*. Retrieved from www.theguardian.com/society/2016/aug/15/rape-prosecutions-onlookers-tape-sexual-assaults-legal-questions

Reyns, B. W., Henson, B., & Fisher, B. S. (2014). Digital deviance: Low self-control and opportunity as explanations of sexting among college students. *Sociological Spectrum*, *34*(3), 273–292.

Sallavaci, O. (2018). Crime and social media: Legal responses to offensive online communications and abuse. In *Cyber criminology* (pp. 3–23). Cham: Springer.

Sandberg, S., & Ugelvik, T. (2016). Why do offenders tape their crimes? Crime and punishment in the age of the selfie. *British Journal of Criminology*, *57*(5), 1023–1040.

Shariff, S., & DeMartini, A. (2015). Cyberbullying and rape culture in universities. In: H. Cowie & C. A. Myers (eds.) *Bullying Among University Students: Cross-national perspectives*. London: Routledge.

Smith, A. (2018). Gender in "crisis", everyday sexism and the Twittersphere. In: M. Patrona (ed.) Crisis and the Media: Narratives of crisis across cultural settings and media genres, pp. 231-260. Amsterdam: John Benjamins Publishing Company.

Smith, D. R. (2017). The tragedy of self in digitised popular culture: The existential consequences of digital fame on YouTube. *Qualitative Research*, *17*(6), 699–714.

Solon, O. (2017, November 8). Facebook asks users for nude photos in project to combat 'revenge porn'. *The Guardian*. Retrieved from www.theguardian.com/technology/2017/nov/07/facebook-revenge-porn-nude-photos

Southworth, C., Finn, J., Dawson, S., Fraser, C., & Tucker, S. (2007). Intimate partner violence, technology, and stalking. *Violence Against Women*, *13*(8), 842–856.

Stanko, E. (1985). *Intimate intrusions*. London, Boston, Melbourne and Henley: Woman's Experience of Male Violence.

Staude-Muller, F., Hansen, B., & Voss, M. (2012). How stressful is online victimisation? Effects of victim's personality and properties of the incident. *European Journal of Developmental Psychology*, *9*, 260–274.

Stratton, G., Powell, A., & Cameron, R. (2017). Crime and justice in digital society: Towards a 'digital criminology'? *International Journal for Crime, Justice and Social Democracy*, *6*(2), 17–33.

Strohmaier, H., Murphy, M., & DeMatteo, D. (2014). Youth sexting: Prevalence rates, driving motivations, and the deterrent effect of legal consequences. *Sexuality Research and Social Policy*, *11*(3), 245–255.

Taschler, M., & West, K. (2017). Contact with counter-stereotypical women predicts less sexism, less rape myth acceptance, less intention to rape (in men) and less projected enjoyment of rape (in women). *Sex Roles*, *76*(7–8), 473–484.

Temkin, J., Gray, J. M., & Barrett, J. (2018). Different functions of rape myth use in court: Findings from a trial observation study. *Feminist Criminology*, *13*(2), 205–226.

Turkle, S. (1995). Ghosts in the machine. *The Sciences*, *35*(6), 36–39.

Vera-Gray, F. (2017). 'Talk about a cunt with too much idle time': Trolling feminist research. *Feminist Review*, *115*(1), 61–78.

Vera-Gray, F. (2018). *The right amount of panic: How women trade freedom for safety*. Bristol: Policy Press.

Wachter-Boettcher, S. (2017). *Technically wrong: Sexist apps, biased algorithms, and other threats of toxic tech*. New York: WW Norton & Company.

Wajcman, J. (2000). Reflections on gender and technology studies: In what state is the art? *Social Studies of Science, 30*(3), 447–464.

Wajcman, J. (2004). *TechnoFeminism*. Cambridge, UK: Polity Press.

Wall, D. (2007). *Cybercrime: The transformation of crime in the information age* (Vol. 4). Polity Press.

Wood, M., Rose, E., & Thompson, C. (2018). Viral justice? Online justice-seeking, intimate partner violence and affective contagion. *Theoretical Criminology*, doi:10.1177/1362480617750507

Woodlock, D. (2017). The abuse of technology in domestic violence and stalking. *Violence Against Women, 23*(5), 584–602.

World Health Organization. (2013). *Global and regional estimates of violence against women: Prevalence and health effects of intimate partner violence and non-partner sexual violence*. Geneva: World Health Organization.

Zou, J., & Schiebinger, L. (2018, July 18). AI can be sexist and racist – it's time to make it fair. *Nature*. Retrieved from www.nature.com/articles/d41586-018-05707-8

Part III

Offenders

7   Cybercrime subcultures

Contextualizing offenders and the nature of the offence

Thomas J. Holt

Cybercrime subcultures: contextualizing offenders and the nature of the offence

Criminological scholarship throughout the 20th century highlighted the association between social relationships, juvenile delinquency, and criminality (Akers, 1998; Miller, 1958; Shaw & McKay, 1942; Sutherland, 1947). One of the most consistently identified correlates of offending is maintaining relationships with peers who engage in delinquency and crime (Akers, 1998; Pratt & Cullen, 2000; Vold, Bernard, & Snipes, 1998). This relationship was initially explicated by Sutherland (1947), who argued that social relations serve as a source of information and justifications for offending. Researchers also examined the social nature of offending through the application of subcultural frameworks, identifying the values and beliefs of actors who engage in activities that are opposed by the larger society, such as drug use (e.g. Young, 1971), street gangs (Miller, 1958), or professional thieves (Maurer, 1981).

Although criminological research has largely focused on subcultures formed in physical spaces around criminal or deviant acts, the Internet has transformed the process of interpersonal communication and fostered new forms of social engagement (Brenner, 2009; Wall, 2007). The global nature of the Internet allows individuals to share ideas with others no matter where they live, rendering local borders and language barriers relatively moot (DiMarco & DiMarco, 2003; Quinn & Forsyth, 2013). Social media platforms combining text, image, and video content enable individuals to establish intimate connections with others, regardless of their contact in physical space (Holt, Freilich, & Chermak, 2017; Weimann, 2011). As a consequence, individuals can now find others who share their interests in a topic, no matter how esoteric or socially unacceptable (Holt & Bossler, 2016; Quinn & Forsyth, 2013).

From a criminological perspective, technology has enabled deviant subcultures to form and operate in ways that were not previously possible (Holt, 2007; Quinn & Forsyth, 2013). Online environments serve as a key resource for deviant and criminal subcultures, as individuals may be introduced to methods of offending and justifications for behaviour without the need for actual knowledge of offenders in offline spaces. The anonymity afforded by technology also allows individuals to discuss interests, attractions, and activities that they would otherwise not talk about in the real world due to legal risks or social rejection (DiMarco & DiMarco, 2003; Holt, 2007; Quinn & Forsyth, 2013). In turn, individuals may be able to engage in crime more efficiently, whether online or offline, and with less risk of arrest or sanctions (Blevins & Holt, 2009; DiMarco & DiMarco, 2003; Quinn & Forsyth, 2013).

At the same time, it is unclear how much virtual and real experiences differentially affect the formation and beliefs of any subculture and the acceptance of its values by participants (Holt, 2007). Similarly, few have considered how subcultures differ based on whether the offence is only possible in physical spaces, such as drug use or violence, or is a form of cybercrime, like computer hacking or digital piracy. Finally, there is limited research considering the commonalities between the norms and values of disparate virtual subcultures generally.

To better understand the impact of technology on subcultures online and offline, this chapter will consider three key issues. First, the criminological theories used to examine subcultures will be discussed and the way in which they situate individual action relative to norms and values. Second, three unique criminal subcultures will be explored to understand the distinctions in norms for offences occurring primarily online, offline, and those that involve actions in both environments. Finally, the chapter concludes with a discussion of future directions for criminological theory and research of subcultures, regardless of where they operate.

Subcultural theories and research in physical and cyberspace

The Internet has transformed the nature of human interaction by partially eliminating the need for physical encounters and changing the temporal boundaries of an exchange. Despite this change, the inherently social nature of criminality has persisted, as individuals appear to use online spaces to discuss not only how to offend, but why it is beneficial and, in some cases, necessary (e.g. Holt, 2007; Quinn & Forsyth, 2013). The dynamic relationship between virtual experiences and the physical nature of many forms of crime presents a challenge for criminologists, particularly those using subcultural frameworks, as they were developed prior to the creation and use of the Internet (Miller, 1958; Short, 1968). Traditional subcultural researchers consider any group with specific values, norms, traditions, and behaviours that set them apart from the dominant culture to be a subculture (Brake, 1980). Individuals coalesce into groups that may become subcultures as a response to individuals' feelings of rejection by the dominant culture (see Miller, 1958) or because a distinct behaviour or activity is not considered important by the larger society (Quinn & Forsyth, 2013; Wolfgang & Ferracuti, 1967).

Subcultural participants emphasize the importance of certain behaviours or activities, or the development of skills that can be used to aid an individual (Maurer, 1981; Miller, 1958). In turn, participants communicate codes of conduct and rules for participants that structure their worldview and shape the ways they interact with others within and outside of their subculture (Foster, 1990; Wolfgang & Ferracuti, 1967). As part of this process, members of a subculture typically develop a specialized language used by members that demonstrates their involvement and knowledge of the group, as well as outward symbols of membership like tattoos or modes of dress (Hamm, 2002; Holt, 2010; Maurer, 1981). Adherence to these values and symbols provides members with ways to assess others' adherence to the subculture and their status and reputation within it.

Membership in a subculture is thought to influence behaviour through a sort of social learning process (see Akers, 1998). Individuals are exposed to beliefs, goals, and values that approve of and justify actions, including crime, by individuals already engaged in the subculture (Herbert, 1998; Holt, 2007). The bonds and relationships between participants ensure the transmission of knowledge and increase the likelihood of criminal behaviour despite the risk of formal and informal sanctions stemming from the behaviour (Miller, 1958; Short, 1968). The process of subcultural information sharing is evident in online spaces and mirrors the interactive experience of real-world encounters through posting in forums, engaging in social media sites, and even videos and interactive livestreaming (Holt, 2007; Holt et al., 2017; Mann & Sutton, 1998; Quinn & Forsyth, 2013).

There is less research considering whether online or offline experiences have greater impact on offender behaviour and the extent to which individuals experience subcultures differently as a result of where they are primarily socialized to its beliefs (Holt, 2007). In this respect, there is no single theoretical orientation within subcultural research because the majority of subcultural theories were developed before the development of the Internet. The foundational literature in this area also has no specific consensus because the theorists differ in their assumptions about individuals' adherence to conventional norms and values. For example, Cohen (1955) argued that a gang subculture operates in direct opposition to the middle-class values espoused by the dominant society. This view assumes that participants completely reject conventional norms and values and wholly embrace a different set of behavioural beliefs.

Other researchers take a more nuanced approach, recognizing that individuals may have greater agency to participate within a subculture while not accepting all of its normative values (e.g. Matza, 1968). For instance, Elijah Anderson's (1999) celebrated work on urban violence argues that there is a code of the streets which espouses the use of violence when responding to threats or social slights. Though all are exposed to this code, individuals differ in the extent to which they internalize its value and actively use violence. As a result, there are variations in the rates of assault and homicides, and individual risk of victimization can be viewed as a function of individuals' situational adherence to the code of the streets (Anderson, 1999).

Research on the role of technology in facilitating deviant and criminal subcultures has not resolved these theoretical differences. A number of studies considered the practices of deviant and criminal subcultures that operate online and involve offences that occur virtually, including computer hackers (Holt, 2007; Jordan & Taylor, 1998; Meyer, 1989; Steinmetz, 2015; Taylor, 1999) and digital pirates (Cooper & Harrison, 2001; Holt & Copes, 2010; Steinmetz & Tunnell, 2013). A larger body of research has examined the online subcultures of groups who engage in deviant behaviours in physical space, including paedophiles (Durkin & Bryant, 1999; Holt, Blevins, & Burkert, 2010; Jenkins, 2001; Quayle & Taylor, 2002) and various forms of sexual deviance (see Denney & Tewksbury, 2013; Grov, 2004; Maratea, 2011; Roberts & Hunt, 2012; Tewksbury, 2006). This research is valuable, as they demonstrate the key role of both factors internal to the individual and that of their peer associations in predicting involvement in offending. These tests also highlight that cybercrimes may be performed alone, but are directly influenced by perceptions and beliefs about the offence that are received in part by involvement in peer networks that engender criminality in online spaces.

The majority of research does not focus on the differences observed in subcultural experiences based on where the participants are exposed to information about the group online or offline (Holt, 2007; Holt et al., 2017). One exception was research by Holt (2007) that utilized data from forums coupled with interviews and observations from a real-world meeting to examine the subculture of computer hackers. His research observed consistent expression of subcultural norms by participants across both virtual and real environments with one exception: online communities place substantial emphasis on the categorization of participants' adherence to subcultural norms (Holt, 2007). As a consequence, there is a need for more careful consideration of the relationships between physical and virtual experiences and variations in subcultural norms expressed by participants depending on whether their offences primarily occur online or offline.

Offender subcultures and cybercrime

To assess the role of technology in both moderating and facilitating deviant subcultures, this section considers three different subcultures focused on online, offline, or hybrid offences. First, the hacker subculture will be explored due to the fact that the majority of hacks can only occur via Internet-connected computers and devices, though offenders interact online and offline (Holt, 2007; Jordan & Taylor, 1998). The subculture of the customers of prostitutes will then be examined, as paid sexual encounters can occur exclusively in physical space, though offenders utilize online spaces to connect and even solicit workers. Lastly, the subculture of extremists will be considered due to the fact that extremist violence may occur offline, though technology appears to have enhanced and expanded the nature of these offences, including victim intimidation and targeting (Holt et al., 2017).

The modern hacker subculture

One of the most common forms of cybercrime that is recognized broadly by both the general public and to a lesser extent the academic community involves computer hacking. Many associate hackers with criminal activity, given the historical coverage of hacking in the popular press and media (e.g. Furnell, 2002; Thomas, 2002). Hacking is, however, a skill set that can be applied for criminal or benign purposes depending on the actor and their motivations (Holt & Kilger, 2012). Several social science investigations of the hacker subculture recognize the diversity of interests and activities among hackers and take steps to identify the extent to which norms and values of the community are present in both criminal and non-criminal actors (e.g. Jordan & Taylor, 1998; Holt, 2007; Steinmetz, 2015; Taylor, 1999).

To that end, research revealed three core concepts which shape the values and beliefs of hackers: (1) technology, (2) knowledge, and (3) secrecy (Holt, 2007; Jordan & Taylor, 1998; Meyer, 1989; Steinmetz, 2015; Taylor, 1999; Thomas, 2002). Though individual studies have identified other concepts influencing behaviour, these three norms appear most consistently across studies and over time. These norms also structure individual action, regardless of the person's criminal or ethical use of hacking techniques, suggesting their value in shaping the experience of being a hacker.

The importance of technology cannot be understated in the hacker subculture, as hackers could not exist without some technological devices. The act of hacking, or manipulating technology, has been observed since the first computer systems were produced in the 1940s (Levy, 1984). As technology evolved, hackers' interests expanded to include telephony, mobile phones, Internet connectivity, video games, and related peripheral devices (Holt, 2007; Jordan & Taylor, 1998; Meyer, 1989; Steinmetz, 2015; Taylor, 1999; Thomas, 2002). The current interests and activities of hackers centre on computer software and hardware, as well as associated devices like electronics, video games, and cell phones (Holt, 2007; Jordan & Taylor, 1998; Turkle, 1984). The importance of understanding the basic functionality of devices is key to being a hacker, as the more an individual knows about computer technology, the more effective their hacks can be in practice (Holt, 2007; Jordan & Taylor, 1998; Steinmetz, 2015; Taylor, 1999; Thomas, 2002).

The central focus of technology among hackers plays an essential role in shaping the common goal of hackers to develop a mastery of computer hardware and software, as well as attendant technologies (Meyer, 1989; Holt, 2007; Steinmetz, 2015; Thomas, 2002). To become a skilled hacker, one must gain an understanding of the ways that computers work and how they may be manipulated to function in ways that were not initially intended by designers and creators. Such knowledge is cultivated through time spent learning through reading and applying their knowledge to actual devices (Holt, 2007; Jordan & Taylor, 1998; Steinmetz, 2015; Taylor, 1999). Hackers are encouraged to learn on their own, though they may also seek help from tutorials posted online and through conferences in the real world. Individuals may also gain information through social network ties, though evidence suggests the majority of individuals engage in hacks on their own or in very small groups (e.g. Holt, 2009; Leukfeldt, Kleemans, & Stol, 2017 Meyer, 1989).

The ability to practically apply one's knowledge of technology is the basis by which individuals are judged and gain status within this subculture (e.g. Holt, 2007; Jordan & Taylor, 1998; Meyer, 1989; Steinmetz, 2015; Thomas, 2002). Individuals who are able to demonstrate their capabilities, whether through public recognition of hacks, posting tutorials, or making conference presentations, garner the most status within the subculture. Such individuals may be called hackers out of respect for their ability and may self-identify as either black or white hat hackers, depending on their ethical leanings (e.g. Furnell, 2002; Holt, 2010; Jordan & Taylor, 1998). Those who engage in poorly executed hacks or have minimal skills but attempt to overestimate their knowledge are often denigrated by others (Holt, 2007; Jordan & Taylor, 1998; Meyer, 1989; Steinmetz, 2015). Participants may refer to such actors as noobs or script kiddies, both of which have negative connotations within the subculture (Furnell, 2002; Holt, 2010).

Finally, there is a distinct tension within the hacker subculture around the ways that individuals garner a reputation while keeping their activities and identities secret from law enforcement (Jordan & Taylor, 1998; Taylor, 1999; Thomas, 2002). Because some hacks violate state or federal laws, hackers must minimize public awareness of their actions to decrease the risk of arrest (Kilger, 2010; Taylor, 1999). Hackers take steps to distance their hacker identities from their actual identity, such as the use of handles or screen names in order to protect their real name and location (see Furnell, 2002; Jordan & Taylor, 1998). A hacker's handle provides a digital persona that they can hide behind to take credit for successful hacks, quality tutorials, and online mischief (Furnell, 2002; Jordan & Taylor, 1998; Taylor, 1999). Handles also follow individuals into the real world, as hackers use these names at conferences and in meet-up spaces to let others know who they may have been interacting with online (Holt, 2007; Kinkade, Bachmann, & Bachmann, 2013; Steinmetz, 2015). These measures help to provide a modicum of privacy for individual identities in an otherwise social subculture based on information sharing and knowledge.

The customers of sex workers

Though the Internet has engendered the distribution of a range of sexual content online ranging from traditional pornographic materials (Lane, 2000) to livestreaming sex shows (Roberts & Hunt, 2012), technology has also facilitated sexual activity in offline environments. Access to computers and the Internet facilitate the practice of paid sex work, specifically prostitution, for both the customer and the provider. There are a range of websites that serve as an advertising space for sex workers and provide methods for contact, vetting, and payment to facilitate paid sexual encounters (Cunningham & Kendall, 2010). It is thought that the Internet has made the practice of sex work safer by minimizing the need for workers to openly seek out customers in the street or in public spaces.

Technology has also revolutionized the experience of being a client of a sex worker by providing an outlet to discuss their preferences and experiences with no fear of social rejection or embarrassment (Cunningham & Kendall, 2010; Holt & Blevins, 2007; Milrod & Monto, 2012; Sharp & Earle, 2003). Paid sexual encounters have existed for millennia, but there is still social stigma surrounding the admission of seeking out the services of sex workers. The faceless nature of technology thus affords customers a space to openly share their knowledge with others who share their interests (Sanders, 2008; Sharp & Earle, 2003).

Several studies have examined the posting and content within online communities used by the customers of prostitutes to consider the nature of their operations. The findings suggest that participants view their actions as non-deviant and value those with knowledge of and experience with sex workers (e.g. Blevins & Holt, 2009; Cunningham & Kendall, 2010; Holt & Blevins, 2007; Milrod & Monto, 2012; Sanders, 2008). Participants within these sites often describe their experiences in detail and allow one another to ask questions about specific sex workers or areas. The quality of information shared becomes a way for participants to judge one another and gauge their expertise with sex workers within a given physical location (Blevins & Holt, 2009; Holt & Blevins, 2007). In fact, participants avoid using stigmatizing terms when discussing their activities, often referring to themselves as mongers, shortening the phrase "whore monger," or hobbyists (Blevins & Holt, 2009; Sharp & Earle, 2003). The use of these phrases reflects the notion that paid sexual encounters can be enjoyable and the pursuit of sex workers constitutes a hobby or lifestyle.

Though customers view their actions as normal, they are keenly aware of the fact that they are engaging in transactional encounters with sex workers. As a result, their discussions around sex workers tend to use language which suggests they view women as commodities rather than people (Blevins & Holt, 2009). The participants typically use specialized language to refer to sex workers, differentiating them based on where they advertise or work, such as the use of the term streetwalker or sw to indicate the person engages in street-based prostitution. Individuals objectify sex workers on the basis of their physical appearance, using a "streetwalker scale" to rate women who engage in sex work compared to those who do not (Holt & Blevins, 2007; Milrod & Monto, 2012; Sanders, 2008). They also use the term mileage to discuss the physical appearance and consequences that participation in the sex trade has had on the worker. In addition, the customers regularly explained the cost of specific sex acts and the negotiation process involved to clearly reflect what the final negotiated price was for a given sexual encounter (Blevins & Holt, 2009).

Additionally, the customers of prostitutes' online discussions focus extensively on sexuality and sex acts due to the nature of sex work generally. Participants in online discussions regularly explain what kinds of sexual acts they perform with prostitutes, as well as the extent to which they were enjoyable or worth the cost (Blevins & Holt, 2009; Cunningham & Kendall, 2010; Milrod & Monto, 2012). To that end, users would regularly discuss their use of condoms when engaging in sex acts and the extent to which that may affect the nature of the encounter. They also used the term girlfriend experience, or GFE, to identify sex workers who provide an experience similar to what may be had in a consensual non-transactional sexual encounter (Blevins & Holt, 2009; Milrod & Monto, 2012; Sharp & Earle, 2003).

Extremist groups

Though research overwhelmingly demonstrates the ways that extremists and radical groups engage in acts of violence against a range of targets (Freilich, Chermak, Belli, Gruenewald, & Parkin, 2014; LaFree, 2010), they have increasingly turned to the Internet as a space to call for physical violence against groups of people (Bartlett & Miller, 2012; Borum, 2013; Hegghammer, 2013). Terrorists and extremist factions have also begun to use social media sites and the Internet as a platform for recruitment and radicalization of vulnerable persons who may be sympathetic to their causes (Borum, 2013; Holt, Freilich & Chermak, 2016; Simi & Futrell, 2010; Weimann, 2011).

The benefit of the Internet for radicals and extremists lies in the fact that people can connect with ideologies across the globe, regardless of the extent to which they are supported by individuals within their local community (Faulk, 1997). This enables individuals to gain access to belief systems and find social support systems from others online, even if those in their immediate family and social network in physical spaces do not value these ideas (McCauley & Moskalenko, 2011; Simi & Futrell, 2010). Additionally, simply posting content may enable individuals to find it, read it, and self-radicalize or accept the ideas without the need for direct social engagement with others online or offline (Hamm & Spaaij, 2017; Pantucci, 2011). Thus, technology affords extremists the ability to promote their ideas no matter how extreme or unusual.

One of the most long-standing extremist subcultures online is driven by the radical far right, an umbrella term recognizing a range of ideological groups with overlapping perspectives, such as white supremacist groups like the Ku Klux Klan, as well as neo-Nazi groups, white nationalists, militia movements, and other ethno–nationist organizations (Borum, 2013; Hamm & Spaaij, 2017; Simi & Futrell, 2010). These groups differ in their ideological beliefs, making it difficult to identify a single subculture that shapes the behaviours of participants (Holt et al., 2016).

Some hold a belief related to the notion that the white race has been threatened by and is actively being sublimated and marginalized by non-white racial and ethnic groups, as well as Jews, Catholics, and Muslims (Hamm, 2002; Simi & Futrell, 2010). Others discuss the need to develop and maintain a robust white race, which may be a function of the perception that whites have been appointed by God to dominate other races generally (Castle, 2011; McNamee,

Peterson, & Pena, 2010). Women actively engaged in online communities often discuss their role in producing and raising the next generation of Aryan children who understand their position in society (Blee, 2002). These messages are frequently communicated through friendly media, such as video games, music, and social media posts (Hamm & Spaaij, 2017). A portion of groups have also developed colouring books and child-friendly content in order to direct their messages and indoctrinate very young people (Holt, Bossler, & Seigfried-Spellar, 2017).

Some of these groups also use overtly inflammatory language about the need to rise up in armed conflict or engage in a "race war" (McNamee et al., 2010). Not all individuals involved in this subculture are willing to engage in violence, though many major and minor harms have been performed by individuals involved in these communities. Those who have committed acts of violence may be held up as martyrs and used as examples in online communities. For instance, Timothy McVeigh is often discussed as martyr for the far right, whether among militia groups or even white nationalist groups (Hamm, 2007; Hamm & Spaaij, 2017; Simi & Futrell, 2010). The actions of individuals like McVeigh have also been used as a source for propaganda and messaging among groups to help promote their agenda (Hamm, 2007). As a consequence, these movements tend to capitalize on violence as a means to further their ideological agenda and aid in the radicalization process.

Discussion and conclusions

Taken as a whole, the Internet is a pivotal resource in the formation and maintenance of deviant subcultures, regardless of whether they involve behaviours occurring online or offline (Hamm & Spaaij, 2017; Holt, 2007; Jordan & Taylor, 1998; Simi & Futrell, 2010). Actors are able to successfully created shared, safe spaces online where they can anonymously discuss their interests and perceptions (Quinn & Forsyth, 2013). The communication of these beliefs and values may also encourage the view that there is nothing inherently deviant or criminal about their actions and potentially increase the risk of future offending.

Examining various subcultures demonstrates that there are some commonalities across offender communities, regardless of the nature of their offence or operation. For instance, subcultures centred in part on real-world offending share the notion that their interests and beliefs have been unfairly marginalized by society. Both the clients of sex workers and individuals interested in extremist ideologies blame the broader culture for delegitimizing the supposedly 'acceptable' nature of their actions, though they differ in their reasons as to why (e.g. Blevins & Holt, 2009; Simi & Futrell, 2010). Similarly, the hacker and prostitution subcultures place an emphasis on knowledge and expertise related to their offences. Both groups also utilize a unique argot to refer to one another and imply status on actors based on their level of expertise (Blevins & Holt, 2009; Jordan & Taylor, 1998; Milrod & Monto, 2012; Taylor, Quayle, & Holland, 2001).

The emergence of technology revolutionized the process of examining deviant subcultures. The use of forums and other social media sources provides a record of the communications between subcultural participants, enabling longitudinal investigations of the values and beliefs of groups and shifts in views over time (e.g. Holt & Bossler, 2016; Quinn & Forsyth, 2013). Scholars have used both quantitative and qualitative methods to examine deviant subcultures and their views (see Holt & Bossler, 2016 for review). The diversity of communications platforms creates a challenge for researchers to fully capture the breadth and depth of subcultural norms (e.g. Dupont, Côté, Boutin, & Fernandez, 2017). For instance, unique social media environments built for individuals with extreme ideological beliefs, such as Gab, may lead them to experience radical subcultures differently from those who only participate in forums and traditional social media.

In addition, researchers frequently utilize data from only virtual or real sources, limiting their ability to identify variations in subcultural experiences on the basis of participants' experiences in both environments (for exceptions see Holt, 2007; Jordan & Taylor, 1998). Future research must find ways to better identify and triangulate multiple data sources in order to better assess the dynamics of deviant and criminal subcultures.

Scholars must also consider how new social media platforms and technologies may foster the creation of new forms of deviance and subcultures operating online and offline. For instance, high-speed Internet access and high-definition video and camera equipment have fostered the growth of so-called "cam shows," where men and women livestream video of themselves engaging in sexual acts (Roberts & Hunt, 2012). There is now a community of individuals who record these shows, referring to themselves as "cappers," because they capture the events and share it publicly (Roberts & Hunt, 2012). This unique subculture would not exist without a range of forums and technology that supports both the production of "cam shows" and an interested audience to consume the content. Thus, researchers must be vigilant in examining these subcultures in order to better document the scope of cybercrime and identify commonalities between offender groups as a whole (Holt & Bossler, 2016).

Law enforcement efforts to crack down on these subcultures have led offenders to displace to different platforms and conceal their discussions from outsiders (see Holt, Blevins, & Kuhns, 2014; Hutchings & Holt, 2017). This creates challenges for researchers to collect data that best reflects the realities of conversation between participants and of the most serious offenders within any given subculture (Holt, 2014). Researchers have found solutions to continue to investigate subcultures as they go further underground, such as the use of leaked datasets that were dumped online of forums and online communications (e.g. Dupont et al., 2017; Yip, Webber, & Shadbolt, 2013). These efforts, however, are incomplete and require constant innovation on the part of the academic community to find better data sources and partners who may give access to participants and subcultures (Hutchings & Holt, 2017).

References

Akers, R. L. (1998). *Social learning and social structure: A general theory of crime and deviance.* Boston: Northeastern University Press.

Anderson, E. (1999). *Code of the street.* New York, NY: Norton.

Bartlett, J., & Miller, C. (2012). The edge of violence: Towards telling the difference between violent and non-violent radicalization. *Terrorism and Political Violence, 24*(1), 1–21.

Blee, K. M. (2002). *Inside organized racism: Women and men in the hate movement.* Sacramento, CA: University of California Press.

Blevins, K., & Holt, T. J. (2009). Examining the virtual subculture of johns. *Journal of Contemporary Ethnography, 38,* 619–648.

Borum, R. (2013). Informing lone-offender investigations. *Criminology & Public Policy, 12*(1), 103–112.

Brake, M. (1980). *The sociology of youth cultures and youth subcultures.* London: Routledge and Kegan Paul.

Brenner, S. W. (2009). *Cyberthreats: The emerging fault lines of the nation state.* New York, NY: Oxford University Press.

Castle, T. (2011). The women of Stormfront: An examination of white nationalist discussion threads on the internet. *Internet Journal of Criminology.* Retrieved from www.internet-journalofcriminology.com/Castle_Chevalier_The_Women_of_Stormfront_An_Examination_of_White_Nationalist_Discussion_Threads.pdf

Cohen, A. (1955). *Delinquent boys* (p. 84). New York: Free Press.

Cooper, J., & Harrison, D. M. (2001). The social organization of audio piracy on the internet. *Media, Culture, and Society, 23,* 71–89.

Cunningham, S., & Kendall, T. (2010). Sex for sale: Online commerce in the world's oldest profession. In T. J. Holt (Ed.), *Crime on-line: Correlates, causes, and context* (pp. 40–75). Raleigh, NC: Carolina Academic Press.

Denney, A. S., & Tewksbury, R. (2013). Characteristics of successful personal ads in a BDSM on-line community. *Deviant Behavior, 34*(2), 153–168.

DiMarco, A. D., & DiMarco, H. (2003). Investigating cybersociety: A consideration of the ethical and practical issues surrounding online research in chat rooms. In Y. Jewkes (Ed.), *Dot.cons: Crime, deviance and identity on the internet.* Portland, OR: Willan Publishing.

Dupont, B., Côté, A. M., Boutin, J. I., & Fernandez, J. (2017). Darkode: Recruitment patterns and transactional features of "the most dangerous cybercrime forum in the world". *American Behavioral Scientist, 61*(11), 1219–1243.

Durkin, K. F., & Bryant, C. D. (1999). Propagandizing pederasty: A thematic analysis of the online exculpatory accounts of unrepentant pedophiles. *Deviant Behavior, 20,* 103–127.

Faulk, K. (1997, October 19). White supremacist spreads views on net. *The Birmingham News,* p. 1. Retrieved from www.stormfront.org/dblack/press101997.htm

Foster, J. (1990). *Villains: Crime and community in the inner city.* London: Routledge.

Freilich, J. D., Chermak, S. M., Belli, R., Gruenewald, J., & Parkin, W. S. (2014). Introducing the United States Extremist Crime Database (ECDB). *Terrorism and Political Violence, 26,* 372–384.

Furnell, S. (2002). *Cybercrime: Vandalizing the information society.* London: Addison-Wesley.

Grov, C. (2004). "Make me your death slave": Men who have sex with men and use the internet to intentionally spread HIV. *Deviant Behavior, 25*(4), 329–349.

Hamm, M. S. (2002). *In bad company: America's terrorist underground.* Boston, MA: Northeastern University Press.

Hamm, M. S. (2007). *Terrorism as crime: From Oklahoma City to Al-Qaeda and Beyond*. New York: NYU Press.

Hamm, M. S., & Spaaij, R. (2017). *The age of lone wolf terrorism*. New York, NY: Columbia University Press.

Hegghammer, T. (2013). Should I stay or should I go? Explaining variation in western jihadists' choice between domestic and foreign fighting. *American Political Science Review, 107*, 1–15.

Herbert, S. (1998). Police subculture reconsidered. *Criminology, 36*, 343–369.

Holt, T. J. (2007). Subcultural evolution? Examining the influence of on- and off-line experiences on deviant subcultures. *Deviant Behavior, 28*, 171–198.

Holt, T. J. (2010). Examining the role of technology in the formation of deviant subcultures. *Social Science Computer Review, 28*, 466–481.

Holt, T. J. (2013). Examining the forces shaping cybercrime markets online. *Social Science Computer Review, 31*, 165–177.

Holt, T. (2014). *Qualitative criminology in online spaces: The Routledge handbook of qualitative criminology* (pp. 173–188). London: Routledge.

Holt, T. J., & Blevins, K. R. (2007). Examining sex work from the client's perspective: Assessing johns using online data. *Deviant Behavior, 28*, 333–354.

Holt, T. J., Blevins, K. R., & Burkert, N. (2010). Considering the pedophile subculture online. *Sexual Abuse: Journal of Research and Treatment, 22*, 3–24.

Holt, T. J., Blevins, K. R., & Kuhns, J. B. (2014). Examining diffusion and arrest practices among johns. *Crime and Delinquency, 60*, 261–283.

Holt, T. J., & Bossler, A. M. (2016). *Cybercrime in progress: Theory and prevention of technology-enabled offenses*. Crime Science Series. London: Routledge.

Holt, T. J., Bossler, A. M., & Seigfried-Spellar, K. C. (2017). *Cybercrime and digital forensics: An introduction*. London: Routledge.

Holt, T. J., & Copes, H. (2010). Transferring subcultural knowledge online: Practices and beliefs of persistent digital pirates. *Deviant Behavior, 31*, 625–654.

Holt, T. J., Freilich, J. D., & Chermak, S. M. (2016). Internet-based radicalization as enculturation to violent deviant subcultures. *Deviant Behavior, 47*, 1–15.

Holt, T. J., Freilich, J. D., & Chermak, S. M. (2017). Exploring the subculture of ideologically motivated cyber-attackers. *Journal of Contemporary Criminal Justice, 33*, 212–233.

Holt, T. J., & Kilger, M. (2012). Examining willingness to attack critical infrastructure on and off-line. *Crime and Delinquency, 58*(5), 798–822.

Holt, T. J., Smirnova, O., & Chua, Y. T. (2016). *Data thieves in action: Examining the international market for stolen personal information*. New York: Springer.

Hutchings, A., & Holt, T. J. (2017). The online stolen data market: Disruption and intervention approaches. *Global Crime, 18*(1), 11–30.

Jenkins, P. (2001). *Beyond tolerance: Child pornography on the internet*. New York, NY: New York University Press.

Jordan, T., & Taylor, P. (1998). A sociology of hackers. *The Sociological Review, 46*, 757–780.

Kilger, M. (2010). Social dynamics and the future of technology-driven crime. In T. J. Holt & B. Schell (Eds.), *Corporate hacking and technology-driven crime: Social dynamics and implications* (pp. 205–227). Hershey, PA: IGI-Global.

Kinkade, P. T., Bachmann, M., & Bachmann, B. S. (2013). Hacker Woodstock: Observations on an off-line cyber culture at the chaos communication camp 2011. In T. J. Holt (Ed.), *Crime on-line: Correlates, causes, and context* (2nd ed., pp. 19–60). Raleigh, NC: Carolina Academic Press.

LaFree, G. (2010). The Global Terrorism Database (GTD): Accomplishments and challenges. *Perspectives on Terrorism, 4*, 24–46.

Lane, F. S. (2000). *Obscene profits: The entrepreneurs of pornography in the cyber age.* New York, NY: Routledge.

Leukfeldt, E. R., Kleemans, E. R., & Stol, W. P. (2017). Cybercriminal networks, social ties, and online forums: Social ties versus digital ties within phishing and malware networks. *The British Journal of Criminology, 57,* 704–722.

Levy, S. (1984). *Hackers: Heroes of the computer revolution.* New York, NY: Penguin.

Mann, D., & Sutton, M. (1998). Netcrime: More change in the organization of thieving. *The British Journal of Criminology, 38,* 201–229.

Maratea, R. J. (2011). Screwing the pooch: Legitimizing accounts in a zoophilia on-line community. *Deviant Behavior, 32*(10), 918–943.

Matza, D. (1968). *Becoming delinquent.* Englewood Cliffs: Prentice Hall.

Maurer, D. W. (1981). *Language of the underworld.* Louisville, KY: University of Kentucky Press.

McCauley, C., & Moskalenko, S. (2011). *Friction: How radicalization happens to them and us.* Oxford: Oxford University Press.

McNamee, L. G., Peterson, B. L., & Pena, J. (2010). A call to educate, participate, invoke, and indict: Understanding the communication of online hate groups. *Communication Monographs, 77,* 257–280.

Meyer, G. R. (1989). *The social organization of the computer underground* (Master's thesis). Northern Illinois University.

Miller, W. B. (1958). Lower class culture as a generating milieu of gang delinquency. *Journal of Social Issues, 14*(3), 5–19.

Milrod, C., & Monto, M. A. (2012). The hobbyist and the girlfriend experience: Behaviors and preferences of male customers of internet sexual service providers. *Deviant Behaviors, 33*(10), 792–810.

Pantucci, R. (2011). What have learned about lone wolves from Anders Bhring Brevik. *Perspectives on Terrorism, 5,* 5–6.

Pratt, T. C., & Cullen, F. T. (2000). The empirical status of Gottfredson and Hirshi's general theory of crime: A meta-analysis. *Criminology, 38,* 931–964.

Quayle, E., & Taylor, M. (2002). Child pornography and the internet: Perpetuating a cycle of abuse. *Deviant Behavior, 23,* 331–361.

Quinn, J. F., & Forsyth, C. J. (2013). Red light districts on blue screens: A typology for understanding the evolution of deviant communities on the Internet. *Deviant Behavior, 34,* 579–585.

Roberts, J. W., & Hunt, S. A. (2012). Social control in a sexually deviant cybercommunity: A cappers' code of conduct. *Deviant Behavior, 33,* 757–773.

Sanders, T. (2008). *Sex work.* London: Willan.

Sharp, K., & Earle, S. (2003). Cyberpunters and cyberwhores: Prostitution on the internet. In Y. Jewkes (Ed.), *Dot.cons: Crime, deviance and identity on the internet* (pp. 36–52). Portland, OR: Willan Publishing.

Shaw, C. R., & McKay, H. D. (1942). *Juvenile delinquency and urban areas.* Chicago, IL: University of Chicago Press.

Short, J. F. (1968). *Gang delinquency and delinquent subcultures.* Oxford: Harper & Row.

Simi, P., & Futrell, R. (2010). *American Swastika: Inside the White Power movement's hidden spaces of hate.* New York: Rowan & Littlefield.

Steinmetz, K. F. (2015). Craft (y) nessAn ethnographic study of hacking. *The British Journal of Criminology, 55*(1), 125–145.

Steinmetz, K. F., & Tunnell, K. D. (2013). Under the pixelated jolly roger: A study of on-line pirates. *Deviant Behavior, 34*(1), 53–67.

Sutherland, E. (1947). *Principles of criminology.* Chicago, IL: Lippincott.

Taylor, M., Quayle, E., & Holland, G. (2001). Child pornography, the internet and offending. *Isuma, 2*, 9–100. Taylor, P. (1999). *Hackers: Crime in the digital sublime*. London: Routledge.

Tewksbury, R. (2006). "Click here for HIV": An analysis of internet-based bug chasers and bug givers. *Deviant Behavior, 27*(4), 379–395.

Thomas, D. (2002). *Hacker culture*. Minneapolis, MN: University of Minnesota Press.

Turkle, S. (1984). *The second self: Computers and the human spirit*. New York, NY: Simon and Schuster.

Vold, G. B., Bernard, T. J., & Snipes, J. B. (1998). *Theoretical criminology*. Oxford: Oxford University Press.

Wall, D. S. (2007). *Cybercrime: The transformation of crime in the information age*. Cambridge: Polity Press.

Weimann, G. (2011). Cyber-fatwas and terrorism. *Studies in Conflict & Terrorism, 34*(10), 765–781.

Wolfgang, M. E., & Ferracuti, F. (1967). *The subculture of violence: Toward an integrated theory in criminology*. New York: Tavistock Publications.

Yip, M., Webber, C., & Shadbolt, N. (2013). Trust among cybercriminals? Carding forums, uncertainty and implications for policing. *Policing and Society, 23*(4), 516–539.

Young, J. (1971). *The drugtakers: The social meaning of drug use*. London: Judson, McGibbon, and Kee.

8 On social engineering

Kevin Steinmetz, Richard Goe, and Alexandra Pimentel

Introduction

In 2015, Central Intelligence Agency (CIA) Director John Brennan's personal email account was compromised by the group "Crackas With Attitude" (CWA) (Franceschi-Bicchierai, 2015b; O'Neill, 2018; Zetter, 2015b).[1] CWA found Brennan's personal mobile phone number and determined that his service provider was Verizon. They then called Verizon and convinced a company representative to hand over Brennan's account information by using a fabricated employee code to pose as company technicians (Zetter, 2015b). Using information gleaned from Verizon, CWA proceeded to call America Online and reset the password to Brennan's email account. With newly minted account credentials, the group accessed his email, downloaded sensitive documents, and publicly shamed both Brennan and the broader U.S. intelligence community. The incident catapulted CWA into the spotlight. They would go on to engage in other high-profile crimes, including illicitly accessing the information of thousands of law enforcement, military, and intelligence personnel; breaching the accounts of other intelligence and law enforcement administrators; and releasing sensitive information over Twitter and WikiLeaks (Dixon, 2018; Franceschi-Bicchierai, 2015a; Zetter, 2015a).

The compromise of systems and information for this many employees and agencies may conjure images of sophisticated technology-based attacks. Although computer systems and networks were certainly involved, the CWA relied primarily on "social engineering," or stated simply, the manipulation of the people involved in information security. The prosecutor in a court case regarding this incident highlighted this fact in explaining that, "The group ... used something known as social engineering, which involves socially manipulating people – call centres or help desks – into performing acts or divulging confidential information" (as quoted in Massey, 2018).

Though certainly headline-grabbing, the CWA is hardly unique in their use of social engineering techniques. In fact, tactics focusing on the human element of information security have long been a significant tool in the offender's toolkit. Despite investing billions in public and private funds toward computer security (Yar, 2008), old-fashioned con-artist tactics are often all that are needed to pry open gaps in security for systems and organizations. Since the early days of phone phreaking – the exploration and manipulation of phone systems – social engineering has been intimately interwoven with hacking and information security. As Thomas (2002, p. 62) explains, "Indeed, oftentimes, social-engineering skills will be the *primary* way in which hackers get system access." For many in the hacking and security fields, "humans are the weakest link in security" is a common refrain. After all, why bother bypassing technical controls when a human can be convinced to hand over login credentials?

Giving a precise definition of social engineering is difficult. For some, social engineering is treated as a synonym for influence or persuasion. For example, Christopher Hadnagy (2014, p. 27) – a well-known hacker and social engineer who runs Social-Engineer.org, the Social-Engineer Podcast, and the Def Con Social Engineering Village – has defined it as "any act that influences someone to take an action that may or may not be in his or her best interest." Others have adopted narrower views. Renowned hacker and social engineer Kevin Mitnick has defined social engineering as a subset of con artistry where a person "uses deception, influence, and persuasion against businesses, usually targeting their information" (Mitnick & Simon, 2002, p. xii). While few in criminology have considered social engineering, Button and Cross (2017, p. 18) give the phenomenon a nod, explaining that "some fraudsters pretend to be someone they are not in order to secure bank account and other personal data . . . this is often known as pretext calling or more commonly as 'social engineering.'"

Although the field of information security often presents the concept of social engineering as through it were a technical designation, the conceptual ambiguity within the term may exist because social engineering is not so much a technical construct as it is a subcultural one. Social engineering bears a resemblance to many subcultural terms, which are often context-dependent and "fuzzy" conceptually. In this way, social engineering may be like pornography, to paraphrase the late U.S. Supreme Court Justice Potter Stewart: we know it when we see it (*Jacobellis v. Ohio*, 1964, p. 197). For the purposes of this chapter, we adopt a working definition more or less consistent with Button and Cross (2017): social engineering is the influence, manipulation, or misdirection of the people involved in information security with the proximal or distal objective being gaining information or system access.[2] Importantly, when we argue that social engineering targets the people involved in information security, we do not simply mean practitioners in the field of information security, such as IT personnel or "C-level" executives like CIOs and CISOs. In this context, the target of social engineering instead refers to anyone (account holder, systems user, receptionist, executive, maintenance worker, mid-level manager, etc.) or any organization (third-party contractor, government agency, private company, school, etc.) that is involved in securing information which can be exploited.

Because little criminological attention to date has been given to social engineering, the current chapter presents an overview of the phenomenon in two parts. The first part provides a historical overview of social engineering. Brief consideration is given to the term's original use as an approach to top-down social reform before situating its contemporary use in the history of phone phreaking and hacking. The second part involves a review of extant literature on social engineering. While other bodies of literature exist on fraud and con artistry, we are interested in tracing academic thought specifically on the concept of social engineering within the context of information security. In general, the literature focuses on two broad areas of social engineering: (1) techniques and strategies employed by social engineers and (2) psychological traits, biases, and tendencies said to be exploited by these fraudsters. These areas are discussed in turn.

History of social engineering

The historical overview of social engineering is presented in four parts. First, this chapter describes the historical use of the term social engineering, which pre-dates the Internet and other computer network technologies. Second, we describe the emergence of a subculture intimately tied to illicit uses of telecommunications networks, the development of hacker culture, and early information security social engineering: phone phreaks. This discussion then breaks from the development of technological subcultures and practices to focus on the history of telecommunications and computer network technologies, which facilitated opportunities for criminal or otherwise alternative uses of such technologies among phreaks and hackers. Finally, we briefly reflect on the kinds of harms contemporary social engineering may cause.

Social engineering as social reform

The term social engineering originally had nothing to do with information security. Instead, it was coined in 1894 in an essay by J. C. Van Marken describing "sociale ingeniurs," or specialists who dealt with the "'human problems' of factories and plants" (Larsson, Letell, & Thörn, 2012, p. 12). Amidst increasing bureaucratization, industrialization, and population expansion that characterized the end of the 19th century, social engineering emerged as one of many visions for rendering intentional societal change through group and institutional controls to be executed by trained professionals (Brownell, 1983; Graebner, 1987; McClymer, 1980). This period was also marked by the emergence of the engineering profession, which tended to view society as ordered by "social laws" similar to the deterministic rules governing technology, which could thus be systematically and scientifically examined and controlled through the judicious actions of trained social engineers (Alexander & Schmidt, 1996; Layton, 1971).

In this spirit, early social engineering advocate Tolman (1909, p. 5) conceived of workers as "animate machines" that could be made more efficient and effective by social engineers, producing profit for the employer while making the worker "an improved man for the improved machine" for the purposes of "industrial betterment." Adopting a broader vision for social engineering,

Edwin Earp (1911, p. 29) extended his view beyond "humans as machines" and argued society itself was a technological system which social engineers could recalibrate and reconfigure for the betterment of all. Social engineering as an approach to social policy endured in the post–World War II period in various forms, including social planning and demography. It also has persisted through government attempts to sway public opinion and augment behaviour. For instance, recent uses of social media to affect democratic elections may be seen as a form of social engineering.

It may seem unusual to elaborate on this early use of social engineering in a chapter focusing on the human factors in information security. Important parallels exist, however, between social engineering as a political project and social engineering as a form of information security fraud. Early social engineers viewed humans and society more generally as operating like machines which could be scientifically tempered and evaluated. Psychology became an instrumental tool used for achieving efficiency and compliance. In the context of information security, social engineering similarly involves the wedding of humans and technology through dependence on psychological manipulation. Though little evidence exists that hackers adopted the term social engineering with these historical significance in mind, there may be at least a degree of coincidental import in the adoption of the term among contemporary technologists.

Phreaks, hackers, and social engineering

In the context of information security and telecommunications networks, the earliest practitioners of social engineering may have been "telephone enthusiasts" or "phone phreaks," predecessors to contemporary computer network hackers who revelled in learning about and manipulating telephony systems (Pfaffenberger, 1988; Taylor, 1999; Turkle, 1984). The significance of phone phreaking to social engineering is two-fold. Notably, the community of phone phreaks served as a large part of the cultural bedrock from which emerged hacker values and techniques regarding illicit uses of technologies. In addition, phreakers were among the first to use the term "social engineering" to describe using social methods to facilitate access to technical systems.

Phone phreak historian Phil Lapsley (2013, pp. 30–36) traces phreaking back to 1955 with David Condon (a pseudonym) who modified a toy flute into a device that could be used to make free calls. Phreaks were also known for producing devices to facilitate their explorations and antics in the phone systems called 'boxes,' most notably "blue boxes" (Coleman, 2012). Using such tools and skills, they would perform feats such as making free phone calls, circumnavigating barriers in the phone system, and even wiretapping, much to the chagrin of both law enforcement and major telecommunications companies.

Multiple events bolstered the popularity of phone phreaking throughout the 1960s and 1970s. The publication of technical details of the telephone networks by Bell helped many phreaks learn about the phone system and identify potential areas to exploit (Lapsley, 2013, p. 38). By 1969, phreaks were coming together over the wires and forming a kind of community (Lapsley, 2013, p. 155). In 1971, phreaking would gain more notoriety following the publication of Ron Rosenbaum's article in *Esquire* which introduced much of the world to blue boxes and Captain Crunch, a now (in)famous phreak whose name is a tribute to the breakfast cereal which used to include a toy whistle that blew the 2600-Hz tone. Among the ranks of the phreaks were soon-to-be leading pioneers of Silicon Valley, including both Steve Jobs and Steve Wozniak (famously known as the founders of Apple) who got their start creating blue boxes after reading the 1971 *Esquire* article (Lapsley, 2013; Levy, 1984; McLeod, 2014; Sterling, 1992; Thomas, 2002).

Phreaking also gained increased attention as a result of its connections to 1960s counterculture through the Yippies or the "Youth International Party." Founded by Abbie Hoffman, the Yippies were a leftist political group who revelled in "a loud and lively policy of surrealistic subversion and outrageous political mischief" (Sterling, 1992, p. 43). They promoted a rip-off culture, which encouraged political resistance by avoiding paying for commercial and government services. Deriving methods for free phone calls, like using "cheap brass washers as coin slugs," were among these rip-off tactics (Sterling, 1992, p. 44). Rip-offs as political resistance were further promoted through the *Youth International Party Line* (*YIPL*) a newsletter created in 1971 by Hoffman and Alan Fierstein, a phone phreak (Lapsley, 2013, p. 186). Lapsley (2013, p. 199) argues that "*YIPL* marked the beginning of the cultural hijacking of phone phreaking" – that phreaking began to pour out of its niche community into other social spheres. As Sterling (1992, p. 44) explains, "ingenious, vaguely politicized varieties of rip-off, which might be described as 'anarchy by convenience,' became very popular in Yippie circles, and because rip-off was so useful, it was to outlast the Yippie movement itself."

YIPL was eventually rebranded as the *Technical Assistance Program* (*TAP*) (Cheshire, 1996). This iteration of the zine mostly shirked its overtly leftist political agenda and focused more on technical aspects of technological rip-offs and disruption, including those for phone systems (Sterling, 1992). It thus served as a resource for phone phreakers and the burgeoning hacker underground until publication ceased in 1984. That same year, *2600: The Hacker Quarterly* began, a prominent hacker zine that derived its name from the infamous 2600-Hz tone (Lapsley, 2013, p. 330). Coleman (2012, p. 105) explains that "largely, although not exclusively, focusing on computers, 2600 paid homage to its phone phreaking roots in choosing its name and spent over two decades lampooning and critiquing AT&T (among other corporations and the government) with notable vigor." A year later, *Phrack* (a portmanteau of "phreak" and "hack") began publication and became one of the most important zines for the hacker underground through the late 1980s and early 1990s. These are just some of the examples that portray how phreaking influenced hacker culture and how phreaking is intertwined with the history of that culture.

The connections between phreaking and hacking were no accident. Though some accounts situate the origins of hacking in institutions like MIT (e.g. Levy,

1984), Coleman (2012, p. 101) instead argues that MIT was "the place where *one variant of hacking* got its start" and that phreakers were another point of origin – one particularly influential on hacker politics and pranks. Genosko (2013, p. 131) similarly asserts that phreaks "are the precursors of information system hackers, and their initiatives establish the route and justification for the hacker chaodyssey." In addition, the "illicit experiments" of the phreaks helped motivate phone companies like AT&T and Bell Laboratories (or "Ma Bell" as many hackers and phreaks called it (Orth, 1971; Rosenbaum, 1971)) to "transition to a digital switching system that couldn't be triggered by tones" (McLeod, 2014, p. 11). This transition meant that computers began to fundamentally restructure the phone system. Thus, throughout the 1970s, phreaks were increasingly required to add computer skills to their repertoire. Additionally, early computer hackers, like the MIT hackers of the 1960s, were connecting computers to the telephone networks and using it "as a computerized blue box" (Lapsley, 2013, p. 313; Levy, 1984, p. 95). In this way, phreaking subculture, which emphasized technical mastery, curiosity, and a love of transgression and prankery, set the stage for the hacker underground that would ensue (Coleman, 2012).

Phreakers also had a tremendous influence on hacker culture through their use of social engineering. Before the term itself was used, however, phreakers referred to the practice as "pretexting" or "calling someone on a pretext to get information or convince them to do something for you" (Lapsley, 2013, p. 372). Lapsley (2013, p. 372) states that this term was borrowed from the Federal Bureau of Investigation (FBI) as they used the technique in their investigations. Some phreaks also used the term 'DT,' named after Denny Teresi who was considered by some phreaks to be the best at talking phone employees into complying with unscrupulous requests (Lapsley, 2013, p. 179). While early phone systems could be manipulated via audio tones and other tricks, there were limits to what could be accomplished on one end of a phone line. Phreaks therefore often targeted telephone company employees (Thomas, 2002, p. 62). For example, an article published in a 1985 issue of *2600* describes how to elicit information from phone company employees:

> Whenever a Bell employee visits your house, feel phree to ask whatever you want, within reason. Most are extremely willing to shoot the bull about almost anything of which they have knowledge. At first, merely joke with them lightheartedly, in order to get them off of their guard . . . They will talk on and on about almost anything, from telecommunications to their home life and their childhood. The possibilities for social engineering are endless. Remember, Bell employees are humans, too. All you have to do is listen.
>
> (The Shadow, 1985, p. 1)

Social engineering was so integral to the phreaking enterprise that Kevin Mitnick has defined phreaking as "a type of hacking that allows you to explore the telephone network by exploiting the phone systems *and phone company employees*" (Mitnick & Simon, 2002, p. x; emphasis added). In fact, for Mitnick, learning to social-engineer was inseparable from learning to phreak (ibid).

Phreaks did not limit social engineering merely to the manipulation of phone company employees. Consistent with other areas of hacking, as well as the antics of any group composed of predominantly young men, they would also use their talents for prankery.[3] Steve Wozniak, for example, used a blue box to "make a prank call to the Vatican, almost getting the pope on the line" (McLeod, 2014, p. 10). Mitnick describes a prank wherein he social-engineered the phone company into changing the phone system classification for his friend's phone line to that of a pay phone, which left the unfortunate phone user being prompted to "please deposit ten cents" whenever attempting to make a call (Mitnick & Simon, 2011, p. 22). In fact, the history of phreaking is also a history of pranking (Coleman, 2012; Lapsley, 2013; McLeod, 2014).

Network technologies and social engineering

The roles of phreaks and hackers in the history of social engineering is firmly situated within the historical context of the rapidly evolving telecommunications technologies during these decades. One of the defining characteristics of the 20th century was the development of telecommunications networks. These systems were instrumental in collapsing spatial and temporal barriers that structured social interactions of previous generations and paved the way to nearly instantaneous communications across the world. Telegraph networks – predecessors for telephone networks – emerged in the mid-1800s (Lapsley, 2013, pp. 15–17). These networks would be transformed and refined through the next century. Other networking technologies began to emerge in the mid-1900s.

In the 1950s, the U.S. military attempted to develop a computerized network called the Semi-Autonomous Ground Environment (SAGE) system, envisioned as an early warning and interception system for enemy bombers (Rid, 2016). In the 1960s, the U.S. military's Defense Advanced Research Projects Agency (DARPA) built on these advances in computer networking systems to create ARPANET, or the Advanced Research Projects Agency Network (Hafner & Lyon, 1996). The architecture of the system was designed in a decentralized manner to ensure that if one point of the network was taken out, data could be rerouted through other avenues to arrive at the intended destination.

These networks and related technologies all paved the way for what would become the modern Internet. Although such networks were tremendously beneficial for many, they also provided new opportunities for offending, including the execution of social engineering frauds, and increased the possible scope and scale of such crimes (Yar, 2013, p. 11). Yet these technological advancements have done more than simply changed structures of opportunity for fraud. Such developments are inextricably intertwined with the trajectories of the hacker scene and broader culture of information security (Levy, 1984; Thomas, 2002, pp. xx–xxii).

Reflections on contemporary social engineering and its harms

From this historical context, social engineering has become an intractable part of the contemporary hacking scene and the broader information security field. Involved is a marriage of old-fashioned con-artistry techniques and technological subcultural sensibilities. The Internet and related technologies, after all, are just as much bundles of social relationships as much as they are networks of wires and signals (Thomas, 2002, pp. xx–xxii). Humans thus provide a constant and consistent point of exploitation. Yet the depictions of social engineering up to this point might give the impression that social engineering is mostly used for political protest or laugh-inducing pranks. Unfortunately, the evolution of social engineering has coincided with its use to produce significant harms as well. For example, social engineering has been used for the purposes of online harassment, like that experienced by independent video game developer Zoë Quinn (2017). In 2014, Quinn's ex-boyfriend began smearing her reputation online and rallying an online mob against her. The result was a persistent sexual harassment campaign that wound up afflicting not only Quinn, but her family, friends, and others in the gaming and media business. In her book *Crash Override*, Quinn (2017) chronicles the various strategies, some of which involved social engineering, used to make her life a living hell. She explains that people can create a fake online presence for the purposes of giving the appearance that the victim is deserving of harassment: "it takes almost no effort to make a convincing fake profile to post incriminating things that coincidentally confirm the mob's talking points" (Quinn, 2017, p. 82). She also recounts that her harassers had called her previous employers under the pretext that they were in the process of hiring Quinn and were looking for references. These calls were ruses intended to glean additional information to use against her.

Social engineering can also cost life and limb in some cases. "SWATing" or "Swatting," for example, involves manipulating 911 operators and the police into dispatching paramilitary police units to an unsuspecting victim's house under false pretenses (Philpot, 2018; U.S. Attorney's Office, 2009). SWATers make a call to 911 services (usually through a 'spoofed' line to prevent their call from being traced back to them) and claim that a fabricated scenario, such as a hostage situation, is taking place at the victim's address. If the social engineering attempt is successful, law enforcement is given the impression that they must act immediately to resolve the situation to prevent loss of life or injury. One notable SWATing case involved Matthew Weigman ('Lil' Hacker' or 'Silence'), a blind kid from Boston, who began phreaking in the late 1990s (Kushner, 2009). To retaliate against a perceived slight, Weigman spoofed a 911 call to make it look like it was coming from inside the victim's house and described an ongoing hostage situation unfolding at the residence (Kushner, 2009, pp. 71–72). According to Kushner (2009, p. 74), Weigman was "a master of what phreakers call 'social engineering'" and used those skills for both laughs and retribution. Although no one died in Weigman's scenario, SWATing has resulted in a small body count. In 2017, Los Angeles resident Tyler Barris SWATed Andrew Harris of Wichita, Kansas (Queally, 2018). Harris was shot dead by one of the responding officers.

Unsurprisingly, social engineering has also resulted in major financial damages to both individuals and organizations. Phishing scams, one form of social engineering, are estimated to cost businesses globally billions of dollars in losses per year, for example (FBI, 2017). While we should be sceptical of such loss estimates because of inaccuracies and biases in reporting (Yar, 2008), these figures still indicate that social engineering can wreak significant financial damages. Social engineering has also been involved in major contemporary data breaches, including the one that hit the Target retail chain in 2013. Malware was installed on the system of a third-party contractor, Fazio Mechanical, which allowed the attackers to gain access to Target's systems. The malware was delivered through a "phishing email" which "duped at least one Fazio employee" into downloading and executing the malicious code (Kassner, 2015). Of course, con artists have worked to deprive people of their resources long before social engineering (Maurer, 1940; Tzanelli, Yar, & O'Brien, 2005). Thus, contemporary social engineering is, in many ways, "same song, different verse."

As demonstrated in this history, the broad technological and cultural origins of social engineering have entailed that particular occurrences of this phenomenon have had a wide range of motivations as their impetus. Consequently, the targets of social engineering, as well as the techniques used by the con artists, may also vary extensively. This chapter now turns to consider a broad overview of some of the more common tactics employed by social engineers.

Social engineering – a literature review

Social engineering techniques

Techniques used by social engineers are variegated. Atkins and Huang (2013) describe these methods as falling within two general categories: "computer-based deception and human-interaction-based deception" (p. 24). Some social engineering strategies involve classic con artistry relying almost exclusively on analog communications (face-to-face, telephone, etc.). Others are facilitated by computer technologies such as email and malware. Some ruses are relatively simple and involve nothing more than a phone call and a couple of well-placed details to establish credibility, whereas other techniques are extraordinarily complicated. Approaches may have to be re-tooled on the fly as new details emerge or as the con artists inadvertently compromise their deception. In addition, some social engineers may be precise in their objectives, focusing on one actor and/or one particular organization. Others, however, may cast a wide net to find a potential target open to manipulation. Social engineering tactics may also be executed by a single offender *or* a group. For example, in one study, Leukfeldt (2014) interviewed prosecutorial and investigative personnel as well as analysed official documentation related to a case of a social engineering group who attempted to defraud two banks and their customers. He demonstrates how social engineering efforts can emerge from relatively sophisticated coordinated group efforts where members drew from each other's strengths to maximize the potential of payoff and to reduce the likelihood of being caught (see also: Leukfeldt, Kleemans, & Stol, 2017). Despite multiple attempts by scholars to create classification schemes for social engineering (see, for example, Ivaturi & Janczewski, 2011), creating a simply typology is an onerous task, as techniques used appear to only be limited by the creativity of their perpetrators.

One common thread in many social engineering frauds is the use of *pretexts*, or fabricated identities or scenarios intended to convey a seemingly credible narrative that will sway a mark into surrendering restricted information and/or access (Applegate, 2009; Atkins & Huang, 2013; Brody, Brizzee, & Cano, 2012; Mitnick & Simon, 2002). To create credible identities and to gain a familiarity with jargon, social engineers will often seek out organizational administrative hierarchy charts, employee manuals, and other documents that will give them some insider knowledge about the chain of command and operations of an organization (Berti & Rogers, 1999; Chantler & Roderic, 2006; Mitnick & Simon, 2002; Tertri & Vuorinen, 2013). The more insider details peppered into a conversation (without sounding forced), the more likely a ruse is to be accepted. Social engineers may go to great lengths to gain access to this information, going as far as sorting through the organization's waste bins (referred to as "dumpster diving" or "trashing") (Applegate, 2009; Brody et al., 2012; Krombholz, Hobel, Huber, & Weippl, 2015; Mitnick & Simon, 2002).[4] Social engineers may also "shoulder surf," or look over a person's shoulder to read information displayed on their computer monitor (Applegate, 2009; Brody et al., 2012; Krombholz et al., 2015). Many social engineers rely primarily on gathering data on readily accessible sources like social media, a process which is described as 'open source intelligence gathering,' or OSINT, a term borrowed from government espionage/intelligence circles (Bazzell, 2018; Wheatley, 2018).

Social engineers may take advantage of multiple vectors of communication to carry out their frauds. In the aforementioned example of the CWA, ruses were carried out over the phone – an approach referred to in security circles as "vishing." Recent times have also seen the emergence of text message–based frauds ("smishing"). In-person social engineering, though carrying a higher risk than other vectors, may also be used by social engineers. Although fraudsters may take advantage of seemingly any method of communication to elicit information or access, the most popular route may well be through the use of email (Huang & Brockman, 2011; Mitnick & Simon, 2002).

Perhaps the most notable email-based social engineering scam is *phishing* where the con artist attempts to pose as a trustworthy actor or organization through email (Applegate, 2009; Atkins & Huang, 2013; Brody et al., 2012; Ivaturi & Janczewski, 2011; James, 2005; Vishwanath, Herath, Chen, Wang, & Rao, 2011; Yar, 2013). These messages are typically aimed at tricking the reader into handing over login credentials. Other social engineering schemes conducted through email may involve social manipulation to convince the victims to unwittingly install malware, which allows the social engineer to have access to the victims' system, for illicit use (Applegate, 2009; Atkins & Huang, 2013; Yar, 2013). Rather than employ boilerplate language applicable to a broad audience, social engineering emails may be tailored to particular organizations or individuals, an approach often called "spear-phishing" or, if these emails target high-ranking officials in an organization, "whaling." The idea underlying this tactic is that if the con artist can invoke insider knowledge in a convincing manner, the mark may be willing to fully cooperate with illicit or otherwise unscrupulous demands.

The vast majority of empirical studies examining the success of social engineering techniques have focused on such scams conducted through email (Bakhshi, Papadaki, & Furnell, 2009; Dodge, Carver, Ferguson, 2007; Greening, 1996; Holt & Graves, 2007; Huang & Brockman, 2011; Jackobsson, Tsow, Shah, Blevis, & Lim, 2007; Jagatic, Johnson, Jackobson, & Menczer, 2007; King & Thomas, 2009; Karakasiliotis, Furnell, & Papadaki, 2006; Vishwanath et al., 2011). Experimental or quasi-experimental designs have been used to examine the susceptibility of students to these email-based scams (Bakhshi et al., 2009; Greening, 1996; Jagatic et al., 2007). For example, Bakhshi et al. (2009) conducted a phishing attack and found they could convince 23% of their sample into surrendering sensitive information. Similarly, Greening (1996) found that 47% of the students in his sample provided valid passwords in response to a researcher-designed phishing inquiry. Jagatic et al. (2007) tested the likelihood of students surrendering sensitive information based on perceived email senders. The authors found that phishing emails that appeared to be from acquaintances duped 72% of students, whereas phishing emails from strangers elicited information from only 16% of students.

Other studies have examined the ability of persons to discern between legitimate and social engineering scam emails. Using a "think-aloud" protocol, Jackobsson, Tsow, Shah, Blevis, and Lim (2007) exposed 17 subjects to both fraudulent and legitimate emails and webpages and evaluated the criteria the participants used to make judgements discerning between scam and legitimate emails/webpages. The authors concluded that emails were more likely to be considered trustworthy if (1) they appeared prototypically professional; (2) had details that closely mirrored those from known legitimate organizations, such as similar web links; (3) invoked well-known companies like Verisign; (4) did not overtly mention money or asked for passwords; (5) were personalized to the recipient; and (6) included telephone contact information for an alternative means to reply. In a similar study, Karakasiliotis et al. (2006) conducted a study where 179 participants of an online survey were asked to discern fraudulent from legitimate emails. Their results indicated that 36% were able to correctly identify legitimate emails, whereas 45% could successfully identity fraudulent emails.

Other studies have specifically examined factors associated with likelihoods of falling for phishing/email scams. A study by Dodge, Carver, and Ferguson (2007) studied the effectiveness of security awareness programs on military cadets in reducing vulnerability to phishing attempts. First, their results indicated that students in their sample were more likely to open attachments in phishing emails (50%) than follow a link (38%) or send private information (46%). Second, the authors found that security awareness increased the longer a person was at the military academy – seniors were far less likely than freshmen to fall for phishing scams. Finally, results indicated that their security awareness program appeared to increase the likelihood persons would report phishing scams the longer they were in the military academy.

Though this section focuses predominantly on email scams, as these are the most common and researched, it should be reiterated that social engineers may take advantage of multiple vectors to execute their frauds. Cutting across these strategies, however, is the fact that social engineering exploits the *human* dimensions of information security through some form of social contact. Many authors argue that one of the key reasons these techniques can be so effective is that they often rely on exploiting certain natural psychological tendencies and traits, including emotional states, perceptions, and cognitive biases (ex: Abraham & Chengalur-Smith, 2010; Applegate, 2009; King & Thomas, 2009; Vishwanath et al., 2011). It is toward these traits and characteristics this chapter now turns.

The psychology of social engineering

Previous research argues that certain human affectual states can be exploited by social engineers, including feelings of trust, fear/urgency, excitement, empathy, greed, sexual arousal, and curiosity as a means of avoiding detection or lowering defences against manipulation (Abraham & Chengalur-Smith, 2010; Applegate, 2009; Goel, Williams, Dincelli, 2017; Huang & Brockman, 2011; King & Thomas, 2009; Kopp, Layton, Sillitoe, & Gondal, 2015; Vishwanath et al., 2011; Williams, Beardmore, & Joinson, 2017). For example, social engineers may sometimes seek a "strong affect," as persons undergoing intense emotional arousal are less capable of making rational judgments about requests or demands (Chantler & Broadhurst, 2006). Emotions also help frame the meanings we have about situations, a fact that can be manipulated to create an affectual scenario that allows a social engineer to appear credible. For example, some advance-fee fraud scams invoke religious language to create favourable feelings in marks, sensations that may cloud the ability of some to recognize the dubious nature of the email (King & Thomas, 2009).

Some research has delved into the emotional aspects of social engineering frauds. Several studies, for example, have focused on exploring the emotional aspects linked to the content of fraudulent email messages (Atkins & Huang, 2013; Holt & Graves; Huang & Brockman, 2011; King & Thomas, 2009). This research finds that these emails often attempt to elicit emotional responses in marks through various pretexts such as official business, religion-laden pleas for help, and promises of great reward (Atkins & Huang, 2013; Holt & Graves, 2007; Huang & Brockman, 2011; King & Thomas, 2009). Such emotionally laden approaches in these emails are important because, as King and Thomas

(2009) describe, "A scammer ... must also create an affectively or emotionally consistent narrative that will avoid setting off an emotional response that alerts the victim to the problematic nature of the situation they are experiencing" (p. 222). Other studies have examined the impact of emotions in security decision making beyond fraudulent email messages. For example, Workman (2007a, 2007b, 2008) published a series of studies examining self-reported measures from a sample of organizational members subjected to both a phishing *and* phone-based pretext scams, the latter of which involved trained actors acting as the fraudsters. Contrary to the assertions of prior research (Holt & Graves, 2007; Huang & Brockman, 2011; Vishwanath et al., 2011), the participants in this study did not seem to react to pressures indicating urgency (Workman, 2007a). He also found support for the power of fear in fraud work, noting that fear of punishment was significant in deterring people against falling for social engineering attempts (Workman, 2008).

Beyond emotions, research has detailed psychological tendencies and biases that may be linked to vulnerability to social engineering exploitation. Many persons, for example, may lack the requisite knowledge to form a conception of legitimate and illegitimate requests for information (Aleroud & Zhou, 2017; Vishwanath et al., 2011). For some in the security field, such knowledge is described as "security awareness," or the ability to read a situation for potential security risks (e.g. Aleroud & Zhou, 2017). For example, Orgill, Romney, Bailey, and Orgill (2004) conducted a security audit and physically infiltrated an organization, posing as employees conducting research. Thirty-three employees were approached to participate in a survey as a pretext. Twenty-six willingly gave their usernames and 19 surrendered their passwords. The auditor also verbally asked them for additional "login information beyond their own network login," and seven complied, thus giving the social engineer researcher access to "company applications containing sensitive data, including financial and human resource systems" (Orgill et al., p. 179). Their observations indicated that employees in isolation, subject to employer or peer pressure, or who were not mindful of security awareness training were more likely to fall victim to the social engineering ploy. In a similar study, Junger, Montoya, and Overink (2017) approached shoppers in a Dutch shopping centre and asked them to disclose sensitive information like email addresses and bank account information. Even when priming questions and warnings were introduced, their analysis indicated that these measures failed to significantly alter disclosure rates, which were relatively high. In other words, people seem willing to disclose a surprising amount of information during in-person engagements.

Social engineers may also seek to engender a *diffusion of responsibility*. (Chantler & Broadhurst, 2006). In other words, they may convince a mark that they will not be held responsible for their actions or, at the very least, that other persons are equally culpable, thus releasing a person from perceptions of obligation and morality. Social engineers may also *overload* their targets (Chantler & Broadhurst, 2006). Most people can only keep track of so much information at any given time. The con artist can therefore bury the mark under a deluge of requests for legitimate information, thereby creating a situation where the target may not notice when an illegitimate request is slipped into the conversation. In terms of email scams, persons who are overloaded in their use of email may tend to automatically reply to requests for information without giving due thought to the potential threat of such requests (Vishwanath et al., 2011). Additionally, social engineers may often take advantage of *hubris*. For instance, "people who fall for cons are often people who have inflated views of their intelligence and competence, and, furthermore, have the 'will to believe' the scenario presented by the con artist" (King & Thomas, 2009, p. 223).

There are also numerous other psychological tendencies and biases said to be exploited by social engineers in the literature. In particular, many authors incorporate insights from the psychology of persuasion, often drawing on the prominent work of Cialdini (2001) in this field, to articulate six key psychological characteristics said to be exploited by social engineers, including:

1   *Authority*: The notion that people have a tendency to comply with reasonable demands made by persons perceived to be in positions of legitimate authority (Applegate, 2009; Chantler & Broadhurst, 2006; Cialdini, 2001; Huang & Brockman, 2011; Karakasiliotis et al., 2006; Mitnick & Simon, 2002; Schaab, Beckers, & Pape, 2017; Workman, 2007a, 2007b, 2008). As such, social engineers will attempt to convey that they are a legitimate person vested with some degree of power or respectability to pry information from a person.

2   *Scarcity:* Persons may become pliable if they believe a coveted item or outcome is in short supply, available for a short period of time, or otherwise under competitive demand (Mitnick & Simon, 2002; Karakasiliotis et al., 2006; Schaab et al., 2017; Workman, 2007a, 2007b, 2008). Such scarcity may "short-circuit" a person's ability to detect a ruse because they are given a sense of urgency about the situation (Huang & Brockman, 2011; Vishwanath et al., 2011).

3   *Likability*: The idea that persons are generally more willing to comply with requests – even if they may go against policy or their own judgement – if they feel an affinity for the social engineer or otherwise see them as compatible with their interests and identity (Mitnick & Simon, 2002; Karakasiliotis et al., 2006; Schaab, Becker, & Pape, 2017).

4   *Reciprocity*: Humans, according to Cialdini (2001), have a tendency to feel indebted to others when given something or when made to believe that some reward is incoming, and this gratitude and sense of obligation can be used to solicit information from marks (Chantler & Broadhurst, 2006; Cialdini, 2001; Mitnick & Simon, 2002; Karakasiliotis et al., 2006; Schaab et al., 2017; Workman, 2007a, 2007b, 2008).

5. *Consistency*: The idea that people generally want to maintain some degree of integrity and consistency in their actions (Mitnick & Simon, 2002; Schaab, Becker, & Pape, 2017; Workman, 2007b). If a social engineer can make the

mark believe they have some commitment or obligation, then this can be exploited.

6   *Social validation*: Finally, humans tend to look toward others to guide their actions, particularly in situations of uncertainty. Social engineers may attempt to construct a scenario where it appears as if other people are behaving in a certain manner – like giving access to a server – thus assuring the mark that they would not be alone in their actions (Mitnick & Simon, 2002).

Scholarship on social engineering frequently draws from Cialdini but, interestingly, little empirical work has been conducted on the psychological components of persuasion in the context of information security.

Some research, however, has been conducted on psychological biases and tendencies in general. Workman's (2007a, 2007b, 2008) battery of organizational-based studies provide examples of such work. One analysis found that *normative commitment* (adherence to norms and customs), *continuance commitment* (consistency/integrity), and *affective commitment* (likeability/emotional connection to others) all positively affected the likelihood of falling for social engineering scams (Workman, 2007b). Higher levels of trustingness and a willingness to kowtow to authority were also significantly associated with fraud vulnerability. Further, social engineering training "was most beneficial for those who had higher levels of commitment and trust tendencies" (Workman, 2008, p. 474), whereas ethics training appeared to have no impact (Workman, 2008). As an aside, his research also found that persons more serious about security were less likely to fall for social engineering scams (Workman, 2007a).

These are just some of the examples given by authors of psychological characteristics exploited by social engineers. Others include *truth bias, miscalculation of risk, choice supportive bias, confirmation bias, exposure effect, anchoring effects, attribution bias, optimism bias*, and the *salience effect* (Atkins & Huang, 2013; Chantler & Broadhurst, 2006; Schaab et al., 2017; Twitchell, 2009). The point, however, is that social engineers are said to take advantage of numerous features of human psychology to conduct their schemes. Despite the attention given to these psychological factors in the literature, very little research has actually been performed on social engineers and the process of social engineering.

Research that outlines the emotional and psychological characteristics exploited by offenders may give the impression that the problem lies with victims. Button and Cross (2017, p. 63) argue that "it is too easy to blame the victim for their own victimization and argue that they should have seen it coming and should have known better." Victims are not uniformly "gullible, greedy, and naïve persons" and, instead, such a view "fails to acknowledge the complexity of how many victims are targeted and the highly skilled offenders who manipulate and exploit victims through sophisticated social engineering techniques" (Button & Cross, 2017, p. 117). Though there may be variability in levels of susceptibility to various social engineering tactics, very few people are without weaknesses that can be exploited by capable fraudsters.

Conclusion

This chapter presented a cursory introduction to social engineering. Although criminology and related fields have investigated fraud and fraudsters in other areas, relatively little attention has been given to the emergence of fraud as an instrumental component of information security compromise and a practice connected to hacker subcultures and technologist subcultures more generally. Thus, we have strived to give the reader a 'crash course' on the subject in three parts. First, attention is given to the history of social engineering, rooting the practice in the history of phone phreaks and hackers. Second, we examine literature exploring the techniques used by such fraudsters – including pre-texting, phishing, vishing, and smishing, to name a few. Finally, we explored the psychological characteristics said to be exploited by social engineers in the research. It is our hope that such information can be used to inform a future research agenda for criminologists interested in the intersection of information security, fraud, and hacker/technological culture. For example, we echo Leukfeldt's (2017) call for more research on cybercrime offenders by urging more research be conducted on social engineering fraudsters. In particular, both qualitative and quantitative research should focus on the processes used by social engineers to conduct their frauds in addition to backgrounds, attitudes, perceptions, and motivations of these offenders. Narrative development and meaning making among social engineers and the broader security scene should also be investigated. Such research may prove invaluable to understand social engineering offending and situate the phenomenon within a broader social structural and cultural context. Further, although much research has been conducted that examines individual victims of fraud (e.g. Button & Cross, 2017; Button, Nicholls, & Owen, 2014; Holtfreter, Reisig, & Pratt, 2008), relatively few criminological studies have empirically examined organizations targeted by social engineering. Future research should focus on how organizations mitigate against and cope with these frauds through both policy and practice. In addition, criminologists may consider evaluating the claims described in the literature regarding the exploitation of emotional and psychological traits and tendencies by social engineers. These are only some possible areas worth investigating, however. The phenomenon of social engineering is a wide-open area for criminological inquiry.

Notes

1   Crackas With Attitude is a play on the early gangsta rap group Niggaz Wit Attitudes (NWA) incorporating "cracker," another name for security and copy-protection hackers, as well as a racial epithet for white people.
2   We will address definitional issues further in future analyses.
3   It is worth highlighting that while phreaks and hackers were generally male, women were not unheard of in these subcultural scenes, and many became very prominent (Furnell, 2002; Genosko, 2013, p. 127; Schell, Dodge, & Moutsatsos, 2002).
4   The practice of trashing dates back to the days of the phone phreakers, some of whom would dig through phone company garbage bins looking for informative technical documents (Lapsley, 2013, p. 286).

References

Abraham, S., & Chengalur-Smith, I. (2010). An overview of social engineering malware: Trends, tactics, and implications. *Technology in Society*, *32*(3), 183–196.

Aleroud, A., & Zhou, L. (2017). Phishing environments, techniques, and countermeasures: A survey. *Computers & Security*, *68*, 160–196.

Alexander, J., & Schmidt, J. K. H. (1996). Social engineering: Genealogy of a concept. In A. Podgorecki, J. Alexander, & R. Shields (Eds.), *Social engineering* (pp. 1–19). Canada: Carleton University Press.

Applegate, S. D. (2009). Social engineering: Hacking the wetware! *Information Security Journal: A Global Perspective*, *18*(1), 40–46.

Atkins, B., & Huang, W. (2013). A study of social engineering in online frauds. *Open Journal of Social Sciences*, *1*(3), 23–32.

Bakhshi, T., Papadaki, M., & Furnell, S. (2009). Social engineering: Assessing vulnerabilities in practice. *Information Management & Computer Security*, *17*(1), 53–63.

Bazzell, M. (2018). *Open source intelligence techniques* (6th ed.). CreateSpace Independent Publishing Platform.

Berti, J., & Rogers, M. (1999). Social engineering: The forgotten risk. In H. F. Tipton & M. Krause (Eds.), *Information security management handbook* (4th ed., Vol. 3, pp. 51–63). New York, NY: Auerbach Publications.

Brody, R. G., Brizzee, W. B., & Cano, L. (2012). Flying under the radar: Social engineering. *International Journal of Accounting & Information Management*, *20*(4), 335–347.

Brownell, B. A. (1983). Interpretations of twentieth-century urban progressive reform. In D. R. Colburn & G. E. Pozzetta (Eds.), *Reform and reformers in the progressive era* (pp. 3–23). Westport, CT: Greenwood Press.

Button, M., & Cross, C. (2017). *Cyber frauds, scams and their victims*. New York, NY: Routledge.

Button, M., Nicholls, C. M., & Owen, J. K. R. (2014). Online frauds: Learning from victims why they fall for these scams. *Australian & New Zealand Journal of Criminology*, *47*(3), 391–408.

Chantler, A., & Broadhurst, R. (2006). *Social engineering and crime prevention in cyberspace*. Brisbane, QLD, Australia: Queensland University of Technology. Technical report retrieved from http://eprints.qut.edu.au/7526/1/7526.pdf

Cheshire, R. (1996). *The TAP newsletter*. Retrieved March 14, 2018, from http://cheshire-catalyst.com/tap.html

Cialdini, R. B. (2001). The science of persuasion. *Scientific American*, *284*(2), 76–81.

Coleman, G. E. (2012). Phreakers, hackers, and trolls and the politics of transgression and spectable. In M. Mandiberg (Ed.), *The social media reader* (pp. 99–119). New York, NY: New York University Press.

Dixon, H. (2018, January 19). British 15-year-old gained access to intelligence operations in Afghanistan and Iran by pretending to be head of CIA, court hears. *The Telegraph*. Retrieved March 6, 2018, from www.telegraph.co.uk/news/2018/01/19/british-15-year-old-gained-access-intelligence-operations-afghanistan/

Dodge, R. C., Carver, C., & Ferguson, A. J. (2007). Phishing for user security awareness. *Computers & Security*, *26*(1), 73–80.

Edwin, E. L. (1911). *The social engineer*. New York, NY: Eaton & Mains.

FBI (Federal Bureau of Investigation). (2017, May 4). Business e-mail compromise e-mail account compromise: The 5 billion dollar scam. Retrieved March 22, 2018 from www.ic3.gov/media/2017/170504.aspx#fn3

Franceschi-Bicchierai, L. (2015a, November 5). Teenage hackers say they've doxed more than 2,000 government employees. *Motherboard*. Retrieved March 7, 2018, from https://motherboard.vice.com/en_us/article/9a39v7/teenage-hackers-say-theyve-doxxed-more-than-3500-government-employees

Franceschi-Bicchierai, L. (2015b, October 19). Teen hackers: A '5-year-old' could have hacked into CIA director's emails. *Motherboard*. Retrieved March 7, 2018, from https://motherboard.vice.com/en_us/article/8q84gx/teen-hackers-a-5-year-old-could-have-hacked-into-cia-directors-emails

Furnell, S. (2002). *Cybercrime*. Boston, MA: Addison-Wesley.

Genosko, G. (2013). *When technocultures collide: Innovation from below and the struggle for autonomy.* Waterloo, Ontario, Canada: Wilfred Laurier University Press.

Goel, S., Williams, K., & Dincelli, E. (2017). Got phished? Internet security and human vulnerability. *Journal of the Association for Information Systems, 18*(1), 22–44.

Graebner, W. (1987). *The engineering of consent: Democracy and authority in Twentieth- Century America.* Madison, WA: The University of Wisconsin Press.

Greening, T. (1996). Ask and ye shall receive: A study in "social engineering". *ACM SIGSAC Review, 14*(2), 8–14.

Hadnagy, C. (2014). *Unmasking the social engineer: The human element of security.* Indianapolis, IN: Wiley.

Hafner, K., & Lyon, M. (1996). *Where the wizards stay up late: The origins of the Internet.* New York, NY: Simon & Schuster.

Holt, T. J., & Graves, D. C. (2007). A qualitative analysis of advance fee fraud e-mail schemes. *International Journal of Cyber Criminology, 1*(1), 137–154.

Holtfreter, K., Reisig, M. D., & Pratt, T. C. (2008). Low self-control, routine activities, and fraud victimization. *Criminology, 46*(1), 189–220.

Huang, W., & Brockman, A. (2011). Social engineering exploitations in online communications: Examining persuasions used in fraudulent emails. In T. Holt (Ed.), *Crime online: Correlates, causes, and context* (pp. 87–111). Durham, NC: Carolina Academic Press.

Ivaturi, K., & Janczewski, L. (2011). *A taxonomy for social engineering attacks.* Proceedings from CONF-IRM '11. Paper 15. Retrieved from http://aisel.aisnet.org/cgi/viewcontent.cgi?article=1015&context=confirm2011

Jackobsson, M., Tsow, A., Shah, A., Blevis, E., & Lim Y. (2007). What instills trust? A qualitative study of phishing. In S. Dietrich & R. Dhamija (Eds.), *Financial cryptographic and data security: 11th international conference, FC 2007, and 1st international workshop on useable security, USEC 2007, Scarborough, Trinidad and Tobago, February 12–16, 2007. Revised Selected Papers* (pp. 356–361). Berlin, Germany: Springer-Verlag.

Jacobellis v. Ohio, 378 U.S. 184, 1964.

Jagatic, T. N., Johnson, N. A., Jackobsson, M., & Menczer, F. (2007). Social phishing. *Communications of the ACM, 50*(10), 94–100.

James, L. (2005). *Phishing exposed: Uncover secrets from the dark side.* Rockland, MA: Syngress Publishing.

Junger, M., Montoya, L., & Overink, F. J. (2017). Priming and warnings are not effective to prevent social engineering attacks. *Computers in Human Behavior, 66,* 75–87.

Karakasiliotis, A., Furnell, S. M., & Papadaki, M. (2006). *Assessing end-user awareness of social engineering and phishing.* Proceedings of the 7th Australian Information Warfare and Security Conference, Edith Cowan University, Perth, WA, December 4–5, 2006. Retrieved from http://ro.ecu.edu.au/isw/12

Kassner, M. (2015, February 2). Anatomy of the Target data breach: Missed opportunities and lessons learned. *ZDNet*. Retrieved March 22, 2018, from www.zdnet.com/article/anatomy-of-the-target-data-breach-missed-opportunities-and-lessons-learned/

King, A., & Thomas, J. (2009). You can't cheat an honest man: Making ($$$s and) sense of the Nigerian e-mail scams. In F. Schmalleger & M. Pittaro (Eds.), *Crimes of the internet* (pp. 206–224). Upper Saddle River, NJ: Prentice Hall.

Kopp, C., Layton, R., Sillitoe, J., & Gondal, I. (2015). The role of love stories in romance scams: A qualitative analysis of fraudulent profiles. *International Journal of Cyber Criminology, 9*(2), 205–217.

Krombholz, K., Hobel, H., Huber, M., & Weippl, E. (2015). Advanced social engineering attacks. *Journal of Information Security Applications, 22*, 113–122.

Kushner, D. (2009, September 3). The boy who heard too much. *Rolling Stone* (1086), 70–97.

Lapsley, P. (2013). *Exploding the phone: The Untold story of the teenagers and outlaws who hacked Ma Bell*. New York, NY: Grove Press.

Larsson, B., Letell, M., & Thörn, H. (2012). Transformations of the Swedish welfare state: Social engineering, governance and governmentality – An introduction. In B. Larsson, M. Letell, & H. Thörn (Eds.), *Transformations of the Swedish welfare state: From social engineering to social governance?* (pp. 3–22). New York, NY: Palgrave Macmillan.

Layton, E. T. (1971). *The revolt of the engineers: Social responsibility and the American engineering profession*. Cleveland, OH: The Press of Case Western Reserve University.

Leukfeldt, E. R. (2014). Cybercrime and social ties: Phishing in Amsterdam. *Trends in Organized Crime, 17*(4), 231–249.

Leukfeldt, E. R. (2017). *Research agenda: The human factor in cybercrime and cybersecurity*. The Hague, The Netherlands: Eleven International Publishing.

Leukfeldt, E. R., Kleemans, E. R., & Stol, W. P. (2017). Criminal networks, social ties and online forums: Social ties versus digital ties within phishing and malware networks. *British Journal of Criminology, 57*(3), 704–722.

Levy, S. (1984). *Hackers: Heroes of the computer revolution*. New York, NY: Penguin.

Massey, N. (2018, January 21). Kane Gamble: Teenager with autism on Leicestershire housing estate took classified information by fooling people into thinking he was FBI boss. *Independent*. Retrieved March 7, 2018, from www.independent.co.uk/news/uk/crime/us-intelligence-cia-fbi-american-government-john-brennan-mark-giuliano-crackas-with-attitude-latest-a8170561.html

Maurer, D. W. (1940). *The big con: The story of the confidence men*. New York, NY: Anchor Books.

McClymer, J. F. (1980). *War and welfare: Social engineering in America, 1890–1925*. Westport, CT: Greenwood Press.

McLeod, K. (2014). *Pranksters: Making mischief in the modern world*. New York, NY: New York University Press.

Mitnick, K., & Simon, W. L. (2002). *The art of deception: Controlling the human element of security*. Indianapolis, IN: Wiley.

Mitnick, K., & Simon, W. L. (2011). *Ghost in the wires: My adventures as the world's most wanted hacker*. New York, NY: Little, Brown and Company.

O'Neill, P. H. (2017, September 8). Member of group who hacked CIA director's email is sentenced to 5 years in prison. *Cyberscoop*. Retrieved March 7, 2018, from www.cyberscoop.com/member-of-group-who-hacked-cia-directors-aol-email-sentenced-to-5-years-in-prison/

Orgill, G. L., Romney, G. W., Bailey, M. G., & Orgill, P. M. (2004). The urgency for effective user privacy-education to counter social engineering attacks on secure computer systems. In *Proceedings from CITE5 '04: The fifth conference on information technology education* (pp. 177–181). Salt Lake City, UT and New York, NY: ACM.

Orth, M. (1971, October 31). For whom Ma Bell tolls not. *Los Angeles Times*. Retrieved March 10, 2018, from www.historyofphonephreaking.org/docs/orth1971.pdf

Pfaffenberger, B. (1988). The social meaning of the personal computer: Or, why the personal computer revolution was no revolution. *Anthropological Quarterly, 61*, 39–47.

Philpot, D. (2018). Symbolic interactionism and technocrime: SWATing as episodic and agentic. In K. F. Steinmetz & M. R. Nobles (Eds.), *Technocrime and criminological theory* (pp. 85–101). New York, NY: Routledge.

Queally, J. (2018, January 26). Fictitious shooting in video game sparked real-life shooting in Kansas swatting case, records show. *Los Angeles Times*. Retrieved March 22, 2018, from www.latimes.com/local/lanow/la-me-ln-kansas-swatting-records-20180126-story.html

Quinn, Z. (2017). *Crash override: How Gamergate [nearly] destroyed my life, and how we can win the fight against online hate.* New York, NY: Public Affairs.

Rid, T. (2016). *Rise of the machines: A Cybernetic history.* New York, NY: W. W. Norton & Company.

Rosenbaum, R. (1971, October). Secrets of the little blue box. *Esquire*, 117–125, 222–225. Retrieved March 10, 2018, from www.historyofphonephreaking.org/docs/rosenbaum1971.pdf

Schaab, P., Beckers, K., & Pape, S. (2017). Social engineering defence mechanisms and counteracting training strategies. *Information & Computer Security, 25*(2), 206–222.

Schell, B. H., Dodge, J. L., & Moutsatsos, S. S. (2002). *The hacking of America.* Westport, CT: Quorum Books.

The Shadow. (1985, January). Wiretapping and divestiture: A lineman speaks out. *2600: The Hacker Quarterly, 2*(1), 1.

Sterling, B. (1992). *The hacker crackdown: Law and disorder on the electronic frontier.* New York, NY: Bantam Books.

Taylor, P. A. (1999). *Hackers: Crime in the digital sublime.* New York, NY: Routledge.

Tertri, P., & Vuorinen, J. (2013). Dissecting social engineering. *Behaviour & Information Technology, 32*(10), 1014–1023.

Thomas, D. (2002). *Hacker culture.* Minneapolis, MN: University of Minnesota Press.

Tolman, W. H. (1909). *Social engineering: A record of things done by American industrialists employing upwards of one and one-half million of people.* New York, NY: McGraw Publishing Company.

Turkle, S. (1984). *The second self: Computers and the human spirit.* New York, NY: Simon and Schuster.

Twitchell, D. P. (2009). Social engineering and its countermeasures. In M. Gupta & R. Sharman (Eds.), *Handbook of research on social and organizational liabilities in information security* (pp. 228–242). Hershey, PA: Information Science Reference.

Tzanelli, R., Yar, M., & O'Brien, M. (2005). "Con me if you can": Exploring crime in the American cinematic imagination. *Theoretical Criminology, 9*(1), 97–117.

U.S. Attorney's Office. (2009, January 29). Individual pleads guilty in Swatting conspiracy case: Defendant faces 13 years in federal prison. Retrieved March 14, 2018, from https://archives.fbi.gov/archives/dallas/press-releases/2009/dl012909.htm

Vishwanath, A., Herath, T., Chen, R., Wang, J., & Rao, H. R. (2011). Why do people get phished? Testing individual differences in phishing vulnerability within an integrated, information processing model. *Decision Support Systems, 51*(3), 576–586.

Wheatley, B. (2018). British open source intelligence (OSINT) and the Holocaust in the Soviet Union: Persecution, extermination and partisan warfare. *Intelligence and National Security, 33*(3), 422–438.

Williams, E. J., Beardmore, A., & Joinson, A. N. (2017). Individual differences in susceptibility to online influence: A theoretical review. *Computers in Human Behavior, 72*, 412–421.

Workman, M. (2007a). Gaining access with social engineering: An empirical study of the threat. *Information Systems Security, 16*(6), 315–331.

Workman, M. (2007b). Wisecrackers: A theory-grounded investigation of phishing and pre-text social engineering threats to information security. *Journal of the Association for Information Science and Technology, 59*(4), 662–674.

Workman, M. (2008). A test of interventions for security threats from social engineering. *Information Management & Computer Security, 16*(5), 463–483.

Yar, M. (2008). Computer crime control as industry: Virtual insecurity and the market for private policing. In K. F. Aas, H. O. Gundhus, & H. M. Lomell (Eds.), *Technologies of insecurity: The surveillance of everyday life* (pp. 189–204). New York, NY: Routledge-Cavendish.

Yar, M. (2013). *Cybercrime and society* (2nd ed.). Thousand Oaks, CA: Sage.

Zetter, K. (2015a, November 6). CIA email hackers return with major law enforcement breach. *Wired.* Retrieved March 7, 2018, from www.wired.com/2015/11/cia-email-hackers-return-with-major-law-enforcement-breach/

Zetter, K. (2015b, October 19, 2015). Teen who hacked CIA director's email tells how he did it. *Wired.* Retrieved March 7, 2018, from www.wired.com/2015/10/hacker-who-broke-into-cia-director-john-brennan-email-tells-how-he-did-it/

9 Contrasting cyber-dependent and traditional offenders

A comparison on criminological explanations and potential prevention methods

Marleen Weulen Kranenbarg

Introduction

Until recently, social scientists have not seen cybercrime prevention as one of their tasks. When comparing the number of cybercrime-related publications in criminology with the growth in Internet users, it is clear that criminological research has not kept pace with the growth in potential cyber-offenders and victims (see Figure 9.1).

Cybercrime prevention has long been the domain of computer sciences only. They develop technical solutions to protect IT systems and prevent victimization. Until recently, criminologists have not contributed much to the prevention of cybercriminal use of IT systems. However, from a criminological standpoint, a focus on the offender is very important, as prevention on the offender side can stop cybercrimes from being committed in the first place. Therefore, some criminologists have started to use traditional criminological explanations to study cyber-offending (for reviews, see Holt & Bossler, 2014; Leukfeldt, De Poot, Verhoeven, Kleemans, & Lavorgna, 2017; Weulen Kranenbarg, Van Der Laan et al., 2017). These studies have provided some very important empirical insights into the applicability of traditional criminological explanations for cyber-offending.

Even though these studies have shown to be very valuable in understanding cyber-offending, possible differences between cyber-offenders and traditional offenders have generally only been addressed in theoretical articles (Grabosky, 2001; Yar, 2005a, 2005b) or case studies (Pontell & Rosoff, 2009). Large-scale empirical comparative research is very rare. This chapter will first discuss cyber-dependent offending and possible differences between cyber-dependent offenders and traditional offenders. Subsequently, it will be discussed how these differences may affect traditional explanations for offending on important domains in criminology: offending over the life course, personal and situational risk factors for offending, and cyber-deviant behaviour in social networks. Afterwards, existing empirical research and some recent empirical comparisons with traditional offenders in these domains will be discussed. The

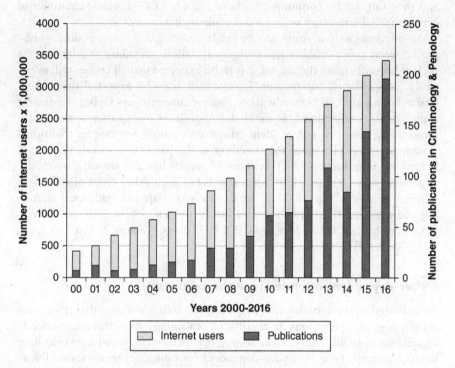

Figure 9.1 Number of Internet users and number of cybercrime-related publications in *Criminology & Penology* between 2000 and 2016

chapter concludes with a discussion of motives for offending and implications for prevention and future research.

Cyber-dependent crime

This chapter will focus on what is called cyber-dependent crime. In general, the literature discusses two categories of cybercrime: cyber-dependent crime and cyber-enabled crime (e.g. Gordon & Ford, 2006; McGuire & Dowling, 2013a, 2013b; Zhang, Xiao, Ghaboosi, Zhang, & Deng, 2012). For cyber-dependent crime, using an IT system is necessary in the commission of the crime. These are new crimes that did not exist before IT systems were introduced. Additionally, the main targets of these crimes are IT systems. Even though there may be human victims who are the owner of the systems, the primary targets are the IT systems. Examples are malicious hacking, malware attacks, distributed denial of service (DDoS) attacks, web defacements, etc. Cyber-enabled crimes, on the other hand, are traditional crimes that now use IT systems in the commission of the crime. These crimes already existed before IT systems were introduced, and they can still be committed without the use of IT systems. Examples of cyber-enabled crimes are online fraud, stalking, harassment, etc.

All offences could in some way be cyber-enabled, which makes distinguishing between cyber-enabled and completely offline offending problematic. As society becomes more digitalized, it is to be expected that all crimes will eventually have a digital component. Therefore, it is to be expected that cyber-enabled crime and other crime will become the same category. Cyber-dependent crime, on the other hand, is more distinguishable from other crime. More importantly, these cyber-dependent crimes are a unique test case for traditional criminological explanations for offending, as the latter were mainly developed before the introduction of IT systems. Research has also shown that cyber-dependent offenders are clearly distinguishable from other types of offenders, whereas cyber-enabled offending shows a large overlap with traditional offending and therefore these are also more similar to those offences (Rokven, Weijters, Beerthuizen, & Van Der Laan, 2018; Rokven, Weijters, & Van Der Laan, 2017; Weulen Kranenbarg, 2018).

Cyber-dependent offenders: are they different?

As indicated in the introduction, empirical research has shown that traditional criminological explanations are valuable in explaining cyber-dependent offending. Elements of life-course criminology, risk factors, and social networks have been empirically linked to cyber-dependent offending (for reviews, see Holt & Bossler, 2014; Leukfeldt et al., 2017; Weulen Kranenbarg, Van Der Laan et al., 2017). These results, which will be discussed in more detail later in this chapter, suggest that cyber-dependent offending is similar to traditional offending. However, as indicated, there are also empirical and theoretical reasons to expect that there are important differences. In this section some overall differences will be discussed, after which the next section will explain how these overall differences may affect explanations for offending in the domains that are the focus of this chapter.

The overarching reason that cyber-dependent offending may be different from traditional offending is that cyber-dependent offences heavily rely on IT systems, as these are the main targets and necessary in the commission of the crime. Crime committed in the context of IT systems could have several unique characteristics that have an impact on traditional criminological explanations for why and how these crimes are committed. This would in turn result in different empirical correlates. The more a crime script relies on the use of an IT system (i.e. if the crime is cyber-dependent), the more prominent these unique characteristics are expected to be.

First of all, the more cyber-dependent a crime is, the more anonymous it can be (Campbell & Kennedy, 2012; Jaishankar, 2009; Suler, 2004). Cyber-offenders can hide their identity and therefore hide their criminal behaviour. This leads to the second difference with traditional offending. As it is hard to trace an anonymous cyber-offender, apprehension rates for cyber-offending are much lower than they are for traditional offending. This means that the anonymity of cyber-offending results in a lower likelihood of getting caught and being prosecuted. Third, it also means that less negative social consequences are to be expected when committing a cyber-dependent crime, compared to when committing a traditional crime. The social environment may not be aware of the online behaviour of a cybercriminal, which means that a cybercriminal may not expect any negative social consequences for his or her behaviour.

In addition to the lower likelihood of both formal and informal (i.e. social) sanctions for cyber-offending, a fourth difference with traditional offending may be that the digital context may also result in what has been called online disinhibition (Suler, 2004). This disinhibition may limit the felt responsibility for online actions. As the digital world feels disconnected from the real world, a person may not feel any responsibilities for online actions, especially not for cyber-dependent crime, as the main target is a computer and the human victim behind that computer may be unknown. This leads to the fifth possible difference with traditional crime, as the consequences for both the victim and the offender may be invisible or perceived to be non-existent (Goldsmith & Brewer, 2015; Jaishankar, 2009; Suler, 2004; Yar, 2013). These all lead to the expectation that the threshold for committing a cyber-dependent crime is lower, as no negative consequences are expected and visible.

However, even if the threshold is low, not everybody will have the opportunity to commit these offences. So as a sixth difference, criminal opportunities for committing cyber-dependent crimes arise in completely different situations from traditional criminal opportunities (Miro Llinares & Johnson, 2018). These are situations where IT systems are present, which is normally not the case in traditional criminogenic settings like on the streets and in nightlife areas. In order to maximize these opportunities, a person also needs the skills to commit cyber-dependent crimes, which is the seventh difference with traditional offences. It should be said, however, that because of cybercrime-as-a-service (i.e. easy-to-buy and -use toolkits for committing cybercrime), even people with fewer IT skills are able to commit these offences. Nevertheless, knowing about these services may still require at least some IT knowledge and skills.

The last difference relates to these skills and the need to be patient in order to learn them. Most traditional offenders have low self-control (Gottfredson & Hirschi, 1990; Pratt & Cullen, 2000). They are less capable of investing in their future. For cyber-dependent offending, on the other hand, patience and investment are required to learn some of the skills that are needed to commit these offences. To some extent, these skills could be socially learned from friends by imitation (Akers, 1998; Holt, Bossler, & May, 2012; Holt, Burruss, & Bossler, 2010; Morris & Blackburn, 2009; Sutherland, 1947). However, trial and error, which requires a lot of time and effort, is often an important part of acquiring these skills (Chiesa, Ducci, & Ciappi, 2008c; Fotinger & Ziegler, 2004; Holt, 2007). In addition, especially for the more sophisticated types of cyber-dependent crime, an offender also needs to be very patient and precise to be able to plan and execute an attack. For example, the offender first needs to find a vulnerability in an IT system and then think of ways to exploit that vulnerability.

Implications for criminological explanations of offending

All eight differences discussed here may have implications for well-established criminological findings on who commits crime and when, where, how, and why these people commit crime. This chapter will focus on the implications of several important domains in criminology, as these are the domains in which cyber-offenders have recently been empirically compared with traditional offenders (Weulen Kranenbarg, 2018). Nevertheless, the discussion section will stress the importance of future comparative research in other domains.

Life course

Life-course criminology is a very important area of research which seeks to identify factors that are related to the onset, acceleration, and desistance in criminal careers. Variation in offending over the life course can be analysed from several different angles. Trajectory analysis indicates different types of offending careers (e.g. Moffitt, 1993), turning points, or life events like marriage may change a criminal career (Sampson & Laub, 1993a), and differences in the strength of social bonds and social control in different life circumstances may explain differences in offending over the life course (e.g. Hirschi, 1969; Laub & Sampson, 1993). This chapter will focus on the latter perspective by discussing how social bonds, social control, and activities in certain life circumstances are related to offending.

When a person has strong social relationships in both personal as well as professional life, that person will be less likely to commit traditional crime (e.g. Hirschi, 1969; Laub & Sampson, 1993). The most important examples of these strong relationships are being married (or living together with a family) and being employed. In these circumstances, there is a lot of both direct and indirect social control of others, for example, family or colleagues. Their presence during daily activities reduces opportunities to commit traditional crime without anyone noticing (i.e. direct social control). Committing a crime may also have very significant consequences when a person has strong social relationships (i.e. indirect social control). Offending may, for example, result in ending those relationships or losing employment. This is likely why these circumstances have been shown to reduce the likelihood of traditional offending (for reviews, see Kazemian, 2015; Lageson & Uggen, 2013; Skardhamar, Savolainen, Aase, & Lyngstad, 2015). However, because of the anonymity and hidden nature of cyber-dependent crime, a person's social environment may be unable to detect any cyber-dependent criminal behaviour. This means that one's social environment may be less capable of exerting direct social control. In addition, as a cyber-dependent offender may expect no negative social consequences, this person may not experience any indirect social control of strong social bonds like family (Weulen Kranenbarg, Ruiter, Van Gelder, & Bernasco, 2018).

Apart from the control theory explanations earlier, another explanation for the protective effect of some life circumstances is that these circumstances generally reduce criminal opportunities during daily activities. For example, when a person has a family and/or if a person is employed, there is simply less time to spend in nightlife areas and other criminogenic settings (e.g. Wilcox, Land, & Hunt, 2003). In contrast, opportunities for cyber-dependent crime arise in situations where IT systems are present. This is the case for most types of employment (Statistics Netherlands, 2015), especially if a person is employed in the IT sector. In short, as both expected social consequences from and opportunities for cyber-dependent offending differ from traditional offending, correlates of offending over the life course may also be different.

Situational and personal risk factors

Traditionally, criminal opportunities arise in situations where offenders and victims meet in place and time in the absence of a capable guardian (Cohen & Felson, 1979). This place has always been seen as a physical place. For cyber-offending there have been some theoretical discussions about the question as to what extent cyberspace could still be seen as a place where offenders and victims converge (Brady, Randa, & Reyns, 2016; Grabosky, 2001; Miro Llinares & Johnson, 2018; Suler, 2004; Yar, 2005a, 2005b, 2013). The general tendency in the literature is that it could still fit in this paradigm. Yet as cybercriminal opportunities also arise in cyberspace, having daily activities in which a person is more exposed to cyberspace can increase risks for victimization and opportunities for offending.

In addition to these opportunities, the more sophisticated a cybercrime gets, the more personal characteristics will also play a role. More sophisticated crimes require greater IT skills and more patience. Traditional offending may require some skills, but the skills needed for cyber-dependent offending are completely different. Additionally, while low self-control is seen as an important predictor of offending behaviuor for traditional offenders (Gottfredson & Hirschi, 1990; Pratt & Cullen, 2000), cyber-offenders may need high self-control in order to learn skills, execute complex attacks, and cover their tracks (Bossler & Burruss, 2011; Holt & Kilger, 2008).

Social networks

With respect to traditional criminal behaviour, same-aged peers tend to be very similar. So, if a person commits crimes, chances are that his or her peers also commit crimes. This similarity in behaviour of social ties is the result of both social learning and selection processes (Haynie & Kreager, 2013; Pratt et al., 2009; Warr, 2002; Weerman & Smeenk, 2005; J. T. N. Young & Rees, 2013). With respect to social learning, the skills and social norms that are needed to commit a crime can be learned through interaction with social contacts (Akers, 1998; Hirschi, 1969; Pratt et al., 2009; Sampson & Laub, 1993b). For cyber-crime, learning specific skills may be even more important. The question is how these skills are learned. If these are learned from social ties, are these traditional strong and offline ties, or online and possibly less strong ties? It may also be the case that skills are not or not only learned from social ties, but from other online or offline sources.

With regard to social selection processes, selecting peers who also commit crimes will reduce the negative social consequences of one's own criminal behaviour. Criminal peers will likely approve that behaviour instead of disapproving it (Flashman & Gambetta, 2014; Hirschi, 1969; Kalmijn, 1998; McPherson, Smith-Lovin, & Cook, 2001). However, a person can easily hide cybercriminal behaviour because of its anonymity. Friends will likely never find out about this behaviour, which means that for a cyber-offender it may is not be necessary to select cybercriminal peers as friends (Weulen Kranenbarg, Ruiter, & Van Gelder, 2019). Both in the light of selection and influence of peers, there are reasons to expect differences in the extent to which peers show similarity in cybercriminal behaviour.

Empirical research on cyber-dependent offenders

In order to evaluate to what extent traditional prevention methods can still prevent cyber-dependent offending, or if new prevention methods should be developed for these offences, it is important to look at empirical evidence for the applicability of traditional explanations of offending for cyber-offending. As discussed in the introduction, a majority of criminological research on cyber-offending to date has focused on applying traditional theories and explanations for offending to cyber-offending (for reviews, see Holt & Bossler, 2014; Leukfeldt et al., 2017; Weulen Kranenbarg, Van Der Laan et al., 2017). This research could provide some insight into the applicability of these explanations. Additionally, a recent empirical study compared cyber-dependent offenders with traditional offenders (Weulen Kranenbarg, 2018). This empirical comparison could indicate if the explanations are just as strong for cyber-offending as they are for traditional offending. This could provide some insight into the expected relevance of traditional prevention methods for cyber-offending. This section will both discuss research about cyber-offending on the domains discussed earlier and the comparison with traditional offending. It will end with a section on motives, which strongly relates to the next section on prevention.

Life course

In life-course criminology, longitudinal data are key to understanding the causal influence of within-individual changes in life circumstances on offending. Detailed survey data over a long period of a person's life are especially necessary to understand exactly how these life circumstances relate to offending.

For cyber-offending, such in-depth, long-term longitudinal data have not yet been collected. The results from a few qualitative empirical studies and some cross-sectional studies, however, provide some initial ideas on which turning points in someone's life may result in desistence from cyber-dependent crime.

Some studies, for example, suggest that people who commit cybercrimes tend to be single, live with their parents, and may stop committing crimes when they get more responsibilities in their lives (Fotinger & Ziegler, 2004; Gordon, 2000; Young, Zhang, & Prybutok, 2007). Others also suggest that moral development plays a role. Just as traditional offenders, cyber-offenders would age out of cyber-offending when they develop their moral reasoning (Gordon, 1994; Rogers, Smoak, & Liu, 2006). Similarly, a longitudinal study based on police data from the Netherlands showed that criminal hackers have a comparable age–crime curve as most traditional offenders (Ruiter & Bernaards, 2013). These results suggest that the life course of cyber-offenders is similar to that of traditional offenders. In contrast, however, with respect to professional life circumstances, the employment effect seems to be less clear. In line with traditional offending, employment may reduce cyber-offending, as most malicious hackers interviewed by Chiesa, Ducci, and Ciappi (2008b) state that they will stop committing crimes when they get a legitimate job in the IT sector. On the other hand, it is suggested that cyber-offending may be more similar to white-collar offending in which employment could actually provide an opportunity to commit crime (Turgeman-Goldschmidt, 2011). In addition, cybercrimes against businesses may be committed by so-called insiders, who are or were employed by that business (Nykodym, Taylor, & Vilela, 2005; Randazzo, Keeney, Kowalski, Cappelli, & Moore, 2005). Similarly, students may find opportunities to commit cybercrimes in their daily use of their school's IT systems (Lu, Jen, Chang, & Chou, 2006; Maimon, Kamerdze, Cukier, & Sobesto, 2013; Xu, Hu, & Zhang, 2013).

In order to find out to what extent the suggested differences between cyber-offending and traditional offending result in different life circumstances that are related to offending or desistance for cyber-dependent crime, a longitudinal dataset was constructed based on Dutch registration data (Weulen Kranenbarg, Ruiter et al., 2018). This dataset contained information on offending registered in the police systems and both the personal life circumstances (i.e. household composition) and the professional life circumstances (i.e. employment or enrolment in education). For each year in the period of 2000–2012, this study conducted within-individual analyses to examine in which life circumstances people tend to commit a cyber-dependent crime or a traditional crime. In line with the studies earlier with respect to personal life circumstances that may reduce offending, this comparison showed that cyber-dependent offences are also less likely to be committed in the years in which a person lives together with a partner or with a family. These crimes tend to be committed in the years in which people live alone or when they are a single parent, which is similar to the personal life circumstances that are related to traditional offending. Furthermore, these effects were even statistically significantly stronger for cyber-offending than for traditional offending.

With respect to the professional life, however, the study found that whereas traditional offenders tend to commit their crimes in years in which they are unemployed and not enrolled in education, for cyber-offending these professional life circumstances were not statistically significantly in relation to offending. Additionally, as this dataset contained the complete Dutch offender population, it was also interesting to see that although the results were not statistically significant, these suggested that employment in the IT sector and being enrolled in education could actually increase cyber-offending instead of decreasing it. As these results were not statistically significant and these analyses were only based on police and registration data, future research should find out to what extent and how employment and education could provide opportunities for cyber-offending, while social control is not able to prevent that offending from taking place. The measures based on registration data used in this study, cannot provide the in-depth information that is needed to test which of these theoretical assumptions explain the relation between certain life circumstances and cyber-dependent offending (Weulen Kranenbarg, Ruiter et al., 2018).

Situational and personal risk factors

As discussed in the previous section, longitudinal data on cyber-offending is very rare. Therefore, when looking at risk factors, it should be noted that these generally are correlates, as the cross-sectional nature of research in this area could not provide any causal evidence of risk factors related to cyber-offending.

Situational risk factors relate to the activities that typically increase exposure to opportunities for cyber-dependent offending. In general, research on routine activities and cybercrime tends to focus on victims. A person is more likely to be victimized if that person spends more time online. For example, online communication and social media use increases hacking victimization (Leukfeldt & Yar, 2016). For offending, however, there has not yet been a clear focus on daily activities that could increase opportunities for cyber-offending. The life-course study discussed earlier, however, suggests that some daily activities, like some forms of employment, may increase those opportunities and risks. Additionally, with respect to knowledge, forums and other online sources of information on cyber-dependent attacks could provide a person the information that is needed to commit these crimes. Therefore, spending more time on these platforms could be related to cyber-dependent offending as well (Holt, Strumsky, Smirnova, & Kilger, 2012; Hutchings, 2014). Some studies also suggest that some online gaming environments provide opportunities to start committing cyber-offences (Blackburn, Kourtellis, Skvoretz, Ripeanu, & Iamnitchi, 2014; Hu, Xu, & Yayla, 2013; National Crime Agency, 2017b), which may also be important in understanding the life course of offenders as discussed earlier.

In addition to these actual activities or situations, when confronted with the opportunity to commit a cyber-dependent crime, a person needs the ability to actually commit that crime. Several studies have shown that IT skills are related to cyber-dependent offending (Holt, Bossler et al., 2012; Morris & Blackburn, 2009). As discussed earlier, this knowledge could be learned from online sources or from peers. Delinquent peers are also a very important correlate of cyber-offending, but these will be discussed in more detail in the next section.

Knowledge is a personal characteristic that enables a person to use an opportunity to commit a cyber-dependent crime. However, there are other personal characteristics that may also relate to cyber-offending. Up until now there is no clear empirical evidence for specific personality characteristics that are related to cyber-dependent offending. Research that has been done in this area has not found any statistically significant results or results that contradict each other (e.g. Rogers et al., 2006; Seigfried & Treadway, 2014). Additionally, although research on this part is limited, there is some empirical work that suggests that some forms of autism may be related to hacking (Harvey, Bolgan, Mosca, McLean, & Rusconi, 2016; Schell & Melnychuk, 2011). One part of personality, however, needs specific attention: self-control. This part of personality is strongly linked to traditional offending (Gottfredson & Hirschi, 1990; Pratt & Cullen, 2000). Some studies have also shown that it is related to cyber-dependent offending, but others have shown that the more sophisticated types of cybercrime may require high self-control (Bossler & Burruss, 2011; Holt & Kilger, 2008; Weulen Kranenbarg, Holt, & Van Gelder, 2017). It is possible that studies that find a relationship between low self-control and offending have a sample of people who commit relatively low-skilled offences, whereas other studies may reflect relatively highly skilled offences.

Studies on victimization generally also include offending as a predictor. These studies show that offending is related to victimization (Bossler & Holt, 2009; Kerstens & Jansen, 2016; Morris, 2011; Ngo & Paternoster, 2011), which means that victimization should also be studied as a correlate of cyber-offending. However, as these studies are generally cross-sectional instead of longitudinal, it is unclear to what extent the relationship between offending and victimization is causal. An overlap between offending and victimization is also observed for traditional crime, and it has been shown that this overlap is only partially causal (for reviews, see Berg & Felson, 2016; Jennings, Piquero, & Reingle, 2012; Lauritsen & Laub, 2007). In addition to a causal relationship, shared risk factors for both offending and victimization explain why one person is more likely to both offend and be victimized. Traditionally, people who are both offenders and victims show the most serious risk profile, which includes risk-taking personality characteristics and risky routine activities. As most of the risk factors for cyber-offending discussed earlier are also risk factors for victimization, it could very well be that the overlap observed for cybercrime is also partly explained by shared risk factors for offending and victimization. In line with that argument, a study by Kerstens and Jansen (2016) showed that both low self-control and online routine activities could explain the overlap between financial cyber-offending and victimization. Additionally, in line with the theoretical differences discussed earlier, they showed that online disinhibition is related to both offending and victimization.

Personal and situational risk factors that are related to both offending and victimization have been compared between cyber-dependent crime and traditional crime (Weulen Kranenbarg, Holt et al., 2017). This study is based on a cross-sectional survey among a high-risk sample of Dutch adults ($N = 535$) who had been suspected of a cyber-dependent crime or a traditional crime in the past. These people responded to a survey which included self-report questions on offending and victimization for both cyber-dependent crime and traditional crime. Additionally, respondents were asked to indicate their online and offline routine activities and their IT skills based on an extended version of the IT skills measure as used in (Holt, Bossler et al., 2012; Rogers, 2001), and their level of self-control was extracted from their answers to the HEXACO (Honesty-Humility, Emotionality, eXtraversion, Agreeableness, Conscientiousness, Openness) personality inventory (De Vries & Born, 2013; Van Gelder & De Vries, 2012).

The first goal was to examine to what extent a victim-offender overlap for cyber-dependent crime also existed in this dataset, which was clearly the case. Second, it was examined which personal and situational characteristics were related to offending-only and victimization-offending. These results showed some very important differences between these two groups. Offenders-only committed the more sophisticated types of cyber-dependent crime, they showed strong IT skills, and there was no significant relationship with low self-control. Additionally, these offenders showed very specific online activities in which they could gain even more IT skills and knowledge on how to commit these more sophisticated types of crime. These characteristics and activities may have also prevented them from being victimized (Weulen Kranenbarg, Holt et al., 2017).

The victim-offenders on the other hand, committed the less sophisticated types of cybercrime. They still had some IT skills, but few than the offenders-only. Additionally, they had low self-control and more general online routine activities in which they could find opportunities to commit cybercrimes, but were also exposed to the risk of being victimized. This group clearly showed the most serious risk profile in both their personal as well as their situational risk factors. The differences between the offenders-only and the victim-offenders are in line with the expectation expressed earlier that studies that find a relationship between, for example, low self-control and cyber-offending may include types of offending that require fewer skills. In particular, the offenders-only seem to differ from traditional offenders (Weulen Kranenbarg, Holt et al., 2017).

When comparing these results to the traditional offenders, it was clear that the victim-offenders were more similar to traditional offenders, and just as traditional offenders, they showed the most serious risk profile. The big difference between cyber-dependent crime and traditional crime was found in the types of situations that were related to offending and/or victimization. As expected, online activities were more important for cybercrime, whereas offline activities were more related to traditional crime (Weulen Kranenbarg, Holt et al., 2017).

Social networks

Social learning has been studied extensively in relation to cyber-offending and also to some extent specifically in relation to cyber-dependent offending. In general, these studies find that cyber-offenders are more likely to have social contacts who also commit cyber-offences (Hollinger, 1993; Holt, Bossler et al., 2012; Holt et al., 2010; Marcum, Higgins, Ricketts, & Wolfe, 2014; Morris, 2011; Morris & Blackburn, 2009; Rogers, 2001; Skinner & Fream, 1997). In relation to self-control, discussed earlier, Holt, Bossler et al. (2012) found that both peer deviance and low self-control predicted hacking behaviour, but that peer deviance was a more important predictor. In addition, in their general model that included cyber-enabled offences, they found an interaction effect: peer deviance mediated and exacerbated the effect of low self-control.

The first goal of the comparative study was to see to what extent cyber-deviance of social ties was also related to cyber-offending in the high-risk sample discussed in the section earlier (Weulen Kranenbarg, Ruiter et al., 2019). The type of network data used in this study also enabled controlling for age and gender similarity of social network members. The study specifically focused on the types of social ties that traditionally show the most similarity in behaviour: strong social ties with whom a respondent discussed important things. In line with the studies discussed earlier, the analyses showed a clear relationship between cyber-deviance of social network members and the cyber-deviance of the respondent. However, the comparison with traditional offending showed a very important difference in the strength of this relationship. The relationship was much weaker for cyber-dependent crime compared to traditional crime. This indicates that strong social relationships are less important when it comes to cyber-dependent offending. It could be that cyber-offenders do not need any social relationship to learn their skills from, as they can easily find all the information they need online, in a more self-direct way (Goldsmith & Brewer, 2015). Additionally, it could be that the deviance of social ties is simply not important, as the offenders do not expect their social ties to find out about their deviant behaviour in the digital world (Jaishankar, 2009; Suler, 2004; Yar, 2013).

Overall, this study indicated that although social ties are still important, they may be less important and different for cyber-dependent crime compared to traditional crime (Weulen Kranenbarg, Ruiter et al., 2019). It should be noted that none of the studies discussed in this section have empirically tested a causal relationship between the offending of a person and his or her peers. Therefore, up until now, it is unknown to what extent the similarity in cyber-deviant behaviour in social networks is the result of selection or influence processes. In addition, specifically studying both selection and influence of new types of social ties, like online social ties, would be an important next step in understanding cybercriminal behaviour in social networks.

Motives

In addition to considering the questions of who commits crime, when, where, and how these people commit crime, it is important to look at the question of why they commit crime. Usually, theories and empirical studies based on those theories simply assume that a person is motivated to commit crime, without asking what that motivation is. The question why people commit a crime is generally only part of the explanations behind an empirical finding, but it is usually not a research topic by itself. Nevertheless, looking at the motives for offending and looking at the differences and similarities between motives for cyber-offending and traditional offending may lead to prevention methods that tap into these motives. If cyber-dependent crime is committed out of different motives, then traditional prevention methods may not be as valuable as they are for traditional crime. New prevention methods, based on these different motives, may be more effective. Therefore, before discussing prevention, this chapter will first discuss the motives of cyber-dependent offenders.

Non-empirical publications generally state that cyber-offences are increasingly committed for financial gain (Grabosky, 2017; Kshetri, 2009; Provos, Rajab, & Mavrommatis, 2009; Smith, 2015; White, 2013). This is in line with the fact that financial transactions in the digital world are growing, which means that opportunities for financially motivated cybercrimes are increasing (Tcherni, Davies, Lopes, & Lizotte, 2016). Nevertheless, most empirical studies show that cyber-dependent crime is not committed for financial gain. These studies indicate that the main motive for committing cyber-dependent crime is related to curiosity, a need to learn, and similar intrinsic motivations (Chiesa, Ducci, & Ciappi, 2008a; Grabosky, 2000, 2001; Grabosky & Walkley, 2007; Holt, 2007; Taylor, 1999; Turgeman-Goldschmidt, 2008; Voiskounsky & Smyslova, 2003; Woo, 2003). Additionally, some studies show that peer recognition may be an important motive for committing these offences (Gordon & Ma, 2003; National Crime Agency, 2017a, 2017b; Taylor, 1999). On forums, for example, showing which targets you have hacked can show your skill level and therefore increase your status in that online community (Holt, 2007; Nycyk, 2010). This may indicate that some form of peer recognition is no longer gained from strong social relationships in the real world, but now from peers that a person may only know in cyberspace. This could partially explain the large difference in the strength of the similarity in deviance in social networks between cyber-dependent crime and traditional crime discussed in the previous section (Weulen Kranenbarg, Ruiter et al., 2019).

The comparative study between cyber-offending and traditional offending (Weulen Kranenbarg, 2018) confirmed these findings from the empirical literature. Almost no cyber-offenders indicated that they committed their crimes for financial gain. Intrinsic motives like curiosity, challenge, educational aspects, and because it just felt good were the most important motives for all cyber-dependent offences. Additionally, Internet-related offences like defacing, phishing, DDoS attacks, and spamming were committed out of extrinsic motives like revenge or anger or to deliver a message. The latter was also quite often mentioned as a motive for hacking and related offences. In contrast to the studies earlier (Gordon & Ma, 2003; National Crime Agency, 2017a, 2017b; Taylor, 1999), impressing others was not often mentioned for these offences. These self-indicated motives are related to the challenge and skills that are specific to cyber-dependent offending and may also be related to the idea that the consequences or criminality of cybercriminal behaviour are not clear to the offender (Goldsmith & Brewer, 2015; Jaishankar, 2009; Suler, 2004; Yar, 2013), as discussed earlier. If the consequences and rules are unclear and a curiosity-driven offender is trying to understand an IT system by attacking it, that person may not be very likely to stop as soon as his or her behaviour is crossing the line of criminality. In comparison with traditional offending, the motives for cyber-dependent offending were most comparable to the motives for vandalism (Weulen Kranenbarg, 2018). Unfortunately, the costs and consequences are generally much higher for cyber-dependent crime in comparison to vandalism.

Prevention of cyber-dependent offending

Both the theoretical differences between cyber-dependent offending and traditional offending and the empirical differences that have been discussed earlier have implications for prevention of cyber-dependent crime. It should be noted that the possible prevention methods discussed next all still have to be empirically tested. Additionally, it is not advisable to base prevention methods solely on theoretically assumed similarities or differences between cyber-dependent crime and traditional crime. For example, some might say that cyber-offenders are comparable to white-collar offenders, but the empirical evidence presented earlier has shown that their motives are not financial (Weulen Kranenbarg, 2018), so prevention of cyber-offending may not benefit from reducing its profit, although that may be a good prevention method for white-collar crime. In addition, most empirical evidence discussed is only based on a small number of studies, so future research (which will also be discussed in the next section) should further test these findings using different samples.

One important opportunity for prevention, which is unique to cyber-dependent crime, is to stimulate potential offenders with high IT skills to use their skills in a legitimate way. As having IT skills is a risk factor for offending (Holt, Bossler et al., 2012; Morris & Blackburn, 2009; Weulen Kranenbarg, Holt et al., 2017) and learning from breaking into systems is an important motive (Chiesa et al., 2008a; Grabosky, 2000, 2001; Grabosky & Walkley, 2007; Holt, 2007; Taylor, 1999; Turgeman-Goldschmidt, 2008; Voiskounsky & Smyslova, 2003; Weulen Kranenbarg, 2018; Woo, 2003), this is an important area to address in prevention. Fortunately, having these skills can also provide opportunities for completely legal professions. Bug bounty programs, coordinated vulnerability disclosure, and several types of employment within the IT sector can provide a challenge and opportunities to enhance skills by testing IT systems without breaking the law. By stimulating potential offenders to take this path as early in their career as possible, future crime may be prevented, as these offenders will not escalate their offending behaviour and criminal careers, and additionally they prevent others from misusing IT systems by finding and patching vulnerabilities in these systems (Weulen Kranenbarg, Holt, & Van Der Ham, 2018).

One important issue should be addressed here. As shown in the discussed life-course study (Weulen Kranenbarg, Ruiter et al., 2018), employment in the IT sector may provide opportunities to commit cyber-dependent crime, and apparently for the offenders in the Dutch population, there was not enough social control in those life circumstances to prevent offending. Therefore, simply helping an offender to get a job in the IT sector may be counterproductive. Ethical guidance in the rules that apply to behaviuor in the digital world is therefore very important. Social control may, for example, be increased by assigning someone to a mentor – for example, a well-known ethical hacker – who can provide a person with information on the rules that apply to vulnerability disclosure, etc. (Weulen Kranenbarg, 2018).

Prevention may also benefit from a focus on the ethics of using IT skills. Nowadays, schools try to stimulate their students' IT skills by teaching them coding techniques. The ethics of using these skills should also be part of this strategy. In that way they are not only teaching students skills to use or even build safe IT systems but also to understand what should and should not be done with these skills (Weulen Kranenbarg, Holt et al., 2018). In this type of training, it may also be valuable to discuss the consequences of cybercrime. As online disinhibition (Kerstens & Jansen, 2016; Suler, 2004) seems to be related to cyber-offending, insight into the consequences of victimization and the formal and informal (i.e. social) consequences of offending may reduce online disinhibition and may reduce the felt anonymity online.

In addition to this type of general training, the situations that provide opportunities for cyber-dependent offending may be used to send messages to a potential offender about the consequences of criminal behaviour or the possibility to report any vulnerabilities without breaking the law. Some criminologists, for example, have started using warning banners in attacked IT systems (Howell, Cochran, Powers, Maimon, & Jones, 2017; Jones, 2014; Maimon, Alper, Sobesto, & Cukier, 2014; Wilson, Maimon, Sobesto, & Cukier, 2015). Even though these have not yet been shown to be extremely effective, these types of situational crime prevention should be further explored to see which messages could persuade a potential offender to abide by the law. In addition to that, minimizing the felt anonymity and lack of consequences may be achieved by so-called 'cease-and-desist' or 'knock-and-talk' visits with first offenders (National Crime Agency, 2017b). By showing them that the police have actually noticed their behaviour and will act upon that if they do not desist may prevent the escalation of the criminal career of first offenders. In such an approach they should be guided in the rules and opportunities of testing IT systems in legitimate ways, as discussed earlier.

Future criminological research

As already discussed, future research should try to replicate the findings of existing criminological research in this area in different samples and test the suggested prevention methods discussed. In addition to that, the main questions that need to be addressed for the domains discussed in this chapter require the use of in-depth longitudinal data. More in-depth data on life circumstances and the specific aspects of, for example, employment that increase the likelihood of offending should be studied in detail. That type of in-depth data would be able to test which theoretical assumptions can explain the relationship between certain life circumstances and cyber-dependent offending. Additionally, in order to find causal relationships between risk factors and offending and between victimization and offending, longitudinal data are key as well. With respect to the social environment of offenders, it is important to find out to what extent selection and influence processes play a role in the observed similarity in behaviour of social network members. In addition, in that area it is very important to study to what extent social network members in the digital world can influence a person to the same extent as social network members in the real world. Lastly, with respect to skills and motives, it is important to use longitudinal data to find out how motives, skills, and types of offending or specialization evolve over the criminal life course.

In relation to that, future research should try to distinguish between high-skilled and low-skilled cyber-dependent crimes. This could provide insight into the extent to which low-skilled offending may be more similar to traditional offending. Additionally, the highly skilled offender may be most different from traditional offenders and may therefore also require the most different prevention approach.

This chapter only discussed the domains in criminology in which cyber-dependent offending has already been empirically compared with traditional offending. Other domains, however, may also benefit from this type of comparison. Not only other domains that try to explain offending but also domains that focus on the effect of punishment or police work may be facing important differences between cyber-dependent crime and traditional crime. For example, differences in the type of evidence, complexity of the crime, and personality characteristics may have a large impact on the way in which a suspect should be interrogated. Similarly, for offenders with strong IT skills, having a criminal record may have completely different effects on their ability to find employment after they served their sentence.

The first empirical comparisons that have been done show that using traditional criminological theories and explanations in understanding cyber-offending is still very valuable, but important differences can also be observed. Therefore, research on both cyber-dependent and cyber-enabled crimes should try to empirically compare their results with traditional offending as much as possible, as that provides strong insight into the extent to which these types of offending or offenders are unique.

References

Akers, R. L. (1998). *Social learning and social structure: A general theory of crime and deviance.* Boston: Northeastern University Press.

Berg, M. T., & Felson, R. B. (2016). Why are offenders victimized so often? In C. A. Cuevas & C. M. Rennison (Eds.), *The Wiley handbook on the psychology of violence* (pp. 49–65). West Sussex, UK: John Wiley & Sons, Ltd.

Blackburn, J., Kourtellis, N., Skvoretz, J., Ripeanu, M., & Iamnitchi, A. (2014). Cheating in online games: A social network perspective. *ACM Transactions on Internet Technology, 13*(3), 1–25.

Bossler, A. M., & Burruss, G. W. (2011). The general theory of crime and computer hacking: Low self-control hackers? In T. J. Holt & B. H. Schell (Eds.), *Corporate hacking and technology-driven crime: Social dynamics and implications* (pp. 38–67). New York, NY: Information Science Reference.

Bossler, A. M., & Holt, T. J. (2009). On-line activities, guardianship, and malware infection: An examination of routine activities theory. *International Journal of Cyber Criminology, 3*(1), 400–420.

Brady, P. Q., Randa, R., & Reyns, B. W. (2016). From Wwii to the world wide web. *Journal of Contemporary Criminal Justice, 32*(2), 129–147.

Campbell, Q., & Kennedy, D. M. (2012). The psychology of computer criminals. In S. Bosworth, M. E. Kabay, & E. Whyne (Eds.), *Computer security handbook* (pp. 12.11–12.33). Hoboken, NJ: John Wiley & Sons, Inc.

Chiesa, R., Ducci, S., & Ciappi, S. (2008a). To be, think, and live as a hacker. In R. Chiesa, S. Ducci, & S. Ciappi (Eds.), *Profiling hackers: The science of criminal profiling as applied to the world of hacking* (pp. 33–56). Boca Raton: CRC Press.

Chiesa, R., Ducci, S., & Ciappi, S. (2008b). Who are hackers? Part 1. In *Profiling hackers: The science of criminal profiling as applied to the world of hacking* (pp. 87–120). Boca Raton: CRC Press.

Chiesa, R., Ducci, S., & Ciappi, S. (2008c). Who are hackers? Part 2. In R. Chiesa, S. Ducci, & S. Ciappi (Eds.), *Profiling hackers: The science of criminal profiling as applied to the world of hacking* (pp. 121–188). Boca Raton: CRC Press.

Cohen, L. E., & Felson, M. (1979). Social change and crime rate trends: A routine activity approach. *American Sociological Review, 44*(4), 588–608.

De Vries, R. E., & Born, M. P. (2013). The Simplified Hexaco Personality Questionnaire and an Additional Interstitial Proactivity Facet [De Vereenvoudigde Hexaco Persoonlijkheidsvragenlijst En Een Additioneel Interstitieel Proactiviteitsfacet]. *Gedrag & Organisatie, 26*(2), 223–245.

Flashman, J., & Gambetta, D. (2014). Thick as thieves: Homophily and trust among deviants. *Rationality and Society, 26*(1), 3–45.

Fotinger, C., & Ziegler, W. (2004). *Understanding a Hacker's mind: A psychological insight into the hijacking of identities.* Retrieved from www.donau-uni.ac.at/de/department/gpa/informatik/DanubeUniversityHackersStudy.pdf

Goldsmith, A., & Brewer, R. (2015). Digital drift and the criminal interaction order. *Theoretical Criminology, 19*(1), 112–130.

Gordon, S. (1994). *The generic virus writer.* Paper presented at the International Virus Bulletin Conference, Jersey.

Gordon, S. (2000). *Virus writers: The end of the innocence?* Paper presented at the International Virus Bulletin Conference, Orlando.

Gordon, S., & Ford, R. (2006). On the definition and classification of cybercrime. *Journal in Computer Virology, 2*(1), 13–20.

Gordon, S., & Ma, Q. (2003). *Convergence of virus writers and hackers: Fact or fantasy?* Retrieved from http://download.adamas.ai/dlbase/ebooks/VX_related/Convergence%20of%20Virus%20Writers%20and%20Hackers%20Fact%20or%20Fantasy.pdf

Gottfredson, M. R., & Hirschi, T. (1990). *A general theory of crime.* Palo Alto, CA: Stanford University Press.

Grabosky, P. N. (2000). *Computer crime: A criminological overview.* Paper presented at the Workshop on Crimes Related to the Computer Network, Tenth United Nations Congress on the Prevention of Crime and the Treatment of Offenders, Vienna.

Grabosky, P. N. (2001). Virtual criminality: Old wine in new bottles? *Social & Legal Studies, 10*(2), 243–249.

Grabosky, P. N. (2017). The evolution of cybercrime, 2006–2016. In T. J. Holt (Ed.), *Cybercrime through an interdisciplinary lens* (pp. 15–36). New York, NY: Routledge.

Grabosky, P. N., & Walkley, S. (2007). Computer crime and white-collar crime. In H. N. Pontell & G. L. Geis (Eds.), *International handbook of white-collar and corporate crime* (pp. 358–375). New York, NY: Springer.

Harvey, I., Bolgan, S., Mosca, D., McLean, C., & Rusconi, E. (2016). Systemizers are better code-breakers: Self-reported systemizing predicts code-breaking performance in expert hackers and naïve participants. *Frontiers in Human Neuroscience, 10*(229).

Haynie, D. L., & Kreager, D. A. (2013). Peer networks and crime. In F. T. Cullen & P. Wilcox (Eds.), *The Oxford handbook of criminological theory* (pp. 257–273). Oxford: Oxford University Press.

Hirschi, T. (1969). *Causes of delinquency.* Berkeley, CA: University of California press.

Hollinger, R. C. (1993). Crime by computer: Correlates of software piracy and unauthorized account access. *Security Journal, 4*(1), 2–12.

Holt, T. J. (2007). Subcultural evolution? Examining the influence of on- and off-line experiences on deviant subcultures. *Deviant Behavior, 28*(2), 171–198.

Holt, T. J., & Bossler, A. M. (2014). An assessment of the current state of cybercrime scholarship. *Deviant Behavior, 35*(1), 20–40.

Holt, T. J., Bossler, A. M., & May, D. C. (2012). Low self-control, deviant peer associations, and juvenile cyberdeviance. *American Journal of Criminal Justice, 37*(3), 378–395.

Holt, T. J., Burruss, G. W., & Bossler, A. M. (2010). Social learning and cyber-deviance: Examining the importance of a full social learning model in the virtual world. *Journal of Crime and Justice, 33*(2), 31–61.

Holt, T. J., & Kilger, M. (2008). *Techcrafters and makecrafters: A comparison of two populations of hackers.* Paper presented at the WOMBAT Workshop on Information Security Threats Data Collection and Sharing, 2008. WISTDCS'08, Amsterdam.

Holt, T. J., Strumsky, D., Smirnova, O., & Kilger, M. (2012). Examining the social networks of malware writers and hackers. *International Journal of Cyber Criminology, 6*(1), 891–903.

Howell, C. J., Cochran, J. K., Powers, R. A., Maimon, D., & Jones, H. M. (2017). System trespasser behavior after exposure to warning messages at a Chinese computer network: An examination. *International Journal of Cyber Criminology, 11*(1), 63–77.

Hu, Q., Xu, Z., & Yayla, A. A. (2013). *Why college students commit computer hacks: Insights from a cross culture analysis.* Paper presented at the Pacific Asia Conference on Information Systems (PACIS), Jeju Island, Korea.

Hutchings, A. (2014). Crime from the keyboard: Organised cybercrime, co-offending, initiation and knowledge transmission. *Crime Law and Social Change, 62*(1), 1–20.

Jaishankar, K. (2009). Space transition theory of cyber crimes. In F. Schmalleger & M. Pittaro (Eds.), *Crimes of the internet* (pp. 283–301). Trenton, NJ: Pearson Education.

Jennings, W. G., Piquero, A. R., & Reingle, J. M. (2012). On the overlap between victimization and offending: A review of the literature. *Aggression and Violent Behavior, 17*(1), 16–26.

Jones, H. M. (2014). *The restrictive deterrent effect of warning messages on the behavior of computer system trespassers.* Ann Arbor: University of Maryland, ProQuest LLC. Retrieved from http://drum.lib.umd.edu/bitstream/handle/1903/15544/Jones_umd_0117N_15230. pdf?sequence=1&isAllowed=y

Kalmijn, M. (1998). Intermarriage and homogamy: Causes, patterns, trends. *Annual Review of Sociology, 24*(1), 395–421.

Kazemian, L. (2015). Desistance from crime and antisocial behavior. In J. Morizot & L. Kazemian (Eds.), *The development of criminal and antisocial behavior* (pp. 295–312). New York, NY: Springer.

Kerstens, J., & Jansen, J. (2016). The victim – perpetrator overlap in financial cybercrime: Evidence and reflection on the overlap of youth's on-line victimization and perpetration. *Deviant Behavior, 37*(5), 585–600.

Kshetri, N. (2009). Positive externality, increasing returns, and the rise in cybercrimes. *Communications of the ACM, 52*(12), 141–144.

Lageson, S., & Uggen, C. (2013). How work affects crime – and crime affects work – over the life course. In C. L. Gibson & M. D. Krohn (Eds.), *Handbook of life-course criminology* (pp. 201–212). New York, NY: Springer.

Laub, J. H., & Sampson, R. J. (1993). Turning points in the life course: Why change matters to the study of crime. *Criminology, 31*(3), 301–325.

Lauritsen, J. L., & Laub, J. H. (2007). Understanding the link between victimization and offending: New reflections on an old idea. In M. Hough & M. Maxfield (Eds.), *Surveying crime in the 21st century* (Vol. 22, pp. 55–75). Monsey, NY: Criminal Justice Press.

Leukfeldt, E. R., De Poot, C. J., Verhoeven, M. A., Kleemans, E. R., & Lavorgna, A. (2017). Cybercriminal networks. In E. R. Leukfeldt (Ed.), *Research agenda: The human factor in cybercrime and cybersecurity* (pp. 33–44). Den Haag: Eleven International Publishing.

Leukfeldt, E. R., & Yar, M. (2016). Applying routine activity theory to cybercrime: A theoretical and empirical analysis. *Deviant Behavior, 37*(3), 263–280.

Lu, C., Jen, W., Chang, W., & Chou, S. (2006). Cybercrime & cybercriminals: An overview of the Taiwan experience. *Journal of Computers, 1*(6), 11–18.

Maimon, D., Alper, M., Sobesto, B., & Cukier, M. (2014). Restrictive deterrent effects of a warning banner in an attacked computer system. *Criminology, 52*(1), 33–59.

Maimon, D., Kamerdze, A., Cukier, M., & Sobesto, B. (2013). Daily trends and origin of computer-focused crimes against a large university computer network: An application of the routine-activities and lifestyle perspective. *British Journal of Criminology, 53*(2), 319–343.

Marcum, C. D., Higgins, G. E., Ricketts, M. L., & Wolfe, S. E. (2014). Hacking in high school: Cybercrime perpetration by juveniles. *Deviant Behavior, 35*(7), 581–591.

McGuire, M., & Dowling, S. (2013a). *Chapter 1: Cyber-dependent crimes.* Retrieved from www. gov.uk/government/uploads/system/uploads/attachment_data/file/246751/horr75-chap1.pdf

McGuire, M., & Dowling, S. (2013b). *Chapter 2: Cyber-enabled crimes.* Retrieved from www. gov.uk/government/uploads/system/uploads/attachment_data/file/246751/horr75-chap1.pdf

McPherson, M., Smith-Lovin, L., & Cook, J. M. (2001). Birds of a feather: Homophily in social networks. *Annual Review of Sociology, 27*(1), 415–444.

Miro Llinares, F., & Johnson, S. D. (2018). Cybercrime and place: Applying environmental criminology to crimes in cyberspace. In G. J. Bruinsma & S. D. Johnson (Eds.), *The Oxford handbook of environmental criminology* (pp. 883–906). New York, NY: Oxford University Press.

Moffitt, T. E. (1993). Adolescence-limited and life-course persistent antisocial behavior: A developmental taxonomy. *Psychological Review, 100*(4), 674–701.

Morris, R. G. (2011). Computer hacking and the techniques of neutralization: An empirical assessment. In T. J. Holt & B. H. Schell (Eds.), *Corporate hacking and technology-driven crime: Social dynamics and implications* (pp. 1–17). New York, NY: Information Science Reference.

Morris, R. G., & Blackburn, A. G. (2009). Cracking the code: An empirical exploration of social learning theory and computer crime. *Journal of Crime and Justice, 32*(1), 1–34.

National Crime Agency. (2017a). *Identify, intervene, inspire: Helping young people to pursue careers in cyber security, not cyber crime.* Retrieved from www.crest-approved.org/wp-content/uploads/CREST_NCA_CyberCrimeReport.pdf

National Crime Agency. (2017b). *Pathways into cyber crime.* Retrieved from www.national-crimeagency.gov.uk/publications/791-pathways-into-cyber-crime/file

Ngo, F. T., & Paternoster, R. (2011). Cybercrime victimization: An examination of individual and situational level factors. *International Journal of Cyber Criminology, 5*(1), 773–793.

Nycyk, M. (2010). *Computer hackers in virtual community forums: Identity shaping and dominating other hackers.* Paper presented at the Online Conference on Networks and Communities: Debating Communities and Networks.

Nykodym, N., Taylor, R., & Vilela, J. (2005). Criminal profiling and insider cyber crime. *Computer Law & Security Review, 21*(5), 408–414.

Pontell, H., & Rosoff, S. (2009). White-collar delinquency. *Crime Law and Social Change, 51*(1), 147–162.

Pratt, T. C., & Cullen, F. T. (2000). The empirical status of Gottfredson and Hirschi's general theory of crime: A meta-analysis. *Criminology, 38*(3), 931–964.

Pratt, T. C., Cullen, F. T., Sellers, C. S., Winfree, L. T., Madensen, T. D., Daigle, L. E., . . . Gau, J. M. (2009). The empirical status of social learning theory: A meta-analysis. *Justice Quarterly, 27*(6), 765–802.

Provos, N., Rajab, M. A., & Mavrommatis, P. (2009). Cybercrime 2.0: When the cloud turns dark. *Communications of the ACM, 52*(4), 42–47.

Randazzo, M. R., Keeney, M., Kowalski, E., Cappelli, D., & Moore, A. (2005). *Insider threat study: Illicit cyber activity in the banking and finance sector.* Retrieved from www.dtic.mil/dtic/tr/fulltext/u2/a441249.pdf

Rogers, M. K. (2001). *A social learning theory and moral disengagement analysis of criminal computer behavior: An exploratory study.* Retrieved from www.cerias.purdue.edu/assets/pdf/bibtex_archive/rogers_01.pdf

Rogers, M. K., Smoak, N. D., & Liu, J. (2006). Self-reported deviant computer behavior: A big-5, moral choice, and manipulative exploitive behavior analysis. *Deviant Behavior, 27*(3), 245–268.

Rokven, J. J., Weijters, G., Beerthuizen, M. G. C. J., & Van Der Laan, A. M. (2018). Juvenile delinquency in the virtual world: Similarities and differences between cyber-enabled, cyber-dependent and offline delinquents in the Netherlands. *International Journal of Cyber Criminology, 12*(1), 27–46.

Rokven, J. J., Weijters, G., & Van Der Laan, A. M. (2017). *Juvenile delinquency in the virtual world: A new type of offedenders or new opportunities for traditional offenders? [Jeugddelinquentie in De Virtuele Wereld: Een Nieuw Type Daders of Nieuwe Mogelijkheden Voor Traditionele Daders?].* Retrieved from www.wodc.nl/binaries/Cahier%202017-2_2699a_Volledige%20tekst_nw2_tcm28-250948.pdf

Ruiter, S., & Bernaards, F. (2013). Are crackers different from other criminals? A comparison based on Dutch suspect registrations [Verschillen Crackers Van Andere Criminelen? Een Vergelijking Op Basis Van Nederlandse Verdachtenregistraties]. *Tijdschrift voor Criminologie, 55*(4), 342–359.

Sampson, R. J., & Laub, J. H. (1993a). *Crime in the making: Pathways and turning points through life*. Cambridge, MA: Harvard University Press.

Sampson, R. J., & Laub, J. H. (1993b). The role of school, peers and siblings. In R. Sampson & J. Laub (Eds.), *Crime in the making: Pathways and turning points through life* (pp. 99–122). Cambridge, MA: Harvard University Press.

Schell, B. H., & Melnychuk, J. (2011). Female and male hacker conferences attendees: Their autism-spectrum quotient (Aq) scores and self-reported adulthood experiences. In T. J. Holt & B. H. Schell (Eds.), *Corporate hacking and technology-driven crime: Social dynamics and implications* (pp. 144–168). New York, NY: Information Science Reference.

Seigfried, K., & Treadway, K. N. (2014). Differentiating hackers, identity thieves, cyberbullies, and virus writers by college major and individual differences. *Deviant Behavior, 35*(10), 782–803.

Skardhamar, T., Savolainen, J., Aase, K. N., & Lyngstad, T. H. (2015). Does marriage reduce crime? *Crime & Justice, 44*(1), 385–557.

Skinner, W. F., & Fream, A. M. (1997). A social learning theory analysis of computer crime among college students. *Journal of Research in Crime and Delinquency, 34*(4), 495–518.

Smith, R. G. (2015). Trajectories of cybercrime. In R. G. Smith, R. C-C., Cheung, & L.Y-C. Lau (Eds.), *Cybercrime risks and responses: Eastern and western perspectives* (pp. 13–34). London: Palgrave Macmillan UK.

Statistics Netherlands. (2015). ICT usage by individuals and individual characteristics [Ict Gebruik Van Personen Naar Persoonskenmerken]. Retrieved January 16, 2017, from Statistics Netherlands [Centraal Bureau voor de Statistiek (CBS)], http://statline. cbs.nl/Statweb/publication/?VW=T&DM=SLNL&PA=71098ned&D1 = 7-14,21-26,69-84&D2 = 8-16,25-28&D3=1&HD=150807-1532&HDR=G1,G2&STB= T&CHARTTYPE=1

Suler, J. (2004). The online disinhibition effect. *CyberPsychology & Behavior, 7*(3), 321–326.

Sutherland, E. H. (1947). *Principles of criminology* (4th ed.). Oxford, England: J. B. Lippincott.

Taylor, P. A. (1999). *Hackers: Crime in the digital sublime*. London: Routledge.

Tcherni, M., Davies, A., Lopes, G., & Lizotte, A. (2016). The dark figure of online property crime: Is cyberspace hiding a crime wave? *Justice Quarterly, 33*(5), 890–911.

Turgeman-Goldschmidt, O. (2008). Meanings that hackers assign to their being a hacker. *International Journal of Cyber Criminology, 2*(2), 382–396.

Turgeman-Goldschmidt, O. (2011). Between hackers and white-collar offenders. In T. J. Holt & B. H. Schell (Eds.), *Corporate hacking and technology-driven crime: Social dynamics and implications* (pp. 18–37). New York, NY: Information Science Reference.

Van Gelder, J-L., & De Vries, R. E. (2012). Traits and states: Integrating personality and affect into a model of criminal decision making. *Criminology, 50*(3), 637–671.

Voiskounsky, A. E., & Smyslova, O.V. (2003). Flow-based model of computer hackers' motivation. *CyberPsychology & Behavior, 6*(2), 171–180.

Warr, M. (2002). *Companions in crime: The social aspects of criminal conduct*. Cambridge: Cambridge University Press.

Weerman, F. M., & Smeenk, W. H. (2005). Peer similarity in delinquency for different types of friends: A comparison using two measurement methods. *Criminology, 43*(2), 499–524.

Weulen Kranenbarg, M. (2018). *Cyber-offenders versus traditional offenders: An empirical comparison* (doctoral dissertation), Vrije. Universiteit (VU) Amsterdam, The Netherlands. Retrieved from http://dare.ubvu.vu.nl/handle/1871/55530

Weulen Kranenbarg, M., Holt, T. J., & Van Der Ham, J. (2018). Don't shoot the messenger! A criminological and computer science perspective on coordinated vulnerability disclosure. *Crime Science*, 7(1), 16.

Weulen Kranenbarg, M., Holt, T. J., & Van Gelder, J-L. (2017). Offending and victimization in the digital age: Comparing correlates of cybercrime and traditional offending-only, victimization-only and the victimization-offending overlap. *Deviant Behavior*, 40(1), 40–55.

Weulen Kranenbarg, M., Ruiter, S., & Van Gelder, J-L. (2019). Do cyber-birds flock together? Comparing deviance among social network members of cyber-dependent offenders and traditional offenders. *European Journal of Criminology*. Advance online publication. https://doi.org/10.1177/1477370819849677

Weulen Kranenbarg, M., Ruiter, S., Van Gelder, J-L., & Bernasco, W. (2018). Cyber-offending and traditional offending over the life-course: An empirical comparison. *Journal of Developmental and Life-Course Criminology*, 4(3), 343–364.

Weulen Kranenbarg, M., Van Der Laan, A. M., De Poot, C. J., Verhoeven, M. A., Van Der Wagen, W., & Weijters, G. (2017). Individual cybercrime offenders. In E. R. Leukfeldt (Ed.), *Research agenda: The human factor in cybercrime and cybersecurity* (pp. 23–32). Den Haag: Eleven International Publishing.

White, K. (2013). The rise of cybercrime 1970 through 2010: A tour of the conditions that gave rise to cybercrime and the crimes themselves. Retrieved from www.slideshare.net/bluesme/the-rise-of-cybercrime-1970s-2010-29879338

Wilcox, P., Land, K. C., & Hunt, S. A. (2003). *Criminal circumstance: A dynamic multi-contextual criminal opportunity theory*. New York, NY: Aldine de Gruyter.

Wilson, T., Maimon, D., Sobesto, B., & Cukier, M. (2015). The effect of a surveillance banner in an attacked computer system. *Journal of Research in Crime and Delinquency*, 52(6), 829–855.

Woo, H-J. (2003). *The hacker mentality: Exploring the relationship between psychological variables and hacking activities*. Athens, Georgia: The University of Georgia. Retrieved from https://getd.libs.uga.edu/pdfs/woo_hyung-jin_200305_phd.pdf

Xu, Z., Hu, Q., & Zhang, C. (2013). Why computer talents become computer hackers. *Communications of the ACM*, 56(4), 64–74.

Yar, M. (2005a). Computer hacking: Just another case of juvenile delinquency? *The Howard Journal of Criminal Justice*, 44(4), 387–399.

Yar, M. (2005b). The novelty of 'cybercrime': An assessment in light of routine activity theory. *European Journal of Criminology*, 2(4), 407–427.

Yar, M. (2013). Cybercrime and the internet, an introduction. In M. Yar (Ed.), *Cybercrime and society* (2nd ed., pp. 1–20). London: Sage.

Young, J. T. N., & Rees, C. (2013). Social networks and delinquency in adolescence: Implications for life-course criminology. In C. L. Gibson & M. D. Krohn (Eds.), *Handbook of life-course criminology: Emerging trends and directions for future research* (pp. 159–180). New York, NY: Springer New York.

Young, R., Zhang, L., & Prybutok, V. R. (2007). Hacking into the minds of hackers. *Information Systems Management*, 24(4), 281–287.

Zhang, Y. P., Xiao, Y., Ghaboosi, K., Zhang, J. Y., & Deng, H. M. (2012). A survey of cyber crimes. *Security and Communication Networks*, 5(4), 422–437.

10 Financial cybercrimes and situational crime prevention

Rutger Leukfeldt and Jurjen Jansen

Introduction

Cybercrime poses a serious threat to Internet users in the current digitized society. Victimization has varying impacts, and some manifestations of cybercrime are quite common. Therefore, it is important to find the means by which cybercrimes can be combatted effectively. One possibility for reducing criminal opportunities to commit cybercrime is situational crime prevention. This chapter focuses on situational crime prevention measures against financial cybercrimes (i.e. phishing[1] and banking malware[2]).

This chapter is based on various empirical studies carried out by the two authors over the past six years. These studies are carried out as part of the Dutch Knowledge Program on Safety and Security of Online Banking[3] funded by and including an analysis of large-scale police investigations, case analysis of incidents registered in a fraud database of a financial institution, interrogations of money mules, a nationwide victim survey, victim interviews, and two survey studies on Internet users, which led to 20 peer-reviewed publications. This chapter takes a holistic view on the results and conclusions from these publications. Unique to this endeavour is that the findings are integrated and translated into measures that can be used to create barriers against cybercriminal networks committing financial cybercrimes.

This chapter is outlined as follows. The second section contains the concept of situational crime prevention. In the third section, the research methods that were used to carry out the various studies are described. The fourth section contains a brief overview of processes and actors involved in phishing and banking malware attacks. First, we devote attention to cybercriminal networks. We describe the processes of the origin and growth of cybercriminal networks: Where and how do cybercriminals meet, and how do they recruit new members? In addition, the structure of networks involved in financial cybercrimes is covered: the composition, key players, and various network layers. In the fifth section, the behaviour of end users and suitable targets is central: Are some end users more at risk than others? This chapter ends by applying the five strategies of situational crime prevention of Cornish and Clarke (2003) to financial cybercrimes. Examples of situational crime prevention measures include making users more cyber-aware (increase the effort of crime), extending guardianship to financial institutions (increase the risk of crime), frustrating online crime markets (reduce the rewards of crime), preventing online hacking subculture from emerging (reduce provocations that invite criminal behaviour), and educating potential money mules about their role in the crime script (remove excuses for criminal behaviour). Although not all of the five strategies seem to be perfectly suitable to creating barriers against cybercriminal networks executing financial cybercrimes, our analyses clearly show that situational crime prevention provides a useful framework for combatting or disturbing financial cybercrimes.

Situational crime prevention

This chapter focuses on financial cybercrimes and the ways to prevent these crimes or to make it as hard as possible for criminals to execute their attacks. This fits within a pragmatic paradigm within criminology: one in which not the causes of crime are central, but the way in which crime is committed and how it can be prevented (see Clarke, 2004). Situational crime prevention fits perfectly within this paradigm. At first, two possible strategies for situational crime prevention were distinguished by Clarke (1980): (1) reducing the physical opportunities for offending and (2) increasing the chances of an offender being caught. Later, these strategies were extended and adapted based on new insights from empirical research (e.g. Clarke, 1992, 1997; Clarke & Homel, 1997; Cornish & Clarke, 2003), resulting in five strategies for situational crime prevention:

- Increase the effort of crime (e.g. target hardening by installing better locks).
- Increase the risk of crime (e.g. extend guardianship by neighbourhood watch).
- Reduce the rewards of crime (e.g. remove targets or identify property).
- Reduce provocations that invite criminal behaviour (e.g. neutralize peer pressure).
- Remove excuses for criminal behaviour (e.g. set rules about (un)wanted behaviour).

Situational crime prevention strategies have been developed for offline crimes. However, Hartel, Junger, and Wieringa (2011) show that these techniques are also applicable to cybercrimes, for example, by increasing the effort required for crime by using password-protected files. To the best of our knowledge, this framework has not been specifically applied to financial cybercrimes.

Data and methods

This chapter focuses on situational crime prevention measures against financial cybercrimes (i.e. phishing and banking malware). In order to identify these measures, insight must be gained into the way in which these crimes are committed and how they can be prevented. Note that applying the situational crime prevention framework was not the main aim of the studies that are presented next.

The first step was to gain insight into the networks that carry out phishing and banking malware attacks. It is a well-known fact that most criminals do not work alone. Therefore, it was vital to understand the processes of origin and growth of these networks: How do criminals meet and select suitable co-offenders, and how are the networks organized? The second step was to gain insight into the structure of the networks: Is there a hierarchy, and are there dependency relationships? Information on these topics helps with developing measures to disrupt criminal networks. Indeed, a different strategy is required to disrupt a mafia-style network compared to a more fluid network. The third and final step was to understand the role of end users: Who are suitable targets for these criminal networks and why?

Thus, this chapter builds on three pillars: (1) insight into the processes of the origin and growth of cybercriminal networks, (2) insight into the structure of cybercriminal networks, and (3) insight into suitable targets. These pillars are based on the various studies of the two authors, which include an analysis of police investigations ($N = 40$), case analysis of incidents registered in a fraud database of a financial institution ($N = 600$), interrogations of money mules ($N = 190$), a victim survey ($N = 10,416$), victim interviews ($N = 30$), and two survey studies on Internet users ($N = 1,200$; $N = 768$). Figure 10.1 shows how these studies are connected to the three pillars. In addition, the methods that were applied to identify situational crime prevention strategies are presented in Figure 10.1.

Large-scale police investigations

Forty large-scale police investigations were analysed in order to gain insight into the processes of origin and growth and the structure of cybercriminal networks. These cases included 18 cases from the Netherlands, 10 from the United States of America (USA), 9 from the United Kingdom (UK), and 3 from Germany. These police investigations contain rich data regarding cyber-criminal networks and their members because of the use of investigative methods such as wiretaps, IP taps, and observation. An analytical framework was used to systematically analyse criminal investigations.[4] The Dutch cases were analysed using actual police records of the criminal investigation (including all information obtained using special investigative powers) and interviews with the public prosecutor and police officers involved in the case. The investigations lasted six months to three years and were carried out in the period 2004–2014. The cases from the UK, Germany, and USA were reconstructed based on an analysis of court documents and interviews with public prosecutors and law enforcement personnel involved in the criminal investigation. For a detailed description see Leukfeldt (2016) and Leukfeldt, Kleemans, & Stol (2017a, 2017b, 2017c, 2017d, 2017e).

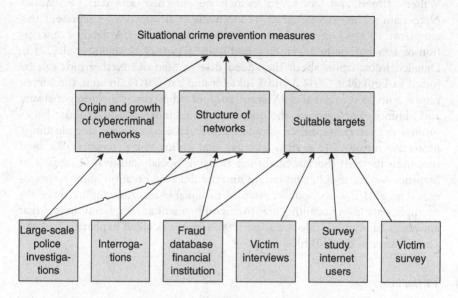

Figure 10.1 Data and methods related to the situational crime prevention measures

Interrogations

The Dutch police records included interrogations with numerous suspects. In order to get insight into the recruitment processes of so-called money mules – persons who play a vital part in cashing stolen money – we analysed all money mule interrogations. In total, we obtained interrogations of 211 money mules. However, because 69 suspects did not cooperate during the interrogations ('no comment') and 30 claimed to be innocent, we have useful information of 112 money mules. More information is available in Leukfeldt and Kleemans (2019).

Fraud case analysis

For the case analysis, we had access to a fraud database of a financial institution in the Netherlands. The database contains information on phishing and malware incidents related to online banking. The data collection took place in 2014 and resulted in 600 phishing and malware incidents, spread over 2011, 2012, and 2013. The purpose was to shed light on the circumstances around bank customers being victimized in phishing and malware attacks and how these attacks manifest in practice. More information on this method can be found in Jansen and Leukfeldt (2015).

Victim survey

In order to identify risk factors related to phishing and malware victimization, we conducted a secondary analysis on the dataset of Domenie, Leukfeldt, Van

Wilsem, Jansen, and Stol (2013), which we enriched with data of Statistics Netherlands. The original survey of Domenie et al. contained a representative sample of 10,314 Dutch citizens aged 15 years and older. A detailed description of data and methods can be found in the report of Domenie et al. (2013). Detailed information about the added data of Statistics Netherlands can be found in Leukfeldt (2014a) and Leukfeldt and Yar (2016). In sum, the survey respondents were asked about victimization of cybercrimes, including malware and phishing. Furthermore, the questionnaire included questions about background characteristics, online activities (e.g. social media use and downloading), protective measures (e.g. virus scanner), and online risk perception. We used files from the SSB (Sociaal Statistisch Bestand, 'Social Statistical Database') of Statistics Netherlands to gain insight into the financial situation of the respondents. The SSB is a non-public database of linkable records, ranging from, for example, data from tax authorities to unemployment agencies, and surveys that are matched. Arts and Hoogteijling (2002) give a detailed explanation of the composition of the SSB files.

Victim interviews

We conducted 30 semi-structured interviews with online banking fraud victims. The purpose was twofold: (1) to gain insight into the behaviour and characteristics of bank customers leading to victimization caused by phishing and malware attacks and (2) to gain insight into the effects and impact of online banking fraud victimizations and how victims cope with the incident. Most interview participants were selected based on police files, but one was recruited via the Fraud Help Desk (the Dutch national anti-fraud hotline). The data were collected in 2014 and 2015 and were analysed using computer-assisted qualitative data analysis software. More information on this method can be found in Jansen and Leukfeldt (2018).

Survey Internet users

The first survey study on Internet users was conducted with 1,200 users of online banking who voluntarily participated in an online survey. The purpose was to compare and test models of precautionary online behaviour in the domain of online banking. The sampling procedure was executed by an external recruitment service of online survey panels. The data were collected in 2015 and were analysed using partial-least-squares path-modelling software. More information on this method can be found in Jansen (2018) and Jansen and Van Schaik (2017, 2018).

The second survey on Internet users used a two-staged approach measuring cognitions, attitudes, behavioural intention, and self-reported behaviour of Internet users on phishing and personal information–sharing behaviour in a one-month interval. The purpose was to gain insight into the effects of fear-appeal manipulations on these aspects and over time. An external recruitment service of online panels handled the recruitment participants who participated voluntarily. In total, 768 participants completed both questionnaires with a net retention rate of 65%. The data were collected in 2017 and were analysed using different statistical techniques. More information on this method can be found in Jansen and Van Schaik (2019).

Cybercriminal networks[5]

Origin and growth

Most criminals do not work alone. This is something criminologists have known for decades (e.g. Shaw & McKay, 1931; Reiss, 1988; Andresen & Felson, 2010). Criminals, however, cannot simply find new 'criminal jobs' in the job advertisement section of the daily newspaper. Therefore, traditionally, social ties play a crucial role in the processes of the origin and growth of criminal networks. Various studies show that recruitment of new criminals is often along the lines of family, friends, and acquaintances who work together and introduce one another to others (Kleemans & Van de Bunt, 1999; Kleemans & De Poot, 2008; Edwards & Levi, 2008; Bouchard & Morselli, 2014). These processes rely heavily on building trust and are strongly related to existing social contacts. These social contacts are limited to, for example, a region or country. So-called 'offender convergence settings' are needed to get into contact with people outside one's initial social cluster (Felson, 2003).

With the digitization of society, new ways have arisen for criminals to meet like-minded people without the traditional restrictions of geographical proximity and existing social networks (e.g. Wall, 2007; Holt & Bossler, 2014). Indeed, the Internet provides new offender convergence settings, such as crypto markets, chat channels, and forums where motivated offenders can meet others (Peretti, 2008; Holt & Lampke, 2009; Lu, Luo, Polgar, & Cao, 2010; Décary-Hétú & Dupont, 2012; Soudijn & Monsma, 2012; Soudijn & Zegers, 2012; Yip, Shadbolt, & Webber, 2012; Dupont, Côté, Savine, & Décary Hétu, 2016). eBay-like rating systems are used to distinguish the trustable criminals from the scammers. Members are able to browse through lists of other rated criminals, each with their own specialization. This means that the ways criminals meet and interact are changing. As a result, the question is if police interventions against such networks should also be changing. Indeed, if, for example, cybercriminals only use crypto markets to recruit others, it makes sense to frustrate these crypto markets and not to focus too much on investigating the social surroundings of cybercriminals. Therefore, an important goal of the analysis of police investigations was to gain more insight into the use of traditional offline social ties, such as family and friends, and new digital ties and offender convergence settings, such as crypto markets and chat channels in recruitment processes.

In order to find out how cybercriminals meet, we analysed 40 cybercriminal networks. The analysis showed that most cybercriminal networks do use new online offender convergence settings. However, unexpectedly, it turned out that almost all networks also rely on traditional social ties. Four types of origin and growth can be identified: (1) completely through offline social contacts; (2) offline social contacts as a base and digital meeting places to recruit specialists; (3) digital meeting places as a base and offline social contacts to recruit local criminals; and (4) completely through online meeting places. In Leukfeldt et al. (2017a, 2017b, 2017c), various cases are used to illustrate these categories. As this chapter is about situational crime prevention methods, we will limit this section to the main findings.

Surprisingly, offline social ties still play an important role in the recruitment processes of cybercriminal networks. Within the networks in category 1 and 2, other suitable co-offenders, such as enablers and money mules, are recruited using existing social contacts. The co-offenders, for example, grew up in the same neighbourhood, went to the same church or soccer club, knew each other from the criminal underworld, or met each other in prison. However, the finding that offline social ties are still important does not mean that online meeting places are not important. Only a few networks managed to execute successful attacks without using online meeting places. The majority of networks use online meeting places one way or another. The networks in which traditional social ties are the base often use online meeting places to recruit specialized enablers, to purchase tools and services, or to sell tools and services themselves. Networks in which online meeting places are the base use online meeting places to meet other suitable core members, recruit enablers, and/or sell criminal services or personal data.

The structure of cybercriminal networks

For law enforcement agencies, it is relevant to understand the structure of criminal networks. Hence, if insight is gained into the structure of a network, it is possible to effectively disrupt that network. A network with a strict military-like hierarchy, for example, needs a different approach compared to a more fluid network of actors that work together.

From the 1950s until the late 20th century, the view of criminal networks, and organized crime networks in particular, was one of a closely knit mafia family with a military-like hierarchy. Empirical studies nuanced that picture: criminal networks were often less hierarchical, less durable, and less fixed in terms of delineation than was assumed (e.g. Fijnaut, Bovenkerk, Bruinsma, & van de Bunt, 1996; Kleemans, van der Berg, & van de Bunt, 1998; Kleemans, Brienen, & van de Bunt, 2002; Kruisbergen, Leukfeldt, Kleemans, & Roks, 2012). This does not mean that networks are completely fluid. There were still dependency relationships; some people are more important and have a more central role than others because they have resources on which others depend, such as money, knowledge, or contacts.

Now over to the cybercriminal networks. At the time the studies were conducted, no empirical analysis was available about the structure of cybercriminal networks. However, studies, often based on data from online forums, showed that online offender convergence settings, such as forms, enable decentralized, flexible networks of loosely organized criminals that are now able to easily collaborate and distribute work (e.g. Peretti, 2008; Holt & Lampke, 2009; Soudijn & Monsma, 2012; Soudijn & Zegers, 2012; Bulanova-Hristova & Kasper, 2016; Odinot, Verhoeven, Pool, & De Poot, 2017; Kruisbergen, Leukfeldt, Kleemans, & Roks, 2018). Although these studies showed that there are still dependency relations, the studies also showed that the role of these central members becomes less important because members of forums are able to get into touch with many other members and are able to expand their own network fast. This raises an important question concerning the structure of cybercriminal networks: Are these cybercriminal networks even more fluid compared to traditional networks? Next, we will give a brief overview of the empirical results about the structure of cybercriminal networks.

When it comes to the composition of networks, different roles can be seen within the networks. All the Dutch cases had three layers: core members, professional facilitators and recruited facilitators, and money mules.

The core members are the brains behind the organization; they initiate and coordinate the attacks. In some networks, a hierarchy can be seen within the group of core members: there is one boss that coordinates everything. In other networks, the core members seem to be equal.

The core members do not have all the skills needed to execute the attacks themselves. Therefore, core members rely on services of criminal enablers. As some enablers are more important than others, a distinction can be made between professional enablers and recruited enablers. Professional enablers offer criminal services to various networks. For example, they develop their own malware or phishing kits, manage botnets, or have networks of money mules in various countries. Recruited enablers are asked (forcefully) by the core members to provide services. This group of enablers usually has an interesting position for the core members because of their work. It might give them access to relevant information or enables them to provide 'simple' services that make the lives of the core members easier. Examples of recruited enablers include employees of call centres of financial institutions (that have access to details about customers) and postal workers (that are able to intercept official post from the bank). Recruited facilitators sometimes receive a small fee for the work or do not get anything at all. They are only used by one particular network.

The bottom layer of the network consists of money mules. These mules are in essence used or abused by the core members to cash money that is stolen from online bank accounts. By cashing the money, the money trail from the victims to the core members is interrupted. Once the core members have access to a bank account of a victim, they will transfer the money to the account of a money mule. The money mule, or someone who controls the money mules, will cash the money as soon as possible. The money is now no longer traceable to the core members. Although this group of offenders is at the very bottom of the network, they do have a very important function for the core members.

Without these money mules, it would not be possible to successful cash money stolen from online bank accounts.

There is a difference between the Dutch networks and the cases in Germany, the UK, and USA. The main difference is that these networks are more diverse when it comes to the composition. The core members of some networks do not need any criminal enablers, because they are able to carry out all the steps of the crime scripts themselves. In these cases, forums play a crucial role. One example is a network of specialized core members who create their own malware and steal large quantities of financial data by hacking into databases and selling data to a handful of trusted wholesalers, who then sell the data on different forums.

Surprisingly, most of the networks within the analysis had a more or less stable group of core members that work together over a longer period of time. Furthermore, all networks clearly had dependency relations. Finally, various roles could be identified. Usually, different roles are needed in order to execute attacks successfully. Only a limited number of networks worked together on a more ad hoc basis for one particular attack. The core members of these networks used forums to actively look for other suitable co-offenders. This is surprising, because Internet and crypto markets facilitate the origin of decentralized, flexible networks of loosely organized criminals that are able to easily collaborate and distribute work based on knowledge and skills. Our analysis, however, showed a different picture: one of cybercriminals that use the advantages that the Internet and crypto markets offer, for example, to buy malware or specific services that are needed, but for a large part resemble much more traditional criminal networks. In sum, members keep on working with people they worked with before and trust.

Another unexpected resemblance with traditional criminal networks can be seen. Offline social ties still play an important role in the process of origin and growth of cybercriminal networks. This is especially true for networks with a more or less stable group of core members; all the ties between the members are usually offline social contacts. Online offender convergence settings, such as forums, are only used to recruit specialists. It should be noted that online social ties seem to be important within origin and growth processes as well.

Most networks in our analysis had a more or less fixed group of core members. However, the composition of networks, including the enablers and money mules, do change constantly. First of all, even though core members form a stable group, it can be seen that subgroups of core members carry out secondary criminal activities, and individual core members sometimes have alliances with criminals outside the network. Furthermore, as the groups have to adapt their modus operandi to the latest security measures of financial institutions, recent awareness campaigns aimed at end users, or police priorities regarding cybercrime, the type of criminal enablers that are needed to fill the knowledge or skills gap of the core members changes regularly. Finally, as money mules are often easily targeted by the financial institutions (which close their bank accounts) or law enforcement agencies (which arrest and interrogate the money mules), a constant flow of new money mules is needed.

Now, back to the question of whether cyber networks are more fluid than traditional networks. As this section shows, that does not seem to be the case. At least, it is not true for the majority of analysed cases. Most networks still have dependency relationships and a more or less stable group of core members. However, online offender convergence settings, such as forums, do enable a more fluid form of cooperation between core members and professional criminal enablers.

It has to be noted that these networks were a minority in our data, but the consequences for the structure and criminal capabilities can be large. Indeed, networks that are able to use the benefits of forums show that short-term alliances to carry out specific attacks are now easily made. Furthermore, it looks like networks with a limited number of core members are now able to become a worldwide operating network relatively fast.

Users as suitable targets[6]

The goal of this section is to clarify the circumstances in which end users are victimized in phishing and malware attacks and how these attacks manifest in practice. This section goes into detail about users as suitable targets and mainly considers (1) who are victims/suitable targets and (2) how and (3) why end users become victims of online banking fraud. In addition, information is provided on (4) precautionary online behaviour of end users and (5) how that can be improved.

Victimization

Based on an analysis of demographic data provided by the case analysis and the interview study, it was found that victims were distributed across genders, age categories, and levels of education. Because the demographic attributes did not provide any explanation for who runs a greater risk for falling for online banking fraud schemes, we investigated the extent to which the routine activity approach might help us in this respect. This approach is commonly used for explaining online fraud victimization (Bossler & Holt, 2009; Choi, 2008; Ngo & Paternoster, 2011; Pratt, Holtfreter, & Reisig, 2010; Van Wilsem, 2011) and predicts that victimization depends on a motivated perpetrator, a suitable target, and the absence of capable guardians in a convergence of time and space (Cohen & Felson, 1979). This approach focuses on daily routines that render individuals more or less suitable for victimization (Bossler & Holt, 2009).

The routine activity approach was operationalized by adopting the components from VIVA. The VIVA acronym stands for value, inertia, visibility, and accessibility. Value means that perpetrators are interested in individuals who are wealthy. Some cybercrime studies demonstrated that there is a correlation between high-income households and victimization of identity theft (Anderson, 2006; Harrell & Langton, 2013). Inertia was not measured, because this refers to the volume of data and technological specifications of computer systems (Yar, 2005), which does not seem to be of relevance when studying online fraud. Visibility refers to online activities. Earlier studies on cybercrime victimization show that certain activities, such as downloading, spending time on social media, opening attachments from unknown sources, clicking on pop-ups, and buying via websites, make targets become suitable because these increase visibility (Bossler & Holt, 2009; Choi, 2008; Hutchings & Hayes, 2009; Ngo & Paternoster, 2011; Pratt et al., 2010). Accessibility concerns weaknesses in software that can be exploited by perpetrators to attack users. Thus, the value, visibility, and accessibility components were measured to determine if a victim could be labelled a suitable target.

The empirical studies using the routine activity approach provided little information on what types of routine activities lead to being more or less prone for online banking fraud victimization. Exceptions were spending more time online and carrying out various kinds of activities, which increased the risk of contracting a malware infection. The value and accessibility components did not provide any evidence for one being more prone to falling for a phishing or malware attack. Although value, visibility, and accessibility do explain victimization for some cybercrimes, the empirical studies, as well as previous quantitative studies, by other researchers fail to agree on universal characteristics. As a last resort, we used a more in-depth methodology, namely victim interviews. However, based on the interview data, the suitability factors from the routine activity approach did not seem to affect online banking fraud victimization either. Moreover, the majority of victims suggested that the perpetrator(s) selected them randomly.

Although the suitability factors from the routine activity approach do not seem to affect victimization, some victims did provide some anecdotal evidence that these factors may have had a connection with online banking fraud victimization. Regarding value, the type of house and suburb victims live in, and the cash flows of their businesses might have attracted perpetrators. For visibility and accessibility, it was less obvious. However, regarding visibility, victims mentioned that having accessed an unsecure website and never logging out of their online banking sessions might have played a role in their victimization. With regard to accessibility, victims mentioned security subscriptions that needed to be extended, computers that had been hacked, business computers that were not equipped with antivirus software, and software updates that were continuously declined to install might have affected their chances of becoming an online banking fraud victim.

Because we were unable to pinpoint any risk-enhancing factors with certainty, based on demographics and criteria from the routine activity approach, we investigated how and why people become victims of online banking fraud. For phishing victimization, the 'how' question can be answered as follows: end users provide their personal information to perpetrators. This is often done by responding to a false email or by filling out information on a phishing website. In some cases, perpetrators called end users and asked them to disclose personal information, including online banking credentials. Note that these actions can also be applied in combination. For malware victimization, end-users' devices were infected with malware that was used to manipulate online banking sessions. Based on the interview study, most devices were automatically infected with malware when they visited websites with outdated security. Based on the case analysis study, we found that malware victimization primarily occurred by responding to a malicious pop-up and by installing a malicious application on a mobile device. We were unable to obtain information on how the malware infection itself was established, though, because this information was absent from the database. Finally, perpetrators monetize the stolen information. These steps are comparable to what is known from earlier studies (e.g. Hong, 2012).

The answer to the 'why' question is similar for phishing and malware attacks. At its most basic form, end users complied with the malicious instructions they saw on their screens or that were instigated by the perpetrator. Perpetrators use a range of psychological tricks in order to gain someone's trust, resulting in that someone giving away his or her personal information. For example, fraudulent messages appealed to trust, authority, and fear and conveyed a sense of urgency, which is also described in the literature (e.g. Vishwanath, Herath, Chen, Wang, & Rao, 2011). By these means, perpetrators create a situation where it is likely for users to make bad decisions. If a fraudulent attempt is in line with the image that a customer has of reality, the risk of becoming a victim increases. An interesting finding is that some of the victims felt that something was not in order but were mentally unable to stop the fraudulent process; they ignored their gut feeling that something was wrong. Somehow, end users do not dare to explicitly doubt that it is the bank that they have contact with. Alternatively, they were simply not paying enough attention at that particular moment. Follow-up research should identify which signals in particular trigger this unsafe feeling and how that feeling can be empowered so people will act upon to it (i.e. start trusting their instincts).

What is interesting is that phishing and malware attacks do not differ much. For example, the goal of phishing and malware attacks (i.e. stealing money from online bank accounts) and the modus operandi of both attack types (i.e. intercepting login credentials, intercepting one-time transaction authentication codes, wiring the money to money mule accounts, and cashing the money) are quite similar. What is different, though, is that phishing attacks often involve direct contact between the victim and the perpetrator, while the contact for malware attacks is indirect.

The conclusion, based on the current findings, is that everyone is susceptible to phishing and malware attacks to some degree; it can happen to anyone. In other words, no specific characteristics of end users could be identified – using different research approaches – that increase the chance of online banking fraud victimization. This holds that victims were equally likely to be male or female; young or old; and low, medium, or highly educated. This leads to the conclusion that the victim population is very diverse. It seems that the way in which the routine activity approach has been applied to online fraud thus far is not appropriate for explaining victimization based on the individual factors that make someone a suitable target.

Moreover, the results suggest that victims have an unintended and sub-conscious, but active, role in the fraudulent process. This counts primarily for phishing victimization, but to a certain extent also for malware victimization. Although malware attacks can be considered a more technical type of attack, end users still had to act for some of these attacks to be successful. Hence, both attack types are similar in many ways, as explained earlier. Therefore, it seems that victimization can be attributed to other factors. Perhaps it is the dragnet method perpetrators usually apply that is highly effective. In this case, victims are not selected because of their suitability factors or routine activities; instead attempts are made to reach them by sending out untargeted bulk emails in the hope that someone will bite. This is complemented by the fact that we did not find any hard evidence that spear phishing – a more labour-intensive type of social engineering – is being applied in online banking attacks. This indicates that target suitability is probably not that important to perpetrators when it comes to online banking, even though this kind of phishing attack seems to have a higher success rate (e.g. Bur35ztein et al., 2014). Another possibility is the context in which fraud takes place. Although not part of the current investiga-tions, anecdotal evidence from the interviews suggests that impactful life events, such as the death of a family member, might explain why some of the victims were not alert or attentive during the fraudulent process.

Precautionary online behaviour

In order to strengthen one of the most essential links in the safety and security of online banking, the end user, two survey studies were conducted. These studies deal with precautionary online behaviour of end users and how that behaviour can be improved. Because it is difficult to pinpoint who runs greater risk for becoming an online banking fraud victim, these studies targeted Inter-net users in general.

Three social cognitive models (i.e. protection motivation theory [Rogers, 1975; Maddux & Rogers, 1983], the reasoned action approach [Fishbein & Ajzen, 2010], and an integrated model comprising variables of these models) were tested with respect to their ability to explain the intentions of precau-tionary online behaviour. Both protection motivation theory and the reasoned action approach make a unique contribution in explaining variance for pre-cautionary online behavioural intention. The integrated model explained most variance in protection motivation ($R^2 = .68$). End users perceive the potential impact of online banking fraud to be severe, but the chances of falling victim themselves to be slim. However, they estimate the chances of others being victimized to be higher. Precautionary online behaviour is largely driven by response efficacy (i.e. the perceived effectiveness of a response in reducing a threat [Milne, Sheeran, & Orbell, 2006]) and self-efficacy (i.e. a user's belief about whether they are capable of performing the recommended response [Milne et al., 2006]).

In the second survey study, the goal was to gain insight into the effects of fear appeal manipulations on users' cognitions, attitudes, behavioural intention, and self-reported behaviour on phishing and personal information–sharing behaviour in a one-month interval. This study demonstrates positive effects of fear appeals on heightening end-users' cognitions, attitudes, and behavioural intentions. However, effects on subsequent security behaviour were not directly observed. Fear appeals show great potential for promoting security behaviour by making end users aware of threats and simultaneously providing behavioural advice on how to mitigate these threats. However, future studies are needed to determine how end-user behaviour can also be positively influenced.

Possibilities for situational crime prevention

Based on the insights into cybercriminal networks, users as suitable targets, and end-user behaviour, we present strategies and measures that disrupt cybercriminals and their schemes as effectively as possible. Needless to say, all strategies have their own pros and cons, and the strategies have to be evaluated in order to prove their effectiveness.

Increase the effort required for crime

Cornish and Clarke (2003) developed five measures that increase the effort required for crime: target hardening, control access to facilities, screen exits, deflect offenders, and control tools and weapons. This section highlights possibilities in terms of target hardening and control tools and weapons.

Target hardening is a means to make it harder for cybercriminal networks to successfully attack financial institutions and their customers. One general measure is identified that increases the effort of crime: financial institutions intercepting fraudulent transaction. This can be realized by monitoring, analysing, and stopping suspicious transactions. This may frustrate criminals because it is harder to acquire the money. Banks should continue to invest in their detection systems in order to stop fraudulent attacks from succeeding. Needless to say, banks should also keep their systems safe and secure and provide end users with a secure Internet connection.

End users have an important responsibility as well. The victim studies show that few variables could be found that increased or decreased the risk of victimization. However, the low-tech attack types rely greatly on social engineering. Target hardening of potential victims for these types of attacks should focus on providing customers of financial institutions with the right information for recognizing how the attacks manifest in practice. Indeed, some of the customers were asked over the telephone to generate and hand over their one-time passwords. These customers might have had a chance to stop the attack if they were aware that financial institutions never ask for these codes over the telephone.

Furthermore, personal risk mitigation measures are important. The challenge is to create a reality that cannot be manipulated when spinning a fraudulent story. This would allow customers to recognize an anomaly more quickly, making them more capable of preventing fraud. Nevertheless, running risks online is comparable to running risks in the physical world. However, in the real world, some personal risk mitigation measures can be taken (e.g. deciding how much cash to carry). This kind of measure could also be taken online; in fact, it is already being applied to some extent (e.g. setting maximum transfer limits and blocking debit cards from being used outside Europe). A variation in limits and usage options makes it potentially more difficult for perpetrators to commit fraud on a large scale. Still, banks could go a step further, for instance, by letting customers block functionality in their online banking that they are not using and by letting them increase the levels of technical security. This may give customers the feeling of being more in control of their online safety, and by doing so they can determine their own risk profile. Moreover, such a solution might be beneficial, because a one-size-fits-all solution does not exist.

Security awareness is not enough; end users should be resilient when online. This means that threat anticipation is not the complete answer. They should also know how to handle such incidents when confronted with them and what to do when things do go from bad to worse in order to recover from it and to minimize impact. Online resilience is not about eliminating risk, but about managing risk. This means that security education and training are important as well. The combination of security education, training, and awareness (SETA) provides an effective barrier against human-related threats to information security according to Parsons, McCormac, Butavicius, and Ferguson (2010). Insights from social marketing/choice architecture can also be used here (e.g. nudges). This is because cybercrime and information security may be very abstract concepts to a large part of the Internet population. An example of a nudge can be a general text on a code calculator saying, 'do not give my codes to anyone.' However, research still needs to provide an answer to which interventions are effective (and lasting) in making end users online-resilient. Nevertheless, our work seems to point in the direction that focusing on underlying cognitive dimensions in SETA efforts is beneficial in order to evoke the right behaviour.

Finally, receiving feedback on how the incident unfolded (e.g. by banks and/or the police) can be helpful to learn from the incident and become resilient regarding future attacks. Considering information security, learning is harder because unwise decisions do not always directly translate into obvious negative outcomes (West, 2008).

High-tech attacks can be frustrated in other ways. First of all, users need to keep their software up to date. The victim survey shows that technical protection (e.g. by a virus scanner) does not necessarily offer protection against cyberattacks. In addition, virus scanners, for instance, do not protect against the latest threats. This does not mean that it is not useful to install a virus scanner and keep your software up to date. Although technical protection might not protect users from the latest threats and against zero-day exploits, it does protect them against known threats. Indeed, cybercriminals who carry out high-tech attacks spend a lot of time online, visiting chat boxes and forums, and share information on known weaknesses and tools. This includes 'old' exploits that might be used by the less skilled criminals to execute attacks.

Target hardening can also be done by so-called 'place managers' (e.g. Internet service providers [ISPs], hosting providers, website owners, and database administrators). This chapter mentioned that spending more time online and visiting all sorts of (legitimate) websites is risk enhancing. This is in line with the routine activity theory: criminals aim their attacks at popular online places. Further risk-enhancing activities are downloading and playing online games. Again, the law of large numbers applies: popular downloads and online games attract many visitors, which makes it attractive for criminals to infect the website in question. Visitors then become potential victims. An analysis of crime scripts of high-tech networks reveals, for example, that networks sometimes do not attack customers directly, but infect the technical infrastructure of third parties. Unsuspicious visitors of these digital places get infected without them knowing. In such cases, it can hardly be concluded that users are the weakest link. Parts of the technical infrastructure that are not well maintained may be closed in order to prevent infection of innocent users. Thus, in order for target hardening to be effective, all responsible parties that are involved in the online banking fraud process should take responsibility. Hence, online safety and security should be considered a team sport.

Finally, measures concerning the control of tools and weapons are of importance. Cybercriminal networks use a range of tools to attack customers of financial institutions. For cybercriminals, it is seemingly easy to purchase malware. Therefore, a way to increase the effort required to successfully attack these customers is to make it harder for criminals to buy malware, for instance, by shutting down forums on which malware is sold.

Increase the risk of crime

According to Cornish and Clarke (2003), the five measures related to increasing the effort required for crime are extend guardianship, assist natural surveillance, reduce anonymity, utilize place managers, and strengthen formal surveillance. We go into more detail on the first and last of these measures.

Guardianship can be extended by financial institutions. This is possible through always initiating criminal prosecution of offenders, reporting offenders to law enforcement agencies, and initiating civil proceedings against money mules as standard practice. Social ties are important in cybercriminal networks; news about arrests will spread quickly among communities, making the recruitment of co-offenders and money mules harder.

A final measure to increase the risk of committing crime is to strengthen formal surveillance. Online meeting places are important for the majority of cybercriminal networks, not only as a marketplace but also as a digital meeting place to recruit co-offenders and enablers. Formal surveillance of these digital meeting places might frustrate the processes of the origin and growth of cybercriminal networks. Furthermore, with regard to international networks, international cooperation is needed from the start of the case. Cases should be screened on at least a European level – as is currently being done on a national level with public–private partnerships such as the Electronic Crimes Task Force in the Netherlands and the USA.

Reduce the rewards of crime

The rewards of crime can be reduced by concealing targets, removing targets, identifying property, disrupting markets, and denying benefits (Cornish & Clarke, 2003). Here, the second and fourth measures are elaborated on.

Concealing targets, removing targets, or identifying property is hard in the case of attacks against customers of financial institutions because those targets are virtual in most cases. However, targets can be removed in those cases in which networks infect websites of third parties or other parts of the technical infrastructure of the Internet. ISPs or hosting providers may, for example, automatically shut down websites with outdated software; see also the measures on target hardening.

A measure to reduce the rewards of crime is to disrupt markets. Large quantities of stolen user credentials and newly developed malware or other criminal tools are sold on forums. These markets need to be monitored and disrupted, for instance, by taking the entire forum offline, feeding the forum with false information in order to break down the systems that enable the building of trust, or by arresting the key actors that are active within the forum (e.g. the administrators or the wholesalers).

Reduce provocations that invite criminal behaviour

This fourth strategy of situational crime prevention includes reducing frustrations, avoiding disputes, reducing emotional arousal, neutralizing peer pressure, and discouraging imitation (Cornish & Clarke, 2003). In this section, the focus is on neutralizing peer pressure and discouraging imitation.

Neutralizing peer pressure and discouraging imitation are measures that can be used to frustrate cybercriminal networks. First, peer pressure can be neutralized with regard to core members, enablers, and money mules. The analysis of criminal investigations shows that core members and enablers have often been active to a great extent in the online world. They are in a world where it is normal to talk about cybercriminal activities and to teach each other ways to commit fraud, abuse weaknesses in software, or carry out distributed denial of service (DDoS) attacks. Awareness campaigns should be aimed at these groups to prevent a subculture in which it is normal to commit cybercrimes.

Furthermore, for money mules, peer pressure seems to be important. It is common that money mules are recruited via existing social networks. Money mules often claim that everybody in their community knows about fraud being committed and that they are often approached to cooperate. Awareness campaigns should be aimed at this group, telling them that they are accomplices to serious criminals and that there are consequences related to their actions, for example, jail time and a debt with their bank because they have to pay back the money cashed from their account.

In conclusion, imitation should be discouraged. In the digital era, forums are used to gain knowledge and skills and replace prisons as the universities for criminals. Loners who experiment with all sorts of technical tools out of curiosity might end up in criminal networks through these forums. More insight is needed into how criminals ended up on forums in the first place in order to disrupt them more effectively.

Remove excuses for criminal behaviour

This final set of measures include setting rules, posting instructions, alerting conscience, assisting compliance, and controlling disinhibition (Cornish & Clarke, 2003). The second and third measure are outlined next.

To remove excuses is to set rules. This can be done by legitimate companies whose employees are used by core members to facilitate certain steps of the crime scripts. These include postal employees who intercept important mails to customers of financial institutions and employees who work at bank call centres and have access to customer data and are able to make changes to user accounts. These companies should be informed about the illegal activities of their employees, and they should communicate clearly that this kind of behaviour is unlawful, that the company actively looks for these kinds of activities, and that the company will press charges when employees are identified executing illegal activities.

Finally, alerting conscience applies to potential core members, enablers, and money mules. These are similar to measures aimed at reducing peer pressure as proposed in an earlier section: make it clear that cybercrimes are real crimes with real victims.

Concluding remarks: applying the situational crime prevention framework to financial cybercrimes

This chapter explored the extent to which the situational crime prevention framework can be used to develop measures against financial cybercrimes, such as phishing and banking malware. It provides a holistic overview of 20 peer-reviewed studies that were carried out under the Dutch Knowledge Program on Safety and Security of Online Banking. These studies focused on both the criminals, victims, and end users. Although we had access to unique datasets and combined insight into criminals, crime scripts, victims, and end users, all studies that underpin the measures presented in this chapter have their limitations. For a detailed description of the limitations, we refer to the particular studies.

In general, the majority of our datasets are Dutch. Furthermore, with regard to the criminals, the most pressing issue is that we only had data about cyber-criminal networks that were known to the police. The biggest limitation with regard to the victims and end users is that we had to rely on self-report studies. In future studies, actual behaviour should also be studied. Indeed, it is well known that attitudes and real behaviour do not always match. Finally, the measures described in this chapter need to be put to the test: Which of the measures work best in practice? How do criminals respond to these measures? And how long do measures aimed at (behaviour) of end users stay effective?

Our analysis clearly shows that the situational crime prevention framework can be applied to financial cybercrimes. Measures can be developed for all five strategies of situational crime prevention. These include 'obvious' measures such as target hardening by monitoring, analysing, and stopping suspicious transactions by financial institutions and by keeping software up-to-date by end users, or reducing the rewards of crime by disrupting online markets. Measures also include increasing the risk of crime by extended guardianship of financial institutions, for example, by always initiating criminal prosecution of offenders and by always initiating civil proceedings against money mules. Furthermore, provocations that invite criminal behaviour can be reduced. Money mules, for example, play an important role in the crime scripts of financially motivated offenders. Money mules often claim that everybody in their community knows about fraud being committed and that they are often approached to cooperate. Money mules can be made more aware of the fact that they are accomplices to serious criminals and that there are consequences related to their actions. In line with this, excuses for criminal behaviour can be removed, for instance, by setting rules by legitimate companies whose employees are used by offenders to facilitate certain steps of the crime scripts, for example, employees of telecommunication companies who are able to perform a sim-swap, which is needed to get one-time security codes sent by banks over Short Message Service (SMS).

Finally, this chapter showed the importance of the human factor in cyber-crime. Some of the proposed situational crime prevention measures are technical in nature, for example, monitoring and having cybersecurity measures in place by end users. Without a doubt, more technical measures are relevant. However, as this chapter shows, measures should also focus on human aspects: either the human as the criminal or the human as the (potential) victim. A good example is making money mules aware of the fact that they are being used by criminals to make a lot of money. It turns out that this seemingly unimportant and interchangeable type of offender that is situated at the bottom of the criminal hierarchy is actually of high importance to core members, because without these money mules, there is no safe way of getting the stolen money from users. Furthermore, end users should install protective technical measures but should also be made more resilient when online. Indeed, they should know how to handle cyber-incidents and what to do when things go from bad to worse in order to recover quickly. Online resilience, therefore, is not about eliminating risk, but about managing risk by people.

Notes

1   Phishing is the process of retrieving personal information using deception through impersonation (Lastdrager, 2014). Phishing often starts with a deceitful email. Fake websites and fraudulent phone calls are also applied to intercept user credentials.

2   Malware is the infection of a device – in this case one that is used for online banking – with malicious software, including viruses, worms, Trojan horses, and spyware, for the purposes of carrying out the harmful intentions of an attacker (Moser, Kruegel, & Kirda, 2007).

3   This programme was funded by the Dutch National Police, the Dutch Police Academy, and the Dutch Banking Association.

4   The analytical framework contained various topics, including case information (e.g. the composition of the investigation team and other parties involved), overview of the investigation (e.g. the starting point for this criminal investigation and the offences that were central in the investigation), the structure of the criminal network (e.g. number of suspects and the composition of the criminal network), the origin of the criminal group and binding mechanisms, and the modus operandi. This framework is published in Leukfeldt (2016).

5   This section is based on Leukfeldt (2014b) and Leukfeldt et al. (2017a, 2017b, 2017c, 2017d, 2017e).

6   This section is based on case analysis of incidents registered in a fraud database of a financial institution (Jansen & Leukfeldt, 2015), victim interviews (Jansen & Leukfeldt, 2016, 2018), a victim survey (Leukfeldt, 2014a; Leukfeldt & Yar, 2016), and two survey studies on internet users (Jansen & Van Schaik, 2017, 2018, 2019; Jansen, Kop, & Stol, 2017).

References

Anderson, K. B. (2006). Who are the victims of identity theft? The effect of demographics. *Journal of Public Policy & Marketing, 25*(2), 160–171.

Andresen, M. A., & Felson, M. (2010). Situational crime prevention and co-offending. *Crime Patterns and Analysis, 3*(1), 3–13.

Arts, C. H., & Hoogteijling, E. M. J. (2002). *Het Sociaal Statistisch Bestand 1998 en 1999* [The Social Statistics Database 1998 and 1999]. Den Haag/Heerlen: CBS.

Bossler, A. M., & Holt, T. J. (2009). On-line activities, guardianship, and malware infection: An examination of routine activities theory. *International Journal of Cyber Criminology, 3*(1), 400–420.

Bouchard, M., & Morselli, C. (2014). Opportunistic structures of organized crime. In L. Paoli (Ed.), *The Oxford handbook of organized crime*. Oxford and New York, NY: Oxford University Press.

Bulanova-Hristova, G., & Kasper, K. (2016). Cyber-OC in Germany. In G. Bulanova-Hristova, K. Kasper, G. Odinot, M. Verhoeven, R. Pool, C. de Poot, . . . L. Korsell (Eds.), *Cyber-OC – Scope and manifestations in selected EU member states* (pp. 165–220). Wiesbaden: Bundeskriminalamt.

Bursztein, E., Benko, B., Margolis, D., Pietraszek, T., Archer, A., Aquino, A., . . . Savage, S. (2014). *Handcrafted fraud and extortion: Manual account hijacking in the wild*. Proceedings of the 2014 Internet Measurement Conference, pp. 347–358.

Choi, K.-S. (2008). Computer crime victimization and integrated theory: An empirical assessment. *International Journal of Cyber Criminology, 18*(1), 308–333.

Clarke, R. V. (1980). "Situational" crime prevention: Theory and practice. *The British Journal of Criminology, 20*(2), 136–147.

Clarke, R.V. (1992). Introduction. In R.V. Clarke (Ed.), *Situational crime prevention: Successful case studies*. Guilderland, NY: Harrow and Heston.

Clarke, R.V. (1997). Introduction. In R.V. Clarke (Ed.), *Situational crime prevention: Successful case studies*. Guilderland, NY: Harrow and Heston.

Clarke, R.V. (2004). Technology, crime and crime science. *European Journal on Criminal Policy and Research*, *1*(10), 55–63.

Clarke, R.V., & Homel, R. (1997). A revised classification of situational crime prevention techniques. In S. P. Lab (Ed.), *Crime Prevention at a Crossroads*. Cincinnati, OH: Anderson.

Cohen, L. E., & Felson, M. (1979). Social change and crime rate trends: A routine activity approach. *American Sociological Review*, *44*, 588–608.

Cornish, D. B., & Clarke, R.V. (2003). Opportunities, precipitators and criminal decisions: A reply to Wortley's critique of situational crime prevention. *Crime Prevention Studies*, *16*, 41–96.

Décary-Hétu, D., & Dupont, B. (2012). The social network of hackers. *Global Crime*, *13*(3), 160–175.

Domenie, M. M. L., Leukfeldt, E. R., Wilsem, J. A. van, Jansen, J., & Stol, W. Ph. (2013). *Victimization in a digitised society: A survey among members of the public concerning e-fraud, hacking and other high-volume crimes*. The Hague: Eleven International.

Dupont, B., Côté, A. M., Savine, C., & Décary Hétu, D. (2016). The ecology of trust among hackers. *Global Crime*, *17*(2), 129–151.

Edwards, A., & Levi, M. (2008). Researching the organization of serious crimes. *Criminology and Criminal Justice*, *8*(4), 363–388.

Felson, M. (2003). The process of co-offending. In M. J. Smith & D. B. Cornish (eds.), *Theory for practice in situational crime prevention* (Vol. 16, pp. 149–168). Devon: Willan Publishing.

Fijnaut, C. J. C. F., Bovenkerk, F., Bruinsma, G. J. N., & van de Bunt, H. G. (1996). *Georganiseerde criminaliteit in Nederland, eindrapport, bijlage VII van: Enquêtecommissie opsporingsmethoden, Inzake Opsporing* [Organized crime in the Netherlands]. Den Haag: du Uitgevers.

Fishbein, M., & Ajzen, I. (2010). *Predicting and changing behavior: The reasoned action approach*. New York, NY: Taylor & Francis.

Harrell, E., & Langton, L. (2013). *Victims of identity theft, 2012*. Washington, DC: Bureau of Justice Statistics.

Hartel, P., Junger, M., & Wieringa, R. (2011). *Cyber-crime science = crime science + information security*. Enschede: University of Twente.

Holt, J. T., & Lampke, E. (2009). Exploring stolen data markets online: Products and market forces. *Criminal Justice Studies*, *23*(1), 33–50.

Holt, T. J., & Bossler, A. M. (2014). An Assessment of the current state of cybercrime scholarship. *Deviant Behavior*, *35*(1), 20–40.

Hong, J. (2012). The state of phishing attacks. *Communications of the ACM*, *55*(1), 74–81.

Hutchings, A., & Hayes, H. (2009). Routine activity theory and phishing victimisation: Who gets caught in the 'net'. *Current Issues Criminal Justice*, *20*(3), 433–451.

Jansen, J. (2018). *Do you bend or break? Preventing online banking fraud victimization through online resilience* (PhD thesis). Heerlen: Open University of the Netherlands.

Jansen, J., Kop, N., & Stol, W. (2017). Internetbankieren: Veiligheidspercepties van gebruikers [End-user perceptions of safety and security of online banking]. *Tijdschrift voor Veiligheid*, *16*(1), 36–51.

Jansen, J., & Leukfeldt, E. R. (2018). Coping with cybercrime victimization: An exploratory study into impact and change. *Journal of Qualitative Criminal Justice and Criminology*, *6*(2), 205–228.

Jansen, J., & Leukfeldt, R. (2015). *How people help fraudsters steal their money: An analysis of 600 online banking fraud cases.* Proceedings of the 2015 Workshop on Socio-Technical Aspects in Security and Trust, pp. 24–31.

Jansen, J., & Leukfeldt, R. (2016). Phishing and malware attacks on online banking customers in the Netherlands: A qualitative analysis of factors leading to victimization. *International Journal of Cyber Criminology, 10*(1), 79–91.

Jansen, J., & van Schaik, P. (2017). Comparing three models to explain precautionary online behavioural intentions. *Information & Computer Security, 25*(2), 165–180.

Jansen, J., & van Schaik, P. (2018). Testing a model of precautionary online behaviour: The case of online banking. *Computers in Human Behavior, 87,* 371–383.

Jansen, J., & van Schaik, P. (2019). The design and evaluation of a theory-based intervention to promote security behaviour against phishing. *International Journal of Human – Computer Studies, 123,* 40–55.

Kleemans, E. R., Brienen, M. E. I., & van de Bunt, H. G. (2002). *Georganiseerde criminaliteit in Nederland. Ttweede rapportage op basis van de WODC-monitor* [Organised crime in the Netherlands. Second report based on the WODC monitor]. Den Haag: WODC.

Kleemans, E. R., & De Poot, C. J. (2008). Criminal careers in organized crime and social opportunity structure. *European Journal of Criminology, 5*(1), 69–98.

Kleemans, E. R., & van de Bunt, H. G. (1999). The social embeddedness of organized crime. *Transnational Organized Crime, 5*(2), 19–36.

Kleemans, E. R., van der Berg, A. E. I. M., & van de Bunt, H. G. (1998). *Georganiseerde criminaliteit in Nederland. Rapportage op basis van de WODC monitor* [Organised crime in the Netherlands. Report based on the WODC monitor]. Den Haag: WODC.

Kruisbergen, E. W., Leukfeldt, E. R., Kleemans, E. R., & Roks, R. A. (2018). *Georganiseerde criminaliteit en ICT Nederland. Rapportage in het kader van de vijfde ronde van de Monitor Georganiseerde Criminaliteit* [*Organized crime and IT. Report based on the fifth round of the Organized Crime Monitor*]. Den Haag: WODC. English summary available at: https://english.wodc. nl/

Kruisbergen, E. W., Van de Bunt, H. G., & Kleemans, E. R. (2012). *Georganiseerde criminaliteit in Nederland. Vierde rapportage op basis van de Monitor Georganiseerde Criminaliteit* [*Organized crime in the Netherlands. Fourth report of the Organized Crime Monitor*]. Den Haag: Boom Lemma. English summary available at: https://english.wodc.nl/

Lastdrager, E. E. (2014). Achieving a consensual definition of phishing based on a systematic review of the literature. *Crime Science, 3*(1), 1–10.

Leukfeldt, E. R. (2014a). Phishing for suitable targets in the Netherlands. Routine activity theory and phishing victimization. *Cyberpsychology Behavior and Social Networking, 17*(8), 551–555.

Leukfeldt, E. R. (2014b). Cybercrime and social ties. Phishing in Amsterdam. *Trends in Organized Crime, 17*(4), 231–249.

Leukfeldt, E. R. (2016). *Cybercriminal networks: Origin, growth and criminal capabilities* (PhD thesis). The Hague: Eleven International.

Leukfeldt, E. R., & Kleemans, E. R. (2019). Cybercrime, money mules and situational crime prevention. In S. Hufnagel & A. Moiseienko (Eds.), *Criminal networks and law enforcement: Global perspectives on illicit enterprise.* London: Routledge.

Leukfeldt, E. R., Kleemans, E. R., & Stol, W. P. (2017a). The use of online crime markets by cybercriminal networks: A view from within. *American Behavioral Scientist.*

Leukfeldt, E. R., Kleemans, E. R., & Stol, W. P. (2017b). Cybercriminal networks, social ties and online forums: Social ties versus digital ties within phishing and malware networks. *British Journal of Criminology.* doi:10.1093/bjc/azw009

Leukfeldt, E. R., Kleemans, E. R., & Stol, W. P. (2017c). Origin, growth and criminal capabilities of cybercriminal networks. An international empirical analysis. *Crime, Law and Social Change.* doi:10.1007/s10611-016-9647-1

Leukfeldt, E. R., Kleemans, E. R., & Stol, W. P. (2017d). A typology of cybercriminal networks: From low tech locals to high tech specialists. *Crime, Law and Social Change.* doi:10.1007/s10611-016-9646-2

Leukfeldt, E. R., Lavorgna, A., & Kleemans, E. R. (2017e). Organised cybercrime or cybercrime that is organised? An assessment of the conceptualisation of financial cybercrime as organised crime. *European Journal on Criminal Policy and Research, 23*(3), 287–300.

Leukfeldt, E. R., & Yar, M. (2016). Applying routine activity theory to cybercrime. A theoretical and empirical analysis. *Deviant Behavior.* doi:10.1080/01639625.2015.1012409

Lu, Y., Luo, X., Polgar, M., & Cao, Y. (2010). Social network analysis of a criminal hacker community. *Journal of Computer Information Systems, 51*(2), 31–41.

Maddux, J. E., & Rogers, R. W. (1983). Protection motivation and self-efficacy: A revised theory of fear appeals and attitude change. *Journal of Experimental Social Psychology, 19*(5), 469–479.

Milne, S., Sheeran, P., & Orbell, S. (2006). Prediction and intervention in health-related behavior: A meta-analytic review of protection motivation theory. *Journal of Applied Social Psychology, 30*(1), 106–143

Moser, A., Kruegel, C., & Kirda, E. (2007). *Limits of static analysis for malware detection.* Proceedings of the Computer Security Applications Conference, pp. 421–430.

Ngo, F. T., & Paternoster, R. (2011). Cybercrime victimization: An examination of individual and situational level factors. *International Journal of Cyber Criminology, 5*(1), 773–793.

Odinot, G., Verhoeven, M. A., Pool, R. L. D., & De Poot, C. J. (2017). *Organised cyber-crime in the Netherlands: Empirical findings and implications for law enforcement.* Den Haag: WODC. Cahier 2017–1.

Parsons, K., McCormac, A., Butavicius, M., & Ferguson, L. (2010). *Human factors and information security: Individual, culture and security environment.* Edinburgh, Australia: Command, Control, Communications and Intelligence Division DSTO (Defence Science and Technology Organisation).

Peretti, K. K. (2008). Data breaches: What the underground world of 'carding' re-veals. *Santa Clara Computer and High-technology Law Journal, 25*(2), 345–414.

Pratt, T. C., Holtfreter, K., & Reisig, M. D. (2010). Routine online activity and internet fraud targeting: Extending the generality of routine activity theory. *Journal of Research in Crime and Delinquency, 47*(3), 267–296.

Reiss, A. J. (1988). Co-offending and criminal careers. In M. Tonry & N. Morris (Eds.), *Crime and Justice. A Review of Research.* Chicago: Chicago University Press.

Rogers, R. W. (1975). A protection motivation theory of fear appeals and attitude change. *The Journal of Psychology, 91*(1), 93–114.

Shaw, C. R., & McKay, H. D. (1931). *Report on the causes of crime* (Vol. II). Washington, DC: Government Printing Office.

Soudijn, M. R. J., & Monsma, E. (2012). Virtuele ontmoetingsuimtes voor cybercrimi-nelen. *Tijdschrift voor Criminologie, 54*(4), 349–360.

Soudijn, M. R. J., & Zegers, B. C. H. T. (2012). Cybercrime and virtual offender convergence settings. *Trends in Organized Crime, 15*(2–3), 111–129.

van Wilsem, J. A. (2011). Bought it, but never got it. Assessing risk factors for online consumer fraud victimization. *European Sociologic Review, 29*(2), 168–178.

Vishwanath, A., Herath, T., Chen, R., Wang, J., & Rao, H. R. (2011). Why do people get phished? Testing individual differences in phishing vulnerability within an integrated, information processing model. *Decision Support Systems, 51*(3), 576–586.

Wall, D. S. (2007). *Cybercrime. The Transformation of Crime in the Information Age*. Cambridge: Polity Press.

West, R. (2008). The psychology of security. *Communications of the ACM, 51*(4), 34–40.

Yar, M. (2005). The novelty of "cybercrime": An assessment in light of routine activity theory. *European Journal of Criminology, 2*(4), 407–427.

Yip, M., Shadbolt, N., & Webber, C. (2012). *Structural analysis of online criminal social networks.* IEEE International Conference on Intelligence and Security Informatics (ISI), pp. 60–65.

11 Modelling cybercrime development

The case of Vietnam

Jonathan Lusthaus

Introduction

The literature on the structure and organization of profit-driven cybercrime has been growing for a number of years. Whereas earlier texts addressed cybercrime as a whole (Wall, 2007; Brenner, 2010; Yar, 2013; Kilger, 2010), some more recent articles have focussed on financially motivated activities (for example Hutchings, 2014; Dupont, Côté, Boutin, & Fernandez, 2017; Leukfeldt, Lavorgna, & Kleemans, 2016; Lusthaus, 2013). In a number of cases, the flowering of these efforts has been tied to the appearance of new forms of data, such as archives and scrapes from illicit online marketplaces (see, for example, Holt & Lampke, 2010; Décary-Hétu & Dupont, 2013; Motoyama, McCoy, Levchenko, Savage, & Voelker, 2011; Dupont, Côté, Savine, & Décary-Hétu, 2016; Hutchings & Holt, 2015).

But there is more to the organization of cybercrime than online organization alone. A niche literature is also beginning to emerge looking at the offline dimension of cybercrime. Leukfeldt and colleagues have studied the importance of 'social ties' – as opposed to digital ties – among groups of cybercriminals (Leukfeldt, Kleemans, & Stol, 2017; Leukfeldt, 2014). Lusthaus and Varese have examined the offline organizational structures of cybercriminals, with a particular interest in the socio-economic contexts in which offenders operate (Lusthaus, 2018a; Lusthaus & Varese, 2017).

Nonetheless, this line of research remains underdeveloped and would benefit from greater investigation, particularly how this offline dimension interacts with geography. The focus of this chapter is on this geographical component: in short, why cybercrime emerges in some locations but not others, and how this process takes place in each instance. The latter concern is more challenging to unpack, both theoretically and empirically, but it is addressed (even imperfectly) in this chapter to move the discussion forward on an important policy-relevant topic. With significant further investigation, understanding the process of cybercrime development, and where certain countries are on this trajectory, could help identify at-risk states so early interventions or responses could be developed.

A number of observers have acknowledged the primacy of Eastern European cybercrime, along with some thoughts on the factors of what led cybercrime to emerge there (see Kshetri, 2013; Kigerl, 2012). This study takes matters one step further by trying to formalize the model of cybercriminal development found in the former Soviet states and to determine if it can be used to predict emerging profit-driven cybercrime hubs in other parts of the world. It takes an exploratory case study of Vietnam for this purpose – a small initial step forward in what is a much larger overall research endeavour.

This chapter proceeds in four sections. First, it outlines a model of cybercrime development from the Eastern European case, drawing on the findings of a major seven-year empirical study on cybercrime, along with other literature in the area. Second, it outlines the data and methods used in this chapter. Third, it sketches the nature of Vietnamese cybercrime. Finally, it applies the model of cybercrime development in Eastern Europe to the case of Vietnam, determining if the same factors are present and if this Southeast Asian country might emerge as a new cybercrime hub.

A model of cybercrime development

This section outlines a model of cybercrime development. It considers both why certain hubs might emerge as key cybercriminal centres and how the development of these hubs might take place. This model is derived primarily from the book *Industry of Anonymity: Inside the Business of Cybercrime*, which involved a seven-year global study of cybercrime in 20 countries with 238 interview participants from law enforcement, private-sector, and cybercriminal backgrounds. Although the book does not explicitly state the model, it provides a number of elements from which it can be elucidated more clearly. In particular, it outlines the development of Eastern European cybercrime, which might be considered the cybercrime hub *par excellence*. This injection of data builds on the work of researchers who have hypothesized different factors driving Eastern European cybercrime, including corruption, Internet penetration, tertiary education, IT skills, a lack of employment opportunities, a lack of enforcement capacity, and support from existing criminal networks (McCombie, Pieprzyk, & Watters, 2009; Kshetri, 2013, 2010). These works form part of a broader, though surprisingly niche, literature on Eastern European hackers and cybercriminals (Holt, Strumsky, Smirnova, & Kilger, 2012; Voiskousky & Smyslova, 2003).

In terms of what factors have led to Eastern Europe, or more particularly the former Soviet states, becoming a major hub for cybercrime, Lusthaus (2018b) identifies four (intertwined) factors: (1) the prevalence of good technical education, tied to a Communist legacy; (2) a large community of hackers and those interested in computing; (3) relatively low salaries and limited employment/ business opportunities; and (4) relatively widespread corruption and limited enforcement against cybercriminal offences.

To begin with the prevalence of technical education, the book argues that this is a key element of why Eastern Europe serves as global cybercrime's technical engine. From early on, it was those from the region who drove innovation in the carding business. In recent times, Eastern Europeans have developed some of the leading malware products within the cybercrime industry. This specialization appears to be linked to social and economic conditions of the former Soviet Union, along with other nearby former Communist nations. Beginning with Lenin, the Soviet Union and a number of these other states invested heavily in the sciences and technology (on the Soviets and science see Bailes, 1978; Graham, 1993, 1998). Part of the effect of this approach was that STEM (science, technology, engineering, mathematics) education was especially good, with both leading universities and a large pool of talented graduates produced in these subjects. Many of these graduates from high school and beyond – including future cybercriminals – would have great proficiency in computing (Lusthaus, 2018b, p. 69).

The second component of the model is that a large pool of hackers and programmers has existed in Eastern Europe. Part of this is tied to the earlier point, but there were other drivers as well. Before the fall of Communism in the region, trade restrictions often meant that Western technology could not be accessed. As a result, there were local efforts in these countries to replicate these pieces of hardware. With regard to software, cracking and piracy also became popular throughout the region, along with many other locations around the globe (Kshetri, 2013, pp. 47–48). One could judge such behaviour negatively, but often the software in question could not be easily acquired by individuals – either because it was not sold in that market or it was far too costly to purchase due to low wages. As a result, a community of skilled crackers developed, who specialized in reverse engineering software. This is a skill set that is well suited to application within the broader cybercrime industry (Lusthaus, 2018b, p. 70).

The third component of the model is low salaries, limited employment opportunities, and a restricted space for entrepreneurialism. A supply of potential cybercriminals is sustained by both a production line of technical graduates and a widespread practice of reverse engineering. But a 'push' into cybercrime is also required. This takes the form of limited opportunities in the legitimate technology sectors of Eastern Europe, and particularly a lack of high-salaried jobs for programmers and others (Kshetri, 2013, p. 48; McCombie et al., 2009, p. 47). Some might take part in cybercrime operations with their eyes open. Meanwhile, others might simply be un(der)employed programmers who respond to online advertisements to assist on projects that they either don't realize are illegal or find it pertinent not to ask the question. At its core, cybercrime is "an aspirational endeavor" (Lusthaus, 2018b, p. 71). In many cases, offenders have both computer access and a considerable amount of education, which moves them beyond drivers of base desperation. Although a number can be relatively poor, for some, making a decent living may not be enough when one seeks to make a fortune like those in Silicon Valley. But the post-Soviet economy is not designed for start-ups and tech entrepreneurs. Unlike the American tech sector, where start-ups can thrive, the tech sector in various Eastern European countries is often controlled by a handful of major and well-protected firms (Lusthaus, 2018b, p. 71). Paradoxically, the Communist heritage of Eastern Europe has created both an enormous reservoir of technical talent and the economic conditions to stifle it: an economy dominated by oligarchs and government interests, with limited entrepreneurial opportunities. Those with a more dynamic instinct are pushed to create cybercriminal businesses instead.

The final component of this model is corruption. This is embedded across Eastern Europe (Varese, 2000; Ledeneva, 2006; McCombie et al., 2009, p. 47). Cybercriminals are only sporadically arrested in the region, despite widespread knowledge about certain individuals. If they can safely navigate the system, this often-corrupt environment can help explain how cybercriminals can operate quite openly (see also Kshetri, 2013). But in some ways, it also explains their career choices when the system is viewed as deeply corrupt, and even legal business is a grey area that often brings a number of moral compromises (e.g. in the form of required bribes and kickbacks). Linked to this reality is often a cybercriminal mentality: inept victims either deserve to be defrauded or are so overly rich that stealing from them is not really criminal (for a cybercriminal perspective see Pavlovich, 2018). There is also a patriotic element with these 'Robin Hood' activities redistributing money back to the former Soviet Union from its old enemies. This links with a widely discussed blurring between business, government, and crime in the region (on post-Soviet society see Galeotti, 2014; Ledeneva, 2006). With intelligent offenders and little fear of punishment, in such terms cybercrime is not shameful.

Although these four factors might define the nature of Eastern European cybercrime, it is also important to understand how the emergence of such a cybercrime hub took place. *Industry of Anonymity* suggests that

> from the 1990s onwards, computers and access to the internet become more widely available for users across the globe, just at the time when increasing amounts of data and commerce are being digitized and finding their way online. All across the world, an economic opportunity emerges to tempt both the technologically adept and those simply looking for new ways to make money.
>
> (p. 36)

A pattern appears to emerge in certain cases, where cybercriminal development takes place in phases. Phase 1 is often centred on students and similar groups who have time to explore and have access to new technology. In this initial phase, profit is not a central driver. But after a period, Phase 2 begins, which might also involve a new generation. This phase is much more heavily driven by profit (Lusthaus, 2018b, p. 36). This new generation may give up on some of the norms of their predecessors: any romanticism is lost and replaced by a strongly profit-driven motivation.

This applies to the Russian-speaking underground as much as it applies to the English-speaking cybercriminal population. The scene was originally far more open and collaborative, but over time the situation changed, and payment is much more likely to be required in place of goodwill or favours (on the evolution of the scene see Poulsen, 2011; Menn, 2010; Glenny, 2011). In contexts like Nigeria or Romania, this pattern might not be as applicable. In these cases, a profit motivation has been a strong feature even during the beginnings of local cybercrime. Nonetheless, in these examples a movement toward more serious criminality, and greater professionalism, is still observed. Romanian cybercrime did begin with students, but it has developed to become increasingly sophisticated and organized, now seeing broader criminal layers getting involved (Lusthaus & Varese, 2017). The Nigerian case also shows cybercrime becoming further driven by profit and increasingly professional and technical over time. The later part of this chapter addresses how well this pattern applies to the case of Vietnam.

Data and methods

As the previous model would suggest, there are suspicions that the prevalence of cybercrime in Eastern Europe is tied to a Communist legacy (Lusthaus, 2018b; Lusthaus & Varese, 2017). This makes the investigation of a current or former Communist country of interest. There is likely some variation within Eastern Europe regarding the prevalence or nature of cybercrime in particular states. But to truly test the relevance of the model, it is important to apply it to a case that differs from Eastern Europe in many respects; otherwise, the model will have little explanatory power beyond a small number of largely uniform cases. It seemed logical that the choice of country would also be a case where cybercrime is believed to be somewhat prevalent. Some current and former Communist nations, such as Cuba and certain African nations, have thus far not displayed a great proclivity towards cybercrime. China and North Korea are regularly mentioned in the media and policy reports, although much of that activity often concerns cyber-espionage on behalf of the state rather than professional cybercrime. Even so, it would be near impossible to research cybercrime in North Korea through fieldwork. Such an approach is possible in China, but the enormous size of the country and the population would require a much larger study beyond the scope of this chapter.

As a result, the case of Vietnam presented itself as sensible choice for a pilot study. Not only is it a Communist country, but it also has a reputation as a rising cybercrime hub. Although some work has been carried out on Asian cybercrime in general (Broadhurst & Grabosky, 2005; Broadhurst & Chang, 2013), case studies of Vietnam in particular are limited (Gohwong, 2017). Fieldwork was carried out in the country in January 2017. Hanoi and Ho Chi Minh City were the sites chosen to base the fieldwork, given that they are major populations with high concentrations of potential interview subjects. This fieldwork was exploratory in nature, meant to offer initial insights in addressing this topic, rather than being an extensive investigation requiring far greater time and resources.

The core of this fieldwork was in person semi-structured interviews. These were conducted in English. Obviously, this is a limitation on the data, as participants who did not speak English could not participate. Luckily the international nature of cybercrime – for attackers and defenders alike – means that a number of those involved in this sphere speak English. Nonetheless, a more detailed investigation of this case would certainly benefit from having a Vietnamese speaker on the research team to broaden the potential participant pool. Participants were primarily sourced through purposive sampling, commonly identified through laborious searches of social media, news articles, and other online information. Following this, direct contact was made, and subjects elected to participate, declined, or did not reply. Some snowball sampling supplemented this approach, with certain participants identified through contacts that had already been developed or were developed through the research process. Interviews were carried out in public places (e.g. cafes), or sometimes in semi-public places like company offices when participant *bona fides* were obvious. Participants were given the choice of being recorded or not; their choice could be either personal or due to their professional circumstances. In other instances, the researcher chose not to record the interview because a loud setting, strong accent, or otherwise suggested that a decipherable recording would not be made. In these cases, detailed notes were taken during the interview, which were fleshed out shortly after each meeting took place.

There were 14 participants in total. These subjects included government agents involved in cybercrime investigation, which are all labelled as law enforcement agents for the purposes of this study, even though some may come from non-policing agencies. This is done in order to not ascribe views to particular agencies. A number of other participants were security professionals from the private sector. One participant was a hacker (although a number of the security professionals may also have fallen into this category at one point or another). Finally, one former cybercriminal was interviewed but this took place through electronic communication, outside of the main fieldwork period. The participants are summarized in Table 11.1.

Table 11.1 Interview participants

No.	Description	Year	Type	Code
1	Vietnamese Hacker 1	2017	In Person/58.13	VN–H–1
2	Vietnamese Cybersecurity Professional 1	2017	In Person/24.25	VN–CSP–1
3, 4	Vietnamese Cybersecurity Profession 2, Vietnamese Cybersecurity Professional 3	2017	In Person/ Unrecorded Interview	VN–CSP–2; VN–CSP–3
5	Vietnamese Law Enforcement Agent 1	2017	In Person/ Unrecorded Interview	VN–LE–1
6, 7, 8	Vietnamese Cybersecurity Professional 4, Vietnamese Cybersecurity Professional 5, Vietnamese Cybersecurity Professional 6	2017	In Person/ Unrecorded Interview	VN–CSP–4; VN–CSP 5; VN–CSP–6
9	Vietnamese Cybersecurity Professional 7	2017	In Person/ Unrecorded Interview	VN–CSP–7

(Continued)

Table 11.1 (Continued)

No.	Description	Year	Type	Code
10, 11	Vietnamese Law Enforcement Agent 2, Vietnamese Law Enforcement Agent 3	2017	In Person/ Unrecorded Interview	VN–LE-2; VN–LE-3
12, 13	Vietnamese Cybersecurity Professional 8, Vietnamese Cybersecurity Professional 9	2017	In Person/ Unrecorded Interview	VN–CSP-8; VN–CSP-9
14	Former Vietnamese Cybercriminal 1	N/A	Written Communications	VN–(F)CC-1

Fieldwork has yet to be widely applied to cybercrime. But there is a long tradition of fieldwork-based studies of various conventional criminal groups (for instance, Sanchez-Jankowski, 1991; Maher, 1997; Levi, 2008). Recent studies suggest that this is a fruitful approach with regard to cybercrime as well (Lusthaus, 2018a; Lusthaus & Varese, 2017). It is particularly useful in exploratory studies, such as the present case, where little is known about a subject and other forms of data are not widely available.

Vietnamese cybercrime

This section explores the nature of cybercrime in Vietnam as important context to the application of the cybercrime development model that follows. It provides background on three key topics within the case of Vietnam: common cybercriminal activities, the cybercriminal community, and the organization of cybercrime.

Cybercriminal activities

Although there are some local peculiarities, Vietnam faces many of the same cybersecurity challenges as other parts of the world. Phishing, malware (e.g. ransomware) and other schemes are experienced by Vietnam as they are elsewhere (VN–LE-1; VN–CSP-1). Vietnamese cybercriminals are also engaged in a broad range of schemes:

> To my understanding and experiences, popular cybercrimes in Viet Nam mostly are: selling stolen credit/debit cards, identities theft, bank accounts, botnet, e-currency exchanger services, ATM cashing out, or buy stuff from big e-commerce sites by stolen credit/debit cards – then resell to get cash money, beside that are: HYIP programs, Affiliate programs, Black SEO, Google Adsense, Hacked accounts (Itunes, Amazon, Dell, Ebay, Paypal, Yahoo, Hotmail, Gmail or any possible value accounts).
>
> (VN–(F)CC-1)

In short, there are a number of different categories of cybercrime in Vietnam. From the interviews carried out, these include (1) Vietnamese who engage in cybercrime for hobby, profit, or both; (2) foreign cybercriminals who target Vietnamese victims; (3) insider threats; (4) patriotic hackers who attack for or against Vietnam as part of broader geopolitical struggles; and (5) agents of foreign states involved in cyberattacks against Vietnamese companies, organizations, and the government, and vice versa (VN-CSP-4;VN-CSP 5;VN-CSP-6; VN-LE-1;VN-CSP-1;VN-LE-2,VN-LE-3). Given the focus of this chapter is on how profit-driven cybercrime hubs emerge, the focus is on the first category of those cybercriminals who are indigenous to Vietnam. Although in some cases there might be an interaction with the second category, whereby Vietnamese collaborate with foreign cybercriminals to target local businesses and individuals.

Some businesses and organizations might make good targets, but it was generally believed that Vietnam was not a target-rich environment, particularly in relation to individuals. Online banking and credit card usage are still not that popular locally, although this is starting to rise (VN-LE-1). Ransomware campaigns are largely targeted to businesses and organizations rather than individuals (VN-CSP-8, VN-CSP-9). Low-level schemes involving mobile telecommunication fraud, such as tricking users into paying for premium texts, are observed (VN-LE-2;VN-LE-3;VN-CSP-4;VN-CSP 5;VN-CSP-6). But more sophisticated and wide-scale cybercriminal activities are rare. One of the few instances of a more serious attack was the 2016 hack of Vietcombank, one of the largest financial institutions in the country. This saw VND500 million fraudulently transferred out of a customer's account, with some of the funds traced to Malaysia (VietNamNet Bridge, 2016). This would not have amounted to a major heist in many parts of the world. The fact that it was mentioned throughout a number of interviews suggested the rarity of such attacks locally. On a far larger scale was the attempted €1 million heist against Tien Phong Bank, which attempted to exploit the SWIFT system in a similar way to the Bangladesh Bank case (Pham, Nguyen, & Finkle, 2016). It is likely that those behind this attack were based overseas rather than in Vietnam.

Conventionally, credit card fraud has been perhaps the major activity of the local Vietnamese cybercriminal community. But this has primarily targeted foreign rather than local victims (VN-CSP-2;VN-CSP-3). Part of this is the reverse of the explanation earlier regarding the limited use of credit cards in Vietnam: foreigners are making much greater use of credit cards and have greater amounts of money to steal. The standard modus operandi has been to compromise online shopping portals in overseas countries like the United States. They can then purchase products online in card-not-present transactions and ship them back to Vietnam, or else sell databases of credit cards online to other cybercriminals (VN-CSP-7). One hacker believed that Vietnam was a leading exponent of credit card hacking, but that they became a victim of their own success. A number of online stores began blocking shipments to Vietnam, as they believed the transactions to be fraudulent. But this simply led to an adaptation: Vietnamese cybercriminals would find mules overseas who could receive products (such as laptops and electronic goods) and then ship them back to Vietnam (VN-H-1). As noted, along with carding, Vietnamese cybercriminals have been involved in affiliate programmes, search engine optimization, hacked accounts (Amazon, PayPal, email, and so on), the sale of compromised personal data, and a number of related activities (VN-(F) CC-1).

Cybercriminal community

The Vietnamese cybercriminal community appears to be tied into the broader hacker community. Although many hackers do not engage in criminality, interviews made it clear that a number still knew carders and were aware of their activities. But carding was also viewed as a less technical pursuit. While one could make a lot of money out of it, some saw it as less challenging than, for instance, discovering 'zero-day' vulnerabilities. Some of those involved in carding did not even require significant skills if they were able to pur-chase tools written by a more skilled hacker (VN-H-1). In a similar vein, some hackers offered a service where they would hack Facebook accounts for paying customers, who might be seeking revenge or have another agenda (VN-CSP-7). This focus on hacking and intrusions appears to distinguish the Vietnamese from parts of the world where malware production is a much greater focus. Whether through the compromise of online shopping websites or otherwise, this appears to be the dominant skill profile of the local cyber-criminal population.

Organization of cybercrime

The organization of Vietnamese cybercrime has both local and international elements. One former cybercriminal described an upbringing where he learned technical skills both from formal education, whether in school or other programmes, and through more informal gatherings with other hackers. This included offline meetings as part of socializing in coffee shops or elsewhere. As he became more senior, the offline meetings continued and were often used as part of illicit trades. This involved other 'high-profile' cybercriminals, who were major vendors of credit card and other data online. In these meetings, the data would be traded for cash (VN-(F)CC-1).

As with other parts of the world, online communications play an important role. A number of interview subjects noted the existence of niche Vietnamese forums. Some forums were serious and difficult to join, whereas other locations appeared to be primarily for 'script kiddies' (for a similar range of forums in broader cybercrime see Dupont et al., 2017; Dupont et al., 2016; Holt & Lampke, 2010). Although carding forums exist, others were more generally focused on discussion/learning, including topics on hacking and website defacement. The former cybercriminal interviewed listed these as some of the early Vietnamese forums: thetindung.tk, Thecorrs, VietHacker, VietExpert, VietMagic, and HCE Group (VN-(F)CC-1). He provided an overview of the scene:

> There are two type of forums in Viet Nam at that time, one focus on sharing knowledge (new vulnerabilities, tools, techniques, tricks, affiliate programs, HYIP, Black SEO and so forth) and showing off skills through hacking and defacing websites, just for fun!. Another focus on sharing knowledge about scams, ways to make money online . . . and of course, a marketplace section for carders, sellers and buyers who are selling any possible value & sensitive information and any possible services for other cybercriminals (stuff like: credit/debit card, bank account, fullz info, ATM cashing out, paypal info, ecurrency exchange services, identity information, dropper service, forwarding service and so forth).

Other than the forums, cybercriminals have also made use of platforms like Yahoo messenger, ICQ, and Skype (VN-(F)CC-1), or have operated in Facebook groups (VN-CSP-8, VN-CSP-9; VN-LE-1). Whereas some believed that Vietnamese-language forums were on the decline (VN-H-1), others thought they still played an important role (VN-CSP-1).

But it is also relatively common for Vietnamese cybercriminals to operate in international forums. These are often English-speaking marketplaces (VN-CSP-7), though some do attempt to join Russian/Chinese-speaking markets with the aid of Google translate (VN-(F)CC-1). Whereas Vietnamese forums are local, international forums allow access to cybercriminals from other countries. This is particularly useful given that a number of companies stopped shipping online deliveries to Vietnam, due to the high levels of card fraud, and these marketplaces allowed access to partners who could reship items to Vietnam (VN-H-1; VN-CSP-4; VN-CSP 5; VN-CSP-6). These forums also provided a market for the illicit goods/service that Vietnamese wished to sell to foreigners, such as credit card and other data, or vulnerabilities (VN-CSP-7; VN-CSP-4; VN-CSP 5; VN-CSP-6).

Vietnam and cybercrime development

This section applies the model for cybercrime development from the Eastern European context to the case of Vietnam. It addresses (1) the prevalence of strong technical education; (2) the size of the hacker community; (3) whether salaries and employment opportunities are limited; and (4) the state of corruption in relation to cybercrime. The following subsection evaluates whether the actual process of cybercrime development found in the former Soviet bloc is mirrored in Vietnam.

With regard to the first point, technical education in Vietnam appears to be solid by regional standards. Interview subjects differed in their assessment of the quality of field in the country, but it seemed that basic concepts relating to computing and security were being taught. One former cybercriminal suggested that there was a strong interest in STEM within Vietnam and that students generally had "strong basic knowledge in STEM" but lacked some of the advanced skills found elsewhere (VN-(F)CC-1). Although there are not many courses on computer science or security, there appeared to be a recent move to expand/update this area within universities (VN-CSP-1; VN-LE-1; VN-CSP-2, VN-CSP-3; VN-CSP-8, VN-CSP-9; VN-H-1). It should be noted that education was relatively strong by regional standards, but it would be considered well below world-class standards. In fact, there seemed to be a 'brain drain' of sorts both with students seeking to study overseas and those being employed by foreign companies (VN-CSP-1). Overall, Vietnamese education in STEM and computing would not meet the standards of Eastern Europe and the model therein.

This feeds into the second component of the model: having a large pool of hackers or other attack-minded technologists. Interviews in Vietnam suggested there was only a relatively small number of cybercriminals but that the hacker community was relatively significant, especially in relation to the rest of the Southeast Asia. Some considered Vietnam to be one of the most powerful hacking nations in the region (VN-H-1; VN-CSP-8; VN-CSP-9). It appeared that certain hackers had university educations in the field, but others were self-taught or informally educated through their interactions with other hackers (VN-CSP-7). The former cybercriminal that was interviewed outlined his experiences with formal education:

> On or about one year in the school, I study well at first, but things get bored again because most of the stuff they teach is not in my interests at all, to me they don't know how to teach computer classes in a right way which will attract student's attention or there're some classes, they don't even know what they are talking about.
>
> (VN-(F)CC-1)

For many, intelligence and aptitude – rather than formal education – was the key (VN-CSP-2; VN-CSP-3; VN-CSP-8; VN-CSP-9). This component of the model might be partially met, but again not on the scale of the former Soviet bloc. The pool of technical talent is simply smaller and weaker in Vietnam.

With regard to employment and business opportunities, Vietnam again appears to buck the trend. In recent decades, Vietnam's economy has been growing at a fast pace (The World Bank, 2018). With that growth has come an increase in economic opportunities for its citizens, including in the IT and security sectors. A number of interview subjects noted that security was an in-demand field, opportunities were growing, and salaries were relatively high (VN-LE-1; VN-CSP-1; VN-CSP-4; VN-CSP 5; VN-CSP-6). As the former cybercriminal put it, the government "got some foreign investments and some other venture capital firms has been helping many new and young start-ups, mostly focus on tech companies. That's a good news for me and for many people in Viet Nam" (VN-(F)CC-1). Others also provided a direct link between employment and cybercrime reduction, suggesting that they knew of people who had past involvement in cybercrime but were tempted away from the 'dark side' into legitimate industry (VN-H-1;VN-CSP-7).

There also appeared to be other pathways out of cybercrime, including working overseas. A number of interview participants noted that the top technical talent in Vietnam was often recruited to work abroad in major companies like Google, Microsoft, and Samsung (VN-CSP-1;VN-CSP-7;VN-(F)CC-1). One hacker regarded these people as "geniuses," often with a particular skill at finding "zero-day" vulnerabilities (VN-H-1). The other pathway out is through forms of licit entrepreneurialism. In particular, a number of Vietnamese aspire to success in mobile app development, following the model of a local programmer who made large amounts of money from a game called "Flappy Bird" (VN-CSP-8,VN-CSP-9).[1]

The final element of the model is corruption. A number of participants noted the continued prevalence of corruption in Vietnam (VN-CSP-4; VN-CSP 5; VN-CSP-6). Some tied this to cybercrime cases in particular, with examples provided of police taking bribes from cybercriminals (VN-CSP-8, VN-CSP-9). The former cybercriminal who was interviewed outlined a number of cases where he and others paid bribes to law enforcement to escape police action or be freed from arrest, whether due to running an underground forum, a money laundering operation, or activities outside of cybercrime. He also noted the value of protection from law enforcement, noting that he spent time around agents for this purpose, and also knew of a big cybercriminal who ran a number of illicit enterprises but never got caught, as he had a "very strong relationship with some of high profiles police." In summary, he believed that "There's so much more to say about corruptions in Viet Nam, from politics to business deals to anything else . . . I want to give it a good 8 of 10 points" (VN-(F)CC-1). On this point, the model of cybercrime development in the former Soviet states is likely met.

There is another point related to corruption that became apparent during fieldwork: law enforcement capacity. In the case of Vietnam, law enforcement capacity and the targeting of cybercrime appears tied to levels of cybercriminality. A point made more than once in interviews was that credit card fraud had decreased in recent years, which was believed to be connected to an increased number of arrests (VN-CSP-8,VN-CSP-9). One hacker believed that in the past, there was a lot of hacking but the police "don't care." But a specialist police unit was formed recently, and carders now have to operate more carefully, wary of talking as openly on forums or meeting in coffee shops (VN-H-1). While cyber-policing appears to be improving in Vietnam, some caution must remain. This is particularly the case with regard to cases involving foreign victims that do not always receive great attention (VN-CSP-7; VN-CSP-8, VN-CSP-9). As one former cybercriminal put it: "Cybercriminals in Viet Nam they don't really concern about the government know their activities, because look like the Vietnamese government don't check those transactions and they don't really care either" (VN-(F)CC-1). This is in keeping with a number of other jurisdictions around the world, including countries in the former Soviet Union. But the more important overall point is that there may often be reasons beyond corruption alone as to why law enforcement in local settings do not intervene in certain cybercriminal cases.

The shift to profit making and organization

This subsection is a secondary focus of this chapter and more speculative. As noted, although it is more empirically and theoretically challenging to bear out, there still seems to be value in tracking the process of cybercriminal development in Vietnam, as it may offer some potential predictive insights as to whether Vietnam might emerge as a greater cybercrime hub in the future. There are questions over whether Vietnam closely matches the Eastern European hub model, but the nature of the cybercrime development that is occurring nonetheless appears to match the steps observed in these other cases. As discussed earlier, in many jurisdictions cybercrime begins with hobby hackers who have an interest in exploring new technologies. But over time, particularly as more profit opportunities such as credit card and other data become available online, there is a shift towards more financially motivated and organized activity. As the former cybercriminal put it in his personal case:

> On those forums I used to hack, deface websites and show off my skills to others, learning and sharing skills. Everything at first, was about fun and entertainment, showing off my skill to others, even sharing stolen credit cards for free or other personal information for free too. (sound childish right!)
>
> (VN-(F)CC-1)

But he eventually saw the money that other hackers were making and the lives they were leading. He went on to explain the development to hacking for profit in both personal and broader terms:

> Everyday, I used to jump from one to another forum, and became a very active member to share and learn from others. At first, in [redacted], mostly people shared anything which they got from hacked websites for free, but things changed shortly because highly skilled hackers saw there's a big demand and value of those information, they started to sell any possible things.
>
> (VN-(F)CC-1)

This shift from hobby to financial motivations to professionalism appeared to apply to the forum scene as well: "In the beginning those forums are operated with no profit, and mostly no required for any vouches or approve, I mean anyone who are interested in, can sign-up for an account" (VN-(F)CC-1).

The transition in Vietnamese cybercrime towards profit has already at least partly taken place. But it is also possible that Vietnam is still within this shift. A number of interviews indicated the continued prevalence of website deface- ments within the country, particularly among students (VN-CSP-2;VN-CSP-3; VN-LE-1;VN-LE-2,VN-LE-3).This is something that harkens back to a past period of hacking in other parts of the world, where it was primarily based around fun and prowess demonstration (see Chiesa, Ducci, & Ciappi, 2009). On one hand, it may be that this type of activity is ingrained within the Vietnamese hacker community, no matter how much profit-driven activity there is along- side it. On the other, there may still be a sizeable proportion of hackers who have yet to engage with the more serious aspects of cybercrime.

It should be noted that in countries like Vietnam, there might be a slight lag in the development of cybercrime, because the Internet and its associated opportunities take greater time to reach and then penetrate some parts of the world. The Internet only formally arrived in Vietnam in 1997, and penetration has still only reached about half the population (VN-CSP-4;VN-CSP 5;VN-CSP-6).Whereas cybercrime activities were well underway in Eastern Europe in the 1990s before significantly ramping up at the turn of the millennium, a number of participants believed that cybercrime only started to become seri- ous in Vietnam around 2005 or even later (VN-CSP-4;VN-CSP 5;VN-CSP-6; VN-LE-1;VN-CSP-2;VN-CSP-3;VN-LE-2;VN-LE-3).This means that the evolution may not have finished, and might still be taking place.

It is also possible that local conditions could change, bringing Vietnam into greater alignment with the model of Eastern Europe in the future and leading to a greater degree of cybercriminal activity there. In fact, it is likely that policy could play a key role in whether more cybercriminals emerge in Vietnam. The government and others are currently on a drive to increase computing edu- cation in the country. As part of this process, it is important to ensure that employment opportunities match the amount of technical talent that is to be produced. If the supply of hackers and programmers exceeds the number of good-paying jobs, the potential pool forced to seek cybercriminal opportuni- ties may grow. This is an important policy concern for both Vietnam and other countries pursuing similar technology skills agendas.

Conclusion

This chapter has attempted to formalize a model of cybercrime development and then use it to predict the emergence of future cybercrime hubs. Vietnam was adopted in this analysis as a case study. This chapter is exploratory in nature and relies on a small pool of data, so its findings are only suggestive. What the findings do suggest is that some elements of the model are present in the case of Vietnam, but that overall the model is not met: (1) although educa- tion in STEM and computing appears to be improving and is relatively strong by regional standards, it falls well below the level found in the former Soviet

Union; (2) there does appear to be a relatively large community of hackers, though the community of cybercriminals is likely considerably smaller; (3) in contrast to the Eastern European model, the Vietnamese economy has been developing over a number of years, and IT is emerging as an area for investment, and employment opportunities are growing considerably; and (4) corruption is the only area where it appears the model is directly matched, with high levels in both Vietnam and Eastern Europe. As the model is not met in this case study, Vietnam is unlikely to qualify as a fully fledged cybercrime hub in the very near future.

This chapter has focused in the case of Vietnam; however, this analysis can also suggest possible improvements to the model of cybercriminal development that has been proposed. For one, it seems sensible to question the direct connection between cybercrime and a Communist legacy. From this case it appears that Communism does not necessarily lead to technical excellence. Vietnamese education in this area is not on par with some former Soviet states. Although China and North Korea are fairly technically advanced, other examples, like Cuba, show some countries with a Communist legacy are well behind in terms of technological development. It seems that this component of the model would be better refined simply by seeking countries that have invested in STEM or computing education, regardless of ideology or the reasons why they have supported these subjects. It is also possible that the cultural and economic isolation of certain Communist countries might be playing a role here and that isolation may also be found in other nations without this same legacy.[2]

Another aspect of the model that could be developed further is around corruption. Implicit in the model and as confirmed in this case study, there appear to be at least two elements involved here: (1) law enforcement corruption that directly prevents or restricts cybercrime investigations and (2) a broader environment of corruption around the political system and society in a given country that might also contribute to cybercriminal hubs forming. It is possible that these two elements are intertwined and will commonly appear together, though that would need to be borne out in specific cases. It is also possible that the component of corruption could be functionally subsumed into a broader "lack of enforcement". This idea has been addressed in broader studies of organized crime (see for example Kleemans, 2018; Paoli, Greenfield, & Reuter, 2009). As seen in the case study, a lack of enforcement may not be due to corruption alone. This broader approach allows for a lack of law enforcement capacity or interest in cybercrime, rather than only corruption, as a factor providing a space for cybercriminals to collaborate without major threats from investigators. Some further conceptual demarcations might be helpful for developing the model in this regard, either through one more clearly defined category or several distinct elements.

Applying the model to further cases would allow it to be refined and also to determine its limits. In future studies, it could also be applied to leading cybercrime hubs (as opposed to suspected emerging ones), including those that are known for less technical cybercrimes, such as advance fee fraud or online auction fraud, which might test its broader applicability. It could also be focused on comparative studies between countries that help isolate components of the model. For instance, cases could be chosen of countries like Poland that might have similarities to other countries in Eastern Europe but have had earlier access to Western economies. Although a country-level analysis offers a good starting point, there can be a local dimension to the concept of hubs, perhaps with direct interactions between offenders and their environments. It may be that further studies should also narrow down into regional or even more micro-level analyses.

Notes

1   See also Williams (2014).
2   With thanks to an anonymous reviewer on this point.

References

Bailes, K. (1978). *Technology and society under Lenin and Stalin: Soviet technical intelligentsia, 1917–1941*. Princeton: Princeton University Press.

Brenner, S. (2010). *Cybercrime: Criminal threats from cyberspace*. Westport: Praeger.

Broadhurst, R., & Chang, L. (2013). Cybercrime in Asia: Trends and challenges. In J. Liu, B. Hebenton, & S. Jou (Eds.), *Handbook of Asian criminology*. New York, NY: Springer.

Broadhurst, R., & Grabosky, P. (Eds.). (2005). *Cyber-crime: The challenge in Asia*. Hong Kong: Hong Kong University Press.

Chiesa, R., Ducci, S., & Ciappi, S. (2009). *Profiling hackers: The science of criminal profiling as applied to the world of hacking*. Boca Raton, London, and New York, NY: CRC Press.

Décary-Hétu, D., & Dupont, B. (2013). Reputation in a dark network of online criminals. *Global Crime, 14*(2–3), 175–196.

Dupont, B., Côté, A.-M., Boutin, J.-I., & Fernandez, J. (2017). Darkode: Recruitment patterns and transactional features of "the most dangerous cybercrime forum in the world". *American Behavioral Scientist, 61*(11), 1219–1243.

Dupont, B., Côté, A.-M., Savine, C., & Décary-Hétu, D. (2016). The ecology of trust among hackers. *Global Crime, 17*(2), 129–151.

Galeotti, M. (2014). *The age of anxiety: Security and politics in Soviet and post-Soviet Russia*. London: Routledge.

Glenny, M. (2011). *Darkmarket: Cyberthieves, Cybercops and you*. London: Bodley Head.

Gohwong, S. (2017). The cyber-attacks in Vietnam during 2010–2016. *Asian Political Science Review, 1*(1), 51–55.

Graham, L. (1993). *Science in Russia and the Soviet Union: A short history*. Cambridge: Cambridge University Press.

Graham, L. (1998). *What have we learned about science and technology from the Russian experience?* Stanford: Stanford University Press.

Holt, T., & Lampke, E. (2010). Exploring stolen data markets online: Products and market forces. *Criminal Justice Studies, 23*(1), 33–50.

Holt, T., Strumsky, D., Smirnova, O., & Kilger, M. (2012). Examining the social networks of malware writers and hackers. *International Journal of Cyber Criminology, 6*(1), 891–903.

Hutchings, A. (2014). Crime from the keyboard: Organised cybercrime, co-offending, initiation and knowledge transmission. *Crime, Law and Social Change, 62*(1), 1–20.

Hutchings, A., & Holt, T. (2015). A crime script analysis of the online stolen data market. *British Journal of Criminology, 55*(3), 596–614.

Kigerl, A. (2012). Routine activity theory and the determinants of high cybercrime countries. *Social Science Computer Review, 30*(4), 470–486.

Kilger, M. (2010). Social dynamics and the future of technology-driven crime. In T. Holt & B. Schell (Eds.), *Corporate hacking and technology driven crime: Social dynamics and implications.* Hershey, PA: IGI-Global.

Kleemans, E. (2018). Organized crime and places. In G. Bruinsma & S. Johnson (Eds.), *The Oxford handbook of environmental criminology.* New York, NY: Oxford University Press.

Kshetri, N. (2010). *The global cybercrime industry: Economic, institutional and strategic perspectives.* Berlin: Springer.

Kshetri, N. (2013). Cybercrimes in the former Soviet Union and Central and Eastern Europe: Current status and key drivers. *Crime, Law and Social Change, 60*(1), 39–65.

Ledeneva, A. (2006). *How Russia really works: The informal practices that shaped post-Soviet politics and business.* Ithaca, NY: Cornell University Press.

Leukfeldt, R. (2014). Cybercrime and social ties. *Trends in Organized Crime, 17*(4), 231–249.

Leukfeldt, R., Kleemans, E., & Stol, W. (2017). Cybercriminal networks, social ties and online forums: Social ties versus digital ties within phishing and malware networks. *British Journal of Criminology, 57*(3), 704–722.

Leukfeldt, R., Lavorgna, A., & Kleemans, E. (2016). Organised cybercrime or cybercrime that is organised? An assessment of the conceptualisation of financial cybercrime as organised crime. *European Journal on Criminal Policy and Research,* 1–14.

Levi, M. (2008). *The phantom capitalists: The organisation and control of long-firm fraud.* Aldershot: Ashgate.

Lusthaus, J. (2013). How organised is organised cybercrime? *Global Crime, 14*(1), 52–60.

Lusthaus, J. (2018a). Honour among (cyber)thieves? *European Journal of Sociology, 59*(2), 191–223.

Lusthaus, J. (2018b). *Industry of anonymity: Inside the business of cybercrime.* Cambridge: Harvard University Press.

Lusthaus, J., & Varese, F. (2017). Offline and local: The hidden face of cybercrime. *Policing,* Online First, pp. 1–11.

Maher, L. (1997). *Sexed work: Gender, race, and resistance in a Brooklyn drug market.* Oxford: Clarendon Press.

McCombie, S., Pieprzyk, J., & Watters, P. (2009). *Cybercrime attribution: An Eastern European case study.* Paper read at Proceedings of the 7th Australian Digital Forensics Conference, at Edith Cowan University, Perth, WA.

Menn, J. (2010). *Fatal system error.* New York, NY: Public Affairs.

Motoyama, M., McCoy, D., Levchenko, K., Savage, S., & Voelker, G. (2011). *An analysis of underground forums.* Internet Measurement Conference 2011.

Paoli, L., Greenfield, V., & Reuter, P. (2009). *The world heroin market: Can supply be cut?* Oxford: Oxford University Press.

Pavlovich, S. (2018). *How to steal a million: The memoirs of a Russian hacker.* Self-Pub.

Pham, M., Nguyen, M., & Finkle, J. (2018). Vietnam bank says interrupted cyber heist using SWIFT messaging. *Reuters,* May 15, 2016 [cited March 20, 2018]. Available from www.reuters.com/article/us-vietnam-cybercrime/vietnam-bank-says-interrupted-cyber-heist-using-swift-messaging-idUSKCN0Y60EN.

Poulsen, K. (2011). *Kingpin.* New York, NY: Crown Publishers.

Sanchez-Jankowski, M. (1991). *Islands in the street.* Berkley and Oxford: University of California Press.

The World Bank. (2018, October 5). *The World Bank In Vietnam.* The World Bank [cited October 15, 2018]. Available from www.worldbank.org/en/country/vietnam/overview.

Varese, F. (2000). Pervasive corruption. In A. Ledeneva & M. Kurkchiyan (Eds.), *Economic crime in Russia.* The Hague: Kluwer Law International.

VietNamNet Bridge. (2018). Vietcombank account holder losses $23,000 in one night. *Viet-NamNet Bridge,* August 16, 2016 [cited February 20, 2018]. Available from http://english. vietnamnet.vn/fms/business/162187/vietcombank-tightens-otp-service-security-after–23–000-account-hack.html.

Voiskousky, A., & Smyslova, O. (2003). Flow-based model of computer hackers' motivation. *Cyberpsychology & Behavior, 6*(2), 171–180.

Wall, D. (2007). *Cybercrime: The transformation of crime in the information age.* Cambridge: Polity Press.

Williams, R. (2018). What is Flappy Bird? The game taking the App Store by storm. *The Tel-egraph,* January 29, 2014 [cited October 15, 2018]. Available from www.telegraph.co.uk/ technology/news/10604366/What-is-Flappy-Bird-The-game-taking-the-App-Store-by-storm.html.

Yar, M. (2013). *Cybercrime and society.* London and Thousand Oaks, CA: SAGE Publications.

12 Humanizing the cybercriminal

Markets, forums, and the carding subculture

Craig Webber and Michael Yip

Introduction

[A] carder can specialise in one or more areas of carding. But there's nobody who does every-thing. Sooner or later that carder will need someone else's services.

– Script[1]

Academic accounts of cybercrime base their theoretical foundation and explanatory analysis on various theoretical constructs such as subcultural theory (Holt, 2007) and social learning theory (Skinner & Fream, 1997). By far the majority of such studies fall within the rational choice/routine activities spectrum, both as explanations for cybercrime and for cybercrime prevention (Holt & Bossler, 2008; Holt, Bossler, & Seigfried-Spellar, 2017; Leukfeldt & Yar, 2016; Cohen & Felson, 1979; Cornish & Clarke, 1987). Few studies utilize an account that explains the thrill afforded by embracing subterranean values or the seductive appeal of 'getting away with it' (Matza, 1964; Katz, 1988; Ferrell, 1999, 2013). Hence, many accounts utilize economic models to explain a phenomena that is against the law, carries risks of punishment, and in many cases, is hardly likely to net the perpetrator more than a well-paid job. In other words, carding is unlike most conventional jobs that rational choice models traditionally seek to explain. Consequently, whilst we do not deny the importance of certain elements of these economic models, we seek to use a more bounded approach to rationality (Kahneman and Tversky, 1979), coupled with an appreciation of the seductive quality of the enterprise of carding derived from cultural criminology (Hayward & Young, 2004; Hayward, 2012; Ferrell, 2013; Hayward, 2016). Aside from learning the techniques of crime, it has long been recognized that it is also necessary to learn from others the "motives, drives, rationalizations, and attitudes favourable to the violation of law" (Sykes & Matza, 1957, p. 664). Therefore, what follows is a discussion of data derived from conversations between carders on one of the earliest and most successful carding forums called Shadow-Crew. These reveal the fluid nature of 'techniques of neutralization' and which undermines any simple attempt at theorizing motivations or over-reading the subcultural affiliations.

Our aim here is not to provide a quantified account where we seek to show the proportion of carders who hold certain views as opposed to others. One aim is to help in the disruption of the social scientific trend to replicate and build on similar work, which leads to an imbalance towards one set of ideas over others. Our hope is to provide a 'pause for thought,' to suggest some other avenues, some of which have already been taken to understand other areas of crime, but rarely in the area of cybercrime.[2] By examining online carding forums, this chapter approaches the subjects of this activity as both flawed and competent humans, some of whom are limited in their abilities, others who have lives that drift between the online and offline world, thus challenging preconceptions about the mythical cybercriminal living alone and interacting with their computer as if they are a character living in *The Matrix* (Webber & Vass, 2010). Unique to organized crime in a web-connected world is the use of social networking tools to facilitate relationships between like-minded individuals through the creation of online discussion forums (Benjamin, Li, Holt, & Chen, 2015; Holt, 2017). This chapter explores one of the earliest and foundational of these social networking platforms and discusses how it acted as an enabler and template for global criminal networking. The key argument is that governments, law enforcement, and security professionals have spent an increasing amount of money and time on chasing technological innovations to restrict, prevent, and disrupt cybercrime. But the evidence suggests that the web is only one aspect of the cybercrime environment and that much of interest is missed when we ignore the human element of the activity. The goal here is to provide a "heuristic device, a rule of thumb" (Wall, 2007, p. 34) for challenging the moral panic surrounding cybercriminals and highlight the influence of criminal and subcultural networking that occurs on carding forums (Cohen, 2002; Holt, 2007; Levi, 2009). Are cybercriminals as 'empowered' as those portrayed in mainstream media? How did they discover the crime and start getting involved? Are they really nothing like 'us'? Using discussions between the carders on the ShadowCrew forum, this chapter examines the perceptions, fears, and triumphs of the carders themselves to get a glimpse of their way of life. This analysis adds to and supports the depiction of cybercriminals as complex, but also flawed human beings; in so doing we are not presenting an analysis that provides easy answers. Our aim is to nudge the discussion on the causes and consequences of cybercrime towards a more nuanced position where risk, thrill, and excitement, as well as tedium and rational procedure, co-exist.

Carding forums and subcultures

The nature of cybercrime has been transformed by the rise of carding (Décary- Hétu & Leppänen, 2016; Hutchings & Holt, 2015; van Hardeveld, Webber & O'Hara, 2017). The earliest successful sites such as CarderPlanet, formed in 2001, and DarkMarket, founded in 2005, and the forum discussed here, ShadowCrew, founded in 2002, have been covered in detail elsewhere (see e.g. Glenny, 2011). But it is accepted that they have become a template for many of the carding forums that have appeared since their demise (Lusthaus, 2018a). Carders are a specialized division of computer crime (Wall, 2007) bringing money into the 'cybercrime ecosystem.' They are mostly separate from, but interact with other branches of this network, such as hackers, spammers, phishers, malware authors, vulnerability finders, money mules, drops, and cashiers (Leukfeldt, Kleemans, & Stol, 2016a, 2016b, 2016c; Lusthaus, 2018a, 2018b). Most of these relationships are only ephemeral and akin to the arm's-length market relationships seen in commercial enterprises (Uzzi, 1997; Brenner, 2002). But, taken together, they give rise to a dark web of offenders, more often referred to as the underground economy (Leukfeldt, Lavorgna, & Kleemans, 2017; Moore, Clayton, & Anderson, 2009). Failed and failing states, mainly from the former Soviet Union, produced eager recruits for these forums (Glenny, 2011). Forum members can gain knowledge of how to 'do' carding, demonstrate their trustworthiness, and possibly move up the scale and into more respected positions. But it is also apparent that there are smaller, localized groups that are culturally linked by shared histories. This is an important observation, because it adds to the argument that we need to see such groups not as some monolithic and homogenized mass, but as smaller, (sub)culturally specific hubs. This shares in common observations that have been made in criminal enterprises when networked technology was, at best, only peripheral (Hobbs, 1998). Hobbs argued that there is a need to question the common analysis of organized crime that crosses borders as 'transnational.' He suggests the need for an analysis that seeks to observe the local cultures of crime. The analysis of the human relationships on carding forums, and other similar networks, supports this contention, albeit with the proviso that networked communication systems allow for a far easier ability to connect with like-minded others and learn the techniques needed to engage in the crime (Lusthaus & Varese, 2017).

Identifying common features on carding forums

So, what can we learn from carding forums? Forums are a unique record of the conversations, business deals, tutorial sessions for self-improvement, and the residual human anxieties of those engaging in the buying and selling of stolen credit cards. It is where the offline and the online merge. Although we have studied many different discussion forums in the underground economy (Webber & Yip, 2018; van Hardeveld et al., 2017), data for this analysis were collected from the ShadowCrew forum, which existed between 2002 and 2004. This forum is used for the basis of this chapter, as the authors were granted access to the complete forum data, including material that was only accessible to forum members when the site was live such as private messages. There are also ethical issues that need to be addressed in any replication of forum posts, but these are lessened with forums that have been taken down and obtained by law enforcement and after ongoing investigations have been completed. There is a small but growing literature on researching on the Internet and forums in particular, as well as the ethics of doing so (Wilkinson & Thelwall, 2011; Hutchinson, 2014; Sugiura, Wiles, & Pope, 2017). The forum discussed in this chapter is historical and no longer active, making this analysis akin to documentary research. In addition to talk of crime, these forums are venues for the discussion of topics that have a more mundane, offline quality, such as where to buy illegal drugs or what protein shake is best for muscle gain. These forums provide insight into the life that is lived outside of carders' computers and outside the purpose of the forum's original creation (Webber & Yip, 2012). There are exchanges that raise questions about the morality of the theft of credit cards; rivalries explored and status negotiated; and fame sought, despite the dangers of raising one's head above the firewall. Of course, it is unwise to only use such forums for data and to treat them uncritically. However, they do have the benefit of being data unsolicited by a researcher.

Forums are generally accessible to all, but carding forums often have the additional element of an invite-only system restricting certain areas of the site to those most trusted. This allows the carders to establish a boundary between them and the rest of the Internet. Inside these 'virtual walls' is a society of carders bounded by the common goal of a profitable return from carding and governed by the forum administrators. In essence, and in an echo of traditional British subcultural theory, a carding forum is "an organized set of social meanings which presumably bear some relation to a larger more inclusive set called 'the culture'" (Clarke, 1974, p. 429). However, we need to be careful not to think of the whole carding subculture as overly homogenous in their values. Aside from a goal of using stolen credit card data to commit fraud, the reasons for doing so can be varied, and so make descriptions of the overly rational and calculating cybercriminal less easy to sustain as a catch-all explanation. The goal of this chapter is to discuss the social meanings within the ShadowCrew carding subculture and to demonstrate how the values are reflective of cultural norms in both criminal and legitimate settings. This is achieved by breaking it down into a set of *normative orders*, defined by Steve Herbert (1998, p. 347) as a "set of generalized rules and common practices oriented around a common value." An order "provide[s] guidelines and justifications" (1998, p. 347) for behaviour, although they are not assumed to be prescriptive, thus highlighting the impact and influence of subcultural membership on the carders. We have arrived at the normative orders through our analysis of various forums and from reviewing the literature in both organized crime and cybercrime. Holt (2007) argued that only three subcultural normative orders have been consistently identified across studies of hacker subcultures:

- *Technology*: An almost intimate relationship with technology, sometimes referred to as an addiction, coupled with the innovative adaptation of technology to novel applications.
- *Secrecy:* Because hacking is illegal, secrecy is a key requirement, but equally reputation is built on successful exploits notified to hacker communities in online forums.

- *Mastery*: The learning of new skills and control over technology and environment.

However, in this analysis, we treat these as underlying narratives in the sense that they are foundational aspects of many forms of cybercrime. We have focused on five factors that we will argue are integral to carding and highlight the difference in this activity to that of hacking for fun, excitement, or challenge. In addition to Holt's three normative orders, our focus is on a further five normative orders: *networking, competence, drive, morality,* and *duality*.

- *Networking*: An essential part of carding, it is important to proactively establish connections with other carders.
- *Competence*: Given the risks associated with carding, it is important for carders to master the techniques of crime. As carding relies heavily on trading, it is also important for carders to be resourceful and have something to offer for trade. Even if one does not possess stolen credit cards for trade, a competent carder could still trade for skills, knowledge, and experience (see Yip, Shadbolt, & Webber, 2013 for a fuller discussion of this).
- *Drive*: Most carders appear to be driven by materialistic goals, but some also find carding a thrilling experience. Key here is the argument that whilst rational economic calculations might be made by some carders, many would still card if they were offered a well-paid job using those same skills for good, not ill.
- *Morality*: Whilst some carders are willing to use whatever means to earn quick money (e.g. scamming college kids), some have shown moral boundaries by only committing carding crimes, as they believe the fraud victims are not the individuals but the big banks, which they blame for seducing the society into financial debt.
- *Duality*: Carding is different from other forms of cybercrime such as hacking, as the crime necessitates the carders to commit crime in real life. This means that carders have a need to be able to maintain composure when they encounter difficulties during criminal acts (e.g. withdrawing from stolen bank accounts).

This chapter is not about how networks grow, but about the ways people behave whilst on carding forums and the fine detail of how they respond to each of these normative orders. Each order works together, but is also mutually exclusive. So, someone can be well connected on a network, but be relatively poor at carding because they do not have the drive or competence. Equally someone may justify their carding through what they perceive as a high moral code, so they only commit fraud against people they think deserve it, whilst others are only motivated by profit, regardless of the target's ability to afford the loss. We also employ a variety of criminological ideas to help us understand the phenomena in question, and do so with an attitude of theoretical promiscuity.

Older theories and more contemporary thinking combine to become a heuristic device to help us think about a phenomenon that shares many characteristics with established forms of criminality, but which in many other ways is also unlike traditional forms of theft or fraud. Therefore, the social network that emerged on ShadowCrew is treated as a cybercriminal subculture, one which provides opportunities for the social learning of the rules of carding through what Edwin Sutherland termed differential association (Sutherland, 1939). But it also provides a support network that enables, encourages, and counsels those who use it.

For those who wish to play in the shadows: the early development of the techniques of carding

The carders of ShadowCrew shared an ethos of play, innovation, and 'gaming the system' with the wider community of hackers, and is epitomized by ShadowCrew's banner: *For those who wish to play in the shadows!* To succeed in carding, it is important to master the 'tricks of the trade.' But key here is the playfulness expressed, the same kind of seduction in the evolving competence that the forums were able to promote through their ability to provide tuition and guidance without parallel in traditional organized crime. Rarely were the techniques of traditional organized crime written down in easily accessible tutorials. Now, the risks of harm from networking opportunities were reduced, in contrast to what might be the case in a late-night discussion of a criminal opportunity in the car park of a pub or bar. But to avoid detection and prosecution, standards still need to be maintained. This section examines two normative orders that are central to carding: *networking* and *competence*.

Networking

One of the most common characteristics in the depiction of cybercriminals is their individualistic nature. Cybercriminals are often represented as talented but lonely individuals who are capable of wreaking havoc. As Wall (2007, p. 40) describes them, they are "lone offenders who exploit networked technology to carry out incredibly complex and far-reaching tasks that can be repeated countless times globally." Based on observations from ShadowCrew, however, such a depiction prevents us from recognizing online criminal networking as one of the most important transformative impacts upon criminality. To highlight the process of financially motivated cybercrime, this section draws upon a carding tutorial that was posted on ShadowCrew in 2002. Forum discussions are based on an instant messaging system that tends to involve slang and typos. Where possible, the original message is kept verbatim and only the layout is altered. Consequently, there will be errors of syntax, grammar, and spelling.

The author began the tutorial with a side note that suggests that the tutorial was originally written for another forum and encourages the readers to correct mistakes. This highlights the sense of freedom carding forum members enjoyed and the sense of community felt among them:

> SIDE NOTE: I originally wrote this C+/B- FAQ for another smaller board, but I dont mind sharing it. I would appreciate it if someone informed me if any statement is made in error on this faq: I dont want to be that kid walking around with a big booger in his nose and instead of telling him, ppl just point and laugh or nod and smile Shocked creepy.
>
> –
>
> This FAQ is intended for educational PURPOSES ONLY. If youre a federalle[3] and youre reading this, you better be educating yourself or I've got a big lawsuit against the United States Govnt. . . . I'll settle for a "get out of jail free" card though :\

The author then proceeds to define what carding is – "the art of credit card manipulation" – and that common motivations for entering the crime include poverty and thrill. This suggests a sense of thrill-seeking, perhaps even a compulsion or addiction, for mastering the crime, rather than just for financial gain:

> – Well, defined loosely, carding is the art of credit card manipulation to access goods or services by way of fraud. But don't let the "politically correct" definition of carding fool you, because carding is more than that. Much more.
>
> Although different people card for different reasons, the motive is usually tied to money. Yea, handling a $9,000 plasma television in your hands and knowing that you didnt pay one red cent for it is definately a rush.
>
> But other factors contribute to your personal reason for carding. Many carders in the scene come from poor countries, such as Argentina, Pakistan, and Lebanon where $50 could mean a weeks pay, on a good day. Real carders (the ones that have been in the scene the longest) seem to card for something more, however. The thrill of cc[4] manipulation? The rush that the federalles could bust down your door at any minute? The defiance of knowing that everyday that you are walking among the public is another day that you've gotten away with a federal crime?
>
> Whatever your personal reason for carding is, this tutorial should answer a few noobie[5] questions and take the guessing out of the entire carding game. The resources and techniques mentioned in this tutorial are NOT, I repeat, NOT the only methods of carding. Experience in carding is key. You have to practice your own methods and try out new techniques in carding to really get a system that works for you. This tutorial is meant to get you on your way.

The author then proceeds to explain how to obtain credit cards either through (1) "ripping," dishonestly trading and defrauding other carders; (2) database hacking; (3) or trading, which is suggested as the easiest way to obtain stolen credit cards:

CREDIT CARDS: *Yes, CCZ. I cant count the number of times someone has messaged me with:*
"do you have any ccz"
"where can I hack CCZ"
"where can I get a list of valid CCZ?"
You need money to make money. Plain and simple. Which means that the only way youre gonna be able to get ccs if you have ABSOLUTELY NO MONEY is if you successfully rip a noobie with 100 cards (but what noobie has 100 cards?), if you have any background in database hacking, if you trade for your shit, or if you know someone thats willing to give you ccz all day.
I know thats a discouraging statement to all of you, but we have to keep shit realistic. The easiest way to get ccz is to purchase them.

Readers are also reminded of the need to be resourceful and always have something to trade:

If youre REALLY strapped for cash, you have to go through the alternative: trade for your resources. you have to be resourceful in carding, meaning you have to use what you got. Got a psybnc[6] admin account? Offer psybnc user for a cc or two. Got shells[7]? roots[8]? Can you make verification phone calls? just ask yourself "what do I have that might be valuable to someone else?" and work with that. It doesn't have to be big, it just has to get you a few cc's in your palms.
Once youve run your first successful cc scam, DONT SPEND ALL YOUR EARNINGS. Save $200 and re-invest back into the carding community. head to SC[9] and get better cards. If you have level 2 cards, I suggest carding C2it/Paypal and using that $$ to buy ccs. (successful C2it/PP scamming techniques will not be discussed in this tut, sorry)

It is important to recognize that trading implicitly requires criminal networking with others, exposing the cybercriminal to the potential danger of encountering rippers, the term used to describe a cybercriminal who rips off or commits fraud against another carder, or undercover law enforcement agents. This shows that unless you have all the skills required for carding, from stealing credit cards to money laundering, trading is inevitable. Who should one trade with? How should one establish trust?[10] The author then introduces ShadowCrew as the venue for trading. ShadowCrew is a place where mistrust is managed and where people with similar criminal dispositions collude. In essence, a forum like ShadowCrew satisfies the two predominant requirements for exploitable criminal ties to emerge (von Lampe, 2003): *meeting individuals with corresponding criminal disposition* and *a common basis of trust*, as shown next.

ShadowCrew reviews all sorts of merchants and sellers of any type of service imaginable (everything from selling full-info cvvs with changeable billing addies[11] to purchasing anonymous bank accounts. If you dont know ShadowCrews forum link, ask someone.)

. . .

ShadowCrew (where the big boys play) is an unreplacable tool for todays carder. ShadowCrew is not for newbies. They discuss everything from cc fraud to anonymous bank accounts, identity theft, scams, fraudulent passports, etc. (The first time I logged on I couldnt believe the amount of fraudulent activity taking place there. I wouldnt be surprised to see Bin-Laden hanging around in there). Their forums are extremely useful and they rate and review their sellers so you know the service youre getting is legit.

Be careful of people out there . . . between federalles and rippers, the carding scene is a shady place. But if you know how to handle yourself and play it smart, you'll get some good results from the dedication you put into carding.

In order to avoid rippers, it is important to be able to validate the credit cards in possession and check the balance of money in the account. The author of the tutorial recommends a few methods, but it appears these are hard to come by:

Knowing whether your cc is valid or not is really important for saving some time and energy. If you live within the USA, theres a phone merchant posted within this forum under (cvv2's and ccs).

The ideal way for checking ccz is through an online merchant. These merchants can verify cc amounts without charging your ccs. Good luck finding one. People on IRC[12] want a ridiculous trade for these merchants (cvv lists, cash). So if you run across a legit merc, dont give it out! even to your best buds! online mercs are gold in the world of carding.

Other methods for verifying cc amounts include registering your cc on an online bank. (You will need at least a level 2[13] card, level 3 for ATM cards). alot of online banks can give you limit, billing addy, etc. etc. but they require at least a level 2 cc (more info on ccz below)

Once valid stolen credit cards are in possession, the next step is to defraud the accounts. This requires personal information about the cardholder. The amount of personal information associated with the stolen credit cards is categorized under three levels:

I want to make something clear right now. The secret to carding is not the number of cards you own, its what you can do with the cards. What do I mean by that? Simple.

Hypotherical situation: My name is Johnny and I have 3 ccs with SSN,[14] DOB, CVV NUMBER, MMN, NAME, STREET ADDRESS, CITY, ZIP, AND BILLING TELEPHONE NUMBER. I have a friend named Billy. Billy has 300 CCCZ with CVV, MMN, NAME, STREET ADDRESS,

CITY, ZIP, AND BILLING TEL. NUMBER. Whos more likely to successfully card something?

Simply put, I (Johnny) am. Why? Because I have more information that can prove that I am the person who owns this CC than Billy does with his 300 CCVZ. Does that mean Billy's not gonna card anything? No, that just means Billy's gonna have a hard time carding anything without verification.

So to sum up this lesson, you have to get information on your mark (the person that youre impersonating.) #1 rule in carding is: the more information you have on a person, the better chances you have for a successful transaction. Here is the information you're looking for (note: the levels of a card is not a technical carding term, I just used L1 L2 L3 to simplify shit throughout the tutorial.):

NAME:
ADDRESS:
CITY:
STATE:
ZIP CODE:
TEL. BILLING NUMBER:
CARD NUMBER:
CARD EXP DATE:
CVV CODE:
(The above is LEVEL 1: REGULAR CVV. If you have this much info, youve got yourself a regular cc. Nowadays you need this much info for carding ANYTHING worth mentioning. If you have any less than this information, youre shit outta luck. :\)

Social Security Number (SSN):
Date Of Birth (DOB):
Mothers Maiden Name (MMN):
(LEVEL 2: (PARTIAL FULL-INFO) If you have this much info as well, your ccz are on another level. With this info, you should be able to card PayPal, C2IT, and other sites without too much of a hassle.)

BANK ACCOUNT NUMBER:
ROUTING NUMBER:
BANK NAME:
BANK NUMBER:
DRIVERS LICENSE NUMBER:
PIN NUMBER (For CC or ATM card)
(LEVEL 3: (true full-info) If you have this info as well as Level 1 and 2, youre cc is ready to card anything your heart desires)

However, the process of fraud cannot begin without adequate protection to preserve anonymity and the ability to eliminate evidence when needed:

Safety is key. No one wants to give the federalles the satisfaction of busting us and shutting down production, so we gotta stay as anonymous as possible.

First let me start off by saying theres no 100% safe way to card. Dont let people fool you into thinking that. You can be behind all the proxies,[15] wingates,[16] socks,[17] and whatever else in the world, but you leave "digital fingerprints" wherever you go. I use a private hidden proxies, and dont really fuck with any other proxies, so I cant comment too much on this topic (maybe someone will paste a separate proxy faq?) As far as I'm told proxies differ from level 1 to level 3, 1 being the most anonymous, 3 being the least.

If you're really serious about carding, this is program, *PoloMint*,[18] you NEED to have installed on your HD[19] at ALL TIMES! Federal agents have several programs that allow them to extract information from your PC, such as the pages you have visited, the files you have deleted, and the emails you have written. Everytime your PC restarts, *PoloMint* kicks in, providing you with the safety of erasing any tell-tale logs and history files. You always want to be prepared for the worse.

Once ready to defraud stolen credit cards, the next step is to find physical addresses (drops) that can be used as delivery addresses for the proceeds of fraud:

> The right drop is essential to your scamming needs. Finding legitimate drops inside and outside of the US is hard. Many people keep your shit and dont send, or some people dont pick up the package at all! (theres nothing worse than watching your hard-earned laptop going back to the store because it was refused by the recipient)
>
> If you live inside (or even outside) the USA, youre better off scoping a drop out on your own. A drop is basically an empty home that looks to be inhabited. This is the shipping address you use for your carding needs. Your items should only picked up at night. As always, be sure to have a coverstory in case someone asks why youre snooping around an empty home. "I'm picking up a package for the person that used to live here" is a legit excuse. Or even "my father is the real-estate agent." is good.

Although this tutorial did not cover every aspect of carding, such as card cloning and money laundering, it has shown enough to demonstrate that making a profit in carding is a process that requires many different kinds of resources, including stolen credit cards and the associated personal information, drops, and secured proxies, as well as knowing which websites to defraud. Evidently, carding is a highly complex crime that requires those engaged in the crime to obtain access to many different types of criminal resources (including intangibles such as techniques and experience). This highlights that there is a limit to what an individual carder can achieve, and so to earn a profit in carding, more than one person is likely to be involved.

Unlike in conventional crimes where access to criminal resources is often restricted by physical and geographical constraints, carding forums allow cybercriminals to meet others anywhere, anytime. Coupled with the instantaneity offered by the Internet (Sandywell, 2010), carding forums greatly expand the resource pool that is immediately available to cybercriminals. This is a critical characteristic of financially motivated cybercrime.

Competence

However, as highlighted in the tutorial, carding is a trading business, and carders have to be resourceful so they have something to offer for trade. Furthermore, carding is a risky business. One wrong decision, and it could result in being caught by law enforcement. Therefore, mastering the techniques of crime is essential to becoming a successful carder. This is evident from the responses to the tutorial described earlier highlighting just how important learning is in carding and the level of commitment some carders have shown:

> Amazing tutorial, I've been covered to most of the things you mentioned by reading hundreds of tutorials, but all of that knowledge in one tutorial is a great save.
> *Hax0r123*
> –
>
> Yea, the only thing I would add is make sure you do your online shopping at a public library, Internet cafe or college library.
> And be ready for a phone call for high dollar stuff.
> Also, knowing the cc balance is key.
> Great post though.
> *MrChill*
> –
> Lovely post, helpful to those starting out. Good starting point.
> I will add a small point that I am noticing alot lately.
> . . .
> I find quite a bit that you will need to talk to the credit or fraud department of the particular shop you are ripping, and convince them of your intentions and identity. For many stores now, they will check the phone number that you have provided (cell or whatever) against a database, including doing an online search for your phone and address. They tell the carder, that phone number is a cell phone. Sorry can't help you. Or your address is coming up as a mail service or box location, even though you checked the drop to see if it is in database, and it wasn't.
> So a lesson or two about this that may or may not be helpful. Instead of using an anonymous cell phone, get a prepaid Master Card or Visa and sign up for a Voice Mail service and leave a message like it is your home number. Advantage;;;;; this number will not show up as belonging to a cell number, it just won't show up. You tell them you have only had the line for less than two weeks, so you might not be listed . . . A little more of a pain is going to pay phones constantly to call in to the vendor or CC company.
> Hope this helps someone.
> *the_unknown*

The responses to the tutorial show that in order to take advantage of new and developing criminal opportunities, carders have to keep up with technological innovation. This is further supported by responses to a thread which calls for a new sub-forum for those who are new to carding:

> just do like most of us here have. read, read, read. start reading the oldest posts here in this forum, and go on. you really learn a lot by just paying attention, and reading all the posts. i'm by no means an expert, but this is how i have learned most of what i know about id's, cards, and creating identities. there are also links to tutorials and long text files in some threads, in addition to the tutorial section. THEN, start asking questions, cause most of it's already out there. good luck!
>
> – Roger–

> There is so much knowledge and talent here … but i think a newbie forum is kinda like free 24 hour room service w/a 5 star 5 diamond menu … come on man.
>
> ˜˜NiHao˜˜

When this tutorial was written in 2002, Amazon and similar websites were still in their early stages of development. High-priced items now need to be signed for, and increasing levels of security are commonplace, rendering an empty drop problematic. Now, a high-priced item is unlikely to be left at a house. Instead, it would likely be returned to the sender or left at a local shop or post office and require a signature and photo identity with an address matching that to which it was sent. 'Cashing-out' credit cards to turn them into usable or sellable goods, or cash, has developed significantly since this period. The buying of cryptocurrency, such as bitcoin, effectively using credit cards in order to turn a stolen identity into anonymous money, has become a more commonplace endeavour than buying goods such as computers and televisions to sell on.

From the contents of the tutorial and the responses relating to learning the 'tricks of the trade,' the learning includes not just the technical skills such as checking the balance of credit cards but also the *argot* of the carding subculture, "a specialized and secret language within a subculture that serves multiple·functions within the group, such as communicating the structure, norms, and values of a given subculture to its members" (Holt, 2010, p. 467). Abbreviated terms such as CCZ, Full-info, and CVVs are some of the terms commonly used and which define this subculture. Carding forums like ShadowCrew serve as venues for carders to meet, trade, and most importantly, engage in dialogue that allows them to share current techniques and experiences.

In order to understand carding fraud and to humanize those behind it, questions are asked of the data such as: Why did they choose to become a carder? Do they have moral boundaries? Are they criminals in 'real life'? In doing this, we will explore the last three normative orders of *drive, morality,* and *duality,* respectively. It will be argued that although there are economic rationalities expressed by the carders to explain their engagement in this fraud, this is bounded by subterranean values of thrill-seeking and resistance (van Hardeveld et al., 2017). From this thread, it can also be seen that there are a number of key recurring themes in the motivation of carders:

- The desire for higher social status and easy money.
- The lack of legitimate ways to achieve higher social status, due to previous wrongdoing.
- Peer recognition.
- Habituation to the lifestyle of the underground economy, often referred to as an addiction. We need to be careful with medicalized terms like addiction. But we report the discussions of the carders who use this term frequently.
- Duality: disconnection from offline society.

Each of these five points will be discussed in relation to the three remaining normative orders: drive, morality, and duality, with ideas derived from cultural criminology used to help form a better understanding of the carders and the influence of subcultural membership.

Drive

From a conversation under the topic "Do you have any regrets" on Shadow-Crew, some answers to the question of what drives and motivates carders can be found, but we also see that these normative orders can overlap in significant ways. Here the drive to commit this form of fraud is often couched in terms of trying to overcome regret at the choice to pursue this activity:

> Some parts of it I love. I'm a total loner outsider, some by choice and some by the fact I've never been the type of guy that gets the girls or anything. Doing what I'm doing kind of makes me feel like I'm doing something . . . something a little risky . . . then when I do something, I still sometimes feel guilty about the people I'm doing it too. I hate that part of it. I'm never going to have a normal life even if I try, so this life, as ShadowCrew says, 'For those who wish to play in the shadows[20]' I love the shadows. I love doing things in the shadows. That's where I'm comfortable'.
>
> *TheDevil–*

> I agree, it gets addictive. There is always that feeling of trying to be the best between your shady friends but appear as the second (because the number one always get caught) . . . Anyway we are free to choose our lifestyle for a while, and most of us are here because we like what we do or what we get from it. That's my opinion
>
> *_cracker_*

In a lot of ways I regret where I am at today. When I was younger I didn't realize the consequences of the shit I was doing – easy money was great. But once you get a record and your chances of a good legit life slip further away the less choice you have in the matter. Now that I am older I wish I had done things differently, but this is the life I chose & as long as I have to live it – I am going to try to take it as far as I can. I am hooked on the rush – there have been times when I could have resumed normal living with a 9–5 job, but I could never bring myself to do it. I need the excitement & the fast cash. The stress is just something I have to live with – that and the isolation from everyone else. With the amount of time that I put into my 'job' there is hardly any time to enjoy life – but it's addicting.

Rupuze79

I agree with Rupuze79: once you get older and get a record, legitimate jobs become that much harder to obtain, thereby making this life that much more attractive. I've concluded that the only way I can make a decent living legit is to own my own business. Since the banks won't give me a loan I have to 'give' myself one. My only regret in this life is doing time. As for it being addictive; everyone needs an exit strategy. Even the Kennedys eventually went legit. Also don't forget where the real money is and where the real crooks are, is in legit businesses.

Dr. P

I try to have the fewest regrets possible. There is nothing you can do to change the past. What's happened has happened. My biggest regret? Not putting in the effort in High School and college. Looking back I wish I had done well enough in High School to go to an ivy league school. From there I could have made contacts and moved into the legit business world much quicker. Once you get a taste of the easy money it's hard to let it go.

JediMaestro

Cybercrime is often suggested to be an easy way to quick money with relatively low risk of getting caught (Wall, 2007). In his thesis on social structure and anomie, Merton argued that certain social structures exert a definite pressure that triggers impulses to break social controls (1938). Two elements are particularly relevant to carders: culturally defined goals and the acceptable processes for achieving those goals. Because cultural goals are often couched in economic terms and cybercrime is often portrayed as a lucrative crime, it is reasonable to hypothesize that cybercrime would appear as an attractive route for those seeking to achieve higher social status through the acquisition of money or high-value goods. As Cloward and Ohlin (1960) argued, however, there is differential access to legitimate routes for achieving culturally accepted goals, and therefore, some choose to pursue criminal routes instead of legitimate ones. This attitude is shown in the response of a carder, ForeverYoung:

> one thing you mention is that carding isn't always that easy, its not like you can roll outta bed and card shit. It does take some prep work, the more the better if you want to stay free.
>
> I would add keeping carded merchandise is bad news, flip it for cash and make sure the belongings in your home are legally yours. I know that if you're young and can't really afford the finer things in life (ps2s, dvds, etc.) carding is just about your only option. Keep any carded items hidden from parents, or find a way to convince them you bought it – "look ma, I bought this x-box at a garage sale!" Instead of carding an entire PC, just stuff your old beat case with the latest boards, no one will ever know.
>
> For the newb its better to take it slow at first, get a feel for it before jumping in with both feet and getting burned.
>
> *ForeverYoung*

In reality then, some carders are the opposite of the deviants commonly depicted in cyberpunk cultures that have "little control over their own eventual fates and are constantly struggling to assert their individuality" (Taylor, 1998, p. 406). Instead, some carders appear to be self-evaluating, reflexive individuals who know what they need to do in order to achieve what they regard as socially accepted goals. Rather than being "constantly struggling to assert their individuality in the face of the identity-threatening technological systems" (Taylor, 1998, p. 406), it appears that some carders use carding as a means to achieve their personal goals. To these carders, carding is just an illegitimate route to the 'American Dream,' or any other national dream of success, and they have made a rational decision to go down such a route. While media-manipulated moral panics require that we see people like the carders as 'others,' the desire of carders to achieve a socially accepted goal (rather than a deviant one) would likely make them more understandable to many. Consequently, in these responses, we see the synthesis of thrill-seeking, consumerism, and neo-liberal wealth accumulation, echoing conventional routes to success. It is Merton's innovative mode of adaptation joined by Matza and Sykes's subterranean values (1961). Indeed, some would argue that this is the very hypocritical nature of exploitative capitalism that we define as deviant those elements of activity that we see as a threat, whilst allowing others to be defined as legitimate despite their social costs (Hall & Winlow, 2007; Winlow & Hall, 2016).

This is not to dismiss the possibility of the loss of individuality entirely. As shown next and in other threads presented in this chapter, there appears to be a common attitude towards carding as a form of addiction, obsession, or dependency (see earlier responses by _cracker_ and Rupuze79), and it is possible that some carders are subsumed by the thrill resulting in a loss of self-awareness and, subsequently, self-control:

> Naah, carding definitely isnt easy, but then again I wouldn't have it any other way. Why is that? simple. That's my adrenaline rush in the madness of things anybody can copy and paste. the real thrill of carding is successfully manipulating the system. Or at least thats my personal interpretation of the enigma ... I'm sure most people card for the money, but I card for the luv.
>
> *Invincible*

The repeated mention of the thrilling sensation of carding is evident from the conversations earlier, and this thrill of carding appears to be one of the defining experiences and emotions of all forms of crime (Ferrell, 1999, p. 404). Some carders, like *Rupuza79*, appear to have gone as far as rejecting legitimate routes and have been fully seduced into committing carding by the moments of "sneaky thrills" (Katz, 1988). This thrill-seeking behaviour has also been seen among computer hacker subcultures as Jordan and Taylor (1998) found:

> [H]ackers often confess to an addiction to computers and/or to computer networks, a feeling that they are compelled to hack. Second, curiosity as to what can be found on the world-wide network is also a frequent topic of discussion. Third, hackers often claim their offline life is boring compared to the thrill of the illicit searches in online life.
>
> (Jordan & Taylor, 1998, p. 768)

In essence, what is evident from the discussion threads examined is that the carding subculture consists of people who have come to carding for a variety of reasons. Some have closed off their legitimate routes to success due to previous convictions; others appear to have limited access to legitimate routes and resort to carding as a way to finance their access to a legitimate route. Some appear to be hooked on the thrill of the crime and express a compulsion to pursue the illegitimate route. This observation concurs with Albert Cohen's remark:

> Those who join hands in deviant enterprises need not be people with like problems, nor need their deviance be of the same sort. Within the framework of anomie theory, we may think of these people as individuals with quite variant problems or strains which lend themselves to a common solution, but a common solution in which each participates in different ways.
>
> (Cohen, 1965, p. 8)

In carding subcultures, members with different backgrounds have found carding as a common solution to their personal problems, and in the process, many encounter the pleasure of an 'adrenalin rush.' Thrill is a significant characteristic of membership in a carding subculture, just like that in a computer hacking subculture (Jordan & Taylor, 1998, 2004; Holt, 2010). It is not possible in this study to determine the significance of thrill in pushing or pulling someone into credit card fraud. Whilst thrill may not be enough to seduce someone into committing credit card fraud in the first place, it may well play a vital role in seducing carders into reoffending (McCarthy, 1995). In other words, the ability of an individual to make a rational choice (Cornish & Clarke, 1986) about committing credit card fraud may differ before and after crime has been committed. Once the individual has had the first taste of carding, the thrilling sensation may overwhelm their ability to self-control (Gottfredson & Hirschi, 1990), thus clouding their ability to reason rationally and assess accurately the risk of being caught by law enforcers and the associated consequences (van Hardeveld et al., 2017). The point is although rational choice and routine activity perspectives are often used to understand how one might prevent cybercrime offending and victimization, they are less well-placed to explain the complexities that drive further offending.

Morality

First introduced by Sutherland (1939) and advanced by Akers (1977; Akers, Krohn, Lanza-Kaduce, & Radosevich, 1979), the theory of differential association argues that criminal behaviour is learned by being in association with other criminals. Indeed, how-to tutorials such as the one described in the previous section are commonly available on carding forums (van Hardeveld et al., 2017), but this is not the only thing that is learned. As Sykes and Matza (1957) argued, juveniles become delinquents only after they have learned the techniques of neutralization to justify their deviant actions. This process of learning to neutralize actions is evident from replies to a topic about scamming college students:

> I agree, scamming college children is plain and simply wrong . . . thats their real hard earned money and there's no way for them to get it back . . . Credit Card fraud, the victim gets all his money back . . . it's a victimless crime, but this is just plain wrong . . . I'm not flaming you, I'm just saying, I'd feel better if you see my point of view and please not do that again. Sorry to put you on the spot like that, but it's just my opinion.
>
> *Fe@r*

> Yeah just cuz the world is immoral doesn't mean we have to feed that fire I personally like to get credit card companies who get the young people dooped (duped) into school loans and credit cards and then not having a way to pay it back. when its time to work and make a living they come for the money and make your life a living hell. so screw them Robin Hood style.
>
> *Camp*

From this dialogue, it can be seen that the carder named Fe@r attempts to "deny the injury" (Sykes & Matza, 1957, p. 667) by claiming that credit card fraud is a victimless crime as the victims are likely to get their money back. Additionally, Camp attempts to "deny the victim" by believing that credit card companies deserve his fraudulent action as they cause young people to be in debt. This dialogue also supports Sykes and Matza's argument that delinquents are at least partially committed to the more widely accepted conventional norms and values, as it appears that carders are in fact driven by goals similar to those of mainstream culture.

Members of the forums are able to read each other's justifications, and this has the effect of reinforcing their own beliefs. Some carders know that their actions are morally wrong; however, the lure of quick cash and the possibility for victims to get compensation is enough for them to justify their actions. It appears that their actions are justifiable as long as the big corporations take the losses and not the individual owners of the credit cards:

> I'm not here to lecture, but I'm interested in the morality of ripping people off in auctions. I can understand why you may want to make £ from large retailers and CC companies, but do some of you feel guilty if you take say a postal order or cheque from a buyer on ebay and don't send an item? I know they have a fraud policy but it only covers low amounts. Personally I wouldn't do anything like this, unless it was perhaps to get back at someone or out of desperation. Another reason is that the more fraud that is committed the tighter the laws and security will become, as long as its worth the company's time and money, not to mention the already long sentences for stealing something which never physically existed. It also makes it harder for people to use it for positive reasons (ie anarchy against a corrupt regime or desperation), which I suppose depends on the mentality and angle of the person. Just a few considerations. Any comments?
>
> The_place

—

> I agree it isnt a particularly nice thing to do to people, but you can get several k[21] from a couple of hours work, so its easy to see why people are doing it.
> If you feel bad about doing it just use paypal then people can file chargebacks with their cc company and visa will eat the loss.
>
> cheers
> fw

—

> At the end of the day its a shitty way to earn a living but like fw said its easy money and if you only accept payments through billpoint/paypal then its the big companies who take the loss. Morally its totally wrong, better to just accept that than trying to justify it with 'positive reasons' (ie anarchy against a corrupt regime or desperation).
>
> Lemon

The moral boundaries exhibited by the carders here and the similarity they have with mainstream societal values show that the carding subculture and the mainstream culture are not distinct from one another, but draw on each other, a finding that has been identified in traditional British subcultural theory (Clarke, 1974). Therefore, carders should not be seen as entirely different from law-abiding citizens; they are simply trying to achieve socially accepted goals using alternative solutions, which in this case is carding.

Duality

Unlike some forms of cybercrime, such as spam and the use of malware, what Wall termed "true cybercrimes" because they could not exist without networked computers (Wall, 2007), carding drifts online and offline. There is a duality to it that makes it more complex (Webber & Yip, 2012). Similar to Matza's (1964) observation that juveniles drift in and out of deviant behaviour, some carders also drift in and out of cybercrime. This is observed in a thread titled "Got barred from college!!!!!":

> Well i really don't see myself carding for a living, ive been thinking about how my life would be if i had 2 paths for me to choose to follow. One would be an educated college degree life with a wife and kids or a life of carding, life of secrecy and constant fear of getting caught. The thing I'm really scared of about carding is getting prostituted in jail. LOL. ive seen those movies with a skinny guy getting prostituted in jail. That would be the lowest of lows.
>
> Chef

> –
>
> You choose your own destiny as we all do, but I really suggest you either change your attitude or quit school or carding. It really sounds like you don't want to live the carder lifestyle and that your just doing it as a hobby in the meantime. Carding is dampening your scholarly abilities, there's no reason to continue unless you plan on making a living off it for a while.
>
> You want to get a good job, you want a stable family that's good. But you need to understand that these other activates your doing are taking away from all this. If carding is not for you, you might as well quit while your ahead. One wrong move and you'll turn this "hobby" of yours into the only descent way to make a living, and even then it'll be hard because your Probation Officer will be on your ass everyday. You think you can quit carding, might as well try now because soon it'll be harder to do soon. The more you smoke it the more you need it.
>
> Good luck with life and its many choices.
>
> Fink3r

carding should be a hobby not your life, unless you dont value your life, and love running from the LE[22] and moving state to state.

chaosm@n

T3la

As shown in this conversation, it is evident that some cybercriminals are not full-time criminals. Rather, they have different identities online and offline and they drift in and out of crime (Matza, 1964). Furthermore, it can be seen that some are using carding as a way to fund access to legitimate routes by, for example, using carding to finance education.

Another example of online/offline convergence is shown in the conversation here in which a carder requested others kill another carder who was suspected of being a ripper, further merging online and offline experiences as a carder:

this motherfucker ripped me off for 3 laptops and 2 monitors.
i'm gonna find this motherfucker and kill him.
i hijacked his yahoo account cuz hes a fuckin idiot and i guessed his password.
his name is ★★★★★ ★★★★★, and if anyone can help me put a bullet in his head,
    i'll give them $1,000
i believe he lives at ★★★ ★★★★★ street, in pittsburg
his girlfriends name is ★★★★★ ★★★★★ i believe.
i also stole his original AIM account, " ★★★★★★★★ "
this motherfucker is gonna get it, and get it hard. no matter what.
please believe it

As can be seen, the carder who was ripped off had published personal details about the ripper and had requested someone kill the ripper in return for money. This shows that the real identity of a carder can sometimes be compromised, highlighting that the flexibility of their online/offline identities are sometimes not as separable as scholars have previously assumed, such as the "identity flexibility and dissociative anonymity" characteristic that forms a main component of Jaishankar's 'Space Transition Theory'" (Jaishankar, 2008). This idea suggests that it is the anonymity afforded by the Internet that encourages crime. However, evident from the conversations earlier, many carders operate on the assumption that they will be identified by law enforcers one day, and many prepare themselves for the moment by having tools available to destroy the evidence.

Perhaps what truly differentiates carding from the more traditional form of computer hacking (Jordan & Taylor, 1998; Yar, 2005; Taylor, 2005; Holt, 2007) is how some aspects of criminality in carding necessitate interactions in real life. This duality is captured by some of the discussions in a thread called "hahaha ups guys r pussys" which was started by someone bragging about their experience with the delivery firm UPS:

dude today was awesome . . . me and my partner were at a drop and the ups guy was givin me shit. . . . asking me questions cause it was an apartment complex and we were just chillin inside . . . anyways the ups guy came with a nice lil package . . . anyways he gave us problems so i took it out of his hands and pushed his ass down and got the hell out of there . . . it was great . . . what a rush.

the_drop

Although this drew the reactions from many members who saw the amusing side in the act, the more serious members saw this as a risk not worth taking:

yea way to draw attention to yourself . . . seriously leave the UPS man alone, the damn guy is just doing his job.

All you did was draw attention to yourself which is the first no no in life. Then you come on here and brag about it like you deserve a cookie.

A real carder can play in smooth, hell I became friendly with the ups man back when i was a big carder . . . we still chill all the time, he doesnt give a fuck that i card or anything . . . hes a good pal to have . . . You play it like your doing nothing illegal and your fine, u start beating on UPS people and taking a package and start running u look like a criminal ! . . . I wish a cop would have seen you so you would have some explaining to do. Then I'd like to see you brag about that one.

Sorry for the rant, but this guy isnt earning any respect with me.

l33t

dude, listen to l33t- get in GOOD with the UPS drivers . . . pissing them off could mean the cops checking out that transaction NOW as opposed to in a few days when the CC comes up bad. If you get in good with the UPS driver, you are all set.

enf0rcer

The responses to this thread highlight not just the online/offline convergence in the crime itself but also the attitude towards risk taking. The responses show that a characteristic among carders that is much respected is *composure*, the ability to maintain control (see Lyng, 1990 for a similar observation among risk-takers). Due to the criminal nature of carding and the need for offline interactions, the ability to maintain control amidst adverse conditions appears to be a particularly important skill for carders, as failure to do so could well expose them to law enforcers. Therefore, whilst duality appears to be a characteristic that separates carding as a distinctive form of deviance from true cybercrimes, the importance of composure, that is, the ability to maintain control amidst adverse conditions, is a characteristic that defines a serious carder.

Discussion and summary

Carding forums like ShadowCrew provide a unique methodological tool to understand carders because forum dialogue is maintained over the entire lifespan of the forum. From these dialogues, we can gain insight into those who engage in carding fraud, the discussions they have, their frailties, triumphs, and the challenges of the everyday. The focus of this chapter was on the carding subculture that emerged on ShadowCrew. In order to enhance our understanding of this carding subculture, five normative orders were examined: *networking*, *competence*, *drive*, *morality*, and *duality*. The evidence presented in this chapter supports the complexity of financially motivated cybercrime and that extensive criminal networking for resources is required for sustainable profits to be made (Lusthaus, 2018b). As carding involves the exploitation of technologies, extensive knowledge sharing is required, and some carders have demonstrated strong commitment in mastering the crime (Leukfeldt et al., 2016c). By examining the content of a carding tutorial shared on ShadowCrew and the responses to the post, it is also clear that forums facilitate not only the social learning of the techniques of crime but also the argots of the carding subculture, that is, the unique linguistic references used among carders, which defines the subculture (Holt, 2007). They are also key resources for the building and maintenance of the level of trust that is required by those engaging in risky behaviours (Yip, Webber, & Shadbolt, 2013) Therefore, this highlights how forums facilitate global criminal networking, a feature of financially motivated cybercrime that distinguishes it from conventional crimes (however, see Leukfeldt et al., 2017 for a discussion of the dissimilarity of cybercrime from traditional organized crime). This chapter has also challenged the mainstream stereotyping of cybercriminals and exposed their human struggle. Rather than being techno-geniuses or super-criminals, they instead engage in the same kinds of discussions that many of us who are not carders have: they worry over their choice of 'career,' the ethics of what they do, and how to do the job better. Dialogues from the forum show that the carders were driven by different motives, but all found carding as a common solution. This provides us with an insight into the nature of criminological theory, because many of the classical theories apply, and many overlap.

A sense of political anarchy is also observed in the discussions and in the pseudonyms they used. For some, carding was a way to 'manipulate the system,' to get one over on the banks, government, and other corporations. Carding is perceived, like so much else on the Internet, as a victimless crime, or at least with little cost. Rather than the offence being against an individual, it is against the banks that will compensate the victim. In the post-credit-crunch world, where worldwide measures of austerity are weighing most heavily on those least able to bear the strain, it should be expected that cybercriminals such as hackers and carders will take on the role of anarchic, anti-establishment anti-heroes. Hacking was the prime example of innovation in the face of the seeming blocks to cherished goals, be they free telephone calls, copyright-protected games, innovative software, or money from banks without the need to work too hard. In carding, individuals appear to be Merton's innovator, retreatist, and rebel combined – a combination that demonstrates that carders cannot be explained in simplistic terms of rational choice or routine activities or written off as just another moral panic. Many of these carders took the line that they were enriching themselves in the face of a system designed to keep everyone down, and they saw themselves as fighting the system and winning. Of course, we all actually pay for these crimes. The sense of rebellion is misplaced, and the thought that the banks are really losing out is misguided. Yet in a discussion about scamming college kids, some carders demonstrate moral values not too dissimilar to mainstream cultural values. Therefore, carders should not be portrayed as 'folk devils' but people just like 'us' who are also trying to accept socially accepted goals. However, the difference lies in the route they have chosen to achieve the goals. Lastly, duality is a normative order that carding necessitates. Evidence from this forum, and elsewhere, has shown that cybercriminals drift online and offline (Leukfeldt et al., 2016a). Examples of offline crimes associated with carding include collecting goods from drop locations and cashing out stolen bank accounts. This brings about a dimension of crime not commonly associated with cybercrime. Another aspect of being a carder is the drifting in and out of crime. Some carders on ShadowCrew had legitimate jobs in real life and found carding as a profitable "hobby," whilst some used carding to finance education, which in other words, was using an illegitimate route to finance access to a legitimate route to a successful education.

This study also examined whether the three common traits among hacker cultures (Holt, 2007), *technology*, *secrecy*, and *mastery*, are also found in carding subculture. The detailed tutorial referenced in this chapter and the corresponding responses show that carders hold an intrinsic relationship with technology and there is a strong need for them to master it. However, it is unclear whether the significance of these values is as defining as those to a computer hacker subculture, or indeed a hacktivist group, mainly due to the differences in personal motivation (Webber & Yip, 2018). Although many carders expressed their devotion to the thrill sensation associated with committing the crime, a testimony to their mastery, many agree that the ultimate end goal is to make a financial profit and avoid being caught. This difference in motivation may well have an impact on the significance of mastery and technology in the carding subculture where it is often just the means to an end, rather than core values of self-identification. In other words, they are learned responses to the risks associated with the crime, and not every carder is willing or able to embed them in their carding activities (van Hardeveld et al., 2017). In contrast, a hacker is defined by the skills they have, which can be employed for any number of reasons and results. In this regard, carders share more in common with hacktivists, who use their knowledge to facilitate explicit results (Webber & Yip, 2018).

Furthermore, although thrill is a sensation experienced by many carders, no evidence has been found to suggest that there were individuals who were seduced into carding by thrill alone. Rather, the materialistic desires caused by structural strains, as well as previous exposure to sanctions, appear to be dominant factors in why individuals engaged in carding. However, this chapter argues that the role of thrill should not be dismissed entirely, as it may have implications on the likelihood of a carder to reoffend after their first taste of carding and their encounter with the thrilling sensation of illicit financial gain. A closer examination into the different stages of a carder's experience in carding is therefore proposed. Based on the responses to a forum thread that was started by a carder boasting about a physical tussle with a delivery firm, secrecy is a highly significant characteristic that is much valued in the carding subculture. This is perhaps not surprising given the inherent criminal nature of carding. However, an interesting observation from the responses to the thread is the characteristic of *composure*, which has not received much attention in cybercrime literature. Composure is a characteristic that has been shown in this chapter to be precursory to the ability to maintain secrecy, which in turn facilitates the thrill and seduction of crime. This is found to be a particularly important characteristic for carders, as carding necessitates committing crimes in the offline world. Consequently, this chapter argues that carding is a unique form of crime that is given complexity through the study of online discussion forums. Any sense that carding, indeed any crime, can be explained or prevented through a rational or routine activities perspective must also countenance the contextual, emotional, and seductive qualities of risky behaviour.

Notes

1 At the end of each forum post the poster's pseudonym appears; we have not changed these names because the forum posts that we use here were publicly available, and several of the forum posters have been discussed elsewhere (see e.g. Lusthaus, 2018b for a discussion on the history of ShadowCrew).
2 Jonathan Lusthaus (2018b) has written a timely study that provides a nuanced perspective of cybercrime, drawing on one of cultural criminology's key inspirations, Jack Katz's (1988) *Seduction of Crime*. Nevertheless, routine activity theory still forms the core theoretical narrative of the book.
3 Slang for Fed or the Federal Bureau of Investigation (FBI).
4 Credit card, also CCz, or ccz, for plural.
5 Slang for anyone who is new to the site or to carding. Alternatives are 'newbie' or similar.
6 A system to allow anonymous internet relay chats, the underlying software that enables discussion forums.
7 Refers to 'web shells,' scripts placed on to a server that would provide an attacker with remote access to the server's operating system.
8 Refers to having root user privilege, which provides the user with unrestricted access to files on the system.
9 ShadowCrew.
10 See Lusthaus (2012) for more on this.
11 Addresses.
12
13
14 These abbreviations are all explained later.
15 Proxies – refers to a proxy, a server designed to receive and relay network traffic to the intended server.
16 Wingate is a particular server application to set up a Windows server as a proxy server.

17   SOCKS is an authenticated proxy server with the ability to relay network traffic of various protocols, including Hypertext Transfer Protocol (HTTP) and File Transfer Protocol (FTP).
18   We have changed the name of the programme for this chapter.
19   HD refers to hard drive or hard disk.
20   This is ShadowCrew's motto and appears at the top of the website page.
21   1,000.
22   Law enforcement.

References

Akers, R. L. (1977). *Deviant behavior: A social learning approach* (2nd ed.). Belmont, CA: Wadsworth.

Akers, R. L., Krohn, M. D., Lanza-Kaduce, L., & Radosevich, M. (1979). Social learning and deviant behavior: A specific test of a general theory. *American Sociological Review*, *44*(4), 636–655.

Benjamin, V., Li, W., Holt, T., & Chen, H. (2015). *Exploring threats and vulnerabilities in hacker web: Forums, IRC and carding shops*. IEEE International Conference on Intelligence and Security Informatics (ISI).

Brenner, S. (2002). Organized cybercrime ? How cyberspace may affect the structure of criminal relationships. *North Carolina Journal of Law & Technology*, *41*(1984), 1–50.

Clarke, M. (1974). On the concept of 'sub-culture'. *The British Journal of Sociology*, *25*(4), 428–441.

Cloward, R., & Ohlin, L. (1960). *Delinquency and opportunity*. London: Collier-Macmillan.

Cohen, A. K. (1965). The sociology of the deviant act: Anomie theory and beyond. *American Sociological Review*, *30*(1), 5–14.

Cohen, L. E., & Felson, M. (1979). Social change and crime rate trends: A routine activity approach. *American Sociological Review*, *44*(4), 588–608.

Cohen, S. (2002/1972). *Folk devils and moral panics* (3rd ed.). London: McGibbon and Kee.

Cornish, D. B., & Clarke, R. V. (1986). *The reasoning criminal: Rational choice perspectives on offending*. The Hague: Springer-Verlag.

Cornish, D. B., & Clarke, R. V. (1987). Understanding crime displacement: An application of rational choice theory. *Criminology*, *25*(4), 933–948.

Décary-Hétu, D., & Leppänen, A. (2016). Criminals and signals: An assessment of criminal performance in the carding underworld. *Security Journal*, *29*(3), 442–460.

Ferrell, J. (1999). Cultural criminology. *Annual Review of Sociology*, *25*(1), 395–418.

Ferrell, J. (2013). Cultural criminology and the politics of meaning. *Critical Criminology*, *21*(3), 257–271.

Glenny, M. (2011). *Dark market: Cyberthieves, cybercops and you*. London: The Bodley Head.

Gottfredson, M. R., & Hirschi, T. (1990). *A general theory of crime*. Stanford: Stanford University Press.

Hall, S., & Winlow, S. (2007). Cultural criminology and primitive accumulation: A formal introduction for two strangers who should really become more intimate. *Crime, Media, Culture*, *3*(1), 82–90.

Hayward, K. J. (2012). Five spaces of cultural criminology. *The British Journal of Criminology*, *52*(3), 441–462.

Hayward, K. J. (2016). Cultural criminology: Script rewrites. *Theoretical Criminology*, *20*(3), 297–321.

Hayward, K. J., & Young, J. (2004). Cultural criminology: Some notes on the script. *Theoretical Criminology*, *8*(3), 259–273.

Herbert, S. (1998). Police subculture reconsidered. *Criminology, 36*(2), 343–370.

Hobbs, D. (1998). Going down the glocal: The local context of organised crime. *The Howard Journal of Criminal Justice, 37*(4), 407–422.

Holt, T. J. (2007). Subcultural evolution? Examining the influence of on- and off-line experiences on deviant subcultures. *Deviant Behavior, 28*(2), 171–198.

Holt, T. J. (2010). Examining the role of technology in the formation of deviant subcultures. *Social Science Computer Review, 28*(4), 466–481.

Holt, T. J. (2017). Identifying gaps in the research literature on illicit markets on-line. *Global Crime, 18*(1), 1–10.

Holt, T. J., & Bossler, A. M. (2008). Examining the applicability of lifestyle-routine activities theory for cybercrime victimization. *Deviant Behavior, 30*(1), 1–25.

Holt, T. J., Bossler, A. M., & Seigfried-Spellar, K. C. (2017). *Cybercrime and digital forensics: An introduction* (2nd ed.). London: Routledge.

Hutchings, A., & Holt, T. J. (2015). A crime script analysis of the online stolen data market. *The British Journal of Criminology, 55*(3), 596–614.

Hutchinson, E. (2014). Researching forums in online ethnography: Practice and ethics. In M. Hand & S. Hillyard (Eds.), *Big data? Qualitative approaches to digital research* (Studies in Qualitative Methodology, Vol. 13, pp. 91–112). Emerald Group Publishing Limited.

Jaishankar, K. (2008). Space transition theory of cyber crimes. In F. Schmallager & M. Pittaro (Eds.), *Crimes of the internet* (pp. 283–301). Upper Saddle River, NJ: Prentice Hall.

Jordan, T., & Taylor, P. (1998). A sociology of hackers. *The Sociological Review, 46*(4), 757–780.

Jordan, T., & Taylor, P. (2004). *Hacktivism and cyberwars*. London: Routledge.

Kahneman, D., & Tversky, A. (1979). Prospect theory: An analysis of decision under risk. *Econometrica, 47*(2), 263–291.

Katz, J. (1988). *Seductions of crime: Moral and sensual attractions in doing evil*. New York, NY: Basic Books.

Leukfeldt, E. R., Kleemans, E. R., & Stol, W. P. (2016a). Cybercriminal networks, social ties and online forums: Social ties versus digital ties within phishing and malware networks. *British Journal of Criminology, 57*(2), 704–722.

Leukfeldt, E. R., Kleemans, E. R., & Stol, W. P. (2016b). A typology of cybercriminal networks: From low tech locals to high tech specialists. *Crime, Law and Social Change, 67*(1), 39–53.

Leukfeldt, E. R., Kleemans, E. R., & Stol, W. P. (2016c). Origin, growth and criminal capabilities of cybercriminal networks. An international empirical analysis. *Crime, Law and Social Change, 23*(3), 287–300.

Leukfeldt, E. R., Lavorgna, A., & Kleemans, E. R. (2017). Organised cybercrime or cybercrime that is organised? An assessment of the conceptualisation of financial cybercrime as organised crime. *European Journal on Criminal Policy and Research, 23*(3), 287–300.

Leukfeldt, E. R., & Yar, M. (2016). Applying routine activity theory to cybercrime: A theoretical and empirical analysis. *Deviant Behavior, 37*(3), 263–280.

Levi, M. (2009). Suite revenge? The shaping of folk devils and moral panics about white-collar crimes. *British Journal of Criminology, 49*(1), 48–67.

Lyng, S. (1990). Edgework: A social psychological analysis of voluntary risk taking. *The American Journal of Sociology, 95*(4), 851–886.

Lusthaus, J. (2012). Trust in the world of cybercrime. *Global Crime, 13*(2), 71–94.

Lusthaus, J. (2018a). Honour among (cyber)thieves? *European Journal of Sociology, 59*(2), 191–223.

Lusthaus, J. (2018b). *Industry of anonymity: Inside the business of cybercrime*. Cambridge, MA: Harvard University Press.

Lusthaus, J., & Varese, F. (2017). Offline and local: The hidden face of cybercrime. *Policing: A Journal of Policy and Practice*, 1–11. doi:10.1093/police/pax042

Matza, D. (1964). *Delinquency and drift*. New York, NY: Wiley.

Matza, D., & Sykes, G. M. (1961). Juvenile delinquency and subterranean values. *American Sociological Review*, 26(5), 712–719.

McCarthy, B. (1995). Not just 'for the thrill of it': An instrumentalist elaboration of Katz's explanation of sneaky thrills property crimes. *Criminology*, 33(4), 519–538.

Merton, R. K. (1938). Social structure and anomie. *American Sociological Review*, 3(5), 672–682.

Moore, T., Clayton, R., & Anderson, R. (2009). The economics of online crime. *Journal of Economic Perspectives*, 23(3), 3–20.

Sandywell, B. (2010). On the globalisation of crime: The internet and new criminality. In Y. Jewkes & M. Yar (Eds.), *Handbook of internet crime* (pp. 38–66). Devon: Willan Publishing.

Sugiura, L., Wiles, R., & Pope, C. (2017). Ethical challenges in online research: Public/private perceptions. *Research Ethics*, 13(3–4), 184–199.

Skinner, W. F., & Fream, A. M. (1997). A social learning theory analysis of computer crime among college students. *Journal of Research in Crime and Delinquency*, 34(4), 495–518.

Sutherland, E. H. (1939). *Principles of criminology*. Chicago, IL: Lippincott.

Sykes, G. M., & Matza, D. (1957). Techniques of neutralization: A theory of delinquency. *American Sociological Review*, 22(6), 664–670.

Taylor, P. A. (1998). Hackers: Cyberpunks or microserfs? *Information, Communication & Society*, 1(4), 401–419.

Taylor, P. A. (2005). From hackers to hacktivists: Speed bumps on the global superhighway? *New Media & Society*, 7(5), 625–646.

Uzzi, B. (1997). Social structure and competition in interfirm networks: The paradox of embeddedness. *Administrative Science Quarterly*, 42(1), 35–67.

van Hardeveld, G. J., Webber, C., & O'Hara, K. (2017). Deviating from the cybercriminal script: Exploring tools of anonymity (mis)used by carders on cryptomarkets. *American Behavioral Scientist*, 61(11), 1244–1266.

Von Lampe, K. (2003). Criminally exploitable ties: A network approach to organized crime. In E. C. Viano, J. Magallanes, & L. Bidel (Eds.), *Transnational organized crime: Myth, power and profit* (pp. 9–22). Durham, NC: Carolina Academic Press.

Wall, D. S. (2007). *Cybercrime: The transformation of crime in the information age*. Malden: Polity Press.

Webber, C., & Vass, J. (2010). Crime, film and the cybernetic imagination. In Y. Jewkes & M. Yar (Eds.), *Handbook of internet crime* (pp. 120–144). London: Routledge.

Webber, C., & Yip, M. (2012). Drifting on and off-line: Humanising the cyber criminal. In S. Winlow & R. Atkinson (Eds.), *New directions in crime and deviancy* (pp. 191–205). London: Routledge.

Webber, C., & Yip, M. (2018). The rise of Chinese cyberwarriors: Towards a theoretical model of online hacktivism. *International Journal of Cybercriminology*, 12(1).

Wilkinson, D., & Thelwall, M. (2011). Researching personal information on the public web: Methods and ethics. *Social Science Computer Review*, 29(4), 387–401.

Winlow, S., & Hall, S. (2016). Realist criminology and its discontents. *International Journal for Crime, Justice and Social Democracy*, 5(3), 80–94.

Yar, M. (2005). Computer hacking: Just another case of juvenile delinquency? *The Howard Journal of Criminal Justice*, 44(4), 387–399.

Yip, M., Shadbolt, N., & Webber, C. (2013). *Why forums? An empirical analysis into the facilitating factors of carding forums*. Paper presented at ACM Web Science 2013, France.

Yip, M., Webber, C., & Shadbolt, N. (2013). Trust among cybercriminals? Carding forums, uncertainty and implications for policing. *Policing and Society*, 23(4), 516–539.

13 The roles of 'old' and 'new' media tools and technologies in the facilitation of violent extremism and terrorism

Ryan Scrivens and Maura Conway

Introduction

Alfred Nobel's invention of dynamite in 1867 was the technological break-through that ushered in the era of modern terrorism; the economy of means it afforded ensured that terrorist bombings proliferated. High levels of illiteracy in 19th-century Europe imposed serious limitations on conventional text-based propaganda. Conversely, 'propaganda by deed' could show, said the French anarchist Paul Brousse at the time, "the weary and inert masses . . . that which they were unable to read, teach them socialism in practice, make it visible, tangible, concrete" (as quoted in Townshend, 2002, p. 55). When the anarchist Albert Parsons was arraigned for his alleged involvement in Chicago's 1886 Haymarket bombing, he proclaimed in court that dynamite "made all men equal and therefore free" (as quoted in Townshend, 2002, p. 5). However, although terrorist attacks may themselves draw attention and by their target choices and other aspects send some kind of message, successful terrorist campaigns must generally also employ speech, text, and visuals in order to seek to legitimize, rationalize, and, ultimately, advertise terrorists' actions. In other words, as Rapoport (1984) reminded us over 30 years ago: "To be noticed is one thing, to be understood is another" (p. 665). 'The media' *qua* the traditional mass media has certainly been employed as a tool by terrorists for these purposes (e.g. 1972 Munich Olympics attack; 1975 Vienna Organization of the Petroleum Exporting Countries [OPEC] siege). That is not what is at issue in this chapter, however; instead, this chapter spotlights the use of media tools directly by terrorists and not 'the media,' in the guise of journalists, as intermediaries. The focus is therefore on the establishment of newspapers and radio and television stations by violent extremist and terrorist organizations rather than press, radio, and television coverage of terrorist attacks. The definition of 'media tools' utilized in the chapter is wider than these, however, encompassing not just 'old' but also 'new' media tools, particularly the Internet, but also incorporating less obvious media tools, such as wall murals and photocopying machines. Underlined in the chapter is that in order to understand new media trends, we must first examine violent extremist and terrorists' 'old' or traditional media forbearers that supply crucial context for contemporary violent extremists and terrorists' online activity, including particularly, the latter's take-up of any and all ready means of communication in whatever era.

In terms of what constitutes 'violent extremism,' we are guided by Berger's (2018) characterization of it as "the belief that an in-group's success or survival can never be separated from the need for violent action against an out-group," which violence may be characterized by the aggressors as "defensive, offensive, or preemptive" (p. 46). Terrorism, on the other hand, may be conceived as "violence – or, equally important, the threat of violence – used and directed in pursuit of, or in service of, a political aim" (Hoffmann, 2006, pp. 2–3). Together, violent extremism and terrorism account for a range of political violence activity by a diversity of actors subscribing to an array of radical beliefs. The media and communication strategies of two particular ideologies are focused on herein: right-wing extremists and violent jihadis – albeit an array of others is referred to also (e.g. nationalist-separatists such as the Irish Republican Army [IRA] and violent Islamists such as Hezbollah). Violent jihadists are inspired by Sunni Islamist-Salafism and seek to establish an Islamist society governed by their version of Islamic or Sharia law imposed by violence (Moghadam, 2008). Right-wing extremists may also subscribe to some radical interpretation of religion, but unlike those inspired by radical Islam, many extreme right adherents are not inspired by religious beliefs per se. Instead, what binds these actors is a racially, ethnically, and sexually defined nationalism, which is typically framed in terms of white power and grounded in xenophobic and exclusionary understandings of the perceived threats posed by such groups as non-whites, Jews, Muslims, immigrants, homosexuals, and feminists. Here the state is perceived as an illegitimate power serving the interests of all but the white man and, as such, right-wing extremists are willing to assume both an offensive and defensive stance in the interests of "preserving" their heritage and their "homeland" (Perry & Scrivens, 2016). With regard to the chapter's structuring, the following sections are ordered chronologically, treating, in turn, early low-tech communication methods or what we term 'pre-media,' followed by other relatively low-tech tools, such as print and photocopying. The high-tech tools reviewed are film, radio, and television, followed by the Internet, especially social media.

Low-tech media tools: pre-media

Over 30 years ago, Rapoport (1984) argued "there can be no politics without publicity" (p. 663). Yet prior to the establishment of 'the media' and easy access to information technology tools, terrorists were restricted in their ability to reach the masses. This did not stop some of the world's earliest terrorists – such as the Shi'a Muslim group that became known as the Assassins (1090–1275) – getting their message across: "They did not need mass media to reach interested audiences, because their prominent victims were murdered in venerated sites and royal courts, usually on holy days when many witnesses would be present" (Rapoport, 1984, p. 665). These witnesses would then travel back to their towns and villages, orally spreading news of the murderous events to which they had borne witness. Complete non-access to means of communication beyond the directly spoken word was and is rare, however. Apart from the latter, wall paintings – graffiti, murals, or other works of art executed directly on walls – are probably the most low-tech communication tools with the capacity to reach a wide audience.

Although primitive in some respects, historically murals have been a powerful communication tool for violent extremist and terrorist groups (Matusitz, 2014), including extreme-right (Heschel, 2008), nationalist-separatist (Rolston, 1991), and Islamist movements (Marzolph, 2003). Plastered on walls, other large permanent structures, and even on the roofs of public buildings, violent extremist and terrorist groups have widely used pieces of artwork or artistic renderings of text for communicative purposes, oftentimes in geographic spaces that are home to clashing ethnic or religious groups (Matusitz, 2014). Murals tend to serve at least two functions: (1) they act as territorial markers: a terrorist group – or those who support the group or cause – will etch out a perimeter, oftentimes in a public space, which they claim control over, thereby also segregating themselves from 'enemy' communities and (2) they act as a form of political communication: instrumental communication devices, or a "landscape of identity" to inform or remind multiple audiences – from the local to the global – about *why* they should take notice of a particular violent extremist or terrorist group or movement (our italics; Matusitz, 2014, p. 167).

Murals in support of right-wing terrorist (RWT) groups or ideologies are not only used to mark or claim territory, they are used to send a message to a particular group of people that they are not welcome. Notable examples include the Nazi terror campaigns in Germany prior to and during World War II and the Ku Klux Klan (KKK) in the southern regions of the United States following the Civil War. To illustrate, in the mid-1930s, the Nazis in Germany used wall murals to mark their 'turf,' on the one hand, and to systematically unite and mobilize the Nazi movement, on the other, oftentimes by painting murals that romanticized their Aryan Jesus as a strong, handsome, muscular, blonde, and pure-hearted figure, while simultaneously depicting Jews and Jewishness as the root of all evil (Heschel, 2008). One of the most active RWT groups in the 20th-century United States was the KKK, which also communicated messages of intimidation and hate through murals. As but one example, in the 1950s, two identical KKK murals, featuring an image of a Klansman riding a black horse and holding a burning cross high in the air as the horse stood on its hind legs, were painted on the north and south walls of a bank in a city in Tennessee (Wilson, 2004).

Such murals did not become extinct with the shift to mass media. Murals, for example, played a role in the Northern Ireland 'Troubles' from the late 1960s. They are still found all over Northern Ireland, but are most prevalent in working-class areas of Belfast and Derry cities. In terms of marking territory, probably the most well-known Northern Ireland mural is located in Derry, where the text "You Are Now Entering Free Derry" was first painted on the side of a house in the Republican Bogside area of the city in 1969. Both the sentiment and technique were emulated by Loyalists who later painted the "You Are Now Entering Loyalist Sandy Row" mural in Belfast. In terms of political communication, it is estimated that throughout the period of the 'Troubles' (1969–1998), some 2,000 murals of varying quality appeared and disappeared. Many of these explicitly supported either Irish Republican or Ulster Loyalist terrorist groups, including the Provisional Irish Republican Army (IRA) and the Ulster Volunteer Force (UVF); others commemorated the perpetrators or victims of terrorist attacks. Not all Northern Irish murals are explicitly political, and it is increasingly common, following 1998's Good Friday peace agreement, for wall paintings undertaken by school and community groups to be non-political or have messages of peace. At the same time, many of the most explicitly hateful and explicit murals have been decommissioned.

Murals are still utilized by some extremist and terrorist groups today. Rather than using the term 'mural(s),' Johnson (2017) refers to 'graffiti' when discussing the Taliban's wall writing activity, which he says "primarily aims to mark territory friendly or sympathetic to the Taliban's cause and objectives, while offensive graffiti (threatening messages) aims at intimidating or 'marking' undecided or pro-government communities" (pp. 102–104). The so-called Islamic State (IS) has also made extensive use of murals in towns and cities controlled by them. Large renderings of their black and white 'logo' were painted on walls and rooftops in Mosul, Raqqa, Tal Afar, and numerous other locations in Iraq and Syria. In a blog post discussing IS murals, Al-Tamimi (2015) supplies a photo of, for example, an IS mural on a double archway stretching over a road showing the IS logo and the text "The Islamic State [Ninawa Province; Locality of Tel Afar] Welcomes You"(p. 2). Similar to the Taliban, many IS murals were wholly text-based, often featuring quotes from prominent jihadi figures or IS slogans, such as the well-known "Remaining and expanding" (Al-Tamimi, 2015, p. 5). The prominence of text-only murals in Afghanistan, Iraq, and Syria can be explained by the prohibition in Islam on depictions of people and animals. Finally, worth mentioning here is that after IS's loss of their Iraqi 'capital,' Mosul, in summer 2017, IS murals were observed "being painted over with Iraqi flags, white doves bearing olive branches and the hashtag 'Make it more beautiful'" (Solomon, 2017, p. 1). Having said this, the commissioning and de-commissioning of wall paintings – a form of 'pre-media' – continues to resonate even in the Internet age.

Low-tech media tools: print and photocopying

Newspapers, magazines, and billboards

In their seminal contribution to the study of terrorism and media, *Violence as Communication* (1982), Alex Schmid and Janny De Graaf point out that:

> Before technology made possible the amplification and multiplication of speech, the maximum number of people that could be reached

simultaneously was determined by the range of the human voice and was around 20,000 people. In the nineteenth century, within one lifetime, the size of an audience was expanded twenty-five to fifty times. In 1839 the New York Sun published a record 39,000 copies; in 1896, on the occasion of President McKinley's election, two US papers, belonging to Pulitzer and Hearst, for the first time printed a million copies. William McKinley paid dearly for this publicity. In 1901 he was killed by an anarchist, Leon Czolgosz, who explained his deed with the words: 'For a man should not claim so much attention, while others receive none.'

(p. 10)

Violent extremists and terrorists of all stripes have exploited the power of the printing press to systematically expand their 'fan' bases, garner new recruits, and gain support amongst broader publics.

The printing press was certainly an enabler in the Nazi Party's transformation of Germany in the inter-war years into a totalitarian state built on racism, hatred, and fear of the 'other' (Herf, 2006; Koonz, 2003; Welsh, 1993). Newspapers were but one of many print-propaganda tools, not only to systematically suppress, instil fear in, and terrorize those who were perceived as less than the Germanic peoples but to unite and mobilize the Nazi movement, as well as recruit new members. In the 1920s, for example, Hitler and his Nazi Party re-established a daily propagandistic newspaper, *Völkischer Beobachter* ('People's Observer') (c. 1920–1945), which disseminated Nazi ideology targeting, amongst other things, the weaknesses of parliamentary government, the national humiliation wrought by the Versailles Treaty, and the evils associated with Jews and Bolshevism. At its height in 1929, the newspaper reached over 26,000 readers daily (Welsh, 1993).

Print magazines were also a staple Nazi media tool. German Nazis used magazines for an array of propaganda purposes during the Third Reich (1933–1945), including, for example, providing magazine editors with guidelines about which topics were appropriate for publication and alerting a wide audience to guidelines about types of race relations that were and were not acceptable (Koonz, 2003). Audience segmentation occurred through the distribution of women's magazines (e.g. *NS-Frauen-Warte*), which supplied a 'better' understanding about what the Nazis were doing for women, as well as guidelines about women's roles in the Nazi state (Rupp & Taylor, 1987). Also worth mentioning here is the biweekly magazine *Signal* (1940–1945), published by the unified armed forces of Nazi Germany as a "slick" and "glossy" propaganda tool designed for readers in neutral, allied, and occupied countries (Meyer, 1976). Appearing in 30 languages, *Signal* published as many as 25 issues and reached as many as 2.5 million readers in 1943. Its contents included an array of relatively high-quality images, alongside detailed information about Nazi Germany and its 'New Order' as the great benefactor of European people, omitting anti-Semitic propaganda (Meyer, 1976).

In addition, front and centre in the Nazi propaganda efforts was an "artistic" yet hateful postering campaign, which – similar to wall murals – marked

German-occupied territories in the 1930s and 1940s. Unlike newspapers and magazines, which one generally had to seek out, posters were difficult to avoid (Rhodes, 1976). To illustrate, from 1936 to 1943, an estimated 125,000 posters were placed in public spaces with a high traffic flow of pedestrians (e.g. train carriages, buses, station platforms, ticket windows) for the purposes of educating and unifying the German people (Herf, 2006). Poster campaigns, which were a blend of political posters, leaflets, newspaper editorials, and tabloid journalism, primarily targeted Jews and the allied countries of Great Britain, the United States, and Russia, all while simultaneously depicting the Aryan race as superior. The visual effect of these posters was striking, as they contained bold lettering and Nazi-influenced colours as a means of capturing the attention of those passing by (Herf, 2006).

Across the Atlantic in the 1920s, RWT groups in the United States were developing their own propaganda machine. In 1921, the second wave of the Klan developed their own press after facing growing criticism from the public about their "hate-propagating tactics and deeds" (Cutlip, 1994, p. 396). The emergence of the U.S. tabloid press at around the same time was viewed by the KKK as a key opportunity for them to showcase their Klan identity and, by extension, present their radical messages to the public by reframing themselves as more "consumable." As Harcourt (2017) explains:

> [T]he Klan publications that were created are revealing. Klan newspapers were shaped by, and reflected, an accommodation to modern press trends – particularly in the tabloidization of news. Perhaps the clearest example of the commingling of these cultural strands was the collision of the Klan's anti-modern rhetoric with the puzzle craze that gripped the emerging consumerist society. The porous boundaries of cultural division in the 1920s were on full display in the popularity of the "Fiery Cross-Word Puzzle."
>
> (p. 31)

What constituted 'news' was changing from traditional broadsheets to tabloid newspapers, and RWT groups in the United States, particularly their public relations teams, took advantage of this development by introducing such newspapers as the *Searchlight* (1921–1924), an Atlanta-based publication that promoted "Free Speech: Free Press: White Supremacy" and was the rival of the official Klan tabloid *The Imperial Night-Hawk* (see Cutlip, 1994).

Magazines were also an important component of the Klan's media and information strategy during this time. Perhaps the most notable output of the Klan's printing presses was the *Fellowship Forum* (1923–1937). This 12-page weekly, unlike its predecessors, was circulated to a national audience, and by 1925 had reached 5 million regular readers – some of whom were international (Harcourt, 2017). Not only did the *Forum* maintain its readership during a period in which the KKK's official press network began to collapse (i.e. c.1925 onward), but it did so in large part because it was developed as a "respectable mainstream weekly" that also tailored itself to Klansmen (Harcourt, 2017, p. 49).

Throughout the 1950s, newspapers continued to be the medium of choice for the U.S. radical right movement more broadly. In 1958, for example, prominent U.S. white supremacist Edward Field launched *The Thunderbolt* (1958), which became a leading white power newspaper, succeeded in the late 1980s by *The Truth At Last*, which only ceased publication in 2008 (Southern Poverty Law Center, 2008). Today, the KKK's official newspaper is *The Crusader*.

The Klan also has a long history of billboard advertising. As far back as Christmas 1923, the corner of a busy street in Des Moines, Iowa, featured a Klan billboard that read "STOP! When you speed you violate the law. Good citizens uphold the law. Knights of the Ku Klux Klan." Comparably, Sims (1996) describes how in the mid-1960s:

> billboards encouraging motorists to JOIN AND SUPPORT UNITED KLANS OF AMERICA INC. became as commonplace as Chamber of Commerce and Rotary Club Greetings. Each year the Klan paid five dollars per sign for a state permit to advertise like Coca Cola and Philip Morris.
>
> (p. 29)

Similar billboards are still observable today in, especially, southern U.S. states. Thomas Robb, the 'National Director' of the KKK, has, for example, erected billboards throughout the area around Harrison, Arkansas, that display messages such as "Diversity is a code for #whitegenocide." Other extreme right groups have followed suit, with the secessionist League of the South erecting billboards in Arkansas and Tennessee urging motorists to "#Secede" (Schulte, 2017).

Historically, Islamist movements, too, have utilized 'old' forms of mass media to disseminate their message widely, recruit new members, and legitimize their cause. The Egyptian Muslim Brotherhood provides a prime example of this propaganda tactic, as they were avid users of the printing press from the 1930s. In 1933, the Brotherhood purchased a printing press and established a publishing company, thus starting a tireless effort to produce various newspapers over the course of the next decade, including launching their own weekly newspaper that was available from 1933 to 1938 and again from 1942 to 1946 and that became a daily from 1946 to 1948 (Ghanim, 1992; Lia, 1998). This print media featured articles that warned its readers about Zionism in general and Jews in particular, drawing distinctions between both groups, but boycotting Egyptian Jews on the basis that they were allegedly financing Zionist groups in Palestine (Lia, 1998; Mitchell, 1993). Funding to support such initiatives was raised by creating a joint-stock company, in which only Brotherhood members were allowed to buy shares (Lia, 1998). The Egyptian Muslim Brotherhood also printed an array of magazines from the late 1930s to the late 1950s, including the weekly magazines *Al-Nazir* (1938–1939) and *Al-Manar* (1939–1940) and the monthly magazines *Al-Shahab* (1947–1948) and *Al-Da'wa* (1951–1957) (Ghanim, 1992). In addition to the Egyptian Muslim Brotherhood, Hezbollah, Hamas, and a range of other Islamist groups have long histories of printing and circulating a variety of daily, weekly, and monthly newspapers and magazines.

Hezbollah's weekly newspaper, *Al-Ahed* ('The Pledge'), was launched on 13 June 1984, for example, and was followed by the weeklies *Al-Bilad*, *Al-Wahda*, *El-Ismailya*, and the monthly *Al-Sabil* (Conway, 2007a).

In terms of IS's media strategy, the vast bulk of attention has been paid to their online activity. IS also established and circulated a weekly Arabic-language newspaper called *Al-Naba* in territory controlled by them from approximately July 2015. *Al-Naba* was also available online from December 2015, but as Mahlouly and Winter (2018) recently noted, "its primary audience, at least between 2015 and 2018, appears to have been civilians and combatants living inside the group's territories in Syria and Iraq" (p. 14). There are more than 100 official IS photographs available showing hardcopies of the newspaper being distributed, oftentimes prior to its appearance online (see Mahlouly & Winter, 2018, pp. 15–16, for a selection of these). As Mahlouly and Winter (2018) further explained: "Al-Naba's structure and form are meticulously consistent: for the most part written in standardized media Arabic, it always features a combination of short and long articles with two full-page infographics" (p. 16). Containing photographs, announcements, military updates, and essays, its 139th issue had appeared at the time of writing (mid-July 2018). Originally 16 pages in length, it was shortened to 12 pages from the 105th edition.

Al-Tamimi (2013) describes IS billboarding as a form of *da'wah*, or Islamic religious outreach or proselytization, and says that those in Raqqa routinely included the text "From your brothers in the *da'wah* office: Raqqa" (p. 5). Unlike its murals, IS billboards often combined text and sophisticated imagery. Al-Tamimi (2015) supplies examples of some of these, including one showing a fighter jet, a missile, IS fighters, and an IS flag, with accompanying text reading "The Messenger of God said: 'Whoever dies and has not launched a raid/ operation or resolved to launch an operation, he has died among the division of hypocrisy" (pp. 2–3). Another very common subject of IS billboards was instruction on correct womanly behaviour and attire. These billboards often showed black woman-type shapes and admonishments to wear the full *niqab*. Many also featured flowers and other feminine design elements, including utilizing a pastel colour palette (see Al-Tamimi, 2013, 2015 for examples). On the other hand, in a twist on this theme, in 2016 American Muslims in Chicago, Phoenix, St. Louis, and elsewhere funded a series of billboards stating, in large black and white lettering, "HEY ISIS. YOU SUCK!!! Life is Sacred (Quran 5:32). From: #ActualMuslims" (Norton, 2016).

Photocopying

Brazilian Leftist Carlos Marighela's *Mini-Manual of the Urban Guerilla* (1969) contains a section on 'Armed Propaganda,' which states:

> [T]he urban guerrilla must never fail to install a clandestine press, and must be able to turn out mimeographed copies using alcohol or electric plates and other duplicating apparatus, expropriating what he cannot buy

in order to produce small clandestine newspapers, pamphlets, flyers and stamps far propaganda and agitation against the dictatorship.

The urban guerrilla engaged in clandestine printing facilitates enormously the incorporation of large numbers of people into the struggle, by opening a permanent work front for those willing to carry on propaganda, even when to do so means to act alone and risk their lives.

(p. 30)

Mimeographs were superseded by photocopiers, so essentially Marighela was advocating for the widespread use of photocopying. And, indeed, the latter's widespread availability from the 1970s, marked the beginnings of 'small' or personal media use for campaigning purposes. Through the simple use of a photocopier, violent extremists and terrorists could mass-produce posters, stickers, or flyers cheaply and at their convenience. Daniels (2009) points to how the extreme-right, amongst other movements, have exploited personal media and information tools both prior to and during the Internet era: "social-movement organizations can and do effectively engage in activism by relying solely on non-Internet-based forms of communication, such as landline telephones and printed materials sent via fax or postal mail" (p. 113). For example, David Lane, an American white supremacist leader and member of the terrorist group The Order, used an office photocopier in the early 1980s to produce thousands of copies of his first pamphlet, 'The Death of the White Race,' which was later distributed around Denver neighbourhoods (Michael, 2009). Similar to 'premedia,' therefore, the employment of low-tech media tools, such as printing and photocopying technology, have been in use by violent extremist and terrorist outfits from when such technologies first became relatively widely available, right up to the present time.

High-tech media tools: sound and vision

Radio

Radio broadcasting gained remarkable popularity amongst the general public in the Western world post–World War I, with the communication strategies of extreme right groups, including the Nazis in Germany (Welsh, 1993) and the Klan in the United States (Harcourt, 2017), in turn shaped by these – in this context – 'new' technologies.

When Hitler became chancellor of Germany in 1933, he saw the radio as an opportunity to disseminate his Nazi message to the masses; soon after, his speeches and Nazi propaganda were being broadcast not only across Germany but also in German-occupied countries and enemy states. In fact, Hitler's speeches were so significant to the Nazi brand that they were widely advertised in weekly postering campaigns and re-printed in book and pamphlet formats. In fear that their audience would not tune in, or worse, Germans would tune in to enemy propaganda broadcasts, the Nazis took active steps to make radio sets cheap to its citizens, as well as broadcast an array of Nazi-leaning programmes with non-propaganda elements, including music, advice, and tips (Koonz, 2003). Nazi propaganda was expected to be aired on restaurant and pub radios across Germany, as well as in the homes of German residents (Bywerk, 2008).

The Klan also exploited the communicative power of radio broadcasting in the post–World War I period. In 1923, for example, the first reported Klansman to contribute to a radio broadcast, Imperial Wizard Hiram Evan, addressed "the Klansmen of the Nation" from station WOQ in Kansas City, Missouri (Harcourt, 2017). In 1924, *Hamilton County Klan* was reported as one of the first Klan programmes broadcast from a government-licensed radio station. It featured lectures by KKK members and 'light' entertainment delivered by Klan musicians (Harcourt, 2017). Klan radio programming became increasingly popular in the United States in the 1920s: "a smashing hit," according to one Klan newspaper. The Klan's *Searchlight* newspaper also regularly published a column aimed at amateur radio enthusiasts (Harcourt, 2017). Klan members even managed to form alliances with one of the most powerful broadcasters in the Midwest, KFKB of Milford, Kansas. In 1925, the station featured Klan members on a fairly regular basis, including KKK lectures and music selections (Harcourt, 2017). But the Klan's most favoured broadcasting station was New York City's WHAP, which three times a week in 1926 broadcast anti-Catholic and anti-Semitic sentiment. Klan newspapers and magazines, including the *Fellowship Forum* and *Kourier Magazine*, praised WHAP for being one of the few stations to spread their message (Harcourt, 2017). From its establishment in 1926, however, the U.S. Federal Radio Commission (FRC) made it increasingly difficult for groups such as the Klan to acquire a broadcast licence and transmit material that was both "undesirable and obnoxious to [. . .] religious organizations" and deemed not in the "public interest, convenience or necessity" (Harcourt, 2017, p. 151).

U.S. talk radio's growth followed decades of deregulation, including the 1987 revocation of the Fairness Doctrine, a way by which the Federal Communications Commission attempted to regulate content produced by licensed broadcasters. The subsequent rise of conservative talk radio had enormous influence and continues to attract millions of listeners daily, well into the Internet age. Some stations and programmes are no longer simply conservative in their orientation, however, but fall squarely into the extreme right category. Contemporary extreme right radio's most conspicuous exponent is InfoWar's Alex Jones. He hosts *The Alex Jones Show* on the Genesis Communications Network, which airs on more than 90 AM and FM stations, and at least one shortwave station, across the United States and also online. Jones is an infamous conspiracy theorist. The aggressively pro-gun Jones is, for example, a Sandy Hook 'truther.' He believes, in other words, that the slaying of 20 six- and seven-year-old children in their elementary school in Connecticut in December 2012 never took place and is an elaborate fake. He has also accused the U.S. government of involvement in 1995's Oklahoma City bombing and the 9/11 attacks. Jones started his career in his hometown of Austin, Texas, with a live, call-in-format, public-access cable television show. In 1996, he switched from television to radio, hosting a show called *The Final Edition* on the former KJFK 98.9 FM, also in Austin. In 1999, KJFK-FM fired him for refusing to broaden his topics beyond conspiracies and similar. He thus began airing his programme online from his home. As far back as 2010, the programme was reported as attracting some 2 million listeners weekly. While Jones has emerged as the most famous U.S. far right radio 'shock jock,' he is certainly not alone. For example, one of the Knights Club of the KKK-sponsored billboards in Harrison, Arkansas, mentioned earlier, features an image of a young girl and the text "It's not racist to [heart] your people," and the URL of White Pride Radio. While the latter URL currently resolves to altrightv.com, which is no longer reachable, a host of other white supremacist radio stations and programmes continue to attract listeners. These include Don Black's long-running *Stormfront* programme, which streams online for an hour every weekday, and National Vanguard Radio, which focuses on "the anti-White agenda," "White survival," and similar topics.

IS's radio station *Al-Bayan*, or 'The Dispatch,' was first heard in early 2015. Originally airing on an FM frequency in Mosul, Iraq, it was shortly also airing in Raqqa, Syria, and, for a short time, in Libya. Described by an Iraqi Joint Operation Command spokesman as "one of the strongest" propaganda tools for the militants in Mosul, the Mosul station reportedly went off air in early October 2016 after it was bombed by Iraqi government jets (NBC News, 2016). *Al-Bayan* had a dedicated website, but it was subject to frequent disruption. IS sought to evade domain takedowns by slightly changing the station's URL each time it reappeared; once a domain such as albayan.com was deleted by authorities, IS would utilize a different but very similar URL, such as by adding an extra character (i.e. albayaan.com), or choose a new domain suffix for the site (e.g.. org). News bulletins were also at different points in time delivered through Twitter and other social media sites. In addition to Arabic-language broadcasts, *Al-Bayan* was known to broadcast in English, French, and Russian, with one English-language news reader described as having "a smooth, male voice with an American accent" (Sharma, 2015, p. 1).[1] Following a February 2017 takedown of the station's website, an updated version was reported as appearing online that included "options for high and low bandwidth playback and a link to a Firefox browser plugin to enable streamlined playback with the click of a button" (Daftari, 2017, p. 1). Earlier, in February 2016, it was reported that AKP files – used to install software on Android systems – for an *Al-Bayan* radio app were circulating on IS-linked social media accounts (Tasch, 2016). The station was widely reported as being played loudly over speakers in public places, such as markets and the like, in areas controlled by IS (NBC News, 2016).

Film and television

The year that witnessed the birth of modern international terrorism, 1968, was the same year in which the United States launched the first television satellite, heralding the second great revolution in mass communications that directly affected extremism and terrorism (Carruthers, 2000; Chaliand, 1985; Hoffman, 2006; Schmid & De Graaf, 1982). In light of these developments, worth noting is that although television marked the birth of modern international terrorism in the late 1960s, roughly 30 years prior, German Nazis took active steps to make their extremist campaign international without the use of television. As early as the 1930s, the Nazi Party exploited film to expand their propaganda efforts and reach an international audience. The KKK also made efforts in this respect at around the same time, but the Nazis were much more successful than the Klan at using film to reach an international audience. Interestingly, no extreme right organization has had the wherewithal to establish its own television station. Prior to IS, the group with the best-known televisual output was Lebanon's Hezbollah and their *Al-Manar* television station.

In addition to radio, in the 1930s, film assisted Hitler's propaganda to reach an international audience (Welsh, 1993). Nazis came to dominate the nascent German film industry, which they viewed as a means of influencing German culture, education, and entertainment. Their nationalistic films, including *Triumph of Will* (1935), featured footage of German soldiers marching to militaristic tunes and speeches from Nazi leaders. They also produced 'documentaries,' such as *The Eternal Jew* (1940), which portrayed Jewish people as cultural hedonists and parasites. German schools were provided motion picture projectors as a means of providing students with "military education" (Rhodes, 1976). In the United States, the Klan also saw the development of cinematography as an opportunity to inject messages of hate into mainstream culture. The movie industry was fast-growing in America in 1915 when the KKK released the film *The Birth of a Nation*, which celebrated the original late 19th-century Klan (Cutlip, 1994). During its height in the 1920s, Klan members developed their own film enterprise, producing feature films such as *The Toll of Justice* (1923) and *The Traitor Within* (1924), both of which were advertised with poster campaigns as well as screened in churches and schools and at outdoor events (Rice, 2015).

Following 'the sanitary decades' (1940s–1950s) (i.e. a period after World War II in which 'fascism' was a dirty word), television played a role in propelling the extreme right message anew (Hoffman, 2006; Schmid & De Graaf, 1982). During the 1980s, for example, television repairman and founder of White Aryan Resistance (WAR), Tom Metzger, developed a cable-access television show called *Race and Reason*, which during its height aired in 62 cities in 21 U.S. states (Southern Poverty Law Center, 2018). Formatted as a 'talk show,' the programme featured interviews with 'Aryan' activists about 'white rights' and other race-related issues (Simi & Futrell, 2015).[2] No group succeeded in actually establishing their own television station, however. Islamist groups like Hezbollah, on the other hand, were pioneers in developing their own stations (Hoffman, 2006).

Al-Manar, the 'Beacon' or 'Lighthouse,' in Arabic, has been described as the "jewel in Hezbollah's media crown" (as quoted in Conway, 2007a, p. 402), but labelled a 'Specially Designated Global Terrorist Entity' by the U.S. government, it was banned by them in December 2004. Live footage of Hezbollah operations appeared for the first time in 1986, with coverage of the invasion of the Israeli-occupied Sujud fort in south Lebanon, and was distributed to those Lebanese television stations in operation at that time. According to Hezbollah's second-in-command, Naim Qassem, "[f]ollowing the first television broadcast of this operation, the camera became an essential element in all resistance operations" (as quoted in Conway, 2007a, p. 402). The establishment of *Al-Manar* followed shortly thereafter; its first broadcast was Iranian revolutionary leader Ayatollah Khomeini's June 1989 funeral. The *Al-Manar* satellite station was launched in 2000 and is now one of the top-ranked television stations in the Arab world. *Al-Manar*, however, has been criticized for, among other things, its anti-Semitic content, circulating the conspiracy theory that Israel was behind the 9/11 attacks and broadcasting a drama series entitled *Al-Shattat* ('The Diaspora'), based on the controversial 19th-century *Protocols of the Elders of Zion*, which depicts a Zionist conspiracy to take over the world (Conway, 2007a). These and other reasons caused it to be banned from broadcasting in, amongst other jurisdictions, France (2005) and the United States (2006), but with this being entirely circumventable via *Al-Manar*'s continuous free live online streaming (Conway, 2007a). The latter was, however, just one of the innovations ushered in by increased access to the Internet by a wide variety of violent extremist and terrorist groups and their supporters from the mid-1990s.

High-tech communication tools: online multimedia

As Ranstorp (2007) put it, "[t]he role of the media as the oxygen of publicity would take on a new added meaning, urgency and complexity with globalization and the instruments of cyberspace" (pp. 1–2). Illustrated in this section is that although the Internet and the ways in which it operates is in some ways quite distinct from 'older' media forms, significant overlaps also exist. Having said this, the Internet's increasing ubiquity is causing us to communicate, think, and ultimately live differently. Indeed, today's world is interactive in ways that are strikingly new in their orders and intensity at all levels (Appadurai, 1996). This has caused some media theorists to describe ours as a 'convergence culture': "convergence represents a cultural shift, as consumers are encouraged to seek out new information and make connections among dispersed media content" (Jenkins, 2006, p. 3). Convergence is occurring at the levels of both production and distribution; newspapers, television, and music once had very different physical productions, but can now be produced via a single high-end mobile phone or other handheld devices, such as tablets. At the distribution level, previously discrete channels are absorbed into a single-networked online process, with news, music, and so on all accessed through the Internet. Convergence is also occurring at the level of content with, for example, news and entertainment being combined and recombined in new ways.

Violent extremists and terrorists have been undeniably quick to adopt and use every emerging online platform at their disposal, exploiting convergence culture through the use of Internet-based media tools. Many journalists and policymakers, however, have only in recent years come to an awareness of the use of the Internet by such actors. This 'discovery' is, by and large, a result of IS's announcement of their so-called 'caliphate' and their release via the Internet of a steady stream of video-taped beheadings of Western hostages and other atrocity footage, including mass shootings, stonings, and crucifixions, beginning in summer 2014. IS's violence, including the Internet's role as its means of dissemination, has attracted significant news media attention globally. Journalists, policymakers, and others have come to view IS's Internet activity as a core mechanism of their 'success,' and that activity has thus taken on something of a mythic status. The terrorism–Internet nexus has a much lengthier history than this, however.

Web 1.0: bulletin board systems, websites, and online forums

Along with a history of violence, the extreme right has a very long online history, dating to the earliest days of the public Internet in the mid-1980s. American white nationalist Louis Beam, an early advocate of 'leaderless resistance,' established and ran a bulletin board system (BBS) known as *Aryan Nation Liberty Net* accessible from at least 1984 via telephone numbers in the U.S. states of Idaho, Texas, and North Carolina. It allowed anybody with a computer and a modem to gain 'dial-up' access to a variety of hate propaganda and to leave their own hate messages. Similarly, the Anti-Defamation League (ADL) described in a 1985 report how:

> [T]he Aryan Nations' network supplies under the heading of "enemies" a listing of the addresses and phone numbers of the Anti-Defamation League's national and regional offices. In the same category are listed what the Aryan Nations refers to as "informers" for the "Zionist Occupational Government," its name for the United States government. Another group of "enemies" is labeled "race traitors" and is accessible, the network claims, only to callers with special clearance.
>
> Also provided are the names and addresses of so-called patriotic organizations, including a variety of neo-Nazi, Klan and armed racist groups such as the Christian Patriots Defense League and the Covenant, the Sword and the Arm of the Lord. The computer supplies dates and locations of their meetings.
>
> (pp. 2–3)

Nor was Beam's service the only such BBS operating at this time; another U.S.-based service known as *Info International* was established and run by George Dietz, the owner of a notorious extreme right publishing company, Liberty Bell Publications (Anti-Defamation League, 1985).

The Internet first became publicly accessible in 1991, and during this time, Florida-based *Stormfront* proudly described itself as "the first White Nationalist site on the Web" (Oldham, 1998, p. 1). As early as 1996, *Stormfront*'s Don

Black asserted that "Organizations have recruited through Stormfront, and through their Web pages that we've linked to" (Kanaley, 1996, p. 1). The original *Stormfront* was more website than forum, containing a 'Quote of the Week,' 'Texts Library' of 'White Nationalist' documents, a letters page, an assortment of cartoons, and a downloadable graphics section. The 'Hot Links' page featured connections to like-minded sites such as those maintained by Aryan Nations, William Pierce's National Alliance, and Posse Comitatus. Some of these websites framed themselves as 'news' (such as 'National Vanguard News' and 'Life Site News') or 'educational' sites (such as 'DavidDuke.com' and 'American Renaissance') (Daniels, 2009) and included links to an array of content and services, from "Whites only" dating services to white power music and racist video games (Back, 2002).

The earliest research into the intersection of explicit terrorism and the Internet focused on the possibility of the emergence of cyberterrorism (i.e. a terrorist attack using or targeting the Internet) (e.g. Collin, 1997; Devost et al., 1997; National Research Council, 1991). By the mid-1990s, however, actually occurring instances of terrorists' Internet use began drawing the attention of researchers, eventually coalescing around five broad types or categories of such use: information provision, financing, networking, recruitment, and information gathering (see Conway, 2006). Influence was identified as an important function, but not singled out at this stage; radicalization was a concept not yet in wide circulation in terrorism analysis (Awan, Hoskins, & O'Loughlin, 2012). In 1998, approximately half of the (then) 30 groups designated as 'Foreign Terrorist Organisations' under the U.S. Antiterrorism and Effective Death Penalty Act of 1996 operated websites, including Hamas, Hezbollah, the Tamil Tigers, and others. These groups oftentimes portrayed their radical content as 'news,' but with the vast majority of the content featuring fierce criticism of Western foreign policy and a focus on violence perpetrated by the groups' adversaries as a means to justify their own use of violence (Seib & Janbek, 2011). Other sites run by supporters of terrorist groups (e.g. 'Kalamullah' and 'Islam Web') were disguised as 'educational' and included provocative speeches from, for example, Anwar al-Awlaki, an American imam who was involved in planning terrorist operations for Al-Qaeda. These early websites fulfilled a largely 'broadcast' function, with website content tightly controlled by the terrorist organizations and opportunities for interaction negligible. The sites nonetheless served as one-stop shops for information on the groups (Conway, 2005).

By the next decade, online forums had become a popular media and information format, especially amongst right-wing extremists and violent jihadis, as forums allowed for much greater levels of interactivity amongst their users (Conway, 2006). The online practices of violent jihadis and their supporters, for example, were subject to increased scrutiny by news media, policymakers, and researchers following the 9/11 attacks (see, for example, Conway, 2007b; Ducol, 2012; Kimmage, 2008; Kimmage & Ridolfo, 2007; Seib & Janbek, 2011). This was unsurprising given both the events of 9/11 and that violent jihadis significantly grew their online presence post-9/11. Dedicated forums were where the global jihad was virtually headquartered throughout this period (Hegghammer, 2014; Zelin, 2013). Not only were the forums important online discussion spaces, but it was also via the forums that new jihadi online content was first advertised and then filtered through to the wider jihadi online community. As late as 2013, Zelin predicted "Twitter is unlikely to supplant the forum architecture because it cannot replace the sense of authenticity and exclusivity created by the forums" (p. 2). Despite increased interactivity, this sense of authenticity and exclusivity was maintained via a significant element of control still in evidence on the forums. An example was a conversation on the English-language *Islamic Awakening* forum in which a member complained of having been ejected from an Al-Qaeda–affiliated forum after commenting on Al-Qaeda in Iraq (AQI)'s killing of Muslims; to this another poster responded that the expelled member deserved it and that the persistence of such questions must be dismaying for the mujahidin (Ramsay, 2009). Such controls notwithstanding, there were five to eight popular and functioning jihadi online forums active in the period 2004 to 2009; by 2013, this had decreased to between three and five. This decrease was probably due to a combination of (1) cyberattacks against the forums from the mid-2000s degrading their functionality and deterring new members and forums and (2) younger adherents shifting to social media platforms (Zelin, 2013, p. 2).

While jihadi online forums have been eroded by a shift to social media, the extreme right is still committed to the use of both general and dedicated online forums. The extreme right became increasingly reliant from the mid-1990s on web forums to facilitate movement expansion by publicizing messages of hatred and connecting with like-minded individuals, both within and beyond domestic borders (Back, 2002; Bowman-Grieve, 2009). A report by the Southern Poverty Law Center (SPLC) alleges that in the period 2010–2014, almost 100 murders could be attributed to registered *Stormfront* users (Beirich, 2014, pp. 2–6). One infamous contributor, for example, was the Norwegian extreme right terrorist Anders Breivik. According to *Stormfront*'s own statistics, the forum had well over 12.5 million posts at time of writing (August 2018), the "most users ever online" on their forum at any one time was 24,066 at 1.52 p.m. on 16 January 2018, and the "total guests" visiting the forum in a 24-hour period in August 2018 hovered around 25,000. In addition to dedicated extreme right forums, a diversity of more general online platforms or forum-like online spaces also host increasing amounts of extreme right content. These include the popular social news aggregation, web content rating, and discussion site Reddit and image-based bulletin board and comment site 4chan.

Web 2.0: digital video and social media

The shift by violent extremists and terrorists over the course of two decades from an overwhelming reliance on websites to a heavy reliance on forums to a wholesale commitment to social media has at least as much to do with transformations in the workings of the Internet as in the workings of violent extremism and terrorism over the period (Hegghammer, 2014). As we have seen, Al-Qaeda had used the Internet for communication and propaganda purposes prior to the 9/11 attacks, but their use of the Internet increased exponentially thereafter. This had two interrelated causes: (1) the loss of Al-Qaeda's Afghan base and the consequent dispersal of its leaders and fighters and (2) the rapid development of the Internet itself, the global spread of Internet cafes, the proliferation of Internet-capable computers and other devices, such as mobile telephones, and the emergence of so-called 'Web 2.0' (Conway, 2012). The latter is character-ized by its emphasis on the integration of digital video, social networking, and user-generated content.

In addition to adopting Web 1.0 and 2.0 technology for violent extremist purposes, the performative nature of terrorism meant that violent jihadis, much more so than RWT groups and supporters, were eager adopters of digital video (Kimmage, 2008; Kimmage & Ridolfo, 2007). AQI's Abu Musab al-Zarqawi was a noteworthy early innovator with respect to the use of digital video con-tent. In May 2004, al-Zarqawi had himself filmed personally cutting off the head of American hostage Nicholas Berg, and posted the footage online. The purpose of this beheading was precisely to videotape it; the images gripped the imaginations of AQI's allies and enemies alike. Al-Qaeda and a diverse range of other jihadis had, for some time, been circulating a range of content online, including particularly text-based (e.g. forum postings, magazines/journals, books, and written statements) and audio (e.g. statements by leaders, sermons by violent jihadi preachers, *nashid* (chants) products). With the advent of easy digital video composition and fast download, large amounts of violent jihad-supporting video began to be produced, distributed, and consumed.

Early genres of jihadi video included political statements, by leaders and (Western) 'spokesmen'; attack footage; 'pre-martyrdom' videos, such as that made of 7/7 bomber Mohammed Siddique Khan; instructional videos, of both theological and military-operational sorts; memorial videos commemorating persons and/or events; 'music' videos; and beheadings. These were produced by a variety of official and semi-official media production houses, such as *Al-Fajr*, the *Global Islamic Media Front*, and *As-Sahab*. These products were "consistently and systematically branded" by the prominent display of graphic logos (Kim-mage & Ridolfo, 2007, p. 1) and made available in a variety of formats, includ-ing those optimized for iPod and cell phone viewing. In terms of production volume, between 2002 and 2005 *As-Sahab* issued a total of 45 video products; there was an exponential increase in 2006, which saw the distribution of 58 productions (Rogan, 2007, p. 91); 2007 too was a banner year, with 97 original productions (Seib & Janbek, 2011, p. 32). Both the number of videos and the quality of the content produced by Al-Qaeda and associated groups came to be eclipsed by IS's video output, however.

It has been estimated that IS produced an average of 46 videos per month in the period between January 2015 and July 2016, which amounted to some 140 hours of digital footage (Milton, 2016). IS's digital video content is notable for its high production qualities with, for example, one video employing aerial drone camera footage in its opening sequence and the 22-minute long production showing the burning of Jordanian fighter pilot, Lt. Muath al-Kasasbeh, containing complicated animations and scene changes. Many videos contained largely Arabic-language content, but were subtitled in English and other languages depending on their content and the audience(s) at which they were targeted. In terms of the nature of the video content, an interesting reversal has taken place over time, with over half of all visual content, including video, being non-military in nature in the first quarter of 2015, but only 15% having this non-martial character in the period January to March 2018 (Milton, 2018). Although video content comprises only a small percentage of IS's overall online output, it is worth underlining that video content probably also has a much greater viewership and thereby also influence than many other types of content (Milton, 2018).[3]

Jihadis and their online supporters had increasing recourse to mainstream social media platforms from 2011, but with a particularly strong swing in this direction from 2013 (Zelin, 2013). Like Al-Qaeda before them, IS does not have a single official website; instead their 'official' online content emanates from IS-affiliated content production entities or so-called 'media departments.' At the height of their 'success' around 2015, official IS media departments included IS's central media bureaus (i.e. *Al-Furqan*, *Al-Hayat*, etc.) and regional media production houses (i.e. *Wilayat Homs*, *Khurasan*, *Sinai*, etc.); semi-official production outlets included *Amaq News Agency* and *Furat Media Centre*; and a variety of unofficial and IS 'fan' online outlets.[4] These media production outlets produce and circulate not just videos, but a host of other types of content, including photo montages, audio, infographics, and magazines. In the period 2013–2016, this content was largely distributed via major and some minor social media and other online platforms. These included prominent IS presences on Facebook, Twitter, and YouTube, but also Ask.fm, JustPaste.it, and the Internet Archive.

Twitter was a platform particularly favoured by IS and their supporters; it was estimated that there were between 46,000 and 90,000 pro-IS Twitter accounts active in the period September to December 2014 (Berger & Morgan, 2015). In IS's Twitter 'Golden Age' in 2013 and 2014, a variety of official IS 'fighter' and an assortment of other IS 'fan' accounts could be accessed with relative ease. For the uninitiated user, once one IS-related account was located, the automated Twitter recommendations on 'who to follow' accurately supplied others. For those 'in the know,' pro-IS users were easily and quickly identifiable via their choice of carousel and avatar images, along with their user handles and screen names. Therefore, if one wished, it was quick and easy to become connected to a large number of like-minded Twitter users. If sufficient time and effort was invested, it was also relatively straightforward to become a trusted – even prominent – member of the IS 'Twittersphere.' Not only was there a vibrant overarching pro-IS Twitter community in existence at this time, but also a whole series of strong and supportive language (e.g. Arabic, English, French, Russian, Turkish) and/or ethnicity-based (e.g. Chechens or 'al-Shishanis') and other special interest (e.g. females or 'sisters') Twitter sub-communities. Most of these special interest groups were a mix of (1) a small number of users actually on the ground in Syria, (2) a larger number of users seeking to travel (or with a stated preference to do so), and (3) an even larger number of so-called 'jihobbyists' with no formal affiliation to any jihadist group, but who spent their time lauding fighters, celebrating suicide attackers and other 'martyrs' and networking around and disseminating IS content (Conway et al., 2017).

External effects, including increased pressure on IS' territory and manpower and direct targeting by Western forces of IS' social media 'experts' and strategists and their cyber apparatus, contributed to a decrease in production of IS online content from late 2015. Disruption by major social media companies of pro-IS accounts began to bite at about this time also. In a February 2016 blog post, titled 'Combating Violent Extremism,' Twitter stated that they had suspended over 125,000 accounts for threatening or promoting terrorist acts, primarily related to IS, since mid-2015. In a follow-up blog post in August, Twitter described suspending an average of c.40,000 IS-related accounts per month in the period between mid-February and mid-July 2016. This ramped up further in 2017, with many pro-IS accounts being suspended within minutes of their appearance, such that in 2018, IS's presence on most major social media platforms is a tiny fraction of what it once was.

While Twitter was once IS's preferred platform, the Telegram messaging application is now its platform of choice. Telegram is as yet a lower profile platform than Twitter – and obviously also Facebook – with a smaller user base and higher barriers to entry (e.g. provision of a mobile phone number to create an account, time-limited invitations to join channels). These are probably positive attributes from the perspective of cutting down on the numbers of users exposed to IS's online content and thereby in a position to be violently radicalized by it. On the negative side, this may mean that Telegram's pro-IS community is more committed than its Twitter variant. Also, although IS's reach via Telegram is less than it was via Twitter, the echo chamber effect may be greater as the 'owners' of Telegram channels and groups have much greater control over who joins and contributes to these than on Twitter. Another aspect of Telegram that is attractive to extremists is its in-platform content upload and cloud storage function(s), which reduces the need for outlinking to other platforms. Although Telegram restricts users from uploading files larger than 1.5 GB – roughly a two-hour movie – it provides seemingly unlimited amounts of storage.

As already mentioned, right-wing extremists have not exploited digital video to the same extent as, for example, IS, but they have nonetheless considerably grown their online presence in recent years. Right-wing extremist groups and sympathizers have a noticeable presence on all major social media platforms, while a new generation of right-wing extremists are also moving to more overtly hateful, yet to some extent more hidden platforms, including 8chan, Voat, Gab, and Discord (see Davey & Ebner, 2017). A cursory Google search also reveals that right-wing extremist groups, unlike the vast majority of jihadi groups, are able to maintain official websites. Davey (2018) chalks up these differences to how social media and technology companies police their platforms, in that a much more concerted effort has been placed on removing Islamist content than content from the extreme right. Less, however, is known about how right-wing extremist groups and supporters are using encrypted communication apps. Some recent reports, however, suggest that *The Daily Stormer*'s Andrew Anglin has taken a page out of IS's playbook by urging his fellow activists to ditch standard online platforms and revert to encryption chat services such as Telegram (Holt, 2018). In 2016, National Action also used Telegram to communicate with other members of the group about a neo-Nazi stickering campaign they were involved in on a university campus (Dearden, 2018), and right-wing extremists in Germany reportedly used encrypted apps to mobilize the movement during the 2017 election (Davey & Ebner, 2017).

Conclusion

Terrorism has always been about communication because, as Schmid and De Graaf (1982) remind us, "Without communication there can be no terrorism" (p. 9). The late British Prime Minister Margaret Thatcher famously described publicity as the oxygen of terrorism. This pronouncement continues to resonate because although it is never their ultimate objective, publicity is what sustains effective terrorist campaigns. It follows from this that violent extremists and terrorists should take every opportunity to get their message out to as large an audience as possible by amplifying their violence via media. What this chapter has shown is that a diversity of groups and movements have been quick to adopt and use every emerging media and information tool at their disposal, seizing on every opportunity to produce and disseminate material and ideas that they desire to resonate with adherents and attract new members.

Two additional points are worth noting as we conclude this chapter. First, although it is clear that the Internet and encrypted platforms have provided violent extremists and terrorists with a centralized space to facilitate interactive communications with like-minded individuals on a global scale, perhaps less obvious to some is that such actors are still drawing upon a wide range of 'old' media tools to further their goals, oftentimes combining them with high-tech communication methods – 'good' examples of this are jihadi online magazines. Second, our mapping of media and information tools exploited by a diversity of violent extremist and terrorist groups and movements, particularly the extreme right and violent jihadis, shows that they have all adopted similar media tactics. What varies between the two movements' use of media tools for violent extremist purposes largely depends on their objectives and the technological, social, cultural, and political context in which they reside. With regard to low-tech communication methods, one terrorist group, such as the Nazis in Germany, for example, who occupy a territory may paint a wall mural on the side of a building in a busy part of town to remind Germans that the Nazi Party is in charge and that residents must adhere to their laws. Another terrorist group, such as Al-Qaeda in Syria, may display wall murals in a public space immediately following a U.S. drone strike, in an effort to drum up local support by reminding residents that the United States is invading 'their' country. Turning to high-tech communication methods, a terrorist group such as IS may have no choice but to turn to encrypted platforms to disseminate their content, in fear that the material will be removed if it is on the open Web. On the other hand, National Action, a RWT group in the UK, may not have to turn to the dark web to spread hatred, but perhaps forced to tone down their rhetoric on their Facebook page, for example, in fear that the social media company will ban them from the site. In short, both movements have used similar communication strategies but at different time periods.

Notes

1   The voice can be heard on a Quilliam Foundation–produced clip about the station entitled 'Islamic State's Al-Bayan radio station' and posted to YouTube: www.youtube.com/watch?v=OUBbwa0FvPs.
2   Metzger also made frequent appearances on national talk shows; his son also appeared on the *Geraldo* television programme, which left Geraldo Rivera, the show's host, with a broken nose after an infamous brawl.
3   Milton (2018) calculates that it never rose above 20% of even their *visual* output between 2015 and 2018.
4   For a graphic representation, see for example Figure 3 and Figure 4 in Milton (2016).

References

Al-Tamimi, A. (2013). The Islamic State of Iraq and ash-Sham billboards in Raqqa [Personal Blog]. Retrieved from www.aymennjawad.org/13960/the-islamic-state-of-iraq-and-ash-sham-billboards

Al-Tamimi, A. (2015). The Islamic State billboards and murals of Tel Afar and Mosul [Personal Blog]. Retrieved from www.aymennjawad.org/2015/01/the-islamic-state-billboards-and-murals-of-tel

Anti-Defamation League (ADL). (1985). *Computerized networks of hate: An ADL fact finding report.* New York, NY: ADL.

Appadurai, A. (1996). *Modernity at large: Cultural dimensions in globalization.* London: University of Minnesota Press.

Awan, A., Hoskins, A., & O'Loughlin, B. (2012). *Radicalisation and media: Connectivity and terrorism in the new media ecology.* London: Routledge.

Back, L. (2002). Aryans reading Adorno: Cyber-culture and twenty-first century racism. *Ethnic and Racial Studies, 25*(4), 628–651.

Beirich, H. (2014). White homicide worldwide. *Southern Poverty Law Center Intelligence Report,* Summer. Retrieved from www.splcenter.org/sites/default/files/downloads/publication/white-homicide-worldwide.pdf

Berger, J. M. (2018). *Extremism.* Cambridge: MIT Press.

Berger, J. M., & Morgan, J. (2015). *The ISIS Twitter census: Defining and describing the population of ISIS supporters on Twitter.* Washington, DC: Brookings.

Bowman-Grieve, L. (2009). Exploring "Stormfront": A virtual community of the radical right. *Studies in Conflict and Terrorism, 32*(11), 989–1007.

Bywerk, R. L. (2008). *Landmark speeches of national socialism*. College Station, TX: Texas A&M University Press.

Carruthers, S. L. (2000). *The media at war*. Hampshire, UK: Palgrave.

Chaliand, G. (1985). *Terrorism: From popular struggle to media spectacle*. London: Saqi Books.

Collin, B. (1997). Future of cyberterrorism: Physical and virtual worlds converge. *Crime and Justice International, 13*(2), 15–18.

Conway, M. (2005). Terrorist web sites: Their contents, functioning, and effectiveness. In P. Seib (Ed.), *Media and conflict in the twenty-first century* (pp. 185–215). New York, NY: Palgrave.

Conway, M. (2006). Terrorism and the internet: New media – new threat? *Parliamentary Affairs, 59*(2), 283–298.

Conway, M. (2007a). Terror TV? Hizbollah's Al Manar Television. In J. Forest (Ed.), *Countering terrorism in the 21st century* (Vol. 2, pp. 401–419). Westport, CT: Praeger Security International.

Conway, M. (2007b). Terrorism and the making of the 'New Middle East': New media strategies of Hizbollah and al Qaeda. In P. Seib (Ed.), *New media in the New Middle East* (pp. 235–258). London: Palgrave.

Conway, M. (2012). From al-Zarqawi to al-Awlaki: The emergence and development of an online radical milieu. *CTX: Combating Terrorism Exchange, 2*(4), 12–22.

Conway, M., Khawaja, M., Lakhani, S., Reffin, J., Robertson, A., & Weir, D. (2017). *Disrupting Daesh: Measuring takedown of online terrorist material and its impacts*. Dublin: VOX-Pol.

Cutlip, S. M. (1994). *The unseen power: Public relations. A history*. Hillsdale, NJ: Lawrence Erlbaum Associates Publishers.

Daftari, L. (2017, February 13). Islamic State's Al Bayan radio station back online. *The Foreign Desk*. Retrieved from www.foreigndesknews.com/world/middle-east/islamic-states-al-bayan-radio-station-back-online/#

Daniels, J. (2009). *Cyber racism: White supremacy online and the new attack on civil rights*. Lanham, MD: Rowman and Littlefield.

Davey, J. (2018, January 13). I work for an anti-extremism organisation and this is the difference between neo-Nazi and Islamist propaganda online. *Independent*. Retrieved from www.independent.co.uk/voices/anti-extremism-islamist-terrorism-far-right-twitter-national-action-scottish-dawn-online-a8157426.html

Davey, J., & Ebner, J. (2017). *The fringe insurgency: Connectivity, convergence and mainstreaming of the extreme right*. London: Institute for Strategic Dialogue.

Dearden, L. (2018, May 9). Neo-Nazis convicted after spreading National Action stickers around Birmingham University and performing Hitler salute. *Independent*. Retrieved from www.independent.co.uk/news/uk/crime/national-action-neo-nazi-stickers-birmingham-aston-university-racist-convicted-a8343596.html

Devost, M., Houghton, B., & Pollard, N. (1997). Information terrorism: Political violence in the information age. *Terrorism and Political Violence, 9*(1), 72–83.

Ducol, B. (2012). Uncovering the French-speaking jihadisphere: An exploratory analysis. *Media, War and Conflict, 5*(1), 51–70.

Ghanim, I. B. (1992). *Al-Fikr al-siyasi lil-imam ḥasan al-banna* [The political thinking of Imam Hassan al-Banna]. Cairo: Dar al Tawzi' wa-al-Nashr.

Harcourt, F. (2017). *Ku Klux Kulture: America and the Klan in the 1920s*. Chicago: The University of Chicago Press.

Hegghammer, T. (2014). *Interpersonal trust on Jihadi internet forums*. Retrieved from http://hegghammer.com/_files/Interpersonal_trust.pdf

Herf, J. (2006). *The Jewish enemy: Nazi propaganda during World War II and the Holocaust*. Cambridge: Belknap Press of Harvard University Press.

Heschel, S. (2008). *The Aryan Jesus: Christian theologians and the Bible in Nazi Germany*. Princeton: Princeton University Press.

Hoffman, B. (2006). *Inside terrorism: Revised and expanded edition*. New York, NY: Columbia University Press.

Holt, J. (2018, April 18). Neo-Nazis are fleeing discord, heading to messaging app popular with ISIS supporters. *Right Wing Watch*. Retrieved from www.rightwingwatch.org/post/neo-nazis-are-fleeing-discord-heading-to-messaging-app-popular-with-isis-supporters/

Jenkins, H. (2006). *Convergence culture: Where old and new media collide*. New York, NY: New York University Press.

Johnson, T. H. (2017). *Taliban narratives: The use and power of stories in the Afghanistan conflict*. Oxford: Oxford University Press.

Kanaley, R. (1996, July 4). Hate groups tap into the Internet. *The Philadelphia Inquirer*.

Kimmage, D. (2008). *The Al-Qaeda media nexus: The virtual network behind the global message*. Washington, DC: Radio Free Europe.

Kimmage, D., & Ridolfo, K. (2007). *Iraqi insurgent media: The war of images and ideas*. Washington, DC: Radio Free Europe.

Koonz, C. (2003). *The Nazi conscience*. Cambridge: Harvard University Press.

Lia, B. (1998). *The Society of the Muslim Brothers in Egypt: The rise of an Islamic mass movement 1928–1942*. Reading, UK: Garnet.

Mahlouly, D., & Winter, C. (2018). *A tale of two caliphates: Comparing the Islamic State's internal and external messaging priorities*. Dublin: VOX-Pol Network of Excellence.

Marzolph, U. (2003). The martyr's way to paradise: Shiite mural art in the urban context. In R. Bendix & J. Bendix (Eds.), *Sleepers, moles, and martyrs: Secret identifications, societal integration, and the differing meaning of freedom* (pp. 87–97). Copenhagen: Museum Tusculanum Press.

Matusitz, J. (2014). *Symbolism in terrorism: Motivation, communication, and behavior*. Lanham, MD: Rowman & Littlefield Publishers.

Meyer, S. L. (1976). *Signal: Hitler's wartime picture magazine*. London: Bison Books.

Michael, G. (2009). David Lane and the fourteen words. *Totalitarian Movements and Political Religions, 10*(1), 43–61.

Milton, D. (2016). *Communication breakdown: Unraveling the Islamic State's media efforts*. West Point, NY: Combating Terrorism Center.

Milton, D. (2018). *Down, but not out: An updated examination of the Islamic State's visual propaganda*. West Point, NY: Combating Terrorism Center.

Mitchell, R. (1993). *The Society of the Muslim Brothers*. London: Oxford University Press.

Moghadam, A. (2008). The Salafi-jihad as a religious ideology. *CTC Sentinel, 1*(3).

National Research Council. (1991). *Computers at risk: Safe computing in the information age*. Washington, DC: National Academy Press.

NBC News. (2016, October 3). ISIS' Al-Bayan radio station in Mosul is bombed into silence by Iraqi jets. *NBC News*. Retrieved from www.nbcnews.com/storyline/isis-terror/isis-al-bayan-radio-station-mosul-bombed-silence-iraqi-jets-n658521

Norton, B. (2016, August 5). Muslim Americans launch "ISIS sucks" billboard campaign: So-called Islamic State "does not represent Islam." *Salon*. Retrieved from www.salon.com/2016/08/05/muslim-americans-launch-isis-sucks-billboard-campaign-so-called-islamic-state-does-not-represent-islam/

Oldham, J. (1998, January 25). Web of hate is growing on the net. *The Jerusalem Post*.

Perry, B., & Scrivens, R. (2016). Uneasy alliances: A look at the right-wing extremist movement in Canada. *Studies in Conflict and Terrorism, 39*(9), 819–841.

Ramsay, G. (2009). Relocating the virtual war. *Defence Against Terrorism Review, 2*(1), 31–50.

Ranstorp, M. (Ed.). (2007). *Mapping terrorism research: State of the art, gaps and future direction.* London: Routledge.

Rapoport, D. C. (1984). Fear and trembling: Terrorism in three religious traditions. *The American Political Science Review, 78*(3), 658–677.

Rhodes, A. (1976). *Propaganda: The art of persuasion: World War II.* New York: Chelsea House.

Rice, T. (2015). *White robes, silver screens: Movies and the making of the Ku Klux Klan.* Bloomington, IN: Indiana University Press.

Rogan, H. (2007). Abu Reuter and the e-jihad: Virtual battlefronts from Iraq to the Horn of Africa. *Culture & Society, 8*(2) (Summer/Fall), 89–96.

Rolston, B. (1991). *Politics and paintings: Murals and conflict in Northern Ireland.* London: Associated Universities Press.

Rupp, L., & Taylor, V. (1987). *Survival in the doldrums: The American women's rights movements, 1945 to the 1960s.* New York: Oxford University Press.

Schmid, A. P., & De Graaf, J. (1982). *Violence as communication: Insurgent terrorism and the western news media.* London: Sage.

Schulte, B. (2017, April 3). The alt-right of the Ozarks. *Slate.* Retrieved from www.slate.com/news-and-politics/2018/07/republicans-changed-the-rules-democrats-need-to-catch-up.html

Seib, P., & Janbek, D. M. (2011). *Global terrorism and new media: The post-al Qaeda generation.* London: Routledge.

Sharma, S. (2015, June 4). Islamic State has an English-language radio broadcast that sounds eerily like NPR. *The Washington Post.* Retrieved from www.washingtonpost.com/news/worldviews/wp/2015/06/04/islamic-state-has-a-daily-english-language-radio-broadcast-that-sounds-eerily-like-it-could-be-on-npr/?utm_term=.ca8b2841a7e6

Simi, P., & Futrell, R. (2015). *American swastika: Inside the white Power movement's hidden spaces of hate* (2nd ed.). Lanham, MD: Rowman and Littlefield.

Sims, P. (1996). *The Klan.* Lexington: University Press of Kentucky.

Solomon, E. (2017, March 5). Mosul medics work to purge legacy of Isis from hospital. *Irish Times.* Retrieved from www.irishtimes.com/news/world/middle-east/mosul-medics-work-to-purge-legacy-of-isis-from-hospital-1.2998670

Southern Poverty Law Center. (2008). *Racist radio, newspaper close up shops.* Retrieved from www.splcenter.org/fighting-hate/intelligence-report/2008/racist-radio-newspaper-close-shops

Southern Poverty Law Center. (2018). *Tom Metzger.* Retrieved from www.splcenter.org/fighting-hate/extremist-files/individual/tom-metzger

Tasch, B. (2016, February 2). ISIS has reportedly released its first Android app. *Business Insider.* Retrieved from https://www.businessinsider.com/isis-releases-android-app-broadcast-al-bayan-radio-2016-2

Townshend, C. (2002). *Terrorism: A very short introduction.* Oxford: Oxford University Press.

Welsh, D. (1993). *The Third Reich: Politics and propaganda.* New York, NY: Routledge.

Wilson, J. (2004, October 12). KKK painting washed away. *The Chattanoogan.* Retrieved from www.chattanoogan.com/2004/10/12/57049/KKK-Paintings-Washed-Away.aspx

Zelin, A. (2013). *The state of global jihad online: A qualitative, quantitative, and cross- lingual analysis.* Washington, DC: New America Foundation.

14 Child sex abuse images and exploitation materials

Roderic Broadhurst

Introduction

The production and distribution of child pornography has a long history, but the advent of the Internet in the 1990s gave new impetus to child pornography offenders. The new technology offered unprecedented anonymity, secrecy, and efficiency for the widespread sharing and selling of what is more aptly termed child exploitation material (CEM) via networks of those sexually attracted to children. It also provided opportunities for child 'grooming' (solicitation and seduction) and the exploitation of vulnerable children. Emerging online criminal networks were trading in CEM (Pierce, 1984; Burgess & Grant, 1988; Flowers, 2001; Jenkins, 2001). The Federal Bureau of Investigation's (FBI) *Operation Innocent Images* launched in 1994 was one of the first to investigate an online CEM group that had shifted its activities to computer bulletin boards and chat rooms to share CEM and groom boys. An 'alarming new trend: sexual exploitation of children via computers' was discovered (FBI Archives, n.d.[1]). *Terre des Hommes* (2019), citing United Nations (UN) and FBI estimates, claims that at any one time 750,000 men worldwide are looking for online sex with children in more than 40,000 public chat rooms.[2]

The victims of these crimes are children who are subject to sexual exploitation or abuse. The terms CEM or child sexual abuse material (CSAM) are preferred to 'child pornography' commonly used in the laws of many jurisdictions because it does not convey the gravity of the sexual assault often associated with the production of CEM. For consistency, CEM is used throughout this chapter and includes the production, distribution, and possession of CEM; online grooming or active sexual solicitation of children; and sexual exploitation and extortion of children (ECPAT, 2018). This type of offending typically "takes place through the Internet or with some connection to the online environment" (ECPAT Interagency Working Group, 2016, p 34). Facilitated online child sexual assault refers both to the sexual abuse of children that are amplified by information and communication technologies and sexual abuse of children that is committed elsewhere and then repeated by sharing it online through images and videos.

CEM is criminalized across the world; however, law enforcement agencies face substantial challenges in suppressing this crime and prosecuting offenders because of the transnational nature of the offences and the difficulties in tracing the origin of the images and identifying victims and offenders.

This chapter first discusses the definitions of a 'child' and the age of consent. We briefly review what is known about the prevalence of CEM, the characteristics of victims and offenders, and efforts to suppress the production and distribution of CEM through the emergence of a growing global web of law enforcement agencies (LEAs), non-government organizations (NGO), industry, academia, and international agreements.

Definitions of a child and legal age of consent to sexual activity

Children are vulnerable to CEM because of their lack of cognitive and social development compared to their often-adult offenders. The relationship between the child and offender during sexual abuse is managed and manipulated by the offender(s) using the authority (and physical superiority) they have over the child victim to gratify their sexual (and monetary) needs (WHO, 1999).

The age of a person determines their status as a child or an adult. Generally, those under the age of 18 are defined as children. The 1989 UN Convention on the Rights of the Child (UNCRC) defines a child (Article 1) as a person below the age of 18, unless the laws of a particular country set the legal age for adulthood younger or higher. The Committee on the Rights of the Child, the monitoring body for the convention, has encouraged states to review the age of majority if it is set below 18 and to increase the level of protection for all children under 18. The 2002 Second Optional Protocol of the UNCRC specifically requires states to criminalize the "producing, distributing, disseminating, importing, exporting, offering, selling or possessing" of CEM. Child sexual abuse is not defined by the UNCRC; however, the World Health Organization (WHO) describes child sexual abuse as:

> [T]he involvement of a child in sexual activity that he or she does not fully comprehend, is unable to give informed consent to, or for which the child is not developmentally prepared and cannot give consent, or that violates the laws or social taboos of society. Child sexual abuse is evidenced by this activity between a child and an adult or another child who by age or development is in a relationship of responsibility, trust or power, the activity is intended to gratify or satisfy the need of another person.
>
> (WHO, 1999, p. 15)

While the age threshold for defining a child is relatively uniform across the world, the legal age of consent to sexual activity varies widely across jurisdictions (from 12 in Angola to 20 years of age in Korea) and may vary within federal systems of government; for example, in Australia, the usual age is 16, but in Tasmania and South Australia, it is set as under 17). Some jurisdictions set a higher age of consent for homosexual relations.

Attitudes to and suppression of sexual activity with children have changed over time and place, and this is reflected in shifts in the age of majority and the age of consent (Foucault, 1990; Toulalan, 2014). For example, the United Kingdom (UK) in the 1885 Criminal Law Amendment Act changed the age of consent from 13 to 16 in response to scandals involving the prostitution of children (Cox, 2017). Over the past century India has changed the age of consent from age 10 to age 12 (in 1892 following the death of an 11-year old bride following rape by her 38-year old husband) then to 16 years (in 1949 driven largely by concerns about maternal and infant health). Following the widely publicized 'gang rapes' of young women in Delhi in December 2012 and Mumbai in August 2013, the Indian Penal Code and related laws were amended to set the age of consent at 18 (Jolly & Khan, 2016).

A number of African and Middle Eastern countries have no minimum age of consent and ban all sexual relations outside of marriage; consent is tied to marriage, and in some cases, children may be married at very young ages. In such jurisdictions and those that define the age of consent for sexual activities at younger ages (e.g. Japan at 13 or the Philippines at 12 years), CEM involving children under 16 but over 12 years of age may be difficult to prosecute, although possession and/or distribution of such images in Australia and many other countries would be unlawful.

Prevalence

Estimating the prevalence of CEM offenders in the population is extremely difficult. Although over ten years old, the U.S. longitudinal National Juvenile Online Victimization study has shed some light on the prevalence of CSA and CEM over time. Fielded in three waves in 2000, 2006, and 2009 (now discontinued), it is based on those arrested for online facilitated sex crimes against children. An increase in arrests (from 2,577 in 2000 to 7,010 in 2006 and 8,144 in 2009) was observed, with half of the arrests being for possession of CEM (Walsh, Wolak & Finkelhor, 2012).

A recent review of online child sex offending by NatCen Social Research (2018) observed a large number of images and active websites. For example, Canadian authorities identified over 5 million CEM images over a six-week period. The Australian Centre to Counter Child Exploitation (ACCCE) estimates that over a million CEM websites are currently active, and Australian Federal Police (AFP) received over 15,857 reports in 2018.[3] The International Criminal Police Organization (Interpol) Child Sexual Exploitation Image Database (ICSE-DB) network of 53 countries holds over a half a million CEM images, which have helped identify around 11,988 victims and nearly 5,617 offenders over the past eight years to December 2017 (Interpol, 2017, p. 28). Analysts working for the NGO End Child Prostitution and Trafficking (ECPAT) monitor webpages every five minutes. They reported that every nine minutes a webpage shows an image of child sexual abuse (ECPAT, 2018). The U.S. National Center for Missing and Exploited Children reported the volume of CEM being shared via videos instead of still images has increased tenfold from 312,000 in 2015 to 3.5 million in 2017 (Langston, 2018). The prevalence of CEM in Tor-like cryptomarkets is unknown.

The UN Special Rapporteur on the sale of children, child prostitution, and child pornography estimates that "the criminal child sexual abuse material-market generates between US$3 billion and 20 billion annually. Other estimates place the market [for CEM] at US$250 million per year" (UNODC, 2015, p. 34).

Nature and severity of CEM offending

Once seized, CEM is a vital resource for the identification of victims and the prosecution of offenders. Describing and classifying the nature of the CEM is crucial to extract full forensic value from the material stored into various national and international CEM databases. The Interpol Child Abuse Image Database (ICAID), the International Child Sexual Exploitation Database (ICSE-DB), and various National Centers for Missing and Exploited Children (NCMEC) and national databases such as the UK Child Abuse Images Database (CAID) provide CEM libraries essential for tracking images and identifying victims and offenders. In addition, the Internet Watch Foundation (IWF) and International Association of Internet Hotlines (INHOPE – an umbrella organization for national Internet hotlines that report online child sexual abuse and CEM) and other NGOs provide reporting and complaint services for individuals, businesses, and others who encounter CEM.

Description of observed CEM

Although it is difficult to assess the scope of the global CEM illicit market, images and other materials monitored and seized by law enforcement and other agencies provide some information on the type of CEM that is produced and circulated. The nature of the images seized has been detailed in a study of 103 online sex offenders arrested by police agencies in Italy, the United States, Australia, and New Zealand during a joint investigation of the Virtual Global Taskforce for Combating Online Child Sexual Abuse (VGT). Eighty per cent of the children pictured on the seized images were female, but male children appeared on 45% of images. Most of the material included children aged between 2 and 12 years, over half pictured teenagers and just under a quarter, infants younger than 2 years. Perpetrators portrayed on the images were predominantly males aged over 25 years. The ethnicity of both children and perpetrators tended to match the suspects' country of origin, suggesting that the images were produced locally and initially exchanged within the offender's national networks. For 35% of suspects, the most serious images in their possession involved sexual activity between children, and for 47%, sexual assault of children by adults, including penetration and sadistic activities. Fewer than 20% of suspects collected images of children not engaged in sexual activity (Bouhours & Broadhurst, 2011).

The IWF (2017, p. 16) reported that CEM content identified from 2014 to 2017 depicted the most graphic and severe forms of child sexual abuse when younger children were involved. The report noted that since 2014 the percentage of children aged 11 to 15 depicted in child sex abuse imagery had increased from 18% to 43%, whilst that of children aged 0 to 10 has decreased from 80% to 55% in 2017; girls remain the primary victims. The increase in imagery of 11- to 15-year-olds may be related to the increase in 'self-produced' or user-generated content created using webcams or during livestreaming and subsequently shared widely online.

The same report noted a decrease in the quantity of images showing sexual abuse of children by adults and other children from 43% in 2014 to 33% in 2017. Images depicting non-penetrative sexual abuse have also shown a decrease since 2014, from 30% to 21%. These fluctuations, however, are poor predictors of trends and may reflect countermeasures taken by offenders such as the increased use of encryption and 'flight' to cryptomarkets rather than a decrease in prevalence.

A recent UK study involving 687 children identified in CEM showed an increase in the number of victims over the 2006–2015 data capture period. Two-thirds of all the images were classified as coercive. Almost two-thirds of the children identified were white females; 44.3% of the images were self-taken, and of these most were taken in a coercive relationship (Quayle, Jonsson, Cooper, Traynor, & Svedin, 2018, cited in ECPAT, 2018, p. 13). Another study of 3,503 18-year-old Swedish youth indicated that for 6.5% of those who reported sexual abuse, the abuse had been documented in pictures or videos; these children also experienced more severe forms of CSA, such as penetrative sex, recurrent sexual abuse, and multiple offenders (Svedin, 2012 cited in ECPAT, 2018, pp. 12)

In a dataset of 1,965 cases (from the UK ICSE, NCMEC database of identified children), 61% of cases involved single victims, whereas images of multiple victims were more likely to involve pubescent children. The majority of cases involved male offenders who were unrelated to the identified child; however, cases with female offenders, younger children, or more extreme content were likely to involve family members. In a study of unidentified victims in the ICSE database, nearly two-thirds (64.8%) of children were girls, 31.1% were boys, and the remaining 4.1% included children of both sexes. Boys were often depicted in content involving more severe abuse. The majority (93.3%) of the children were white. Where age could be determined, the largest group was of pre-pubescent children (56.2%). Across the available databases the proportion of infants abused varied between 6.5% and 12.4% of all cases (ECPAT, 2018, p. 13).

CEM severity

A number of CEM classification schemes are in use, but the classification and coding process is fraught with problems of reliability and consistency across classifiers, particularly with respect to the age of persons and the degree of indecency (Kloess et al., 2019). The most widely used system across the English-speaking world is the COPINE classification and its variants. The COPINE project (Combating Paedophile Information Networks in Europe) was developed in the 1990s for therapeutic and psychological purposes and was used initially to distinguish between child 'erotica' ('artistic' posing with no sexual activity) and child pornography. It was then adapted to categorize child abuse images in research and legal settings within ten levels of severity (Taylor, Holland & Quayle, 2001).

The (UK) Sentencing Advisory Panel (SAP) then reduced the ten-level COPINE classification to five categories and provided sentencing guidelines based on these categories – sometimes referred to as the 'Oliver Scale.'[4]

The Oliver (SAP) classifications

The five categories of the Oliver scale, as originally devised, are:

1   Erotic posing with no sexual activity.
2   Sexual activity between children, or solo masturbation by a child.
3   Non-penetrative sexual activity between children and adults.
4   Penetrative sexual activity between children and adults.
5   Sadism or bestiality.

The Australian National Victim Image Library (ANVIL) is a reference holding of CEM that has adapted the Oliver SAP scale as a means of classifying the severity of CEM and uses a version of Microsoft PhotoDNA to track and identify new CEM. The ANVIL classification system incorporates an additional three categories covering material that is not illegal but is connected to CEM. Category 6 encompasses material featuring any of the activities described by Categories 1 to 5 of the Oliver scale but is not a genuine photograph or does not feature a real child. This includes animé, cartoons, and drawings depicting children engaged in sexual poses or activity. Categories 7 and 8 cover material directly connected to the exploitation of a child but not illegal in itself and adult pornography. The classification assists courts to assess an accused's sexual interest in children.

Victims of CEM: risk factors

Research shows that sex, socioeconomic factors, and social networking presence affect the risk of victimization; however, poverty is the mediating factor. Generally, victims of CEM are financially poorer than offenders and often live in disadvantaged locations. The available evidence suggests that numerous cases of child sexual abuse and exploitation occur in developing countries. A typical example is the comparatively wealthier Western sex tourist who travels to, say, Southeast Asian countries and engages in child sex offences with local children (Australian Federal Police, 2015). A lack of social security, entrenched inequalities, and ineffective child protection practices affect the marginalized populations across the region, where up to one-third of citizens live below the poverty line (United Nations Development Program [UNDP] & ASEAN, 2017). Poor parents perhaps not able to support their family may be driven or enticed into the role of producer of CEM using their own children or paid for access to their children. The sacrifice of a child in return for money may sometimes appear necessary for the survival of the child's family. Yet the visibility of child sexual abuse in Southeast Asia does not discount its existence amongst other regions (notably West Africa, where the age of consent may be as low as 11 years of age), as well as developed countries.

Hernandez et al. (2018) reviewed English news articles published between 2011 and 2015 and referring to cybersex cases involving children in the Philippines. They identified 55 articles that reported on cases of live streaming, CEM, and 'sextortion' involving children from 18 months to 17 years of age. They noted that 72% of victims were female, 24% male and female, and 4% exclusively male. Seven of the cases involved family-run operations, 27 hidden 'cybersex dens' mostly in slum areas, and 8 cases were associated with fake call centres that engaged in online chats or businesses that sold CEM. All the clients were male. One-third of the offenders were foreigners.

> Cybersex operations involved uploading sexually explicit images of children, nudity in front of a webcam, and live sexual performances with children or among children. In one operation, snapshots of naked children cost USD50, nudity in front of the webcam cost USD100, and a live sex show among children cost as high as USD500. The children, or parents, got USD10-USD18 per show. Sudden show of increased wealth would arouse suspicion in the community but did not always prompt reporting.
>
> (Hernandez et al., 2018, p. 39)

Impact of CEM on victims

Few studies of children who have experienced sexual assault are reported due to ethical concerns. A survey of survivors by the Canadian Centre for Child Protection (2017) found that the online sharing of images and videos of crimes committed against them intensified feelings of shame, humiliation, vulnerability, and powerlessness. One survivor explained: "The abuse stops and at some point, also the fear of abuse; the fear of the material never ends." Another lamented:

> The hands-on was horrible. But at the very least it is over and done with. The constant sharing of the abuse will never end; therefore, the reminder of its existence will never end. . . . If you ask me, a crime that will never end is worse than one that is over; no matter how much more serious it may appear. That this is something inescapable. That there will never be total absolution.
>
> (Canadian Centre for Child Protection, 2017, p. 149)

Survivors of CEM often display behaviour consistent with post-traumatic stress disorder (PTSD) (Hannan, Orcutt, Miron, & Thompson, 2015). Images can be replicated and shared again. Victims experience anxiety using the Internet because their image may reappear and they will be traumatized again. This constant re-victimization process and stress affect day-to-day functioning, degrade quality of life, increase potential physiological and mental harm, and negatively affect the life course (Canadian Centre for Child Protection, 2017). CEM survivors tend to experience high levels of mental illness, heart disease, lower immune system response, behavioural problems, alcohol or drug addiction, and certain cancers and diseases such as liver disease, which often results in shorter average lifespan (Gewirtz-Meydan, Walsh, Wolak, & Finkelhor, 2018; Hannan et al., 2015).

CEM offenders

Research about online sexual offending is relatively new and has focused on potential links or differences between online and offline child sex offending (e.g. Brown & Bricknell, 2018; Henshaw, Ogloff, & Clough, 2015; Elliot, Beech, Mandeville-Norden, & Hayes, 2009; Endrass et al., 2009; Webb, Craissati & Keen, 2007), sexual addiction (e.g. Henshaw et al., 2015; Young, 2008), childhood sexual abuse experiences and online access to CEM, online grooming behaviours (e.g. Jayawardena & Broadhurst, 2007) and studies of victims (e.g. Babchishin et al., 2018; DeHart et al., 2016). Samples of offenders are often small and limited to a handful of countries.

Richards (2011, p. 1) argued "perpetrators of sexual crimes against children are not, contrary to widespread opinion, a homogenous group. Rather, there are a number of varied offending profiles that characterize child sex offenders." In part variation occurs because some offenders engage in contact sexual offences, including production and/or distribution, whereas others only view and/or collect CEM (i.e. non-contact child sex offenders). Online-only offenders may become child sex contact offenders, and exposure to CEM may play a role in shifting their offending. The assumption that child sexual abuse (CSA) offenders are mostly or exclusively paedophiles (i.e. sexually aroused only by a child) is not borne out by the variety of sexual predation observed.

The notion of a specific 'type' or 'profile' of online CEM offenders is not supported; however, offenders tend to be white, young, single, and unemployed (Babchishin et al., 2011), although other studies (Brown & Bricknell, 2018) found offenders more likely to be employed. Babchishin et al. (2011) conducted the first review of 27 studies (mostly North American/English-language studies released up until 2009) addressing the question of whether online offenders differ from offline offenders. They found that *online* offenders displayed higher sexual deviancy and experienced more psychological barriers to acting on these deviant interests but also exhibited greater victim empathy than contact child sex offenders. Online offenders may be less likely to act on their sexual deviant interests because they wish to avoid the connection or closeness associated with real-life relationships and prefer the emotional distance of images or other material. Noting the novelty of research about online offenders, the authors suggest:

> One line of inquiry would explore the inhibitors and self-control mechanisms that limit the extent to which online offenders act on their deviant interests. Another line of inquiry would explore the extent to which the emotional distance inherent in pornography use is a core feature of the sexual preference of online offenders.
>
> (Babchishin et al., 2011, p. 110)

They reiterated the findings about the "tendency for men to prefer sexual partners of the same race . . . a change in the racial distribution of child pornography victims will likely signal an expansion of this deviant market into more racially diverse segments of the male population" (p. 110). However, this finding may reflect the limitations of studies largely restricted to the English language and may also be further obscured by the forensic awareness of online child sex offenders (Bouhours & Broadhurst, 2011; ECPAT, 2018).

Brown and Bricknell (2018) reviewed recent literature about those who view and collect CEM. They identified 49 peer-reviewed studies that provided quantitative data – drawing on official criminal justice data about convicted offenders and online convenience samples. These studies examined demographic (age, ethnicity, marital and parenting status, education, and employment) and psychological factors (mental health, cognitive distortions) and offending characteristics (prior offending and recidivism risk). CEM offenders were predominantly white males, tended to be older than the average offender (i.e. between 35 and 45 years of age) but younger, more often single, and better educated than contact sexual offenders. Very few had prior offences for contact sexual offences and generally were less likely to re-offend than contact child sex offenders. The evidence also suggested that CEM offenders "tend to be less assertive, less dominant and under-socialized" and "show higher levels of sexual deviancy than contact or mixed sexual offenders and are more likely to fantasize about children." The study concluded that the 'profile' of CEM offenders "may be different to that of other types of sexual offenders, especially those who commit contact sexual offences against children" (Brown & Bricknell, 2018, p. 9).

Despite inconsistent evidence to support a causal relationship between online and offline sexual abuse of children, various typologies for online and offline sexual offenders have been developed in an attempt to clarify key differences and similarities in their profiles and predicted behaviours. For example, Webster et al. (2012) proposed that some offenders are 'intimacy-seeking' and view their communication with children as a consenting relationship compared to 'hypersexualized' offenders who quickly proceed with sexual communication (see also Armstrong & Mellor, 2013; McGuire & Dowling, 2013). Other typologies focus on the offender's actions and distinguish between collection, distribution, and use of CEM (Corriveau & Greco, 2012; McNally, 2016); or contact versus fantasy-driven offenders (Merdian, Moghaddam, Boer et al., 2016). Although there are several ways of differentiating online offenders, both compared to each other and to offline offenders, a major challenge is determining the difference between offenders who use the Internet as a means of satisfying sexual needs (i.e. offline sexual abuse) and those who use cyberspace to consume and engage in online CEM instead of in real life. Viewing online CEM could provide a 'safer' outlet for individuals to fantasize and virtually experience their deviant sexual interests (Corriveau & Greco, 2012). Generally, research highlights the *disinhibiting effects* of the Internet that helps facilitate offending behaviuor (Merdian et al., 2016).

Overall research suggests that situational and environmental factors (and the relevance of situational crime prevention strategies) are as important as the probable pathology of offenders for the prevention of CEM online (e.g. Elliot et al., 2009; UNODC, 2015; Wortley & Smallbone, 2006).

CEM: modus operandi

Victim recruitment

Computer applications (apps) and online games are easily available on a range of devices that younger children (8 to 13 years) use routinely. They include communication apps (e.g. instant messaging services), gaming apps, social media (e.g. Facebook, Instagram) apps, or a combination of these. Most apps have a messaging or chat feature, which provides a way for adults to hide their identity and reach hundreds of children by pretending to be one of their peers (Keating, 2015). Children may be more inclined to share information or content, as they feel it cannot be traced back to them through their anonymous account. For example, online gaming platforms *Minecraft*, *League of Legends*, and *Fortnite* were used by offenders to communicate directly with children in an attempt to obtain CEM (Boyd, 2018; Cimpanu, 2019; Nurse, 2018).

Games may also be hacked by offenders to allow them to gain access to child players. The 2016 *Pokémon Go* quickly attracted malware that looked like the real game but was in fact used to groom and lure children. *Pokémon Go* used a location function, which was useful for offenders, who could arrange to meet their victims in real life (Office of the Children's eSafety Commissioner & ACMA, 2016, July 20).

In February 2017, the Canadian Centre for Child Protection issued a warning about the online multi-player gaming site *Roblox* following multiple reports of luring or grooming and sexually explicit chat messages and requests to meet received by younger children on the game's chat feature. *Roblox* reviewed the game and added chat-filtering software to find and flag offensive language; used a moderator network to review each image, audio, and video file uploaded to the site; and made sure that the accounts of all users under the age of 13 were defaulted to communicate exclusively with friends (CBC, 2017). Similar warnings about grooming attempts via *Roblox* have been issued in the United States, Australia, and the UK (International Centre for Missing & Exploited Children, 2017).

Although strangers often try to contact children and youth through apps and games, the danger can also come from peers and acquaintances. In 2016, young women and underage girls from at least 70 Australian schools were targeted by users of an online pornography website. While the site was hosted overseas, most of the users were local, some attending the same schools as their victims. Users were largely young men and teenage boys attempting to obtain nude images as well as identifying information of specific 'targets' (name, phone number, school and home address, etc.) to view and share. The AFP and the Australian Office of the Children's eSafety Commissioner worked together to take down the site, which hosted thousands of images, some falling into the CEM category (Funnell, 2016).

User-generated CEM

User-generated CEM consists of images produced and shared willingly with a few trusted persons that is then stolen and shared online without the consent of the person who produced the material and sometimes without their knowledge. Many LEAs and INHOPE hotlines now report that the misuse of user-generated images is among the most common complaints handled. The rise of social media is integral to the production and distribution of user-generated CEM material, and all content uploaded to networks such as Facebook, Instagram, or Snapchat could be considered 'user-generated.' Parents may upload 'innocent' photos of their children with the intent of showing them only to family and friends; however, these photos and videos can become accessible to others who may be able to subsequently identify young CEM targets (Battersby, 2015). Online predators often collect sensitive information from social network profiles and use it to contact vulnerable children (Maxim, Skinner, Orlando, & Broadhurst, 2016).

Sexting and CEM

A key factor for online CEM is the common user-generated act of 'sexting,' which involves the sharing of 'sexually suggestive, nude or nearly nude photo[s]' (ACMA, 2013, p. 11) of oneself or a girlfriend/boyfriend or another person via a photo app on a smart phone or computer (Keating, 2015). It is not uncommon for older children to engage in this behaviuor, and 13% of 16- and 17-year-old Australian teenagers reported having engaged in sexting (ACMA, 2013).

Even the consensual sharing of explicit images can constitute an offence and pose legal risks if a child is involved. In many jurisdictions including states of the United States and Australia, 'Romeo and Juliet' provisions provide a defence to a child sex offence if the participants are teenagers of a similar age in a consensual relationship. Age-difference laws usually specify an age gap (e.g. a two- to four-year age gap) but varied greatly, as Bierie and Budd (2018) observed in a review of U.S. federal and state laws. However, consensually shared or 'stolen' sexualized images distributed via various apps may inadvertently or otherwise enhance and facilitate online CEM (Wolak, Finkelhor, Walsh, & Treitman et al., 2018). In addition, sexting may lead to 'sextortion,' where victims are convinced to provide sexualized user-generated material and, then, under the threat of exposure, are compelled to continue providing such images to the offender (Europol, 2013; IOCTA, 2015). Sextortion directly facilitates the production of CEM, as it provides offenders with more material and vulnerable targets (UNODC, 2015).

Between October 2013 and April 2016 1,428 reports of sextortion were recorded by the U.S. NCMEC CyberTipline, and 78% involved female child victims and 15% involved males, with the remaining 7% the gender was unknown.[5] In a study of 78 U.S. prosecuted cases all offenders were male, often with prolific repeated offending, and although victims were mostly females, many child victims were male (Wittes, Poplin, Jurecic, & Spera, 2016). In 2016, a Californian offender, Luis Mijangos, orchestrated many acts of sextortion on multiple victims. He obtained sexual videos and images from his victims by threatening to expose indecent images or content obtained through deception. He had convinced his victims to download malware that provided him access to their files and assumed control over their device microphones and web cameras, thus gaining remote access to their private lives (Wittes et al., 2016).

Finally, hacking and phishing are also an avenue for the production and distribution of online CEM. The hacking of 'big data' sites and websites provides hackers with content such as personal images or online conversations to sell and distribute to others through niche virtual private networks (VPNs) and other encrypted online platforms. Children are placed at risk if they divulge personal information, private images, or videos through these apps and websites because they lose control of the content once it has been sent or uploaded (Maxim et al., 2016).

Emerging technologies

New technologies such as high-speed Internet, file compression, increased computer processing unit (CPU) speed, livestreaming, and virtual reality (VR) have improved the quality of CEM and the ease of distributing videos, which have begun to replace photographs. These new technologies make possible the ability to request almost instantaneous, customized material.

Webcamming and livestreaming

Livestreaming of child sexual abuse continues to evolve, and clients are able to order and pay online for criminal services such as customized online child sexual abuse 'on demand' (IOCTA, 2015; Wolak, 2015). Evidence of the growing monetization of online CEM suggests the emergence of criminal organizations that avoid tools such as web crawlers and hash and URL lists that have traditionally provided ways to identify CEM and to block and/or blacklist illegal content from the Internet.

Livestreaming offences take place in real time and do not require the offender to store the material, making it more difficult for law enforcement agencies to acquire digital evidence (Europol, 2013, 2015; Thorn, 2016). Perpetrators and producers avoid detection by conducting multiple payments of smaller amounts that do not arouse the suspicion of financial monitoring programs (Europol, 2015). Furthermore, the act of solely 'viewing' streamed material (not storing it) may not always fulfil the legislative requirements of 'possession or production' of CEM material in all jurisdictions (Europol, 2013).

The demand for new 'fresh' material and a customized experience is crucial in understanding the popularity of CEM streaming. Prices of on-demand material (e.g. livestreaming or video files) are still significantly higher than dated or generic material but are falling (Europol, 2013; ECPAT, 2017; IWF, 2018). "Live-streamed abuse is not only increasingly common, but also increasingly affordable. Five or six years ago, access to live-streamed abuse cost in the region of $US50 Today, it is available for $US15–20. LEAs predict costs will continue to decrease" (WeProtect Global Alliance, 2018, p. 12).

Virtual reality

The purpose of VR is to live the experience without actually being there, and it has the potential to transform the pornographic industry. With the advent of Google Cardboard and Oculus Rift, the VR experience has now become affordable, and pornography consumers are among early adopters of this technology (Hussey, 2016; Takahashi, 2016). Rather than the typical voyeuristic, third-person standpoint in traditional pornography, VR pornography is a first-person point-of-view system that delivers an intimate viewing experience for users (Takahashi, 2016). Additional sexual peripherals (i.e. sex toys that re-create the sense of touch) increase the sense of intimacy and realism and can be programmed to respond to an individual's movements or the feedback from a video or livestream (Cooper, 2015).

Research into the viewing of CEM by non-contact paedophiles has suggested that they are less likely to offend in the real world because of moral, personal, and legal constraints (Brown & Bricknell, 2018). The VR CEM enhanced experience of intimacy and realism may break down these barriers and entice an online offender to become a child sex contact offender (Rutkin, 2016; Maras & Shapiro, 2017). Although VR or child sex dolls could be useful as a treatment for paedophilia, it may also encourage some offenders to enhance their experience by incorporating livestreaming of actual child abuse with the tactile experience promised by such technologies. Brown and Shelling (2019) in a review of the limited literature on the therapeutic benefit of child sex dolls, including robotic versions, note there is "no empirical evidence to support the assertion that sex dolls (whether adult or child) reduce the likelihood of sexual violence."

Distribution of CEM

Little is known about CEM networks and their relationships with other criminal enterprises or how trust is acquired and maintained in the virtual world. Illicit markets, such as that for CEM, require consumers to trade tools or illicit images before accessing the network.

The IWF remarked, "criminals are increasingly using masking techniques to hide child sexual abuse images and videos on the Internet" (IWF, 2016, p. 19) and:

> [O]nline-facilitated CSA are increasingly disguising digital pathways leading to indecent and illegal content online through legitimate and legal Internet sites. . . . This reflects a trend for illegal content being hidden more professionally, shifting away from peer-to-peer networks into deeper parts of cyberspace, with a higher volume of CSA material being shared and published in forums on the darknet.
>
> (NatCen Social Research, 2018, p. 15)

The 'darknet' or Tor-based crypto markets are now among the major platforms used by online offenders due to the enhanced anonymity provided for creating and distributing online CEM. Many large crypto markets such as Dream Market prohibit the posting or sale of CEM on their sites and peer-to-peer VPNs, and niche Tor-like markets will continue to be preferred methods to communicate and distribute CEM despite LEA efforts to de-anonymize these illicit networks and identify offenders. Cryptocurrency block-chain ledgers have been recently identified as a means of storing and concealing CEM (Sward, Vecna, & Stonedahl, 2018; Matzutt et al., 2018).

Responses to CEM

International law enforcement cooperation

Differences in legal definitions of offence and in the age of consent confound cross-national and international efforts to suppress CEM because many states require legal equivalence before providing mutual legal assistance (MLA). The quickening of MLA and the creation of common legal definitions of CEM are essential to respond to the cross-national nature of many CEM offences, as is typical of cybercrime offences in general. This is because the offender, victim, and CEM may be located in different jurisdictions.

The first international treaty seeking to harmonize national laws and increase cooperation to address cybercrime was signed in 2001 and came into force in 2004. The Council of Europe (CoE) Convention on Cybercrime (Budapest Convention) outlawed 'child pornography' (Article 9) by requiring member states to make it illegal to produce, distribute, offer, procure, or possess child pornography via computer or media storage devices. The Budapest Convention is a key instrument for international law enforcement cooperation and provides for the extradition of suspects, the disclosure and preservation of computer and traffic data, real-time traffic data collection, transborder access to stored computer data, and the interception of CEM.

The Budapest Convention has been adopted by 67 states around the world, including all 47 states in Europe. However, China, Brazil, the Russian Federation, and India, among others, have not signed the convention, limiting its scope in assisting with CEM offences that may involve offenders and victims from these jurisdictions.

Since the Budapest Convention, concerns about the increasing availability of child pornography and other serious forms of sexual abuse and sexual exploitation of children through the use of new technologies and the Internet have intensified. To keep pace with new technologies the CoE in 2007 strengthened laws aimed at suppressing all forms of CEM, enacting the Convention on the Protection of Children against Sexual Exploitation and Sexual Abuse, or the Lanzarote Convention. The Lanzarote Convention focuses on ensuring the protection of children through the prevention of abuse and exploitation, assistance for victims, punishment of perpetrators, and promotion of national and international law enforcement cooperation. Crucially the convention stressed the increased use and inherent danger of information technologies in the exploitation of children. The Lanzarote Convention for the first time in an international treaty established the offence of solicitation or grooming of children for sexual purposes as a stand-alone offence, considering the Internet and mobile phones among the most dangerous methods of grooming children (International Centre for Missing & Exploited Children, 2017).

Following the initiative of the Lanzarote Convention, the European Parliament and the Council of the European Union passed in 2011 a European Union (EU) Directive on combating the sexual abuse and sexual exploitation of children and child pornography (2011/92/EU) to strengthen efforts to suppress child sex abuse and CEM. The EU's Directive on CEM and child sex abuse provides a comprehensive description of the proscribed behaviours or offences and seeks to improve protection based on a greater understanding of the risks of CEM facilitated by the Internet.

The United States, UK, Australia, Canada, New Zealand, and many other states have long-established laws aimed at suppressing child sex abuse and CEM and regularly update laws to keep pace with changes in information communication technology (ICT), in particular, responding to the increasing presence of encryption in messaging, social media, and Voice over Internet Protocol (VoIP) services. The AFP report that 90% of telecommunications information now intercepted by them uses some form of encryption (Australia, Minister for Home Affairs, 2018). In response to the rapid uptake of encrypted ICT by terrorists and other serious offenders such as producers of CEM, a controversial new Australian law, The Telecommunications and Other Legislation Amendment (Assistance and Access) Act, was passed in 2018 to provide law enforcement with additional powers to decrypt communications between high-risk offenders via computer access and search warrants. The Assistance and Access Act increased penalties for suspects who decline to provide passwords or de-encryption keys and requires assistance from telecommunication companies in Australia and abroad. Enhanced computer access powers will enable Australian LEAs to assist overseas partners connected through Australia's mutual legal assistance framework because "computers, communications and encryption are now global and perpetrators of crimes and terrorist acts have a global reach through these mediums" (Australia, Minister for Home Affairs, 2018). There were, however, widespread objections from the cybersecurity and ICT industry, who claimed that the risks inherent in 'backdoor' de-encryption access could also assist criminals and drive offenders to non-commercial encryption methods (Hayman, 2018).

The absence of a universal treaty on CEM is a significant barrier but is partially addressed by the UN Transnational Organized Crime Convention (UNTOCC), or the Palermo Convention, that came into effect in 2003 and was signed by 147 states, including China, Russia, India, and Brazil, who, as noted, are not signatories to the Budapest Convention on Cybercrime. The UNTOCC is the key multi-lateral treaty addressing organized crime and can be invoked in cases where an organized crime group uses CEM. However, the offences to which it applies must attract a penalty of four years or more in prison in the countries affected. This threshold limits obligatory cooperation to only the most serious CEM production offences, although police-to-police cooperation in less serious matters often occurs informally. Three additional protocols extend the remit of the UNTOCC. These address trafficking in firearms, people smuggling, and trafficking in persons. The Protocol to Prevent, Suppress and Punish Trafficking in Persons, Especially Women and Children signed by 117 countries, including China, Russia, India, and Brazil, focuses on the exploitation of trafficked persons and includes "the exploitation of the prostitution of others or other forms of sexual exploitation, forced labour or services, slavery or practices similar to slavery, servitude or the removal of organs" (UNTOCC, Article 3). The UNTOCC combined with the efforts of Interpol and regional LEAs suggest that a seamless web of law enforcement cooperation to suppress CEM is possible.

The apprehension of offenders and suppression of CEM

Law enforcement officials attribute CEM offences to specific individuals by connecting the offence to a particular digital device and the user of the device and then tracing illicit acts back to the source, such as an IP address and a person. However, anonymity and encryption make the identification of the devices and/or persons responsible for the cybercrime difficult (Lin, 2016).

CEM offences do not usually involve computer trespass, but rather the presence of illegal content. Consequently, covert strategies are useful to identify and disrupt the criminal conspiracies and enterprises that drive CEM online networks. Proactive policing, such as police posing as CEM offenders to gain access to distribution and collector sites or posing as vulnerable children, has been fruitful (Jayawardena & Broadhurst, 2007) but has become less effective over time. More recent network investigation techniques and undercover investigations have become the norm (Walsh et al., 2012). These new methods play an increasingly important role in the suppression of CEM as cases such as Playpen, Sweetie, and Child's Play illustrate.

Sweetie

The Dutch children's rights organization Terre des Hommes sought to address the growing problem of webcam sex tourism through the *Sweetie* operation in 2013. Terre des Hommes created a ten-year-old Filipino girl Sweetie as a fictional online vulnerable child whose role was to collect data (e.g. detect IP addresses) from individuals who contacted Sweetie to solicit webcam sex. She engaged in discussion with potential child sex predators but was not programmed to undress, perform sexual acts, or show sexual organs and thus did not meet the legal elements of a child sex offence in most jurisdictions (Schermer, Georgieva, Hof & Koops, 2016, p 83). The *Sweetie* 'sting' operation ran for three months and led to the investigation of around 1,000 potential offenders from 71 countries (Açar, 2017; Schermer et al., 2016). Following amendments to the Netherlands Criminal Procedure Law in 2016, Dutch police were able to use a 'virtual child' in CEM investigation and adapted methods that avoid legal challenges associated with entrapment. The legality of lures is less crucial in common law jurisdictions (Australia, United States, Canada, New Zealand, and the UK) because matters of subjective intent (i.e. *mens rea*) are given more weight, and interaction with an avatar or similar may result in offences of attempted child sex offending.

Taskforce Argos and Child's Play

Queensland police specialist child protection unit Taskforce Argos was established in 1997 and conducted successful operations against child pornography because of its extensive legal powers. Similar to a 'controlled operation' commonly used to suppress illicit drug importation and distribution, these powers allow investigators to undertake undercover operations that involve 'controlled' criminality. This enabled Taskforce Argos to undertake operations against CEM networks by joining and engaging with the criminal conspiracies engaged in the production and distribution of CEM. Argos was able to use a uniquely powerful investigative strategy not available in other jurisdictions (Bleakley, 2018; Høydal, Stangvik, & Hansen, 2017).

A common investigative method was to impersonate persons less than 18 years on online chat sites that allow users to 'randomly' chat or socialize with strangers without the need to register such as Omegle or Chatroulette. If their conversational partner attempted to groom or coerce the investigators' child persona and arranged to meet with the Argos agents' child persona, the agents contacted the local authorities, and the predator was apprehended by police assigned to observe the meeting (Bleakley, 2018). However, Argos also employed a more controversial investigative techniques, such as the brief but potent covert takeover of a CEM website.

In 2017, Taskforce Argos conducted a covert operation that removed Child's Play and Giftbox, two large CEM distribution websites operating in Tor crypto markets. Child's Play had been operational in 2016–2017 and at its peak had over 1 million registered users sharing and viewing content (Høydal et al., 2017). Argos agents were able to identify and quietly arrest the leaders of both websites, Benjamin 'WarHead' Faulkner and Patrick 'CrazyMonk' Falte, and obtain their administrative passwords. Argos officers assumed the identity of Faulkner and actively published CEM to the website to allay any suspicion. During active posting as CEM distributers, Argos investigators were able to participate in and view private conversations between users to build a profile of individual members and the likely locations. After several months, Argos removed the website and the information obtained in the clandestine operation led to the arrest of many more people than would otherwise have been possible. Child's Play had 3,000 to 4,000 active users and over 100 producers of CEM and led to the rescue or identification of over 100 children (Knaus, 2017). However, controversy remains because Argos, for a short time, operated a CEM market and potentially re-victimized the children involved. This was also the case of the earlier FBI takedown of *Playpen*, an operation that also raised questions about the methods used by law enforcement in searches of hidden encrypted websites.

Playpen and network investigative techniques

Operation Pacifier, an FBI investigation applying similar methods used by Taskforce Argos, led to the shutdown of a notorious Tor-based CEM website, Playpen, that operated between August 2014 and February 2015. Playpen hosted over 20,000 sexual images or videos of children from a server in Virginia, and featured on its home page "two images depicting partially clothed prepubescent females with their legs spread apart" (*U.S. v. Kim*, p 4; note 15[6]). The FBI operated the site for two weeks after identifying the site owners' IP address. Malware-enabled network investigation techniques (NITs) were used to hack the computers of visitors accessing the CEM via Tor, leading to 900 arrests and the conviction with lengthy sentences of three of the principal operators, including the website creator, Steven Chase.

Apart from criticism that the FBI operation required the continued distribution of child pornography, the nature of the NIT warrant has been challenged by a number of alleged Playpen users (some 60 cases in all with only a few successful in excluding evidence). Justice P. K. Chen in November 2017 further addressed the validity of the NIT warrant in *U.S. v. Kim* in the New York District Court. The defendant, Yang Kim, sought to suppress the evidence obtained using these NITs for his indictment for the possession of child pornography from Playpen, claiming they constituted a breach of his Fourth Amendment constitutional right to not be subject to unreasonable search and seizures. It was further argued by the defendant that the warrants obtained by the FBI misrepresented the grounds for probable cause. Although the defendant's suppression motion was denied, the FBI declined to reveal the full details of the techniques used to search and transmit information to the FBI server from computers logged into the Playpen website. The methods enabled the identification of the computer's actual IP address, host name, timestamp, and media access control (MAC) address, as well as the type of operating system and username on the computer.

Other methods of identifying CEM offenders through malware, such as Torsploit, that identify a user's real IP address and forward it to an FBI server with a timestamp, can also be used with NIT to assist in the tracing of CEM online users (Cimpanu, 2019). These methods force CEM distributors to become more cautious and invest in methods to identify LEA malware on the darknet. The combination of honeypot, technical 'hacks,' anticipation of displacement, or migration of users and vendors to new darknet markets, combined with attempts to disrupt and undermine trust in these markets, illustrate the complexity of the measures needed to suppress such resilient darknets (Afilipoaie & Shortis, 2018).

In 2017 *Operation Bayonet*, a joint FBI, Dutch National High Tech Crime Unit, and Europol taskforce, used similar infiltration methods to take over the then largest darknet market AlphaBay and briefly operate Hansa, a smaller related market. As these markets focused on illicit drugs, malware, stolen credentials, and other contraband rather than CEM, these methods did not attract the level of controversy associated with Playpen or Child's Play.

A global regulatory challenge

The suppression of Internet-driven CEM is a major challenge for law enforcement agencies across the globe and a leading example of the response to the transnational nature of cybercrime. Effective alliances have been formed across nations to share intelligence and prosecute the most serious CEM offences. NGOs such as INHOPE and ECPAT, along with increasing engagement from industry, have begun to increase the risks of detection for CEM offenders. In 2015, INHOPE launched ICCAM (I-'See'(C)-Child-Abuse-Material) that allows the hotline's network to process complaints from the public about illegal CEM. Complaints that identify a suspicious URL are entered into the ICCAM system, which then crawls the URL, captures CEM images, and passes them to a centralized database provided by Interpol's ICSE-DB. Cases are then investigated and evidence identified through image analysis, specialists, and routine policing (McKay, Swaminathan, Gou, & Wu, 2008; Dalins, Tyshetskiy, Wilson, Carman, & Boudry, 2018).

The VGT is another example of a global response to CEM. Established in 2003 to help respond to and investigate serious CEM cross-border cases, VGT coordinates investigative responses to multinational child exploitation material cases and uses information provided by INHOPE, ECPAT, and other civil society groups, as well as Interpol's ICSE-DB. Over 1,000 investigations have been completed to date. Fourteen agencies including Interpol and Europol are actively engaged, often in collaboration with the FBI's Violent Crimes Against Children (VCAC) unit, as well as LEAs in Australia, New Zealand, Italy, the UK, Switzerland, Canada, Republic of Korea, the Netherlands, Colombia, Philippines, and the United Arab Emirates. Promising new image recognition technology, network investigation techniques, and web monitoring tools could further strengthen the capacity of LEAs and NGOs to suppress CEM.

Enhancing forensic data capture of CEM

The ICSE-DB, now in its fourth iteration, has been enhanced to improve connectivity across national CEM databases. The ICSE-DB allows LEAs, especially child protection specialists, to use image comparison software to identify victims, offenders, and likely places through the forensic analysis of images and hashes. The expansion of the ICSE-DB to more countries is needed, especially in the developing world; however, many jurisdictions also need to reform the law in relation to child sexual abuse and CEM. Many poorer nations require technical assistance to create the computer infrastructure, connectivity, and expertise needed to operate a national CEM database. As more jurisdictions become capable of identifying victims and offenders, it is likely that offenders will shift their operations to the most vulnerable jurisdictions and populations.

Although CEM perpetrators embrace new technologies that allow them to escape detection, law enforcement has also benefited from recent developments in image recognition. Microsoft's PhotoDNA is designed to recognize similar images and has been widely used by police agencies across the world to identify victims found in CEM since 2009. PhotoDNA and a recent enhancement, PhotoDNA Video, have become widely used by online services, media providers, and law enforcement, who apply the tool to seized CEM stored in databases to help identify and trace offenders and victims of child sexual assault. The method developed by the Dartmouth College vision laboratory computes a specific hash value (similar to a fingerprint) for images, video, and audio files, allowing CEM images to be uniquely identified. The PhotoDNA hash allows law enforcement to match the hash value with images held in CEM databases across the world and to prioritize cases that are new and/or involve ongoing abuse (Farid, 2016).

The application of deep machine learning to CEM image recognition and classification enables researchers using a variety of approaches, notably the Convolutional Neural Network best suited to analyse visual images, to manage the increasing scale of CEM available online (Dalins et al., 2018). The application of artificial intelligence (AI) to enhance data capture from child sex abuse images could enable LEAs to improve the availability of forensic intelligence and evidence for the first time on a sufficient scale to affect CEM distribution networks. These novel approaches have the advantage of reducing human exposure to risks of tertiary victimization through the need for INHOPE, Interpol, and local LEAs to repeatedly view and classify CEM.

Conclusion

A daunting challenge for LEAs, educational institutions, communities, and parents is how the overlap between licit 'adult' pornography and the child sex abuse (and child 'erotica' [sic]) business can blur boundaries and normalize some forms of CEM. Implicit in responding to the risk of CEM is the need for the education of parents, children, and the community. The work of NGOs such as INHOPE, ECPAT, and others is crucial in the education process and can be amplified through new institutional responses, such as Australia's E-Safety Commission and UNODC's initiatives such as the E4J (Education for Justice initiative) project that promotes the training of cybercrime investigators and the production of child-friendly e-safety materials.

In a recent review of law enforcement efforts to suppress CEM, ECPAT recommended more investment in the development and maintenance of a national database of CEM in each country and the routine analysis of national and transnational trends in CEM. A critical step in improving the monitoring of CEM is the need to standardize the variables that are collected, stored, and analysed, and to create uniform metrics that effectively measure change in the prevalence, frequency, nature, and risk of CEM, especially in highly vulnerable countries increasingly becoming the target for CEM criminal enterprises. This requires constant dialogue across communities about what constitute key metrics on CEM (ECPAT, 2018). A positive step would be to continue to promote participation in research by LEAs and to invest in novel uses of new technologies that can help address the rapid scaling up of CEM now encountered. These include methods to help de-anonymize CEM crypto markets and the cryptocurrencies used to purchase CEM, computer vision and image recognition techniques that enable rapid forensic extraction of evidentiary material, and research that explores the countermeasures or 'forensic awareness' of the producers and distributors of CEM.

The scale and depravity of online child sexual exploitation images may be at its zenith, but the risks of detection of the criminals have increased. Regardless of the source of these images, crimes of domination remain entrenched and continue to offer opportunities for abuse and profit. A broad approach linking government, NGOs, industry, LEAs, and academia with community engagement in child safety has emerged. Albeit imperfectly, the comity realized by these cooperative endeavours at the international and local level have improved awareness and helped disrupt the activities of CEM producers and distributors. As with other crimes, displacement to more vulnerable jurisdictions are likely as criminal enterprises seek out 'fresh' CEM and new Internet safe havens.

Acknowledgements

I am grateful for the assistance of Brigitte Bouhours, Peter Grabosky, Shanmuk Kandukuri, Katrina Pinn, and the anonymous reviewers in the preparation of this chapter.

Notes

1   www.fbi.gov/history/famous-cases/operation-innocent-images
2   www.terredeshommes.nl/en/programmes/sweetie-20-stop-webcam-child-sex
3   See www.accce.gov.au/
4   From a leading UK case: *R v. Oliver, Hartrey and Baldwin* (*Times Law Report*, 6 December 2002).
5   See www.missingkids.com/theissues/sextortion
6   U.S. v. KIM, No. 16-CR-191 (PKC) available from www.leagle.com/decision/infdco20171113f28

References

Açar, K.V. (2017). Webcam child prostitution: An exploration of current and futuristic methods of detection. *International Journal of Cyber Criminology, 11*(1), 98–109.

Afilipoaie, A., & Shortis, P. (2018). Crypto-market enforcement-new strategy and tactics. *Policy, 54,* 87–98.

Armstrong, J., & Mellor, D. (2013). Internet child pornography offenders: An examination of attachment and intimacy deficits. *Legal and Criminological Psychology, 21*(1), 41–55.

Australian Federal Police (AFP). (2015). Annual Report 2014–15, Commonwealth of Australia, Canberra. Retrieved from www.afp.gov.au/~/media/afp/pdf/a/afp-annual-report-2014-2015.pdf

Australia (Minister for Home Affairs). (2018). Explanatory Memorandum – Telecommunications and other legislation amendment (Assistance and Access) Bill 2018. Commonwealth of Australia. Retrieved from www.legislation.gov.au/Details/C2018A00148

Australian Communications and Media Authority. (2013). Like, post, share: Young Australians' experience of social media. Retrieved from www.acma.gov.au/-/media/mediacomms/Report/pdf/Like-post-share-Young-Australians-experience-of-social-media-Quantitative-research-report.pdf?la=en

Babchishin, K. M., Hanson, K. R., & Hermann, C. A. (2011). The characteristics of online sex offenders: A meta-analysis. *Sexual Abuse: A Journal of Research and Treatment, 23,* 92–123.

Babchishin, K. M., Merdian, H. L., Bartels, R. M., & Perkins, D. (2018). Child sexual exploitation materials offenders. *European Psychologist, 23*(2), 130–143.

Battersby, L. (2015, September 30). Millions of social media photos found on child exploitation sharing sites. *The Sydney Morning Herald.* Retrieved from www.smh.com.au/national/millions-of-social-media-photos-found-on-child-exploitation-sharing-sites-20150929-gjxe55.html

Bierie, D., & Budd, K. (2018). Romeo, Juliet, and statutory rape. *Sexual Abuse: A Journal of Research and Treatment, 30*(3), 296–321.

Bleakley, P. (2018). Watching the watchers: Taskforce Argos and the evidentiary issues involved with infiltrating Dark Web child exploitation networks. *The Police Journal: Theory, Practice and Principles.* Retrieved from https://journals.sagepub.com/doi/full/10.1177/0032258X18801409

Bouhours, B., & Broadhurst, R. (2011, December 15). On-line child sex offenders: Report on a sample of peer to peer offenders arrested between July 2010-June 2011. Retrieved from SSRN: http://dx.doi.org/10.2139/ssrn.2174815

Boyd, C. (2018, October 2). Fortnite gamers targeted by data theft malware. Malwarebytes LABS. Retrieved from https://blog.malwarebytes.com/cybercrime/2018/10/fortnite-gamers-targeted-by-data-theft-malware/

Brown, R., & Bricknell, S. (2018). *What is the profile of child exploitation material offenders?* Trends & Issues in Crime and Criminal Justice, No. 564. Canberra: Australian Institute of Criminology.

Brown, R., & Shelling, J. (2019). *Exploring the implications of child sex dolls.* Trends & Issues in Crime and Criminal Justice, No. 570. Canberra: Australian Institute of Criminology. Retrieved from https://aic.gov.au/publications/tandi/tandi570

Burgess, A.W., & Grant, C.A. (1988). *Children traumatized in sex rings.* Arlington, VA: National Center for Missing & Exploited Children.

Canadian Centre for Child Protection. (2017). Survivors Survey – Full Report 2017. Retrieved from www.protectchildren.ca/pdfs/C3P_SurvivorsSurveyFullReport2017.pdf

CBC News. (2017). Child protection group warns parents about luring, explicit chat on game site Roblox. *CBC News.* Retrieved from www.cbc.ca/news/canada/manitoba/winnipeg-roblox-luring-warning-1.3997258

Cimpanu, C. (2019, January 16). Fortnite security issue would have granted hackers access to accounts. *Zednet.* Retrieved from www.zdnet.com/article/fortnite-security-issue-would-have-granted-hackers-access-to-accounts

Cooper, D. (2015). Adult themes: The rise and fall of America's first digital brothel. *Engadget.* Retrieved February 1, 2019, from www.engadget.com/2015/02/26/adult-themes-digital-brothel/

Corriveau, P., & Greco, C. (2012). Online predators and cyberspace. *Media Kit on Sexual Assault.* Retrieved from www.inspq.qc.ca/en/sexual-assault/fact-sheets/online-pedophilia-and-cyberspace

Cox, P. (2017, August 17). Blamed for being abused: An uncomfortable history of child sexual exploitation. *The Conversation.* Retrieved from http://theconversation.com/blamed-for-being-abused-an-uncomfortable-history-of-child-sexual-exploitation-82410

Dalins, J., Tyshetskiy, Y., Wilson, C., Carman, M. J., & Boudry, D. (2018). Laying foundations for effective machine learning in law enforcement. Majura – A labelling schema for child exploitation materials. *Digital Investigation, 26,* 40–54.

DeHart, D., Dwyer, G., Seto, M., Moran, R., Letourneau, E., & Schwarz-Watts, D. (2016). Internet sexual solicitation of children: A proposed typology of offenders based on their chats, e-mails, and social network posts. *Journal of Sexual Aggression, 23*(1), 77–89.

ECPAT Interagency Working Group. (2016, January 28). Terminology guidelines for the protection of children from sexual exploitation and sexual abuse: Adopted by the Interagency Working Group Sexual Exploitation in Luxembourg. Retrieved from http://luxembourgguidelines.org/english-version/

ECPAT International. (2017). *SECO Manifestations – Live streaming of child sexual abuse in real-time.* Bangkok. Retrieved from www.ecpat.org/wp-content/uploads/legacy/SECO%20Manifestations_Live%20streaming%20of%20child%20sexual%20abuse%20in%20real-time_0.pdf

ECPAT International. (2018, April). Trends in online child sexual abuse material. Bangkok: ECPAT International. Retrieved from www.ecpat.org/wp-content/uploads/2018/07/ECPAT-International-Report-Trends-in-Online-Child-Sexual-Abuse-Material-2018.pdf

Endrass, J., Urbaniok, F., Hammermeister, L. C., Benz, C., Elbert, T., Laubacher, A., & Rosseg-ger, A. (2009). The consumption of Internet child pornography and violent and sex offending. *BMC Psychiatry, 9*, 43–49.

Elliot, A., Beech, A. R., Mandeville-Norden, R., & Hayes, E. (2009). Psychological profiles of Internet sexual offenders: Comparisons with contact sexual offenders. *Sex Abuse: A Journal of Research and Treatment, 21*(1), 76–92.

Europol. (2013). *Threat assessment of child sexual exploitation and abuse*. Child Exploitation and Online Protection Centre [CEOP]. Retrieved from www.norfolklscb.org/wp-content/uploads/2015/03/CEOP_Threat-Assessment_CSE_JUN2013.pdf

Europol. (2015). *Copyright European financial coalition against commercial sexual exploitation of children online*. EUROPOL. Retrieved from www.europol.europa.eu/publications-documents/commercial-sexual-exploitation-of-children-online

Farid, H. (2016). *Digital forensics*. Cambridge, MA: MIT Press.

Flowers, R. B. (2001). The sex trade industry's worldwide exploitation of children. *The Annals of the American Academy of Political and Social Science, 575*(1), 147–157.

Foucault, M. (1990). *The history of sexuality: An introduction* (Vol. I, R. Hurley, trans.). New York, NY: Vintage.

Funnell, N. (2016, August 17). Exclusive: Students from 71 Australian schools targeted by sick pornography ring. *News.com.au*. Retrieved from www.news.com.au/lifestyle/real-life/news-life/students-from-70-australian-schools-targeted-by-sick-pornography-ring/news-story/53288536e0ce3bba7955e92c7f7fa8da

Gewirtz-Meydan, A., Walsh, W., Wolak, J., & Finkelhor, D. (2018). The complex experience of child pornography survivors. *Child Abuse & Neglect, 80*, 238–248.

Hannan, S., Orcutt, H., Miron, L., & Thompson, K. (2015). Childhood sexual abuse and later alcohol-related problems: Investigating the roles of revictimization, PTSD, and drinking motivations among college women. *Journal of Interpersonal Violence, 32*(14), 2118–2138.

Hayman, L. H. (2018). Australia's encryption-busting law could impact global privacy. *Wired*. Retrieved from www.wired.com/story/australia-encryption-law-global-impact/?mbid=email_onsiteshare

Henshaw, M., Ogloff, J., & Clough, J. (2015). Looking beyond the screen: A critical review of the literature on the online child pornography offender. *Sexual Abuse: A Journal of Research and Treatment, 29*(5), 416–445.

Hernandez, S. C. L. S., Lacsin, A. C., Ylade, M. C., Aldaba, J., Lam, H. Y., Estacio, R., Jr., & Lopez, A. L. (2018). Sexual exploitation and abuse of children online in the Philippines: A review of online news and articles. *Acta Medica Philippina, 52*(4), 305–311.

Høydal, H. F., Stangvik, E. O., & Hansen, N. R. (2017). Breaking the dark net: Why the police share abuse pics to save children. *Verdens Gang*, pp. 1–28. Retrieved from http://nodabase.net/cases/breaking-the-darknet-why-the-police-share-abuse-pics-to-save-children/

Hussey, M. (2016, February). A deep dive into the business of virtual reality porn. *The Next Web*. Retrieved from.https://thenextweb.com/evergreen/2017/09/05/a-deep-dive-into-the-business-of-virtual-reality-porn/?

International Centre for Missing & Exploited Children. (2017). *Online grooming of children for sexual purposes: Model legislation & global review* (1st ed.) [ebook]. The Koons Family Institute on International Law & Policy. Retrieved from www.icmec.org/wp-content/uploads/2017/09/Online-Grooming-of-Children_FINAL_9-18-17.pdf

Internet Organised Crime Threat Assessment, Europol. (2015). *Online child sexual exploitation*. Retrieved from www.europol.europa.eu/iocta/2015/online-child-exploit.html

Internet Watch Foundation. (2017). *Trends in online child sexual exploitation: Examining the distribution of captures of live-streamed child sexual abuse*. Retrieved from www.iwf.org.uk/sites/

default/files/inlinefiles/Distribution%20of%20Captures%20of%20Live-streamed%20 Child%20Sexual%20Abuse%20FINAL.pdf

Interpol. (2017). *Interpol Annual Report 2017*. Retrieved from www.interpol.int/ News-and-media/Publications2/Annual-reports2

IWF. (2016). *Annual report*. Cambridge: IWF.

IWF. (2018). *Trends in online child sexual exploitation: Examining the distribution of captures of live-streamed child sexual abuse*. Cambridge: IWF.

Jayawardena, K., & Broadhurst, R. (2007). Online child sex solicitation: Exploring the feasibility of a research 'sting'. *International Journal of Cyber Criminology, 1*(2), 228–248.

Jenkins, P. (2001). *Beyond tolerance: Child pornography on the internet*. New York: NYU Press.

Jolly, J., & Khan, U. (2016). *Rape culture in India: The role of the English-Language Press*. Shorenstein Center on Media, Politics and Public Policy, Harvard Kennedy School Discussion Paper Series #D-102. Retrieved from https://shorensteincenter.org/rape-culture-india-english-language-press/

Keating, F. (2015, October 29). Online grooming: New trends in online sexual abuse. *International Business Times*. Retrieved from www.ibtimes.co.uk/online-grooming-new-trends-online-sexual-abuse-1526146

Kloess, J. A., Woodhams, J., Whittle, H., Grant, T., & Hamilton-Giachritsis, C. E. (2019). The challenges of identifying and classifying child sexual abuse material', *Sexual Abuse, 31*(2), 173–196.

Knaus, C. (2017, October 7). *Australian police sting brings down paedophile forum on dark web*. Retrieved from www.theguardian.com/society/2017/oct/07/australian-police-sting-brings-down-paedophile-forum-on-dark-web

Langston, J. (2018). How PhotoDNA for Video is being used to fight online child exploitation. *Microsoft on the Issues*. Retrieved January 31, 2019, from https://news.microsoft.com/on-the-issues/2018/09/12/how-photodna-for-video-is-being-used-to-fight-online-child-exploitation/

Lin, P. (2016). Is it wrong for victims of cyber-crime to hack back? *World Economic Forum*. Retrieved from www.weforum.org/agenda/2016/09/is-it-wrong-for-victims-of-cyber-crime-to-hack-back/

Maras, M. H., & Shapiro, L. R. (2017). Child sex dolls and robots: More than just an uncanny valley. *Journal of Internet Law, 2017*(x), 1–21.

Matzutt, R., Hiller, J., Henze, M., Ziegeldorf, J. H., Müllmann, D., Hohlfeld, O., & Wehrle, K. (2018, February). A quantitative analysis of the impact of arbitrary blockchain content on bitcoin. In *Proceedings of the 22nd International Conference on Financial Cryptography and Data Security (FC)*. New York: Springer.

Maxim, D., Skinner, K., Orlando, S., & Broadhurst, R. (2016, November 4). *Online child exploitation material – Trends and emerging issues*. Research Report of the Australian National University Cybercrime Observatory and Office of the Children's eSafety Commissioner, Canberra. Retrieved from SSRN: https://ssrn.com/abstract=2861644 or http://dx.doi.org/10.2139/ssrn.2861644

McGuire, M., & Dowling, S. (2013). Cyber-enabled crimes – Sexual offending against children. In *Cybercrime: A review of the evidence*. Research Report 75 (pp. 1–25). Retrieved from https://assets.publishing.service.gov.uk/government/uploads/system/uploads/attachment_data/file/246754/horr75-chap3.pdf; www.gov.uk/government/publications/cyber-crime-a-review-of-the-evidence

McKay, C., Swaminathan, A., Gou, H., & Wu, M. (2008, March). *Image acquisition forensics: Forensic analysis to identify imaging source*. 2008 IEEE International Conference on Acoustics, Speech and Signal Processing, pp. 1657–1660.

McNally, A. (2016). *Every picture tells a story. A study of those who gather and accumulate legal and illegal images* (PhD thesis). Nottingham Trent University.

Merdian, H., Moghaddam, N., Boer, D., Wilson, N., Thakker, J., Curtis, C., & Dawson, D. (2016). Fantasy-driven versus contact-driven users of child sexual exploitation material: Offender classification and implications for their risk assessment. *Sexual Abuse: A Journal of Research and Treatment, 30*(3), 230–253.

NatCen Social Research. (2018, January). *Behaviour and characteristics of perpetrators of online-facilitated child sexual abuse and exploitation.* Retrieved from www.natcen.ac.uk/news-media/press-releases/2018/january/new-report-on-online-child-sexual-abuse-identifies-most-at-risk-children/

Nurse, J. (2018, August 30). Fortnite is setting a dangerous security trend. *The Conversation.* Retrieved from http://theconversation.com/fortnite-is-setting-a-dangerous-security-trend-102294

Office of the Children's eSafety Commissioner & ACMA. (2016, July 20). *Are you GO-ing Pokemon crazy?* Retrieved from www.esafety.gov.au/about-the-office/newsroom/blog/are-you-going-pokemon-crazy

Pierce, R. L. (1984). Child pornography: A hidden dimension of child abuse. *Child Abuse & Neglect, 8*(4), 483–493.

Quayle, E., Jonsson, L., Cooper, K., Traynor, J., & Svedin, C. (2018). Children in identified sexual images – Who are they? Self- and non-self-taken images in the International Child Sexual Exploitation Image Database 2006–2015. *Child Abuse Review, 27*(3), 223–238.

Richards, K. (2011). *Misperceptions about child sex offenders.* Trends & Issues in Crime and Criminal Justice, No. 429. Canberra: Australian Institute of Criminology. Retrieved from https://aic.gov.au/publications/tandi/tandi429

Rutkin, A. (2016, August 2). Could sex robots and virtual reality treat paedophilia? *New Scientist.* Retrieved from www.newscientist.com/article/2099607-could-sex-robots-and-virtual-reality-treat-paedophilia/

Schermer, B. W., Georgieva, I. N., Hof, S., & Koops, B. J. (2016). *Legal aspects of sweetie 2.0.* Center for Law and Digital Technologies, Leiden University, Faculty of Law. Retrieved from https://research.tilburguniversity.edu/en/publications/legal-aspects-of-sweetie-20

Sward, A., Vecna, I., & Stonedahl, F. (2018). Data insertion in Bitcoin's blockchain. *Ledger, 3.* doi:10.5915/LEDGER.2018.101

Svedin, C. G. (2012). *Victims assistance.* Launching Conference on Global Alliance Against Sexual Abuse Online. Brussels: EU. Retrieved from www.ecpat.org/wp-content/uploads/2016/05/Emerging-Issues-and-Global-Threats-Children-online-2017-1.pdf

Takahashi, D. (2016, April 13). Naughty America tries to get VR porn just right. *Venturebeat.* Retrieved from https://venturebeat.com/2016/04/13/naughty-america-tries-to-get-vr-porn-just-right/

Taylor, M., Holland, G., & Quayle, E. (2001). Typology of paedophile picture collections. *The Police Journal, 74,* 97–107.

Thorn. (2016). The intersection of child sexual exploitation and technology. Retrieved from www.wearethorn.org/child-sexual-exploitation-andtechnology/

Toulalan, S. (2014). "Is he a licentious lewd sort of a person?" Constructing the child rapist in early modern England. *Journal of the History of Sexuality, 23*(1), 21–52.

United Nations Development Plan & ASEAN. (2017). *ASEAN-China-UNDP report on financing the sustainable development goals (SDGs) in ASEAN: Strengthening integrated national financing frameworks to deliver the 2030 agenda.* Retrieved from www.asia-pacific.undp.org/ . . . /launched-publication-on-financing-the-SDGs.html

United Nations Office of Drugs and Crim (UNODC). (2015). *Study on the effects of new information technologies on the abuse and exploitation of children.*Vienna: UNODC. Retrieved from www.unodc.org/documents/Cybercrime/Study_on_the_Effects.pdf

Walsh, W., Wolak, J., & Finkelhor, D. (2012, September). *Methodology report – 3rd National Juvenile Online Victimization Study (NJOV3): Prosecution study.* Retrieved from http://unh.edu/ccrc/pdf/CV293_NJOV3%20Prosecution%20Study%20Methodology%20Report_1-18-13.pdf

Webb, L., Craissati, J., & Keen, S. (2007). Characteristics of internet child pornography offenders: A comparison with child molesters'. *Sex Abuse: A Journal of Research and Treatment, 19,* 449–465.

Webster, S., Davidson, J., Bifulco, A., Gottschalk, P., Caretti, V., & Pham, T. (2012). *European online grooming report: European Commission, safer internet plus programme* (pp. 1–152). Retrieved from www.researchgate.net/publication/257941820_European_Online_Grooming_Project_-_Final_Report

WeProtect Global Alliance. (2018). *Working together to end the sexual exploitation of children online. Global Threat Assessment 2018.* Retrieved from https://static1.squarespace.com/static/5630f48de4b00a75476ecf0a/t/5a83272c8165f5d2a348426d/1518544686414/6.4159_WeProtect+GA+report.pdf

Wittes, B., Poplin, C., Jurecic, Q., & Spera, C. (2016). *Sextortion: Cybersecurity, teenagers, and remote sexual assault.* Center for Technology at Brookings. Retrieved from www.brookings.edu/research/sextortion-cybersecurity-teenagers-and-remote-sexual-assault/

Wolak, J. (2015). Technology-facilitated organized abuse: An examination of law enforcement arrest cases. *International Journal for Crime, Justice and Social Democracy, 4*(2), 18–33.

Wolak, J., Finkelhor, D., Walsh, W., & Treitman, L. (2018). Sextortion of minors: Characteristics and dynamics. *Journal of Adolescent Health, 62*(1), 72–79.

World Health Organisation. (1999). *Report of the consultation on child abuse prevention* (p. 15). Geneva: World Health Organization. Retrieved from https://apps.who.int/iris/handle/10665/65900

Wortley, R., & Smallbone, S. (Eds.). (2006). *Situational prevention of child sexual abuse.* New York, NY: Criminal Justice Press.

Young, K. (2008). Understanding sexually deviant online behaviour from an addiction perspective. *International Journal of Cyber Criminology, 2*(1), 298–307.

Part IV

Policing

15 Policing cybercrime

Responding to the growing problem and considering future solutions

Cassandra Dodge and George Burruss

Introduction

The police are the first responders to criminal events, civil unrest, natural disasters, and civic matters; it would follow, then, that cybercrime victims would call the police when they discover a crime has occurred. However, cybercrime victims are often unwilling to make a call for services. Similarly, in offline fraud and other kinds of white-collar crime, victims either believe the police cannot or will not do anything to resolve the crime (Huff, Desilets, & Kane, 2010). Also, white-collar crime and cybercrime victims often are unaware of their victimization because offenders use deception or because victims lack technical expertise needed to detect the crime. Nevertheless, as cybercrime grows in prevalence for citizens and businesses, touching on almost every kind of transaction and mode of communication, the police are increasingly called to address the cybercrime problem.

Despite this pressing need for a systematic response to cybercrime, it is not clear local police departments have the means, training, or ability to respond effectively. Four aspects of cybercrime make the local law enforcement response problematic. First, cybercrime offenders hide their crimes through anonymous interactions with victims' devices or accounts, often through spoofed or anonymized networked connections. This makes identifying the offenders virtually impossible, thus hindering investigation, arrest, and prosecution. Second, even if the offender is identified, the fact that cybercrimes are not limited by geography restricts the local police's jurisdiction. For example, it would be unlikely a Brazilian police officer could arrest a French hacker for a one-on-one theft of credit card data occurring in Rio de Janeiro. Third, the asynchronous nature of cybercrime means the offence may have occurred months before the victim is even aware of the cyberattack, further hindering investigation. Fourth, front-line officers are unlikely to possess the expertise to collect, store, or process the chain of custody for digital evidence. Although police departments have invested in such expertise and technology, they are typically deployed in high-level cases or those involving Internet crimes against children, not standard calls for service for fraud or stolen credit card information.

Given the challenges that cybercrime presents to law enforcement, criminologists have begun to examine various aspects of policing vis-à-vis cybercrime – training, attitudes, and capabilities. In this chapter, we begin by discussing cybercrime's prevalence and growth. By understanding the scope of the problem, we can put into context the strains required of policing to respond to cybercrime. Next, we look at research on police attitudes and perceptions toward cybercrime followed by the various work hazards facing cybercrime investigators. Knowing this will help us understand to what extent line officers and administrators might embrace policies and practices intended to improve their handling of such cases. We follow with a discussion of some organizational strategies employed to improve agencies' response to cybercrime, specifically the use of the multi-agency task force. We then discuss how law enforcement has partnered with private organizations and businesses to improve enforcement effectiveness. Finally, we speculate on how law enforcement might incorporate various strategies in responding to the growing problem of cybercrime.

Prevalence

There is little disagreement about the prevalence of cybercrime, as governments, businesses, and individuals have been victimized. However, reports of the extent of cybercrime, and its associated costs, vary among sources. According to the FBI's Internet Crime Complaint Center (IC3), cybercrimes were credited with a loss value of $1.4 billion in the United States in 2017 (FBI, 2017). In 2013, security software manufacturer Symantec Corp. reported $110 billion in international losses to Internet users, while their competitor, McAfee, Inc., estimated the losses to total approximately $1 trillion in that same year (Hyman, 2013). Levi (2017) found that 12% of the population of the European Union had experienced online fraud. The United Kingdom reported 3.8 million fraud incidents, with over half being cyber-related. In the Netherlands, between 134 and 228 million euros were illegally withdrawn from victims' bank accounts between 2010 and 2012. In 2015, Hong Kong reported 6,862 reported cases of computer crime resulting in a financial loss of over 1.8 trillion Hong Kong dollars (Levi, 2017). The major discrepancy between these numbers is most likely the result of one of four factors: a failure of victims to report, self-selection bias, no standard for estimating loss, and undetected losses.

As already noted, some cybercrime victims may not report the crime to authorities. Current estimates are only based off of reported cybercrimes, so it is possible that the figures presented are significant underestimations. This is particularly true for the IC3 estimation, as it is based off official reports as opposed to corporate surveys. The United States Attorney's Office (2015) estimates that only 15% of fraud victims report their crimes to law enforcement. Dutch victims of identity theft, consumer fraud, and hacking reported their victimization less often than victims of traditional crimes. Those who were victimized multiple times were less likely to report to police, but they were more likely to report their victimization to other organizations. This may be due to dissatisfaction with previous police investigations (van do Weijer, Leukfeldt, & Bernasco, 2018). For some victims, admission of victimization may be embarrassing. Cybercrime victims experience emotional harm, including feelings of betrayal, isolation, and loss of personal and financial security. Cross, Richards, and Smith (2016) found cyber-fraud victims in Australia, the United Kingdom, and New Zealand suffered from significant emotional and psychological impact, including responses of shame, distress, sadness, and anger. One participant admitted to experiencing a nervous breakdown.

Corporations may never report their victimizations to law enforcement simply because it is bad for business. Admitting that a cyber-incursion had occurred could affect business and possibly corporate stock value. Rather than allowing for a public investigation, these organizations may investigate these incursions internally through their own cyber-security or information technology units. In cases of major losses, a full legal investigation could still occur, but many smaller incursions remain private.

One of the primary sources for cybercrime prevalence and overall loss estimates are derived from surveys of businesses and organizations. Although these reports may be helpful in lieu of official reports (which fail to capture a majority of cybercrimes), they, too, are problematic. Anderson and colleagues (2013) identified over 100 sources of data on cybercrime. However, each of them was considered insufficient and incomplete. Over- and under-reporting varied depending on the source of the data. In some cases, over-reporting could be intentional (e.g. security vendors artificially inflating numbers) or unintentional (e.g. poor research methodology). Cybercrime reports based off of self-report losses have been criticized as inaccurate, as self-selection allows for biased participation (Florencio & Herley, 2013). Organizations experiencing little to no loss are more likely to respond to the survey. Conversely, businesses experiencing larger losses are less likely to respond, leading to lowball estimates. When significant losses are reported, it is likely they are concentrated within a small population. In other words, reports of large losses could be an outlier, artificially inflating the reports. "A single individual who claims $50,000 losses, in an N = 1,000 person survey, is all it takes to generate a $10 billion loss over the population. One unverified claim of $7,500 in phishing losses translates into $1.5 billion" (Florencio & Herley, 2013, p. 35). Ultimately, one must consider the source of these reports because the cyber-security industry has a reason to establish cybercrime as costly problem (Wall, 1998).

Each of the prior issues assumes the crime has been detected by the victim. This is not always the case. Individual victims may have no idea that they have been successfully targeted, confounding detection and response. Even after an intrusion is detected, there is no way to be certain that data have been stolen or how much has been taken. Unlike terrestrial crime, digital theft does not require the removal of data; copying information is sufficient for nefarious purposes. It is not until that data are used or made available elsewhere that those victims are able to confirm the loss.

Crime committed through digital means has become more prevalent and will continue to evolve with technological innovation. Law enforcement agencies at the local, state, and federal levels will likely be asked to investigate these crimes at some point, if they have not already. The more prevalent cybercrime becomes, the more pressure the public and politicians will place on law enforcement agencies to do something about the problem. At the same time, the complications associated with responding to digital crime suggest the police will continue to resist efforts to become the first responders, especially those involving digital financial transactions. We next explore how individual officers perceive cybercrime and how they view their ability to respond to it. Against the backdrop of cybercrimes' prevalence, the attitudes of line officers provide insights into the likelihood of initiating successful policies.

Police attitudes and perceptions of cybercrime

Police officers, like the public, perceived some crimes to be more serious than others. This is important because it influences officer motivation to investigate and process specific crimes. This perception also influences the distribution of resources available to investigators. For example, cyberstalking and harassment occurs more frequently than does child pornography (Hinduja, 2004), but child pornography is perceived as more serious by both law enforcement and community stakeholders. The allocation of resources aligns with the perception of seriousness rather than frequency to appease stakeholders while still lining up with officers' views.

In 2004, Senjo surveyed officers, asking them to rank five cybercrimes by severity: paedophilia, credit card fraud, electronic theft, copyright infringement, and espionage. Unsurprisingly, paedophilia was ranked the most severe while copyright infringement was ranked the least severe. In their 2011 study, Holt and Bossler took the ranking a step further, asking line officers to rank 12 traditional crimes and cybercrimes by seriousness. Paedophilia was still the highest-ranked cybercrime, coming second to armed robbery. Terrestrial and cyber-thefts were all ranked closely together, with cyber-specific crimes of viruses and malware as well as cyber-harassment falling in the middle of the rankings. However, when asked to rank the frequency of individual crimes, officers believed traditional crimes were more common. Cyber-harassment was actually ranked as the least frequent, even though it is among the most common cybercrimes reported (Holt & Bossler, 2011).

Although the seriousness of some cybercrimes is recognized by law enforcement officers, this is not true across the board. In Holt and Bossler's (2011) survey of line officers, cyber-harassment was perceived as an offence equal to traditional harassment by approximately two-thirds of the respondents. Between 11.1% and 25.8% of the responding officers perceived online harassment to be a less serious offence. Cyberbullying, arguably a related offence, has been met with some derision by law enforcement. In the aptly titled article, "'Just Being Mean to Somebody Isn't a Police Matter': Police Perspectives on

Policing Cyberbullying," 12 officers were interviewed about their experiences with cyberbullying (Broll & Huey, 2015). Overall, the officers perceived the issue to be primarily non-criminal, and criminalizing cyberbullying would unnecessarily increase the strain on the criminal justice system. If and when the issue escalated to the point of harassment or threat of harm, existing laws would already address the issue. Officers acknowledged the online component of cyberbullying extended the problem outside of schools, limiting school administrators' ability to address the problem. As a result, parents would report incidents to law enforcement because they felt there was no other authority to turn to, but officers would consider them non-criminal, interpersonal incidents.

As a result of these perceptions, police administrators have resisted allocating resources to cybercrime over more traditional crime. Research in this area has been mixed. Some findings indicated that officers believe cybercrime diverts attention away from traditional crime investigations, which were arguably more important and certainly more common (Hinduja, 2004). However, in a more recent study, 63% of surveyed patrol officers indicated cybercrime investigations were not a drain on resources (Bossler & Holt, 2012). The eight-year difference between studies may indicate a shift in the perception of cybercrime. In 2004, cybercrime was novel, which could explain the initial resistance to supporting cyber-investigations. By 2012, cybercrime may have been perceived as normal; the police may now agree cybercrime-specific resources are necessary and routine.

There appears to be a shift towards accepting cybercrime as a legitimate concern for law enforcement, though the perception of traditional crime as more important is still strong. For example, 24% of surveyed line officers believed investigating violent crimes should receive more recognition for case closure than for investigating cybercrimes (Bossler & Holt, 2012). If they can get more respect pursuing offline crime, officers may lack motivation to train in digital forensics or other cyber-investigation techniques.

The perception of cybercrime's importance appears to vary depending on officer rank and roles. Upper-level management in both law enforcement and government organizations appear to have stronger opinions regarding the importance of developing cybercrime response programmes and units. Police Executive Research Forum (PERF) Executive Director Chuck Wexler stated, "Local and state governments must recognize that the crime-fighting successes of these past 50 years are not preparing us for the new crimes of this millennium" (PERF, 2014, p. 2). Upper-level management must work with and respond to concerns of community stakeholders. High-profile cybercrimes often make media headlines, increasing the pressure on management to address community concerns. Agencies have been working with organizations such as PERF to develop best practices for dealing with cybercrime. Director Wexler described the discussion at the 2013 Cybercrime Summit: "Police chiefs and other experts stood up, one after another, to tell us that cybercrime is changing policing, because it allows criminals on the other side of the world to suddenly become a problem in your own back yard" (PERF, 2014, p. 1).

Although upper management may be trying to address cybercrime, there appears to be a disconnect between upper management and line officers. Research has shown that line officers have little knowledge of how the issues were being addressed by police administrators, if at all (Bossler & Holt, 2012). A lack of communication and implementation of solutions has led to a lack of confidence in officers' ability to investigate these crimes, as well as a lack of motivation. Even though line officers are typically the first officers to respond to calls for service, most believe local law enforcement should not be the primary investigating agency for cybercrime. A majority (72.8%) of surveyed officers believed cybercrimes should be reported directly to specialized investigative units (Bossler & Holt, 2012). Regardless of their differences, line officers and police administrators appear to agree that cybercrime is changing policing. More than half of the line officers surveyed by Bossler and Holt believed that cybercrime will dramatically change policing as we know it.

The stress of handling cybercrime cases

Because line officers perceive cybercrime as less serious than traditional crime, they may also feel those tasked with responding to cybercrimes are not doing real police work. Certainly, investigating digital crime is less dangerous than offline crime, given most of the legwork is done in cyberspace. Digital investigators, like their traditional counterparts, however, are subjected to stressors as a result of their roles. Analyses of digital investigators' job stress found they experience levels of stress comparable to those experienced by other law enforcement officers (Holt, Blevins, & Burruss, 2012). Job specialization does not appear to create additional stress, though the sources of stress vary. Some of the sources of stress unique to the role are a shortage of qualified staff and a lack of standardized investigative procedures.

Cases involving Internet child exploitation, or ICE, are more stressful than typical law enforcement activity (Krause, 2009). ICE investigators experience high rates of burnout and are at high risk for secondary traumatic stress disorder. Because investigators must observe media (pictures, sound, videos) depicting abuse rather than hearing about it second-hand, this trend is not necessarily surprising (Perez, Jones, Engler, & Sachau, 2010). Interviewed officers consistently stated video with audio as the most disturbing. The age of the victim is also a factor for investigators (Krause, 2009; Perez et al., 2010).

Research on ICE investigators by Bourke and Craun (2014) indicated one-quarter of respondents experienced severe or high levels of traumatic stress; nevertheless, more than half of the respondents were coping with the stressful environment. Similar research reported high levels of professional efficacy; that is, the officers felt their work made a positive impact in spite of the difficulties it presented (Perez et al., 2010). For those unable to cope, common stress reactions included anxiety, mood changes, withdrawal from family and social circles, distrust, and cynicism (Krause, 2009).

To mitigate stress, officers need to implement adaptive coping mechanisms. These mechanisms are intended to allow officers to exert some form of control over their experiences, with the primary goal of establishing emotional distance (Krause, 2009). Ideally, investigators should limit or reduce their exposure to disturbing media, though this is not always feasible (Krause, 2009; Perez et al., 2010). Exposure reduction may be achieved through the use of automated software that can scan and match digital images to those already known to ICE investigators. Of course, if the files have not been previously identified, they still have to be analysed by investigators (Perez et al., 2010). Some agencies limit the amount of time an investigator can remain in an ICE assignment, rotating them out before they burn out or develop a traumatic stress disorder. Ideally, officers should not be assigned to ICE units or investigations on a permanent basis (Perez et al., 2010).

Strong social support, especially from supervisors, appears to have a strong relationship with lower secondary traumatic stress experiences (Bourke & Craun, 2014). Although social support of families and friends is also beneficial, seeking comfort from these groups is more difficult due to the subject matter (Burns, Morley, Bradshaw, & Domene, 2008). Supervisors already have knowledge of ICE investigations and the difficulties faced by officers. Professional counselling may be necessary for officers to process their experiences in a proactive way. Psychologists and counsellors need to have a familiarity with policing culture and norms, so the officers' frame of reference is understood. It would be better if the service providers had an idea of what ICE investigations involve (Burns et al., 2008). Perez and colleagues (2010) suggested implementing training for officers, supervisors, and members of the social support system. Training cantered on developing prosocial coping skills should be offered to ICE investigators. Supervisors need to be taught how to recognize signs of distress so they may intervene appropriately. Members of officers' social support system may need to be educated on what exactly their loved ones do and have to deal with so officers can feel comfortable approaching them when they need support.

In sum, officers assigned to ICE cases face the possibility of experiencing vicarious trauma. The perception that cybercrime investigation is not real police work makes coping with the potential stress, burnout, and secondary trauma all the more difficult, as officers cannot rely on the traditional mode of commiserating with colleagues. Even in non-ICE cases, cybercrime investigators often work outside of the traditional role of law enforcer. Given the other issues dealing with cybercrime that we have discussed, officers responding to cybercrime face many challenges; nevertheless, several innovative strategies have been adopted to improve efficacy with regard to cybercrime. We discuss those next.

Response strategies

Despite the problems that police face in responding to cybercrime, the law enforcement field as a whole has been successful with various strategies. The establishment of a task force devoted to extending the abilities of one agency to others is one such strategy. In the United States, the USA PATRIOT Act of 2001 established 35 national Electronic Crime Task Forces (ECTFs). The ECTFs bring together local, state, and federal law enforcement agencies along with prosecutors, private-sector companies, and academics to investigate cyber-attacks on financial and critical infrastructures. International investigations are typically handled by federal agencies, and domestic crimes are worked collaboratively with state and local agencies. Ultimately, ECTFs attempt to address cybercrimes using the strengths of the individual agencies to the best effect (PERF, 2014).

Working with the private sector is critical for accurate intelligence-based investigations. Information sharing allows for offender and victimization patterns to be recognized. Victimization is not restricted geographically, and most cyber-attacks are not isolated incidents. For example, attacks on one financial institution could very easily be replicated on another by the same offender or offenders. Without sharing intelligence, an actor may not be identified as connected to multiple crimes. Much of this information is controlled and identified by private-sector companies. Relationships developed though ECTFs allow for mutual benefits in both the investigative and prevention efforts.

ECTFs are useful for cybercrimes that fall under the purview of financial and critical infrastructure, and other similar task forces exist for other cyber-crimes (e.g. Internet Crimes Against Children Task Force). However, some cybercrimes are investigated solely by local law enforcement agencies, many of which are struggling to address and respond to those calls. Chief Douglas Middleton explains,

> [F]ederal agencies have done a lot to help us deal with our cybercrime issues, but I still see a gap in how we're going to handle the cases that are the responsibility of local agencies. My officers are the ones with their boots on the ground, responding to the calls for service. When they answer a call and someone wants to file a complaint about being the victim of a cybercrime, we take the report and do our best to resolve it, but we aren't responding as well as we should be to those complaints.
>
> (PERF, 2014, p. 18–19)

One method agencies have used to address local complaints is the establishment of specialized cybercrime units. These units can be implemented at the local level, allowing agencies to investigate cybercrime in-house. Members of these units are specifically trained, possibly including digital forensic professionals. The number of cybercrime units have tripled between 2000 and 2013. However, this still only accounts for 27.5% of agencies nationally in the United States. Agencies instating cybercrime units tend to be larger, more technologically inclined, and have other specialized units as well (Willits & Nowacki, 2016). In other words, these agencies have the resources available to fund such initiatives. Additionally, large municipalities have more suitable targets such as banking and finance firms, large hospitals, or government agencies. Large-scale investigations need more specialized resources. It is no surprise that state agencies also reported operating a large number of cybercrime units (Willits & Nowacki, 2016). These agencies not only investigate crimes within their specific purview but also act as a resource for agencies who lack the expertise or tools to investigate cybercrime.

ECTFs and specialized units have been useful organizational responses to the growing cybercrime problem. These enterprises are typically done within the law enforcement community, multiplying the capabilities of units with resources to less able organizations. Although somewhat successful, much of the technical capabilities to address cybercrime lies outside of the law enforcement industry. A collaboration between law enforcement, businesses, and the technology sector would seem to be a prudent avenue to explore. In the next section, we discuss some of those public–private partnerships (PPPs).

Public–private partnerships

Policing serves two primary goals: investigation of crimes and the regulation and enforcement of behaviour (Avina, 2011). Unfortunately, the complexity and diversity of information and communication technology (ICT) lead to an uncertain and unstable environment for policing cybercrime. Police may lack the technical know-how or resources to deal with ICT. Wall (2007) called for collaboration between the police and the private sector to legitimize their role in cyber-security and crime prevention. The 2013 Cybersecurity Strategy of the European Union reads, "the private sector owns and operates significant parts of cyberspace, and so any initiative aiming to be successful in their area has to recognize its leading role" (p. 2). PPPs can address these challenges in a way that is beneficial to all stakeholders (Christensen & Petersen, 2017). Simply defined, PPPs are collaborative relationships between public-sector organizations (e.g. law enforcement, governmental agencies) and private-sector entities (e.g. equipment manufacturers, software developers, Internet service providers) for the purpose of achieving a mutual goal (Leppänen, Kiravuo, & Kajantie, 2016).

Leppänen and colleagues (2016) analysed the loose PPP network that included the Computer Emergency Response Team (CERT) of the Finnish Communications Regulatory Authority (FICORA), the police, and private companies. Criminal investigations were handled by the police, who requested evidence collected by CERT through a court order. Communication, however, was not automatic within the Finnish legal structure. Although successful PPPs should result in a long-term commitment, Leppänen and colleagues (2016) found the cooperation between the public and private sectors was not continuous: the majority of these relationships were established and activated ad hoc.

Developing PPPs can be difficult for policing entities that are unfamiliar with ICT industries. They may not know how to approach the issue in a way that encourages "buy-in" from organizations whose priorities differ (Avina,

2011; Hodge & Greve, 2007). Although there is supposed to be a mutual benefit between these groups, PPPs face challenges when a lack of trust and goal discontinuity between public and private partners do not allow for clear communication. Legal constraints may result in pertinent information being withheld. Additionally, private organizations are businesses; profits and finances are priorities in ways that are not important to public-sector agencies (Bures, 2017). Even though the importance of the private sector was acknowledged in the 2013 Cybersecurity Strategy of the European Union, concerns regarding prioritization of security over finances were also addressed:

> A high level of security can only be ensured if all in the value chain ... make security a priority. It seems however that many players still regard security as little more than an additional burden and there is limited demand for security solutions.
>
> (p. 12)

Christensen and Petersen (2017) acknowledge that this argument may have merit; however, they posit that changes in corporate risk management ideologies are shifting businesses away from the consideration of economic interests to reputational risk. This shift may align well with public interests which, along with loyalty (patriotic, professional, or personal), may strengthen PPPs.

The European Union has debated the possibility of adopting legislation that would mandate the sharing of information from private entities to policing and governmental agencies, fundamentally forcing private organizations into PPPs. Detractors claim this undermines the very foundation of PPPs, which are characterized as voluntary relationships (Bures, 2017). Many PPP relationships are already perceived as asymmetric, with the private partner shouldering the majority of the burden (Pinguelo, Lee, & Muller, 2012; Tropina & Callanan, 2015). Attempting to mandate cooperation from private organizations will likely meet resistance, even if it is for the greater good.

Issues in policing cybercrime

One of the first obstacles faced in policing cybercrime is the question of jurisdiction. Who is responsible for the investigation? As already addressed earlier in the chapter, many officers believe the majority of cyber-investigations should be referred to specialized units at the state or federal level. Additionally, it is common for victims and offenders to be separated geographically, causing jurisdictional issues (Brenner, 2006). According to data from ten states reported to the Internet Crime Complaint Center in 2010, victims and offenders were located in the same state in 20% to 35% of Internet-based fraud cases. Although such cases are not as complicated jurisdictionally, this does mean multiple agencies could be responsible for each case. Initial investigations are likely to be based where the offence was reported, but completion of these investigations requires cooperation between agencies. Dealing with international investigations creates additional complications, especially regarding legal or technical constraints.

Even when jurisdiction is clearly defined, investigators still face the challenge of accessing evidential data controlled by Internet service providers and other corporations. With public concerns over the privacy of their data, businesses do not want to be seen as too cooperative with government agencies, especially in cases that could have major implications for customer privacy. For example, following the 2015 San Bernardino terrorist attack, the FBI obtained a court order to force Apple, Inc., to develop software that could bypass iPhone security features that allow only ten attempts to crack the passcode lock before wiping data from a device. Apple, Inc., refused over larger user privacy concerns. The resulting court case was dropped when a third party developed the capability to crack the iPhone's security (Tanfani, 2018).

Another series of high-profile cases stirred debate about data storage. In particular, in the case of *Microsoft Corp. v. United States*, Microsoft argued that data stored on a server in Ireland could not be subject to a warrant issued under the Stored Communications Act (SCA), as it only applied domestically. Arguments were heard by the Supreme Court in February 2018. However, before a decision could be rendered, the Clarifying Lawful Overseas Use of Data Act was passed by Congress, rendering the Supreme Court Case moot. As of March 2018, federal law enforcement agencies can subpoena data from U.S. technology companies even if the data are stored overseas (Nakashima, 2018).

Before a crime can be investigated, it must be reported. Under-reporting, as stated earlier, is a huge concern when addressing the problem of cybercrime. Questions regarding jurisdiction over cybercrime can also lead to confusion for victims, who may not know who to contact (Bossler & Holt, 2012). In 2014, the Australian Cybercrime Online Reporting Network (ACORN) website was implemented to serve as a central hub for victims to report cybercrime, as well as provide information to the public regarding cyber-threats. It was intended to make reporting cybercrime easy and convenient. ACORN operates in a manner similar to the IC3 in the United States. Information reported through the system, which is maintained by the Australian Criminal Intelligence Commission, is then disseminated to state and territory policing agencies.

An evaluation of the system was completed in 2016, finding it had largely failed to meet its goals: it did not appear to have any significant effect on reporting rates nor public awareness of cybercrime. In fact, only 14% of citizen respondents surveyed were even aware of ACORN's existence (Australian Institute of Criminology, 2016). The low reporting rates make sense under this lens. Victims are not going to report to these systems if their existence is not common knowledge. To be successful, any new reporting initiative should therefore advertise its services.

Many cases were never investigated even when victimization was reported through ACORN (AIC, 2016). Like the IC3 system, there is no guarantee that a complaint will be investigated by any agency. The role of the reporting system is to collect the information and then forward it to the relevant agencies. It is up to those agencies to follow up. It is not unusual for reports to "go into a black hole" (Nott, 2018, n.p.). One possible explanation for the discrepancy with ACORN is incompatibility of the ACORN system and those used by local agencies. ACORN (and potentially IC3) may collect data, but its utility for investigators may be limited. In August 2018, the Australian government announced its plans to phase out ACORN, utilizing a new platform operated by the Australian Cyber Security Centre (Nott, 2018). Hopefully, the findings from the 2016 evaluation of ACORN were considered when designing the new system. Improved functionality and public relations will be key in creating a successful system. Future evaluations may be fruitful in the development of best practices.

Even successful takedown operations lose effectiveness over time. *Operation Onymous* targeted the drug cryptomarkets Cloud-Nine, Hydra, and SR2. The operation initially had a deterrent effect on fellow crypto markets Angora and Evolution, whose number of dealers dropped in the time frame immediately following *Onymous*. However, the number of dealers recovered to pre-operation levels within a month. Additionally, consumption numbers were double the pre-operation amount (Décary-Hétu & Giommoni, 2017). In another example, Armenian police successfully arrested and sentenced the hacker in control of the Bredolab botnet; however, the botnet was operational within two days, as it was taken over by other hackers based out of Russian servers. The malicious software was already present in millions of victims' computers. Without removing the botnet infrastructure, there is no way to prevent further problems (Dupont, 2017). The Coreflood takedown of 2011 managed to do just that. Following court approval, the U.S. Department of Justice set up a server to communicate with compromised systems. The machines were directed to uninstall the botnet software, resulting in the cleaning of 95% of infected systems (Dupont, 2017).

As technology used in crime becomes more sophisticated, so, too, do the tools available to law enforcement. However, agencies need to consider the legal and ethical implications of the application of these tools. Unfortunately, statutory law is slow to change, allowing for legal loopholes that tempt offenders and law enforcement alike (Chan, 2001). This issue is not new; the need for updated cybercrime legislation was identified in a National Institute of Justice study from 1998 (Stambaugh et al., 2001).

The 2018 Supreme Court decision in *Carpenter v. the United States* is a good example of how investigative decisions and tactics made using technology may be subject to legal challenge. The case involved cell-site location information (CSLI) of robbery suspects obtained by police through the wireless carriers in pursuant of a court order under the SCA rather than utilizing a search warrant. The defence argued that CSLI should have been protected by the U.S. Constitution's Fourth Amendment, specifically an individual's reasonable expectation of privacy. A warrant therefore should have been used to acquire the data. The defence further argued the court order required a lesser standard of 'reasonable grounds' rather than a standard of 'probable cause' required by a search warrant. In a 5–4 ruling, the Supreme Court agreed. Even though the evidence was proof that Carpenter was present at the robberies, the data were improperly obtained and should not have been used against him. Although this case was not associated with cybercrime or digital investigation, it did involve the use of emerging technology in a police investigation. Cybercrime investigations occur in an environment that is underregulated. Officers have to make decisions that could be challenged, so it is in their best interest to proceed with caution and get legal advice before proceeding.

Some countries address the grey area in cybercrime investigations through statutory law that would protect the use of technology in criminal investigations. In 2013, the Dutch government proposed the Computer Crime Act III, allowing criminal investigators to hack into computers, install spyware, and destroy or disable access to data. The controversial legislation has been criticized for infringing on the right to privacy as well as other human rights. Pool and Custers (2017), reviewed the proposed legislation through the lens of the European Convention of Human Rights (ECHR). Article 8 of the ECHR lays out the requirements for interfering with the right to privacy, specifically citing that the interference occurs in accordance with the law, it has a legitimate aim, and it is necessity in a democratic society. Although Pool and Custers (2017) agreed the first two criteria were met, they believed that the effectiveness of the legislation was questionable and the benefits did not outweigh the risk of abuse.

Future of law enforcement and cybercrime

Cybercrime is increasing in prevalence and expanding in scope; local law enforcement must take up this growing problem. As we move into the future, it is important to acknowledge and address policing deficiencies in this area. First and foremost, law enforcement agencies need to invest in cyber-investigation training for line officers. Agencies must train officers to safeguard the evidentiary integrity of a digital crime scene because digital evidence can be incredibly volatile. Line officers need to have enough knowledge of cybercrime and digital forensics to ensure that valuable evidence is not lost, while still being able to make educated judgement calls if normal procedures are not feasible (e.g. the circumstances under which a computer should be shut down before a digital forensics expert is available). Some common issues may not require a full investigation, but if an officer lacks digital competency, they may miss important information when responding to calls for service, or lose important evidence.

Research in this area has resulted in several recommendations for agencies to expand the training for officers and recruitment of subject matter experts. Reform, an independent think tank from the United Kingdom, advocated for the establishment of a digital academy capable of training 1,700 cyber-specialists a year with a goal of 12,000 specialists working in the UK (Evenstad, 2017). In her recommendations for Indiana law enforcement, Cummins Flory (2016) called for the inclusion of a training module on digital evidence collection and identification in the police academy. This would ensure all officers have at least a foundational knowledge of cybercrime investigation.

Cummins Flory (2016) also recommended offering additional advanced courses at the academies, giving interested officers an opportunity to increase their expertise. If localized training is not feasible, the National Computer Forensics Institute (NCFI), operated through the U.S. Secret Service, has offered training to local and state officers since 2008. As of 2014, over 3,000 officers had received training at NCFI. An officer may be able to explain their investigation in court, but if neither the prosecution nor the presiding judge understands the fundamentals, the officer's testimony may not be particularly helpful. As a result, NCFI has also expanded their training to include prosecutors and judges (PERF, 2014). For officers who choose to pursue an education through private sources, a number of certification and degree programmes specializing in cybercrime and digital forensics are available through universities and certifying organizations. Although training is the priority for the future of policing cybercrime, agencies need to ensure standard operating procedures are consistent across training curriculum and are appropriate for their local laws (Cummins Flory, 2016). There are many other such training initiatives across the globe; academic standards for cybercrime training would be a useful policy to implement.

Because cybercrime affects more than just law enforcement, agencies must partner with businesses to better respond to and investigate cybercrime. Interestingly, several large banking corporations have actually applied lessons from law enforcement in their own cybercrime response plans. Cyber-fusion centres, based on anti-terrorism fusion centres, serve as a hub for banking institutions to track and prevent cyber-attacks while sharing information with affiliated businesses. One such fusion centre also conducts training scenarios. The 2017 iteration of the biennial exercise Quantum Dawn brought together 900 participants from banks, banking regulators, and law enforcement to role play responses to a major malware infection. By practicing responses with all stakeholders, including law enforcement, it is the hope of these organizations to come up with feasible plans of action in advance rather than if and when something actually occurs (Cowley, 2018). The after-action reports from the exercise are available to the public online.

One of Reform's recommendations to the Home Office was to increase recruitment for cyber-volunteers. In the UK, volunteer constables are part-time and unpaid, though they still retain full legal powers of their full-time counterparts. These individuals hold regular jobs, assisting and supplementing local constabularies as needed. To recruit volunteers with cyber-specialization, Reform appeals to civic-mindedness through requests for assistance with specific projects. Some may volunteer because of their distaste for a particular type of crime; others may just enjoy the challenge (Evensted, 2017).

PERF agrees with Reform in that agencies should actively recruit technologically inclined candidates, though with the goal of hiring them as full-time officers. The difficulty is retaining these individuals. Officers with advanced technical skills often leave law enforcement for more lucrative job opportunities in the private sector. However, they argued that this high turnover may not be as large of a concern as it seems. The digital world is quick to change, so training must be constantly updated. The officer leaving may have outdated knowledge, so it may be in the best interest of the agency to hire someone with more up-to-date skills. The training would have to happen in either situation, so the loss is minimal (PERF, 2014).

Up to this point, most policing of cybercrime has been reactive. However, proactive approaches are easy to implement. Although some cybercrimes affect victims without needing user interaction, crimes such as fraud, phishing, malware, or grooming require the victim to engage with the offender or a malicious application or code. Community education programmes and outreach are key in training potential victims to recognize red flags and prevent unsafe online behaviour. For example, teaching individuals that emails beginning with "Dear customer" instead of including their name should not be trusted is a simple way to prevent malware or phishing scams. Considering the difficulty of regaining financial losses from these types of crimes, it is infinitely preferable to avoid victimization all together.

The Madison Area Council on Cyber Safety for Children is an example of a strong community education partnership. Created in 2011, the Madison Police Department in Wisconsin partnered with local businesses, health organizations, and schools to expand upon cyber-safety initiatives already in practice. One of the key takeaways from the Madison model of community education that stands apart from other similar programmes is its constant development. At their Youth Cyber Detective Camp, officers work with youth on case studies of cyber-bullying and teen suicide. Rather than just disseminating information to the participants, the youth are encouraged to teach the officers about social media applications they currently use and how they may apply to the issues discussed. Officers allow themselves to be trained by the children about technology they may not have encountered up to this point and are able to implement this new information immediately, expanding the safety training to include information relevant to their audience. A DVD produced early in the programme is being updated and integrated into a phone app (PERF, 2014). Community education programmes must be updated frequently to ensure they remain effective.

Conclusion

In this chapter we discussed the growing prevalence of cybercrime and its potential impact on policing. Although the data to examine the police response to cybercrime are meagre, available research suggests police officers and administrators are beginning to see the need for a reasoned response to the problem. Surveys of officers are showing a healthy respect for the problems cybercrime presents to society, though they still may not see it as falling under their main mission of safety and traditional law enforcement. In addition, the growth in specialized cybercrime units suggests an operational response to the problem, but these typically only address Internet crimes against children and not the wider problem of fraud, intrusion, or identity theft.

We would expect that as cybercrime continues to embed in almost every aspect of our social, financial, and workday lives, the police will need to become involved. Recommending a way forward becomes problematic when we lack basic data on the prevalence and response to cybercrime incidents. Although in the United States, the National Incident-Based Reporting System (NIBRS) data do capture information on computer-related crimes, currently data collection is crude for understanding the various facets of the offence, offender, victims, and police response. The FBI's IC3 provides specific information about cybercrime, but the scope of the dark figure of cybercrime remains unknown. Improving the data collection on cybercrime incidents and the law enforcement response is paramount in being able to recommend positive changes to the current system.

The research on police officers' and investigators' perceptions of cybercrime has been useful to understand how any proposed changes might be accepted by the current policing culture. The results suggest there is much work to be done on educating officers and administrators about the need for a complete response from line officers – from responding to calls for service to linking with digital evidence handlers and prosecutors. Part of this education is technical: they need the expertise to detect that a cybercrime has happened, collect the digital evidence, and convey the details of the criminal event in a report. Another important aspect is understanding the limitations of jurisdiction and the nature of cybercrime that might affect making and arrest and putting a case forward difficult. Also, educating officers about the harm victims face would seem to be an important element to any policy recommendation. Like white-collar crime, cybercrime victims often take actions that facilitate their own losses. This can cause responding law enforcement agents to be unsympathetic, thus limiting the response.

We also need to understand how organizations respond to cybercrime. For traditional policing, we know how agency attributes and policies affect the efficacy of crime reduction and community–police relations. For example, the utility of preventative patrols (foot or vehicle) has been well studied. Efforts to understand and improve how the police patrol neighbourhoods has been proffered, evaluated, re-tooled, and further evaluated. This has led to a change in the way police departments deploy officers, especially in crime hot-spots. Given the nature of cybercrime, however, a spatial/temporal response would seem unfeasible. Nevertheless, by understanding the nature of the cybercrime problem and then evaluating how the police respond, we can begin to formulate effective policies that should, at the very least, improve how the police relate to cybercrime victims.

A useful tool to employ in the policing response to cybercrime is the SARA method from the problem-solving policing paradigm (Eck & Spelman, 1987). SARA stands for scanning, analysis, response, and assessment. Ideally, police officers tasked with reducing crime in a particular area will scan for root causes of a problem. For example, an officer might examine the distribution of calls for service in a neighbourhood and discover an increase in thefts from vehicles during the late afternoon. Analysing the problem, a typical response might include increased patrols, but the root cause of the problem might come from somewhere else, such as a neighbouring community high school that dismisses a large number of students around the same time as the thefts. Rather than simply increasing patrols, the officer might coordinate with the school to stagger the release of students walking home or have officers monitor students as they leave school. Once a plan has been enacted, the officer then assesses whether the response reduced car thefts following its implementation and whether it resulted in any unanticipated consequences such as crime displacement.

For cybercrime, the SARA method would be useful to detect patterns in identity theft complaints within the community, say among elderly citizens. Partnering with banks and other financial institutions, the officer's response might include a door-to-door educational campaign to alert potential victims. The officers could provide information about how to respond to victimization and who to contact at their banks to add digital security measures. Then assessing the impact, the officer would track the change in reported identity theft and adjust the response accordingly. In sum, the SARA method seems particularly useful for a cybercrime response because the root causes may be quite disparate and uncoordinated in a local community; however, by focusing on the victimology, the police may be able to help alleviate the problem. Interested readers should consult the U.S.-based Center for Problem Solving Policing (n.d.) for more information about SARA and its implementation.

The SARA method also offers another useful avenue to address cybercrime and its root causes, namely technology. The analysis stage of SARA might suggest a particular technology – for example, credit card skimmers – has become a major cause of theft in a jurisdiction. At the response stage, the police could partner with various interested stakeholders (public and private) to devise a technical solution, for example, gas stations and banks where skimmers are commonly placed, computer engineers, and ethical hackers. The partnership could devise some type of digital detection for skimmers, crime prevention through environmental design, or improved surveillance of card accounts of persons known to live in skimmer hot-spots. If successful, the response and assessment could be disseminated to other agencies and through the cybersecurity industry.

The challenges cybercrime poses to law enforcement will only continue to escalate in the foreseeable future. Without any reasonable ability to track the prevalence and changes in cybercrime trends, criminologists and policing officials will be unlikely to formulate a cogent response. In this chapter, we highlight some of the current and important research on the subject. Although it is common to make a self-serving call for more research, in this particular area that call is past due.

References

Anderson, R., Barton, C., Böhme, R., Clayton, R., van Eeten, M. J. G., Levi, M., . . . Stefan, S. (2013). Measuring the cost of cybercrime. In R. Boehme (Ed.), *The economics of information security and privacy* (pp. 265–300). Berlin: Springer.

Australian Institute of Criminology. (2016). *Evaluation of the Australian Cybercrime Online Reporting Network*. Australian Institute of Criminology. Retrieved from https://eprints. qut.edu.au/121532/1/acorn_evaluation_report_%281%29.pdf.

Avina, J. (2011). Public-private partnerships in the fight against crime : An emerging frontier in corporate social responsibility. *Journal of Financial Crime, 18*(3), 282–291.

Bossler, A. M., & Holt, T. J. (2012). Patrol officers' perceived role in responding to cybercrime. *Policing: An International Journal of Police Strategies & Management, 35*, 165–181.

Bourke, M. L., & Craun, S. W. (2014). Secondary traumatic stress among internet crimes against children task force personnel: Impact, risk factors, and coping strategies. *Sexual Abuse: A Journal of Research and Treatment, 26*(6), 586–609.

Brenner, S. W. (2006). Cybercrime jurisdiction. *Crime, Law and Social Change, 46*, 189–206.

Broll, R., & Huey, L. (2015). 'Just being mean to somebody isn't a police matter:' Police perspectives on policing cyberbullying. *Journal of School Violence, 14*, 155–176.

Bures, O. (2017). Contributions of private businesses to the provision of security in the EU: Beyond public-private partnerships. *Crime, Law and Social Change, 67*(3), 289–312.

Burns, C. M., Morley, J., Bradshaw, R., & Domene, J. (2008). The emotional impact on and coping strategies employed by police teams investigating Internet child exploitation. *Traumatology, 14*, 20–31.

Carpenter v. the United States, 585 U.S. (2018).

Center for Problem Solving Policing. (n.d.). Retrieved from https://popcenter.asu.edu/

Chan, J. (2001). The technological game: How information technology is transforming police practice. *Criminology and Criminal Justice, 1*, 139–159.

Christensen, K. K., & Petersen, K. L. (2017). Public – private partnerships on cyber security: A practice of loyalty. *International Affairs, 93*(6), 1435–1452.

Cowley, S. (2018, May 20). Banks adopt military-style tactics to fight cybercrime. *The New York Times*. Retrieved from www.nytimes.com/2018/05/20/business/banks-cyber-security-military.html?partner=applenews&ad-keywords=APPLEMOBILE&region=written_through&asset_id=100000005907680

Cross, C., Richards, K., & Smith, R. G. (2016). The reporting experiences and support needs of victims of online fraud. *Trends & Issues in Crime and Criminal Justice*, (518), 1–14.

Cummins Flory, T. A. (2016). Digital forensics in law enforcement: A needs based analysis of Indiana agencies. *Journal of Digital Forensics, Security & Law, 11*, 7–37.

Décary-Hétu, D., & Giommoni, L. (2017). Do police crackdowns disrupt drug cryptomarkets? A longitudinal analysis of the effects of Operation Onymous. *Crime, Law and Social Change, 67*(1), 55–75.

Dupont, B. (2017). Bots, cops, and corporations: On the limits of enforcement and the promise of polycentric regulation as a way to control large-scale cybercrime. *Crime, Law and Social Change, 67*(1), 97–116.

Eck, J. E., & Spelman, W. (1987). *Problem solving: Problem-orientation policing in Newport News*. National Institute of Justice and Police Executive Research Forum, US Department of Justice, Office of Justice Programs,

European Union. (2013). *Joint communication on the cybersecurity strategy of the European Union: An open, safe and secure cyberspace* (JOIN(2013) 1 final). Retrieved from http://eeas.europa. eu/policies/eu-cyber-security/cybsec_comm_en.pdf

Evenstad, L. (2017, August 24). Policing revamp needed to tackle rise of digital crime, says Reform report. *Computer Weekly*. Retrieved from www.computerweekly.com/news/450425095/Policing-revamp-needed-to-tackle-rise-of-digital-crime-says-Reform-report

Federal Bureau of Investigation (FBI). (2017). *Internet crime complaint center: 2017 Internet crime report*. Retrieved from https://pdf.ic3.gov/2017_IC3Report.pdf

Florencio, D., & Herley, C. (2013). Sex, lies and cyber-crime surveys. In B. Schneier (Ed.), *Economics of information security and privacy III* (pp. 35–53). New York, NY: Springer.

Hinduja, S. (2004). Perceptions of local and state law enforcement concerning the role of computer crime investigative teams. *Policing: An International Journal of Police Strategies and Management, 3*, 341–357.

Hodge, G. A., & Greve, C. (2007). Public – private partnerships: An international performance review. *Public Administration Review, 67*(3), 545–558.

Holt, T. J., Blevins, K. R., & Burruss, G. W. (2012). Examining the stress, satisfaction, and experiences of computer crime examiners. *Journal of Crime and Justice, 35*, 35–52.

Holt, T. J., & Bossler, A. M. (2011). Police perceptions of computer crimes in two Southeastern cities: An examination from the viewpoint of patrol officers. *American Journal of Criminal Justice, 37*, 396–412.

Huff, R., Desilets, C., & Kane, J. (2010). *National public survey on white collar crime*. Fairmont, VA: National White Collar Crime Center.

Hyman, P. (2013). Cybercrime: It's serious, but exactly how serious? *Communications of the ACM, 56*(3), 18–20.

Krause, M. (2009). Identifying and managing stress in child pornography and child exploitation investigators. *Journal of Police and Criminal Psychology, 24*, 22–29.

Leppänen, A., Kiravuo, T., & Kajantie, S. (2016). Policing the cyber-physical space. *The Police Journal: Theory, Practice and Principles, 89*(4), 290–310.

Levi, M. (2017). Assessing the trends, scale and nature of economic cybercrimes: Overview and issues. *Crime, Law and Social Change, 67*(1), 3–20.

Microsoft Corp. v. United States, 585 U.S. (2018).

Nakashima, E. (2018, March 31). Justice Department asks Supreme Court to moot Microsoft email case, citing new law. *Washington Post*. Retrieved from www.washingtonpost.com/world/national-security/justice-department-asks-supreme-court-to-moot-microsoft-email-case-citing-new-law/2018/03/31/e3c46e60–34f6–11e8–8bdd-cdb33a5eef83_story.html?noredirect=on&utm_term=.9e0cccf086ef

Nott, G. (2018, September 5). 'Revolutionary' cybercrime reporting site ACORN a flop finds internal report. *CIO*. Retrieved from www.cio.com.au/article/646246/revolutionary-cybercrime-reporting-site-acorn-flop-finds-internal-report/

Perez, L. M., Jones, J., Engler, D. R., & Sachau, D. (2010). Secondary traumatic stress and burnout among law enforcement investigators exposed to disturbing media images. *Journal of Police and Criminal Psychology, 25*, 113–124.

Pinguelo, F. M., Lee, W., & Muller, B. W. (2012). Virtual crimes, real damages part II: What businesses can do today to protect themselves from cybercrime, and what public-private partnerships are attempting to achieve for the nation of tomorrow. *Virginia Journal of Law & Technology*, (1), 75–87.

Police Executive Research Forum. (2014). The role of local law enforcement agencies in preventing and investigating cybercrime.

Pool, R. L. D., & Custers, B. H. M. (2017). The police hack back: Legitimacy, necessity, and privacy implications of the next step in fighting cybercrime. *European Journal of Crime, Criminal Law & Criminal Justice, 25*, 123–144.

Senjo, S. R. (2004). An analysis of computer-related crime: Comparing police officer perceptions with empirical data. *Security Journal*, *17*, 55–71.

Stambaugh, H., Beuapre, D., Icove, D. J., Baker, R., Cassaday, W., & Williams, W. P. (2001). *Electronic crime needs assessment for state and local law enforcement: Research report.* Washington, DC: National Institute of Justice, US Department of Justice, Office of Justice Programs, National Institute of Justice.

Tanfani, J. (2018, March 27). Race to unlock San Bernardino shooter's iPhone was delayed by poor FBI communication, report finds. *Los Angeles Times*. Retrieved from www.latimes.com/politics/la-na-pol-fbi-iphone-san-bernardino-20180327-story.html

Tropina, T., & Callanan, C. (2015). *Self-and co-regulation in cybercrime, cybersecurity and national security*. Heidelberg: Springer.

United States Attorney's Office. (2015). Financial fraud crime victims. Retrieved from www.justice.gov/usao-wdwa/victim-witness/victim-info/financial-fraud

van de Weijer, S. G. A., Leukfeldt, R., & Bernasco, W. (2018). Determinants of reporting cybercrime: A comparison between identity theft, consumer fraud, and hacking. *European Journal of Criminology*, 1–23.

Wall, D. S. (1998). *The Chief Constables of England and Wales: The socio-legal history of a criminal justice elite*. Aldershot: Dartmouth.

Wall, D. S. (2007). Policing cybercrimes: Situating the public police in networks of security within cyberspace. *Police Practice and Research: An International Journal*, *8*(2), 183–205.

Willits, D., & Nowacki, J. (2016). The use of specialized cybercrime policing units: An organizational analysis. *Criminal Justice Studies: A Critical Journal of Crime, Law and Society*, *29*, 105–124.

16 Responding to individual fraud
Perspectives of the fraud justice network

Cassandra Cross

Introduction

> *I don't think these organisations are set up to catch anybody. We contacted five or six organisations and I don't understand who is responsible to pursue them [offenders].*
> *I don't know, where do other people go to report it [fraud]? I mean it was made pretty clear to me that there weren't many places that were actually interested in your story anyway.*
> — *(fraud victim quotes taken from Cross Richards, & Smith, 2016a, p. 43)*

Fraud victimization is an increasingly prevalent issue globally. Each year, millions of individuals are victims of fraud, which can cause devastating harm across both financial and non-financial aspects of their life (Button, McNaughton Nicolls, Kerr, & Owen, 2014; Deem, 2000; Ganzini, Bentson, McFarland, & Cutler, 1990; Kerr, Owen, McNaughton-Nicolls, & Button, 2013; Marsh, 2004; Ross & Smith, 2011). Reports indicate that billions of dollars are lost to fraud across many countries and that this is on the increase (ACCC, 2018; CAFC, 2015; IC3, 2015; ONS, 2016).

Consequently, many of these victims will attempt to report their victimization to agencies within the criminal justice system, as well as an array of other relevant agencies. Fraud is unique, in that it is not simply the police who can take a complaint. Rather, there are many organizations to which victims can legitimately report their incident. To recognize this, Button, Lewis, and Tapley (2013) term the phrase 'fraud justice network' (FJN) to illustrate the multitude of potentially relevant agencies across areas such as law enforcement, finance, banks, consumer protection, government, and non-government agencies (to name a few) (Button et al., 2013). The complexity in attempting to navigate the FJN can leave victims overwhelmingly angry, frustrated, and disappointed with their response. This is clearly illustrated in the opening quotes taken from victims in an Australian study (Cross et al., 2016a). The concept of the FJN is returned to later in the chapter.

The literature highlights a large disparity between the expectations of what victims hope to achieve in their reporting of fraud, compared to the reality of what agencies can actually provide (Cross, 2018a). For many victims, this discrepancy is a source of additional trauma and suffering, which exacerbates that which they have already suffered at the hands of their offender (Button et al., 2009a, 2009b; Cross et al., 2016a). To date, existing research has solely focused on the victim perspective of reporting through the FJN and highlighted their largely negative experiences (Button et al., 2009a, 2009b; Cross et al., 2016a). However, there has been no research which has directly sought the perspectives of the organizations themselves in order to gain their perspectives on the issues and ways to improve the system.

This chapter contributes to this identified gap. It explores the perspectives of professionals across the FJN and their insights into the interactions of their organizations with fraud victims. As stated, there is no known research which has sought to document and understand the ideal outcomes of organizations when interacting with fraud victims and the challenges and barriers they face in seeking to achieve this. There has also not been any work that has asked organizations what they think victims want to determine if this is consistent with identified victim needs.

In order to achieve this, the chapter is divided into a number of sections. The first details the concepts relevant to this context through an examination of the FJN globally and also established research on the reporting of fraud and victim expectations. Second, the chapter outlines the methodology used to conduct the interviews that underpin this chapter. Third, the chapter details the insights provided by participants as to their ideal organizational outcomes when interacting with fraud victims, as well as what they believe are the ideal outcomes of the victim themselves. Consequently, the last section of this chapter uses this as a foundation to provide a critical analysis of the tension and disparity that exists from the organizational perspective.

Overall this chapter highlights that organizations have a solid understanding of victims needs and desires; however, their own ideal outcomes do not correspond to these. Rather, there is a tension between the reactive approaches anticipated by victims which are met with a largely proactive, future-driven response by organizations. The difference in timing and focus of these priorities is therefore exacerbating the difference in expectations held by victims and contributing to their overwhelmingly negative experiences with the FJN and large levels of dissatisfaction with their outcomes.

Defining (online) fraud

Definitions of fraud generally revolve around notions of deception, cheating, and lying. Fraud collectively involves offences of dishonesty (Smith, 2008), achieving a result through false pretences (Fletcher, 2007, p. 195). For example, the Collins Dictionary defines fraud as "the crime of gaining money or financial benefits by a trick or by lying," as well as "a fraud is something of someone that deceives people in a way that is illegal or dishonest." Fraud is not new; however, the evolution of technology has exponentially increased the ability for offenders to access and target potential victims globally (Yar, 2013). In this way, a large amount of fraud is now perpetrated through the Internet and other technological means.

Consequently, online fraud can be understood as the following:

> The experience of an individual who has responded through the use of the Internet to a dishonest invitation, request, notification or offer by providing personal information or money which has led to the suffering of a financial or non-financial loss of some kind.
>
> (Cross, Smith, & Richards, 2014, p. 1)

There are an endless number of "plotlines" used by offenders to target victims (Cross & Kelly, 2016). Additionally, offenders will use a variety of communication platforms to establish the trust necessary to defraud individuals. This includes (but is not limited to) email, telephone, text messages, chat/messenger services, and face-to-face interactions. In this way, there is a growing recognition of needing to break through and challenge "the binary of online/offline and real/virtual barriers" (Stratton, Powell, & Cameron, 2017, p. 22). Consequently, although a large amount of fraud referred to throughout this chapter has been perpetrated online, it is important to also acknowledge the complexity of many victimization experiences and the multitude of platforms used by offenders to gain their financial reward.

Reporting fraud

Compared to other categories of crime, fraud is known to have one of the lowest rates of reporting to police (Button et al., 2014; Copes, Kerley, Mason, & van Wyk, 2001; Van Wyk & Mason, 2001). There have been several studies globally that assert less than one-third of all fraud is reported to authorities (Mason & Benson, 1996; Schoepfer & Piquero, 2009; Smith, 2007, 2008; Titus, Heinzelmann, & Boyle, 1995). There are clear reasons for why victims of fraud choose not to report, which include not recognizing their own victimization, not being sure of whether an offence has occurred, a sense of shame and embarrassment about being a victim, a lack of knowledge about who to report the incident to, a sense of guilt and personal responsibility in their circumstances, and a belief that nothing can be done about it (Button et al., 2013; Kerley & Copes, 2002; Schoepfer & Piquero, 2009; Smith, 2008; United Nations, 2013).

In contrast, there is limited research which seeks to explore demographic characteristics between those who report and those who do not (Copes et al., 2001; Mason & Benson, 1996; Schoepfer & Piquero, 2009). In most cases, there is a lack of evidence to support any relationship (Van Wyk & Mason, 2001, p. 332). However, a few other studies have found factors such as education, social support, legal capital, and the seriousness of the offence to be relevant (Copes et al., 2001; Mason & Benson, 1996; Schoepfer & Piquero, 2009).

Further, there is limited research that attempts to document the reasons why victims *choose* to report, or at least attempt to report in the first place. Cross

(2018b) argues that victims report for two main reasons: the first is concerned with an individual notion of justice, and the second revolves around altruistic notions of protecting others. In both cases, victims expect to get some sort of action from the relevant agency, and a lack of action is perceived to be a failure from their perspective (Cross, 2018b).

For those who do attempt to report fraud, the difficulties and challenged associated with this are immense (Button et al., 2013; Cross, 2018b; Cross et al., 2016a). Although a large amount of dissatisfaction stems from the aforementioned issues surrounding the complexity and diversity of the FJN, there are also other factors at play. Critically, there is evidence of a large disparity between the expectations of victims in reporting fraud compared to the reality of the response they are likely to receive from authorities (Cross, 2018a). The inability of authorities to deliver on these expectations, despite their unrealistic nature, fuels a large amount of anger and frustration and overall leads to additional trauma and suffering on the part of the victim. A recent evaluation of the Australian Cybercrime Online Reporting Network (ACORN) supports this, with four out of five cybercrime victims (including fraud victims) expecting an investigation to arise from their report, but only one in six reports actually leading to the initiation of an investigation (Morgan, Dowling, Brown, Mann, Voce, & Smith, 2016). As a result, the evaluation found that more than three-quarters of individuals were dissatisfied with the *outcome* of their report (Morgan et al., 2016).

Despite evidence to indicate the unrealistic expectations of victims towards the FJN, Cross, Richards, & Smith (2016b) are clear in articulating the needs of victims, based on their interviews with 80 fraud victims in Australia (similar results were found in Button et al., 2009a, 2009b). They concluded that victims desire the following:

- To be listened to and treated with respect and dignity when reporting to authorities, rather than blamed for their victimization.
- To receive an acknowledgement that a crime has been committed against them.
- To have access to clear channels of reporting and be directed to appropriate agencies as quickly and simply as possible.
- To have access to agency staff who are trained in dealing with victims of fraud and who know how to handle cases appropriately.
- To be openly and honestly supported by friends and relatives
- To know what support services are available, how and where these can be accessed and at what cost.
- To have access to trained professional support that addresses not only the consequences of financial victimization but also the factors that precipitate such victimization such as relationship difficulties or addictions. (Cross et al., 2016b, p. 11)

The existing research provides a somewhat bleak picture as it relates to fraud, from the lack of reporting in the first place, to an overwhelmingly negative experience for those who do report or attempt to report through the FJN.

Therefore, it is imperative to better understand the organizational perspective of fraud victimization and what the ideal outcome is as it relates to the agency, as well as what organizations believe is important to victims. This can then be contrasted to what is known from victims to provide evidence of the areas that require improvement. Before detailing the findings from the professionals across the FJN, it is valuable to outline the methodology of the current project.

Methodology

This chapter details one part of a larger study examining ways to improve the response to fraud victims by the FJN. Thirty in-depth, semi-structured interviews were conducted with 31 fraud justice professionals across England and Canada in October and November 2017. The research was approved by Queensland University of Technology's Ethics Committee on 14 September 2017 (Approval number #1700000730).

Sampling and recruitment

A targeted and purposive sampling technique was employed to recruit participants for the current study. Given the strong existing networks of the author in both countries, direct email invitations were sent to relevant individuals outlining the purpose of the overall project and the details of participation. Respondents emailed the author directly to organize participation. Second, participants were also recruited through the suggestion of existing networks. Third, the author approached relevant organizations directly to ascertain the appropriate person to communicate with and to determine if they were interested in participation. The combination of these strategies resulted in a diverse sample of professionals across the FJN in both countries.

To be eligible for the current study, participants had to be aged 18 years or older, be capable of providing informed consent to participate in the project, and be currently employed within an organization across the FJN. Given the nature of employment of many of the participants and the organizations they are part of, both confidentiality and anonymity were assured. In this way, it was the personal perspectives of the participants that were sought, rather than the official position of any agency they worked for. As a result, participants were therefore willing to provide their frank and open insights into the issues at hand.

Data collection

The author travelled to England and Canada in October–November 2017 to conduct the interviews. The majority of the interviews ($n = 25$) were conducted in person, at either a workplace or a local coffee shop (depending on the preference of the participant). The remaining interviews ($n = 5$) were conducted over the telephone. This enabled greater participation from individuals who were physically located outside of both London and Toronto, as well as for convenience in other circumstances. Participants were each asked a range of questions regarding their perspectives on the ways that their organization interacts with fraud victims. A small number of demographic questions were also completed by the majority of participants. With permission, all interviews were digitally recorded.

Data analysis

All interviews were transcribed verbatim and imported into NVivo (version 11), which is a computer-assisted qualitative data analysis tool. Thematic coding was undertaken by the author around the questions contained in the interview schedule. This utilized a general inductive coding approach, where no predetermined themes were applied to the data. Rather, in reading the transcripts, categories were created based on what was read.

The current chapter explores responses to the following four questions:

1   From an organizational perspective, what is the ideal outcome for someone who has experienced fraud?
2   What (if any) are the barriers to achieving this?
3   What do you think the victims themselves want when dealing with your organization?
4   What (if any) are the barriers to achieving this?

Responses to these four questions were coded thematically to encompass the variety of ideas put forward. As will be illustrated, in several cases, the challenges to achieving the ideal outcome from both an organization and victim perspective overlapped significantly.

The participants

Thirty interviews were conducted with 31 participants (one interview comprised two participants). Twenty interviews were conducted in England and ten interviews were conducted in Canada. Of the participants, 25 were male and the remaining 6 were female. Of those who provided their age ($n = 24$), the average age was 47 years (min = 26 and max 62).

A diverse array of agencies across the FJN was represented. Twelve were from police agencies (including a mixture of both sworn and unsworn staff), five were from consumer protection agencies, four were from the financial sector, three were from a non-government agency, and two were from an advocacy organization. Further, there was one representative from a government agency, a not-for-profit, the private sector, victim support, and one agency that did not fit into any of the other descriptions. When asked about the number of years each had been in their current job, the average response was 11.6 years (min = less than 1 year, max = 39). When asked about the number of years each had been involved across the FJN, the average was 15.3 years (min = 3, max = 43).

Overall, the current sample provided a diverse range of insights from across the FJN. In addition, it is clear that there was a variety in the experience of participants. Although some were relatively new to the area, others brought with them many decades of experience and knowledge on the topic at hand.

Given that both anonymity and confidentiality were assured to participants in this project, direct quotes will be used throughout the remainder of the chapter to highlight individual perspectives, but only an interview number and a country will be provided.

A note on the 'fraud justice network'

As stated, compared to other offences, fraud is unique in that it can be reported to a multitude of agencies, including but not restricted to law enforcement. The term 'fraud justice network' is a concept advocated by Button et al. (2013) which encapsulates this characteristic and the large number of agencies who may be relevant to a case of fraud victimization. This obviously includes the criminal justice system, but can also extend to the civil system, other statutory systems, and private systems (Button et al., 2013, pp. 42–43). The term 'fraud justice network' is intended as an umbrella term to capture the variety of agencies legitimately involved in fraud and to highlight its complexity. It also seeks to demonstrate how the scope of an official response to fraud goes well beyond the police and the criminal justice system.

Victim trajectories for those who experience fraud can be fraught with difficulty and frustration as they attempt to navigate the complex FJN they are confronted with. For example, in their research of fraud victims, Button et al. (2013, p. 49) outline a detailed list of bodies that victims in the United Kingdom may approach to report fraud. This includes from the public sector: Action Fraud, the police, Serious Fraud Office, Consumer Direct, Location Authority Trading Standards, Financial Services Authority, Office of Fair Trading, and Companies Investigation Branch. From the private sector, it includes banks and other credit providers, Banksafeonline, CIFAS, credit reference agencies, and Crimestoppers. There are also advisory boards such as Citizens' Advice Bureau, Federation of Small Businesses, Fraud Advisory Panel, and Help the Aged/Aged Concern who may be relevant. Lastly, a number of online reporting mechanisms are available. Although extensive, this is still not an exhaustive list of agencies relevant to fraud in the UK and may also include the Charities Commission, telecommunications service providers, and others.

A similar situation is highlighted in Australia. Cross, Richards and Smith (2016a) in their research list the large number of organizations that victims of online fraud approached in an attempt to report an online fraud incident. This included (but was not limited to) law enforcement (state, federal – national – and international), banks (local and international), consumer protection agencies (state based and international), remittance agencies, the Australian Investments and Securities Commission (ASIC), mobile telecommunications and Internet service providers, trade bodies, consular services and embassies (both Australian and other international jurisdictions), private investigators, private solicitors and lawyers, website providers, dating agencies, ombudsmen (state and federal), civil and administrative tribunals, and politicians (at various levels) (Cross, 2018b, p. 555). There are also a number of online reporting mechanisms available to victims, which includes both Scamwatch (run by the Australian Competition and Consumer Commission) and ACORN (hosted by the Australian Criminal Intelligence Commission).

Although there is no research that documents the FJN in Canada or other countries, a similar situation arguably exists. Every country has a combination of police, financial institutions, consumer protection, government, non-government agencies, and private-sector organizations that are relevant to those experiencing fraud and who may be contacted by an individual seeking a response in the aftermath of their victimization.

Limitations

There are a number of limitations of the current study to be acknowledged. First, the sample is not intended to be a representative group of FJN professionals across either country. Although there is diversity in the sectors represented, the findings are not generalizable to the FJN more broadly.

Second, those interviewed were self-selecting, and many have been involved in fraud for a long time. In this way, their responses may be more favourable and attuned to victims compared to others across the FJN. This is particularly the case for police, whereby existing research clearly identifies levels of victims blaming and negative stereotypes (see Button et al., 2009a, 2009b; Cross et al., 2016a, 2016b). Having said that, the responses given by professionals contain much diversity in their thoughts, and as will be illustrated, are not synchronized with victim wants and needs.

Third, the insights provided by professionals were not triangulated with any other sources. Interviewees were taken at their word. This may reflect at times a disparity between what they believe is occurring compared to the lived realities of victims experiencing the FJN.

Fourth, approximately half of the interviewees were known to the author prior to this interview through previous work and interactions in the area of fraud. This may have influenced their responses to the questions posed. However, the other half of the respondents were recruited through cold calling/email or through suggestions and had no prior knowledge of, or communications with, the author.

It is also important to note that the views sought were those of the individuals themselves and not of the organization that they worked for/represent. Despite these limitations, it is believed that the data present some valuable insights into the interactions between victims and the FJN and highlight some important areas for reform and further consideration.

Perspectives from professionals across the fraud justice network

The following section presents some of the themes that were evident in participants' responses to the four questions posed earlier. Each perspective (organizational and victim) will be addressed separately.

Ideal outcomes from the organizational perspective

All participants were asked what they thought was the 'ideal outcome,' or what they were trying to achieve as it related to their organization interacting with an individual fraud victim. Despite the variety of sectors represented across the FJN, there were some consistent themes evident in the responses. These fell into four notable categories: assessing harm and protecting the victim, initiating action, helping the victim to move forward, and maintaining a positive image. Each of these will be detailed in turn.

Assessing harm and protecting the victim

One of the most prominent responses from FJN professionals ($n = 17$) focused on the need to assess the level of harm experienced by the victim and put in place measures to protect the victim. A few interviews spoke of the need to first establish what has happened prior to making any further decisions.

> *Well first of all as law enforcement you need to understand exactly what's happened. If they've reported a fraud to you, first of all you need to understand what type of fraud they're talking about, how it's happened and what they've lost.*
>
> *(Interview 16, UK)*

> *Obviously we want to clarify our details in order to be able to best address what has happened.*
>
> *(Interview 21, Canada)*

Unsurprisingly, a large focus was on the financial element of fraud and stopping the victim from sending more money in the immediate future. Often, despite reporting an offence, victims can still be involved in a fraudulent situation and at risk of sending further amounts of money.

> *There's a number of things we're trying to do – (a) we're trying to prevent any more losses, is the first thing.*
>
> *(Interview 6, UK)*

> *One of the problems is convincing them first of all that they've got to stop sending the money abroad because they're not going to win the money. So for us a positive outcome would be that they'd stop doing that.*
>
> *(Interview 9, UK)*

> *The ideal outcome is to stop them from sending any more money. To stop them from responding to the scams.*
>
> *(Interview 19, UK)*

The type of harm experienced by the victims was also recognized not simply as financial loss but also included physical threats. This is illustrated in the following.

> *First issue is to protect them [victim], because . . . they [are] themselves . . . [at] a physical risk . . . many of them are engaged closely with the criminals, they become embedded. So there are the physical issues. There's the economic risks, that they put themselves at risk by being drawn into it, not only their own but they've drawn other people into it.*
>
> (Interview 3, UK)

The need for protection was not just identified as the immediate threat, but also longer-term strategies to prevent future revictimization.

> *[It is important to] help them understand how to protect themselves in future.*
>
> (Interview 4, UK)

> *In this role, it isn't really the clean-up. It's more the making sure the bad thing doesn't happen second, third, fourth time around.*
>
> (Interview 8, UK)

> *We want to have the person protected from what we know will be follow-up scams.*
>
> (Interview 26, Canada)

The focus on prevention through education was important for several professionals, which included the need to explain to victims how they may have been targeted and defrauded. The aim of this information is arguably to strengthen their resilience to future approaches.

> *But the more they get their head around what the issues are and the threats that they're under, the safer they can become.*
>
> (Interview 7, UK)

> *Number two is to then educate them and to provide them with some – some knowledge about what scams are, how to identify them.*
>
> (Interview 19, UK)

> *So making sure that they're educated to recognise what frauds are I guess and that knowing that you could be a victim of a recovery scam now or another scam. Your name is on a list, you've sent money, the scammers are going to keep trying.*
>
> (Interview 25, Canada)

The sentiment across many of these quotes encompassed a recognition of the importance and need to prevent fraud from recurring.

Ultimately the outcome that you're trying to get people to arrive at is it's far easier to do things to prevent it than it is to actually deal with the incident that's there.

(Interview 7, UK)

Overall, these comments illustrate that in responding to victims, a large focus is on stopping the threat from fraud and the harm inflicted across both immediate and ongoing time frames. This was predominantly centred on financial loss but also recognized non-financial elements. Further, education was seen as key to helping the victim understand their current circumstances as it related to fraud but to also reduce their likelihood of repeat or ongoing victimization.

Moving forward

The second theme evident from the FJN professionals was focused on the recovery of victims and their ability to move forward from their victimization experience (*n* = 16). This goal was expressed in several ways. The first was reassurance. This is explicit in the following comments:

The second thing is to try and reassure the victim that we're protecting what's left.

(Interview 6, UK)

I think in relation to the victim it's to reassure them, make them feel valued, safe and secure.

(Interview 20, UK)

My goal is to reassure them and be really honest about what they can expect.

(Interview 28, Canada)

The idea of assisting the victim to recover was also highlighted in some interviews.

It would always be our teams [goal] to work out how to help clear up the damage and then enact prevention.

(Interview 8, UK)

[Our goal is] To get them to move beyond the crime … It's trying to help them come to terms with that, how can they get their life back on track, what does their life look like going forward? … The ideal solution is that somebody at the end of all of this has their life back on track.

(Interview 13, UK)

In addition, the desire to help the victim cope with their loss was mentioned.

> *But it's hard . . . because once you've felt the pain, you've suffered the harm, haven't you? So it's then just more of a case of how do you minimise that and not have it as a long standing issue?*
>
> (Interview 7, UK)

> *The ideal resolution is to just help them deal with the reality of what they've lost and to contextualise it in their own lives. That's about it.*
>
> (Interview 22, Canada)

There was also the idea from one participant of attempting to restore the victim to the point prior to the fraud occurring.

> *You get back to the point that you were before it happened . . . you kind of want to rewind the clock. You want it to go like one minute before it actually happened and whatever took place in that next minute, doesn't occur.*
>
> (Interview 7, UK)

Each of these comments indicates how several professionals articulated their ideal outcome in terms of addressing and minimizing the ongoing effects of the fraud on the victim. This recognizes the impact on individuals and is based on a similar to the previous discussion around the protection of the victim.

Initiating action

The third outcome detailed by professionals across the FJN relates to taking action of some sort, predominantly through an investigation (*n* = 11). This is evident in the following.

> *Once you've understood what's happened then you have to obviously start building a case and doing the investigation.*
>
> (Interview 16, UK)

> *So the [police organisation] have three options, as does any police force in the country. They can either take the crime that's being reported and retain it as a force and investigate it themselves, or deal with it in whichever matter they feel themselves.*
>
> (Interview 17, UK)

> *What I hope to achieve is that we will get as much information from this victim as possible and we can use that information, firstly, to do our best to solve the crime. With solving the crime we're hoping that we can bring whoever is responsible to justice.*
>
> (Interview 23, Canada)

> *Well ultimately it's [the goal] to seek justice. So in our case it's identifying the perpetrators, potentially arresting and charging them and hopefully getting some form of restitution for the victim. That's the ideal outcome and it's all I've achieved.*
>
> (Interview 24, Canada)

In addition to an investigation, the notion of gathering intelligence from the victims was discussed.

> *Ultimately what we're hoping to achieve is to capture the victim's information about the fraud case.*
>
> *(Interview 25, Canada)*

> *Well, from the law enforcement side of it we want to extract as much information as we can on the scam itself or as much detail, phone numbers, e-mail addresses, websites, bank accounts, names, money [that] is being sent to by Western Union and MoneyGram and whatever, all of that good stuff.*
>
> *(Interview 26, Canada)*

Although the ability to recover lost money to the victim is unlikely, it was still a stated goal by a few organizations.

> *To ensure that we identify the offender and we bring the offender to justice and any loss, we compensate them for their loss.*
>
> *(Interview 20, UK)*

> *We're hoping that we can get some type of remuneration for the victim. Although in the Canadian system it's rare, it's still sometimes possible. It's still definitely a goal. Sometimes that will be the goal. Sometimes we will do that – sometimes that will happen over – that will take precedence over, for example, conviction because it's a better result for the victim.*
>
> *(Interview 23, Canada)*

Overall, the goal of organizations to initiate an investigation and attempt to recover lost funds for victims was evident across a number of the professionals. The ability for them to actually achieve this is a point that is returned to later in the chapter.

Maintaining a positive image

In addition to goals clearly focused on the victims directly, there were limited comments that focused their ideal outcome on the organization themselves ($n = 6$). First, this was evident through maintaining positive relationships.

> *From my experience, the banks are – see it as a customer experience, so they're keen for that person to feel like they've been treated well by their banks, even if the outcome isn't necessarily what they wanted.*
>
> *(Interview 15, UK)*

> *I want the victim to also leave with the impression that [police agency] is working for them, is doing the best that they can for the victim. I hope to leave that impression on the victim as well.*
>
> *(Interview 23, Canada)*

> *The ideal outcome is to make it as positive an experience as possible as a customer, for the purposes of retaining them.*
>
> > (Interview 29, Canada)

The focus on the relationship with the victim then also feeds into the desire to mitigate any reputational risk as a result of the fraud.

> *[A goal is also to have] reputation intact ... So that that individual, one would hope that that individual doesn't think that it is a reflection on the institution and that they, that they still have, because it is a huge reputational risk.*
>
> > (Interview 2, UK)

> *There's a reputational thing around their business, if this was to become known what would be the long-term harm to their own reputation and the reputation of the business?*
>
> > (Interview 3, UK)

In combination, these comments illustrate that the ideal goal for organizations can focus on both the victim and their own organization.

Summary of the ideal outcomes from the FJN

The previous section has sought to highlight the main themes that were evident across interviews with the professionals in the FJN. Four main themes were discussed, which are articulated as the focus of organizations across the FJN in their interactions with individual fraud victims.

It is clear from this that a large number of professionals put forward goals that focus on the future wellbeing and protection of fraud victims across both financial and non-financial areas of their lives. Although there was still a focus on investigations, it was not as dominant as the support and prevention aspect of fraud. Lastly, there were a few considerations of the organization itself and how to maintain a positive relationship with both the victim themselves as well as the community more broadly.

Having outlined what professionals across the FJN advocated in terms of their desired outcome in their interactions with fraud victims, the next section examines the challenges that these professionals advocated in attempting to achieve these goals.

The challenges of meeting organizational goals

Professionals articulated a large number of challenges that they face in attempting to achieve their earlier-stated ideal outcome with victims of fraud. Despite the variety of their responses, these can be categorized into two main categories: factors associated with the victim individually and factors associated with the system. Each of these is explored in turn.

Factors associated with victims

Overall, 18 of the interviews touched upon some of the difficulties associated with victims themselves in being able to achieve the ideal outcome of the organization. The most common challenge revolved around the need to manage victim expectations.

> *There is this expectation I think of the public that the bank will step up and refund them. Perhaps in some cases it is appropriate but in lots I think there is this need to get the message out to people to understand that fraud can happen to them.*
>
> *(Interview 5, UK)*

> *So I think if the general public or the victim profile were more informed over what we've got to play with, then that may well better align their expectations in what can be done.*
>
> *(Interview 18, UK)*

> *And also try to . . . manage their expectations . . . in my ideal scenario, I always say I would much rather forgo a conviction . . . I would much rather get the persons money back. So we'll often try to use that as a lever in many cases can we get this offender to pay restitution in return for it. So we try to do that but we also try to manage the expectations.*
>
> *(Interview 21, Canada)*

> *By the time it gets to me, usually the people – ideally I want to lower their expectations, I would start by saying that.*
>
> *(Interview 28, Canada)*

Although several talked about the need to explicitly lower expectations, others noted how difficult this can be.

> *Getting it [reality of the situation] over to the victim and understanding where the victim comes from, it's really personal and sometimes a long and difficult conversation on the phone or in person.*
>
> *(Interview 14, UK)*

Further, several struggled with the fact of how to manage the expectations in a way that the victim was satisfied even if the outcome was not their desired one. A large part of this was the recognition of honesty in communication.

> *I mean it's a really interesting one because it's one we've been wrestling with for a while, about how we can get better – so people come away with an expectation that, okay, even if it isn't the outcome they initially wanted, but actually they feel like they've been able to do what they can and that they've been taken seriously.*
>
> *(Interview 15, UK)*

> *My goal is to reassure them and be really honest about what they can expect. Meaning I don't want to promise a resolution or their money back or anything like that, because in most cases, that is not possible. I tell them that they will contribute greatly to resolving the issue and that their time is really valuable and their input is really important.*
>
> *(Interview 28, Canada)*

Although these quotes speak to the importance of open communication between the victim and the organization, for some professionals, it was being able to convince the victim of their circumstances that posed the greatest challenge. This is illustrated by the following:

> *It's convincing them that what they're doing is not just a little gamble but it is actually detrimental and that they're running a risk of being targeted by other people – so persuading them to stop can be really tricky sometimes.*
>
> *(Interview 9, UK)*

> *It's explaining that to them, the nature of the scam and explaining . . . Then you're left with a person who sometimes, well, I'd say more often than not, will still continue to deny that that's the case for – for maybe a few more visits before they start to realise. That's the biggest challenge, is the denial.*
>
> *(Interview 19, UK)*

> *In terms of things like romance frauds and so on, it's difficult to get them to even realise they've been defrauded.*
>
> *(Interview 24, Canada)*

In addition to the denial of some victims, professionals detailed how the shame and stigma of fraud works against the organization in being able to appropriately respond.

> *A lot of victims blame themselves, they feel embarrassed by it . . . It's getting them to come to terms with that as well as their own internal feelings of guilt, shame, embarrassment and everything else that goes with that and to feel able to share it.*
>
> *(Interview 13, UK)*

> *The victimology is no different from any other criminality . . . So they'll be victimised by fraud, then they come to you by whatever mechanism and then you want to help them and they don't want to be helped. They're like, oh don't tell my family, don't tell this, don't tell that. Then you're just powerless.*
>
> *(Interview 22, Canada)*

This has highlighted a number of factors associated with victims themselves that present a barrier to organizations being able to achieve their ideal outcome in the aftermath of fraud. However, there are several system factors which impede this, outlined in the following section.

System factors

A myriad of factors was identified by professionals in relation to the FJN itself which prevent organizations from being able to deliver successfully on their ideal outcome to fraud victims. This was captured across 13 of the interviews.

First, it includes a lack of resources available to organizations in the response to fraud.

> Well, I think you've got the problem that there are too many victims or potential victims and there aren't enough resources to probably deliver the kind of service that these people need.
>
> *(Interview 11, UK)*

> But inevitably, if you've got less than half of what you had and the game has moved on as well, the threats have changed, the problems have changed, you're not going to be able to deliver really a lot – you're going to fall short of a lot of people's expectations, including our own. It's just inevitable. It's a costly thing. Especially when it comes to fraud. It's a costly thing to investigate.
>
> *(Interview 18, UK)*

> So I think one of the reasons that it is very challenging, I think you can put austerity, lack of financing, lack of resources [as contributing factors].
>
> *(Interview 20, UK)*

The comments about a lack of resources (including general funding and police) were specific to interviews conducted in the UK. This is reflective of the recent historical context, where successive governments have implemented austerity measures across departmental budgets and agencies across the FJN have invariably suffered cuts as a result. This also feeds into a perception that fraud is not a priority for governments and therefore lacks the ability to gain adequate resources.

> I think there's also an attitudinal problem. Fraud isn't a priority. I think it's more than attitudinal. I think there's a kind of organisational – the organisational or even the political level it's not prioritised. That kind of filters down to practitioners on the ground.
>
> *(Interview 11, UK)*

> From a local police force point of view where do you put your money? Counter-terrorism? Historical child abuse? Fraud? They can't put money in all of the boxes so they have to decide on their priorities. We would like fraud to be a much higher priority.
>
> *(Interview 13, UK)*

[For] other police forces the challenge is priority setting for fraud against other high harm crimes and being able to illustrate harm in fraud has historically been more difficult than physical harm crimes . . . and they all exist.

(Interview 17, UK)

The lack of priority given to fraud in the UK is not a new phenomenon, with a substantial amount of research supporting this assertion (Button, 2012; Levi, Doig, Gundur, Wall, & Williams, 2017; Levi, 2008; Levi, 2003; Gannon & Doig, 2010; King & Doig, 2016; Levi, Doig, Gundur, Wall, & Williams, 2015; Doig, Johnson, & Levi, 2001; Frimpong & Baker, 2007). There were also several other observations which support known challenges in responding to online fraud offences (see Cross & Blackshaw, 2015; Cross, 2016 for examples) through the current operation of the FJN.

They [victims] don't know where to go. There's a lot of different places you can land. For a lot of people it's really – not a poor service, but it's way below what they expect . . . we see quite a lot of the correspondence that goes to ministers. It seems to be a lot of that is just driven by an annoyance that despite provide a fair amount of detail, they've just been summarily dismissed.

(Interview 15, UK)

This points in part to the complexity of the FJN and the inability of victims to find an agency who is willing to listen and perhaps take their complaint. Further, the issue of jurisdiction was apparent.

Well in many cases it's very difficult to identify the perpetrators, for jurisdictional reasons . . . especially the web-based investigations; they're [offenders] very difficult to identify, let alone charge.

(Interview 24, Canada)

The systemic challenges noted by the professionals as barriers to their ability to respond to fraud victims mirror those established within the existing literature that examines the policing of fraud and cybercrime more broadly.

Summary of challenges in delivering the ideal organizational outcome

The earlier section highlights many difficulties that are encountered by professionals and organizations across the FJN when interacting with fraud victims. These barriers were identified into those relating to the individual victim compared to those relating to the system itself. Many of these are not new and are well established in the existing research examining the policing of fraud and cybercrime. Their presence in these excerpts seeks to demonstrate the reality of these challenges and how they affect daily the ability of the FJN to deliver their desired level of service to victims of fraud.

Having detailed the ideal outcomes from an organizational perspective as well as the perceived challenges in delivering these, the following section seeks to provide an understanding of what organizations perceive victims are hoping to achieve in their interaction.

Organizational perspectives on the ideal outcome of victims

Having established the ideal outcome of organizations in their interactions with fraud victims, professionals across the FJN were asked what they perceived to be the ideal outcome on the part of the victims themselves. The responses to these formed three main categories: getting their money back, justice, and an acknowledgment of victimization. Each of these will be detailed in turn.

Getting their money back

The desire for victims to get their money back was the most prevalent and direct response by those across the FJN ($n = 18$). This is illustrated in the following.

> People naturally . . . want their money back. They've lost money. It's really important to them and they want to get it back any way they can, sort of push the buttons to get it. I would do the same.
>
> (Interview 6, UK)

> So many people just want restitution. That's the most important thing. That's your life savings. You want your life savings back. There are significant amounts of money, life-changing amounts of money that are lost in those types of circumstances.
>
> (Interview 12, UK)

> I do think a victim expects their money back, especially the larger the amount and the quicker they report it.
>
> (Interview 17, UK)

> Well I think first and foremost, most victims hope that they'll be able to get something back monetarily. Typically you're talking about a monetary loss and they're hoping to get some or all of their funds back.
>
> (Interview 24, Canada)

> Victims are looking for their money back.
>
> (Interview 30, Canada)

Unsurprisingly, this was the most common goal articulated by professionals. However, the ability of agencies to achieve this is limited, as explored further in the chapter.

Seeking justice

Associated with the recovery of any financial loss, professionals were also clear in the idea that victims want to see justice served, predominantly through the traditional criminal justice system ($n = 14$). In most cases, this is arguably achieved through an investigation, arrest, and prosecution.

> *Most people coming to the police, that's what they want. Because they expect the police to investigate, identify and arrest. If that person can be prosecuted – but very rarely does that actually happen.*
>
> (Interview 1, UK)

> *I presume some still want justice in that kind of sense, criminal justice. In terms of what – I think there's probably a sense that they still expect to receive the same as they would get if they recorded any crime.*
>
> (Interview 11, UK)

> *I still think the victims expect investigations because that's traditional policing.*
>
> (Interview 17, UK)

> *They are naturally expecting some form of comeuppance, some sort of justice, something to happen to the criminals, you know, for them to be arrested and put in prison.*
>
> (Interview 19, UK)

> *I would say . . . some people want a measure of justice.*
>
> (Interview 21, Canada)

> *There are a lot of times when they do believe that we are going to find these people.*
>
> (Interview 27, Canada)

The relationship between victims wanting to get their money back and seeking justice was not straightforward. On one hand, there were those who argued that they were intertwined.

> *I think individuals are, their gut reaction is they want revenge. They want some punitive action to be taken, to be demonstrated, but they want their money back as well.*
>
> (Interview 5, UK)

> *Of course, if we have an investigation and we're able to identify people that are responsible and we're able to charge them and bring them before the courts, victims seem happy about that. Of course, if we can get some type of compensation for the victims, they're happy about that.*
>
> (Interview 23, Canada)

In contrast, others believed that it was either one or the other, usually with the money taking precedence.

> *Money back is really high up . . . I want the police to know so that if there's any money I can get back . . . whether they want someone to go to prison for it I think that comes way down the line. Not something they — not something that everyone considers when they first report it — is the Court process and prison for anybody.*
>
> *(Interview 14, UK)*

These quotes indicate the complexity that is perceived to exist for victims of fraud. Although it is argued that many victims expect a policing response similar to what they would receive from any other type of crime, the reality of this is questionable. The priority given to getting money back over a criminal justice response in some circumstances is also notable.

Acknowledgement

A few professionals spoke of the desire by victims to simply be acknowledged as a victim, as well as to be treated accordingly ($n = 6$). This is reflected in the following.

> *In that interaction, there's got to be a degree of empathy with the individual and there's got to be helping, as far as possible, to put things right.*
>
> *(Interview 12, UK)*

> *They want someone to — I think they want someone to know that it's happened. I think that's probably as equal with getting their money back, is to know that I've been scammed here. I want someone to know that I've been scammed. I might not [want] my friends to know I've been scammed but I want someone to know. I want the police to know so that if there's any money I can get back. More importantly I want someone to know.*
>
> *(Interview 14, UK)*

> *In my experience I generally find that most victims initially, their initial instinct is generally that they wish to be heard. At least feel like they've been heard. . . . But the biggest thing . . . is give them the sense that is not only they've been heard but that they're understood and that effectively they are understood to be victims.*
>
> *(Interview 21, Canada)*

> *Certainly in many cases too they're hoping for some acknowledgement that they actually matter, so what has happened to them actually matters to society. So that can come at the judicial end as well, so at least some sort of validation or recognition that they've actually suffered something that they shouldn't have suffered.*
>
> *(Interview 24, Canada)*

These comments indicate a recognition of the nature of victimization experienced by individuals and their desire and need to have that acknowledged in an appropriate manner.

Summary of perceived victim goals

Overall, this section has highlighted the perceived goals of the victim as articulated by the FJN professionals in their interactions with their organizations. Obtaining their money back was the top priority highlighted, followed by the desire to see justice served. The need for acknowledgement of their victimization was also mentioned as a desired outcome. Similar to the organizational goals, professionals were asked about the challenges and barriers that they faced in being able to achieve these victim goals. These are explored in the following section.

The challenges of meeting victim goals

Having outlined the perceived expectations of victims, professionals were then asked to describe what they thought were the barriers and challenges to achieving this. Notably, the responses provided to this question somewhat mirror the factors previously advocated in terms of barriers to the organization achieving its ideal outcomes. These focused predominantly on victim expectations and factors associated with the system itself. Each of these will be detailed next.

Managing victim expectations

Similar to the previous section, many professionals articulated the challenge of managing expectations as a challenge in meeting the desired outcomes of fraud victims ($n = 14$).

> They think they can come to us and we can sort it all out for them, but we can't. We can only . . . be one part of the mosaic, of the mess that has been made.
>
> (Interview 4, UK)

> It is realistic that subjectively, you want your money back. Of course, that's your perception as a person, isn't it? Is it a realistic prospect of it happening on every case? No.
>
> (Interview 6, UK)

> I think initially the expectation is quite high. I think initially they're hoping that we'll be able to get their money back for them . . . I think they will often have an expectation that we will be able to dig into our unlimited pit and to give them their monies back. The first conversation we have is to try and get them to understand that that's not our role.
>
> (Interview 13, UK)

There are some victims who just demand to get their money back. Even when we explain to them what we can and cannot do, or what we can do mostly for the victim, they still just – all they care about is they want their money back. Really, that's unreasonable.

(Interview 23, Canada)

There are a lot of times when they do believe that we are going to find these people, so making sure they are aware of the [organisational] mandate and the fact that we are here to gather and collect intel on fraud is a really big thing. So I don't want anyone to feel that we have let them down, so I tell the mandate to 95% of the calls that we do receive.

(Interview 27, Canada)

The challenge in being able to manage victim expectations around the recovery of money and the realities of what each agency within the FJN can reasonably do was a strong focus across the professionals.

System issues

Further to this, the same issues regarding the system, such as jurisdiction and a lack of resources, were also readily apparent (*n* = 6).

You do everything in your power to go away and to investigate that particular crime until there are no more avenues that you can investigate. Hopefully by that time you'd have identified the person and you'd be in a position to arrest them. Now that's slightly different when you do stuff online because you could be in any jurisdiction in the world, and that is a huge problem.

(Interview 16, UK)

But sometimes the officers will explain to the victim what we can't do or what we don't do. The victims don't really want to hear that. I'm not sure why the officers do it. The victims want to know what we can do, and they have a high expectation of the police, especially because of what they see on TV and in the news. To tell a victim we're not capable of investigating something doesn't really make sense to victims. They expect the police to be capable.

(Interview 23, Canada)

Lastly, there was recognition of the confusion victims must feel at having to confront the FJN in the first place. Particularly in the UK, there has been a lot of change across the relevant agencies, and it was noted that this would have an impact on the victims themselves.

You've had huge [structural and organisational] change and to think you can have that change and the change required a huge amount of energy and – for things to – for people to know where to go, it – they've got to be pretty up to date with what actually is in place. Where you don't – if you go out of the country and came back, it would just be changed. It would be different. It would be – it is – it's hard for the professionals, so I can imagine the victim or the end user of ours . . . services would find it quite confusing.

(Interview 18, UK)

This illustrates the complexity of the system in and of itself and how the ongoing change poses an additional layer of challenge to those victims seeking to access support.

Summary of barriers to achieving desired victim outcomes

The previous comments illustrate many of the same issues previously articulated by professionals in the ability to deliver both on their ideal goals as well as achieve those of the victim. The most prominent challenge is the managing of expectations, and this is clearly evident in the literature as well (see Cross, 2018a).

Having provided in-depth insights from the professionals across the FJN, the last section of this chapter starts to look critically at these themes and what can be learnt by having a clearer understanding of the organizational perspective of individual fraud victimization.

What can be learnt from the organizational perspectives?

The previous sections have provided insights into how professionals across the FJN perceive fraud victims, both in terms of their ideal organizational response compared to that desired by the victim. Further, they have articulated the many challenges they face across both areas in being able to successfully deliver on these goals. A number of points of interest are generated by these results. Overall, much of what has been said accords with the known existing research in the area. This is particularly the case with knowing what victims want, the challenge of managing victim expectations, and the issues surrounding the policing of fraud. However, there is an important context to these points, explored next.

Organizations have a clear understanding of what victims want

When asked what professionals across the FJN believed the ideal victim outcome was, there was consistency and accuracy in their observations. In agreement with the literature, they articulated three main goals: a desire to get their money back, a need to see justice served, and an acknowledgement of their victimization. This is consistent with much of what is known from fraud victims directly (see Button et al., 2009a, 2009b; Cross et al., 2016a) and accords with the main reasons why victims attempt to report fraud in the first place (Cross, 2018b). In this way, there is no divergence in understanding between what fraud victims say they want and what organizations across the FJN believe the victims want. So the question remains: If there is no divergence in this understanding of ideal victim goals, why is there still such a large level of dissatisfaction with reporting fraud (for example, see Morgan et al., 2016) and why do victims experience such overwhelmingly negative experiences through the FJN (see Button et al., 2009a; Cross et al., 2016a)? Potential answers to these questions are explored next.

The ideal organization goal versus the ideal victim goal

It is clear that both victims and organizations are consistent in their understanding of ideal victim goals. However, the responses provided by organizations as to their own ideal goal were very different. The initiation of action (usually through an investigation) was one of the goals stated, and this does match with what victims want and their expectations of each organization and what is stated in the literature (Button et al., 2009a, 2009b; Cross et al., 2016a; Cross, 2018b). Nevertheless, the other two themes of assessing harm and protection, as well as helping victims to move forward, are quite unique and different from anything that victims advocate. They are also not apparent in the limited research that has examined the needs of fraud victims (for example, Button et al., 2009a; Cross et al., 2016a).

The desire to protect the victims from immediate harm as well as future harm is important and positively reflects the willingness of the organizations to assist the victims in whatever ways they can. The same can be said for organizations who advocated their goal to help victims move beyond the fraud that has occurred. The problem with these two goals being at the forefront of an organizational response relates to timing. When victims seek assistance and report to agencies across the FJN, they are focused on the situation they currently find themselves in and the fraudulent situation that has just occurred. They are seeking a response to what has already happened – in other words, they desire a reactive approach to their current circumstances.

The ideals of seeking to protect victims from ongoing and future harm, as well as to help them move beyond what they have experienced, is focused on the future. It is a proactive stance that focuses attention not on the event itself that has occurred, but on ways to stop it from happening in the future. Although not ignoring the fraud, it does not adequately address the current context that victims are in and perhaps seeks to move them forward prematurely. Victims are very much focused in the present and past and unable to see into the future. This then becomes a point of tension for victims who are expecting a response to their current circumstance.

In terms of the likely reasoning behind this, it is easily identifiable why organizations appear to be future focused. As acknowledged by the professionals themselves and what is strongly supported by the current research, the ability of the FJN to respond to fraud is limited (Cross & Blackshaw, 2015; Cross, 2016). There are severe constraints on agencies being able to successfully investigate, arrest, and prosecute fraud offenders. The issues of jurisdiction, resources, knowledge, appropriate skills, and adequate legislation are well known across the FJN and cybercrime more broadly (Brenner, 2006; Burns, Whitworth, & Thompson, 2004; Button, 2012; Cross & Blackshaw, 2015; Cross, 2016; Finklea, 2013). Many of these issues were clearly articulated by professionals in previous sections. If the professionals know with certainty that their ability to successfully achieve an outcome is highly unlikely, then it makes sense that they would instead prioritize a response to victims which seeks to prevent them from being revictimized in the future and to limit the harm that they have already experienced.

The problem with this approach is that victims do not have the same level of understanding and knowledge on the constraints and limitations placed on the FJN. When they report, they are seeking an outcome, regardless of whether it is focused on their own need for individual justice or whether they want to protect others (Cross, 2018b). They still expect agencies to be able to identify the offender and take action, both as a symbolic action and a practical one. Most victims are unaware of the realities of fraud, the prevalence in which it is perpetrated, and the complexities that exist from a law enforcement perspective or that of the wider FJN. When they do not receive an expected response, they perceive the FJN in a negative light (Cross, 2018a; Morgan et al., 2016).

The current data demonstrate it is not the lack of understanding that is the problem. Rather, it is the tension that exists between the reactive approach sought by victims compared to the future-oriented approach taken by organizations. This disparity exists for a number of legitimate reasons on the part of organizations, yet is not understood by the victims themselves. This is further elaborated next.

The challenge of managing victim expectations

The most pressing challenge articulated by professionals across the FJN was the managing of victim expectations. This was identified as a barrier in both delivering on the organizational ideal goal as well as that of the victims. The importance of this is highlighted in the previous section and cannot be underestimated.

The fact that organizations can identify this as one of their most pressing issues is positive. It demonstrates a reflective understanding of their interactions and communications with fraud victims. It shows that they are aware of the issue at hand. However, despite their own attempts to address the gap in expectations versus reality and the need to be open and honest with victims, this continues to be a great source of anger, frustration, and additional harm to victims (Cross, 2018a). Many victims report being traumatized first by the offender and then again at the hands of the FJN (Cross, 2018b). Although those who participated in the current study all have a strong grasp of the issues faced by organizations in responding to fraud victims, this may not translate to the front-line workers that victims communicate with on a daily basis. There are many documented instances of shame, humiliation, and victim blaming experienced by victims by those in the FJN (Button et al., 2009a, 2009b; Cross et al., 2016a; Cross, 2015). In this way, the knowledge and understanding of those professionals in this study may not be as prevalent across the entire FJN. As highlighted by one professional in the current study, "as with all things you are at the mercy of whoever it is you're dealing with" (Interview 21, Canada). This finding may also reflect one of the limitations noted in the current study whereby those interviewed may have a detached view of what is happening at the coalface of their organization.

Taking action for the future

The current chapter has explored the ideal outcomes of organizations across the FJN in their response to individual fraud victims. It has also explored the perceived ideal outcome from victims themselves. The results of this analysis indicate that although organizations have a solid understanding of victims' desires and needs, this does not translate into the priority of their goals with respect to interacting with victims. Rather, organizations appear to be focused on the future and events beyond the current fraud incident, whereas the victims are focused on their present circumstances and what has already happened to them. The future-oriented focus of organizations is understandable based on the many genuine challenges associated with achieving a successful criminal justice outcome (such as identification of the offender, arrest, and prosecution). The tension between these approaches to fraud is a strong basis for unmet expectations on the part of victims, leading to additional anger, frustration, and trauma.

It is arguable that neither party is right or wrong in their desired approach to fraud victimization. The underlying premise of wanting both a response to the offence that has occurred as well as seeking to prevent future offences and support recovery are genuine needs. The current point of contention is the disparity between victim expectations and the inability for organizations to successfully communicate the reasoning behind their inability to respond to the current offence and therefore their focus on both prevention and recovery. It is also questionable as to how successful they are in achieving these goals around prevention and recovery, but that is beyond the current chapter. It also speaks to the wider issues of achieving justice for these victims when the traditional criminal justice system does not seem to be equipped or able to counter these offences in the same way as other offence types; however, this topic is also beyond the scope of the current chapter.

What is readily apparent is the need to account for the human factor in responses to victims across the FJN. A large amount of suffering appears to be the result of a lack of effective communication between organizations across the FJN and victims themselves. This highlights a need to target an awareness and education campaign across society as a whole, outlining the reality of fraud victimization and the ability of the FJN to respond. Although organizations themselves are attempting to do this on a case-by-case basis with individual victims at each interaction, it is arguable that a larger-scale effort is needed. This may help to overcome some of the unrealistic expectations placed on agencies within the FJN and seek to counter some of the beliefs held by victims about what agencies can and should do for them in the aftermath of fraud. Much like what has occurred in public health, there is the need to put forward a campaign focused on fraud across both the prevention and response to victimization. Further, although the professionals in the current study spoke openly of a proactive approach to victims and a desire to help them recover and move beyond their victimization, this is not the lived experience of victims, who openly assert a lack of support from both their family, friends, and authorities (Button et al., 2009a, 2009b; Cross et al., 2016a).

This chapter has demonstrated that there is a need for a conversation which better communicates the reality of fraud victimization and the limits of the FJN to society as a whole. This is not to say that individual organizations themselves are absolved of responsibility in their interactions with fraud victims. There is arguably always room for improvement, and existing research would support this. Nor does it advocate that organizations should just give up and not pursue an investigation. This is by no means the case. Rather, this acknowledges that the current levels of suffering and trauma experienced by victims as a result of their experience with the FJN can be partially attributed to factors which can be addressed through targeted measures. Action to address these could, and should, be taken.

References

Australian Competition and Consumer Commission. (2018). *Targeting scams: Report of the ACCC on scam activity 2017*. Retrieved from www.accc.gov.au/publications/targeting-scams-report-on-scam-activity/targeting-scams-report-of-the-accc-on-scam-activity-2017

Brenner, S. (2006). Cybercrime jurisdiction. *Crime, Law and Social Change, 46*(4–5), 189–206.

Burns, R., Whitworth, K., & Thompson, C. (2004). Assessing law enforcement preparedness to address internet fraud. *Journal of Criminal Justice, 32*, 477–493.

Button, M. (2012). Cross-border fraud and the case for an "Interfraud." *Policing: An International Journal of Police Strategies and Management, 35*(2), 285–303.

Button, M., Lewis, C., & Tapley, J. (2009a). *A better deal for fraud victims*. London: Centre for Counter Fraud Studies.

Button, M., Lewis, C., & Tapley, J. (2009b). *Support for the victims of fraud: An assessment of the current infrastructure in England and Wales*. London: Centre for Counter Fraud Studies.

Button, M., Lewis, C., & Tapley, J. (2013). The "fraud justice network" and the infrastructure of support for the individual fraud victims in England and Wales. *Criminology and Criminal Justice, 13*(1), 37–61.

Button, M., McNaugton Nicolls, C., Kerr, J., & Owen, R. (2014). Online frauds: Learning from victims why they fall for these scams. *Australian and New Zealand Journal of Criminology, 47*(3), 391–408.

Canadian Anti-Fraud Centre. (2015). *Annual Statistics Report 2014*. Retrieved from www.antifraudcentre-centreantifraude.ca/reports-rapports/2014/ann-ann-eng.htm

Copes, H., Kerley, K., Mason, K., & van Wyk, J. (2001). Reporting behaviour of fraud victims and Black's theory of law: An empirical assessment. *Justice Quarterly, 18*(2), 343–363.

Cross, C. (2015). No laughing matter: Blaming the victim of online fraud. *International Review of Victimology, 21*(2), 187–204.

Cross, C. (2016). Using financial intelligence to target online fraud victimization: Applying a tertiary prevention perspective. *Criminal Justice Studies, 29*(2), 125–142. http://dx.doi.org /10.1080/1478601X.2016.1170278.

Cross, C. (2018a) Expectations vs reality: Responding to online fraud across the fraud justice network. *International Journal of Law, Crime and Justice*. Online first. doi:10.1016/j. ijlcj.2018.08.001

Cross, C. (2018b). Victims' motivations for reporting to the "fraud justice network." *Police Practice and Research, 19*(6), 550–564.

Cross, C., & Blackshaw, D. (2015). Improving the police response to online fraud. *Policing: A Journal of Policy and Practice, 9*(2), 119–128.

Cross, C., & Kelly, M. (2016). The problem of "white noise": Examining current prevention approaches to online fraud. *Journal of Financial Crime, 23*(4), 806–828.

Cross, C., Richards, K., & Smith, R. (2016a). *Improving the response to online fraud victims: An examination of reporting and support.* Canberra: Australian Institute of Criminology.

Cross, C., Richards, K., & Smith, R. G. (2016b). The reporting experiences and support needs of victims of online fraud. *Trends and Issues in Crime and Criminal Justice, 518*, 1–14.

Cross, C., Smith, R. G., & Richards, K. (2014). Challenges of responding to online fraud victimization in Australia. *Trends and Issues in Crime and Criminal Justice, 47*, 1–7.

Deem, D. (2000). Notes from the field: Observations in working with the forgotten victims of personal financial crimes. *Journal of Elder Abuse and Neglect, 12*(2), 33–48.

Doig, A., Johnson, S., & Levi, M. (2001). New public management, old populism and the policing of fraud. *Public Policy and Administration, 16*(1), 91–113.

Finklea, K. (2013). *The interplay of borders, turf, cyberspace and jurisdiction: Issues confronting US law enforcement.* Congressional Research Service Report for Congress. Washington, DC: Congressional Research Service.

Fletcher, N. (2007). Challenges for regulating financial fraud in cyberspace. *Journal of Financial Crime, 14*(2), 190–207.

Frimpong, K., & Baker, P. (2007). Fighting public sector fraud: The growth of professionalism in counter-fraud investigators. *Crime Prevention and Community Safety, 9*, 130–137.

Gannon, R., & Doig, A. (2010). Duckling the answer? Fraud strategies and police resources. *Policing and Society: An International Journal of Research and Policy, 20*(1), 39–60.

Ganzini, L., Bentson, H., McFarland, M., & Cutler, D. (1990). Prevalence of mental disorders after catastrophic financial loss. *The Journal of Nervous and Mental Disease, 178*(11), 680–685.

Internet Crime Complain Centre (IC3). (2015). *2014 internet crime report.* Retrieved from www.ic3.gov/media/annualreport/2014_IC3Report.pdf

Kerley, K. R., & Copes, H. (2002). Personal fraud victims and their official responses to victimization. *Journal of Police and Criminal Psychology, 17*(1), 19–35.

Kerr, J., Owen, R., McNaughton-Nicolls, C., & Button, M. (2013). *Research on sentencing online fraud offences.* London: Sentencing Council.

King, J., & Doig, A. (2016). A dedicated place for the volume fraud within the current UK economic agenda? The Greater Manchester police case study. *Journal of Financial Crime, 23*(4), 902–915.

Levi, M. (2003). The Roskill Fraud Commission revisited: An assessment. *Journal of Financial Crime, 11*(1), 38–44.

Levi, M. (2008). Organized frauds and organising frauds: Unpacking the research on networks and organization. *Criminology and Criminal Justice, 8*(4), 389–419. doi: 10.1177/1748895808096470/

Levi, M., Doig, A., Gundur, R., Wall, D., & Williams, D. (2015). *The implications of economic cybercrime for policing.* London: City of London Corporation. Retrieved from www.

cityoflondon.gov.uk/business/economic-research-and-information/research-publica-tions/Documents/Research-2015/Economic-Cybercrime-FullReport.pdf

Levi, M., Doig, A., Gundur, R., Wall, D., & Williams, M. (2017). Cyberfraud and the implications for effective risk-based responses: Themes from UK research. *Crime Law and Social Change*, *67*(1), 77–96.

Marsh, I. (2004). *Criminal justice: An introduction to philosophies, theories and practice*. London: Routledge.

Mason, K., & Benson, M. (1996). The effect of social support on fraud victims' reporting behaviour: A research note. *Justice Quarterly*, *13*(3), 511–524.

Morgan, A., Dowling, C., Brown, R., Mann, M., Voce, I., & Smith, M. (2016). *Evaluation of the Australian Cybercrime Online Reporting Network*. Canberra: Australian Institute of Criminology.

Office for National Statistics. (2016). *Overview of fraud statistics: Year ending March 2016*. Retrieved from www.ons.gov.uk/peoplepopulationandcommunity/crimeandjustice/articles/overviewoffraudstatistics/yearendingmarch2016

Ross, S., & Smith, R. G. (2011). Risk factors for advance fee fraud victimization. *Trends and Issues in Crime and Criminal Justice*, *420*, 1–6.

Schoepfer, A., & Piquero, N. (2009). Studying the correlates of fraud victimization and reporting. *Journal of Criminal Justice*, *37*, 209–215.

Smith, R. G. (2007). Consumer scams in Australia: An overview. *Trends and Issues in Crime and Criminal Justice*, *331*, 1–6.

Smith, R. G. (2008). Coordinating individual and organizational responses to fraud. *Crime Law and Social Change*, *49*, 379–396.

Stratton, G., Powell, A., & Cameron, R. (2017). Crime and justice in digital society: Towards a "digital criminology?" *International Journal For Crime, Justice And Social Democracy*, *6*(2), 17–33.

Titus, R., Heinzelmann, F., & Boyle, J. (1995). Victimization of persons by fraud. *Crime and Delinquency*, *41*(1), 54–72.

United Nations. (2013). *Comprehensive study on cybercrime – Draft report*. Vienna: United Nations Office on Drugs and Crime, Retrieved from www.unodc.org/documents/organized-crime/UNODC_CCPCJ_EG.4_2013/CYBERCR IME_STUDY_210213.pdf

van Wyk, J., & Mason, K. (2001). Investigating vulnerability and reporting behavior for consumer fraud victimization: Opportunity as a social aspect for age. *Journal of Contemporary Criminal Justice*, *17*(4), 328–345.

Yar, M. (2013). *Cybercrime and society* (2nd ed.). London: Sage.

17 The ecology of cybercrime

Benoît Dupont

Introduction

Cybersecurity remains a puzzle. While human societies are in the midst of a digital revolution that is proving as transformative and disruptive as the two industrial revolutions that preceded it, the complex problem of how to safeguard new emerging technosocial assemblages against a broad range of manufactured online risks proves extremely challenging (Giddens, 1999). Alarming headlines remind us daily that the personal and financial data that we entrust to employers, insurers, banks, retailers, or online service providers are being plundered on a systematic basis by hackers who exploit a broad range of technical vulnerabilities or human errors (Verizon, 2018). The revelations made by Edward Snowden also highlighted how the intelligence agencies that were supposed to protect us against such threats were in fact busy developing a massive bulk-surveillance apparatus (Bauman et al., 2014). Meanwhile, police organizations are facing severe budgetary constraints and can hardly hire, train, and retain the specialized investigators and forensic experts required to prosecute local and international cybercrimes (Council of Canadian Academies, 2014). In this fast-evolving and uncertain environment, private companies see attractive business opportunities marketing a broad range of products and services, from cybersecurity insurance policies to antivirus solutions or new authentication technologies (for a comprehensive description of this growing market and its multiple components, see MarketsAndMarkets, 2018). The global cybersecurity market was estimated by Gartner to be worth $77 billion in 2015 and will grow to $156 billion by 2019 if forecasts prove correct (Gartner, 2017). Yet despite these massive investments, the situation does not seem to improve and cybersecurity remains an elusive objective.

This unique mix of rapidly transforming criminal risks, government crime-control institutions that seem unable to innovate at the required pace and whose capacities are being shaped by expanded national security mandates, and private interests bent on profiteering from this highly uncertain context creates substantial and complex policy challenges. The main one is arguably the coordination of collective action among a plural set of institutional actors pursuing diverging objectives, operating under different rationalities and responding to singular incentives. Although many fields of research are producing valuable new knowledge on this emerging cybersecurity ecosystem, their insights remain all too often fragmented. Computer scientists focus on the technical dimension of systems' vulnerabilities with limited interest for the psychological and behavioural forces at work (Anderson, 2008; Leukfeldt, 2017), while criminologists and sociologists examine the social organization and career trajectories of individual online offenders without always focusing on how technical and economic decisions made by private and public stakeholders might facilitate cybercrimes (Holt & Bossler, 2014). Legal scholars, for their part, study legislative and regulatory approaches in the digital domain, but with a clear preference for access and privacy issues over security considerations (Lessig, 2006). Some forums created by computer scientists have sought to build bridges with the social sciences (in particular, psychology and economics) and are yielding promising results (see for example the Symposium on User Privacy and Security or the Workshop on the Economics of Information Security, both held annually, or the Cambridge Cybercrime Centre, hosted by the Computer Laboratory in collaboration with Cambridge's Institute of Criminology and Faculty of Law). Social scientists, however, have erected fewer similar interdisciplinary tents, despite their unique expertise in the complex craft of designing institutions that can manage and mitigate a broad range of societal risks (Braithwaite, 2014). Among the few examples that come to mind, one can mention Berkeley's Center for Long-Term Cybersecurity in the United States or University College London's Department of Crime Science in the UK.

Generally speaking, cybersecurity could be defined as the constellation of policies, practices, and systems put in place to address the digital risks that have become so prevalent in today's societies, including the various forms of cybercrime. Despite the fact that we do not yet have the tools to measure the scope and impact of cybercrime with the same degree of precision as those used for traditional crime (Tcherni, Davies, Lopes, & Lizotte, 2016; Caneppele & Aebi, 2017), the limited data published by national statistics institutions and a few specialized companies confirm the exponential growth of this phenomenon (Levi, 2017). Although the Internet only became a part of our daily lives a quarter of a century ago, cybercrimes now represent the largest source of property crimes, while having profoundly altered most other forms of crime. This profound transformation can be attributed to three foundational features of the Internet, the most disruptive technology to enter our lives since electricity. First, the Internet and its underlying technologies operate as a decentralized infrastructure of continuously evolving machines, communication networks, data streams, and computer applications that can process massive amounts of data. This unique technical architecture has made it possible for a new economic model to emerge, offering everyone novel and inexpensive ways of communicating and automating social interactions (Benkler, 2006). In other words, offenders have now access to the same resources Silicon Valley start-ups used to disrupt industries like retail, tourism, telecommunications, print media, etc. They can leverage these resources to innovate and industrialize their criminal activities.

The second feature is that this collection of technologies is mainly designed, produced, distributed, and governed by private interests such as telecommunications companies, computer equipment manufacturers, content producers, social media platforms, and online transaction brokers. From the moment the Internet became a viable commercial enterprise, these key players have been resistant to regulation and have implemented a relatively autonomous system of governance (Castells, 2001; DeNardis, 2014). This predominance of private interests and their preference for profit and universal accessibility over user security complicates cybercrime regulation.

The third and final aspect is the global reach of the Internet and its inherent lack of borders, which poses a significant challenge to the sovereignty of states trying to react locally and with limited resources to a universal phenomenon (Castells, 2001). This mainly applies to democratic states though, as authoritarian states have no qualms about sequestering their residents in walled and highly censored systems, which are often, coincidentally, designed in the West (Deibert, 2013). The thriving trade in surveillance and censorship technologies illustrates how even the most authoritarian regimes feel threatened by the Internet.

These three structural features explain in large part why it is so difficult for security institutions to address digital risks, whether they be traditional crimes made easier though the creation of the Internet, such as online fraud; entirely new crimes, like hacking and denial of service attacks; or crimes that use the Internet as a vehicle for the mass distribution of illicit content (Wall, 2007). In other words, the automation of certain forms of crime on a global scale, combined with the new interdependencies that link together technological systems, social institutions, and our relentless data-sharing habits, represent a major challenge for local law enforcement organizations that were born during the industrial revolution and were intended to preserve public order in urban settings. The challenge of low-impact but high-volume crimes faced by police services that are designed to deal with high-impact low-volume crimes (such as homicides) is by extension a challenge to the theoretical and methodological frameworks used by those who study how security is understood and delivered. In a context where complexity reigns supreme, criminology and the related disciplines need an extended and enhanced toolbox to analyse how technology helps transform the criminal practices and the solutions security institutions forge and implement to address these practices.

Norbert Elias's work on the concept of figuration (which he defines as webs of interdependence) provides some interesting insights into this topic. He attributes a great deal of importance to the interdependencies of individual actors within larger social groups trying to overcome sociology's false dichotomy of person and society as two discrete levels of analysis. He also expresses the need to simultaneously study relationships of conflict and cooperation, which characterize any sphere of social activity (Elias, 1978). By urging us to think in an integrated way about how diametrically opposed groups (banking institutions, Internet fraudsters, and the police, for example) are intertwined and inexorably connected through the shifting, yet balanced, relationships that make up a single process, his concept of figuration also allows us to build theoretical and empirical bridges between interconnected fields of criminological study such as the sociology of deviance, security governance, situational crime prevention, and victimology. Elias's analytical framework is particularly compatible with the ecological metaphor, on which I'll rely extensively to describe and analyse the various forms of interdependencies that bind together diverse categories of actors such as large multinational corporations, cybercrime groups, and public and private security providers. Ecology is the "science of relationships" (Haeckel, 1866, as cited in Lévêque, 2003, p. 2). Dating back to as early as the second half of the 19th century, the ecological approach anticipated the importance of studying organisms holistically by also considering the communities they embed themselves into and interact with, as well as the environment they take their resources from, which also restricts their ability to function. My approach is not about naturalizing criminology by trying to discover universal laws that would allow us to create models for criminal behaviour. That would likely prove futile. Instead, the idea here is to leverage ecology's well-stocked toolbox in order to borrow concepts and metaphors that could help interpret the interdependent relationships and organizational complexity that characterizes cyberspace by focusing on cyber-risks and the security measures implemented to manage them.

Because of the approach I am taking, I have divided this chapter into two sections. The first one covers the three main communities in the cybersecurity ecosystem: the industrial community, the criminal community, and the security community. This section will also analyse the entities that comprise these communities and the way each one functions. The second section focuses on the three relational modes – competition, predation, and cooperation – that regulate the way these communities operate internally and interact with each other.

The three cybersecurity communities

In the ecological approach adopted in this chapter, cybersecurity is understood as the product of constant interactions between three interdependent communities: an industrial community, which is the source of a major technological revolution launched some 20 years ago that has also spawned major digital risks; a criminal community, which was able to capitalize on this revolution to take advantage of criminal opportunities on an unprecedented scale; and, a security community, which has struggled to effectively manage cybercrime. This first section examines the main characteristics of each community and their various actors.

The industrial community

The Internet's transformation from a basic communication tool reserved for academic researchers to a digital nervous system used by half of the world's population (and nearly 80% of people living in developed nations, according to the International Telecommunications Union) was mostly made possible thanks to the development of new information technologies and the intense innovation efforts of telecommunications companies. Whether they be network service providers like AT&T, Bell, or Orange; device manufacturers such as Apple or Samsung; software and operating system designers like Microsoft; or even platform resources offering services and content such as Google, Amazon, and Facebook, these companies – and the thousands of start-ups trying to gain the same stronghold in the digital economy – have become household names and represent the cornerstone of the Internet revolution. More established industries such as the media, professional services, and finance sectors have also embraced this technological shift, leveraging it to enhance their productivity and reinvent their business models (Gandhi, Khanna, & Ramaswamy, 2016).

Although there is no denying the social and economic benefits generated by companies of all sizes in this industrial ecosystem, their explosive growth and focus on innovation explains, in large part, why the security of their products and services is often an afterthought. In fact, as Castells (1996) pointed out, for a product or service to be quickly adopted, it must have new features that sets it apart from the competition. This forces the immediate release of any innovation, even when its features remain incomplete or unstable, in order to capture market advantage and exclude potential competitors. More recently, these practices of accelerated product development have been formalized in 'Lean' or 'Agile' methodologies, which has shaved off a few months from the time a product is designed until it is launched. Although these approaches may promote a permanent technological and economic effervescence, they also create conditions favourable to underlying and recurring security problems that can be exploited by cybercriminals.

This explains why even the most renowned companies' products have structural security issues. A quick search in the U.S. National Institute of Standards and Technology's (NIST) National Vulnerability Database (NVD) will reveal more than 108,000 problems on all types of software, of which 16% have been deemed critically severe based on the Common Vulnerability Scoring System.[1] By doing a keyword search with the word 'Apple,' the database will return some 6,092 vulnerabilities linked to the company's software since 1996. If we were to do the same search with the word 'Microsoft' instead, it would produce comparable results: 5,825 vulnerabilities.[2] In some emerging markets that have not yet reached maturity, like the Internet of Things (IoT), few companies make the effort to ensure the security of the devices they sell, despite the growing number of cybercriminals exploiting flaws in their technology (Krebs, 2016a). Other segments of the digital market tolerate high levels of fraud, such as online advertising, which was a $66 billion market in 2016. It is believed that fraudsters have been able to hijack 20% of online advertising revenues by selling fake clicks or traffic of dubious origin (The&Partnership, 2017). More established firms in the financial or professional services sectors are submitted to higher levels of regulatory and market oversight, but they are not immune from the same cybersecurity pathologies that plague information technology companies. Because of those intense competitive pressures and its general indifference to security issues, the industrial community offers many alluring opportunities for the criminal community.

The criminal community

Online crime is different from traditional crime, in that certain acts can be automated on a very large scale and reach thousands, or even tens or hundreds of thousands, of victims with limited human resources. However, this industrialization of crime requires some relatively rare technical, entrepreneurial, and social skills (Copes & Vieraitis, 2008; Dupont, 2013). Technical skills reflect the ability of online criminals to programme malware, infiltrate computer systems, or operate compromised computers to get access to personal data and confidential information while remaining undetected (Macdonald & Frank, 2017). Entrepreneurial skills refer to the ability to convert this personal data or intellectual property into criminal profits and to convert electronic financial flows into hard cash (Custers, Pool, & Cornelisse, 2018; McGuire, 2018). Because technical and entrepreneurial skills are usually held by distinct individuals, the social skills that bring them together and facilitate cooperation are crucial. Offenders who master these social skills usually display above-average abilities to assess trustworthiness and in turn elicit trust from strangers in an environment where the costs of betrayal or defection are very low (Holt, 2012; Allodi, Corradin, & Massacci, 2016; Décary-Hétu & Leppänen, 2016).

The skill distribution among participants in the criminal community implies that each individual plays a specific role. A number of studies have detailed a long list of functions that are needed to sustain the cybercrime ecosystem (Ablon, Libicki, & Golay, 2014; Hutchings & Holt, 2015; Grabosky, 2017). Each major function branches off into as many smaller, more specialized, tasks to be executed either in the virtual or real world (Leukfeldt, Kleemans, & Wouter, 2017a; Maimon & Louderback, 2019):

- Administrators of illegal online marketplaces, where people with various expertise can connect with each other and products and services can be bought and sold (Leukfeldt, Kleemans, & Wouter, 2017b).
- Programmers, whether they be responsible for identifying vulnerabilities, developing malware, encrypting malware to make it undetectable, distributing malware that infects thousands of devices, or even ensuring the criminal infrastructure is being maintained.
- Intermediaries who distribute mass email phishing campaigns, sell or rent out access to compromised devices, sell personal information such as credit card numbers, or manage call centres allowing fraudsters to circumvent security measures put in place by financial institutions.
- 'Mules' who more or less deliberately loan out their identities to facilitate money transfers from a victim's to a fraudster's account for a share of the profit.

These typologies, which are not exhaustive, illustrate to what extent the cybercrime community has left behind the picaresque and craft modes of organization that characterized traditional acquisitive crimes for more project-structured and business-oriented types of crime that form complex supply chains (McIntosh, 1975; Bhalerao, Aliapoulios, Shumailov, Afroz, & McCoy, 2018; Lusthaus, 2018). This transformation has helped in planning more complex crimes targeting companies and organizations that handle dematerialized assets but that also have implemented tougher countermeasures. This leads us to the question of the place held by organized criminal groups in this ecosystem. Despite the alarming statements made by many police organizations (see, for example, Europol's annual "Internet Organised Crime Threat Assessment" report), and the exception of a few rare documented incursions (Choo & Smith, 2008), nothing leads us to believe that traditional mafias have colonized the cybercrime ecosystem (Levi, Doig, Gundur, Wall, & Williams, 2015; Leukfeldt, Kleemans, & Wouter, 2017c). This could very well be explained by the difficulty of maintaining strong hierarchical relationships, the lack of monopolies over certain territories or criminal markets, or even the material impossibility of using physical violence as a method of coercion (Lusthaus, 2013).

The security community

As with the two previous groups, the security community is characterized by its diversity. As anyone would imagine, this community contains police organizations, which have been forced to adapt to changing crime trends by creating specialized cyber-investigation units (Levi et al., 2015; Harkin, Whelan, & Chang, 2018). By and large, these units lack the resources to combat the transnational crime affecting millions of people globally. The reality is that police organizations are a product of the industrial revolution and were created to maintain public order, which was being threatened by the frantic rate of urbanization at the time. Their territorial jurisdiction and focus on criminal neutralization do not equip them well to help millions of victims repair the damage done by cybercriminals from across the world. Initiatives that aim to facilitate international police cooperation are slowly being implemented and are increasingly involving players from the non-government and private sectors (Dupont, 2018).

Many security companies have flooded the highly profitable cybersecurity market, which had an estimated value of $US86 billion in 2017 (Gartner, 2017). These companies offer their clients technical solutions to protect them against cyber-intrusions in addition to incident-response and security breach investigation services. The names of some of these companies such as Symantec or Kaspersky are fairly familiar, but they also include innovative start-ups that claim to have discovered the new cybersecurity silver bullet (artificial intelligence is a strong contender at the moment) and small and medium-sized enterprises (SMEs) that employ a handful of consultants. Like in physical security, some large corporations also have their own internal teams made up of seasoned experts, particularity in the banking and telecommunications industries, as well as among defence companies and critical infrastructure operators. By comparison with their public police counterparts, private cybersecurity actors are clearly able to leverage more resources and technical expertise, while also being able to negotiate easier access to the data and systems targeted by cybercriminals and being less exposed to legal constraints, particularly when international efforts need to be coordinated. In that respect, they could be deemed more effective than police organizations in the fight against cybercrime, especially at the prevention and mitigation stages. However, they represent narrow corporate interests that do not necessarily align with the common good, and can therefore have different priorities than tackling the most-pressing harms threatening the digital ecosystem.

Beyond the traditional dichotomy composed of public and private actors, a detailed survey of the organizations active in fighting cybercrime at the national and international levels has also shed light on the significant role played by various non-governmental organizations (NGOs) and professional associations. These organizations play an underrated role in consolidating the expertise needed to address specific cybercrimes or cyber-harms such as the sexual exploitation of children (for example, the International Association of Internet Hotlines), phishing (for example, the Anti-Phishing Working Group), or cyberbullying (for example, the UK's Royal Foundation Taskforce on the Prevention of Cyberbullying).

These four groups of actors, if we include international organizations such as Interpol, Europol, or the International Telecommunications Union, tend to focus their attention and actions on specific cybersecurity issues, such as online financial fraud, child abuse, or destructive cyberattacks. This functional specialization is certainly convenient from an organizational perspective, but it contributes to an artificial scattering of expertise and capacities in a field where risks frequently overlap (petty cybercriminals often recycle the leaked tools and tradecraft of government hackers) and where the technological and organizational systems connecting the industrial, criminal, and security communities are interdependent.

These three communities should not be construed as mutually exclusive categories separated by hard organizational or social boundaries. On the contrary, they sometimes overlap and let individuals or the organizations that employ them occupy dual roles. It is not uncommon, for example, for cybersecurity professionals to also dabble in cybercrime activities (or vice versa, for cybercriminals to offer security services) (Solon, 2017), for the industrial community to resort to hacking practices in order to gain a competitive edge (Nicas & Bensinger, 2017), or for industry players to initiate takedowns and civil litigations against cybercriminal gangs (Dupont, 2017). The industrial, criminal, and security communities are therefore ideal types that help us understand the various forms of interactions at work in the cybersecurity ecosystem.

The three cybersecurity interdependencies

The actors that make up these three communities – whether they be companies selling technology products or services, criminal networks, or public and private organizations responsible for securing IT systems – are in constant interaction with each other based on three main relational modes, which determines the beneficial or harmful nature of these relationships. These three modes are competition, predation, and cooperation. They influence both the interactions among actors from the same community (intraspecific interdependencies) and between actors from different communities (interspecific interdependencies).

Competition

Often presented as a virtuous and necessary condition to breed a culture of innovation accelerating the pace of technological development, competition has often conflicted with the implementation of effective security practices, which are viewed as obstacles to obtaining new market shares and profitability. We saw earlier how the vitality and economic incentives that characterize the industrial community favour innovation, convenience and the rapid marketing of new products and services over security features, which often prove a burdensome afterthought.

The intense competitive pressures that shape this constantly changing environment, where the fear of losing clients frequently trumps the need to protect the latter, can lead to disastrous decisions for millions, or even billions, of users. This was for example the case for Yahoo!, whose infrastructure was compromised in 2010 by hackers probably employed by the Chinese government. Following this incident, upper management ignored requests from Yahoo!'s IT security team to reinforce the company's defence mechanisms. These decisions were based on the costs associated with the proposed fixes and fears of inconveniencing users, who had started to flock to new competitors such as Google. In a similar vein, when two major data breaches were disclosed to the public in 2016 (the first one having occurred in 2013 and the second in 2014), it appeared that Yahoo! had decided not to force its users to change their passwords when those incidents were discovered – a common industry practice – to help prevent email users from leaving for a different company. Another concern was that reinforcing security measures would prevent the company from accessing the content of its users' inboxes, thereby limiting the amount of targeted advertising the company could deliver (Perlroth & Goel, 2016). As we learned in October 2017, these considerations are by no means trivial, as they likely affected more than 3 billion users (McMillan & Knutson, 2017). This interference of competitive pressures on healthy security practices is not systematic. Google is proof of this. The search giant also faced a massive hack by the same group of Chinese attackers in 2010. However, Google decided to make security one of its organizational priorities by investing hundreds of thousands of dollars into that aspect of its business (Perlroth & Goel, 2016).

Google is a particularly interesting example. The company's move illustrates how competition can *a contrario* improve security practices when actively promoted by a key player in an industry. It shows how competitors can be compelled to adopt the same security practices to avoid being framed as a company neglecting its users' safety. Google has since implemented several 'naming and shaming' programmes, where they publicly reveal the vulnerabilities of their industry partners and competitors. In Google's transparency report, which was published for the first time in 2014, the company started revealing a list of its competitors that had not activated a default encryption feature for email accounts (Luckerson, 2014). In January 2017, this practice was extended to websites that asked their users to provide passwords or credit card numbers without using default encryption through the Transport Layer Security protocol (Francheschi-Bicchierai, 2016). In 2014, Google also launched 'Project Zero.' The project consists of a group of specialists responsible for identifying unknown security vulnerabilities in its competitors' products and publicly revealing them if they are not rectified within a reasonable time frame (Hackett, 2017). Although the aim of these initiatives is to improve security practices throughout the community, sometimes they are manipulated to inconvenience a competitor or to maintain market leadership. Software updates are a good example of this tendency to weaponize security activities that are generally presented as desirable for more dubious ends. These days, updates are no longer only meant to improve incrementally the security of applications and equipment. They can also be used to add new features to an application and thereby neutralize the efforts of potential competitors, or even block features of a competitor's software installed on the same device (Shuler & Smith, 2017). Thus, competition in the industrial community interferes with the implementation of security measures that benefit the whole cybersecurity ecosystem.

Of course, competition is not limited to the industrial community, and relationships among groups belonging to the criminal community are also determined by this form of interaction. For example, in the early 2010s, a rivalry erupted between the creators of two different banking fraud malware programs. One of the two added an uninstall feature that removed his competitor's program when it was found on a machine that had just been infected by his malware (Krebs, 2010). Cybercriminal networks that sell malware on underground forums also compete intensely over sale prices, features, and the quality of their technical support. They do not hesitate to disparage the reputation of their competitors on specialized criminal marketplaces, or even to leak the source code of their competitors' products to prevent them from profiting from their efforts (Dupont, Côté, Boutin, & Fernandez, 2017).

Competition figurations can also be found in the security community, where the publicity associated with the disruption and takedown of cybercriminal networks sometimes leads police services and security companies to make hasty moves without first coordinating with other security actors that may also have infiltrated those networks to monitor their activities. Takedowns in those circumstances disrupt criminal networks, but they also terminate access to intelligence sources that help cybersecurity experts understand how the threat landscape is evolving and what protective measures they should advise their clients to adopt (Lerner, 2014, p. 251).

Predation

Whereas competition defines the interdependent relationships between actors within an ecosystem, predation, on the other hand, is more prevalent between groups of actors from different communities. Predation occurs when one group of actors attacks another to seize its resources (such as personal information, sensitive data, or intellectual property) or neutralize the group (through arrest, the disclosure of personal information enabling the removal of anonymity – the practice of 'doxing,' or the disruption of a technical infrastructure used to commit cybercrimes). Unlike predation in the physical world, where each species usually has a fixed place in a food chain and the roles of predator and prey rarely change, the interactional symmetry that characterizes cyberspace introduces the novel concept of predatory reciprocity. In this perspective, the predatory relationship is not coloured by the inherent moral dimension so frequent in criminology and is mainly concerned with its security and survival implications for the actors subjected to it.

This means that predatory relationships are not limited to cybercrimes committed by actors from the criminal community on those from the industrial community and their users. They also include actions taken by the security community to permanently disrupt and disband cybercriminal networks. The interactional symmetry mentioned earlier also means that members of the criminal community can attack actors from the security community, for example, by infiltrating their computers to reveal confidential information, such as the personal contact details of police officers (Turnham & Lyon, 2012), the identities of police informers and undercover agents (Cox, 2016), secret surveillance practices and methods (Constantin, 2012), or even questionable business practices performed by some cybersecurity companies (Hern, 2015).

Predation sometimes also takes more subtle forms, for example, when cyberoffenders take advantage of the automated platforms offered by the industrial community to market their goods and services through advertising exchanges, or when their activities are protected from disruptions by the anti–distributed denial of service (DDoS) services provided freely to them by companies such as Cloudflare (Krebs, 2016b). In ecological terms, this symbiotic relationship oscillates between commensalism and parasitism: the companies that unwillingly provide their services are not directly harmed by criminal predators – which explains why they are often reluctant to take action – while the general population of digital users suffers the brunt of these abuses.

The various predation figurations that were just outlined never stop evolving, based on the vulnerabilities cybercriminals detect in the flow of digital products and services that enter the market, the innovations these actors develop to convert these vulnerabilities into crime profits, and the security mechanisms implemented when companies have reached the limit of losses they can tolerate or when their consumers' confidence is fading. As a result, and in contrast to ecological theories, the process of co-evolution between predator and prey in the cybersecurity ecosystem is characterized by compressed time scales. The capacity of various actors to innovate constantly and with unpredictability changes the dynamic of interdependencies and introduces accelerated sequences where figurations reach a new balance of tensions (Elias, 1978, p. 132).

In ecology, a predatory relationship is not associated with a normative judgement because it provides a positive contribution to ecosystems' natural balance by helping control populations size and limiting the pressure they exert on their environment (Odum, 1997). This is a major distinction from criminology, which as a social science cannot disregard the fate of individuals to only focus on the level of analysis of populations or ecosystems. However, we can legitimately ask the question of the collective benefits unintentionally generated by cybercriminals and their victims when they help identify poorly secured technologies and services and encourage the targeted organizations to respond to attacks by enhancing their investments in security engineering. As Killias (2006) illustrated, while the adoption of new technologies leads to vulnerabilities for criminals to exploit, these vulnerabilities are just as quickly fixed by technical and legal solutions implemented when the harms caused threaten the stability and growth of an economic sector or a business community. In other words, we could formulate the following hypothesis: the difference in size between criminal predators and their industrial preys certainly favours the former by giving them more agility and flexibility to identify exploitable vulnerabilities and profit from them, but this advantage is short-lived. As industrial prey closes the breaches that are brought to their attention by cybercriminals, they increase the protection of millions of users and contribute to improved levels of cybersecurity . . . until new offending opportunities emerge.

Cooperation

While the two previous interactional modes are mainly perceived as delivering negative externalities for the industrial and security communities, and ultimately Internet users, the concept of cooperation, on the other hand, which comprises a significant proportion of interactions between actors from the three communities, has a more positive connotation – except for the mechanisms that allow cybercriminals to collaborate with each other.

Because of the complexity involved in the technologies that need to be mastered and the security systems that are bypassed in the process, cybercrime relies on a division of labour to coordinate the various complementary skill sets required by transient criminal projects. But the dilemma that all cybercriminals face is whether to trust the critical co-offenders they need for their projects to succeed. This kind of decision has to be made in a digital environment where anonymity is the default state; where the near-irrelevance of geography and dematerialization of exchanges have almost eradicated face-to-face interactions; and where failures, mistakes, or malfeasance can hardly be deterred or punished by coercive means (Tilly, 2005). In this context, cooperation is both essential to becoming a successful offender and one of the hardest interactional modes to establish and maintain, mainly due to the trust deficit that characterizes relationships between cybercriminals. Hence, deceit is often much more profitable than cooperation, which explains why small groups of hackers (including the most dynamic online criminal markets) suffer from an endemic climate of mistrust and uncertainty that erodes their performance (Herley & Florêncio, 2010; Dupont, 2013). In order to overcome this sense of mistrust and to promote cooperation, reputation management mechanisms inspired by those available on major e-commerce platforms such as Amazon and eBay have been developed with variable rates of success (Lusthaus, 2012).

Although cooperation within the criminal community contributes to its members' improved performance, the collaborative ties that increasingly link members of the industrial and security communities reflect a more defensive approach. For them, cooperation aims to compensate for the shortcomings generated by intense intraspecific competition and the incapacity of police organizations to adapt to this new criminal environment. Nascent cooperation patterns between Internet companies, cybersecurity vendors, and the police have helped establish a web of legal, technical, and organizational capacities that were fragmented until very recently. This network provides innovative solutions to the challenges posed by the industrialization of cybercrime. For example, the problem of botnets, which now provide the basic infrastructure for most cybercrimes, has helped generate original cooperation figurations between these three categories of actors, spurred in particular by Microsoft's efforts (Dupont, 2017). Unlike more traditional approaches to cooperation, where a single category of actors (the public police) attempts to manage transnational crime through arrest and incapacitation, this polycentric form of cooperation is defined by institutional diversity and the establishment of a network of organizations that are not used to collaborate with each other, but leverage complementary capacities to reduce harms (Dupont, 2018).

The two main cooperation figurations outlined here do not only differ because they display very variable implementation capacities, stretching from the most rapid (often witnessed in criminal cooperation) to most sluggish paces (more characteristic of institutional cooperation). The thorny question of accountability, which is obviously of no concern to criminal co-operators, is a crucial aspect of cybercrime prevention and enforcement. If these two activities are henceforth delivered by hybrid cooperation networks composed of organizations pooling very intrusive technical expertise and legal powers, what transparency, privacy, and oversight mechanisms will apply to ensure these new security figurations remain compatible with the democratic principles of justice and equality? In other words, how do we make sure more structured private interests do not capture the few public resources available so that these security figurations remain committed to the common good?

The competition, predation, and cooperation interactions come together to create a large web of interdependencies connecting the various actors from the three communities. Table 17.1 summarizes the intraspecific interactions of each community (grey boxes), as well as interspecific linkages between pairs of communities. The direction of the relationship is obtained by reading the table starting from the top row and matching one of the three communities with its counterpart in the left-hand column. For example, we can see how actors from the security community maintain a relationship of cooperation with the industrial community and that this relationship is reciprocal heading in the other direction. On the other hand, interactions between security actors and criminal actors are not as diametrically reciprocal: if the security community defines its relationship with the criminal community as a predatory one, focusing on arrests and disruption, the criminal community responds to this mode of interaction mostly through avoidance, and in rare cases that can prove costly through predation. Avoidance is the absence of interaction, and, as such, does not appear to require further development.

Conclusion

This chapter provides an ecological framework of the risks associated with cybercrime. This approach is intended to be more metaphorical than literal, in contrast to other attempts at applying concepts and resources from the natural sciences to criminology (Felson, 2006). The ecology of cybersecurity takes a more modest approach to borrowing a few of the main concepts from biology to try to better understand the complexity of the relationships that now exist between humans, machines, and algorithms.

This goal is attained by combining some core notions such as ecosystem, competition, predation, and cooperation with sociological theories compatible with the profound transformations and hyper-connectivity introduced by the digital revolution, particularly Norbert Élias's (1978) works on figurational sociology.

Table 17.1 Intraspecific and extra-specific modes of interaction between the three communities

Direction of the relationship	Industrial community	Criminal community	Security community
Industrial community	Competition Cooperation	Predation	Cooperation
Criminal community	Avoidance	Cooperation Competition Predation	Predation
Security community	Cooperation	Avoidance Predation	Cooperation

Although it was not used in this chapter for lack of space, Bruno Latour's (2007) work on actor–network theory is also highly relevant to that approach, especially in light of its interest for understanding how non-human entities such as botnets act, and make humans act, in those cybercrime figurations (van der Wagen, 2015). Now that the conceptual foundations for this cybersecurity ecology have been laid, empirical studies will be required to refine the scope of these concepts and their utility to help us better understand the source of digital risks, their impact on contemporary societies, and the most promising governance strategies.

The ecological approach advocated in this chapter could lead, for example, to longitudinal studies of figurations that result from interactions between criminal innovation and situational crime prevention to better understand how the three communities mutually adapt to changes introduced by their adversaries and partners. The evolution of specific types of online fraud could be tracked over extended periods of time (10 to 20 years) to identify what specific measures taken by industrial and security community members led to inflections in the victimization rate and what industrial or criminal innovations spurred higher levels of exposure to criminal risks. Targeted case studies could also teach us why actors from certain communities prefer competition at the expense of cooperation. Similarly, case studies could also be conducted to understand the technological and organizational parameters that trigger predation. The outcomes of these two types of very detailed empirical research would support the design of policies and interventions that incentivize and enhance cooperation across the industrial and security communities while decreasing predatory opportunities. Security impact assessments could be conducted when new technologies or processes are introduced by the industrial community and pre-emptive mitigation measures involving cooperative arrangements could be implemented. The emergent effects that this complex web of interactions will inevitably produce will also need to be forecasted, tracked, and assessed to account for the new, unpredictable, and non-additive features such as synergies and negative externalities that will appear as a result (Corning, 2002). This research programme will naturally draw on well-established criminological approaches, such as situational crime prevention, security governance, and victimology, while incorporating knowledge from ecology, economy, computer science, regulatory studies, and the sociology of risks (Maimon & Louderback, 2019), in the continuation of the long tradition of integration in the field of criminology.

Notes

1 https://nvd.nist.gov/general/nvd-dashboard
2 These figures were valid on 12 June 2018.

References

Ablon, L., Libicki, M., & Golay, A. (2014). *Markets for cybercrime tools and stolen data: Hacker's bazaar*. Santa Monica, CA: RAND Corporation.

Allodi, L., Corradin, M., & Massacci, F. (2016). Then and now: On the maturity of the cyber-crime markets. The lessons that black-hat marketers learned. *IEEE Transactions on Emerging Topics*, 4(1), 35–46.

Anderson, R. (2008). *Security engineering*. Chichester: Wiley.

Bauman, Z., Bigo, D., Esteves, P., Guild, E., Jabri, V., Lyon, D., & Walker, R. B. J. (2014). After Snowden: Rethinking the impact of surveillance. *International Political Sociology*, 8(2), 121–144.

Benkler, Y. (2006). *The wealth of networks*. New Haven, CT: Yale University Press.

Bhalerao, R., Aliapoulios, M., Shumailov, I., Afroz, S., & McCoy, D. (2018). Towards automatic discovery of cybercrime supply chains. *arXiv:1812.00381v2 [cs.CR]*, 1–16. Retrieved from https://arxiv.org/abs/1812.00381

Braithwaite, J. (2014). In praise of tents: Regulatory studies and transformative social science. *Annual Review of Law and Social Science*, 10, 1–17.

Caneppele, S., & Aebi, M. (2017). Crime drop or police recording flop? On the relationship between the decrease of offline crime and the increase of online and hybrid crimes. *Policing: A Journal of Policy and Practice*. doi:10.1093/police/pax055

Castells, M. (1996). *The rise of the network society*. Cambridge: Blackwell Publishers.

Castells, M. (2001). *The internet galaxy: Reflections on the Internet, business and society*. Oxford: Oxford University Press.

Choo, K.-K. R., & Smith, R. (2008). Criminal exploitation of online systems by organised crime groups. *Asian Journal of Criminology*, 3(1), 37–59.

Constantin, L. (2012, January 10). Father's attempt at parental control resulted in hacked German police system. *NetworkWorld*. Retrieved from www.networkworld.com/article/2184610/network-security/father-s-attempt-at-parental-control-resulted-in-hacked-german-police-system.html

Copes, H., & Vieraitis, L. (2008). The risks, rewards and strategies of stealing identities. In M. McNally & G. Newman (Eds.), *Identity theft and opportunity, crime prevention studies* (Vol. 23, pp. 87–110). Monsey, NY: Criminal Justice Press.

Corning, P. (2002). The re-emergence of "emergence": A venerable concept in search of a theory. *Complexity*, 7(6), 18–30.

Council of Canadian Academies. (2014). *Policing Canada in the 21st century: New policing for new challenges*. Ottawa: Council of Canadian Academies.

Cox, J. (2016, May 13). A 2005 FBI hack exposed a secret list of informants and hunted cybercriminals. *Motherboard*. Retrieved from https://motherboard.vice.com/en_us/article/wnxxdy/fbi-hack-in-2005-exposed-names-of-wanted-cybercriminals

Custers, B., Pool, R., & Cornelisse, R. (2018). Banking malware and the laundering of its profits. *European Journal of Criminology*. doi:10.1177/1477370818788007

Décary-Hétu, D., & Leppänen, A. (2016). Criminals and signals: An assessment of criminal performance in the carding underworld. *Security Journal*, 29(3), 442–460.

Deibert, R. (2013). *Black code: Surveillance, privacy and the dark side of the internet*. Toronto: Signal.

DeNardis, L. (2014). *Global war for internet governance*. New Haven, CT: Yale University Press.

Dupont, B. (2013). Skills and trust: A tour inside the hard drives of computer hackers. In C. Morselli (Ed.), *Illicit networks* (pp. 195–217). Oxford: Routledge.

Dupont, B. (2017). Bots, cops and corporations: On the limits of enforcement and the promise of polycentric regulation as a way to control large-scale cybercrime. *Crime, Law and Social Change*, 67(1), 97–116.

Dupont, B. (2018). The global anti-cybercrime network: Mapping the polycentric regulation of online harms. In L. Chang & R. Brewer (Eds.), *Criminal justice and regulation revisited: Essays in honour of Peter Grabosky* (pp. 163–185). New York, NY: Routledge.

Dupont, B., Côté, A.-M., Boutin, J.-I., & Fernandez, J. (2017). Recruitment patterns and transactional features of "the most dangerous cybercrime forum in the world". *American Behavioral Scientist, 61*(11), 1219–1243.

Elias, N. (1978). *What is sociology.* London: Hutchinson & Co. Publishers.

Felson, M. (2006). *Crime and nature.* Thousand Oaks, CA: SAGE Publications.

Francheschi-Bicchierai, L. (2016, September 8). Google Chrome will start shaming unencrypted websites in January. *Motherboard.* Retrieved from https://motherboard.vice.com/en_us/article/xyg55z/google-chrome-shaming-http-unencrypted-websites-january

Gandhi, P., Khanna, S., & Ramaswamy, S. (2016, April 1). Which industries are the most digital (and why)? *Harvard Business Review.* Retrieved from https://hbr.org/2016/04/a-chart-that-shows-which-industries-are-the-most-digital-and-why

Gartner. (2017, August 16). Gartner says worldwide information security spending will grow 7 percent to reach $86.4 billion in 2017. *Gartner.* Retrieved from www.gartner.com/newsroom/id/3784965

Giddens, A. (1999). Risk and responsibility. *Modern Law Review, 62*(1), 1–10.

Grabosky, P. (2017). The evolution of cybercrime 2006–2016. In T. J. Holt (Ed.), *Cybercrime through an interdisciplinary lens* (pp. 15–36). New York, NY: Routledge.

Hackett, R. (2017, June 23). Google's elite hacker SWAT team vs. everyone. *Fortune.* Retrieved from http://fortune.com/2017/06/23/google-project-zero-hacker-swat-team/

Harkin, D., Whelan, C., & Chang, L. (2018). The challenges facing specialist police cybercrime units: An empirical analysis. *Police Practice and Research: An International Journal, 19*(6), 519–536.

Herley, C., & Florêncio, D. (2010). Nobody sells gold for the price of silver: Dishonesty, uncertainty and the underground economy. In T. Moore, D. Pym, & C. Ioannidis (Eds.), *Economics of information security and privacy* (pp. 33–53). New York, NY: Springer.

Hern, A. (2015, July 6). Hacking team hacked: Firm sold spying tools to repressive regimes, documents claim. *The Guardian.* Retrieved from www.theguardian.com/technology/2015/jul/06/hacking-team-hacked-firm-sold-spying-tools-to-repressive-regimes-documents-claim

Holt, T. (2012). Examining the forces shaping cybercrime markets online. *Social Science Computer Review, 31*(2), 165–177.

Holt, T., & Bossler, A. (2014). An assessment of the current state of cybercrime scholarship. *Deviant Behavior, 35*(1), 20–40.

Hutchings, A., & Holt, T. (2015). A crime script analysis of the online stolen data market. *The British Journal of Criminology, 55*(3), 596–614.

Killias, M. (2006). The opening and closing of breaches: A theory on crime waves, law creation and crime prevention. *European Journal of Criminology, 3*(1), 11–31.

Krebs, B. (2010, April 1). SpyEye vs. Zeus rivalry. *Krebs on Security.* Retrieved from https://krebsonsecurity.com/2010/04/spyeye-vs-zeus-rivalry/

Krebs, B. (2016a, October 1). Source code for IoT botnet 'Mirai' released. *Krebs on Security.* Retrieved from https://krebsonsecurity.com/2016/10/source-code-for-iot-botnet-mirai-released/

Krebs, B. (2016b, October 19). Spreading the DDoS disease and selling the cure. *Krebs on Security.* Retrieved from https://krebsonsecurity.com/2016/10/spreading-the-ddos-disease-and-selling-the-cure/

Latour, B. (2007). *Reassembling the social: An introduction to Actor-Network-Theory.* Oxford: Oxford University Press.

Lerner, Z. (2014). Microsoft the botnet hunter: The role of public-private partnerships in mitigating botnets. *Harvard Journal of Law & Technology, 28*(1), 237–261.

Lessig, L. (2006). *Code version 2.0.* New York, NY: Basic Books.

Leukfeldt, R. (Ed.). (2017). *Research agenda: The human factor in cybercrime and cybersecurity.* The Hague: Eleven International Publishing.

Leukfeldt, R., Kleemans, E., & Wouter, S. (2017a). A typology of cybercriminal networks: From low-tech all-rounders to high-tech specialists. *Crime, Law and Social Change, 67*(1), 21–37.

Leukfeldt, R., Kleemans, E., & Wouter, S. (2017b). Cybercriminal networks, social ties and online forums: Social ties versus digital ties within phishing and malware networks. *The British Journal of Criminology, 57*(3), 704–722.

Leukfeldt, R., Lavorgna, A., & Kleemans, E. (2017c). Organised cybercrime or cybercrime that is organised? An assessment of the conceptualisation of financial cybercrime as organised crime. *European Journal on Criminal Policy and Research, 23*(3), 287–300.

Lévêque, C. (2003). *Ecology: From ecosystem to biosphere.* New York, NY: CRC Press.

Levi, M. (2017). Assessing the trends, scale and nature of economic cybercrimes: Overview and issues. *Crime, Law and Social Change, 67*(1), 3–20.

Levi, M., Doig, A., Gundur, R., Wall, D., & Williams, M. (2015). *The implications of economic cybercrime for policing.* London: City of London Police.

Luckerson, V. (2014, June 4). Google shaming email providers into offering encryption. *Time.* Retrieved from http://time.com/2822100/google-email-encryption/

Lusthaus, J. (2012). Trust in the world of cybercrime. *Global Crime, 13*(2), 71–94.

Lusthaus, J. (2013). How organised is organised cybercrime? *Global Crime, 14*(1), 52–60.

Lusthaus, J. (2018). *Industry of anonymity: Inside the business of cybercrime.* Cambridge, MA: Harvard University Press.

Macdonald, M., & Frank, R. (2017). The network structure of malware development, deployment and distribution. *Global Crime, 18*(1), 49–69.

Maimon, D., & Louderback, E. (2019). Cyber-dependent crimes: An interdisciplinary review. *Annual Review of Criminology, 2,* 191–216.

MarketsAndMarkets. (2018). *Cybersecurity market by solution (IAM, encryption, UTM, antivirus/antimalware, firewall, IDS/IPS, disaster recovery, and DDOS mitigation), service, security type, deployment mode, organization size, industry vertical, and region – Global forecast to 2023.* Pune: MarketsAndMarkets.

McGuire, M. (2018). *Into the web of profit: Understanding the growth of the cybercrime economy.* Cupertino, CA: Bromium.

McIntosh, M. (1975). *The organisation of crime.* London: Macmillan Press.

McMillan, R., & Knutson, R. (2017, June 13). Yahoo triples estimate of breached accounts to 3 billion. *The Wall Street Journal.* Retrieved from www.wsj.com/articles/yahoo-triples-estimate-of-breached-accounts-to-3-billion-1507062804

Nicas, J., & Bensinger, G. (2017, December 15). Uber hacked and surveilled rivals, alleges ex-manager in letter. *The Wall Street Journal.* Retrieved from www.wsj.com/articles/uber-hacked-and-surveilled-rivals-alleges-ex-manager-in-letter-1513389333

Odum, E. (1997). *Ecology: A bridge between science and society.* Sunderland, MA: Sinauer Associates.

Perlroth, N., & Goel, V. (2016, September 28). Defending against hackers took a back seat at Yahoo, insiders say. *The New York Times.* Retrieved from www.nytimes.com/2016/09/29/technology/yahoo-data-breach-hacking.html?_r=0

Shuler, R., & Smith, B. (2017). Internet of Things behavioral-economic security design, actors & cyber war. *Advances in Internet of Things, 7*(2), 25–45.

Solon, O. (2017, August 11). Marcus Hutchins: Cybersecurity experts rally around arrested WannaCry 'hero'. *The Guardian*. Retrieved from www.theguardian.com/technology/2017/aug/11/marcus-hutchins-arrested-wannacry-kronos-cybersecurity-experts-react

Tcherni, M., Davies, A., Lopes, G., & Lizotte, A. (2016). The dark figure of online property crime: Is cyberspace hiding a crime wave? *Justice Quarterly, 33*(5), 890–911.

The&Partnership. (2017). *What happens next: How to reverse the rising tide of ad fraud.* Retrieved from https://theandpartnership.app.box.com/s/qt8ahj4led6h77b2dsbsa1bnu07wxqcm

Tilly, C. (2005). *Trust and rule.* Cambridge: Cambridge University Press.

Turnham, S., & Lyon, A. (2012, January 13). *Cop watchers: Anonymous vs. police.* Retrieved from www.cnn.com/2012/01/13/us/cnnpresents-anonymous-vs-police/index.html

Van der Wagen, W. (2015). From cybercrime to cyborg crime: Botnets as hybrid criminal actor-networks. *British Journal of Criminology, 55*(3), 578–595.

Verizon (2018). *2018 Data breach investigations report.* Basking Ridge, NJ: Verizon Enterprise.

Wall, D. (2007). Policing cybercrimes: Situating the public police in networks of security within cyberspace. *Police Practice and Research: An International Journal, 8*(2), 183–205.

18 Displacing big data

How criminals cheat the system

Alice Hutchings, Sergio Pastrana, and Richard Clayton

Introduction

In this chapter, we consider how commercial organizations are using 'big data' processing to detect and prevent cybercrime. Typically, a large dataset is created to hold information about how customers interact with the organization. Known instances of crime are then considered, with the aim of determining what differences in behaviour can be identified when comparing criminals with all the legitimate customers. Going forward, the organization will use these differences to flag up behaviour which matches the criminal profile with a view to preventing further crimes. Although this type of big data approach is used by national security and policing agencies (Chan & Moses, 2017), we focus on established uses by financial institutions and technology companies.

Displacement occurs when offenders or crime changes as a direct result of preventative actions and can result in crime changing and evolving (Cornish & Clarke, 1987). Online, offenders do not have to physically relocate in order to displace their activities. Smith, Wolanin, and Worthington (2003) characterized the different types of displacement that can occur online. These include moving to new locations, times, targets, methods, offenders, or offence types.

Displacement has been noted in relation to a number of cybercrime types as a direct result of prevention measures. For example, offenders providing denial of service attacks for a fee (known as 'booter services') have come across a number of obstacles designed to stymie their activities, such as patching the servers being used to reflect traffic and blocking the accounts they use to receive payment. In these situations, offenders have displaced by changing the methods used for denial of service attacks (Hutchings & Clayton, 2015) and accepting new forms of payment such as bitcoin (Karami, Park, & McCoy, 2016).

Displacement is very evident following website takedown, a popular disruption method for a number of cybercrime types, most notably phishing (Moore & Clayton, 2007). Hutchings, Clayton, and Anderson (2016) explored the displacement effects observed following website takedown. These include displacing to new domain names or new hosting providers, including 'bulletproof' and abuse-tolerant providers. Offenders also selected different targets, such as different brands, and diversified phishing targets away from financial institutions towards other online services. New methods included technical approaches to make takedowns harder. As well as displacing, websites are simply replaced, reappearing in the same location. This typically occurs with malicious pages hosted within compromised websites, when the vulnerability that led to the initial compromise is not fixed. As a result, takedown is often described as a 'whack-a-mole' approach, as websites tend to pop back up soon after (Hutchings et al., 2016; Chia, Chuang, & Chen, 2016).

Some crimes that are commonly detected using big data solutions, such as fraud detection systems, have also been seen to displace in response to intervention. For example, credit card fraud used to be the main method for fraudulently obtaining airline tickets. However, as detection of these unauthorized transactions improved, offenders changed their operations, including compromising loyalty point accounts, phishing travel agencies for their access credentials for booking systems, and compromising business accounts (Hutchings, 2018b).

Although these are relatively straightforward examples of displacement, in this chapter we instead focus on more complicated ways that criminals have designed ways of circumventing big data systems to avoid detection. We demonstrate the practical limitations of machine learning and big data approaches in adversarial settings. To do this, we explore how online crime and crime prevention techniques have co-evolved over time.

Cybercrime risks and big data approaches

The systems we describe here use algorithms to detect unusual activity that may point to active instances of particular types of cybercrime, namely the use of compromised credit cards, access to compromised accounts, malicious communications, unauthorized access to computer systems, malware infection, and denial of service attacks.

Machine learning approaches may use one of a variety of techniques, including supervised, unsupervised, and reinforcement approaches (Robert, 2014). Supervised approaches require training data that have been pre-labelled. Unsupervised learning involves a fully automated approach without any pre-labelled training data, with the aim of identifying interesting patterns. Reinforcement learning involves reward or punishment signals.

Although many of the specifics of how these systems work are the 'secret sauce' of the commercial organizations that provide them, we do know that many use big data approaches, typically learning from what 'normal' behaviour looks like (and therefore detecting unusual behaviour), as well as 'red flags,' or activities that are indicative of crime.

We start by describing the crimes and detection systems. We will later demonstrate how these mitigations can be circumvented by motivated offenders, leading to displacement and offence evolution.

Use of compromised credit cards

Credit cards can be compromised in a number of ways, both online and offline. Methods include data breaches, skimmers installed on point-of-sale terminals and automated teller machines (ATMs), malware, phishing, theft, and physical mail interception. Depending on the methods by which it is obtained, credit card data can come in a variety of forms. 'Dumps' include the data read from the magnetic strips on the back of cards, obtained by skimming, and can be used to create card clones. Credit card numbers, expiry dates, and card verification values, found on the back of the card, are required to process card-not-present payments. 'Fullz' refers to the full information associated with the account, including data relating to the account holder, such as name, address, and date of birth (Hutchings & Holt, 2015).

Stolen data markets provide platforms for the sale of compromised credit card data (Franklin, Paxson, Perrig, & Savage, 2007; Holt & Lampke, 2010; Hutchings & Holt, 2015; Motoyama, McCoy, Levchenko, Savage, & Voelker, 2011). Cloned and stolen cards can be used over the counter or at ATMs if personal identification numbers (PINs) are also obtained. However, card-not-present transactions require data that can be obtained without physical contact with the card, and can be completed online, by phone, or by mail order. The main objective is to monetize the compromised cards, such as by selling on purchased goods and services (Hutchings & Holt, 2015).

Fraud detection systems

Fraud detection systems are used to detect credit card fraud at the time of the transaction (Abdallah, Maarof, & Zainal, 2016; Phua, Lee, Smith, & Gayler, 2010). These systems use algorithms to score the potential risk. They identify patterns that do not match the cardholder, such as the Internet Protocol (IP) address and location, address provided, browser, language setting, and spending patterns. They also identify patterns that match known frauds, such as the type of purchase and associated variables. A risky transaction can then be reviewed and attempts can be made to confirm its legitimacy by making enquiries with the cardholder. If there is confirmed fraud, or significant doubt, the transaction may be cancelled or another payment method requested.

Fraud detection systems may be used by the merchant, as well as by financial institutions attempting to detect fraudulent transactions on their cards. Third-party vendors and payment processors may also have their own fraud detection systems. Multiple parties operating their own fraud detection systems is beneficial, because while one party, such as a merchant, may see deeply into fraud on their own systems, another party, such as a bank or third-party vendor, may see more breadth, with attempted transactions across multiple targets (Hutchings, 2018b).

Access to compromised accounts

A variety of accounts may be compromised, such as bank, email, social media, merchant, and gaming accounts. There are also a number of ways accounts can be compromised, either at scale or by targeting particular account holders. For example, data breaches may provide access to large numbers of online accounts. Furthermore, if username and password combinations are breached, these may be checked against other online systems to gain access to accounts where credentials have been reused. Therefore, accounts may be compromised due to opportunity, as well as through targeted attacks. Accounts may also be compromised through the use of malware or phishing (Onaolapo, Mariconti, & Stringhini, 2016). Account recovery systems can also be misused to gain access to particular accounts, particularly where 'secret' questions can be inferred through other public or known information.

Some account credentials are offered for sale in online criminal markets, whereas others may be released publicly on websites such as Pastebin (Onaolapo et al., 2016). However, accounts can also be used by those that obtained them or their accomplices. Accounts can be used to commit other types of offences, such as email and social media accounts for the purpose of sending malicious communications (as detailed in the following section).

Onaolapo et al. (2016) monitored the way compromised Gmail accounts are used by purposely leaking accounts under their control and observing the subsequent activity. Most visitors appeared to be simply curious and did not perform any further actions after accessing the accounts. However, other visitors using the leaked credentials searched for potentially sensitive information that could be monetized or they sent email spam, and some attempted to lock out the account holder by changing the password.

Behavioural analysis

The Messaging, Malware and Mobile Anti-Abuse Working Group (M³AAWG) is an industry group that develops cooperative approaches for the purpose of combating cybercrime. Among their 'best practice' guides, M³AAWG (2014) have recommendations for detecting the types of unusual activity associated with compromised accounts. They recommend using systems that require big data solutions, which can then detect unusual account activity, such as access from different locations or devices. Whereas this analytic approach compares activity to the usual behaviour of the account holder, other approaches compare behaviours with the activity that typically occurs after compromise.

Indications that an account may be compromised may differ by account type. For example, for email accounts, indications could include sending messages to all contacts or the deletion of sent mail. For some other account types, a typical pattern associated with compromise is immediate steps to lock out the account holder. Changing passwords and associated email addresses rarely occurs spontaneously, which facilitates detection.

Malicious communications

As identified earlier, some accounts may be compromised for the purpose of sending malicious communications. Other accounts may be specifically set up for this purpose. Malicious communications can be sent on many different platforms and can take the form of email, chat, text messages, or social media posts. The malicious purpose of the communication may include disseminating spam or phishing URLs, distributing malware, or attempts at social engineering for fraudulent purposes.

Moore and Clayton (2015) analyse how malicious communications have spread across instant messaging and social media systems. The messages analysed contained URLs, and when the website was visited by the recipient, they could also be infected with malware, and those in their contact lists were in turn sent a copy of the malicious message. By monitoring the command and control (C&C) channel that was issuing instructions to the malware, they found that offenders changed their methods in response to efforts made to take down websites that the URLs directed to, such as using URL shorteners for malicious links.

One way to detect malicious communications is to measure behaviour that is different from that of the purported sender (Egele, Stringhini, Kruegel, & Vigna, 2017). In addition to the behavioural analyses that may indicate that an account has been compromised (as discussed earlier), anomalous patterns can be identified in the messages that are sent, and the associated metadata.

Patterns can also be detected for similar messages to known malicious communications. For example, for malicious messages sent over social media, this could include the message content and the presence of suspicious URLs (Egele et al., 2017). Additional factors may include attachments, and for email, 'spoofing' (a term used in computer security to refer to events in which an attacker masquerades as another party) the header information to make it appear it had been sent by a legitimate organization (Fette, Sadeh, & Tomasic, 2007).

Unauthorised access to computer systems

Remote exploitation mechanisms rely on system vulnerabilities to gain unauthorized access to a computer system. Exploitation usually consists of three phases: scanning the network, sending the exploit, and post-exploitation. Prior to triggering an exploit, offenders usually scan networks (or the whole Internet) to find vulnerable machines. Once a vulnerability is discovered, a crafted network packet containing the corresponding exploit is sent. The post-exploitation phase usually involves the compromised system connecting to a remote server (also known as a C&C server) for further instructions, for example, to download additional malware which will persist after the machine reboots.

Another way of gaining unauthorized access to a machine is by means of escalation of privileges, where users with restricted permissions gain access to unauthorized assets within the same system or network. Vulnerable machines, weak passwords, and weak security policies (e.g. those that do not enforce access control or have configuration flaws) are the most common causes that allow for escalation of privileges (Affinity IT Security Services, 2017).

Intrusion detection systems

Intrusion detection systems (IDS) are one of the oldest security mechanisms used to protect systems and networks (Denning, 1987). These systems look for patterns of malicious behaviour in either the network (network IDS, or NIDS) or the host activity (host IDS or HIDS). An IDS will trigger alarms when any suspicious activity is monitored. Prior to exposing the alerts to human operators for further inspection, IDS alarms might be further correlated with other activity gathered from the systems or networks, such as system or router logs, or even other IDS alarms in Security Information and Event Management (SIEM) systems.

IDSs are typically classified based on their detection mode. *Anomaly-based* IDSs compute a model of normal behaviour and trigger alarms when they monitor activity that does not fit within the model. *Signature-based* IDSs analyse the monitored activity looking for malicious patterns which are encoded in a predefined set of rules or 'signatures.' The main challenge for an anomaly-based IDS is to compute a model that represents faithfully the normality, due to the current complexity of current systems and networks. This paradigm leads to a higher false-positive rate (i.e. normal activity being tagged as suspicious). On the contrary, signature-based IDSs are more precise when detecting known attacks but are ineffective at detecting so-called zero-day exploits (i.e. attacks that have not been seen previously and for which there are no known signatures).

The use of big data technologies for IDSs is widespread. This is mainly due to the large number of network packets and system events that need to be processed. Example analytical approaches include machine learning, graph analysis, and clustering, which have previously been applied to characterize traffic sent to and from C&C servers (Gardiner & Nagaraja, 2016). Additionally, the increased use of 'Internet of Things' devices and mobile sensors poses additional challenges which require big data approaches. Previous studies showed that intrusion detection for mobile ad-hoc networks (MANETs) can be performed by means of evolutionary computation techniques (Sen & Clark, 2011) or machine learning classifiers (Pastrana, Mitrokotsa, Orfila, & Peris-Lopez, 2012).

Malware infection

Malware, or malicious software, poses a number of risks. Malware infections can result in stolen data and compromised credentials (Hutchings & Clayton, 2017). Malware can create botnets, whereby the connected machines can be controlled to perform acts in concert, such as denial of service attacks or phishing campaigns. Malware known as 'ransomware' encrypts data, demanding payment of a ransom if the victim wants to regain access. Attackers using malware to compromise victims' machines may have additional motivations, such as accessing the webcam for voyeurism.

Antivirus software

Antivirus programs constantly run in the background of systems looking for evidence of malware infection. Commonly, antivirus companies manage a list of known bad applications, such as fingerprints of malicious files, blacklists of IP addresses, or malicious programs that are known to be loaded by malware. These lists must be periodically updated by the antivirus program from the antivirus company server to prevent infection from new pieces of malware.

Antivirus companies receive a large number of new samples to analyse every day. There are two approaches for binary analysis: static and dynamic analysis. Static analysis focuses on the binary itself, analysing the contents without executing it to detect suspicious activity (i.e. without installing and running the software). Dynamic analysis is performed by executing the malware in a 'sandbox.' The term sandbox refers to a controlled machine where the binary can be safely executed and its behaviour can be analysed (Gandotra, Bansal, & Sofat, 2014).

According to Panda Labs (2017), up to 285,000 suspected malware programs were analysed daily during 2017, though such information should be analysed critically (Anderson et al., 2013). Given this threat scenario, big data approaches are necessary to rapidly classify the analysed binaries. There is a large volume of research applying machine learning for the purpose of classifying malware samples. For example, Rieck, Trinius, Willems, and Holz (2011) applied clustering algorithms to group malware samples into families and detect botnet campaigns based on the responses from the Domain Name System (DNS) server. Dash et al. (2016) used machine learning to classify Android malware into families, based on the activity monitored during the execution of the samples in a controlled environment.

Denial of service attacks

Distributed denial of service (DDoS) attacks involve overloading a website or computer system with bogus traffic, thereby blocking legitimate access. DDoS attacks have a wide range of targets, such as corporations, governments, and gaming servers (Karami & McCoy, 2013). The targets may vary with the purpose of the attack, such as extortion (demanding payment for 'protection' against further attacks), and protest. Booter services provide DDoS attacks as a service, which is primarily advertised towards gamers, offering them an advantage against their adversaries (Hutchings & Clayton, 2015).

At one time, DDoS attacks were primarily carried out using botnets, following malware infection. However, 'amplification' or 'reflection' methods allow attackers to have greater power with limited resources. Amplification attacks involve spoofing the victim's IP address and sending a query to another server. As it appears the question was sent by the victim, the response is returned to them. Because the responses are larger than the requests, the attacker has amplified the amount of traffic sent to the victim, reflected from another server, compared to the resources they actually deployed (Thomas, Clayton, & Beresford, 2017).

Denial of service attack protection

There is now a substantial industry providing DDoS mitigation services. The basic idea is to place a device 'in front of' the systems to be protected and inspect the incoming traffic. Malicious traffic is discarded, but 'good' traffic is passed on to the service, which can then respond as normal. This will keep the service available for legitimate users, provided the detection is accurate and provided that the malicious traffic does not exhaust the available bandwidth. Complex arrangements to reroute traffic are used to deal with bandwidth issues and indeed just to arrange that the filtering device can be put 'in front of' the system to be protected. Further information about the type of systems involved can be found in the survey by Zargar, Joshi, and Tipper (2013) and the book by Yu (2014).

Filtering systems originally depended on simple heuristics or used custom filters specially created by a human to deal with the particular attack. Recently considerable academic work has been done on machine learning systems that use a wide range of traffic characteristics to determine whether or not traffic is malicious (and whether or not there is an attack going on at all) (Mayhew, Atighetchi, Adler, & Greenstadt, 2015; Sommer & Paxson, 2010; Zuech, Khoshgoftaar, & Wald, 2015). However, the actual devices are made by commercial companies, and they provide no details of their technology.

Cheating the system

During the course of our research careers, we have identified a number of ways criminals have cheated big data systems in order to circumvent detection. In some of the case studies we outline next, we acknowledge we are deliberately vague about certain details in order to protect specific organizations and industry types and to avoid further malevolent development of these approaches.

Fraud detection systems are not fool-proof. In particular, they have mainly been developed to detect fraudulent credit card transactions, so few will detect more elaborate frauds. Many merchants use fraud detection systems within their online shops where there is a wealth of data that can inform fraud risk, such as IP addresses and device fingerprints. However, some merchants may also operate call centres that do not use such systems, and even if they did, there is far less data to go on.

Some types of transactions are time sensitive. However, confirming fraud can take time. When fraud is identified or suspected, merchants will usually check with the bank to verify a transaction is not authorized. This introduces delays, especially when crossing international borders, as there can be time zone and language differences. This issue is compounded when there is no incentive for the issuing bank to detect fraud themselves or respond in a timely fashion. If the purchase is fraudulent, they suffer no financial loss, with the merchant generally liable for the chargeback for card-not-present transactions.

Tutorials are available on underground forums and markets which teach others how to circumvent fraud detection systems. Tutorials found on stolen data markets by Hutchings and Holt (2015) detailed how to imitate genuine cardholders, including using virtual machines to change the operating system; changing settings, such as language and time zone, for operating systems and browsers; and changing the IP address to one near the victim's usual residence by using proxies, anonymity networks such as Tor, or virtual private networks. An example extract from such a tutorial, translated from Russian, reads:

> [V]ery simple while working you have to fU . . . k the security system and for this reason your comp must be American and namely the language, time and even the username everything should be like it is with a real americosa. in order to reduce suspicion against you to a more acceptable level take this seriously here every detail is important, the winda language, socks, browser language even the time must be completely set for the state in wich we are working. (In certain situations it is necessary to pay attention to what's time it is nooww in the cardholder's country and not type too late or too early).

Other research has found support for the idea that offenders will imitate genuine account holders. Onaolapo et al. (2016) found that when the location of leaked account holders was known, some offenders would connect to the account using IP addresses in nearby locations. Others disguised their browser 'user agent' string, which provides a website with information about the visitor's browser and operating system.

Another way to imitate a user is through the use of cookies. Cookies are small pieces of data stored in the web browser. Some malware will steal users' cookies. These can be used to fool websites into treating an attacker as a logged-in user (Hutchings & Clayton, 2017).

Future ways to imitate include building accurate video and audio models of targets. Some organizations are investing in voice and facial recognition systems in order to positively identify customers. However, in the future attackers may use the same types of data that are used to train recognition systems for impersonation of selected targets (Riek & Watson, 2010).

Appear innocuous

Ways to appear innocuous include changing what is being purchased from something that is not suspicious, but the offender does not really want, to the real target after the fraud detection system checks have been completed. This technique can be used for transactions that are likely to be flagged as high risk. The offender first completes a transaction that does not raise a red flag. Once the order has been confirmed, they can then contact the merchant, still posing as the genuine cardholder, and change the order to reflect what they actually do want.

Another way of avoiding red flags is to tailor the order to make it appear less suspicious. Fraudulently obtained airline tickets tend to be booked shortly before departure, so as to limit the likelihood that the transaction will be flagged before the flight departs. This resulted in one-way flights being booked for each route, with bookings for return or subsequent destinations being made separately. However, one-way flights then became a red flag for flights. Subsequently, Hutchings (2018b) found there is often a return flight booked, even if there is no intention of flying it. As the booking is made using fraudulent means, the second flight doesn't come at a cost to the traveller.

In relation to malware, there are techniques to make the software appear innocuous in the eyes of antivirus signatures. Packing refers to compressing malware executables in order to obscure their contents. This makes it harder for antivirus software to detect the malware. However, packers can be detected, and some antivirus software will flag everything that has been packed. More advanced techniques are possible, such as those that change the morphology of the binaries so they are not detected, without encrypting the entire file (Kruegel, Kirda, Mutz, Robertson, & Vigna, 2005).

A common approach to evading IDSs requires acquiring knowledge about how they work. This can be done by means of probe attacks, where the attacker queries the IDSs and analyses their responses (Pastrana, Orfila, & Ribagorda, 2011). This information allows offenders to create exploits that mimic regular network traffic and bypass detection (Vigna, Robertson, & Balzarotti, 2004; Fogla, Sharif, Perdisci, Kolesnikov, & Lee, 2006; Pastrana, Orfila, & Ribagorda, 2010). Some researchers have proposed the use of random detection functions to combat these mimicry attacks (Wang, Parekh, & Stolfo, 2006). However, such randomized schemes are still vulnerable if the adversary is able to interact with the detector for a longer period of time and infer randomization patterns (Pastrana, Orfila, Tapiador, & Peris-Lopez, 2014).

Insiders

The use of insiders can help offenders circumvent fraud detection systems entirely or learn how to reverse-engineer and avoid them. Offenders may seek to obtain employment at targeted organizations. On one stolen data market, Hutchings and Holt (2015) found suggestions that specialist knowledge could be learnt by applying for employment at a company offering fraud detection systems. There were indications that the news and developments relating to organizations of interest were being closely followed for the purpose of seeking such opportunities, for example, the following post related to a consumer credit reporting agency, which was moving offices and advertising for new staff:

> *Another change that will be occuring within* [company] *is the closeure of all of their regional offices.* [The company] *is going to consolidate to one fixed location in* [city]. *The reason they are doing this is, and I quote, "To lover overhead costs, and also to increase security." So don't be too overly suprised if* [the company]

seems to be learning a few new tricks. The plan is to be completed within 2–3 years, with most of the outlying sites already closed. One nice note to this . . . If you live in [city], *look in the want adds,* [the company is] *hiring Data Entry personnel . . . Hmmmm. . .*

Offenders may also target employees and contractors to either corrupt or blackmail them into providing assistance. In another post, it was suggested that employees with knowledge of fraud detection systems and "morals that are questionable" should be targeted in order to learn about how to avoid detection:

Right now I would like to get a hold of the [. . .] *program that all the check cashing places use. With this we could figure out EXACTLY how there system works, and there is NEVER a callback with the program. If anyone works for a place that uses this software, or knows someone who has morals which are questionable, please contact me. I will make it very worthwhile for you to do so. . .*

Target the unprotected

Larger organizations will have significant resources available to implement systems that will reduce the amount of crime they experience. They benefit from economies of scale due to the amount of trade that they do. However, smaller companies are less likely to be able to pay for fraud detection systems, and there are indications that fraudsters know this. When studying the trade in fraudulently obtained airline tickets, Hutchings (2018b) found that offenders recommended purchasing tickets from smaller travel agencies to avoid detection:

its better to go through smaller companies that cant pay for the extra fraud detection

Unfortunately, smaller companies are also less likely to be able to withstand the losses arising from fraud, particularly if they are repeatedly targeted within a short period of time. Some small family-run companies have gone out of business for this reason (Hutchings, 2018a), contributing to the monopolization of trade and shutting down competition (particularly independent organizations).

Adversarial machine learning

Many of the crime detection techniques rely on a model which is constructed using a training dataset which informs the machine learning algorithms what should be considered 'good' or 'bad.' In the case of anomaly detection, this model represents what is normal, and the algorithm aims to detect outliers. In the case of signature-based detection, this model is a classifier of events into either malicious or regular events (spam vs. regular email, intrusion vs. normal traffic, malware vs. benign software, etc.). In recent years, researchers have identified a weakness in the use of machine learning under adversarial scenarios.

Because these algorithms have not been designed with security in mind, a sophisticated adversary might be able to cheat the system.

A seminal paper by Barreno et al. questioned for the first time the security of machine learning (Barreno, Nelson, Sears, Joseph, & Tygar, 2006), leading to a number of researchers working on this problem. Huang, Joseph, Nelson, Rubinstein, and Tygar (2011) presented a taxonomy of potential attacks against machine learning algorithms with three main aspects: the influence (causative, if the adversary targets ('poisons') the training data, or exploratory, if the attacker targets the system once it is trained); the security violation (availability, integrity, or privacy of the data); and the specificity (targeted or indiscriminate). Biggio, Fumera, and Roli (2014) enriched this taxonomy by adding the set of adversarial capabilities regarding its knowledge about the algorithm or capabilities to modify the system both before and after it is trained.

In the literature there are examples on how adversaries can bypass spam filters (Biggio et al., 2014) or malware classifiers (Biggio, Rieck et al., 2014) that make use of machine learning. In both cases, the adversary is able to evade the classifier by first acquiring knowledge about how it works and then a very small number of modifications to the attacks so as to bypass detection (e.g. by adding or removing specific words from spam messages). However, in the real world it may be rather more complicated. Miscreants may find it difficult to obtain sufficient knowledge about the system and its capabilities and may be unable to run enough tests to scope out its training and detection processes, so they will not be able to trick the detectors.

Discussion and conclusion

Big data solutions that aim to detect cybercrime rely on humans behaving in relatively predictive way. Attempts to commit cybercrime will tend to generate distinctive patterns, and so the good and the bad can each be identified. Offenders will try and cheat the system by trying to make their behaviour blend in, but the edge for big data solutions is that the business employing them is in a position to know far more about the behaviour of its customers than the bad guys ever will.

One of the key features of these big data solutions is the use of continuous feedback so that the systems learn and adapt in response to known criminal activity. However, the systems continually need to know the 'ground truth,' and it is necessary for a certain amount of malicious activity to be detected by the system or by other monitoring so the system can track and adapt accordingly.

This feedback is why reporting spam leads to improved spam detection, and the reports are used to train the system as to what is or is not spam. However, this means that the definition of spam is no longer 'bulk unsolicited email' but becomes 'email the user does not want in their inbox today.' This leads to two problems. First, the bad guys know the feedback votes matter, so they submit incorrect votes about their own emails. The response is to build another machine learning system to identify false votes and eliminate them before training the main system. Second, it is essential to whitelist particular types of mail, such as boarding passes, electricity bills, and so forth; otherwise, a small number of people reporting these as spam will cause the machine learning system to treat these as spam for everybody.

These big data solutions are treading a delicate balance between false positives and true negatives. For example, although spam detectors want to ensure account holders do not receive unwanted emails, they also want to ensure that the email account holders do want to receive gets through. Fraud detection systems want to ensure that fraudulent transactions are blocked, but also that genuine transactions are quickly processed. If genuine transactions are blocked or fraudulent ones are processed, there is not only immediate financial loss, but increased expenditure in staff time and more annoyed customers. If switching costs are low, customers may go elsewhere in the future.

Offenders are evidently learning techniques to circumvent big data solutions. As we show in this chapter, some of this learning is facilitated by discussions that occur on forums and marketplaces. There is also self-learning, through trial and error, reverse-engineering the systems to identify what methods work and what does not. Resources are available online for individuals to learn cybersecurity skills for defensive purposes; however. technically inclined offenders can also avail themselves of these opportunities. As identified, insiders provide another way to learn about the algorithms powering these systems.

However, the methods used for cheating the system can eventually be identified, either by the machine learning algorithms themselves or by those that operate them identifying that criminal activity has been overlooked. The solution is to re-engineer the system and retrain it, whilst ensuring that the quality of the results is maintained. Software packing hides the malicious payload of an executable program, but once the system learns to identify packers, it will rapidly learn to treat them as a red flag. But here again, there is a delicate balance. Offenders may learn that if they buy time-sensitive orders at the last minute, they can avoid the process required to confirm if a transaction is genuine. However, if buying at the last minute becomes a red flag then the organization will have to weigh up the cost of inconvenience to genuine customers with the potential fraud risk. It may be more profitable to allow some fraud to occur rather than turn away genuine customers.

Financial incentives play an important part in everything we have discussed. For example, merchants usually carry the cost of fraud for card-not-present transactions, such as those that occur online. If they suspect a transaction is fraudulent, the normal process is to verify this with the cardholder's financial institution. To the financial institution, this is often not a priority (as they won't carry the cost of the transaction, the merchant will). Hence, verification can take time, particularly if the cardholder is not immediately available, and if there are communication barriers, such as different languages and time zones.

Finally, the most important thing to understand is that the use of machine learning against adversaries is quite unlike the use of machine learning for other types of prediction, such as the weather. Thunderclouds do not cheat and change their behaviour just because you have worked out where they are. In Lewis Carroll's book *Through the Looking Glass*, the Red Queen tells Alice "Now, here, you see, it takes all the running you can do, to keep in the same place. If you want to get somewhere else, you must run at least twice as fast as that!" These big data approaches represent a Red Queen's race. Running non-stop is required to stay in one spot.

Funding

This work was supported by the UK Engineering and Physical Sciences Research Council (EPSRC) [grant EP/M020320/1] for the University of Cambridge, Cam- bridge Cybercrime Centre. The opinions, findings, and conclusions or recommendations expressed are those of the authors and do not reflect those of the aforementioned funder.

Acknowledgements

We thank our colleagues at the Cambridge Cybercrime Centre, in particular, Dr Daniel Thomas for his insightful feedback and comments. We also thank the anonymous reviewers for their helpful suggestions and advice.

References

Abdallah, A., Maarof, M. A., & Zainal, A. (2016). Fraud detection system: A survey. *Journal of Network and Computer Applications, 68*, 90–113.

Affinity IT Security Services. (2017). *What is privilege escalation?* Retrieved June 14, 2018, from https://perma.cc/MAP3-HUXK

Anderson, R., Barton, C., B¨ohme, R., Clayton, R., Van Eeten, M. J., Levi, M., . . . Savage, S. (2013). Measuring the cost of cybercrime. In *The economics of information security and privacy* (pp. 265–300). New York: Springer.

Barreno, M., Nelson, B., Sears, R., Joseph, A. D., & Tygar, J. D. (2006). *Can machine learning be secure?* Proceedings of the 2006 ACM Symposium on Information, Computer and Communications Security, pp. 16–25.

Biggio, B., Fumera, G., & Roli, F. (2014). Security evaluation of pattern classifiers under attack. *IEEE Transactions on Knowledge and Data Engineering, 26*(4), 984–996.

Biggio, B., Rieck, K., Ariu, D., Wressnegger, C., Corona, I., Giacinto, G., & Roli, F. (2014). *Poisoning behavioral malware clustering.* Proceedings of the 2014 Workshop on Artificial Intelligent and Security, pp. 27–36.

Chan, J., & Moses, L. B. (2017). Making sense of big data for security. *British Journal of Criminology, 57*(2), 299–319.

Chia, P. H., Chuang, J., & Chen, Y. (2016). *Whack-a-mole: Asymmetric conflict and guerrilla warfare in web security*. Proceedings of the 15th Annual Workshop on the Economics of Information Security.

Cornish, D. B., & Clarke, R. V. (1987). Understanding crime displacement: An application of rational choice theory. *Criminology, 25*(4), 933–947.

Dash, S. K., Suarez-Tangil, G., Khan, S., Tam, K., Ahmadi, M., Kinder, J., & Cavallaro, L. (2016). *Droidscribe: Classifying Android malware based on runtime behavior*. Security and Privacy Workshops (SPW), IEEE, pp. 252–261.

Denning, D. E. (1987). An intrusion-detection model. *IEEE Transactions on Software Engineering, 2*, 222–232.

Egele, M., Stringhini, G., Kruegel, C., & Vigna, G. (2017). Towards detecting compromised accounts on social networks. *IEEE Transactions on Depend- able and Secure Computing, 14*(4), 447–460.

Fette, I., Sadeh, N., & Tomasic, A. (2007). *Learning to detect phishing emails*. Proceedings of the 16th International Conference on World Wide Web, ACM, New York, NY, pp. 649–656.

Fogla, P., Sharif, M. I., Perdisci, R., Kolesnikov, O. M., & Lee, W. (2006). *Polymorphic blending attacks*. USENIX Security Symposium, pp. 241–256.

Franklin, J., Paxson, V., Perrig, A., & Savage, S. (2007, October 29–November 2). *An inquiry into the nature and causes of the wealth of internet miscreants*. ACM Conference on Computer and Communications Security (CCS), Alexandria.

Gandotra, E., Bansal, D., & Sofat, S. (2014). Malware analysis and classification: A survey. *Journal of Information Security, 5*(02), 56.

Gardiner, J., & Nagaraja, S. (2016). On the security of machine learning in malware C&C detection: A survey. *ACM Computing Surveys (CSUR), 49*(3), 59.

Holt, T. J., & Lampke, E. (2010). Exploring stolen data markets online: Products and market forces. *Criminal Justice Studies, 23*(1), 33–50.

Huang, L., Joseph, A. D., Nelson, B., Rubinstein, B. I., & Tygar, J. (2011). *Adversarial machine learning*. Proceedings of the 4th ACM Workshop on Security and Artificial Intelligence, pp. 43–58.

Hutchings, A. (2018a). Flying in cyberspace: Policing global travel fraud. *Policing: A Journal of Policy and Practice*, advanced access. doi:10.1093/police/pay063

Hutchings, A. (2018b). Leaving on a jet plane: The trade in fraudulently obtained airline tickets. *Crime, Law and Social Change, 70*(4), 461–487.

Hutchings, A., & Clayton, R. (2015). Exploring the provision of online booter services. *Deviant Behaviour, 37*(10), 1163–1178.

Hutchings, A., & Clayton, R. (2017, April 25–27). *Configuring Zeus: A case study of online crime target selection and knowledge transmission*. APWG Symposium on Electronic Crime Research (eCrime), Arizona.

Hutchings, A., Clayton, R., & Anderson, R. (2016, June 1–3). *Taking down websites to prevent crime*. APWG Symposium on Electronic Crime Research (eCrime), Toronto.

Hutchings, A., & Holt, T. J. (2015). A crime script analysis of the online stolen data market. *British Journal of Criminology, 55*(3), 596–614.

Karami, M., & McCoy, D. (2013). Understanding the emerging threat of DDoS- as-a-service. In *Presented as part of the 6th USENIX Workshop on Large-Scale Exploits and Emergent Threats*. Washington, DC: USENIX.

Karami, M., Park, Y., & McCoy, D. (2016, April 11–15). *Stress testing the booters: Under- standing and undermining the business of DDoS services*. International World Wide Web Conference (IW3C2), Quebec.

Kruegel, C., Kirda, E., Mutz, D., Robertson, W., & Vigna, G. (2005). *Automating mimicry attacks using static binary analysis*. Proceedings of the 14th Conference on USENIX Security Symposium, USENIX, Baltimore, MD, Vol. 14, pp. 162–176.

Mayhew, M. J., Atighetchi, M., Adler, A., & Greenstadt, R. (2015). *Use of machine learning in big data analytics for insider threat detection*. MILCOM, IEEE, pp. 915–922.

Moore, T., & Clayton, R. (2007, October 4–5). *Examining the impact of website take-down on phishing*. APWG 2nd Annual eCrime Researchers Summit, Pittsburgh.

Moore, T., & Clayton, R. (2015). *Which malware lures work best? Measurements from a large instant messaging worm*. APWG Symposium on Electronic Crime Research (eCrime), Berlin.

Motoyama, M., McCoy, D., Levchenko, K., Savage, S., & Voelker, G. M. (2011, May 26–29). *An analysis of underground forums*. ACM SIGCOMM Conference on Internet Measurement, Barcelona.

Onaolapo, J., Mariconti, E., & Stringhini, G. (2016). *What happens after you are pwnd: Understanding the use of leaked webmail credentials in the wild*. Proceedings of the 2016 Internet Measurement Conference, ACM, New York, NY, pp. 65–79.

Panda Labs. (2017). *2017 in figures: The exponential growth of malware*. Retrieved May 23, 2018, from https://perma.cc/R5FG-73YR

Pastrana, S., Mitrokotsa, A., Orfila, A., & Peris-Lopez, P. (2012). Evaluation of classification algorithms for intrusion detection in MANETs. *Knowledge-Based Systems, 36*(0), 217–225.

Pastrana, S., Orfila, A., & Ribagorda, A. (2010). *Modeling NIDS evasion with genetic programming*. Worldcomp 2010: Security and Management, pp. 444–448.

Pastrana, S., Orfila, A., & Ribagorda, A. (2011). *A functional framework to evade network IDS*. Hawaii International Conference on System Sciences (HICSS'11), IEEE, Koloa, HI, pp. 1–10.

Pastrana, S., Orfila, A., Tapiador, J. E., & Peris-Lopez, P. (2014). Randomized anagram revisited. *Journal of Network and Computer Applications, 41*, 182–196.

Phua, C., Lee, V., Smith, K., & Gayler, R. (2010). A comprehensive survey of data mining-based fraud detection research. *arXiv preprint*, arXiv:1009.6119.

Rieck, K., Trinius, P., Willems, C., & Holz, T. (2011). Automatic analysis of malware behavior using machine learning. *Journal of Computer Security, 19*(4), 639–668.

Riek, L. D., & Watson, R. N. M. (2010). The age of avatar realism: When seeing shouldn't be believing. *IEEE Robotics & Automation Magazine, 17*(4), 37–42.

Robert, C. (2014). *Machine learning, a probabilistic perspective*. London: Taylor & Francis.

Sen, S., & Clark, J. A. (2011). Evolutionary computation techniques for intrusion detection in mobile ad hoc networks. *Computer Networks, 55*(15), 3441–3457.

Smith, R. G., Wolanin, N., & Worthington, G. (2003). *Trends & Issues in Crime and Criminal Justice No. 243: e-Crime solutions and crime displacement*. Canberra: Australian Institute of Criminology.

Sommer, R., & Paxson, V. (2010). *Outside the closed world: On using machine learning for network intrusion detection*. IEEE Symposium on Security and Privacy, IEEE Computer Society, pp. 305–316.

Thomas, D. R., Clayton, R., & Beresford, A. R. (2017). *1000 days of UDP amplification DDoS attacks*. APWG Symposium on Electronic Crime Research (eCrime), pp. 79–84.

Vigna, G., Robertson, W., & Balzarotti, D. (2004, October). *Testing network-based intrusion detection signatures using mutant exploits*. Proceedings of the 11th ACM Conference on Computer and Communications Security, ACM, Washington, DC, p. 21.

Wang, K., Parekh, J. J., & Stolfo, S. J. (2006). *Anagram: A content anomaly detector resistant to mimicry attack*. International Workshop on Recent Advances in Intrusion Detection, pp. 226–248.

Yu, S. (2014). *Distributed denial of service attack and defense*. New York: Springer.

Zargar, S. T., Joshi, J., & Tipper, D. (2013). A survey of defense mechanisms against distributed denial of service (DDoS) flooding attacks. *IEEE Communications Surveys and Tutorials*, *15*(4), 2046–2069.

Zuech, R., Khoshgoftaar, T. M., & Wald, R. (2015, February 27). Intrusion detection and big heterogeneous data: A survey. *Journal of Big Data*, *2*(1), 1–41.

Index

Note: Page numbers in *italic* indicate a figure and page numbers in **bold** indicate a table on the corresponding page.